Translated for the first time into English in their enti... . . ладimir Bronevskiy describe the actions and movements o... ...ин Admiral Dmitriy Senyavin's squadron and the infantry at his disposal in the Adriatic and Aegean Seas between the years of 1805 and 1810. The story moves from Kronstadt to Corfu, to the siege of Ragusa and battle at Mount Athos, to the chaotic reshuffling of alliances with the signing of the Treaty of Tilsit and the ill-fated dispersion of the fleet among the British, French, and Austrians.

Straddling the Wars of the Third and Fourth Coalitions and the Russo-Turkish War, Senyavin carefully manoeuvred around multiple threats from all sides with limited resources and came through with minimal losses, though political circumstances ultimately robbed him of the laurels.

Told from the perspective of a midshipman aboard the frigate *Venus*, but augmented and expanded with archival data and interviews with his comrades and acquaintances, Bronevskiy illuminated an often-overlooked theatre of war and sought to teach his readership about the myriad cultures and rich history of the region, transforming his personal journals into a comprehensive history of the campaign. His scope varies from personal interactions with civilians and tours of local landmarks to the diplomatic correspondence of general and admirals and the combat actions of whole squadrons and corps.

Unabridged, illustrated with all the original engravings, featuring newly translated maps and annotated throughout with notes and corrections, Boland's translation brings Bronevskiy to a new, wider audience in a faithful but approachable presentation.

Darrin Boland is a translator and amateur historian from Hamilton, Ontario, Canada with a particular interest in Russian military history and the Napoleonic Wars in general. He has previously published a collection of Russian Napoleonic memoirs in the From Reason to Revolution series with Helion and several primary documents through the Nafziger Collection.

# Northern Tars in Southern Waters

## The Russian Fleet in the Mediterranean, 1806-1810

Vladimir Bogdanovich Bronevskiy
Translated and annotated by Darrin Boland

 Helion & Company Limited

Helion & Company Limited
Unit 8 Amherst Business Centre
Budbrooke Road
Warwick
CV34 5WE
England
Tel. 01926 499 619
Email: info@helion.co.uk
Website: www.helion.co.uk
Twitter: @helionbooks
Visit our blog http://blog.helion.co.uk/

Published by Helion & Company 2019
Designed and typeset by Mary Woolley (www.battlefield-design.co.uk)
Cover designed by Paul Hewitt, Battlefield Design (www.battlefield-design.co.uk)

Notes, Commentary, and Maps © Darrin Boland, 2019
Front cover: Ivan Ayvazovskiy, 'Frigate underway', 1838, oil on canvas (St. Petersburg, Central Naval Museum). Rear cover: 'View of the Citadel in Corfu, illustration from original publication.

ISBN 978-1-912866-71-7

British Library Cataloguing-in-Publication Data.
A catalogue record for this book is available from the British Library.

For details of other military history titles published by Helion & Company Limited contact the above address or visit our website: http://www.helion.co.uk.
We always welcome receiving book proposals from prospective authors.

# Contents

# List of Plates

# List of Maps

# Translator's Foreword

The following is an English translation of Vladimir Bronevskiy's *Memoirs of a Naval Officer in the Campaign on the Mediterranean Sea under the command of Vice-Admiral Dmitriy Nikolayevich Senyavin from 1806 to 1810*, originally published in four parts between the years 1818 and 1819 by the Naval Printing Press in St. Petersburg. Part military journal, part travel log, and part general history, Bronevskiy sought to produce a holistic and broadly informative description of not only his personal experiences but also of the whole campaign and the geography in which it was set. Enjoying the patronage of the Russian Academy and access to naval archives, he was able to describe both those events he personally experienced as well as contemporary events seen by other detachments with a fair degree of accuracy, but augmented these with personal encounters and shared anecdotes, tours of churches and museums, attempts at geographical survey and anthropology, summaries of European history, and anything else that struck his fancy. Besides the highlights of the campaign such as the siege of Ragusa and the Battle of Mount Athos, he also attempted to summarize the culture and government of Montenegro, give a historical background for Sicily, dispel misconceptions of his day about the Turks (while perhaps reinforcing others) and give ponderous praise of English democracy with a dim prognosis for its survival. Most prominently and consistently throughout the work is a defence of Admiral Senyavin's tactical and diplomatic abilities and a celebration of those feats of the Russian Navy which he regarded as exceptional but belong to a lesser known campaign that had been overshadowed by the larger political context and decisive land battles of the era. In that capacity, his memoirs are invaluable and provide an unparalleled level of detail to the events in the Adriatic and Aegean, albeit while concerned only with the Russian perspective.

The author was born in 1784 to a large noble family in the Smolensk Governorate, descending from Belorussian nobility originally under the arms of Tarnawa. His father, Bogdan, had served in the bombardier company of the Preobrazhenskiy Regiment of the Imperial Guard before retiring with the rank of guard ensign and went into the civil service as an assessor for the government of Tver. Bogdan married Serafima Alekseyevna née Levshina and had seven sons and one daughter, five of whom enrolled in the Naval Cadet Corps.[1] Vladimir Bogdanovich entered the corps in 1794 and underwent voyages around the Gulf of Finland and along the coast up to Åbo (Turku). In 1802, he was commissioned as a midshipman and served on the frigate *Schastlivyy* and the 100-gun ship *Gavriil*. Joining Senyavin's squadron in the Mediterranean, he conducted commerce raiding aboard the frigate *Venus* and was a participant of the siege of Ragusa (Dubrovnik), the Battle of Castelnuovo (Herzeg Novi), the skirmish in the Dardanelles and the siege of Tenedos (Bozcaada) between 1806 and 1807. At Tenedos, he was wounded and was awarded the Order of Saint Vladimir, 4th Class.[2] After the conclusion of the Mediterranean campaign and his return to Russia, he was promoted to lieutenant and transferred to the Black Sea Fleet in 1811, cruising aboard the *Pobyeda* in 1812 before taking command of the brig *Lavrentiy* and performing fire watch duties at Feodosia. In 1816, he retired from the navy with the rank of captain-lieutenant and the Order of Saint George 4th Class and began to write his diary and general history of the Mediterranean campaign. Around the same time they were published, he became an inspector of classes at the Alexandrovskiy Noble Military Academy in Tula. He was awarded the Order of Saint Anne, 2nd Class in 1822 and in that same year published a review of the shores of Crimea. In 1824, he produced a Russian translation of Sir Walter Scott's novel *Guy Mannering or the Astrologer* and, a year later, he published a second travel log detailing the 1810 overland march those crews stranded in the Adriatic were forced to make from Trieste to the Russian frontier. In 1828, he became an assistant director and inspector of classes for the Corps of Pages. He retired from service in 1833 with the rank of major-general and shortly after produced a history of the Don Cossack Host and description of the Don region in four volumes. Vladimir Bronevskiy died in 1835.[3] Records attest that he could speak Italian, French, and English in addition to his native Russian. He was survived by his wife Evdokiya Pavlovna and two sons, Valerian and Vladimir.

This translation reproduces the original four volumes in their entirety and original format, with the addition of a timeline so that the reader can easier follow

---

1   Дмитрий Броневский, 'Воспоминания Броневского,' *Русская Старина* 6 (1908), pp.537-543. [Dmitriy Bronevskiy, 'Bronevskiy's Recollections,' *Russian Antiquity* 6 (1908),pp.537-543.]

2   *Придворный Месяцеслов на Лето от Рождества Христова 1808* (St. Petersburg: Императорская Академия Наук, 1808), p.370. [*Courtly Menologium for the Year of Our Lord 1808* (St. Petersburg: Imperial Academy of Sciences, 1808), p.370.]

3   *Общий Морской Список*, vol. 6 (St. Petersburg: Типография Морского Министерства, 1893), pp.457-459. [*Complete Naval Roster*, vol. 6 (St. Petersburg: Press of the Naval Ministry, 1893), pp.457-459.]

the overlapping events and a partial reproduction of the Russian Empire's Table of Ranks for cross-referencing the naval, army, and civil service ranks which appear throughout. Place names in the Adriatic are almost all exclusively given in Italian in the original work and this was common as well in contemporary English works, but this translation provides the Serbo-Croat-Bosnian or Greek equivalents in parentheses whenever they first occur, in the Latin alphabet with diacritics as necessary, and likewise for Greek islands now in Turkish possession. When the author refers to the language of the southern Slavs as 'славянский', I have rendered this as 'Slavonian.' Certain uses of 'English' have been changed to 'British,' 'Turkish' to 'Ottoman' and 'Greek' to 'Orthodox' where appropriate, but much of the original diction and even sentence structure is preserved wherever possible. The names of Russian naval vessels are transliterated and italicized, as most sources do not translate vessels' names, but a list of translations with the original Cyrillic is provided as an appendix. For the battle of Mount Athos, Bronevskiy provided a list of Turkish or Arabic vessel names for the Ottoman squadron in Cyrillic and their Russian translations and I have rendered these in the Latin alphabet according to the list given in John Tredrea and Eduard Sozaev's *Russian Warships in the Age of Sail, 1696-1860*, but with a few modifications to maintain Bronevskiy's names. As a result of consulting different dictionaries and wrestling with multiple alphabets, there may be inconsistencies or grammatical errors with the Ottoman vessels. Whenever the author references obsolete or false information about various subjects, I have attached a footnote to correct him, but the information is still otherwise presented as it was originally written and allusions to literature, mythology, and scripture are annotated as well, to the best of my ability. Dates provided by the author are in the pre-reform calendar of the Russian Empire, which for the 19th Century entails adding 12 days to produce the Western or New Style date, and such conversions are provided in square brackets. This is maintained in the footnotes and appendix timeline as well for consistency. Square brackets are also used for any other editorial insertions. The original footnotes from the Russian publication are prefaced with 'Bronevskiy's note:' and enclosed with quotation marks. The engraved illustrations from the original Russian publication are included, but several maps have been redrawn with more accurate shorelines in addition to being translated. Measurements in obsolete systems are presented as-is followed by a Metric conversion given in square brackets. The Russian *funt* appears in two forms, the mercantile *funt* at 409.52 grammes, and the artillery *funt* at 491.4 grammes. The author establishes the use of Italian miles (one minute of latitude at the equator, nearly equal to the modern nautical mile) early in the text for measuring distances at sea, and so whenever distances at sea are given simply in 'miles,' the Italian mile is assumed for its metric conversion.

Darrin Boland, 2019

# Author's Dedication

To his Excellency the gentleman Vice-Admiral, State Councillor, permanent member of the State Admiralty Department, President of the Imperial Russian Academy, honorary member of the Imperial Academy of Sciences, University of Kharkov and Kazan and many other educational institutions, Knight of the Order of Saint Alexander Nevskiy, Knight First Class of the Order of St. Vladimir Equal to the Apostles, and Knight First Class of the Order of Saint Anne,
Aleksandr Semyonovich Shishkov

Dearest Sir!
Aleksandr Semyonovich!

While presiding in the temple of the Russian Muses like Maecenas or the Nestor of the Russian word, turning your attention to every vital exercise in the national literature, Your Excellency does a great honour to my endeavour. This book, which illustrates the glory of our navy and army, is solely for your approval and petition for publication.

You taught in the Naval Cadet Corps, served in the fleet and encouraged and took under your special patronage the first fruit of my labours: for all this I find the courage to dedicate this edition in your esteemed name. Receive this favourably as a sign of the zeal and gratitude of the one who presents that honour with perfect admiration and equal devotion.

Your obedient servant,
Vladimir Bronevskiy

# To the Reader

Serving in the fleet from the beginning to the end of the campaign, sailing from Kronstadt through the Sound, the English Channel and the Atlantic Ocean to the Mediterranean, I set foot on the greater portion of the islands of the Greek Archipelago and Dalmatia, surveyed Sicily, Malta and Sardinia, returned from the Dardanelles to Lisbon, and finally for a third time passed through the Strait of Gibraltar, departed from Trieste over land through Carinthia, Styria, Hungary and Poland to return to Kronstadt. By circumnavigating Europe thus, I saw the best of its countries, famous for the glorious episodes of their antiquities, enlightenment and science. I kept daily notes about those incidents to which I was an eyewitness and whatever else seemed worthy of my attention and curiosity.

The exploits of the Russian Navy on the waters of the Mediterranean and the boundless triumph of the small contingent of ground forces over a skilful enemy, superior in numbers and methods, placing new unfading laurels on the victorious Russian arms glorify the name of their famous commander Vice-Admiral Senyavin throughout all of Europe, despite the fact that according to the circumstances of the time and unexpected events, this glorious campaign did not have brilliant consequences corresponding to its deeds. Drinking to the unshakable love for the fatherland and acting in the gentle spirit of his monarch, Senyavin was not only the soul of his subordinates but acquired the unlimited trust of Russia's devoted people. Even his enemies esteemed him, as shown by the leniency of the British government and the ample and personal respect of Admiral Cotton, who helped Senyavin in trying circumstances to preserve the fleet and save the honour of the flag which had not been defeated. The convention at Lisbon will remain in military history as a monument and testament to his merits, but these deeds are known to only a few, for true courage stands with modesty; a clean service without deceptions and a sound character without arrogance does not seek a single bauble or momentary celebration, but rather finds reward in his own deeds and hope in the love and remembrance of his subordinates.

These notes, like several others, were to remain in my possession for I had no means to publish them, but upon my arrival to Petersburg, his Excellency Loggin

Ivanovich Golenishchev-Kutuzov, under whose command I was educated at the Naval Cadet Corps, was always merciful and accommodating to me in my labours and now, finding my manuscript worthy of attention, he informed the gentleman President of the Russian Academy, whose intercession and positive response ensured the acceptance of this book under the auspices of the Russian Academy and State Admiralty Department to be printed. Additionally, an order from the Admiralty has allowed me access to the relevant acts and all necessary cases from the Archives in order to produce from them the most accurate descriptions.

In the full hope of the charity of the nation's public, I offer a historical narrative of this memorable journey together with my observations, thoughts and impressions laid out in chronological order. I would happily praise myself if the enlightened reader should honour this first work of mine and if I might bring joy to the officers who then served in the fleet and in the 15th Infantry Division on Corfu with the descriptions of those battles in which each of them had an integral part in their glory.

# 1

# Preparations for the campaign – Departure from Kronstadt – Sailing to Reval

For half of the year 1805, the political horizon of Europe was clouded. The immense ambition of Napoleon Bonaparte gave great cause for preparations for war. Russia, Britain and Austria took active part in it. As a result, to bolster our previous forces[1] which defended the Ionian Republic, it was ordered to send five ships of the line and one frigate. Command of this squadron was entrusted to Rear-Admiral Dmitriy Nikolayevich Senyavin, who then was simultaneously promoted to vice-admiral of the red flag with the authority of commander-in-chief over the naval and land forces stationed in the Mediterranean. At the same time, an auxiliary army under the command of the famous General Mikhail Illarionovich Golenishchev-Kutuzov marched to the borders of Austria. Another corps under Lieutenant-General Count Pyotr Aleksandrovich Tolstoy was tasked with liberating Hanover, then occupied by the enemy.

At the beginning of August, Kronstadt was alive with unusual activity. A fleet consisting of 11 ships, 9 frigates and 300 English transports and small war craft occupied the whole anchorage and harbour. Admiral George (Yegor Yegorovich) Tate, the commander of this fleet, received the order to take on forces encamped near Oranienbaum and land them on the island of Rügen. The transfer of regiments began on the 20th of August [1st of September]. The infantry officers were amazed at the vastness of the *Gavriil*, the 100-gun ship of the line on which I served. In fact, our *Gavriil* constituted a whole city in miniature. Imagine a massive building, 32 *sazhen*s [68.3 m] long, 10 [21.3 m] in width, 40 [85.3 m] tall

---

1   Bronevskiy's Note: 'This consisted of the [future] 15th Infantry Division under the command of Major-General Heinrich Reinhold [aka. Roman Karlovich] Anrep, and 5 ships, 4 frigates, 6 corvettes and 6 brigs under the command of Captain-Commodore Aleksey Samuilovich Greig.'

Dmitriy Nikolayevich Senyavin. Vladislav Koval, 1987, excerpt from 10-kopeck postage stamp, Postal Service of the Soviet Union.

in three storeys with 110 guns of 48- [23.6 kg], 24- [11.8 kg], 18- [8.85 kg] and 12-*funt* [5.9 kg] calibres, containing seven months of provisions, water and all kinds of spare and necessary items for the journey; that this fortress afloat on the water was home to thousands of men who ruled and protected it must amaze and astonish the human mind.

A deputy of the Admiralty Collegium conducted an inspection of the squadron on the 25th of August [6th of September] to send us off on the long journey. The Sovereign Emperor,[2] as an expression of his good will, granted the officers and servicemen half a year's salary. The spectacle of honours displayed at sea upon the appearance of the Standard,[3] the flag which indicated the monarch's presence, was so magnificent that it nearly had no equal: the fleet's ships of various size and type were decorated with a multitude of colourful flags and stood in a line seven *versta*s

---

2    Alexander I Pavlovich reigned as Emperor and Autocrat of All Russia from 1801-1825.

3    The Emperor's Standard was pale yellow with the black, two-headed eagle, thrice crowned and bearing the arms of Moscow (St. George on horseback lancing a dragon) over its breast. In its beaks and talons it held four maps meant to represent the White, Baltic, Black and Caspian Seas. *Полное Собрание Законов Российской Империи*, collection 1, vol. 24 (Moscow: II Отделение Собственное Его Императорского Величества Канцелярии, 1830), pp.384.; Ibid., col. 1, чертежи и рисунки к собранию, p.33. [*Complete Collection of Laws of the Russian Empire*, collection 1, vol. 24 (Moscow: II Department of His Imperial Majesty's own Chancellery, 1830), pp.384.; Ibid., col. 1, drawings and diagrams for the collection, p. 33.] No. 17,833.

[7.47 km] long. The Emperor's boat passed with the standard flying before the long row of vessels under the silken flags of the admirals of the three divisions.[4] When His Majesty passed each ship, the sailors arranged along the yards and masts resounded with a loud 'ura!'.[5] When coming aboard and departing again from each vessel, the fortresses and ships greeted the Emperor by firing all of their guns at once.

The squadron bound for the Mediterranean consisted of the following:

1. the *Yaroslav* of 74 guns under the flag of the commanding vice-admiral and under the personal command of Captain Fedot Mitkov;
2. the *Moskva* of 74 guns under Captain Yegor Hetzen (Gettsen);
3. the *Svyatoy Pyotr* of 74 guns under Captain Ilya Baratynskiy;
4. the *Selafail* of 74 guns under Captain Pyotr Rozhnov;
5. the *Uriil* of 84 guns under Captain Mikhail Bychenskiy;
6. the frigate *Kildyuin* of 32 guns under Captain-Lieutenant Yegor Razvozov.

The first three of the ships and the frigate were built by the master shipwright A.M. Kurochkin in Arkhangelsk, and although they were not so beautiful in appearance, they had all the good qualities of a warship. The last two were built in St. Petersburg by the masters I.P. Amosov and V.A. Sarychev and were distinguished by the fineness of their finish and their ease of movement. Our navy today is built by Russian shipwrights and staffed by Russian admirals, captains and officers. Peter the Great had accepted foreigners to construct and helm the ships when founding the navy, but he did not need to rely on them for long: the Russians themselves soon became skilled in their construction and navigation.

On the 28th of August [9th of September], according to the records of the Collegium, I was transferred from the *Gavriil* to the *Svyatoy Pyotr*. After acquiring everything necessary for a long voyage and gaining a capable wind, the

---

4  The ensigns of the three squadrons were: for the 1st, the blue saltire of St. Andrew on a white field; for the 2nd, a blue ensign with St. Andrew's flag in the canton; the 3rd had a red ensign with St. Andrew's in the canton. The white, blue, red seniority mirrors the Russian tricolour, and differs from the British system where red was senior, white was second and blue was junior. *Complete Collection of Laws*, col. 1, vol. 28, pp.327-329. No. 21,300.

5  'Ypa' – a traditional Russian war cry and cheer, equivalent to the English 'hooray,' German 'hurrah,' etc. The etymology is uncertain but may come for the Tatar 'Ур" (ur') meaning 'strike; hit; blow.' It was still used in the world wars of the 20th Century and can be heard today during Russia's Victory Day celebrations. И. Е. Андреевский, К. К. Арсеньев and Ф. Ф. Петрушевский (eds.), *Энциклопедический Словарь Брокгауза и Ефрона*, 1st ed. (St. Petersburg: Ефрон, 1890), s.v. 'Ура.' [I. E. Andreyevskiy, K.K. Arsenyev and F.F. Petrushevskiy (eds.), *Brockhaus and Efron Encyclopedic Dictionary*, 1st ed. (St. Petersburg: Efron, 1890), s.v. 'Ura.']

Emperor Alexander I of Russia (reigned 1801-1825). François Gérard, 1817, oil on canvas, St. Petersburg, State Hermitage Museum.

vice-admiral's ship weighed anchor at noon on the 10th [22nd] of September and the whole squadron followed behind him.

He with white wings flapping
Soared and behind him foamed the moats!
-Derzhavin[6]

A slow, changing wind kept the squadron in sight of Kronstadt all day. It seemed as though the ships were not willing to leave their beloved fatherland, however this feeling of regret was tempered by the hope to return, and the delightful prospect for a young man to see distant lands and all the curiosities they might present him. At least for myself I can say that on that day it bore the most joyous prospects.

6    A paraphrased quote from the poem 'The Fleet' by Gavriil Romanovich Derzhavin. Гавриил Державин, *Сочинения Державина с Объяснительными Примечаниями Якова Грота*, vol. 1 (St. Petersburg: Императорская Академия Наук, 1864), pp.689-691. [Gavriil Derzhavin, *The Compositions of Derzhavin with Explanatory Notes by Yakov Grot*, vol. 1 (St. Petersburg: Imperial Academy of Sciences, 1864), pp.689-691.]

Before sunset, a fortunate wind picked up and we sailed fourteen *versta*s [14.95 km][7] in an hour; no longer did our ship feel like it was standing still. The dark night did not prevent us from safely passing between many islets, shallows and underwater rocks scattered throughout the Gulf of Finland. The sea was calm, the wind was blowing upward, and besides the slight noise produced by the motion, a tranquility was preserved.

We leave the ships to calmly continue their journey. Let us make a small digression for the uninformed to understand how such great masses, such as ships, are safely conveyed over the wet and capricious swells and a brief explanation of navigation which will give some idea of the art that reliably pilots them from province to province, country to country. The magnificent canopy of the heavens surely drew the attention of the earth's first inhabitants, especially in the fortunate countries where the air is always clear and inviting them to gaze at the stars. Contemplating the continuous circulation of the celestial firmament, their courses were observed for several centuries in Asia, the first dwelling of humanity and the cradle of all sciences. Chaldea, Egypt, Persia and China were the first to broach the subject of astronomy, though imperfectly. These facts revealed the sea to the Phoenicians and the science of maritime navigation emerged. They were the first to sail on weak boats only in the day and in sight of the coasts, on which they landed each night, but when by chance they were forced from the shore by a storm, they sailed by the sun in the day and by the stars at night. These means were quite inadequate since cloudy skies could conceal these guides for long periods of time. Their successors were the Carthaginians who, although acquiring great knowledge in the science of navigation, still went no further than the sight of their shores allowed and were still subjected to great difficulties and dangers. In such a state remained that science until the invention of the compass by the Neapolitan Flavio Giola around 1300 AD.[8] Seafarers, receiving a tool by which they could always find their place and direct their course, yearned for a long time to leave their coastlines and sail across the open seas. The spirit of discovery, excited by the hopes of greedy self-interest, was then entrusted to great enterprises. In the beginning of the 15th century, Prince Henry of Portugal invented the first marine

---

7    Bronevskiy's Note: 'Or eight knots corresponding to eight Italian miles, of which 60
     constitute a degree, or in other words each mile consists of one and three-quarters *versta*s
     [1.87 km].'
8    The first application of the compass for maritime navigation is now believed to have
     been at least as early as 1119 AD in Song Dynasty China, though European usage of
     the compass developed independently. Helaine Selin (ed.), *Encyclopedia of the History
     of Science, Technology and Medicine in Non-Western Cultures* (Dordrecht, Netherlands:
     Kluwer Academic Publishers, 1997), s.v. 'Magnetism in China.'

maps.[9] He also, with the help of other mathematicians, taught to observe the sun and the stars with astronomical instruments, astrolabes and nocturlabes. Led by these imperfect implements, the Portuguese unlocked the great expanses of the west coast of Africa, circumnavigated the cape of storms (Cape of Good Hope), opened communication with the East Indies and thereby deprived the Venetian and Genoese of the monopoly on trade with India through the Red Sea. They ascended to the highest degree of glory and became the rulers of the seas, acquiring great riches. At the same time the Genoese Christopher Columbus, a man skilled in navigation and astronomy, reflecting on the image of the globe, was greatly convinced that from Europe to the west could be found a new landmass whose adjoined shores would lead to India or China. For a long time he vainly presented this belief and offered his services to the various sovereigns of Europe in order to undertake such a voyage. At that time, no one wanted to believe the earth was round,[10] but finally Ferdinand and Isabella, the sovereigns of Castile and Aragon, granted him three ships on which he travelled to one of the islands of what are now called the Bahamas,[11] lying in a whole new region of the world and made the first step towards its exploration. Soon after, seafaring encompassed the whole globe and its science gradually improved.

Though all sciences gradually ascend to perfection, none made such hurrying leaps and strides as did the science of navigation. Its improvement belongs to the 18th century, rightfully called the great age of discovery. The precise definition of the flow of magnetized materials, the laws of gravity formulated by the great Newton, new discoveries in astronomy, the measurement of the earth's degrees, the mapping of the true shapes and dimensions of landmasses, the study of the tides and currents of the oceans, and finally the improvements in cartography named after their inventor Mercator,[12] all guaranteed, expedited and proliferated travel at sea.

---

9    Bronevskiy's note: 'These maps were useful in low latitudes close to the equator or only for short distances between the tropics and the polar circles.'

10   It is a myth that the belief of a flat earth was prevalent during Columbus's day. Rather, Columbus asserted that the circumference of the Earth was much smaller than geographers calculated, and that a journey across the Atlantic to Asia would be shorter and more feasible than his naysayers predicted. The discovery of America salvaged his expedition from a false hypothesis and perhaps saved his crews from death by dehydration were they to sail the whole length of the Atlantic and Pacific combined. Jeffrey Russell, *Inventing the Flat Earth: Columbus and his Modern Historians* (New York: Praeger, 1991), pp.1-26.

11   Bronevskiy's note: 'Columbus struck the island of Guanahani, which he named San Salvador.'

12   Bronevskiy's note: 'In Mercator's map, the distances of the meridians are expanded in proportion to the parallel circles' distance from the equator. The map represents the whole sphere of the earth unwrapped into a plane on which the distances and positions of places

For calculating a course and determining one's position on the map, the following means are used: the compass, the simplest tool, is the most necessary for the control of the ship at all times. It is divided into 32 parts called rhumbs, each of which had a name to signify the different directions of wind, and the same rhumbs gave their names to the sections of the horizon. By the map, one could locate places over spans of several thousand miles. By this system, one defines a line by which the ship must sail from one port to another. Near the coastline, having noticed two landmarks on the compass, and having drawn from them opposite rhumbs on the map, the location of the ship can be located on the map by triangulation. Speed is measured by a chip log. This tool is nothing more than a wooden plank in the shape of a quarter-circle attached to a long thread measured at intervals of 48 English feet [14.63 m], denoted by knots. Throwing the log into the water from the stern and unravelling the thread, if the knots are unspooled every half a minute with a consistent strength of wind in the sails, then the ship will traverse an Italian mile [one minute of latitude at the equator or approximately 1.86 km] in an hour. For example: if two knots transpire in half a minute, then the ship will cover two Italian miles or three and a half *versta*s [3.73 km] in an hour. Using a quarter of the compass circle drawn at the stern for observation, the drift or leeway of the ship from its true course is measured by however many degrees the track of the ship deviates from the line drawn along the length of the ship. Each half hour, recordings are taken of the wind, the direction of the course, the speed and the drift so that they can be reckoned and every four hours the ship will be relocated on the map. In so far as these means are subject to error, especially over long-term periods without seeing land, verification by astronomical means is employed. Octants, sextants and chronometers – the first two, refined to the most possible perfection, served to observe the height of the sun and the stars according to which the latitude of the location was determined with mathematical precision when these objects are on our meridian; the last, accurate to within a third (one sixtieth of a second), serves to calculate the longitude. With latitude and longitude so determined, a ship can still be located on the map even on broad seas where land cannot be seen.

Those three implements, along with the compass, log, sandglasses,[13] and tracking the sun and stars allow the helmsman to locate the ship on the globe at any time. With the accuracy of the map, the navigator arranges for the ship to enter harbours along the way to the final destination to give the crew frequent

are preserved in the same shape as they have on the ground. These maps have an advantage over their predecessors in that they could be used with absolute accuracy at all latitudes and across broad spaces.'

13  Bronevskiy's note: 'These glasses are in denominations of hourly, half-hourly and quarter-hourly.'

rest and resupply their provisions. Columbus undoubtedly deserves to be named among the greatest sailors, for without the means we have today, he crossed a vast ocean on only mathematical deduction and estimation; but today an ordinary helmsman, sailing around the world, can reliably reach wherever he intends.

At night, a favourable wind increased and by the evening of the 11th [23rd] of September, the squadron already reached the height of Reval (Tallinn), but as the southwesterly wind prevented travelling between the islands of Nargen (Naissaar) and Wulf (Aegna), the admiral led the ships through a different straight and bypassed Nargen to drop anchor in the dark night between that island and the Suurupi lighthouse. At dawn, the tall bell tower of St. Olaf's Church appeared in the light and the squadron beat windward[14] closer to the city and dropped anchor again.

14    Bronevskiy's note: 'Beating refers to turning sharply one way and then another [or tacking] in a zig-zag to catch the wind in one's sails when the ship's course runs contrary to the wind's direction.'

## 2

# Reval – 12th [24th] of September

Reval, like Kronstadt, has a harbour and arsenal for the navy. Reval's harbour, by virtue of its poor breakwaters and embankments, offered little protection for the vessels against the northerly winds and could not hold more than 15 ships. Furthermore, as Kronstadt's harbour was noticeably shallower, it was intended to leave older vessels in Reval for commerce and construct a new harbour that could accommodate the entire Baltic Fleet. Two wings of the new embankments were already finished. They cost many millions and their solidity and craftsmanship will stand as a monument to the reign of Alexander I. The uniformly Gothic buildings and the aged architecture of its tall churches, decorated in place of the cross with roosters to represent the rejection of Christ by Saint Peter, gave the old city the appearance of venerable antiquity. The cleanliness of the beautiful homes of the suburbs from the first glance demonstrated the taste of the Germans. Few places can compete with Reval in the beauty of their surroundings; on all sides one can find pictures pleasing to the eye. After the day's exercises, I went ashore in the evening and, as it was Sunday, visited the elegant public garden at Katharinenthal.[1] I met many people out walking along the lengthy, shaded avenue leading to the shore. Further, in the courtyard, I followed the sound of music and entered the summer gallery. The slender, blushing and elegantly dressed wives of the artisans, swirling about in waltzes, seemed to forget the labours of the working day; their husbands, with a filled mug of beer in hand, conversed among themselves or played bowls. This was the way of life and good nature of Reval! Outside the holidays, everyone sat at their work and the city was as quiet as a small village.

---

1   Kadriorg Palace, an estate built in the Petrine Baroque style for Empress Catherine I between 1718 and 1725. Today it is owned by the Art Museum of Estonia. Andreyevskiy et al., *Brockhaus and Efron Dictionary*, s.v. 'Екатеринентальʼ. [Andreyevskiy et al., *Brockhaus and Efron Dictionary*, s.v. 'Katerinenthal.']

A multitude of English transports arrived in the harbour to convey our soldiers to the island of Rügen. The people, looking on the conspicuous soldiers climbing aboard the vessels, crowded in and covered the whole embankment, hearing the bitter sobbing of the women and looking on the courageous men, but the sorrowful faces of the soldiers penetrated every heart with a remorseful compassion. It seemed as if the whole of Russia, at the wave of her monarch's hand, was headed off to curb the ambitions of Napoleon. His spirit was all-destroying, unceasingly contriving new wars, his love was only of himself, having no virtue particular to truly great men, and he trampled over all rights and privileges and neglected the well-being of the people who elected him as their leader, becoming the tyrant of France!

Emperor Napoleon I of France (reigned 1804-1814 and again in 1815). Jacques-Louis David, 1812, oil on canvas, Washington D.C., National Gallery of Art.

Taking on some cargo we lacked in Kronstadt and bringing our crew to its full complement with new men, we set off on our voyage again on the 17th [29th] of September.

# 3

# Sailing the Baltic Sea

The convoy with the landing force which departed with our squadron was barely visible by evening, having passed the Odensholm (Osmussaar) lighthouse, and on the 18th [30th] of September, bypassing the Cape of Dagerort (Kõpu), the westernmost extreme of Russia's territory, we entered the open sea. In our eyes we saw only gloomy clouds, driven by the north wind, and snowy white waves. At midnight when I came on duty, I admired the swift run of the ship bursting through the waves under its bow like a boisterous waterfall. The whistling of the wind was occasionally interrupted by the voice of the lieutenant on watch, whose vigilance was entrusted with both the pace and course of the ship. The sailors were in a state of perfect inactivity: some sat on the rigging telling tales of their past campaigns, others perched at the tops of the masts were chanting out long drawn songs, and some entertained their comrades with amusing jokes and anecdotes. What caused such carelessness? Trust in the knowledge of their commanders and confidence in the ability and durability of their ship.

The invention of shipbuilding is in truth the most important and useful invention created by the human mind. The degree of improvement it has obtained today belongs also to the previous century. By the principles of higher mathematics it was found what kind of shape a ship's draught (the submerged portion) should have: how wide it must be for a ship of a certain size, how far it must be submerged, how much rests above the water, how much cargo it can hold, how many masts, sails and other accoutrements are required, and all the necessary qualities for the fastest, easiest and most reliable sailing. Deep experimentation in this fashion, gradually improving, traced the ideal structure of the ship, whose perfection amazes the most daring imagination. The structure of each seagoing ship is so designed that neither waves nor winds can capsize it, and a brave seaman, separated from death by a single board floating on the sea, is unafraid of either the bottomless depths of the ocean or the turbulent hurricanes and all the fierce and fickle elements. One cannot help but be amazed at the difference in structure and command of our vessels compared to the ancients'. The monstrous galleys of the Romans with three or four tiers of oars, having small, thin and weakly fixed sails, moved only by the hands of the oarsmen, and without a dependable timepiece, being unable to measure their own speed, could hardly stray from the coastline. What a danger such ships were on rough waters! How troubling they were to turn about! On the contrary, today a 100-gun ship of the line twice as large as the galleys of old and taking on many thousands of pounds can sail from the Old World to the New in a few weeks by the hand of the helmsman alone. The rigging on the ship is just as amazing as its hull. Even the smallest rope has its name and is as vital as any link in a chain, whose removal will undo the whole. The height of the mast itself is great and holds many sails so balanced that in a calm wind, by the immensity of its height it could capture the largest area, but when the wind grows stronger, it trims its sails to protect them from harm. Of each of the three great spars, set one on top of another, the upper two being able to rise and fall, the highest is called the royal mast, the middle is the topmast, and together with the lower mast they can have a height of 40 *sazhen* [85.3 m] on a 100-gun ship. Forty sails stretched over 12 yards (cross-beams on the masts), hanging one over the other in perfect balance, always compensate for every direction of the wind and capture such a force over their surfaces that no matter how adverse the conditions, the navigator can bring the ship to his desired port.

The wind blew consistently and our fortune did not falter. We passed Gotland on the 20th of September [2nd of October] and then Öland in the night, and approached Bornholm on the 21st [3rd]. Soon we saw the white shores of Møn mingling with the blue sea, creating a dazzling melange of colours. Rounding the cape of Falsterbo, we could reach Copenhagen in an hour, but suddenly the wind changed and became poor and we were forced to stop at the village of Dragør within 30 *versta*s [32 km] from the capital.

The strong foul wind lasted from the 23rd to the 30th of September [5th to the 12th of October]. Through the tedium of being anchored in bad weather so close to the capital, we tried to liven up our moods with debates and discussions. As the crew on our ships were for the most part recruits, then for their instruction, once the wind abated, the admiral gave a signal and the *Uriil* and *Kildyuin* weighed anchor. The concept of signals, by which the fleet is controlled, deserves special attention. Ten different brightly coloured flags signifying the numbers 0 to 9 conveyed all the orders of the admiral by way of numbered written instructions kept in special books. The upper flag represented the ones-column, the next flag below it represented the tens, and third the hundreds, et cetera. With these flags, all possible commands, news and the like can be transmitted. At night and in thick fog, signals are made by cannon shots and lanterns. Telegraph signals are shown by balls and flags and form a lexicon containing the alphabet as well as numbers and up to three thousand of the most common words. Additionally, there are the so-called identification signals, which are agreed upon to differentiate friendly ships from enemies encountered on the sea. These and secret signals given to admirals and captains are not printed out before they are needed and are state secrets.

# 4

# Copenhagen

---

The harbour of Copenhagen was always filled with ships and the market was packed with merchandise brought there from all the ends of the earth. The Danes managed to profit from their neutrality and knew how to amass wealth while other European nations fell into ruin, and now they were the only rival to the English in trade. Trading companies, in which, like with the Swedish and English, the King himself participated, were a great benefit to them. The merchant ships belonging to the crown were distinguished by the royal cypher emblazoned on their flags. An embankment divided the harbour into two parts: one containing 30 warships and the other 300 merchant vessels. The military harbour, Admiralty and shipyard can serve as an example of taste, order and economy. The magazines were filled with everything required for arming ships, with reserves ready to last several years. The [marshy] forests are not utilized for construction until they are perfectly drained. The platforms on which the ships are constructed are covered with roofs, as are the ships chained to the piles in the water and covered on all sides with canvas to shield them from the sun. It should therefore be no surprise that some Danish ships have served for 50 years or more. This prudent thrift certainly saved the state treasury millions. Each ship is set next to a magazine in which sails, tackle and all its accoutrements are organized and stored so that the craft does not need to travel here and there to be outfitted. The Danish navy almost never sailed the seas and half its sailors were released on leave to serve on merchant vessels, acquiring not only essential knowledge of seamanship but also personal wealth. The other half stayed on, working in the Admiralty, learning how to fire the batteries and pursuing handicrafts in the market on their days off. After a few years, they are replaced by the first half and so, rotating between obligated service and liberal employment, they become experienced and skilful sailors. The arsenal, in which the Admiralty was also located, had a beautiful exterior and was large enough to house the arms of an army 100,000 strong. In one special chamber they displayed antique helmets, coats of plate, maces and shields. Some of the panoplies weighed as much as 4 or 5 *puds* [65.52-81.90 kg]. One heavy sword preserved there bore an inscription in gold on the flat of its blade: 'Peter the Great visited this arsenal in the year 1718'.[1]

The trading house, located behind the Admiralty, draws attention with its huge and Gothic appearance. It had the form of a great hall, always filled with people, where terrible carts drawn by 12 horses are driven in and merchandise of every sort is laid out across countless tables, under tents, in special stores built along the side walls, and hanging overhead, accessible by staircases. The entrance and exit of this building were covered with porticos of stout columns. The long sides were broken by disproportionately high windows in which the panes of glass were round and multi-coloured. The whole roof from corner to corner was lined with dormer windows.

The main street and two squares were decorated with two equestrian statues of the Kings Christian V and Frederick V. The first square was octagonal and with picturesque homes all of equal height constructed along its faces.[2] The private estates of Copenhagen cannot be compared with St. Petersburg; they present a mixture of Gothic and modern architecture but interspersed with a multitude of stores, shops and cellars that prove how Copenhagen produces a much more significant commerce than our capital. The palace and library which had beautified the city unfortunately burned down. The royal museum is revered as among the best in Europe; it is divided into eight halls filled with all sorts of rarities. Mammals, birds, fish, plants, and minerals collected from all the countries of the world filled a rich chamber of natural wonders. Of the artificial specimens, I consider the most noteworthy to be: a human skeleton reproduced in ivory with all the most minute veins and arteries; a model of a ship with masts and sails; watches made of ivory and finished with surprising precision; a marble table with a naturalistic depiction of the crucifixion on it; a wooden goblet containing a hundred others which are carved so thin they bend like paper from the slightest touch; in an ordinary needle case was built a miniature carriage, harnessed by six horses and driven by a coachman, a postilion and a servant, which are so expertly carved that they survive the scrutiny of a microscope; a mechanical orrery which simulated the movements of the celestial spheres according to the model of Copernicus; clothes and weapons from numerous peoples; several Indian and Egyptian idols made from wood, porcelain and ivory; and various writings on papyrus paper. Finally in the picture gallery there was one painting which attracted particular attention: set

---

1    The blade may have been inscribed long after his visit, since Peter I of Russia did not take on the moniker of 'the great' until 1721. *Complete Collection of Laws*, col. 1, vol. 6, pp.444-446. No. 3,840.

2    Amalienborg Square.

in a dark corner, it portrayed an old man in glasses sitting near a table surrounded by his family and reading a book by the light of a candle. The diffusion of the light is so excellent that only Gérard alone could paint the flame to be so uncannily lifelike. Alas, the artist of this painting is unknown. Experts consider the use of shadow and light as an exemplar of representational painting.

# 5

# The Sound

After a long delay, the wind finally shifted and the squadron on all sails was launched by diverging channels into the Sound. This was dangerous enough that although the shores on both sides were indicated by bright red paint and landmarks, all the ships departing took on pilots. The wind was quite lively and we quickly raced past the Danish capital. Its towers and steeples, its harbour swollen with vessels, its coastal fortresses and behind them the terrific buildings of Copenhagen created a beautiful view from the sea. The coast of Sjaelland, which was very close, was dotted with villages and country houses. Gardens, groves and meadows perfectly decorated the landscape. On the other side of the Sound was the coast of Sweden. It seemed more sparsely populated and barren in décor, but its golden fields of grain were richly bearing in their fruit. Within two miles from Helsingør stands a small royal estate with a flat roof.[1] It is said that it was built on the very spot where Hamlet's father lived and near the garden where that unfortunate man was poisoned. No Englishman will pass up the chance to visit it – such is the powerful talent of the glorious Shakespeare! With such charming views, sailing through the Sound was like a pleasant stroll. In this straight, constrained by two resplendent shores, one always met, as on a highway, large caravans of ships of various size and shape. Everyone was moving back and forth: one flew, another ran, a third was barely moving, some rushed along with the wind and currents while others fought against them to slowly advance.

Some travellers tell a tale that the island of Hven, lying in the Sound, drew the attention of Peter the Great and he supposedly offered to purchase it for however many silver rubles as could fit on the island. If that were the case, he was undoubtedly joking, and meant to say that with so many vessels annually passing through the Sound, and with the island secured with a fortress and collecting

---

1    Marienlyst Castle.

duty from them all, such an outlandish purchase would quickly pay for itself. It is currently half-owned by both Sweden and Denmark and barely has a population of 200 or 300 people, whose only boon is trading in prohibited goods.[2]

2    The island of Hven was ceded entirely to Sweden in 1660 by the Treaty of Copenhagen. 'Freden i København, 27. Maj 1660,' *Danmarkshistorien – Aarhus Universitet*, http:// danmarkshistorien.dk/leksikon-og-kilder/vis/materiale/freden-i-koebenhavn-1660/, last modified 25 August, 2011. ['The Treaty of Copenhagen, 27 May 1660,' *Danish History – Aarhus University*, http://danmarkshistorien.dk/leksikon-og-kilder/vis/materiale/freden-i-koebenhavn-1660/, last modified 25 August, 2011.]

# 6

# Helsingør – 30th of September [12th of October]

At four o'clock, the squadron flew through the Sound and stopped at Helsingør. That port was always home to a great gathering of ships from nearly all the countries of the world, for every vessel entering the Baltic and coming back again had to stop there and pay dues. The sea was full of flags and pennants of every colour. The ships were departing ceaselessly and when the sounds of cannon shots and the cheers of the working sailors reach your ears, they had such a charm that you would never want to leave the quarterdeck. The town, sitting on the low shore, appeared through the dense array of masts as if behind a thick forest.

After the typical visitations and congratulations on our arrival, the officers were allowed to go ashore. There was a light rain and the streets were slick but such crowds of foreigners were out and about that we were forced to duck into the first coffee house. When the sun came out, we left that choking tavern and the Gypsies smoking their pipes within and instead of standing about to read the posted newspapers, we went walking. Finding a guide, we ordered him to lead us to the town proper. We only passed a few streets before the whole town was before us! The houses were high and had only three or four windows on their façade, and below them all were shops and businesses. Reaching the gates of Kronborg, a courteous officer of the guard led us into the courtyard of the castle, which stood like a rectangular tower. The church with its Gothic belltower was locked so we went down into the casemates where the criminals were held. They had fresh air, the prisons were clean, the prisoners were busy with work and only murderers were held in chains at night. The walls of the castle were of natural stones hewn into shape, very thick and armed with several cannons. The best of its defences, the naval batteries, were constructed outside the walls. These could harm ships, but a fleet breaking through the strait could not be stopped, especially with a fresh wind in their sails. Lord Nelson in 1801 proved to the Danes that their Sound was not impenetrable.[1]

---

1    When the League of Armed Neutrality threatened to violate Britain's blockade of France

Kronborg. Illustration from the original publication.

The officer of the guard suggested that we visit the royal gardens and ordered one of his soldiers to escort us there. It was a holiday and the streets were full of women's clothing. Men were walking back and forth with measured steps and now removed their hats before us when earlier it was better to bump into us and blow smoke in our faces. Although the leaves had fallen and little greenery remained, the garden was located on a hill near the sea, so it seemed very pleasant to me. From the balcony of the summer home, built on open ground, the view of Helsingør and its surroundings made for a pretty panorama. The noisy Sound separating this image from the formidably steep cliffs of Sweden, in stark contrast, was all the more captiviating to the eyes.

in 1801 during the War of the Second Coalition, the British responded by sending a fleet under Admiral Hyde Parker and Vice-Admiral Horatio Nelson to engage the Danish fleet at Copenhagen and threaten to bombard the city, which ended in an armistice and the dissolution of the league. A. W. Ward, G. W. Prothero and Stanley Leathes (eds.), *Cambridge Modern History*, Vol. 9 (Cambridge: University Press, 1907), pp.42-50.

Since the wind was adverse for sailing to England and the day was beautiful, we boarded a boat with some comrades, crossed the Sound in half an hour and went ashore to Helsingborg. Two streets under a hill, a collapsed windmill on its summit and the tall red roofs of the houses were all that could be seen in that small town. No one bothered us on the road, for we had not met a single person until we reached the centre of town. When we did come across someone, they could not understand us and everyone passed us by smiling while we had no idea where to go. By the portrait of Galen[2] on a shop sign we recognized a pharmacy and entered. Hoisted up to the ceiling was a terrifying stuffed crocodile! What a discovery! In the clean cupboards along with medicine stood confectionery in neatly stacked banks. We quickly purchased some, since one needs a reason to enter a pharmacy. Finally we were shown a tavern bestrewn with sand and tastefully decorated with spruce and we were happy to find there playing billiards some handsome and conspicuous Swedish officers of the Yellow Hussars.[3] They treated us like lords, we became very well acquainted, dined together and departed as friends.

2    Claudius Galenus or Galen of Permagon was a prominent Greek medical researcher, practising surgeon and philosopher of the second century whose treatises contributed to numerous branches of medicine. Andreyevskiy et al., *Brockhaus and Efron Dictionary*, s.v. 'Гален, Клавдий.' [Andreyevskiy et al., *Brockhaus and Efron Dictionary*, s.v. 'Galenus, Claudius.']
3    No such regiment existed at the time, but it is possible Bronevskiy encountered men from the Mörner Hussars, who had yellow mirliton caps, or the Scanian Dragoons, who wore yellow coats with blue lapels. John Elting and Herbert Knötel, *Napoleonic Uniforms*, vol. 4 (Rosemont, Illinois: Emperor's Press, 2000), pp.616-619.; Magnus Olofsson, 'The Swedish Army in the Napoleonic Wars – Regular Army Units in 1805,' *The Napoleon Series*, http://www.napoleon-series.org/military/organization/Sweden/Army/Organization/c_swedisharmy2.html, last modified April 2008.

# 7

# Sailing the North Sea

On the 3rd [15th] of October, the squadron weighed anchor during a calm southeasterly wind. Due to our windward course, during the night we barely managed to pass the peninsula of Kullaberg and the dangerous island of Anholt, which is surrounded by shoals. On the next day the wind turned to the east and became very strong, our ships now able to achieve 22 *verstas* [23.47 km] an hour, and we spanned the whole Kattegat in 14 hours. When the sun began to set, we were passing the gloomy and wild rocks at Lindesnes, the last cape of Norway, and by nightfall the squadron had entered the North Sea. A tempestuous and dark night created a magnificent sight: the ship cut through the waves and heaved up and down with them, beating its course against them and spraying up foam and mist as it did. Along the crests of the waves, the wake and churning rudder spat out streams of lava which wriggled like fiery serpents giving chase to the vessel. The water shined like gold and the ship appeared to float on molten metal. Under the bow where the resistence was the strongest, the waves crushed by the hull of the ship rose up like the typhonic column, towering high and raining fire down onto the deck.[1] The sight was terrible and beautiful all the same. The sea water, containing countless particles of salt, phosphorus and other substances, seemed to flare from the friction against the flanks of the hull and apparations sometimes appear on a dark night when sailing at a fast pace.[2]

---

1   In Greek mythology, the serpent-giant Typhon was imprisoned under a mountain, later conflated with Mount Etna, the 'pillar that held up the sky,' and its volcanic activity was credited to his restless stirring. William Smith, *A New Classical Dictionary of Greek and Roman Biography, Mythology and Geology* (New York: Harper and Brothers, 1871), s.v. 'Arimi'; ibid., s.v. 'Typhon.'
2   Several types of dinoflagellates, single-celled organisms with long whip-like appendances for mobility that can dwell on the surface, are known to briefly emit a blue or green light at night when disturbed as a defence mechanism to confuse predators. Steven Haddock,

The next day, when we were in the middle of the open sea, we pitied the tedious, flinty Norwegian shores. The bare rocks raised the question of what the inhabitants subsisted on. Merciful Providence gave the camel to the Arabs and the reindeer to the Lapps, but for the Norwegians he led herring to their doorstep in such quantities that the desolation of the earth was wholly compensated by the bounty of the ocean. In 1800, I saw a herring fishery in Bergen and another at Kungsbacka[3] in 1804, a curious and charming sight. When the herring entered the bay, the sea shone as brightly as a mirror, changed colour and flashed with fish scales. The heads of sharks, whales and orcas continuously broke through the surface. The northern Atlantic true whales, a kind of small whale, having throats as vast as Iceland, are the worst enemy of the herring. They drive them to the shore with the beating of their tails and the ones they stun with these blows fall into their mouths. Fishing boats drawn up in two lines sail through scooping up fish with buckets and pales, or even with the fishermen's own hands. The fishing is always more successful at night because the fish strive for the lights lit on the shore and on the vessels and massive schools swim into the nets stretched from boat to boat. During a successful catch, one enterprising sailor can secure in a night as much as his family would need for a year. The Dutch, immediately after taking the herring out of the sea, gut them, wash them with salt water, cure them with salt and store them in barrels and probably for that reason, their herring is better than others'. The English, Swedish and our own fishermen of Arkhangelsk wait some time before cleaning them.

The eternal wisdom concerning the preservation of life in all creatures is also observable in the mind of the herring, if that hidden motivation or instinct is what compels them to journey all at once to certain latitudes in order to return to their homeland, the North Pole, where they might live in safety from predators under its ice.[4] Here is the route they take: at the beginning of the year, the army of herring favours the south. In March, they reach Iceland and split into two corps. The first head to Telerife by several detachments and the other turns to Norway and passes the peninsula of Lindesnes to split into two more columns. One heads though the Sound and the other through the Belt to enter the Baltic Sea where they reach the Swedish skerries and turn back to reconverge on the coast of Holland. The

Mark Moline and James Case, 'Bioluminescence in the Sea,' *Annual Review of Marine Science* 2 (2010), pp.443-493.

3    Bronevskiy's note: 'The bay, convenient for ships, lies 30 *versta*s [32 km] to the [south] of Gothenburg.'

4    Atlantic herring migrate between spawning, nursery and feeding grounds, which include shallow bays where fishers can easily trap them but none of which typically lie above the Arctic Circle. 'Atlantic Herring (Clupea Harengus),' *Newfoundland and Labrador Department of Fisheries and Aquaculture*, http://www.fishaq.gov.nl.ca/ research_development/fdp/pdf/herring.pdf, accessed 20 October, 2017.

western army, always prey to predatory fish, pass the Shetland and Orkney Islands, reach the shores of Britain and Ireland, turn into the Engish Channel and detach a column to enter the Atlantic, rarely swimming farther than the Bay of Biscay. Having scattered throughout the whole of the northern seas, they reunite in the North Sea and in the late fall, return to their homeland. Natural scientists seeking the reason for such regular migration patterns in the herring consider the search for worms to feed on, of which the nothern seas are full.

This migration seems to the observer as curious as it is amazing. Ahead of their army is a vanguard and in its main corps is the king who differs in size and can extend as long as an *arshin* [71.12 cm].[5] This king governs all the movements and typically in the sea the herring swim in a line formation but when they have to pass through a strait, they ploy into a column. If someone happens to catch the king, they throw him back into the water, believing that his leadership is essential to their prosperous catches and the most predatory fish are likewise believed to spare him for that reason. The herring, as the eloquent Comte de Buffon said, executes his manoeuvres without the least confusion. On their campaigns, no one ever leaves his place, no one deserts and no stragglers fall behind; they continue on their route without stop or delay and always return to their home at the determined time.

On the 5th and 6th [17th and 18th] of October, the wind regained its former strength and the sea became a field of snowy hills. The ships all achieved an equal speed and we had no delays waiting for the rear. The most autumnal nights followed: shrouded, cold and rainy. The clouds raced overhead, flashing occasional glimpses of the moon. The darkness, hiding objects, seemed to embolden the wind which howled terribly in the rigging. The ship was rolling side to side like a light boat and when the wind blew from the stern, the ship began to pitch in a most distressing fashion which was harmful to the hull. In this fashion, our voyage was only so pleasant and fair.

On the 7th [19th] of October, the wind abated somewhat and we passed an English squadron anchored in the middle of the sea on the Dogger Bank. This bank smoothly and proporitonately rises in the middle such that when you reach it, you can determine your place on the map by sounding the depth with a lot (a leaden weight) and graduated line. On the 8th [20th], the clouds cleared and the sea calmed down. The day became beautiful and flocks of seagulls were already passing overhead, which indicated our proximity to shore. Soon a sailor on watch shouted 'land ho!' Everyone with a telescope rushed to look for themselves. One

---

5    The 'king of herrings,' oarfish or streamer fish belongs to a wholly different taxonomic order than the herring and has no real influence on the latter's migration patterns. They can reach lengths in excess of 10 metres. William Richards (ed.), *Early Stages of Atlantic Fishes*, vol. 1 (New York: CRC Press, 2005), p.1009.; Culum Brown, Kevin Laland and Jens Krause (eds.), *Fish Cognition and Behavior* (Oxford: Blackwell Publishing, 2006), p.282.

Dover. Illustration from the original publication.

needs to be at sea to fully understand the joy of land's first appearance. The transition from the drab view of the sea to a blossoming greenery is incomparable. With greedy anticipation one jumps at the slightest shades to be the revelation of an object and one's elation wells up as the objects grow, sprouting out of the sea on the horizon, little by little disrupting the boring monotony of the sky and the water. Soon these hints and glimpses split into a plethora of places and things that move, materialize and unveil to the eye such a challenge that it cannot bring anything but tremendous happiness. We first saw the North Foreland lighthouse.[6]

On one side stood England and on the other was France, whose two lands are as opposed as the rivalry between their peoples. The white rocky shores of Albion are elevated a little and covered in greenery. All the visible spaces were divided by commons, meadows, groves and dotted with towns, villages and beautiful small

6   Bronevskiy's note: 'It should be noted that the English pilots at night point mirrors toward
    the lighthouse so that not only the fire but also all the surrounding objects on the horizon
    can be very clearly seen at distances of 25 *versta*s [26.67 km].'

houses. Dover's harbour was filled with ships and beyond it to the north stood a large military fleet in the Downs. The opposing Calais lies sadly on a sandy spit on a barren waste where you cannot see any trees, meadows or even a single ship or fishing boat in the harbour. A beautiful night and a favourable wind took us through the English Channel. On the 9th [21st] of October, at dawn, the squadron reached Portsmouth.

# 8

# Portsmouth – October

As soon as the squadron dropped anchor, a dinghy from a 100-gun ship which flew the flag of Admiral Sir George Montagu, commander-in-chief of Portsmouth, hailed the *Yaroslav* to congratulate us on our arrival and confer the details of a salute, in which the British flag demanded an advantage over all other colours in the port. For some time however they became lenient with Russian admirals and now after 15 shots from our guns, they replied with an equal number. We hardly managed to remove the sails when a crowd of curious people already came aboard the ship: stout, finely dressed merchants swaying on the flanks of small skiffs came selling fresh greens, bread, cream and fruit. One of the visitors admired the Russian construction of the ship and the cheerful sight of the crew. Another invited us to his tavern which he called the best in the town. One merchant bowing elegantly before us offered a handbill which gave instructions for finding his shop and listed goods for sale with their prices. A theatre manager invited us to pay a visit to his production and promised to light the boxes magnificently in honour of the Russian officers. Finally a hundred beautiful and strikingly dressed women came wishing to come aboard and see the Russian seamen, but we could not admit them and were forced to refuse a visit which would have been a great pleasure for us.[1] One boat with water[2] and another with meat and vegitables soon reached the squadron and the attention of the British government was so accomodating that we acquired everything we needed without ever leaving the ship.

---

1   Bronevskiy's note: 'According to the Naval Regulations, only wives were allowed to visit their husbands and then only before the striking of the tattoo [at sunset] in their port.' *Книга Устав Морской*, 6th ed. (St. Petersburg: Императорская Академия Наук, 1780), p.20. [*Book of the Naval Regulations*, 6th ed. (St. Petersburg: Imperial Academy of Sciences, 1780), p.20.]
2   Bronevskiy's note: 'The water is dumped into the hold plated with lead [for a ballast] and, with the aid of pumps, can be quickly and easily poured into barrels for storage.'

## Spithead

Spithead is the name given to the large roadstead which lies between the town of Portsmouth and the Isle of Wight. It can comfortably fit up to 5,000 ships. As the main assembly area for military and mercantile ships, the harbour behind becomes impossible to see when so many souls converge there from every corner of the globe. There was a squadron or two there at all times tasked with patrolling the channel. Transports from the East and West Indies arrived there to obtain convoys and be cleared of quanrantine. I could not count the number of ships that stood in the water, their masts so close together they nearly touched, and likened the spit to a large inhabited city in which everything was in motion without pause. The Solent Strait lies on the northern side of the Isle of Wight and the ebb and flow of the tide every six hours allows ships to come and go at all times, which is of the greatest advantage to a military port. Its depth is from 5 to 15 *sazhen*s [10.67-32.0 m] and is exposed to southerly winds.

## A Glance at the Town

Cloudy, rainy weather, fog and thick plumes of smoke covered the town. The stench of coal wafted out to us. On the third day when the weather cleared, with great impatience, I boarded a boat with three comrades and went ashore in town. Having just put a foot on land, I had my first reception and first incident – a drunken red-headed sailor requested that we let one of our rowers fight him with fists. The embroidery on our uniforms seemed to draw attention from the mob.[3] The crowds running up before us surrounded us endlessly and compelled us to force our way through them onto the wider street. Crossing the pavement and wandering about not knowing where, we were met on a parade square by many handsome youths with bags and books in their hands. They came running and jumping before us shouting: 'Russian *dobra!* Russian *dobra!*'[4] A spendid greeting, but since this was the only word the English could say in Russian, it sometimes took on the opposite meaning. Behind them came little English women in bonnets and straw hats and with baskets in hand, scarcely few blushing as we passed them. A guilded sign offering services to Russian officers caught our attention and stopped us. We stepped onto the porch and into a spacious entryway. Several boys ran up, some to clean our boots and others to brush our uniforms, and for

---

3    Russian officers of the sailing fleets wore a golden embroidered anchor with fouled rope on both sides of the collar and three smaller foul anchors on each sleeve cuff underneath its buttons. *Complete Collection of Laws*, col. 1, vol. 44, part 2, appendix 'Decrees on Uniforms', p.77. No. 20,743.

4    A corruption of the Russian 'добрый – *dobryy*' meaning 'good, fine, kind.'

such a service they asked for a shilling. Taking a hold of the door handle, we heard a bell ring and on the very threshold stood a handsome man in shoes and silken stalkings, combed and sprinkled with perfume and seemingly wearing two watches or perhaps only two chains. He bowed courteously. We would have been at a loss for what to make of this dandy if his taciturn, deferential and anxious face did not betray his profession as a tavern servant. He bowed again and showed us to a room with newspapers scattered over the tables, windowsills and everywhere else. The occupants in hats were deep in their reading. No one paid any mind at our entrance though the host bowed silently to them. A merry noise on the other side of the building drew us into a room where we found officers from almost the entirety of our squadron. It is not necessary to comment about the cleanliness and good order of English taverns and inns, but it should be noted that in them at every step one needs to take out his wallet, which no matter how heavy it was soon became light. At six, they served dinner and the host himself, a polite and trustworthy old man, waited on us and with each dish asked 'was it good? Did you enjoy it?' His agility was amazing: he alone served 30 men and never lost pace with us. We spent the night there and in the morning, breakfast and fresh gazettes were served with tea. Journals and broadsheets are elemental for the Englishman, as necessary as air. They engage in political debates all morning long and even their women know geography so firmly that they can show on a map the site of any battle and trace the movements of the armies.

A foreigner who comes to England for the first time will be amazed by its liveliness, industriousness and cleanliness. From morning to evening, you will see everyone about their work; you will see an energy in the city which is rarely found anywhere else, everyone rushing to their places by wide strides that seem to stimulate their thoughts. Here you will not be crushed by a galloping carriage and even the ladies are not ashamed to travel on foot and this safety on the road generally improves health. The façades of the homes, the pavements and walkways were all surprisingly pristine by continuous sweeping and washing. The houses had such clear windows that the glass almost appeared to be absent from the frame and though few are plastered over, their neatly formed and laid bricks were no poor sight. Some homes were built from wood but cannot be distinguished from the stone ones and their lime-washed exteriors are covered in crushed flintstones which, when doused with water in the mornings, shine like precious gems in the sun. Red or lacquiered wooden doors surmounting staircases make up the entrance to every home. The lower floors were occupied by endless rows of the finest shops with their goods spread out behind large pane windows so skillfully that one is involuntarily drawn in and compelled to make a purchase. Entering a fabric store, the merchant handed me a book of sample swatches and prices withour saying a word. We made a choice and paid silently, and when you asked what you wanted sewn and how long it would be finished, the answer was: 'frock – 2 o'clock,' and rest assured everything will be ready when you come back at the appointed time.

## The Admiralty

Portsmouth is considered the best fortification in England and consists of three sections or quarters: Portsmouth, Portsea, and Southsea Castle. The mouth of the river, serving as a harbour, was protected by the round fortress of Monckton. In Portsea, lying near Portsmouth and on the same side of the island, was the Admiralty, which is perhaps the best and most extensive admiralty in the world. The harbour and docks are always occupied by ships being built or repaired, terribly large buildings are filled with every necessity of the fleet and alive with a masterful and uninterrupted industry. I will not speak of the beautiful buildings, whose sturdiness and convenience is obvious, nor will I mention the countless reserves of every variety, which filled the arsenals and magazines. I need not expound on the strength and beauty of the vessels, which as everyone knows are perfect, but I will note here that it seemed they did not know how to do anything wrongly – every craftsman was a master in his field. A simple carpenter can work a piece of wood to be laid onto the deck of a ship with just a compass, ruler and protractor. It seems excessive. Our carpenter having no other tool but his axe finishes his work sooner than three Englishmen and even if it is not as elegant, it fits just as squarely. Where we use sheer manpower, here they utilize machines, fire, water and horses. The clatter and thunder of wheels and the hissing and crackling of fire and steam, in continuous movement, replace several hundred workers, improve the product and shorten its required time. It cannot be described all the myriad mechanisms whose design might surprise even the most learned mechanics. I will speak of one of the workshops where, with the help of eight men and four boys, 600 pulley blocks can be produced in a day. The Frenchman who invented the machinery was awarded fairly generously: he is entitled to two pence (4 kopecks) for every block produced until the day he dies.[5] How can one calculate how many thousands of blocks will be manufactured per day in all of Britain and how many thousands of rubles he should receive in his life? With this method, the government's servant

---

5    Marc Isambard Brunel is credited with devising and installing at partial personal expense the block-making machinery at Portsmouth Block Mills in 1803, which became one of the first truly mechanized manufactories in the United Kingdom. The Admiralty Board did not pay Brunel on a regular basis and the estimation of expenses was complicated by fluctuating prices over several years and the Navy's growing requirements. After several other unprofitable endeavours, he accrued debts severe enough to be imprisoned in 1821. Richard Beamish, *Memoir of the Life of Sir Marc Isambard Brunel* (London: Longman, Green, Longman and Roberts, 1862), pp.55-170.

has achieved the perfection of all production! The spirit of the English people is to seek wealth and to multiply abudance and surplus; and the government, nourishing this zeal, rewards the generous diligence of not only its own citizens but even foreign innovators. The French have an advantage in the mechanical arts – their lively imaginations enable that – but complex machinery in which geometric accuracy is required cannot be achieved anywhere except England, as the French without the patience of the English do not achieve perfection in such works which require constant diligence.

From the Admiralty, we crossed by skiff to the town of Gosport. In the middle of the river sat old disarmed ships with entangled anchors. Some poor Frenchmen peeked out of the windows while others danced on the upper deck. 'Is that a fine way to keep prisoners?' I asked the pilot. He said it was the very same way their men were kept in France. This fact was very distressing. And a Frenchman could answer my question with: 'just as in England.' Whom can one believe? It is only known that the British Government sends princely sums to France for the care of their countrymen taken as prisoners of war and Bonaparte does not waste a penny of it.

## The Hospital

Having observed in Gosport the Haslar Naval Hospital, the nearby botanical garden and the anatomical theatre, everyone should agree that in England they spare no expense on their humanitarian institutions. The building has a simple exterior, while its interior is comfortable and peaceful. Entering the long halls, you breathe in air as clean as in the gardens. The curtains and windows, linens, dishes, furniture, all neat and in good order, will not let you notice that you are in fact in a hospital. In one room the wounded are placed in beds with cranks which enable the patient to be moved without touching their wounded arm or leg. In the ward for the greviously wounded I examined everything with particular satisfaction and tarried there longer than in the others. The beds are placed a few paces apart from one another. In front of each is a table of medicines and on a blackboard hanging at the head of the bed is the date when the patient was admitted. The patients have the consolation of being surrounded by their relatives on their deathbed and their last breath will move a sensitive heart. Look at what gentle emotion shimmers in the eyes of this girl as she helps a weak old man to drink! Look at the tenderness of this woman's prayer and into her friend's heart she pours a balm of comfort! Two doctors sit at a table, always ready to give care – what a mercy! Nurses go about the sick and wounded administering medicines and food with such care and cleanliness. In front of the façade in a vast courtyard flows a fountain from which, via pipes, water is carried into the kitchen and throughout all the chambers. With pleasure we can say that the care and hygiene in our hospitals are not the least inferior to the English ones. The hospital for junior officers formerly in Kronstadt can serve as a model.[6]

## A Women's Club

One foul evening, while sitting around the tea table beside a roaring fireplace, James, the tavern serveant, announced the director of an aristocratic women's club. The young, rosy ward of the ladies, making several excessively deep bows according to the etiquette of dance, invited us to a ball to be held that evening. How could one refuse such an offer? Honouring the gentleman director in Russian and granting him with a very pleasing response, we then worried over how to bring our clothing from the ship. The darkness and strong winds prevented sending a boat across. The punctual James saved us from our anxiety: in an hour, for several guineas, several tailors and perruquiers provided everyone with everything they needed. Carriages were provided and we all arrived at the club and entered the hall together as a party. During a thundering march, the director, with a flattened tricorne under his arm, received us at the entrance. The hall was barren in decoration save for its clean white walls and several lamps which brightly lit its length. At the opposite end from the doors sat the ladies on chairs arranged in rows, all dressed in dazzlingly white dresses, while the gentlemen stood behind in the distance. The director introduced us to some of those seated in the front row and we were immediately seated between the girls – I say girls because I never heard anyone addressed as 'lady,' everyone was a 'miss' and all were in the full bloom of youth. These customs were wholly new for Russians! Here the girls are provided with full freedom and the women, the mothers of these families, on the contrary sit at home and very rarely appear in these large gatherings. Presently serving officers were dressed in tailcoats, because as I was told, in such societies the name of a citizen is preferred to his military rank. A boy in a top hat and a girl in a short dress, as beautiful as two Cupids, opened the ball with a minuet and a jig, and in the latter this girl with the most courageous movements kept her delicacy and decency. Then began the sophisticated quadrilles in twelve pairs from which we abstained, but the ladies wished to see us dance and volunteered to teach us a little something English. One girl invited me to be her partner all evening and this special indulgence was only with the Russians. Each of us had our special lady.

---

6    English travellers such as John Howard, the philanthropist and prison-reformer, indeed remarked on the quality of the Kronstadt naval hospital and other facilities like it in St. Petersburg proper, Moscow, and most of the provincial capitals, but their poor proliferation across the vast Russian Empire meant that their impact on public health was narrow. William Tooke, *View on the Russian Empire During the Reign of Catherine the Second*, vol. 2 (London: Longman and Reese, 1799), pp.164-251.

After the quadrilles came écossaises, in which the slimness of the waists would present for painters and sculptors the most inspiring models and muses. In a short time we learned that those who could speak English were surrounded by ladies. Those who knew other languages could also hold an audience, but their language was certainly preferred to foreign ones, especially French. Among themselves, everyone spoke English. That language which was prior so poor and rude to the ear became soft and gentle from the mouths of women, and the Englishman always tries to explain himself firstly in his native tongue as best he can, otherwise he might sound ridiculous here in a women's club and to be ridiculous here of all places would be most unfortunate. A few Russian words memorized by the enterprising girls caused a commotion in the group; one would teach another how to pronounce it, they would laugh, and then trip over their tongues in trying to say it, multiplyng their collective amusement.

At midnight, the ladies disappeared and we remained with the gentlemen who proceeded to torture us with politics and current events. What were the ladies doing? Changing gowns, stockings, shoes and gloves. Half an hour later, the door opened and the ladies brought in tables and tableware, three or four together hauled in a gigantic samovar along with as much tea and snacks as the assembly could need. We rushed to help but were forbidden. In a moment, the hall was furnished with tables and filled with ladies busily worrying over the preparation of tea. When they sat down in their chairs, from behind each table came one girl who each took at first all of the Englishmen before splitting us up individually and treating us just like family. After that pleasant supper, the écossaises continued until dawn. At the behest of the members of the club, we were given tickets inviting us to future meetings. That ball provided the warmest acquaintances for some of our officers.

## The Outskirts of Portsmouth

Intending to take a stroll and choosing a clear October day, we took three postal carriages and two riding horses and set out. I was mounted on one of the latter, but as a bad rider, I soon feel behind my comrades. Having left the city and fallen behind the carriages, I rode at a slow walk along the beautiful, smooth and flat road. Both sides were densely planted with rose and blackberry bushes. The lanes through the plain were lined with wire fences so that no traveller could cut through the fields. Diligent labour could be seen at every step, for not an inch of the land had gone unworked. Every cottage had a drainage ditch dug and trimmed back trees. The farmer's house here was an exemplar of comfort, good taste and purity. Everything was finely arranged, rich in abundance and contentment and nowhere could I see signs of poverty. A peasant could be seen labouring on a handsome horse while his hearty cattle and sheep grazed in the meadows. I could not find a flaw in anything that I saw.

After two miles [3.22 km, assuming English miles], I was stopped at a boom gate. A legless invalid manning the post, upon learning I was a Russian, did not want to extract the toll equivalent of a few kopecks for road maintenance from me. On the fourth mile, the horse stopped on its own reflexively at the postal station. Unconcerned by who I was or what I was riding, a new mount was brought out to me and three postmen offered me their hands. Each briefly and firmly announced his demand: the first offered the horse, the second cleaned the saddle and the third brushed my hat. The fiery steed which he did not dare keep quickly brought me to another station, and there I learned carriages did not pass and having separated from my friends, I had to return to the town without any amusement, riding back and forth nearly 16 miles [25.75 km]. Descending from the saddle where I was unaccustomed, tired and especially hungry, I entered a road kitchen and asked for a quickly prepared capon. The hostess refused because it had been prepared according to the order of another gentleman who was soon to arrive. A servant intervened in our dispute and agreed to stick another bird on a spit to roast and serve to me. As soon as I sat down at a table, a carriage rolled up to the entrance. The hostess came running to take away my roast and the servant, holding her arms, tried to stop her. Meanwhile, an elderly man in a uniform entered the room and, finding the source of the disturbance and discovering that I was a Russian foreigner (as the innkeeper called me), reassured that he would be more pleased if she awarded me his entire meal. Then, turning to me, he asked if I would dine with him. I hardly had time to thank him for his generosity and courtesy before a young girl in a straw hat ran into the room. 'This is my daughter,' said the colonel, 'Betsy.' Turning to her he said: 'I present to you a Russian officer. He will be dining with us. Go and see if you can get us something better here and two bottles of a good wine.' At the table, the colonel opened up on current events and in frank terms extolled the selflessness of our Emperor, which pleased me greatly; all the more so because the English do not give compliments easily. He drove me to the village where luckily I found my friends, who were beginning to worry about me and would have sent someone to search for me after returning to town.

## The Isle of Wight

Although October was nearly over, the weather was clear and fairly warm. Wishing to take advantage of our free time from duty, eight of us agreed to travel to the Isle of Wight and visit the major town on the island, Newport, which is 21 *versta*s [22.4 km] from the Spithead. In order to gain more time, we crossed to the village of Cowes early in the morning, from which our ships were not far. The owner of a coffee house, on making our acquaintance, took it upon himself to arrange for carriages and served us tea in the meantime. A shepherd's horn called me to the balcony to see the fields where every hostess and girl, accompanied by a dog, drove out the cattle. The breed of these shepherding dogs deserves attention: it is known that in England all predatory beasts have been extinguished, especially in places where livestock are most populously bred and kept, and these dogs are so clever and well accustomed to cattle that in almost all cases they can replace their human masters as shepherds. Leaving Cowes, we climbed a small mountain and the Isle of Wight unveiled a gorgeous panorama before our eyes! All visible space was filled by long rows of green hills covered with groves and gardens and separated by meadows on which grazed large herds of every kind of livestock. Passing further, we met new, ever more captivating views with each step. Alternations between meadows and tilled fields, orchards and gardens, noble manors and manufactories, and clean farmhouses scattered in the shade of trees, create such a work of art that Wight seemed to be rightfully called 'the garden of England.' Even the fruitless places here are decorated with more green than what Nature herself chose to bestow. A tasteful and diligent labour worthy of praise could be appreciated everywhere one looked. A swamp, a sandy field, a small brook or a rocky hill, although at a great cost, can bring some benefit. The convenience and tidiness of the farmers' cottages is so surprising that only those who have been to England and been amongst them can agree that the English peasants live noble lives. Passing one grove, we saw a simple ploughman sitting under the shade of a bush while his wife poured him tea. A tall, fat horse nibbled on the grass beside its plough. When we approached the man, he offered us rum, tea and cheese without moving from his place. The King of France, Henry IV, wished that the poorest of his peasants had at least a chicken in their pot every Sunday. If the good sovereign believed that was the extent of the well-being of his people, then the Russians have achieved it and the English enjoy an excess. Is not our good *gorelka*[7] the same as rum? Cheese, tea and various seasonings weaken one's strength which only simple foods can restore, and if it is undisputed that the English are the richest people in Europe, then they have passed into decadence by exceeding their needs.

On the outskirts of the town, on the small river of Medina which flows into the narrow bay, floated flocks of many domesticated birds and their sight convinced us that there was hardly enough space to supply all the ships moored on the Spithead. Newport is not very large, consisting of several straight streets crisscrossed with very level and smooth paving. The peaceful major and captain of the local militia honoured us with their company for dinner. The owner of the inn first took us downstairs, but when he was ordered to prepare a good meal, we were transferred

---

7    Or 'horilka' – a synonym of 'vodka' used in southern Russia, Belarus and Ukraine.

to the best accommodations where he himself appeared with a diamond ring on his hand and his hair made up. The table and all its fixings beyond all expectations asked for only a small fee. After the meal, we called on the leaders of the town who, on account of the fact it was Sunday, suggested we take a walk out of town and visit the castle of Carisbrooke, 4 or 5 *verstas* [4.27-5.33 km] from Newport. Various wagons and carriages harnessed to stately horses and driven by beautiful women rolled along the smooth road to the garden which lies at the foot of the hill on which the castle stands. Down two boulevards and through the alleys we walked and, forgoing a vehicle, continued on foot up to the castle.

A curving, distressing, narrow road carved into the stone of the hill led to the gate, through which we came to a courtyard overgrown with grass and littered with piles of stones marking the places of fallen buildings. Seeing the household of the invalid belonging to the castle's garrison, whose task was to open and close the gates with the passing of visitors, and having seen the former structures and the disrepair of the curtain walls, I confess I regretted the exertion of climbing to such a height. But the invalid there, an old infantry sergeant, began to tell me about the memorabilia of Carisbrooke. He told us that the oak gates stood for 800 years and you can see how they are still strong – such oaks grew then in England! Those ruins served as a refuge for Charles I, who was later executed by Cromwell, and in the surviving chapel there, his daughter Princess Elizabeth was buried. The learned invalid then showed us a well which had a depth of 170 *sazhens* [362.71 m]. At first this seems incredible but the well is excavated from atop a hill which took us half an hour to ascend and judging by the sound of dropped stones, which took 36 seconds to reach our ears, the depth must be true. The well water was so clean and clear that when a lamp was lowered in, at a depth of 2 *sazhens* [4.27 m] even the stones on the floor were visible.

Leaving the castle through a collapsed portion of the tower, we descended straight down the slope and did not arrive too late to pass through all the curving alleys of the garden, which were filled with pedestrians. Musicians were playing in the gazebo; children as adorable as Cupids jumped and skipped around the trees; a family sat on blankets and drank tea; another party in a circle drank a porter ale; others played bowls; but most of them, folding their hands behind their backs, pulled their hats over their eyes and walked with rapid paces from alley to alley without paying anyone their mind. The damp, cold evening air compelled us to leave this charming, simple garden. Returning to the town, we hurried back to Cowes and, though it was late, we managed to board the ship on the same day.

## Thoughts and Remarks

In the character of the Englishman, in their very appearance, there is something special which belongs to them. Their love of country and everything in it produces in the English a notorious arrogance. In neatness, craftsmanship and wealth, they exceed all other Europeans. The common people call foreigners by a common name: 'French dog'; only Russians alone are exempt from this pejorative, for they call us 'Russian *dobra*,' which is to say that the Russian is a good man. Our sailors get along with the English in an amazing fashion, seeming to be made for each other. When they meet for the first time in their lives, they shake hands and if one has a penny in his pocket, they head to a tavern, drink zealously, erupt into a fist fight and then depart as the dearest of friends. There is nothing more amusing than listening to their speech, which is a twisted patois of Russian and English half-words that is clear to one sailor but unintelligible to another. Often they will both speak together, one in English and the other in Russian, without stopping and for several hours discuss a wealth of important subjects. Through intelligible words that are not found in any language, the sailors communicate their thoughts to every foreigner and are understood much better than, for example, their officers. All foreign names, nautical terms and names for equipment on ships are transformed by our sailors by conflating them with similar words, such as the corvette *Pomona* becoming *Pomora*;[8] the *Melpomena* became *Little Pomora*;[9] the *Amfitrida* became the *Afrosinya*,[10] and so on.

Since the time of Queen Elizabeth, England began to enjoy the benefits of trade and demonstrated a special ability in this new field. A passion for accumulating wealth, the spirit of commerce, gradually increased and was confirmed liberally. When all the governments of Europe wished to possess colonies in other parts of the world in order to enrich their fatherlands with gold, the English showed the greatest activity. In a few years, their merchant vessels grew significantly in number, their military vessels could be seen on every sea, the richest French, Spanish and Dutch settlements had been conquered and in our time Britain gained a domination at sea which raised her people to the highest degree of prosperity. The division of crafts, with the constant care of the government, brought every art and product to a state of perfection. The King himself, being a participant and patron of the trading societies, encouraged the affluent nobility to entrust them with their capital, which in turn enjoyed such entrepreneurial revolutions that their profits were guaranteed and their losses were inconsequential. Buying commodities from such people whose handicrafts were still in their infancy and processing them in their factories, they could, by a concession in price, make

---

8   Помора or Поморы – *Pomory*. A term that literally means 'by the sea' to refer the sailors and settlers of the White Sea coast and the rivers that empty into it throughout north-western Russia.

9   Малая Помора – *Malaya Pomora*.

10  From the Greek Euphrosyne. This particular Greek name is better known to the enlisted men than the others because it passed into Russian as a woman's name.

English goods a necessity in Europe. Presently, 20,000 vessels transport goods to all the countries of the world and the benefits of recent years have increased so quickly so that in 1783, the export of their own and foreign-made products was worth 14,741,000 pounds sterling, and in 1802 it reached 57,520,000 pounds.[11] By these means, especially their entrepreneurship, honesty and diligence, England sees all treasure float into her harbours, and as long as elegance, durability, taste and purity belong exclusively to British products, then the gold of all trading nations will be in the hands of these international merchants.

Tacitus, describing a constitution similar to the English one, wrote that the theory is beautiful but its application is nearly impossible.[12] Experience has proven that he was mistaken; their free monarchy has existed for roughly 500 years. Liberty, subject to the law, constitutes the lasting prosperity of their subjects. The British King is truly a god on earth! He grants mercy and rewards; has the full power to do good; and with one law he punishes criminals and halts abuses of power. Trial by jury is the chief advantage and unshakable bastion of liberty for the British people. These jurors are independent of the influence of ministers and subject to no authority. The offender is regarded as an innocent man until the twelve jurors can unanimously agree on his guilt. Then only the King can forgive him and yet still, not always.

In England, as a free land, during peace there stands only a small army. Naval power however, as necessary for the colonies and the most favourable to liberty, is maintained in the finest order. In the beginning of the year 1800, the British navy consisted of 224 ships of the line, 200 frigates, 478 sloops, brigs and other small military vessels – 902 craft in total. With such a force, when all the maritime powers cannot even send half of this number, Britain can undoubtedly be said to rule the waves. The inhabitants of this island, avoiding participation in wars on terra firma, are kept completely safe from an invasion by their powerful enemy by the protection of these floating fortresses, despite being separated from the French by only a narrow strait.

---

11   The figure of 57.52 million comes from a parliamentary speech made by Chancellor of the Exchequer (aka. Prime Minister) Henry Addington on 10th [22th] June, 1802 and was a calculation for the previous year of 1801. William Guthrie, *A New Geographical, Historical and Commercial Grammar*, 21st ed. (London: Hamilton, Weybridge and Surry, 1808), p.159.
12   In the fourth book of his *Annals*, Tacitus asserted that all states are ruled wholly by either a democracy, an aristocracy, or a tyranny of one man. Further he asserts that a hypothetical model government which balances the interests of all three is unfeasible and doomed to collapse. The legislature of the United Kingdom however, consisting of the House of Commons, the House of Lords and the Crown, resembles that disparaged model of three estates. Alfred Church and William Jackson (eds.), *Annals of Tacitus* (London: Macmillan and Co., 1876), p.128.

The British government expends great sums for the poor. Experience shows that the size of this sum has increased as much as the number of poor. Although the English beggar is poorly dressed, he is always clean. Cleanliness is an inherent property of the English people. The English beggar would be ashamed to appear in the street in dirty rags, for he is convinced that a tidier appearance will garner more sympathy from the pedestrians.

Free printing and the fine organizations of public schools have expanded education in every category. Everyone but the lowest of the rabble has learned to read and write. The enlightenment and all the luxuries it brings have deeply taken root and have already quite changed the customs of the Englishman. It seems that they have ascended to the final degree possible in human institution. Having opened the book of the history of kingdoms, we will see that universal enlightenment is a precursor of the fall. The sailor, soldier and day labourer, if criticizing the government, interpreting politics and law for themselves and acting in accordance with their own will, can cause great disturbances. No matter how glorious the constitution of England may be, and no matter how much the citizens prosper, sooner or later a fatal blow will befall them. 'None shall escape the fall, and with new heights shall they fall further. Eternal alone is God, who alone made the world. To the works of the hands of the omniscient Creator and to the soul do we turn our thoughts in supremely high ascendance'.[13]

## Celebrations for the Victory at Trafalgar

On the 25th of October [6th of November], news of the Battle of Trafalgar reached Portsmouth. I should try in vain to describe the joy of victory and the sadness of the loss of Nelson! Even those who had occasion to see the rapture of the English can only imagine their inner feelings. From the earliest morning, pages[14] were brought along the streets describing the battle and the death of Nelson; everyone's

---

13   This may be a paraphrasing of St. Nilus of Sinai's 'On the Eight Evil Spirits', specifically the description of avarice or worldly possessions in general weighting down the believers in their ascent toward God and causing them to stumble. Нил Синайский, 'О Восьми Духах Зла', *Добротолюбие*, 2nd ed., vol. 2 (Moscow: Типо-Литография И. Ефимова, 1895), pp.238-249. [Nilus of Sinai, 'On the Eight Evil Spirits', *Philokalia*, 2nd ed., vol. 2 (Moscow: Type and Lithographic Press of I. Yefimov, 1895), pp.238-249.]

14   Bronevskiy's note: 'I came from the Admiralty once and saw a woman handing out leaflets and shouting: "a glorious victory by the Russians over the French". I approached her, took one and asked: "how must do I owe you?" She asked for a guinea. Why so expensive! She said a Russian can pay for a victory which brings him such honour (referring to Krems, fought on the 30th of October [11th November], 1805). I replied: "If one pays a guinea for each, he will need a hefty wallet for keeping up with all the victory announcements". The woman thought that that was a perfect answer and handed me several leaflets, saying they should fetch 2 guineas but would let me have them for 4 pence. The same day, our

face wore a mixture of grief and triumph and everywhere exclamations were heard: 'long live Nelson!' Firing from ships and fortresses lasted all day and the city was illuminated magnificently at night. The finer houses were decorated with transparent paintings in their windows. One depicted Nelson in the moment a bullet struck his chest and he collapsed into the arms of his comrades. Another showed the mournful personification of Britain accepting the laurels of victory. The streets were full of crowds at night; the garrison was standing at arms, and the regimental musicians were playing the national song 'Rule, Britannia!' Should we not agree that a glorious death in battle is better than to remain alive, having gained such an important victory, for it affords the greatest envy and honours and all petty doubts are put to rest by the complete and unqualified glory of the deceased victor!

The Battle of Trafalgar is one of the most glorious ever fought at sea. On the 2nd of October [14th October], a combined French and Spanish fleet consisting of 33 ships of the line, under the command of Admiral Pierre Villeneuve, left Cadiz and sailed into the Mediterranean. Vice-Admiral Horatio Nelson with 27 ships of the line, making use of a weak wind from the west, overtook the enemy fleet near Cape Trafalgar. Forming two columns and leaving behind a reserve, Nelson attacked the centre of the combined fleet with the wind on his side, cut through it and surrounded both halves with a superiority of force, and before the enemy's rear guard could rush to their aid, their whole fleet was in disarray. The Franco-Spanish vanguard, having attacked the British reserve, was also defeated. At four o'clock, the battle ended in the complete defeat of the combined fleet, of which 19 ships struck their colours and were captured. The Spanish admiral, Don Federico Gravina, returned to Cadiz with only nine ships. Five French ships which had been in the reserve and nearly did not participate in the battle were captured by Rear-Admiral Strachan.[15] This decisive victory destroyed the last naval powers of France and Spain. Britain suffered a major loss however: its navy lost its beloved, brave and merry leader. This hero was always triumphant in all his 104 naval battles and his last victory attained for his fatherland an unlimited command of all the seas of the world. The fatal bullet fired from a musketoon aboard the *Santísima Trinidad*[16]

---

conversation was published in the Portsmouth gazettes. Such was the passion for news in that country!'

15    Sir Richard Strachan was only a captain when he fought the Battle of Ortegal on the 23rd of October [4th November] and was promoted to rear-admiral of the blue as a result of his victory. He only fought and captured four ships, not five: the *Formidable*, *Scipion*, *Duguay-Trouin* and *Mont Blanc*. 'The Monthly Register for November 1805,' *The Scots Magazine and Edinburgh Literary Miscellany* 67 (1805): pp.873-874.

16    Bronevskiy's note: 'A 140-gun Spanish ship of the line, [largest in the world at the time,] on which flew the flag of Admiral Gravina.' Translator's note: Its full name was *Nuestra Señora*

pierced the epaulette, shoulder and chest of the illustrious Nelson. He lived for only a few hours. When they carried him below deck to treat him, and when the doctors could not hide the severity of his wounds, he called for his flag captain. The battle was still raging around them.

Entering into the cabin, the captain said: 'congratulations, Your Excellency! 19 ships have been taken and the *Trinidad* has been sunk.'[17]

'My friend,' Nelson replied, 'I have always wished to fall in battle and now I will die peacefully. Ask Collingwood (the next senior in command) to drop anchor for the night. Here are my last orders… I regret that I could not do more for my country!' In the arms of his friend he soon gave his last breath. And so died the hero who in the cruel moment of death did not lose his presence of mind and saved the victorious British fleet in the final moments of his life; for as he had foreseen, a storm arose in the night which sank or crashed ashore all the captured ships that were not anchored in time.

The British do justice to the bravery of the Spanish. They fought bitterly and resisted much longer than their enemies expected. Napoleon for a long time could not believe that his fleet ceased to exist. The sad truth assured him finally that for the sake of his honour, several thousand Frenchmen died terribly. In this battle, several mistakes were made, the most important of which was explained to me by an English officer as follows: the allied [Franco-Spanish] fleet could have attacked the British with the wind on the same day they left Cadiz, the latter having then only 25 ships to bear. The combined fleet closed its line so well that if they opened fire on Gravina's instruction, they would not have let the British columns close and the battle would not have turned decisively so soon, yet Villeneuve ordered to open fire when Nelson's ships were already within range of grape and canister. The first salvo was terrible and the advance ships, the *Victory* and *Royal Sovereign*, were dismasted but they had already sailed close enough to effectively join the battle. The British reserve began to fire at the French vanguard opposite, only reaching them with solid shot, and as a result, the French van was already half defeated before reaching the British line. The main mistake was that the fleet was entrusted to Villeneuve and not to Gravina. The French admiral may have been brave, but he was not as skilful as his revered Spanish comrade and did not command the confidence of his own or the Spanish officers and sailors. The English themselves admit that the courageous and experienced Gravina could compete with the valiant and fortuitous Nelson. Under his leadership, the allied fleet at least would not have been completely broken by 4 o'clock.

de la Santísima Trinidad (*Our Mother of the Most Holy Trinity*); this was not Gravina's flagship, nor was it the ship from which was fired the shot that killed Nelson.

17    The *Santísima Trinidad* was captured and not sunk during the battle, but was scuttled the next day. 'The Monthly Register for November 1805,' *The Scots Magazine* 67: pp.869-871.

# 9

# Saint Helen's Road

The brigs *Feniks* and *Argus* purchased in London, the first having 16 carronades and the second with 12, sailed to the roadstead at the same time locks[1] were fitted to the guns and provisions were taken on. The squadron left Portsmouth on the 16th [28th] of November but when they circled the Isle of Wight at nightfall, there blew such a cruel wind from the southwest and the sky became so dark with clouds that at dawn, the Admiral was forced to return and anchor at the southern tip of Wight on St. Helen's Road. Three days later, the frigate *Kildyuin* arrived there and the ships *Selafail* and *Uriil* separated from the squadron on the first night and remained at sea. Powerful, terrible winds continued throughout the remaining days of that month, at the end of which the admiral sent the *Kildyuin* to Plymouth to inquire whether the separated ships had taken shelter there.

On the 3rd [15th] of December, with a fresh north-easterly wind, the squadron set out. As we departed, the 12 most damaged vessels from the Battle of Trafalgar were heading onto the anchorage. The magnificent 100-gun ship *Victory* was carrying the body of Lord Nelson. The flags and pennants at half-mast, splintered masts with small sails, and hulls pierced with shot aroused our curiosity and instilled a deep sense of respect for that fearless hero of England. Our admiral's ship saluted them with 15 shots and the *Victory* replied with equal number. A swarm of skiffs and boats set out from Portsmouth to meet the victorious fleet and a cannonade erupted; the Spithead was blanketed in a thick smoke while our squadron rounded Wight and flew under full sails along the shores of Hampshire. The next day, as we approached Plymouth, the frigate *Kildyuin* reunited with

---

1    Bronevskiy's note: 'Gun locks have the advantage of allowing a cannoneer, watching the movement of the ship and pulling the trigger's cord at the right moment, to ensure an accurate shot on a distant target; but in battle at close ranges however, the hammers are inconvenient because shattered flints cannot be changed quickly. Even still, the pan primed with powder can still be set off with a linstock.'

us and told the vice-admiral that the separated vessels set out into the ocean without stopping anywhere else, for which reason we continued along the shores of Devonshire and Cornwall. Aligning ourselves with Lizard's Point, we sent out pilots and confirmed the ship's location on the map by bearing, then arranged the ships in a sailing order and set out into the open ocean.

# 10

# Sailing the Atlantic Ocean

The ships ran on all sails with a fresh *voor de wind*, that is, the most favourable wind blowing directly astern. As we strayed farther from the shore, the wind grew stronger, the waters grew choppy and the grey foam of the waves covered the whole surface of the ocean. The charming coast of England gradually sank into the abyss and already the rolling ridges of water were as high as its green hills, until they were overtaken and we became orphans in the midst of that vast ocean, surrounded by nothing but the gloom of the sky and the rustling waves. The setting of the sun preceded the worst of the weather: black clouds raced after us from the north and a light misty rain began to fall. Nature's dark appearance did not frighten me, but poured sadness into my heart. The swift transition from pleasantries to danger filled the imagination with depressing thoughts and when the English coast vanished, all joyous fancies evaporated like a dream. I looked out at the terrible portent of the storm and the heavens sinking lower and lower until the horizon shrank into a tight circle.

The rain forced me into the wardroom, which represented a living space where the company of our willing family gathered. Some of the men were playing a game of Boston, chess or lotto, while others sang as best they could as a quartet, others still were reading and a few were preparing tea. Lighting a pipe and sitting in a chair by the fireplace, I admired the scarlet flame, which flared up and then died down, grew again and withered again… Finally the calm faces and pleasant preoccupations of my comrades dispelled my boredom. But it is not so easy for someone who is seeing the sea for the first time: the horrible sight, at that time, is felt all the stronger, and he involuntarily sinks into despair as his imagination is painted over in dark and opaque films which spread before him with every step.

Despite the dull and rather cold weather which covered the 3rd, 4th and 5th [15th-17th] of December, the officers did not retire from the quarterdeck all day and delighted in the view of our hasty journey. Our ships sailed at 18 *verstas* [19.2 km] per hour. Despite the rough waves and the strong winds on the open ocean, everyone was calm and quiet. One commanding voice from the lieutenant on watch repeated from time to time to adjust the sails and keep the ship under control, protecting her from the rapid deviations in course which might subject us to danger or even disaster. The duty of the lieutenant on a ship is the most important. The captain manages and assigns tasks regarding safe navigation, but the execution of his orders falls to the lieutenant and moreover, he is responsible for protecting the ship from sudden, often instantaneous events during which even the slightest lapse in judgement can lead to inevitable misfortunes. I loved to watch how my experienced watch officer, standing on the ratlines or on the bow, quickly glancing around at everything ahead, behind, above and below, with his booming voice would rouse everyone into motion and without a moment's hesitation prevented every danger, of which he no longer had any fear. Naval service was a natural school for military men, for it nurtured that spirit of adventurousness and courage that one needed in battle. The naval officer who is prompt and prudent in managing the ship during a storm or disaster will assuredly not cower from being the first to enter an assault. Experienced sailors, overcoming every peril and horror in the course of their service and spending the longest and greatest part of their lives *in the jaws of death*, so to speak, take on a dour, gloomy and silent countenance which one can use to identify them, dear reader! If you happen to come across a Russian seaman with this appearance, pay him justly your attention and be sure that he is a brave and courageous man, who perhaps more than once has saved the lives of thousands of your compatriots.

On the night of the 5th and 6th [17th and 18th] of December, the British frigate *Pegasus*, approached the *Moskva* and informed us all that the French squadron at Rochefort, consisting of 7 ships and several frigates, had left port and was tasked with preventing our passage into the Mediterranean, and that they were dispatched by Admiral Lord William Cornwallis to warn us and ascertain the location of that enemy squadron. Shortly after noon on the 6th, several masts belonging to the enemy ships rose up on the horizon. Although from our side we did not have a proper declaration of war on France, and the army had fought in Austria under the designation of auxiliaries, naturally the French admiral possessing such a powerful force would not miss the opportunity to attack us. The *Yaroslav* hoisted the signal to set all possible sails and our squadron turned toward Ferrol, which was being blockaded by a British force. The enemy, 11 vessels strong, moved to intercept our course, hoping to prevent our unification with the British. They drew close and it seemed impossible to avoid a battle, but the artful direction of our admiral deceived the enemy and the coming darkness of night concealed our movements so that we slipped out of their grasp. During sunset the following signals were raised: 1) douse the lights; 2) at 8 o'clock, change course without signals due west; 3) at midnight, turn to a southern course; 4) prepare for battle. At daybreak, we could no longer see the French. Since we met the French on the day of Saint Nicholas the Wonderworker, our sailors were eager to fight. When the batteries were ready and everyone had taken up their places, then in order to keep the men occupied, they were told to sing and dance, and then were given something to drink for encouragement, toasted to the health of the Sovereign with an extra cup of wine. The navigation students, youths and barbers – that is to say, the literate people – formed a stage out of flags and performed the opera *The Miller* which was fairly entertaining for its audience.[1] After the theatrical performance, a horn and tambourines led numerous choirs of soldiers, sailors and artillerists vying for supremacy over one another. Everyone was singing and dancing without a care for the nearby threat. In the wardroom, after a full dinner which would have satisfied a stout Muscovite vintner, the officers danced until dawn, despite the slight swaying of the vessel.

The favourable wind was strong enough that by the 7th [19th] of December, we had already passed Finisterre, that cape where Julius Caesar erected a column to mark land's end, which still stands to this day.[2] As we sailed south, we found warmer weather, the sky cleared above us and the wind began to die down, becoming completely silent by the heights of Lisbon. A new swell came from the west and cleared away the previous waves to produce a restless, irregular oscillation that swayed and surged our ships about in all directions and left us with little control. Waves rose and fell to crown our vessels and let us peer deep into the abyss. The creaking of the masts, the snapping of ship components and the endless flapping of the sails and rigging created an indescribable din. My head was spinning, and many men were nauseous. Sea sickness is so excruciating that men suffering from it cannot eat or drink, nor can any medicine assuage them. Men both strong and weak were equally susceptible to it without distinction. Habitual sailing weakens the effects of the illness and some never feel it at all, while others with even the slightest wave will never be free from it. The fate of these latter sorry people is worth a comment: a strong fever grows throughout the body, and then under the scorching rays of the sun, the stricken sailor begins to shiver as if from cold, the mouth becomes parched, they feel incessantly nauseous, their skin turns

---

1    *The Miller who was a Sorcerer, Cheater and Matchmaker* was a popular comedic opera which premiered in 1779 in Moscow. Its libretto was written by Aleksandr Onisimovich Ablesimov, while its score was written by Mikhail Matveyevich Sokolovskiy and Yevtigney Ipatyevich Fomin. Анатолий Соловцов, *Книга о Русской Опере* (Moscow: Молодая Гвардия, 1960), pp.32-33. [Anatoliy Solovtsov, *Book of Russian Opera* (Moscow: Young Guard, 1960), pp.32-33.]

2    The great Roman edifice on the Galician coast is the Tower of Hercules lighthouse, erected in the 2nd century AD during the reign of Emperor Trajan rather than Julius Caesar, and it lies beside La Coruña rather than on the Cape of Finisterre. Richard Ford, *A Handbook for Travellers in Spain and Readers at Home*, vol.2 (London: John Murray, 1845), pp.651-653.

yellow and the sufferer weakens until they are nearly coldblooded.[3] Sadness and hope are felt in equal measure, and the past and future become irrelevant in his present anguish. In this extreme situation, the sick must be fed black bread soaked in vinegar or kvas[4] and lemons to suck; for this is the only food they can stomach without terrible upset. Fresh air, warm clothes and gentle movements for some or perfect stillness for others also alleviate the illness. Once the rocking stops however, the illness passes without any lasting harm to their health. It should also be noted that pregnant women and children never get motion sickness.

On the 8th and 9th [20th and 21st] of December during a weak wind, strong waves and fog, we were in a most precarious position but during the afternoon of the 10th [22nd], the fog lifted and the waves subsided, and a fresh wind carried us to the Strait of Gibraltar. The warmth, to which we were unaccustomed in December, and the soft, pleasant breezes soon brought an end to our previous anxieties. A new spectacle surrounded us: flocks of seagulls and all sorts of marine birds swirled through the air; orcas and dolphins frolicked around our ships; polyps, jellyfish, nettles and turtles slowly glided over the shifting surface of the water; the very sea seemed animated and all its inhabitants came out to enjoy the fresh air. On the 11th [23rd] by evening, we finally saw land: the Cape of Saint Vincent. Establishing our place on the map from that landmark, we found a noticeable divergence from our assumed course, due to the strong currents, which could not be measured amidst the heavy waves, but the sea became calm again when we neared the Strait of Gibraltar on the 13th [25th].

Being in view of a port one eagerly wishes to enter and yet being unable to move is a dilemma that only occurs at sea. Our impatience was akin to the thirst of Tantalus.[5] Finally on the 14th [26th] of December, the wind picked up and the squadron entered the strait to anchor off the coast of Gibraltar, where we found the *Selafail* and the *Uriil*. Our voyage over the ocean was merry and rushed, for despite three windless days where we could scarce traverse a mile, the distance we managed to cover in ten days spanned nearly 3,500 *verstas* [3733.8 km] in a straight line.[6]

---

3    It sounds as though Bronevskiy is conflating motion sickness with other illnesses like yellow fever or malaria.

4    A thick alcoholic beverage made by fermenting bread, sometimes with the addition of fruits or honey. *Kvas* was a staple of traditional cuisines across Eastern Europe and is still popular in Russia today. Andreyevskiy et al., *Brockhaus and Efron Dictionary*, s.v. 'Квас.' [Andreyevskiy et al., *Brockhaus and Efron Dictionary*, s.v. '*Kvas*.']

5    In Greek myth, Tantalus was fated to an eternal afterlife in which he would stand in a pool of water which receded whenever he tried to cup a drink with his hand and under a branch of fruit which hung just high enough that he could not grasp it. Smith, *A New Classical Dictionary*, s.v. 'Tantalus.'

6    A straight line from Lizard's Point in Cornwall to the harbour of Gibraltar is closer to 1,540 km.

# 11

# Gibraltar

---

Seeing nothing for several days but sky and water, we looked with relish at those Pillars of Hercules which signified the end of the ancient world. The towering rocky cliff of Gibraltar seemed poised to fall onto my ship and was the first to demand our attention as soon as we saw it, like all great and powerful landmarks. At the summit of its nigh heavenly altitude could be seen a semaphore telegraph with a small house beside it, flickering in view behind the passing clouds. To its north sloped the green coast of Andalusia along the narrow sandy isthmus which barely compared with the great granite bulk of the Rock of Gibraltar. The vast bay is roughly 30 *verstas* [32 km] in circumference from the fortifications to the west, curving in a semi-circle and open at the south toward the African coast. On the banks of this bay one can see many villages, forts and towns; one could trace a straight line as if by a shot of the cannon from Gibraltar through the Spanish forts of San Felipe and San Roque behind it. Directly across from them lies Algeciras, in whose harbour floated several French corsairs and Spanish gunboats that attacked convoys when the straits were quiet, even from the furthest edges. Gibraltar withdrew her merchant vessels at night. To the north, in the distance, one can see the blue mountains of Andalusia and to the south lies the coast of Africa, adorned as well with huge mountains. Abila, the tallest of them, constituted the second pillar of the Herculean gate. The Spanish fort lying on the Berber shore, Ceuta, was Gibraltar's counterpart, so to speak.

A few narrow, crooked streets make up the small town and a thick wall runs along the south, west and north and encloses it so that it is obscured from both the sea and the Spanish fortresses. The houses were nearly built to the English tastes and make a perfect contrast with the old Spanish architecture, whose flat roofs and four-sided towers called mirandas[1] or miradors are more appropriate both

---

1    Bronevskiy's note: 'Miranda in Spanish means to "marvel" or "be astonished"'.

in the dreary wilderness and in the great heat of this climate than the merry and handsome English homes. For two days we wandered the heights, climbing up to the clouds, descending into the chasms and clambering back out along its steep slopes. The unassailability of Gibraltar is obvious from first sight, and on a closer examination that impression is only strengthened. Imagine a granite mountain whose northern and eastern faces are completely vertical, while its western and southern faces are slightly more sloped but still steep. The sea at the foot of the mountain is strewn on both sides with submerged rocks, and the waves that form about them produce breakers, warning ships of the danger under keel. The New Mole[2] is the only place where troops can be landed, as the whole western side is covered with batteries.

The fortifications on the northern side deserve attention. A few paces from the cliff there was built a straight earthwork with a ditch and a ravelin which spans the whole isthmus and is only interrupted at some distance from the glacis by a canal with water locks which allows the Spanish to flood the whole ground before their line in the event of a siege. From here, up a staircase hewn deeply into the steep mountain, climbing to a height of 200 *sazhen*s [426.72 m], we entered through a doorway into glorious galleries cut into the womb of the rock. Each casemate housed a 48- or 24-pound [21.77 or 10.89 kg] gun and could accommodate 30 soldiers. The walls are roughly 4 *sazhen*s [8.53 m] thick. The embrasures cut into them provided both light and air circulation. Behind the casemate, carved even deeper into the mountain is a powder magazine and a chamber for storing all the ammunition allotted to the gun. Walking around several of the chambers, I thought that we would have to descend down the old, dangerous staircase, but instead we were led up and entered a second gallery similar to the first. After it was examined, we had to ascend three more times, following the light passing through the small windows carved in the side of the mountain. After spending some time inside the rock, at an altitude of 300 or 400 *sazhen*s [640.02 or 853.44 m][3] and passed through all the galleries and stairwells, we exhausted the great mass of the height and came to a point from which the town, harbour and Spanish line all appeared as if laid out in a diagram. At that terrible height on the precipice, from which one cannot look down without a sinking heart, heavy guns were laid and mortars behind them. From the Mediterranean side, at the corner of the cliff, nature formed a sort of rounded column named the Devil's Tower. It is not possible to calculate how much capital, labour and time those galleries costed;

---

2    Bronevskiy's note: 'A stone embankment serving to protect the ships in harbour from the wind'.
3    The Rock of Gibraltar's highest point is only 426 metres above sea level. *The World Fact Book: 2010 Edition* (Washington D.C.: Potomac Books, 2010), s.v. 'Gibraltar.'

neither solid shot nor shells could do any harm against their garrison and it is impossible to imagine undermining and collapsing more than a *versta* [1.07 km] of stone. Gibraltar is the only fortress in the world where 5,000 soldiers, should they have the necessary reserves, could oppose 100,000 in a siege. After resting on a mortar platform, we descended along the slope of the mountain into the town lying on the eastern side.

Departing from the town through the southern gate, our guide showed us a wall built on the edge of a deep ravine which stretches from the mountain top to the town's ditch. If an enemy captured the New Mole, this wall, defended by just one musket, could stop his advance, and this side of the town and galleries cannot be attacked due to the pits, crevices and steep slopes. To our surprise, we saw by the town several trees, vineyards and other greenery, yet until now we had not seen a single blade of grass. We asked our guide how these plants survived. The Scotsman told us that the soil had been brought over from the opposite coast, pointing to Africa.

On the next day, having agreed to observe the rest of the Rock of Gibraltar, we began to climb up the spiralling road. Up to a certain altitude one can ride a horse or in a light wagon, but beyond that the road becomes more treacherous. Fatigued, we rested halfway up to the slope in an artificial hollow carved in the face where benches had been set down. Continuing just a little up the road, our guide stopped us to show us the Cave of Saint Michael. After taking a few steps down, we entered a vault with the proportions of a great looming hall, which was adorned by the skilful hand of Nature with a marvellous splendour. The black arch was reinforced by supports of every size and type, some of which were an *arshin* [71.12 cm] in diameter. The walls, where light entered through the opening of the cave, shone with crystals in formations resembling men, birds and quadrupeds. Heavy stones like icicles hung down from the ceilings and crept along the walls. The water tricking through the pores of the earth and falling ceaselessly from the vaults, drop by drop, deposited sediments and formed clear and cloudy white stalactites. These stones, gradually increasing in thickness and length, formed crooked pillars and wondrous images and for centuries they will probably continue to grow until they fill the whole cave. The guide assured us that the cave ran so deep that no one had yet descended to the very bottom. My comrades wished to descend as far as possible but, with neither rope nor a torch, they did not dare go any farther. This cave lies 185 *sazhens* [394.72 m] above sea level. Besides these stalactites, Gibraltar has brought lovers of rarities other items no less important. In 1788, while blasting the northern rock for the construction of the galleries, fossilized animal bones were discovered. Some were delivered to a British museum undamaged. How did these skeletons fall into the belly of a rocky mountain? This question gave rise to various debates and hypotheses between scholars, which seem to be humbled by the recognition of the universal deluge.

From the cave to the summit, there was no real footpath; one clambered over rocks excessively steep which crumble under foot and it was so difficult to progress that we frequently rested. Finally, not far from the top, we saw a gate on which was written the English: 'Passage from the Ocean to the Mediterranean Sea' in large letters. We emerged through an arch cut into the mountain and saw the Mediterranean right under our feet. Waves swirled around the base of the mountain, attacking the rocks and rebounding as foam and spray, but their crashing was scarcely like the rustling of the wind when it reached our ears. Imagine yourself at that terrible height, hanging just above the water, and it will make you dizzy and want to hurry back with us. Under the arch on the walls were written many names in every language, some had been worn off and others were hard to parse. I saw too the French rhyme: *'les noms des fous se trouvent partout'* – the names of fools can be found everywhere. The guide told us to descend back to the cave and then from there climb out to reach the telegraph.

Wishing to reach it more directly, the three of us separated from the group and climbed first to the very top of the mountain where the majestic spectacle rewarded our considerable exertion. Not only Gibraltar and all its fortifications, the shores of Andalusia and Granada with all their towns and forts and not only Alpujarras and the snowy mountains of Africa holding up the clouds, but the whole strait and a considerable portion of the Atlantic and Mediterranean were all in view, laid out like the glistening brushstrokes of a great panoramic painting. The clear rays of the sun gilded its various subjects below. It seemed impossible for even the most skilled artist to exactly depict such a multitude of picturesque places exactly as they appeared from there. As we made our way to the semaphore along the mountain ridge, we came to such a deep and steep ravine that we were forced to abandon that road and descend directly to the New Mole. In that ravine we saw several monkeys – it is not clear what they eat to survive in that place. Sloes and fragrant dry grasses grow upon the mountain in places. At the governor's garden, we again reunited with the rest of our comrades and retired together to the ship exhausted.

Gibraltar was previously named Mons Calpe; then the Saracens built a fortress on the mountain and named it Jabal Tariq or Tariq's Mountain after one of their generals, and from that the present name of Gibraltar emerged. This fortress was alternatively controlled by the Spanish and the Moors, until it was finally seized from the former by a combined English and Dutch fleet commanded by George Rooke in 1704, not by force but by accident. The Prince of Hesse-Darmstadt, landing troops on the isthmus, was assured that the attack was not possible from the northern side. The fleet fired 15,000 shots but did not inflict the slightest harm on the fortifications. The only way to force the castle to surrender was by starvation, but the English effected a much sooner conclusion. A party of sailors, having drunk an extra share of their grog, approached the New Mole on two or three boats and daringly went ashore to attack the small number of Spanish residing there. The fleet then immediately dispatched all its men, and since the fortress had no wall on that side, it was overrun and forced to surrender. In 1713 with the Treaties of Utrecht, Gibraltar formally passed over into the possession of Great Britain. The Spanish made several attempts to reclaim it. The last siege was by a combined force of Spain and France from both land and sea and made famous the name of General George Augustus Eliott, who, with a small garrison, repelled the besiegers and inflicted terrible losses on them. The Prince of Nassau, being then a lieutenant-general in the Spanish Army,[4] built newly devised floating batteries but they were sunk and 300 large guns fell to the British. Gibraltar, lying on the road from Britain to Malta, serves as the main assembly of their merchant and military fleets, defends the Levantine trade and observes Cadiz and Cartagena, where the Spanish squadrons are held in blockade.

4    Karl Heinrich (Carlos Enrique) von Nassau-Siegen held the rank of colonel during the siege of Gibraltar and was afterward promoted to lieutenant-general as a reward for his brave conduct. Narciso Oliva (ed.), *Diccionario Historico o Biografia Universal*, vol 9 (Barcelona: Antonio y Francisco Oliva, 1833), s.v. 'Nassau-Siegen, Carlos Enrique Nicolás Oton, principe de.' [Narciso Oliva (ed.), *Historical Dictionary of Universal Biography*, vol 9 (Barcelona: Antonio and Francisco Oliva, 1833), s.v. 'Nassau-Siegen Carlos Enrique Nicolás Oton, prince of.']

# 12

# Sailing the Mediterranean Sea

On the 17th [29th] of December, the whole squadron weighed anchor except for the brig *Argus* which remained at St. Vincent. Despite a calm wind, the ocean's current flowing into the sea helped our progress and we sailed at 10 *versta*s [10.67 km] per hour. The Strait of Gibraltar has two currents. Closer to the African coast the water tends to flow from the ocean in, while along Europe it spills out. The ocean's current in the middle of the strait is so strong that, with poor wind, ships can actually be carried backward. The ocean water enters far and preserves its darker colour before mixing in with the Mediterranean, for which the latter is known to many as 'the white sea.' For a hundred *versta*s [106.68 km], the western current acts with almost the same force. Easterly and westerly winds blow the most often in the strait, because of the high narrow banks which reflect and hone in the oceanic and sea winds, compelling them to follow the directions of the strait, whereas on the open water no such obstacles exist.

The 18th [30th] of December was a beautiful day, like the kind we have in May, decorated by an even more pleasant sail by the shore. With each hour, new objects approached, passed and disappeared. Far off on the very edge of the horizon a distant shore showed itself as a thin blue line and in a few minutes time it transformed until after an hour it appeared as tall as a mountain. Calm sailing in good weather by the coast is more pleasant and quiet than a journey over land. Standing on the deck, you span a tremendous distance without fatigue and you are surrounded by a charming society; and unlike riding in a carriage where your arms and legs are shackled in a confined position with dust flying up your nose, in your mouth and in your eyes which barely lets you look out the window at the passing views, onboard a ship you have the clear and clean sea air and all the space you might need.

On the 19th [31st] of December, the rising sun gilded the bright azure of the sky, and not one cloud tarnished its clear vault. A light breeze scarcely disturbed the sea and soon a perfect silence fell. A silent sea for the simple traveller is peaceful, but for the navigator it is a frustrating setback in the accomplishment of his goals. For three days by the small and bare stone of Alborán we were tormented by an agonizing and restless expectation of the wind, hoping by some luck that it would blow from any direction, at any speed. Every cloud, every mottled spot in the sky, seemed to us to portend a coming wind, but our hopes were in vain – the mirror surface of the sea was motionlessly smooth. After target-shooting with muskets and exercising the cannon crews, the men passed the time with singing, handicrafts and fishing. The cabin boys[1] barely had to cast their lines fully before hauling up two or three fish at once, however when they left the lures floating on the water, they caught seagulls instead. Flocks of these birds hovered in circles above the ships, taking pieces of bread that we threw out or fighting for a fish caught, squawking and screeching in the water and then suddenly fluttering into the air. Since the day was very hot, the men were allowed to swim, for which they lowered dinghies, and for those who could not swim they stretched out sails on ropes at the side of the ship, on which they could bathe just like in a tub.

Leaving the fatherland in the autumn, in a few days we moved to southern England where the beauty of the landscape still lasted, and when it began to rain and fog over and all the green life of nature withered there, in stormy December we fled to the hot climate of [southern] Europe. There we were reunited with the most beautiful summer again. The whole earth was draped with greenery, everything around us bloomed and the air rustled with thousands of insects. Without seeing snow, frosts, or any cold signs of winter, should not a Russian sailor be charmed completely? Should not the freshness of the air and its extraordinary warmth be striking for a people accustomed to living in the harsh north? The beautiful day was followed by an even more beautiful night, but these nights could become rather cold and even with condensing dew, that could be harmful to one's health. The rapid transition from hot to cold produces chills and scurvy, but acting in accordance with instructions given to us for the preservation of the men's health, our crews were not subject to these diseases.[2] The hold[3] of the ship, being the most contaminated with stagnant air, was ventilated regularly. The decks were daily fumigated with vinegar and gunpowder. The hygiene and neatness of both the ship

---

1    Bronevskiy's note: 'Juvenile sailors.'
2    It was a prolific belief in the 18th century that scurvy was a result of climate, yet was treatable with fresh fruits and vegetables. It is now understood that the disease is caused by a deficiency of Vitamin C (ascorbic acid), which is a matter of diet exclusively. The British Navy had already recognized the utility of citrus juices in combating scurvy as early as 1796. Kenneth Carpenter, *The History of Scurvy and Vitamin C* (Cambridge: Cambridge University Press, 1988), pp.54-96.
3    Bronevskiy's note: 'A large cellar at the bottom of the ship where the ballast, wooden boards, barrels of water and other supplies were laid.'

and the crew were monitored with the fullest accuracy. Most of all, the men were observed to prevent passing in the open air with uncovered heads and sleeping in wet clothes. Lack of fresh water, spoiled meat and other poor provisions can sometimes be more lethal to the men than strenuous and unceasing labour and disturbances. The water stored in barrels in the hold, especially during hot months, begins to spoil on the fourth day and soon develops a stink. Dripstones and filtering machines cannot prepare enough water for 800 men each day. All other methods and contrivances for producing fresh water onboard a ship are found to be impractical and not fulfilling their required outputs, therefore a lack of fresh water is the primary inconvenience to life aboard. With the frequent changing of water and acquisition of fresh supplies however, we do not lack anything essential. By the extreme diligence of our commander-in-chief[4] in the safeguarding of the men throughout the duration of the campaign, not one of our ships suffered from those diseases that stem from rotten food that rage like bloody war among sailors.

After the windless still, a quiet easterly wind came in on the night of the 20th of December [1st of January, 1806] by the Cape of Gata near Almeria and we met with a British flotilla of 15 ships under the command of Vice-Admiral Cuthbert Collingwood, which we were told was heading to the West Indies to search for France's Brest squadron, with which travelled Jerome Bonaparte, brother to Napoleon.[5] At Cartagena, this fleet had trapped and blockaded eight ships, three of which were 100-gun ships of the line. Taking all precautions and preparing for a battle, we passed Cartagena with a fresh and fair wind and approached Sardinia on the 27th [8th of January], until finally beating through a strong northerly wind to anchor at Cagliari on the 29th [10th of January].

4    Vice-Admiral Senyavin
5    Future King of Westphalia (1807-1813). In early 1806, he was the captain of the 74-gun ship *Vétéran* in the squadron of Vice-Admiral Jean-Baptiste Willaumez. 'Historical Affairs,' *The Scots Magazine* 68 (1806): pp.795-796.

# 13

# Cagliari

---

The poor capital of the King of Sardinia lies on a steep hill surrounded by two rings of stone walls and many depressions, salt lakes and swamps. At the bottom of this town is a small harbour. Tall mountains which dot the whole island stand a certain distance away. To the north, a long dam separates a large lake from the anchorage. The Gulf of Cagliari, which has a current flowing from south to north, is uncomfortable in the winter because of the brutal gusts from the north which exposes ships to violent crossing forces, as there is no cover from the sea. Mooring on one anchor dropped to the northeast and another to the northwest becomes necessary. A good muddy floor and a depth from 4 to 18 *sazhen*s [8.53-38.4 m] make for a safe anchorage at other times of the year.

Our large ships were hardly noticed in the city. A few dirty boats of the kind they use to sail to their villages, filled with musicians and beggars, came to our vessels and both asked for payments in exchange for their congratulations on our safe arrival and for the labours they underwent to reach us and appease us with their clownish shouting and ridiculous antics. Bare foot, unkempt and never-washed hair, dressed in soiled rags; the whole appearance of these Sardinians garnered sympathy. We endured a three-day quarantine, during which we went ashore and were then strongly prohibited from communicating with the anchored vessels. However, all of our necessities were delivered to us by boats. The low cost of fruits surprised us: for ten oranges we paid just one kopeck and for two *pud*s [32.76 kg] of almonds, only a thaler.

When the quarantine ended, everyone hurriedly rushed ashore. Stepping on to the pier, the crowd of people removed their red caps respectfully and followed behind us. Wherever we turned, the mob greeted us with a bow. We asked in Italian where the best inn was, and a multitude of voices which had before only whispered now all shouted together 'here is the best!' pointing with both arms outstretched at a house standing opposite. We stepped into a dark room and found a full game of billiards set up but no one was there. We entered a second dwelling and its host, wearing a greasy apron, looked astonished and tore off his cap.

'What can I do for you?' he asked hurriedly. 'Please sit down. I assure you mine is the finest tavern in town and we have many foreigners stay here – all of them satisfied'.

Ordering a meal, we went into town to walk and a few peddlers approached us asking if we would like to buy anything. 'We want to see the town before us', one of us said.

'As you command, Your Excellency!' which was their common address for foreigners. Immediately one of those advanced ahead of us in great theatrical strides though the others followed behind us at a respectful distance.

Excellently built houses with flat roofs surrounded by lattices set with vases of flowers make for a striking contrast with the filth of the streets. At first glance over this Italian town, laziness, negligence and their friend poverty were represented everywhere. At every step we were met by beggars barely covered in torn pieces of linen. They surrounded us and constantly pestered us for alms, assuring us that they had not eaten for days. With a disgusted look, they pointed to the sky and said that it was their only shelter and that nothing protected them from the severity of the weather. The clarity of the air and the fertility of the soil here never brought prosperity to these people. The industrious Norwegian does better for himself in a barren land than the lazy Italian in a country flourishing with all the gifts of nature. The lower rows of homes are occupied by the shops of craftsmen. There was a tailor, a cutter, a carpenter, a smith and a cooper all sitting at their work with open windows and doors. The Italian enjoys seeing other people and being in the open air unceasingly, even at the expense of the cleanliness of his home. From the narrow alleys separating one house from another a foul smell emanates: dirty walls, crumbling plaster, red blemishes on the windows and stairs, puddles that pour down from the upper tiers, dead cats and dogs rotting in the streets; altogether so much infects the air that we had to cover our noses with handkerchiefs and hastened to ascend the hill in the hopes of escaping the miasma. Up the steps carved into the hillside, we entered a fortress located at the top of the hill which was still located inside the town. Here, we were shown a deep well which provided fresh water for the whole municipality. The well is inside a building vaulted with such thick ceilings and walls that it seemed impossible to pierce with a bomb. The fortress walls which faced out to the open country were not in good condition, while the bastions facing the sea were armed with heavy artillery. Cagliari lies on a height surrounded by defending neighbourhoods however, and can therefore resist a siege for a long time.

We entered a cathedral and were surprised at the magnificence and opulence of its ornamentation. The dark ceilings, fine paintings and massive pillars supporting the great heft of the building inspired a reverence for this old temple. The monks led us through all the chambers of the church and on one altar, in a golden urn, they displayed the head of Saint Saturninus. We eagerly revered this relic and laid a few coins there on the plate beside it. The astonished Franciscans, looking at each other, seemed to want to say something, but after looking at the idle crowd walking behind us, they humbly lowered their eyes, bowed and made an appeal to heaven without saying a word.

A foul odour in the room in which we were to eat dampened our appetites. On the walls, windows and everywhere else there were cobwebs and dust, the dirty brick floor had not been swept, but only sprinkled with water. Instead of a tablecloth, a thick rag was laid out. The meal, even the roast and cake, were drizzled with olive oil and so we were content with only salad, fruits and whatever had not been prepared by the cook. It is hard to imagine anything sloppier than an Italian tavern; only in their best cities can you find a decent establishment.

After dining, we were taken to a silk factory. Here we could see the national character of the Italians. The hall was filled with a few dozen looms on which silk was unwound and woven. Guess who spun them all so quickly – turkeys, roosters and hens. They were unleashed between two levers inserted into a winch by which, with the transferal of gears, the wheels are spun. The turkey lets down its tail, spreads its wings and runs gobbling along the pallets as quickly as it can until it inevitably keels over with its feet in the air. A boy and girl wrangle another bird while the exhausted worker is sent to a tavern, and it is said that they are more delicious than the slaughtered variety. Dogs, squirrels, rabbits, marmots and many other small animals barking, yelping, and screeching were running at full speed inside of wheels. These poor animals were frantically keeping up with themselves for fear of falling onto their backs and inadvertently drove the looms with the greatest force. The silk flowed out into the second room, and finished in a third room. On their steel, mechanized razors, a single worker can trim two dozen stockings in a day. Despite the ridiculous proposition of the looms, their work was successful, durable and cheap. Once this machine was started, its output and maintenance were very inexpensive.

From the factory we descended to the harbour, where there sat a galley and two demi-galleys, comprising the whole naval power of the king.[1] His incomes were so small that he had just three or four thousand soldiers, who were so poorly dressed that had they not a banner and bullet holes in their hats, they would be

---

1    Victor Emmanuel I, who ruled Sardinia from 1802 to 1821 and would have the Duchy of Savoy restored to him by the Congress of Vienna in 1814, in addition to the annexation of Genoa. Edward Hertslet, *The Map of Europe by Treaty*, vol. 1 (London: Buttersworths, 1875), p.18.

unrecognizable. There was nothing more to see in the harbour, so we went out of town. Our guide took off his shoes and threw a jacket over one shoulder, proudly stepping out ahead of us. Outside of town there was nothing but vegetable gardens and thin cabins which did not elicit a glance. The sandy earth, saltmarshes and swamps soon bored us and we reached a collapsed old church and decided to turn back. Learning that the gate to the fortress was being locked up at sunset, and then hearing that it was dangerous to stay in the town, due to the poor who could sometimes kill a foreigner for a few kopecks, we did not hesitate to return to the ship.

Despite the laziness of its inhabitants, Sardinia is very fertile. In addition to wine, oil, fruits and all kinds of grain are grown in abundance. In the mountains can be found silver and iron ores and marble. Salt generates a significant income for the King. Corals are harvested off the coasts. Trade, besides the aforementioned commodities, consisted of silk stockings and red woollen caps, while the rest of Italy wore black. The air on the island was unhealthy, due to the many swamps. Sardinia was a place of exile during the time of the Romans and in the present kingdom when it still possessed Piedmont. The Sardinians speak a broken dialect of Italian mixed with Spanish. The island is assured to be without poisonous reptiles and with the exception of foxes, there are no predatory animals. A small animal like a frog, called the *mafrone*, properly belongs to Sardinia.[2]

In antiquity, the Greeks likened the shape of the island to a sandal or footprint, naming Sardinia 'Sandaliotis' and 'Ichnusa.' The present name, some claim, comes from Sardus, a son of Hercules. The first inhabitants lived in isolation and wandered the forests. The Greeks established a colony in Sardinia and henceforth the native inhabitants have been subject to alien masters of one origin or another. The Carthaginians, ruling the Mediterranean for 400 years, owned this island until the end of the First Punic War. A Roman army under the command Tiberius Gracchus sacked Cagliari, then called Cavalis, during a time of peace and soon conquered the island, possessing it until the fall of the Western Empire. The ancient inhabitants of Sardinia were known as skilled slingers. In the first century after the birth of Christ, Cagliari already had its own bishops, among whom Lucifer was renowned for his passionate opposition to Arius and though he himself was

---

2    Bronevskiy is incorrectly paraphrasing the geographer Patrick Gordon who claimed that the 'mafrones or mastriones' was unique to Sardinia, and that the island was also home to a 'solifuga,' which resembled a frog. In actuality, 'mafrone' in several Italian dialects refers to a variety of sea bream or porgy which is not unique to the waters of the island, while the solifugae are arachnids which bear no resemblance at all to a frog or a toad. Patrick Gordon, *Geography Anatomized or a Complete Geographical Grammar*, 15th ed. (London: Knapton, Midwinter, Bettesworth and Hitch, Ward, Birt, Longman, Brotherton, Ford and Clarke, 1737), pp.234-235.

later accused of heresy, he is venerated and recognized as the patron saint of the island. Around 800AD, the Saracens at various times attacked the island, finally conquering it in 852 and driving its inhabitants to Italy. They held it peacefully for three hundred years. The Pope at this time, as a token of gratitude for their services, awarded Sardinia to the Republic of Pisa, which conquered it from the Saracens. After a century, as soon as the Pisans managed to fully subjugate the island and establish themselves there, another Pope gave it to James II, the King of Aragon, who conquered it and secured it for his descendants. After the extinction of his line [and inheritance by the monarchs of Castile], the territory fell to the Kings of Spain.[3] In 1708, the English took possession of the island but were driven out again in 1717, and finally in 1718, after the Treaty of Utrecht, the Duke of Savoy exchanged the island of Sicily for Sardinia with the Austrian Emperor, and from that time, Sardinia belonged to the House of Savoy with the rank of a kingdom.[4] In 1798, Bonaparte attempted to take Cagliari on his route to Egypt, but the hastily assembled peasantry routed the army that had landed. The conquest of Malta compensated him for his first failure. In 1801, in accordance with the Treaty of Amiens, the King of Sardinia was left with only one island and Piedmont was annexed to France.[5]

The king lived in Rome for some time and his brother Charles Felix, the Duke of Geneva, ruled as his viceroy. Our admiral required an audience with His Highness, which was to take place in his country home upon arrival, which delayed us somewhat in Cagliari. By the will of our Sovereign Emperor, the admiral offered assistance to protect Sardinia and this new gesture of friendship was accepted by the viceroy with heartfelt gratitude.

---

3    The extinction of James II's successors first resulted in the Compromise of Caspe in 1412, which installed a branch of the Trastamara dynasty to the throne of Aragon. The intermarriages between Castile and Aragon would not result in a single monarch holding both titles de jure until Charles I (Charles V of the Holy Roman Empire) in 1516. E. Michael Gerli (ed.), *Medieval Iberia: An Encyclopedia* (New York: Routledge, 2003) s.v. 'Caspe, Compromise of'; Ibid., s.v. 'Catholic Monarchs, Isabel I of Castile and Fernando II of Aragon.'

4    The trade of Sardinia and Sicily was effected in the Treaty of London of 1718 when Savoy joined the Quadruple Alliance against Spain. John Tyndale, *The Island of Sardinia* vol. 1 (London: Richard Bentley, 1849), pp.7-8.

5    France occupied the Duchy of Savoy (Piedmont) and County of Nice in 1792 and negotiated their annexation in the 1796 Treaty of Paris, not at Amiens in 1801-2. Tyndale, *The Island of Sardinia* vol. 1, pp.28-29.

# 14

# Sailing from Cagliari to Messina

At noon on the 7th [19th] of January 1806, we left Cagliari and sailed around Cape Carbonara, passing dangerous stones under the water at a depth of 20 feet [6.1 m]. Small vessels passed through safely during calm waters, but when the wind picks up, many perish. The voyage to Messina was a most pleasant period, riding a fine quiet wind that barely moving our ships or ruffled the waters. On the 8th [20th], the island of Sicily revealed itself and then the Aeolian Islands became distinguishable shortly after. Sicily appears as a high mountain rising gradually in the form of an amphitheatre covered from top to bottom in forests. The sight of the Aeolians was even more beautiful. Although they are volcanic, they are covered with green and prolific groves which proudly rise above the waves of the sea. We slowly and closely sailed past these hesperid gardens where the various beauties attracted the eye in so many directions one was bewildered by where it should stop, and the taste of their ripe bountiful fruits dazzled one with innumerable choices.[1] A small village on the rocky coastline appeared in the bright mirror of the water and the rays of the sun falling on every earthly object drew new images with each step. Of these islands, some spew forth buried fire from the bottom of the sea and others disappear below the waves to become sunken hazards. Because of their extinct or still smoking volcanoes, like the conjoined namesake islands of Vulcano and Vulcanello, some of the islands were uninhabited. Ash enriched the soil so fruitfully that the crops here reached the final degree of perfection. The Malvasia delle Lipari wine challenges the glory of the Lacryma Christi. In addition to these wines and a host of other fruits, especially dates, these islands provide a large amount of sulphur, vitriol, volcanic stones and pumice.

---

1    The Hesperides in Greek mythology are the nymphs which tend to and guard the golden apple orchards of Hera and Zeus somewhere in the distant west. Smith, *A New Classical Dictionary*, s.v. 'Hesperides.'

On the 10th [22nd] of January, we approached Stromboli. Providence wisely placed this volcano on the sea along a straight line between Vesuvius and Etna and its eternal eruption which began with the dawn of time and continues today relieves the belly of the earth of all its combustible substances, in such quantities between the three of them that they could blanket the ruins of Sicily and the whole lower half of Italy. The throat of Stromboli was not at the summit of the mountain like other volcanos, but stood like a foothill attached to the higher mount. In the daytime, the mountain seemed peaceful, one house topped its peak, and only the sea near the shore fumed. But at night, we were shown a most wonderful and amazing sight, with which no other found in nature can compare. The sea was calm, the sky was shaded over gloomily, and a tiny moon stole occasional glimpses below. The volcano opened up for us like a great horn blown with bellows and belching up sparks. Eruptions ceased and resumed almost every 10 minutes and flashed like bright lightning animated by a terrible desire to escape from the earth. The flames gradually increased to form a massive pillar of fire which roared like approaching thunder or the crackling of massive timbers as a building collapses. The brilliance of the volcano illuminated the clouds with all the colours of a rainbow: scarlet, bright purple and the finest shades of azure. The sky appeared as if it were on fire from the view of our ships. The shores of Calabria and Sicily glowed beautifully in the distance. We watched this magnificent natural phenomenon in silence; the booming, crackling and bubbling of the underground thunder and red hot stones falling into the sea and casting up tall sprays of foam and steam inspired in us a reverence for the greatness of God. At the sight of the eruption, it seemed the most stubborn atheist would be convinced of the omnipotence of the Creator.

The Island of Stromboli has a circumference of 10 Italian miles [18.6 km]. Its view from the sea is of a steep and uninhabited rock with a unique hill of cooled lava on its south side and its entire western face from the sea to the mouth is covered with ash so deeply that it is inaccessible. On the northern side, where several homes stood, grapes are grown for Malvasias which fetch very high prices here. Their currants, wine fruits and dates are considered superb.

On the 11th [23rd] of January, with a fresh wind in the morning, the squadron entered the strait called the Faro di Messina. The hazards of Scylla and Charybdis, glorified by the poets of Greece and Rome and which were so terrifying to the ancients, were of little concern to us.[2] During the infancy of seafaring and with the imperfections in ancient ship construction, they were terrifying, but today not

---

2    Two sea-monsters alleged to dwell in the Strait of Messina, later conflated with whirlpools and hidden rocks. Smith, *A New Classical Dictionary*, s.v. 'Scylla.'

even the *sparonaras*[3] fear a whirlpool there. We passed them on a brusque wind, however when we crossed the Faro, the ships' course noticeably slackened. These eddies came from two strong currents, one called Scylla which came from the south and flowed north along the coast of Calabria and the second was Charybdis, called Garofalo by the local inhabitants, which flowed conversely along the coast of Sicily. A great sum of water flowed from the west, north and south to converge in the narrow strait only two and a half *verstas* [2.67 km] wide, rebounding off both banks without enough space to dissipate and with such force that they produced many competing currents and turbulences. Should a ship enter the strait when the wind dies out and is unable to anchor itself on the deep floor, it will be carried back and forth until finally being thrown onto the shores of Calabria or on that sandy spit where a lighthouse stands. When the air is still, the strait is wavy, and at its most narrow point the water boils up and rushes to the shore. The whole space of the passage is animated with small waves from the conflicting currents which spin and swiftly stream in different directions. Prudence requires pilots to be taken when entering the strait who know the directions of these extraordinary currents by vast experience and should disaster strike due to their negligence, they answer with their lives. The ebb and flow do not correspond to those found on the ocean. They change here every 4 hours, between which for two hours the currents are all in disarray. Such disorder begins an hour before the rising and setting of the moon, during which time there is a low tide in the centre of the strait but high water along the shores, a bizarre phenomenon named *il Bastardo*. When we entered, the current flowed down the middle. On a new moon and during the equinox, the whirlpools rush with great force, yet on the morning of the new moon they are calm enough that by keeping closer to the lighthouse and the Sicilian coast, one can safely pass through the strait without a pilot. In the event that the wind dies out, without delay one must drop anchor and moor[4] the stern of the ship to the shore, which, despite being low and muddy, abruptly drops out to a depth of 15-20 *sazhen*s [32-42.67 m] a short distance away. Despite the considerable abyss in the water at the lighthouse, from the town of Messina 12 *verstas* [12.8 km] away they are imperceptible.

The view of the Messina strait was incredible! The ship sailed between gardens so close that it seemed a sailor could pluck a flower off the branches. On the left side of Reggio is a low coast evenly transitioning into the adjoined conical, pyramidal and hemispherical mountains, piled on one another, topped with white snow and covered on their slopes with dark forests. A little Gibraltar in the fortress of Scilla,

3    Brovenskiy's note: 'Boats used in Italy, which glide extremely quickly both under sail and
     by oar.'
4    Bronevskiy's note: 'To tie the ship to shore with ropes'.

Aleksey Samuilovich Greig.
Vikentiy Brioski, 1831, oil on
canvas, St. Petersburg, The
State Russian Museum.

clinging to the top of an unhewn rock, hangs over an abyss and appears poised to tumble in. On its northern face, the steep bank reveals its granite walls. On the right side of the strait, at the tip of a low sandy spit stands the lighthouse of Faro with its beautiful colonnade, seeming to sink into the water and be carried away. From the lighthouse to the town of Messina, along the shore, grow brightly coloured rows of oranges and lemons enclosed by the turquoise-green of countless vegetables. These lands slope up in shelves like a flight of stairs toward the low mountains of the island and are neatly delineated as if deliberately carved. The mountains are covered with olive, almond and myrtle forests. On the shores of the strait which flows like a majestic river and gradually expands until it merges with the sea, three fortresses and numerous country homes, monasteries and villages are seen. The pier at Messina is always filled with ships moored, entering and leaving, its activity creating a wonderful picture that seemed to be purposefully set in the midst of a dense and eternal greenery. The colossal blue Etna stood in the distance, lending a new brilliance to the rays of the sun with its snowy peak while its mouth exhaled a straight pillar of smoke that rose above the clouds. She is now slumbering, and perhaps, I thought at the time, gathering new strength with which to burst out again and destroy the vicinity and swallow up thousands of unfortunate victims.

The thunder of cannons ushered in our approach to Messina. All the ships flew into harbour to within no more than 30 *sazhen*s [64 m] from the shore, following in the wake behind their admiral with all sails set. A vast brass band, accompanied by a few shots from the *Yaroslav*, responded to the salutations of the ships of the squadrons of Commodores Aleksey Samuilovich Greig and Aleksandr Andreyevich Sorokin,[5] returning from Naples with ground forces aboard. The *Argus*, having lagged behind in St. Vincent and whom we thought of as lost, as there were rumours in Gibraltar that the Spanish had seized it, was standing in the harbour despite all expectations. Its red flag was the reason that Spanish gunboats had fired several shots at it, but when it was changed for white, the Spanish captain apologized for mistaking our flag of the third division for a British ensign and then escorted the brig out of the strait, as they were not permitted to allow it to proceed to Gibraltar. As soon as we entered the gate of the harbour and cast two anchors northward and southward, we immediately moored the ship to the embankment with thick ropes.

---

5    Greig and Sorokin were both promoted to rear-admiral of the red flag on the 27 December 1805 [8 January 1806] but word had yet to reach the Mediterreanean. *Общий Морской Список* (St. Petersburg: Морская Типография, 1806), p.37. [*The Complete Naval Roster* (St. Petersburg: Naval Press, 1806), p.37.]

# 15

# Messina, 11th [23rd] of January

A narrow sandy spit gives the port of Messina the appearance of a round basin in which 500 ships stand near the embankment itself, safe from the winds. Charybdis rages noisily on the other side of this natural dam, but just a hundred paces into the port it becomes as quiet as a garden pond. Here, nature seemed to want to prove the insignificance and imperfection of human art. The view of the harbour full of ships from every trading nation except for France was captivating: innumerable masts like a dense forest grew out of the water, adorned with a dazzling collection of flags and pennants in every colour. The military and merchant vessels were nestled in tightly one behind the other, coupled together by their yards and tethered with flags, and seemed to hug each other in a pledge of friendship.

The earthquakes in 1783 destroyed the best portion of the city around the port. Despite this, the embankments of Messina have something special – its ruins surpassed anything I had hitherto seen. It does not matter that the glorious Palazzata or La Calata, which encompassed the port like a crescent moon and formed a handsome boulevard two *verstas* [2.13 km] in length along its sweeping façade, is still unrestored, as by its remaining columns, balconies and porticoes one can surmise and admire its graceful architecture. The city itself, between a harbour below and a castle above, surrounded by jagged, half-collapsed walls, like Jerusalem, occupies the ledges of several separate mountains with a vast array of homes and churches. The stately domes in the Gothic style together with the façades of the palaces facing out to sea formed an amphitheatre of structures, standing in rows one above another. Looking at it all from a ship, you have the impression you are standing on the stage. The beauty of Messina is such that the eye wanders from one object to another always in awe.

A 16-day quarantine was to be imposed on the squadron, but at the insistence of the commander-in-chief, it was lifted on the same day as our arrival. In the evening when the embankment was full of pedestrians out for a stroll, we went ashore. Black taffeta dresses are the ordinary attire for the local women; many monks could be seen in white, black and brown cassocks; the costumes of Turks, Greeks, Slavs and Italians altogether made such a motley as can rarely be seen elsewhere. The red uniforms of the British infantry, the unusual dress of the Scottish highlanders in their busily-coloured skirts,[1] the manly and courageous appearance of our grenadiers in their bullet-riddled mitre caps embossed 'God is with us'; all of these contrasts captivated their spectators in the most charming way. The lively gaiety of the crowd, amused by a puppet comedy and harlequin, produced a greater noise and movement than usual. I was very pleased to hear how cheerfully and affectionately our moustached soldiers conversed with the Italians: such is the ability of the Russian to quickly fall in love in any land he sets foot. His politeness and generosity were especially appealing to the Italians. Here it was preferable to the Russian to order every available service where possible. These all costed money naturally, but where is anything done without the use of that manmade idol? Observe the Italian when he receives a few coins and see the ecstasy written on his face; he is not so much pleased with the copper as the opportunity to serve a Russian. The Frenchman and Englishman, if they do not abuse the poor, at least wish to seem superior to him. The Russian does not seek such an advantage and wishes to meet him on equal terms. For that key reason, the Italian rabble shouts at us: '*evviva moscoviti!*' – long live the Russians. In Italy, in order to seem like a typical foreigner and not a Russian and be left alone peacefully, one must hide. For that reason we came ashore covered in frocks, since our uniforms would attract a crowd.

Acquiring tickets to the opera, I asked when the performance would begin and I was told it would be at 'two o'clock at night'. Although late, I went at the appointed time but to find the theatre was closed and locked, and only then remembered that in Italy the hours of night are counted from sunset, and the hours of the day from sunrise. The wide main street running from south to north behind the Palazzata was lined with four-storey uniform houses, paved with great broad slabs and had sidewalks of marble and lava stones. Some of the churches, of which there were many, deserve special attention not for their exterior, but for their interior decoration. In the ancient building of a cathedral, the throne and bas-reliefs by the Italian sculptor Gagini are in the most exquisite style. The mosaic on the central altar is formed by gem stones and when seen from a distance, its figures and shadows blend flawlessly with its surroundings. The frescos painted by the hand of Quagliata, also a Sicilian native, are equal in quality with Tintoretto. Gold and silver vessels kept among the treasures of the church were shown to us with pride and for their great rarity, for on one was the work of Gabriello, the famous Roman artist who was born in Messina, and the inspiration of that singular genius,

1    Tartan kilts.

without imitating any other, attained perfection. Generally all the local churches are too burdened with gilding and marble works. The Monastery of Saint Gregory is considered to be the most opulent, and the Jesuit College, to which one must climb several staircases and terraces, can be justly proud of its beautiful condition and its paintings by another Messinese, Raphael of Sicily;[2] in their composition, fine details and studiousness, the images united a refined taste with a striking pleasantness. Of the many statues that adorn the city, the white marble fountain on the waterfront representing Neptune, reining in Scylla and Charybdis with chains, depicted as sea monsters with seven heads as they were described by the ancient poets, built in the style of Michelangelo's school, is simply excellent. After all these, the monument of Don John of Austria standing by the governor's manor seems very mediocre.

Under the present circumstances, when all of [continental] Italy is dominated by the French, Messina has become an important trading port and a refuge for many voluntary exiles. In their factories, they produce moveable type, silk stockings, corsets and taffeta, known to us [in Russian] as *noblesse*. Besides fruits – especially oranges, wine, oil and chicken, the primary commodity traded was salt.

On the night of the 12th [24th] of January, the frigate *Nazaret* with four British transports ran aground at the Faro, as did the brig *Letun* at the Messina lighthouse. Fortunately the stillness of the wind lasted two days; the frigate, brig and three transports were removed from the shallows with no harm by men dispatched from the squadron. The fourth transport breached its bottom and was forced to remain. The 13th Jäger Regiment, which was aboard these ships, was transferred to our squadron and we were held up until finally leaving Messina on the 16th [28th] of January.

---

2    Or the Raphael of Messina, a nickname given to Girolamo Alibrandi. Ralph Wornum (ed.), *The Biographical Catalogue of the Principal Italian Painters* (London: John Murray, 1855), s.v. 'Alibrandi, Girolamo'.

# 16

# Sailing from Messina to Corfu

When we rounded Spartivento, the southern cape of Calabria, a strong wind agitated the waves and our ships were travelling close-hauled,[1] swaying about like thin canoes. On the night of the 16th and 17th [28th and 29th] of January, after a brief thunderstorm, the fore-topmast[2] on the *Uriil* was damaged. The admiral left the *Selafail* and *Feniks* with her and reached the southern strait with the remainder of the vessels by the evening of the 18th [30th]. The wind was fresh and rather abrupt and the strait was crowded with shallows and hidden rocks. The admiral surprised us with his determination and skilful knowledge of these places. As the sun set, the signal was given to close the line and follow behind his ship. Through the impenetrable darkness, we safely passed every danger and by midnight the squadron dropped anchor under the walls of Corfu, the main goal of our expedition. The journey from Kronstadt to Corfu, counting only the time underway, took 38 days. Two hours later we were joined from the Neapolitan anchorage by the commodore's ship *Retvizan*.[3]

When sailing from Messina to Corfu during a southerly wind one should keep to the island of Santa Maura (Lefkada); but during a northerly wind, keep to the northern extremity of Corfu since in the Ionian Sea the current together with the wind tend either toward the Adriatic or to the south along the coasts of Morea. Entering the southern strait, one must keep close to the island of Paxos, because from Cape Bianco the shallows stretch across half the passage. Another sandy

---

1   Bronevskiy's note: 'The points of sail closest to windward.'
2   Bronevskiy's note: 'The middle span of the foremast.'
3   From the Swedish 'Rättvisan' – Justice. The ship was captured from the Swedish in 1790 during the Vyborg Gauntlet and its name was retained by the Russian Navy. Феодосий Веселаго, *Список Русских Военных Судов с 1668 по 1860 год* (St. Petersburg: Морское Министерво, 1872), p.748. [Feodosiy Veselago, *The List of Russian Military Vessels from 1668 to 1860* (St. Petersburg: Naval Ministry, 1872), p.748.]

shoal runs from Punto de Saline to the northeast for half a mile [3.72 km], which along with other shoals on the eastern side of Corfu, require keeping close to the Albanian coast until one reaches the town. The shallows from the point to a depth of 20 *sazhens* [42.67 m] stretch for 10 miles [18.6 km], at which the town of Corfu opens up its island, but when approaching, you will see a fortress on the tip of the cape. The northern strait is roughly 3 *verstas* [3.2 km] wide, and excluding one stone which stands equal with sea level, it is free of hazards. The anchorage at Corfu is located between the city and the island of Vido, with a depth of 8, 10 and 12 *sazhens* [17.06, 21.34, 25.6 m], muddy soil, and provides ships with a safe haven. The advantage of this port is that the fleet can exit into the sea by one strait or the other regardless of the wind. At Lazaretto, the island to the west of Vido, vessels stand in quarantine. Small military vessels stand in the Mandraki harbour, which is beside the citadel and shipyards. The Venetian docks and the canal in Gouvia remain, but the buildings which cost several millions are now all in ruin.

# 17

# Corfu

---

At sunrise, the thunder of cannons from the squadrons of Greig and Sorokin ushered in the arrival of the new commander-in-chief, and the senior officer's ship *Retvizan* greeted the vice-admiral with nine shots, the republican fortress saluted him with 15, and the merchant ships of various nations gave him 3, 5 and 7 shots. All the military vessels, as a sign of coming under Senyavin's command, lowered the white ensign and hoisted the red instead. Meanwhile, as the *Yaroslav* answered these salutes and congratulations, Major-General Anrep with his staff and Commodore Greig with his captains on boats under flags came from all sides to the admiral's ship, which accompanied the arrival and departure of these visitors with a band playing with thundering snare and kettledrums. The strength of the ground forces now under the command of Vice-Admiral Senyavin reached 13,000 and consisted of the following regiments: the Kura, Kozlov, Kolyvan and Vitebsk Musketeers; the 13th and 14th Jägers; and the light infantry Albanian Legion formed from Epirote Greeks. The Siberian Grenadier Regiment, accompanying the former commander-in-chief General of the Infantry Boris Petrovich de Lacy, soon returned to Russia.

The naval forces, besides the five ships of the line, one frigate and two brigs which came from Kronstadt, consisted of the following:

1. the *Retvizan*, 64 guns, under Commodore Greig;
2. the *Svyataya Yelena* of 74 guns under Captain Ivan Bychenskiy;
3. the *Svyataya Paraskeva* of 74 guns under Commodore Sorokin and Captain Ivan Saltanov;
4. the *Aziya* of 74 guns under Captain Henry Baillie;
5. the *Svyatoy Mikhail*, without guns for the transport of ground forces, under Captain Teodoro (Fyodor) Lelli.

The frigates:

1. *Venus* of 50 guns under Captain-Lieutenant Yegor Razvozov;
2. the *Mikhail* of 44 guns under Captain-Lieutenant Mark Snaksaryov;
3. the *Avtroil*[1] of 32 guns under Captain-Lieutenant Ivan Backman;
4. the *Grigoriy Velikoy Armenii* serving as a floating hospital.

The corvettes:

1. the *Diomid* of 24 guns under Captain-Lieutenant Anastasios Palaiologos;
2. the *Kherson* of 24 guns under Lieutenant Yakov Chaplin;
3. the *Altsina* of 18 guns under Lieutenant Vasiliy Titov;
4. the *Dnyepr* of 18 guns under Lieutenant Dmitriy Balzam;
5. the *Grigoriy*, a large military transport of 24 guns;
6. the *Pavel* of 18 guns.

The brigs: the *Oryol*, the *Aleksandr*, the *Bonasorte*,[2] the *Letun*, the *Bogoyavlensk*; and the schooner *Ekspeditsion*,[3] each of 16 guns.

The whole fleet consisted of 10 ships of the line, 5 frigates, 6 corvettes, 6 brigs and 12 gunboats. On all of these ships stood 7,908 sailors, naval soldiers,[4] and artillerists, and 1,154 cannon. Additionally there [will be] taken from the French

---

1    From the Swedish 'Af Trolle', named after General-Admiral Henrik af Trolle. It was captured from the Swedish in 1789 during the first Battle of Svensksund and its name was retained by the Russian Navy. Veselago, *The List of Russian Military Vessels*, p.745.

2    From the presumably Italian 'Bona Sorte' – Good Fortune. It was captured from the French in 1799 at Ancona and its name was retained by the Russian Navy. Veselago, *The List of Russian Military Vessels*, p.755.

3    From the French 'l'Expédition'. It was captured from the French in 1799 at Corfu and its name was retained by the Russian Navy. Veselago, *The List of Russian Military Vessels*, p.754.

4    Marines. Russia's naval infantry was organized into four numbered regiments and one independent battalion. The first three naval regiments were nominally attached to the Baltic Fleet, the 4th regiment to the Black Sea Fleet, and the independent battalion to the Caspian Flotilla. In the Mediterranean, the Russians deployed four companies of the 1st Regiment, two companies of the 2nd, four companies of the 3rd, and four companies of the 4th. The ten companies of the Baltic Fleet's regiments were consolidated and formally re-designated the 2nd Naval Infantry Regiment on 10 [22] November 1806, while in Russia the remaining companies were used to re-form the 1st and 3rd Regiments. Сергей Попов, Армейская и Гарнизонная Пехота Александра Первого (Moscow: Русские Витязи, 2010), pp.64-75.; Александр Кибовский and Олег Леонов, *300 Лет Российской Морской Пехоте*, vol. 1 (Moscow: Русские Витязи, 2008), pp. 119-141. [Sergey Popov, *Army and Garrison Infantry of Alexander the First* (Moscow: Russian Knights, 2010), pp.64-75.; Aleksandr Kibovskiy and Oleg Leonov, *300 Years of the Russian Naval Infantry*, vol. 1 (Moscow: Russian Knights, 2008), pp. 119-141.]

the xebecs *Azard*[5] and *Zabiyaka* both of 16 guns, and from the prize vessels the following corvettes: the *Dyerzkiy* of 28 guns under Captain-Lieutenant Konstantin Saltiy and the *Versona* of 22 guns under Lieutenant Orest Krichevskiy.

Our first day staying in Corfu was spent with mutual visitations and boats proceeded without interruption from ship to ship, cross-crossing through the harbour, as everyone hurried to see a friend, comrade and brother. These are the titles I give to my fellow cadets. Naval officers, with a few exceptions, are all reared in the Naval Corps like a communal cradle and by sharing customs and needs from veritable infancy, we are bonded in friendship. On the slippery path of life, in the martial service, where envy often breaks down the strongest ties, comrades remain faithful until old age. Examples in our service are not rare, even when one man becomes a commander and another the subordinate. From the corps come fleet and artillery officers who constitute the most harmonious society. The benefit of a public education here is obvious. On the ships, in the army and everywhere else where the greater portion of officers were commissioned from the cadets, there is a clearly superior cohesion.

The next day, I managed to visit the casino, the *spianata* or promenade, strolled along the ramparts around the city and went to the theatre, but I must admit that my ignorance of the language robbed me of much entertainment. For this reason, I decided to learn Italian as quickly as possible so that I could see all the memorabilia of Corfu in close detail as soon as possible. At the opera, when they spoke in recitativo, I was bored in the extreme, and when they sang, it seemed strange that a dying hero would continue to bellow so loudly. The ballet was composed of the best Italian dancers and seemed excellent to me, and I had to agree that until then I had merely been watching figurants. The local jumpers were even better, more courageous and surprising with their death-defying leaps (*salto mortale*). The first male dancer and his beautiful female counterpart, Gaetani, truly flew across the scene. Their pantomime, in its lightness, dignity and synchronous musical accompaniment, was simply perfect.

In order to demonstrate to the dear reader how important for our policy our stay there was, and what benefits the island of Corfu presented to the trade of our fatherland, I offer a brief overview. Peter the Great, having built a fleet, wanted to place Russia among the naval powers to enrich his subjects with the spread of shipping, which is known to be more profitable than caravan trade over land. The seas that belonged to Russia then were inadequate for the extensive ambitions of our wise illuminator. He sought to acquire possession in remote though small

---

5    From the French 'Hasard'. It was captured from the French in the Bay of Kotor on 16 [28] February 1806 and its name was retained by the Russian Navy. Veselago, *The List of Russian Military Vessels*, p.755.

lands, in order to establish a fleet there and prepare that corps of seafarers which he would require in the future. To that end, the squadron was dispatched to the island of Madagascar by the south of Africa but returned to port unsuccessful after being damaged in a storm. Catherine II followed in the footsteps of the Greatest of the Tsars and during her profitable war with the Turks, she sought in 1770 to purchase the island of Corfu from the then declining Venetian Republic, but with the death of Joseph II of Austria, peace was concluded with the Turks by Leopold, and the sour relations with England, Prussia and other mediocre powers in the world prevented this plan. Finally when the children of the French Revolution, with dreams of liberty and the rejection of God Himself, threatened to overthrow the legitimate authorities and unleash the horrors of anarchy and the old ignorance of the medieval epoch; when three mighty powers united; when Suvorov liberated Italy and restored the faith and kings,[6] then Admiral Fyodor Fyodorovich Ushakov commanded the combined Russian and Turkish fleet that subdued Corfu, expelled the French from Naples and Rome, and on the 13th [25th] of March, 1802, at the Congress of Amiens, the republic of the seven united Greek islands was recognized under the auspices of Russia and Turkey.[7]

The Ionian Republic, by its geographic location, is the key to Italy and the gate to ancient Greece. Corfu, having an infantry division and ten ships of the line, was not only safe from enemy invasion but also became an important point of observation between the northern and southern powers. The peoples of Italy, oppressed by a foreign yoke and rejecting the influence of the other competing states, awaited liberation from Corfu. On the other side, the Greeks who live in Morea, Albania

---

6    Generalissimo Aleksandr Vasilyevich Suvorov, Count of Rymnik and Prince of Italy, was Russia's most successful and celebrated military leader and is credited with never having lost a field battle. In 1799 he commanded a combined Russo-Austrian army and defeated the French at Cassano and Trebbia, drove them back to the Riviera and occupied their Italian client states. His later Swiss campaign ended in failure, though his retreat across the Alps by the St. Gotthard Pass with minimal losses was a martial feat in its own right. He was withdrawn to Russia in 1800 and his accomplishments in northern Italy were reversed in his absence. Andreyevskiy et al., *Brockhaus and Efron Dictionary*, s.v. 'Суворов, Александр Васильевич'; Ibid., sv. 'Итальянский поход Суворова'; Ibid., s.v. 'Швейцарский поход Суворова'. [Andreyevskiy et al., *Brockhaus and Efron Dictionary*, s.v. 'Suvorov, Aleksandr Vasilyevich'; Ibid., s.v. 'Suvorov's Italian Campaign'; Ibid., s.v. 'Suvorov's Swiss Campaign'.]

7    The Septinsular Republic or Republic of the Seven Islands was a state that encompassed the seven Ionian islands: Corfu, Paxos, Lefkada or Santa Maura, Cephalonia, Ithaca, Zakynthos or Zante, and Kythira or Cerigo, which had all previously belonged to the Republic of Venice, and was established after Russo-Turkish intervention in 1799. *Le Tre Constituzioni delle Sette Isole Jonie* (Corfu: Tipografia di Nicolaides Filadelfeo, 1849), pp.41. [*The Three Constitutions of the Seven Ionian Islands* (Corfu: Press of Nicolaides Filadelfeo, 1849), pp.41.] Article 3.

and the Archipelago dreamed of liberty in the presence of our meagre forces. The Slavs living on the eastern shore of the Gulf of Venice [and Adriatic Sea], being proud of our common heritage and faith, considered Corfu to be their capital. The gentleness of the government and the goodness and righteousness of our monarch united in our favour the various peoples and although we were surrounded by the enemy then, we found ourselves as safe as in Moscow itself. The disposition of the Italians, the religion of the Greeks,[8] the common language and customs of the Slavs, and the completely sincere love and devotion of the people served us as a reliable and most flattering shield.

Corfu is necessary for trade in the Black Sea. Being in the middle of the Mediterranean, it represents a safe haven for the reliable storage and protection of goods. The benefits our fatherland enjoyed from this port is proven by the fact that in 1806 and the first half of 1807, the number of merchant vessels, excluding those of the Bokez,[9] increased fourfold. In the Mediterranean, the Russian flag prevailed over all others. In another respect, Corfu represents the most important advantage. Russia was revered as the second naval power, sailing the Black Sea alone all year long, the Baltic for five months while it is open, and having also Corfu, circulating 10,000 naval officers and sailors with extensive knowledge of foreign waters. By this, the dream of Peter and the ambition of Catherine had been fulfilled.

8    Eastern Orthodox Christianity.
9    The Slavs who inhabit the Bay of Kotor ('Boka Kotorska' in Serbo-Croatian, hence 'the people of the bay'). They are also known in period literature as the Bocchesi, from the Italian 'Bocche di Cattaro'.

# 18

# New Ragusa, 30th of January [11 of February]

During the general deployment, with sorrow I had to part with the officers of the *Svyatoy Pyotr* and transfer to the frigate *Venus*, that glorious Venus who had no equal in her ease of flight; not only among our navy but even in the English Navy it was known as a preeminent glider. Its advantage for naval officers was so renowned and sought that it was considered an honour to serve on the *Venus*. Captain Robert Crown[1] (presently a vice-admiral) captured her from the Swedish in 1789 with the cutter *Merkuriy* and then, aboard the *Venus*, he captured the *Retvizan*. I consider it necessary to note here that the British have in their fleet 108 French vessels, which constitute a ninth of their entire naval force; at the end of the war with Sweden in 1794, we had 34 enemy vessels, constituting a fifth of our navy. Honour and glory to the Russian people!

The admiral, having no news of the events transpiring on land, instructed the captain of the *Venus* to receive State Councillor Carlo Pozzo di Borgo and Collegiate Assessor Cousin, officials of the Foreign Collegium,[2] in order to land them in Ragusa so that the latter of the two could proceed to Russia with dispatches. On route, we were especially tasked with learning the movements of the enemy. On the 24th of January [5th of February], besides these officials, we took onboard a Colonel Mackenzie in British service, son of the famous explorer of Northwestern America,[3] and then set sail.

---

1   Known in Russian as Roman Vasilyevich Kroun. He was promoted to vice-admiral of the blue flag on 10 [22] February, 1804. *The Complete Naval Roster of 1806*, p.36.

2   The predecessor to the Ministry of Foreign Affairs, which continued to exist after 1802 as a department of that ministry. *Complete Collection of Laws*, col. 1, vol. 27, pp.243-248.

3   Sir Alexander Mackenzie, the explorer, fur trader and member of the Legislative Assembly of Lower Canada, did not marry before 1812 and had no sons before 1818. Francess Halpenny and Jean Hamelin (eds.), *Dictionary of Canadian Biography*, vol. 5 (Toronto: University of Toronto Press, 1983), s.v.'Mackenzie, Sir Alexander'.

A still air stopped us at Fano (Othonoi), the purported island of Calypso. Homer and Fénelon covered it with cool groves of sweet and bitter oranges and cypress trees. Those who, despite such eloquent writers, still believe that Fano is a lonely, uninhabited crag do not properly represent it, save for its whitish rocks. Strabo believed that Calypso's island was closer to the coast of Malta and this is more probable considering Homer's description: 'Ulysses set sail with a tailwind and after 18 days he saw the shores of Korkyra' which is at most 20 *versta*s [21.35 km] from Fano, demonstrating that Fano cannot be Calypso's abode.

A slow and foul wind delayed our voyage. On the 30th of January [11th of February] when we reached the height of New Ragusa, it became still. At the insistence of the State Councillor Pozzo di Borgo, who had special assignments, we fired a shot while raising the merchant's flag[4] and requested the consul, and Mister Fonton did not delay in his arrival.[5] He immediately returned to the city with both diplomats. At midnight, the frigate entered the gulf of Santa Croce or Gravosa (Gruž), which forms the harbour of Ragusa.

The next day, the rector (head of government for the republic) sent us his congratulations on our safe arrival and asked to receive the customary gifts of vegetables, fruits and wine. The captain went into the city to pay his respects in person to the rector and invited the other officers to accompany him. Not finding him at home, we met him in the square. His princely mantle and large wig which left only a part of his face visible gave him a strange and authoritative appearance. It seemed as though we were seeing a living shadow of the Doges of Venice who had already vanished from the earth. The rector took several measured steps toward meeting us and began with dignity a favourable conversation about the city and its lands, the glory of Russia and finally about the grace of our monarch, who was so beloved everywhere, and finished by saying: 'what a happiness it is to be Russian'. With a low bow, thanking him for his flattering reception, we bid him farewell and went to tour the city, but it was so small that a mere two or three streets and a few houses constituted the capital of the republic. Their construction was beautiful and the city was very clean. The square walls with embrasures could only protect the city from the sea, as on land the high mountain of Sergio (Srđ) provides a

---

4    Russia's flag for merchant vessels was the same as its national flag today: a horizontal tricolour of white at the top, blue in the centre and red at the bottom. *Complete Collection of Laws*, col. 1, vol. 28, pp.327-329. No. 21,300.

5    Charles (Karl Karlovich) Fonton, Russia's consul general to Ragusa, Cattaro and later Fiume from 1801 to 1815. Алексей Нарочницкий (ed.), *Внешняя политика России XIX и начала XX века*, series 1, vol. 2 (Moscow: Государственное Издательство Политеческой Литературы, 1961), p.709. [Aleksey Narochnitskiy (ed.), *The Foreign Policy of Russia of the 19th and Beginning of the 20th Century*, series 1, vol. 2 (Moscow: State Press of Political Literature, 1961), p.709.]

favourable position for a besieging enemy. The surroundings of Ragusa – called Dubrovnik by the Slavs – are decorated with gardens and rustic houses built in the English style. The people of Ragusa, dwelling on a mountainous and barren land, practice in trade. They are as ubiquitous throughout the Mediterranean as the English are throughout the world. Being under the auspices of the Ottoman Porte and taking advantage of their neutrality in the midst of the tumultuous events of Europe, they amassed a great sum of wealth in a short time. This small republic had 600 vessels on which they exchanged a small quantity of their own products for a far greater quantity of smuggled goods. Lacking their own armed forces and being forced to seek protection from others, Ragusa had temporarily paid considerable sums to the Ottoman Sultan, the King of Naples, the Pope and the Emperor of Austria. Sometimes they took from different nations two or three certificates for a single ship, for which they were reproached with the moniker '*di sette bandiere*'.[6] The vessels of Ragusa are very beautiful and appropriate both for taking on great cargos and for fast and safe navigation. The government of the republic is in the hands of the nobility, who elect the rector monthly. During his tenure, he lives in the palace and when it is concluded, he is expelled from it rather abruptly. In general, the republicans are so jealous of their freedom that they fear the slightest attack and lock the fortress gates as soon as the sun goes down. The republic is stable and calm due to the wisdom of its laws, which resemble those that governed the Venetian Republic. The nobility profess the Catholic faith, but the common people are Slavs of the Greek confession. The first class of citizens, the nobility, have many advantages while the second have none. The common language is a variation of Slavonian, although it is intelligible to a Russian. Italian is also used with equal familiarity.

In Ragusa we received reliable news that Dalmatia had been occupied by French forces, for which reason the courier could not travel from here to Russia, and of how our diplomatic officials completed their other missions. The frigate then weighed anchor on the 1st [13rd] of February and responded to a salute from the walls of Ragusa with two shots fewer than those received.

---

6    Italian for: 'of seven flags'.

# 19

# Sailing the Adriatic Sea

On the night of the 2nd [14th] of February, the wind picked up and became rather fresh and the waves became restless but regardless the frigate ran downwind and achieved a great speed, for the captain had reason to hurry. We continued all night long between the rocks and islands on our course, despite rain and an overcast sky. During that night we passed the dangerous island of Lagosta (Lastovo) and threaded between the islands of Isto and Lussino (Lošinj). At first light the long ridge of islands of the Dalmatian Archipelago sprang into existence on our starboard side. Enjoying the ever-changing vistas scrolling by, we soon passed a great open space and by noon on the 2nd, we were approximately opposite Ancona. Toward evening, we saw a dismasted ship left unattended, waves lapping over the deck, alternatingly concealing and revealing it to us. Approaching closer, several men onboard began waving at us with their scarves and hats. The wind was strong and the waves terrible, but how could we refuse to help the drowning? The frigate approached closer and was lain to,[1] then we lowered a dinghy off the side. A boatswain with six of the bravest sailors rushed onto the boat and rowed off into the engulfing waves. Not without joy emerging from the struggle, I watched the effort with which the sailors rowed, struck the hull and climbed aboard. Then, pulling a thin rope taken from the frigate, they hauled over a thicker cable and lashed it to the bow, thereby saving the wrecked vessel. The seven men aboard were Venetians – subjects of France. They could hardly speak from fear and cold and had no food or water for three days, so they were taken aboard the frigate and handed over to the doctor. Upon inspection of the vessel, which was of a type called a trabaccolo, it was found to be in good condition; the captain ordered that it be pumped out, its masts and sails repaired, in accordance with the law which

---

1    Bronevskiy's note: "'To lie to" means to turn into the wind and furl the sails to hold the ship in place'.

states that if an enemy ship runs aground or suffers any disaster at sea and calls for help, then she must be assisted and granted passage. Thus, when the trabaccolo was repaired and the wind quieted, the captain ordered that the skipper, Bartolomeo Pizzoni, be informed he could go where he pleased. The Italians did not want to believe it, but when adequate water and provisions were loaded onto their boat, they thanked the captain and officers with the utmost gratitude. The skipper was touched by this unexpected mercy and said in parting: 'for having let me go free, I willingly remain your prisoner, being sure that in my country I can scarcely find friends as generous as you who are unfortunately my enemy'. You must believe that a good deed never goes unrewarded, and I later discovered that this same Bartolomeo, being in Ancona, offered his services to the captured Russian soldiers who were compelled to serve in a French regiment; he exposed himself to danger and sacrificed his life to release some of them from captivity and transport them to Corfu in his trabaccolo.

Since we were to disrupt the enemy who was safely transporting armies from Venice to Dalmatia, we then sailed from Ancona to Senigallia and from there to Istria, finally stopping at the major thoroughfare of communication by the island of San Pietro dei Nembi (Sveti Petar). In order to deceive the enemy regarding the number of ships, we raised different flags everywhere; one moment our own, the next English, then Swedish and so on. Because the enemy took precautions or for some other reason, during the span of two days we saw only one ship sailing under Austrian colours, to which we hailed with a cannon shot and signalled to approach, but it moved away through a field of stones and disappeared behind an island.

On the 5th [17th] of February, while approaching the islands that covered the entrance to Fiume (Rijeka), we learned first-hand of the wind, called here the 'bora,' which is so strong that it can be compared to a terrible hurricane. The haze obscuring the tops of the mountains is a sure sign that the bora is approaching. The wind, with an apparent aspiration and an extraordinary strength, burst forth from behind the mountains, raising clouds of dust, tearing out trees and peeling the roofs off houses. The sea near the shore was seething but was not wavy; the wind tore up water from the surface and carried it as a mist, and these sprays of water often reached a height of five *sazhens* [10.67 m]. The bora always blows from the northeast and can last two or three consecutive weeks. It brought small vessels from Dalmatia to Italy where almost all the ports were open to attacks from the wind. Since the Earth's beginning, many ships have perished during the bora and sailing the Adriatic in these months is very difficult. The strength of the wind by the shore is incredible; anchored ships often lose their masts. Yet the wind softens out into the sea such that the local sailors move away from the coasts to the islands, though not one sail can be unfurled.

Despite the indications of the experienced pilot who showed us the mountains covered with light, fluctuating clouds to assure us that the *bora* was still ongoing and that we were about to endanger ourselves if we pressed on, the captain had orders to land in Fiume or Trieste the officials of the Foreign Collegium with important dispatches for the Sovereign Emperor, and relying on the fact that the wind in the sea was relatively quiet and the sky was clear, he ordered to reef[2] the topsails and head to Fiume. Behind Ossero (Osor) and in the strait opposite Mount Maggiore (Učka), we encountered such a strong squall that the frigate broached into the wind, rolled onto its side and stopped in a position like being held down in the water. Cracking masts, toppling tables and furniture in the wardroom, flying scraps of torn sail, and our lieutenant's desperate voice: 'hard a-starboard! All hands on deck!' nearly scared our passengers to death, and in fact, while we were righting the frigate, we were at risk of losing a mast; yet a new even more obvious problem threatened us. A flat submerged rock covered only by four feet of water lay in the middle of the strait, incorrectly indicated on the map and unknown to the pilot in its fullest extent. The surface of the sea was as white as snow and so the breaking of the water around the stone could not be seen. The hoarse, choking shout of the commanding lieutenant; the embarrassed expression of the captain, perplexed as to where to steer the frigate; the hasty disorder of the officers, who searched in vain with telescopes for the underwater stone and argued over the discrepancies between the map and the lay of the strait around us, which made each man turn pale; and the sullen faces of our passengers formed for the next few minutes the spectacle of our most desperate situation. Meanwhile, the frigate without sails unpredictably flew with the wind close to the steep banks where hanging rocks seemed to threaten to crush us and the submerged hazard was nearly under the bow already: but 'God, without Whose Will the hairs on our heads do not perish,'[3] brought us safely into the open sea. At night we dropped anchor by the island of Sansego (Susak) to make repairs. The wind blew hard above but below it only occasionally came in gusts, and waves came at us from both sides as they rebounded off the island which created an irregular rolling. To alleviate that effect, we took down the upper masts and lower yards. The empty and uninhabited island of Sansego had a spring of fresh water on its southern side, which was a treasure trove for seafarers. Flocks of seabirds blanketed its shores so densely that hunters did not need to expend their powder; the birds were so fearless and sat so close that they could be beaten with sticks and children could catch them with their bare hands. We immediately found several turtles. These amphibians were exceptional animals: without food and only a spraying of sea

2    Bronevskiy's note: 'This means to reduce the sail's area and secure it with ropes called ties'.
3    A paraphrase of Matthew 10:27-31.

water, they could live for a very long time, but they will eat any sort of fresh grass and rusk bread after it has been soaked. Their eggs are laid in pits at such a distance from the sea that the waves cannot flood them. In such pits we found fifty or more turtle eggs, not much smaller than a chicken's, carefully covered with sand. Turtle meat is white, fatty and, as it is known, very useful for curing scurvy.

On the 6th [18th] of February, when the wind was quiet, while anchoring off the island of San Pietro (Sveti Petar), we saw a vessel slowly cruising. Although the wind only filled the upper sails, the frigate reached 7 miles [13.02 km] an hour and soon we looked on a large galley not unlike the designs of antiquity. Because of the dead calm by the shore, she was rowing with oars and the frigate under sail quickly closed the distance. Almost immediately we began to fire solid shot and one ball fell into its mast, another into the stern, but after crossing the belt of the wind and entering the still air, the frigate slowed to a stop. The galley then retreated to a distance outside our guns' range, and with a cannon shot, unfurled the sails and hoisted the flag of the new Kingdom of Italy. Rounding a cape, the galley entered a bay where we could not attack it due to the shallowness of the water and also, because of batteries protecting this harbour, we could not attempt to send a boarding party in our boats.

On the 6th and 7th [18th and 19th] of February, when the sea was quiet, the *bora* raged on at Mount Maggiore; it was for this reason that the strait leading to Fiume had the nickname of the Devil's Mouth. Each time we were deceived, and every night we were forced to return to Sansego, which provided safe cover from the wind for anchoring. On the 8th [20th], anchored on the western side of the island at a depth of 30 *sazhens* [64 m] and with the topmasts and yards taken down, we saw to the south at 8 o'clock in the morning a large three-masted vessel. In half an hour we restored our masts and the frigate was already under all sails and in three hours we caught up to that vessel which nearly escaped below the horizon. It sailed under an Austrian flag and was travelling from Odessa to Trieste with a cargo of wheat. The skipper assured us that no vessel dared to approach the Devil's Mouth during the *bora*. For that reason, the captain decided to land the courier in Trieste, but when approaching Istria, the terrible storm again drove us to Sansego, where it was surprisingly peaceful.

On the 9th [21st] of February, the skipper of a Turkish ship which left Trieste announced that the entire Austrian coast from Trieste to Fiume was occupied by French forces and that a squadron was ready in Venice to transport an army into Dalmatia after the *bora* passes. Thus in learning the enemy's intentions and being able to do him much harm, the captain ordered to turn into the wind and sail to Corfu. By nightfall, the wind grew so strong that with the wind blowing us along the 12th rhumb [southeast by south], the frigate nearly plunged forward into the water. At dawn on the 10th [22nd], we were forced to remove the upper sails again.

The clear sky, rough sea and floating frigate would make for an image worthy of the brush of Vernet; yet how can one convey those golden rays of the sun that reflected and mixed with the whiteness of the waves, following us into the deep rolling furrows? How to reconcile the calm azure of the celestial vault with the terrifying sight of the sea below? What paint should be chosen in order to properly capture those swirling, breaking and engulfing waves at the bow, which like a destructive flood pour into it, and how can one imagine that churning whirlpool behind the stern?

On the 13th [25th] of February, as the wind was whistling by the island of Fano, we met with the *Aziya* and the schooner *Ekspeditsion*, who requested to speak with our commander with the first signal, during which he learned that he had been assigned to the squadron of Captain Baillie on a secret assignment; but since the diplomatic officials onboard had information for the admiral, Captain Baillie ordered us to continue to Corfu and hasten to rendezvous with him again at Ragusa. The varying wind interspersed with moments of dead silence did not allow us to enter the northern strait by night. Passing through that strait on the 14th [26th], we met the frigate *Mikhail* which was also assigned to Baillie's squadron. We reached Corfu by evening after tacking windward all day.

## 20

# Sailing from Corfu to Cattaro

We stayed in Corfu until the 15th [27th] of February and saw the most beautiful morning and the most terrible storm. A dense morning mist paired with a fine rain disappeared like a phantom when the sun arose, and a clear day set in with the clearing of the clouds. But by noon, the mountains were shrouded in darkness and the sea began to vibrate unusually. The mountain of San Salvador (Pantokrator), the highest peak lying on the northern end of the island, suddenly flashed and flared with lightning, which tore up the sky and stabbed at its peak one after another. This lightning spread from right to left and soon the whole horizon appeared on fire. In the distance the thunder resembled the rumbling of gunfire. The radiance increased steadily and I looked on with fear at these streams of light spilling across the gloomy sky and dazzled with serpentine fibres. But when the clouds closed around us and the storm arrived, the terrible thunder, like the volleys of warring fleets or a small earthquake striking a town, shook the air and with it our frigate swayed and trembled. The blows increased continuously until the whole sky turned into a blue vault shining with iridescent colours. Sparks like those drawn down by Franklin's kite string were descending into the sea and scattering across the deck; the fire pumps could not extinguish them, since sea water contains many bitter salts and combustible particles which are greatly electrifiable and only serve to further enflame the glowing invaders.[1] Although the powder magazine was kept at the very bottom of the ship and carefully closed from outside air, the

---

1   A phenomenon known as Saint Elmo's Fire, a discharge of plasma resulting from strong electrostatic charges during storms, has long been regarded as a good omen for sailors, despite the necessary conditions bringing with them the danger of a lightning strike. It is typically seen on the tips of masts and yards, where the charge is concentrated into a narrow space and can ionize the surrounding air. Madeleine Bonsma, 'Weird and Wonderful Manifestations of Electromagnetism: Past and Present,' *University of Waterloo Phys13 News* 149 (Fall 2014): pp.3-5.

sparks underfoot made everyone anxious regardless. This thunderstorm cost the squadron several men killed or deafened. Finally the lightning subsided, the clouds began to thicken and the day seemed to turn to night with the pouring rain, which was heavy enough that it did not drain overboard. An hour later everything was silent and the black clouds blew by with the easterly wind to unveil the delightful surroundings. The sun returned in full splendour and everything took on a new tranquil appearance.

On the 16th [28th] February, the captain received a secret order, which was to be published upon arrival in Ragusa, and commanded us to weigh anchor. The officials from the Foreign Collegium came with us. For the whole day, we could not pass the White Road (Strada Bianca), which was so called because of the curve of a white strip visible on the slope of a mountain. It is noted that at this place there is almost always a still air and from here to Corfu the *bora* does not exist, for the position and height of the mountains indeed serve as an obstacle to cover the water from the wind. Often when a fresh wind blows on the open sea, the strait at the Strada Bianca is calm, yet when the wind comes from the shore and the sea appears calm, strong and sudden gusts can dismast ships.

On the 17th of February [1st of March], a stormy southwesterly wind brought us to the height of the Bay of Cattaro (Kotor), but then not far from Ragusa the *bora* began again, lasting three days. I can scarcely imagine a more severe storm. The pilot was the first to notice the round cloud on the mountains, crying out with great concern and fear: 'quick, take down the sails!' The men only had time to disperse along the yards. The fore-topsails, being half-secured, were torn to shreds and the main-topsails threw three sailors from the yard, of which one was killed, another broke his arm and the third miraculously escaped with only light bruises. Regardless of this regrettable loss, we took solace in having managed to remove the other sails which otherwise could have broken the masts. One by one we raised the storm staysails but they tore like sheets of paper and flew away on the wind. We remained without sails and were carried by the sheer force of the wind, roaring so violently that one could not hear the screaming of another man from 3 *sazhen*s [6.4 m] away. In the evening, when the *bora* slightly relented and allowed us to lie to under the mizzen-staysails, I went below deck. The sight of a coffin and the quiet singing of psalms stopped me. The deathbed, the covering with the flag, the sadness worn on the faces of the men surrounding the body of the deceased, the dim light of the lamp and the faint voice of the grey-haired monk singing 'give rest with the saints' all poured into the soul a reverential awe. In my heartache I forgot about the storm outside, I forgot about myself, and prayed, as they say: 'he that will learn to pray, let him go to sea'. The seafarer cannot be a freethinker, for at every step he faces perilous dangers and stands before death, where all godless thought evaporates and all the depraved customs of imagined philosophy, when the candle is set before the icon, fall silent and turn to soulful prayer.

On the 20th of February [4th of March], when the wind stopped, the courier Kozen was sent to Ragusa on a boat provided by the consul, and in four hours he returned with a message for the captain, who then immediately ordered all sails to be set and to head south. The weak wind tried our patience. An inaccurate map and inexperienced pilot led us to Antivari instead of Cattaro, forcing us to return north and by evening we saw threatening clouds on the high mountains which closed off the Bay of Cattaro from us. Despite an opposing wind blowing in gusts, we flew all night in deep darkness under reefed topsails to reach the mouth of the bay and pass between the steep cliffs, small islands and submerged rocks scattered there. On the 21st [5th], even before dawn, we anchored on the roadstead before Castelnuovo (Herceg Novi) in a thick fog as the wind came to a stop. Here we found the *Aziya*, the *Svyatoy Mikhail*, the schooner *Ekspeditsion* and the xebec *Azard*. The last of these was captured from the French as follows: on the 16th [28th] of February, Captain Baillie, having arrived in Cattaro, found the xebec floating beside the fortress. Despite the protection of the Austrians, the local people forced her to retire from the fort. Lieutenant Aleksey Sytin with five rowing boats under the cover of the *Ekspeditsion* conducted a boarding action at night in the pouring rain and caught the French so unaware that they did not fire a single shot. She was armed with 16 guns of various calibre and crewed by 60 men.

**21**

# The Occupation of the Bay of Cattaro – 21st of February [5th of March]

The mystery of our journey here was revealed and we were happy to learn that the admiral's endeavour was met with success. For a better explanation of the events of this day, we must pay attention to the connection of political events.

In Corfu, when the rumour was confirmed that the Emperor of Rome had made peace with Bonaparte at Pressburg and conceded Venice and Dalmatia to France;[1] and when it became known that the French government had dealings with Ali Pasha so that this unruly subject of the Ottoman Sultan would bow to the reception of their armies;[2] the reliability of this news led the vice-admiral to a difficult situation but also gave him the fortuitous idea to take advantage of the following circumstances. During his previous service in the Mediterranean, he learned of the devotion of the Slavic peoples, especially those of Cattaro and Montenegro, and then upon receiving high command though without concrete instructions, upon the return of our armies from Austria to our borders, and when we found ourselves continuing hostilities with the French state based on deeds committed by their side; he then decided to take Cattaro in order to assert control over the Adriatic Sea, divest the French from such close proximity to Corfu and prevent them from recruiting to their cause the Greeks who always hungrily search for an opportunity to throw off the Turkish yoke. The commander-in-chief established himself so as not to lose his opportunity or waste any time and began to proceed to an immediate execution, although he met a new obstacle. The former commander,

---

1   Francis II and I reigned as Holy Roman Emperor from 1792 to 1806 and as Emperor of Austria from 1804 to 1835.

2   Ali Pasha of Tepelina ruled the territory of Yanina in western Greece and Albania nigh independently from 1788 to 1822. Andreyevskiy et al., *Brockhaus and Efron Dictionary*, s.v. 'Али-паша'. [Andreyevskiy et al., *Brockhaus and Efron Dictionary*, s.v. 'Ali-Pasha'.]

General de Lacy, was ordered to only leave for the protection of the Ionian Republic those garrisons necessary to occupy the fortresses and withdraw the rest of his force to the ports of the Black Sea. Senyavin entreated him to try and convince him of how important it was for the fatherland that the French be prevented from establishing themselves in Dalmatia and Albania and how difficult it would then be to hold the Ionian Republic against superior forces and moreover the cunning of an enterprising conqueror. The two shared a lengthy correspondence. Finally, by persistent insistence, de Lacy agreed to leave most of the army behind and returned to Russia with only the Siberian Grenadier Regiment.

On the 9th [21st] of February, Captain First Rank Baillie with a ship, two frigates and a schooner received the order to assume a position at the mouth of the Bay of Cattaro to communicate with Mister Sankovskiy who was an individual in Montenegro entrusted with giving the people of Cattaro hope of our patronage and aid,[3] and then, having established a blockade in the channel of Calamotta (Koločep) and between the islands of Meleda (Mljet) and Lagosta to deny the French access to Cattaro, he waited to ascertain if the people wished to be freed from the enemy and take the appropriate measures to occupy the surrounding country. Captain Baillie deserved such an important assignment after his previous service. He was known as a skilful and enterprising naval officer and especially distinguished himself in the war of 1799. After detaching from the fleet of Admiral Ushakov and landing in Brindisi, Baillie took 500 sailors and unexpectedly marched on Naples opposite 10,000 French, seized a forward post, captured two guns on the bridge and bravely assaulted their vanguard. At that time, Cardinal Fabrizio Ruffo had armed a mob and the enemy withdrew into the fortress before laying down their arms at a handful of Russian sailors. When Emperor Paul I received the report,[4] he remarked 'Baillie has surprised me, so I will surprise him'. He was promoted to captain-lieutenant and awarded the Order of Saint Anne, first class.

The people of the Bay of Cattaro have constituted an independent republic for ages, voluntarily recognizing the protection of the Venetians under the seventh article of their treaty with them (in which it reads 'if the republic is not able to defend the region, then the people are within their right to remain independent'), and they did not wish to recognize the authority of the Holy Roman Emperor who unfairly gained the province in the Treaty of Campo Formio in 1797. The Viennese

---

3    Stefan Andreyevich Sankovskiy served as Russia's consul general to Montenegro from late 1805 until the Treaty of Tilsit and French occupation of Kotor in 1807. Gabriel Frilley and Jovan Vlahović, *Le Monténégro Contemporain* (Paris: E. Plon et Cie., 1876), pp.43-51. [Gabriel Frilley and Jovan Vlahović, *Contemporary Montenegro* (Paris: E. Plon and Co., 1876), pp.43-51.]

4    Paul I Petrovich reigned as Emperor and Autocrat of All Russia from 1796-1801.

court was compelled to confirm the former rights of the people and accept the region on the same terms as it had once belonged to Venice. The Bokez have learned that now, contrary to their rights, they have been conceded to France, who then intended to deprive them of their trade, freedom and prosperity. The Austrian government oppressed the most prominent citizens due to their amicability towards Russia. One of them raised his voice one Sunday and said to the people: 'Awaken from inaction, this sorrow doesn't suit you, my brothers! We stand on the brink of death, the abyss is under our feet, the fatherland is in peril and only one path leads to freedom – your sword and bravery will show it to you'. Every man in that church with despair in his heart and a fervent love for his homeland regained his strength and endeavoured to either oust the French or die. Cries of 'who is a warrior?' and 'to arms, brothers!' instantly inspired the fallen spirits. In a few hours, like a sweeping wildfire, everyone armed themselves. Even in that fortress of Cattaro in the presence of the Austrian governor they rang the alarm and told him that all the people were unanimously ready to defend their liberty to the last drop of blood. Not only devotion to Russia, but common and private interests were the cause of this amazing unanimity. It was only necessary to show the Russian flag and the whole people armed themselves, not one man remained idle or refused and no one doubted the protection of the Russian Emperor. Many of the Bokez with experience in Russian service wanted this change more than anyone. The community elders in Risan and Castelnuovo, Counts Sava Ivelić and Đorđe Vojnović, were the most zealous and ready to liberate their country. The retired Lieutenant-General Count Marko Ivelić, a native of Risan who lived in his home there as a private citizen, probably played a role as well in inspiring the people to such a bold venture due to his former assignment of being the Emperor's liaison to Montenegro and commanding the respect of his fellow citizens. The elders of the people, the captains of the districts, assembled without any outside suggestion and endeavoured not only to seek protection but to definitively swear allegiance to the Orthodox and august monarch of Russia. As a result, the people sent deputies to Mr Sankovskiy and the Metropolitan of Montenegro. The former was assured of the vice-admiral's intention to give assistance for the defence of the region and did not reject their claims, which made them believe we were worthy of their loyalty and love. The Metropolitan Petar Petrović-Njegoš, head of the Montenegrin people who for 97 years recognized themselves as a subject of Russia, on the 15th [27th] of February at a general assembly in Cetinje, decided with the consent of the princes and chiefs to not only fight against the French but also to drive out the Austrian forces. Assuming command of the combined forces of the Montenegrins and Bokez, he first enveloped Castelnuovo. The timely arrival of Baillie's squadron on the anchorage on the 16th [28th] shielded the people from the terrible revenge of the Austrians. Negotiations began, during which on the 21st of February [5th of March], the Metropolitan told the commandant that if he did not wish to give up the fortress to the people, it would be taken by storm. Baillie, who was requested by the Austrian governor, fired just one cannon and then the governor surrendered, turning over the keys to the fortress to the elders of the communities who then assumed local authority during the occupation of the Bay of Cattaro. It must also be noted that the Austrian forces here were now defending a foreign territory, as the deadline for relinquishing the territory to the French expired already on the 29th of January [10th of February]. The Austrian Emperor's emissary, Filippo, the Marquis de Ghislieri, consented to these proposals. Thus the brave people regained their liberty and in all eight fortresses replaced the Austrian garrison without opposition.

At 9 in the morning, the Metropolitan arrived onboard the *Aziya* with the elders and then returned to shore with Captain Baillie and a company of naval infantry to be met by the clergy with a cross, blessings, bread and salt. The people joyfully exclaimed 'long live Alexander!' At the Savina Monastery, where more than 10,000 people gathered, the clergy performed a service of supplication, after which the Metropolitan blessed the banners which were assigned to the fortresses and handed them to the elder captains of the districts. He spoke briefly in these strong terms: 'your wish has come true, brave Slavs! You see before you the long-awaited brothers who are yours in birth, faith, bravery and glory. The mighty Russian monarch welcomes you into the numbers of his children! Oh blessed be the Providence of the Lord! May this joyous and fortunate day be memorable to you! Before we give these blessed banners to you, you must take an oath to protect them with all your strength to the very end'. The people repeated the oath unanimously and in the ancient custom of the Slavs, shook their naked swords in the air and swore on the ashes of their ancestors to be faithful until death. During the procession into the town, the enthusiasm of the people was a touching sight. Boys in festive outfits showered the soldiers with flowers and the throngs of adults came to kiss the hems of our coats or reverentially clasp our hands. Amid thunderous exclamations for our good Tsar's health and long reign we raised the Russian banner in Castelnuovo and the fortress of Espanola. The ships of the squadron and all the merchant vessels blossomed with flags of every hue and together with the fortresses fired a salute from 101 guns. From then until the darkest of night, in the whole region muskets and cannons fired unceasingly, and not only the merchant ships but all the homes and sloops too flew the blue saltire on white – Saint Andrew's flag. The populace knew no limits to their joy and treated the soldiers to all the best luxuries, embraced them, shed tears in their heartfelt gratitude and every face was sincere through that day's most magnificent celebrations.

The Cattaro region together with Montenegro, being adjacent to Slavic peoples loyal to Russia, separated itself from the independent Republic of Ragusa in

Dalmatia, and through Herzegovina connected with Serbia to constitute an excellent military position for our army and a key acquisition for the political relations of that time. Herzegovina and the brave Black George, leader of the Serbs, made it easier to receive aid from Russia, in the event it proved necessary to unite and halt all of Bonaparte's ambitions in the region, thereby preserving the integrity of the Ottoman Porte which was allied with us.[5] Having in Cattaro a safe harbour in the middle of the Adriatic, Senyavin bolstered his strength with the 12,000 brave Bokez and Montenegrin warriors and transferred the theatre of war from Corfu to Dalmatia, cut it off from Italy with a tight blockade at sea, and forced the delivery of troops and provisions through Austrian territory and over impenetrable mountains where there were no roads, against the will of the local inhabitants – all of this placed the French generals in a precarious situation and Napoleon hastened to declare his claims to various cities in Albania[6] which had belonged to the Venetian Republic, seeing that his plans aimed at Greece and especially Corfu were destroyed from the onset. The ambitious and self-interested Ali Pasha, learning of the occupation of Cattaro and the measures taken to maintain his neutrality after several experiences demonstrating his unwillingness towards us, he began to seek Senyavin's acquaintance and became a good neighbour and friend, thereby destroying Bonaparte's last hope of overthrowing the Turkish Empire. The occupation of the Ragusan Republic, which had been under the auspices of the Sultan, as an endeavour to conquer the Cattaro region with cunning politics and force of arms, clearly proved how important this point alone was for the future plans of the conqueror. For these reasons, the occupation of Cattaro [by Russia] made a great commotion. The convergence of French and Turkish forces was denied, the prospect of seducing the Greeks and Slavs was dashed, and this first step taken under Senyavin's command justified the wise choice of His Majesty in his appointment. All the measures and orders serving to guard the province were approved and the admiral received the monarch's

---

5    Black George (Karađorđe) Petrović who ruled as the leader of the Serbs from 1804 to 1813 was in open rebellion against the Ottoman Empire. This apparent contradiction in Russian foreign policy would be resolved however in November of 1806 when Russia and the Ottomans went to war over the fate of the Danubian Principalities. Andreyevskiy et al., *Brockhaus and Efron Dictionary*, s.v. 'Карагеоргиевичи'; Александр Михайловский-Данилевский, *Описание Турецкой Войны в Царствование Императора Александра, с 1806 до 1812 года*, vol. 1 (St. Petersburg: Штаб Отдельного Корпуса Внутренней Стражи, 1843), pp.1-41. [Andreyevskiy et al., *Brockhaus and Efron Dictionary*, s.v. 'the Karađorđević'; Aleksandr Mikhaylovskiy-Danilevskiy, *Description of the Turkish War in the Reign of Emperor Alexander from 1806 to 1812*, vol. 1 (St. Petersburg: Staff of the Independent Corps of the Interior Guard, 1843), pp.1-41.]

6    Bronevskiy's note: 'Butrinto, Parga, Santiquaranta (Saranda) and Antivari (Bar), the first three of which lie opposite Corfu'.

favour, expressed to him in a flattering rescript. As it was known that the Ragusan Senate, partly by its own volition and partly out of an inability to resist, permitted French forces through its territory and provided them with provisions and boats for transportation from Stagno (Ston) to Ragusa; in order to compel the senate to keep its proper and complete neutrality, the Metropolitan sent a detachment of his Montenegrins to appear on their border while Captain Baillie sent our frigate to the Calamotta channel to prevent the enemy from crossing the sea to Ragusa. Count Vojnović, the chief of the Castelnuovo district, accompanied us to induce the senate to withdraw their support for the French. We weighed anchor at the same time the schooner *Ekspeditsion* departed for Corfu with reports to the admiral.

# 22

# The Calamotta Channel

During a fresh wind at 5 o'clock, we sailed from Castelnuovo to Ragusa and stood in the middle of the Calamotta channel at a depth of 15 *sazhen*s [32 m]. As a frigate in a light wind cannot chase smaller vessels, the captain sent me to the nearby islands from which it was more convenient to observe ships passing both through the channel and over the open sea. Taking provisions for four days, I went to the neighbouring islet and circled around its northern side to reach a small bay protected on both sides by high capes; in this place, we were well covered from the sea and not a single boat travelling to Ragusa could avoid passing us. I went ashore to inspect the location. With each step forward, I pushed through uneven stones and occasionally clambered up steep slopes with thorny bushes and the branches of fallen trees for handholds. For roughly half a *versta* [533.4 m] we ascended in this fashion until we reached the island's summit where, taking out a telescope, I scoured the horizon and under the shorelines for ships. Apart from a great snowstorm and violent waves, nothing was discovered. Looking closer, I saw that the channel is comprised of a large ridge of islands running parallel to the coast at a distance of two or three miles [3.7-5.56 km] from it. A pilot assured me that the depth between these islands is unfathomable but since the passages between them are so narrow, only three are convenient for warships. Far to the north were the islands of Curzola (Korčula) and Meleda and to the south, the giants of Cattaro were covered with snow.

Posting a guard on the height, I descended toward what I thought to be the middle of the island. The cold wind forced me to put on a cloak and if I had not, my uniform would have been shredded by thorns. Finally we reached a ravine which led us to a pool surrounded by trees formed by the rainwater streaming down the heights into the shallow depression. This reservoir seemed like a significant discovery for pilgrims like us who of course rarely come here. This island, to which no one has ever given a name although many millions of people may have set foot on it before me, consisted of a hard horizontal slab covered with only a few inches of earth. In this thin layer grew crooked juniper trees, large shrubs of sage and roses and although I am not much of a botanist, I noticed much rosemary, a kind of wild laurel, wilting stems of lilies and other flowers that only grow for us in greenhouses. Large crevices visible all over the island made us think there had been earthquakes and maybe all of these islands were broken off from the coastline. Finding no settlement and only wild donkeys and a herd of sheep wandering freely, we returned to the shore with torn up boots and scratched hands and legs for our trouble. On the way, I heard a musket shot and looked up at the height where the guard was posted to see a signal informing me of the appearance of a ship. I began at a walk, broke into a run, rolled down the hill and immediately jumped into the boat, casting off into the open sea.

The sky was overcast and the sea was covered with foam. Paddling past the tip of the island, there came into view a large tartane running south with wind astern. We set sail on a close-hauled course. The boat began to flood with the waves and two sailors were continuously pouring out water. When we were close enough, I ordered a shot from our swivel gun, which prompted the tartane to immediately turn from the shore toward the sea and unfurl its sails. I also loosened the reefs and, turning slightly away from the wind, we began to noticeably gain on them. Meanwhile it was already beginning to grow dark and a light rain began to fall, while the sky vacillated between clear and cloudy. The pilot assured me that there would be a *burrasca* (storm) that night and predicted that on such a light craft, it would endanger the lives of the 30 men. In the hope that I would sooner overtake the tartane than reach the shore while the sky was still light, I did not listen to his warning and continued the pursuit. After a heated argument, when the pilot was forced to give up and be quiet, my assumption was confirmed in just a few minutes. The skipper of the tartane, frightened by another ball shot his way, led into the wind, hoisted the flag of Ragusa and lay to. To climb aboard and enter the cabin was a matter of one minute and a few paces. There in that clean cabin I found for myself a better refuge from the storm than on our frigate's boat and my spirits were lifted, however I internally reproached myself for the foolishness of taking to the sea at night. When I was presented with the vessel's passport, I saw that the skipper was carrying rich cargo belonging to a French merchant from Ancona to Ragusa. He then calmed down and with a merry spirit and cheer immediately dispatched his men to their places, tied our boat on their towline and in a beam reach with all sails set, we headed straight to Santa Croce. The pilot's prediction came true, for as the sun went down and the night became its darkest, a torrential rain began. Despite an increased wind, I kept all the upper sails, from which the tartane was blown nearly onto its side, the masts cracked, and the skipper in a desperate fear began to recite his '*ave maria*' and '*padre nostro*' although I safely navigated through the rocks (called *petini*), passed all dangers and came to drop anchor beside the frigate at 10 o'clock.

A cutter was brought to the Dalmatian trabaccolo at dawn, but the captain, in deference to the residents' loyalty to us, let it pass without delay. From the skipper we were informed that all of Dalmatia was now occupied by the enemy, for which reason we should increase our caution. The captain, sending me again to the same island, ordered me not to stray too far from the frigate. Making my way through a very narrow and absolutely violent channel between two high, steep islands, I took shelter on a third, considering my experience the day before. We made a circuit of the island and found neither a settlement nor a drop of water; the whole island was overgrown with small bushes of every kind, one of which bore dried berries like our strawberries and had a very pleasant, tart flavour. The Slavs call this berry 'gloginja' and it has the dark-red appearance of wild strawberries, four seeds in the centre, and a round, firm cup at the end. Mounting a guard above as usual, we made a tent out of sails and I settled down for the night. At sunset the sky darkened and a pouring rain fell, soaking every thread we wore, and for two hours thunder roared overhead. The wind began to roar and the storm began in earnest, blowing out our fire, while all the sailors huddled together in the small tent singing songs. The next day, I learned why they had been so merry: a share of wine intended for four days was drank to the last drop in one night.

In the morning of the 24th of February [8th of March], I wanted to try to return to the frigate, but with hardly any effort I rounded the cape and proceeded 300 sazhens [640 m] ahead when a wind and current carried us back and I was forced to land on the eastern side of the same island. The site where we landed was open, with waves crashing against the rocks of a strong breaker for which I ordered the boats to be pulled ashore and a hut built under a nearby rocky overhang. We were not discouraged that day, and although there was no luck in the hunt, for we only saw where the goats graze, the time was spent cheerfully and we were content with raw corned beef and biscuit. By evening they became tired and collected broken branches, climbed into their hut and built a fire. Another thunderstorm and downpour came with nightfall.

With the rising of the sun, we read good and bad omens like Peruvians from its light, which failed to penetrate the dense clouds blanketing the sky in all directions. Powerful waves crashed on the sea driven by a southerly wind and in the distance it was so dark you could scarcely find the horizon between the sky and the water save for the white crests of the waves; again we could not return to the frigate. I became displeased when our scant provisions ran out at breakfast and the hunt again ended empty-handed. Not a plant on the island could be eaten except for the berries. Some of the men became tormented by thirst. I became desperate, thinking fate had determined that we would die there from hunger. By evening, when we gathered in our bivouac, it was no longer a jovial affair; the sailors had no desire to sing and sat around the fire quietly, often going out to look at the clouds and confirming time and time again that the storm had not abated before lying down on the wet ground with grief. I did not close my eyes all night and walked about the boats along the shore despite the rain. In my strong agitation, I felt as though I had been cast out from the world and my soul was exhausted by a thousand thoughts, the faint light of hope not at all easing my sad disposition. For several minutes I stood numb, staring out both to heaven and at sea. From my strong desire, during the crashing waves and whistling wind, it seemed to me sometimes to be silently still and on one occasion I entered the hut to wake the peacefully slumbering men but came to my senses and held my head in despair, seeing the horror of starvation.

Unable to wait until morning, I roused the sailors and just before dawn ordered them to launch the boats. Some were amazed by such an endeavour but according to the strict subordination particular to the Russian soldier in all cases, they silently obeyed and put the boats to water, despite the terrible surf. Deciding not to stay any longer in such a desolate place and patiently wait for the weather to change, I intended to cross over to the side of the channel where a house could be seen. We cast off, set our sails at half, and shortly thereafter the wind rolled us so far over we began to ladle up seawater. The boat would have capsized if our sail did not tear open. Then turning into the wind, we would only hope to tack towards another island which was as untamed and uninhabited as the first. Forced to sail with extreme danger, we strayed no more than 200 *sazhens* [426.72 m] from shore when we saw before us a small bay very well covered from the southerly wind. I was grateful to see that our boats could be left anchored and it would not be necessary to pull them onto the beach.

Leaving a guard by the boats and laying a heavy blunderbuss on the shoulder, I set out with 30 armed sailors searching for some kind of dwelling or settlement. Silently and with measured steps we ascended to a small hill and what did we find? A large village nestled in a beautiful valley covered with trees and surrounded by vineyards. No words can express our rapture and joyfully we crossed ourselves and cried 'glory to God!' before taking off at a run. When I came to the first house, I remembered that every meal asks for money and when I reached into my pockets, there was not a single kopeck. I asked the sailors but they too were penniless. We stopped and stood searching ourselves and laughing at the circumstances. In the first home we approached, we found an old man who told us that the island was named Giuppana (Šipan), that a chancellor, governor, senator and landowner lived there, and led me to understand that all four titles belonged to one individual. I sent to him a *garde de marine*,[1] asking permission to stock ourselves with provisions

---

in the belief that by military right he would aid us on a single signature. Rather, the senator requested to see me in person and met me at the gate, gently took me by the arm, and brought me into his home. In a conversation at first too long for my hungry stomach, he began to explain the difficult position of the republic between two powerful empires. To my joy, his wife soon entered in a beautiful morning gown and served me a very small cup of coffee without bread and told her talkative husband that she had learned through the maid that it was necessary to feed my people as soon as possible. The husband left. I stood up and passed a mirror to see my torn boots and face smeared with campfire soot. With great embarrassment, I expressed my gratitude to the wife for her attention. I presented the most lamentable image of a knight, sitting before her on a high and narrow chair in an awkward position, hiding my boots, adjusting my cravat, buttoning up my jacket, and from her compassionate glance I became even more timid. Despite this however, our conversation with the help of several Italian words written in my book, which I was forced to consult, and a few borrowed utterances from Scripture, I was gradually revived. I was already laughing when the senator returned. The policy of his poor republic again changed my countenance however and I would certainly have become ill if his beautiful, wise and educated wife did not hurry to have breakfast served.

My men were also fed. The hospitality of the Slavs, delighted by guests they could understand, anticipated the governor's care, and the men under my command who came to me with a cheerful face to notify me that the wind was beginning to subside seemed to be already physically and emotionally restored. At noon, when I had time to eat a lunch after a full breakfast, the wind turned toward the frigate and it carried us back safely.

In the final three days of this month, the weather was fine and my reconnoitres were more successful: three trabaccolos with full loads worth 100,000 rubles fell into our hands. A tartane belonging to a Ragusan merchant was released with its goods placed on other craft, and by the time Count Vojnović had completed his assignment in Ragusa, they were sent to Cattaro. On the 3rd [15th] of March, when the frigate *Mikhail* relieved us of our position, we went out to sea on a light wind and captured a rich prize. During this favourable voyage, we pursued all the ships that showed themselves to us, but they were all henceforth Austrian and permitted to pass. On the night of the 6th [18th], we entered the bay of Fiume during a fog and anchored at a depth of 35 *sazhen*s [74.68 m].

corps proper. *Complete Collection of Laws*, col. 1, vol. 44, part 1 (1711-1799), pp.45-53. No. 10,062.

# 23

# Fiume

---

Fog and rain did not prevent anyone from going ashore. Seafarers in a hurry to enjoy the pleasures of the city and its people, who were not out walking the streets in the bad weather, inspected the buildings and surveyed the surrounding area. Finding the home of Russian Consul Fonton, we visited together with him the Austrian governor, who advised us to beware of the French now crossing into Dalmatia. In the company of State Councillor Pozzo di Borgo and Collegiate Assessor Kozen with us, who carried dispatches for Russia, and at the invitation of our passenger Mackenzie, we went to dine at the best restaurant. The host met us on the stairs, turned pale and said 'all of our chambers are full!' But on closer inspection and realizing that we were not French, he then admitted us and joyfully opened three beautiful rooms. Entering, he quietly whispered in Slavonian: 'what a pleasure it is to receive Russians in my house. I have never seen any before, but I hear that they are good gentlemen who do not offend poor and gracious innkeepers. If you really are Russians, then it would be impossible for me pass up such guests, can't you see?' Those words, along with the advice of the governor, prompted us to occupy the most remote room. We were only served breakfast before we were notified of some commotion on the wharf. As if anticipating our reaction, people ran from all sides to the embankment asking what the cause was, and we were told 'the Russians have beaten a Frenchman'. Pushing through the crowd to our boats, we were reassured by an officer of the Hungarian hussars that our sailors were in the right. The reason for the brawl was that three of our rowers were walking along the sidewalk when a French sergeant-major, wishing to pass them, pushed one into the dirt and then another, but this sailor guardedly threw the Frenchman in the mud face first. Angry in his humiliation, he drew his sabre. The sailors, being unarmed, rushed and grabbed the weapon from the Frenchman's hands and badly pummelled him. Thirty French soldiers ran to his screams and, were it not for the hussars' arrival, this useless quarrel could have ended badly for us. Returning to the inn, we were met in the hall by two French generals who for one thing or another scolded the trembling innkeeper and ordered his servants to harness their horses. They looked us up and down with a terrible, arrogant gaze.

Fiume lies on a flat plain below a bare ridge of mountains which form a semi-circle. The *bora* blows from them occasionally, knocking people off their feet, overturning carriages and tearing the roofs off houses. For that reason, the anchorage is completely deserted in the winter, as ships take shelter in Buccari (Bakar) and Porto Re (Kraljevica), 8 and 15 *versta*s [8.53 and 16 km] away. The town is well built with broad streets, houses all consistent and with a most pleasant appearance. By the number of incomplete buildings, it can be seen that the town will grow to be quite extensive. The occupation of the French is significant here, as the shops and magazines were empty and mostly locked up, left penniless with only their walls, as the residents say. On the southern side where the river[1] flows, the bank is built up with huge stores. Vessels arriving are loaded quickly and conveniently there. The mouth of the river provides a safe harbour for smaller craft. Fiume, as a free port, could soon be equal to the best commercial cities, but its proximity to the rich Trieste and its poor anchorage deprives it of greater prosperity. However, as all the industry of Hungary has no other outlet to the Mediterranean than Fiume, trade with Malta, Sicily and smuggling with the blockaded harbours of Italy prove to be sufficient.

When the rain stopped, we crossed to the other side of the river and there, following for two *versta*s [2.13 km] the path hewn into a rocky hill, we stopped at a waterfall whose noise could be heard in town. The river was constrained by two steep cliffs, flowed through several rapids and spilled over heights of five or seven *sazhen*s [10.67 or 14.94 m] into a ravine, on the steep slopes of which stood mills built practically on top of one another. Below the rapids which fell over ledges and steps were anchored floating mills. The view from the mountain was charming. Water falling from the upper wheels onto the lower ones and foaming about the stones drenched the roofs of the works with a fine rain and sprayed up like a small cyclone. The whining and clattering of the wheels, the thunder of water tumbling into the silvery overflows, a multitude of boats driving hard against the awful winding water to reach the floating mills, and several pack mules descending along the steep paths formed such a quaint, majestic and altogether menacing spectacle. From here begins the glorious road that will give to posterity the names of Emperor Francis and General Josef Philipp Vukasović who built it. It cuts through a chain of the impassable Croatian mountains and, as I was assured, is of no inferior durability or elegance than the ancient roads of the Romans. Before this road was laid, goods were transported on packhorses and taken up the slopes

---

1    Bronevskiy's note: 'The river is called the Fiume, from which the town derives its name. In the Italian language, 'fiume' means river'.

with great difficulty and risk; but now large carriages hauling 500 *pud*s [8.19 t] of luggage can drive straight from Hungary to Fiume smoothly and conveniently.

On the 9th [21st] of March, with the arrival of Titular Councillor Laskari from St. Petersburg with dispatches to the admiral, we weighed anchor within the hour. On the same boat as the courier, the consul sent an escort of three Russian soldiers who were then forced to serve in an Austrian regiment that had recently arrived in Fiume.

## 24

# Sailing from Fiume to Cattaro – Port Carboni – Nighttime Debarcation

During a period of still and gloomy weather, we were forced to anchor for the night and then at dawn on the 10th [22nd] of March, we set sail and reached the mouth of the bay where we seized two Italian ships sailing from Fiume for Ancona and Senigallia. Light winds slowed our journey and as the frigate kept close to the Dalmatian islands, an armed boat was prepared to attack enemy vessels that might be hiding in the small and narrow bays. In the channel between the island of Meleda and the coast of Ragusa, a strong foul wind and a chain of rocks lying on the northern side of the island of Lagosta imperilled us in the night, compelling the captain to turn to the open sea; but here the wind grew even stronger and the frigate barely progressed at all. On the 15th [27th], we reached the small bay of Carboni (Zvirinovik) and dropped anchor in the mud at a depth of 35 *sazhen*s [74.68 m]. Here we found a single tartane. The skipper, as usual, came aboard the frigate with his papers and as he was a Bokez, the captain returned his Austrian certificate, saying: 'your papers are inappropriate for you; you need to exchange them for Russian ones'. The skipper did not understand and turned pale as he thought he was being taken prisoner. But when he was told that the Russian flag was flying over Cattaro and that his fatherland was free, you might easily imagine his astonishment and delight. He immediately went down to his boat, changed the flag and returned to the frigate to request that he and his crew be administered an oath of allegiance. After this, forgetting about his trade, he suggested to the captain that we should seize a French magazine located in a certain village. Towards evening, another Bokez trabaccolo came to us and its skipper offered his services, volunteering to be our guide.

The sun had already set when we anchored. The night was supremely dark and pouring rain fell on us. Five rowing vessels, of which two were armed with swivel guns, with 80 sailors, soldiers and Bokez were entrusted to me. We set off from the frigate at 9 o'clock. When we reached the shore, the skipper took us close to the embankment. Arriving this way to the pier, we moored our boats with a guard of several men and then ascended onto the street with the remainder. The Bokez could not find the home of the French captain in the dark and so were forced to enter the nearest house with a light shining. Through the loosely fixed door they saw inside four old men dining by a fading fire in the hearth. On a wobbly table before them one could see cheese, bread and chestnuts. One man held a jug in his hand, the others smoked cigars and were laughing over some topic of conversation. 'God keep you, good people,' I said as I stepped into the room and they looked back but became frightened by the sight of our soldiers and their glistening bayonets. 'Don't be afraid, we don't mean you any harm' … but they did not seem to understand me and became mute and frozen before me.

When a Bokez skipper said to them: 'have no fear, brother, these are our *moshkovi*', these words changed their fear into joy like the touch of a magic wand and they rushed to kiss me and my soldiers. One wanted me to drink his wine, another called his wife and children to furnish us with everything they had, but when we explained that we came to take the French, the son of the host fetched a musket and volunteered to show us the captain's house and their magazine. The old men went out to warn the residents about our arrival and to forbid them from leaving their homes, in order to avoid confusion.

Walking through the village, I heard a gunshot, then another, and ran to find that the sailors attached to a *Garde de Marine* Baskakov were already in the house, however no one was taken prisoner; its former French occupants had dived out the windows on the other side of the building. The locals assured me that they fled to a fortress which was six hours away. In the impenetrable darkness, we could not pursue them, so we turned to the destruction of their magazines. The sailors, with the aid of the residents, loaded onto two trabaccolos all of the enemy's accessories, several barrels of wine, vodka, bread and flour. The remainder, for which we had no room, was distributed among the locals and the barrels of red wine, which constituted 300 *vedros* [3.94 kL] or more, were assembled in one place and smashed open. At dawn we returned to the frigate with fine booty and celebratory songs.

On the 16th [28th] of March, when we weighed anchor, a vessel with a rich cargo was taken. The 17th [29th] brought a strong adverse current and a calm foul wind which together forced us to retire and anchor at a depth of 19 *sazhens* [40.54 m] in the bay of Greater Carboni. This harbour is located between the three islands of Carboni and the western side of the island of Curzola, covered from all winds, with clear entrances and a convenient site for even 100-gun ships of the line. On the 18th [30th] of March, we again went out to sea and for the same reasons were repelled and upon our return we found in port a Danish merchant brig and corsair from Cattaro flying our flag, which informed us that the admiral was now in Castelnuovo. On the 21st of March [2nd of April], the captain ordered me to take four prize vessels back to Cattaro. Hauling up its anchor, the frigate moved further seaward and with its squadron I departed by the canal between the island of Meleda and the hard shore.

A northeasterly breeze served us for only a few hours and by noon it became calm and waves previously from the south mercilessly jostled us. One trabaccolo was overloaded with cargo and sagging in the water and if the waves did not calm down by evening, I would have been forced to break open and dump the barrels of cheap olive oil standing on its deck. The sun set as pleasantly as in the summer, the sea became as smooth as a mirror, the sky appeared as a dome of crystal beset with shining jewels over a night as clear as day and we floated in place just as if we stood on shore. Nature was in perfect tranquillity, everyone slept except for me and an Italian sailor at the wheel who sang in a strange voice one of his nation's songs. Ordering him what course to hold and by what wind, I wrapped myself in a cloak, lay down on the deck and did not awake until dawn. My trabaccolo was so close to the shore that in a light northerly wind it was difficult to evade the cape of Meleda while entering the channel. Reprimanding the helmsman who forgot to inform me that he decided to approach the shore, I ordered the launch of a dinghy with a towline and quickly entered the channel. Another trabaccolo in the same position also traversed the cape by oars and my whole squadron calmly reached the eastern shore of Meleda.

I cannot remain silent about the good Bokez named Spiridaro, who was given to me as a pilot from a boat accompanying the frigate in the port of Carboni. He presented himself as a man of the world and was literate although he did not read books, but often visited the theatre in Venice and could recite verses from Pietro Metastasio for me. I was learning the Italian language then and he proudly translated the meaning of the words for me. His servility and observation of the strictest laws of subordination was tiring and no matter how hard I tried to treat him kindly and without ceremony, he always stood on my left with a respectful bow and took my every word as an order. I could forcefully convince him not to kiss my hand, the floor or the hem of my coat, but he did not want to give up his deep and ridiculous bowing. Gaetani, the owner of the trabaccolo, when I told him that he would be released and paid for the cargo, was calm and caressed me but did not bother with any excessive courtesy. I had to spend time with these people and perhaps it would have been tolerable if I were not concerned with the poor condition of all four prizes. Due to the sparse knowledge of navigation among my fellows, who had a poor compass and no maps, a distrust in me took hold: I was on the deck constantly and if, when exhausted, I closed my eyes, I would awaken every minute and even while I slept, I heard everything said and done around me. My stomach was also deprived of good food but what I had was nutritious:

beans in lamp oil with bitter vinegar, black bread and sweet beans; these were the extensive, luxurious dishes to which I was treated.

All day, we rode on a weak breeze and nothing better presented itself. The water flowed completely calmly alongside us. I sat on an overturned barrel secured at the entrance of the cabin, in which there were only two beds, and in a merry disposition conversed with Spiridaro when suddenly a cannon ball flew past our stern. No painter could depict the surprise on our faces. I jumped up, grabbed the telescope and looked around while the sailors feebly looked at each other and stayed fixed in their places. Another ball flew over our heads and broke a sail, the Italians screamed and fell on their faces, and my six sailors rushed to arms and began to load the two swivel guns. Then I saw a small boat with sails fore-and-aft, which came out from behind the rocks covering the port of San Paolo on Meleda and sailed straight at us – her ensign could not be seen behind her sails. The three other trabaccolos formed up closely with me on my signal. Wishing to make them think we were peaceful merchants, I ordered the Austrian flag be raised and sent Spiridaro in a skiff to assure the enemy that we were sailing from Trieste to Ragusa, while in the meantime encircling them so that we might capture them in a boarding action. The pilot did not completely cross the gulf to the boat before returning and shouting out: 'relax, commander, they're ours! They're ours!' I did not know whether to believe it or not and continued to advance. The gunners brandished their burning matches and the sailors lay down on the deck with their muskets and blunderbusses at the ready. Finally they sent out a boat of their own with a troop of armed men who did not attack me but asked if I was a Russian. I answered in Russian that there could be no doubt about it, naming the frigate on which I served, where I came from, and so on. They did not seem to trust me and I was convinced by their dialect that they were Bokez. My sailors began to talk with them and they immediately came aboard. The captain of the corsair was exceptionally rich with weaponry and came to kiss my hand while the others touched the skirt of my coat and bowed humbly like Spiridaro. He showered me with a thousand apologies and pleaded that they could not see our flag and presumed we left Curzola, therefore being enemies. He informed me that Stagno and the port of Zuliano (Žuljana) have fallen to French corsairs. To ask him about other circumstances, I ordered a glass of wine for everyone and invited the captain to accompany me to Ragusa. He requested a written order so I wrote him a small note on a scrap of paper torn from a notebook and further instructed him to keep his vessel close to mine and raise a lantern on his mast at night. We parted with mutual courtesies. The Bokez rowed away and fired a salute from all their muskets, shouting 'evviva nostri!' – long live our own. I ordered a shot from a swivel gun and shouted 'ura!'

At noon the wind picked up and we navigated successfully all night. In the morning of the 23rd of March [4th of April] however the wind died out and the current began to drag us backward. My squadron was close to the southeastern tip of Meleda where a small cove surrounded by a low shore was no more than a mile [1.86 km] away. The luxury of such a position seduced me and since it was useless to stay in the open sea, I turned toward the cove and fired a shot to signal the other trabaccolos to follow behind me. All five boats stood around me and the men went ashore. No water was found, but a chestnut grove gave my sailors cause for rejoicing. They filled ten bags for the most part with fallen and rotten chestnuts and found that they tasted similar to those in the mountains and one pointed out that on Wednesdays and Fridays one can eat them without sin.[1] The Bokez shot two goats and a ram and brought various game while the others caught several fish. Immediately a fire was lit but the wind forced us to give up our bountiful dinner and weigh anchor. With a jolly ruckus we sailed until the northeasterly wind stopped and then we very quickly turned to run downwind. Passing Zuliano, a corsair came under our stern and saluted me with all of its muskets and cannons and all its crew cried 'long live Alexander!' in a booming volume we had never before heard and once we were nearly deafened, they sailed on to their post. The wind served me until Old Ragusa, which I was forced to enter on the 26th of March [7th April] by the dying breeze and lack of fresh water.

---

1    On most Wednesdays and Fridays of the year, Orthodox Christians fast from meat, fish, eggs, dairy and oils. The 23rd of March, 1806 fell on a Friday in the Old Style calendar. *Месяцослов с Росписью Чиновных Особ или Общий Штат Российской Империи, на Лето от Рождества Христова 1806*, vol. 1 (St. Petersburg: Императорская Академия Наук, 1806), p.iv. [*Menologium with a List of the Ranking Individuals or a General State of the Russian Empire in the Year of Our Lord 1806*, vol. 1 (St. Petersburg: Imperial Academy of Sciences, 1806), p.iv.]

## 25

# Old Ragusa

---

The port of Old Ragusa (Cavtat) lies from north to south over a span of the sea covering 20 *verstas* [21.34 km]. Its only entrance was covered by two bridges of bare stones called the *pettine* (comb). The depth in the bay was sufficient for warships but as it was not very wide and a northerly wind blew straight in from the entrance making it difficult to leave, typically only trabaccolos and other light craft took refuge here. The town consisted of two streets on the eastern headland of the harbour. A wall with four guns was built on a narrow isthmus to protect from the overland route, but no fortifications face the sea. A short distance away is the assumed site of the ancient Epidaurum. The town's mayor greeted me with respect and invited me ashore. I accompanied him to a poor coffee house where they served me a small cup of coffee, a pipe of tobacco and a glass of rosolio. I and many others were compelled to eat and drink against our will and I was surprised when everyone paid for themselves. Of course as a Russian I was charged double, which I did not condemn as it is the custom everywhere. I warned the other men of this fact. Hospitality, the holy benefactor of our fatherland, was not known here and everyone had his own price written in the corner. On the next day, the mayor ordered his boats to lead my trabaccolos out to sea. Taking advantage of a quiet northerly wind on the 27th of March [8th of April], I arrived at Castelnuovo where I turned over the papers entrusted to me to the newly established Court of Prizes.

# 26

# The Arrival of the Commander-in-Chief in Cattaro

---

Although the state of affairs on our home shores and the system which our Imperial court intended for us to follow were not yet known to the admiral, the commitment of the people gave hope not only to hold Cattaro but also to disrupt the French in Dalmatia itself, so for the first time the two battalions of the Vitebsk Regiment with four guns under the command of their chief, Major-General Pavel Klavdiyevich Musin-Pushkin, were sent to occupy the fortresses at Cattaro and Castelnuovo. For the personal implementation of everything, the admiral on board the *Selafail* arrived in Castelnuovo on the 13th [25th] of March and on the next day made for Cattaro by boat. This procession was a real triumph, men all along the shores firing off muskets and merchant vessels ceaselessly firing off cannons. The clergy with a cross and civil officials with the keys to the town came to meet the admiral on the pier. Mr Sankovskiy, on behalf of the people, gave a speech expressing devotion to our sovereign, happy and grateful to be rid of the French. For three days it could be said that Senyavin fascinated the people. His accessibility, affection and amazing leniency delighted everyone. His house was surrounded by crowds. The Montenegrins deliberately came down from the mountains to be honoured with the privilege of kissing his coat, his entryway was always full of them and they were never turned away. They seemed to have forgotten their Metropolitan and Senyavin's orders were executed with zeal and an astonishing preparedness.

The admiral personally made sure of the sincere devotion of the inhabitants, freed them from every duty, established communication with Herzegovina and established a convoy for the protection of trade to Trieste and Constantinople. For such favours and care the Bokez were not ungrateful. The elders presented the admiral with a letter of gratitude on the behalf of the people and offered their life and property at his complete disposal. In several days the inhabitants had armed themselves and went out to sea with 30 ships armed with between 8 to 20 guns, which were a great help to a fleet lacking in small craft. This action was more useful than if taxes were simply levied. The mercy and gentleness of our government was in perfect contrast with the rule of our neighbour Napoleon.

The admiral, having learned of the devotion to us of the people of Dalmatia and their occupation by 6,000 French soldiers, undertook the endeavour of liberating that people from their oppressive circumstance. Captain Baillie with 3 ships, 2 frigates and 4 brigs was commanded to take possession of the islands which run opposite of the Dalmatian coast.[1] The Metropolitan, instead of a requested thousand men, promised to assemble 6,000 warriors and volunteered to lead them himself, for which reason the admiral went to Corfu on the 25th of March [6th of April] and took necessary steps in the event of the enemy's intentions. He gathered 3 battalions of Jägers and intended on uniting with Baillie and the Dalmatians to drive the French out, but upon arriving in Corfu, he received a personal order dated from the 14th [26th] of December, 1805 calling for all naval and land forces to be withdrawn to the Black Sea, a location from which any enterprise he had intended would be undoubtedly futile. The commander-in-chief began making preparations for sailing and kept the order a secret, so that a premature announcement would not alarm the locals unnecessarily. When Count Mozzenigo notified him that according to his dispatches,[2] General de Lacy commanded the naval and land forces, the admiral, to dispel his bewilderment, decided to open the letters bearing de Lacy's name wherein he found to his delight that all the forces must remain in the Mediterranean. The admiral sent a brig to return those forces that were with General de Lacy but he was no longer in Constantinople, and on the 19th of April [1st of May] with two ships and a frigate, the admiral himself relocated six companies of Jägers to Cattaro where he then learned that the French forces in Dalmatia had been reinforced. Receiving no instructions from the Emperor, he decided to act only defensively and protect the bay of Cattaro and the occupied island of Curzola. Finally on the 15th [27th] of May, the Emperor expressed his monarchical favour to the admiral with all new orders for the occupation of Cattaro as well as the authority to open instructions in General de Lacy's name as commander-in-chief and act according to his own prudent thinking, in accordance with previous instructions and however the lay of the land and present circumstances should allow.

The joyful cries of the people did not stop, the name of Alexander was repeated endlessly and by its echo, it seemed as though the very hills were booming in rapture. In the churches, as soon as the priest began to read the very first words of

---

1    Bronevskiy's note: 'Regarding the second [southern] half, encompassing the island of Curzola and so on'.

2    Count Giorgio Mozzenigo or Mocenigo was Russia's minister plenipotentiary to the Septinsular Republic from 1802 to 1807. *The Foreign Policy of Russia of the 19th and 20th Centuries*, series 1, vol. 2, p.706.

the announcement, 'the most pious sovereign,' everyone from young to old fell to the ground in prostration. In a school which I happened to enter, the students stood up and all greeted me with one voice. To the teacher's question of to whom they should worship, they answered: 'to God alone'. Next the teacher asked to whom should they serve until their last drop of blood? 'To Alexander alone'. Whom do they hate? And so on. Here was the catechism of a brave nation. Children barely old enough to speak repeated Alexander's name and recited it to everyone they met. Boys constantly shot off pistols and shouted 'long live our Tsar Alexander; may the infidel perish!'

# 27

# My Exploration of the Surroundings of Castelnuovo

After handing over the vessels to the commission and while waiting for the frigate to arrive from Corfu, having no duties or affairs, I took a musket in my hand and wandered around the countryside, hunting and enjoying its beautiful mountainous vistas rarely found outside Switzerland. The ridges of the high, bare mountains surrounding the bay have a savage and bleak appearance. Large stones torn from the flinty peaks are visible along the slopes, but on the sea shore one is treated by pleasant green gardens in the shade of beautiful houses with little sheds and barns. White walls and red tiled roofs with green flora create a pleasing mixture of colours. A beautiful spring had bloomed. Every day I chose a different place to stroll and so with each day I learned something new about my surroundings. With the aid of the Italian language and a few Slavonic words, I was not a mute. The hospitality of one good Slav, whose home stood behind a prize vessel entrusted to me, entertained me for many fine moments. The sight of the small church of St. Elijah the Prophet standing on top of a mountain draped with clouds was especially striking to me, and my considerate host offered to take me there with his children for a mass on the first Sunday. His eldest daughter with one relative and two boys 8 and 9 years old accompanied me soon after the sun rose. The road with each passing minute became steeper, the sites more perilous and the climb more terrifying. After passing several valleys and handsome places, a narrow path led us along a stone wall, then over a deep abyss and under a canopy of rock. Moving from mountain to mountain, we ascended higher and higher and at a certain height, we heard the noise of water falling in the distance. In a few more paces the most beautiful sight revealed itself: a small mountain stream (not far from the mouth of which is built a mill and a stone dam), cramped with rocks, trickles, bends and rolls over stone after stone and spills into a fine white mist, especially during rainy periods, and washes clean the gardens, the trees and heavy boulders below. Two meagre boards laid over the frightening chasm, at the bottom of which the stream was raging, offered us a dangerous bridge. I went ahead and brought across behind me, hand in hand, the others. With difficulty we finally reached the summit of the mountain, but the mass had already concluded and the church was locked. Its position was at such a height, almost touching the ceiling of the clouds, that it seemed to be the best and most respectable site for a temple to this prophet, revered by the common people as the patron of storms and thunder. The cold wind forced us to leave the mountain top without hesitation, but we chose to return by a different road. Not passing the Savina Monastery, we came to another source which formed a striking waterfall. Spilling down from a height of two or three *sazhens* [4.27 or 6.4 m] onto black mossy stones, the stream showered the dense overshadowing forest, curved between the centuries-old oaks, nut and mulberries, quietly and smoothly flowed through the green meadows and by many bends and branches watered the gardens and orchards before finally emptying into the sea near the quarantine. Here was where I came most often to shoot doves. Sometimes while walking alone, I ascended to the high and sharp rocks hanging over the abyss and, indulging in fancies, created a new world for myself, wandering through that country's sunrays and finding myself in a heavenly bliss.

## Celebration of Easter

It is known that in Catholic lands, the Christians of other confessions suffer humiliating oppression. When our presence in the province of Cattaro liberated the Greek faith there, the first celebration of Easter was marked with great festivity. On Saturday in the evening, the people gathered at two monasteries, the Savina and the Topla.[1] A regimental priest was sent to the former to assist the abbot with services, and the regimental singers sang at the latter in the wings. The people listened with great attention to the speech of the Russian priest, and the harmonious singing of the regimental choir led the Slavs into a state of rapture. At the end of the matins, without distinction of class or rank, they began to kiss one another and exchanged the traditional greeting 'Christ is risen' and 'truly he is risen' with such zeal and joy that these embraces of the Russian and Bokez people, united as one, represented the true triumph of faith. After the mass, the grey-haired abbot, inspired by the admiration of his countrymen, made a short speech which was simple but very effective, after which he fell to his knees and raised his hands to heaven, praying for the health of our Emperor and his army with tearful eyes. He begged the all-merciful Creator to preserve the dominion of the Russians in their country until the end of time. His weak, trembling voice and deep emotion

---

1    Holy Saturday in 1806 fell on March 31 [April 12] in the Eastern Orthodox churches, with Easter proper being April 1 [13]. *Menologium with a List of Ranking Individuals in 1806*, vol. 1, pp.vi-xvi.

expressed on his face would have moved even the coldest heart. Many in the crowd genuflected and remained on the ground for several minutes after the speech. Sobbing could be heard everywhere. It is impossible to describe the sensations evoked by such a sincere expression of love from those people. The procession was accompanied by a narrow file of Russian soldiers which was joined en route by the Catholic clergy and made for a complete triumph for our fellow Orthodox. All prior grievances and restrictions on freedom of worship were forgotten and everyone went home completely satisfied.

Early in the morning of the next day, Easter, the bells were rung and cannons fired to usher in the procession. Crowds of villagers appeared on the heights, some climbed up the mountains and others descended the valleys. Each parish visited the next and the next in turn. Boys in white robes, decorated with flower wreathes, carried a cross on a long pole also bestrewn with flowers from village to village. Under the cross was attached the Russian flag of the first squadron,[2] but there were no other images besides this. When the procession passed from one church to another and stopped at every house, singing 'Christ is risen,' muskets and pistols were shot off again. Finally all the banners converged at the main monastery of Savina. The residents of the town at each passing greeted them with shots from their muskets and cannons. The monastery, standing in the middle of the woods under a canopy of rocks and by the seashore dotted with a multitude of merchant vessels, which deliberately approached the structure on this occasion, made for a stunning image. After mass, the abbot blessed the *paskhas*[3] and everyone dispersed through the woods. Each family sat in a circle around a carpet or blanket on which were laid the *paskha*, hot and cold dishes, wine and fruits. Everyone without exception mingled from circle to circle, greeted one another, kissed, sat down and tasted everything prepared before moving on. Our soldiers with difficulty conceded to join in and every family tried to keep them at their blanket as an honoured guest. The women, especially the oldest, remained seated and looked after the food. After dinner, games were played. On a high oak tree, after removing a band of bark, a target was made and opposite it at an agreed distance was positioned a bound rooster. Elders selected as judges sat on the sides of the target and young men set out by twos and soon aimed and shot at the target by one, and the rooster by the other. If a bullet struck the target, the spectators would congratulate the shooter with a loud shout but if he missed, they laughed, and the old people took

2    The blue saltire of Saint Andrew on a white field.
3    Paskha is an Easter dish made of foods forbidden during the fast of Great Lent (especially cheese) which is molded into a truncated pyramid and typically decorated with monograms pertaining to the passion and resurrection. Andreyevskiy et al., *Brockhaus and Efron Dictionary*, s.v. 'Пасха (у великороссов)'. [Andreyevskiy et al., *Brockhaus and Efron Dictionary*, s.v. 'Paskha (Great-Russian usage)'.]

a fine from him of two coins, in addition to the one every shooter must pay to participate. If someone can make several shots without a miss, he will receive a small reward. The fees and fines levied are shared with the poor and pay for the dead birds. The most skillful shooters hit eggs and apples thrown up into the air. Leaden and wooden mugs and balls also served as targets for games. Young boys engaged in running and shooting with pistols. What interested me more were the songs recited by the elders which retold the glorious feats of their ancestors. The stories of Prince Marko[4] and the brave Đorđe Kastriotić[5] were heard with great attention. Swings set up by the soldiers greatly fascinated the Bokez. For a week the festivities continued, and where one crowd dispersed another formed in its place.

## Journey into the Mountains

After the Prize Court's consideration of the papers and certificates of those vessels captured by the *Venus*, and having no affairs or duties to occupy me, I travelled around the Cattaro province and Montenegro. Arriving first in Cattaro, I rode from there to Dobrota, Perasto, Risan, Persano (Prčanj) and Teodo (Tivat) and then after returning to Castelnuovo, I spent a profound week at the Savina Monastery in fasting, prayer and Christian humility. On the third day of Easter,[6] with the Bjelodinović family, I went to Cattaro for a second time and since I could not find a single tavern in the regional capital where I could spend the night, I approached the widow of Archpriest Petrović, who was recommended to me by the Bjelodinoviches. I cannot help but boast of the hospitality, diligence and goodwill of this venerable eldress. Belonging to the dynasty of the Petroviches, she was respected and had a fortune and property, but lived alone in modesty. She had neither servants nor maids and her daughter, Marija, whom I met prior at the home of a mutual acquaintance in Castelnuovo, carried out every chore with a surprising speed that could overtake even the servants of England's taverns. She cleaned the rooms, cooked in the kitchen, served coffee to guests, had time to dine, was as handsomely dressed as any lady and was all the while very attentive. On one occasion, the old widow loved me. She had received a letter from her son

---

4   Marko Mrnjavčević reigned as King of Serbia from 1371 to 1395 and is much mythologized in Southern Slavic folklore for his doomed struggle against the Ottoman Empire. Tanya Popovic, *Prince Marko: The Hero of South Slavic Epics* (New York: Syracuse University, 1988), pp.1-29.

5   George Castriot or Skanderbeg, the 15th century Albanian noble who fought a 25-year long rebellion against the Ottoman Empire from 1443-1468. Andreyevskiy et al., *Brockhaus and Efron Dictionary*, s.v. 'Кастриот Георг'. [Andreyevskiy et al., *Brockhaus and Efron Dictionary*, s.v. 'Kastriot Georg'.]

6   Or more precisely, the Tuesday of Bright Week, which fell on the 3rd [15th] of April in 1806.

in Smyrna (Izmir) and with great impatience waited for the next day when a labourer would come for some service or another, at which point she would send him to fetch a priest in order to read her the letter. Returning from the fortress for dinner, my hostess, like a typical mother, bragged to me about the dignity of her son and as proof that he was very learned, gave me his letter. I read the address and the old woman with hands clasped asked joyfully: 'do you already know your letters? When did you learn to read Slavonian?' I answered the first question in the affirmative and unfolded the letter in which, besides a few words, I could barely understand anything. The next day, she invited me to a modest dinner with all of her friends and tearfully introduced me to everyone, assuring them that I was a great person and even knew how to read!

My good hostess gave me an opportunity to visit Montenegro. Father Spyridon, her parish priest, found a guide for me and according to my instructions made little preparations, as I was in haste. He took with him ten *funts* [4.09 kg] of powder and purchased flints, beads, glasses and cups, blue glass, and put a few pieces of sugar in his pocket in order to give as keepsakes to those hosts with which I would spend a night. During the gathering of my provisions, the Metropolitan visited the town and I considered it my duty to ask for his permission. His High Eminence willingly agreed to my request and urged me to indulge in the customs of his people 'with all the heart and soul of a Russian,' to summarize his words. He ordered a warrior from his guard, nearly a *sazhen* [2.13 m] tall, to escort me everywhere I wished to go and also assured me that I would be received with zeal and due respect by his people. My first guide did not want to surrender the honour of guarding me to the Metropolitan's man and they argued for a long time, became angry, and were somehow reconciled by Father Spyridon though I know not how.

To attain a more military demeanour, I took a greatcoat, girded myself with a long sabre which could cut off a nose from a *sazhen* away, and a dagger thrust through the belt. On Bright Thursday,[7] toward evening, on foot and with a walking stick in my hands, I set off with a single sailor, who was very intelligent and agile and on whose bravery I could absolutely rely; I mention the latter because the Montenegrins like to meet their dear guests with musket shots so close that the bullets whistle past one's ears. In the village of Škaljari, lying in the most beautiful valley by Cattaro, they gave me a hinny and we began to climb the mountain whose summit rested against the clouds. Along the path winding up like a conch, we reached the fortress of Trinita, or more accurately the square tower, which stood on the border of Montenegro and protected the road from Cattaro to Budva. The mountain we were meant to climb thence was even taller than the first and its summit could not be seen through the ceiling of clouds. The sun set and it grew

---

7    5th [17th] of April, 1806.

dark. Up to Cetinje, where our evening lodgings were to be, there were still 18 *versta*s [19.2 km] of road to cover and the footing was so steep and passed by such horrifying precipices that I lay on the neck of my mount, swaying over the edge of the bottomless abyss, my head spinning. I asked to stop at the first village. The guide was assuring me that there was no place to spend the night besides Cetinje when suddenly we heard wild piercing cries. My companion answered in the same voice and an involuntary fear seized me, increasing even more when we caught up with the source, called a *krvavac*,[8] a party of Montenegrins carrying merchandise from Cattaro; they surrounded me and one asked if I was a Russian. Another asked if I was a Christian. A third wanted to know if I was Catholic. Being satisfied with my answers and the assurances of the Metropolitan's guardsman, they wanted me to mount one of their donkeys, kiss my hands and the hem of my coat and meanwhile dragged me down and then began arguing with one another; I was nearly sure a fight would break out before they put my sailor on a donkey and I was left with the hinny still. We set off and calmly continued our journey. Around 10 o'clock, my escorts fired several shots and everyone gave a shout together, then notified me that we would soon stop at the village of Mirac. As we approached it, we heard confused screams in the dark night and I was glad to see nearby several lit candles: a crowd of boys holding bundles of burning straw. When entering the village proper, they hampered me and stopped my animal. The first person to approach me was a *knjaz* or prince (the title used by their rural chieftains) who decisively announced to me that I should spend the night at his home.

I had no reason to argue and obeyed his command to follow. The prince stopped me at the gate, entered the house and soon returned to take my hand and lead me inside. To my amazement, the interior was very similar to our peasants' *izba*.[9] I was put in the corner beneath an icon, while beside me was the sailor who was constantly getting up from the bench though I forcibly reiterated that we must do as we are told here. A young woman entered (the youngest in the home was his sister-in-law) and placed a wooden bowl of water at my feet, bowed timidly, kissed my uniform and the hand of my sailor. He was so shocked he leapt up and nearly

8    Literally 'a bloody person,' either a heroic warrior or a murderer and villain. Perhaps these trading caravans inherited their appellation from raiding parties or Bronevskiy has mistakenly conflated the two. *Речник Српскохрватског Књижевног и Народног Језика* (Belgrade: Институт за Српскохрватски Језик, 1978), s.v.'Крвавац'. [*Dictionary of Serbo-Croatian Literary and Folk Language* (Belgrade: Institute for the Serbo-Croatian Language, 1978), s.v.'*Krvavac*'.]

9    A small cabin of logs or wattle and daub containing one or two chambers and shelves or lofts. The central feature of the peasant abode was a large masonry oven that was used for baking, heating, waste disposal and even a platform to sleep on. Andreyevskiy et al., *Brockhaus and Efron Dictionary*, s.v. 'Изба'. [Andreyevskiy et al., *Brockhaus and Efron Dictionary*, s.v. 'Izba'.]

laughed. She knelt down and took off my boots, looked at them curiously, then took off my stockings and with some word to me and the sailor, she began to wash my feet. After this, the prince offered me some *paskha* which was laid on the table and his whole family came to kiss me three times and my companion equally. They washed their hands, lit a candle before the icons, brought out a boiled chicken and smoked mutton and prayed. One host sat between us at the table, the children served and the guests looked at us and spoke among themselves. After dinner, they immediately put us to sleep in a sort of special pantry on boards covered with a carpet. The prince lay beside us and his son, laden with weaponry, undressed at the door without stumbling, then both of them were quickly snoring. For a long time I could not sleep and looked at the roof through which the wind was whistling. Every movement of my hosts terrified me though I know not why. I clutched my long sabre closely and was ready to defend myself, but fatigue closed my eyes and I slept very heavily for three hours.

Early with the sun, the loud voice of the prince woke me up. He asked if I slept well. Considering it as an order, I jumped onto my feet and followed him to immediately set out on the next leg of my journey, but I was mistaken and soon profited nothing by it. Several of the household elders from the village were expecting me in the yard and as soon as I appeared, they asked me to honour them with a visit. I followed the first that came to me and the sailor followed another. I was only just spared from another foot washing and was then fed an omelette and delicious bread baked from wheat. Imagine my shock when it became clear I was expected to visit all 20 households and always sit down to a meal or at least sample everything they had to offer me. When entering and leaving a house, I had to kiss the whole family and if I gave a child a piece of sugar, then everyone would kiss me again. I was passed from house to house, hand to hand, like some precious thing beholden as the apple of one's eye. Finally, after kissing the whole village several times over, I was given a little hinny, helped into the saddle, wished a good journey and seen off with gunshots. My sailor had gotten so drunk that he had to be thrown over the back of a donkey crosswise.

The road to Cetinje ran past many frightening pits and ravines where vineyards, small gardens and patches of grain were visible, already a *chetvert* [17.78 cm] tall, and on the left and right Koložun and Lovćen were the highest of the mountains, whose flinty chain with hanging rocks at every step presented difficult defiles and were, so to speak, the impenetrable strongholds guarding the liberty of the Montenegrins. I arrived at noon at the Cetinje Monastery, the seat of the Metropolitan, and stopped at the home of my first escort. Despite a compelling invitation from the monks, I could not visit them at first as they had been called to vespers. Cetinje lies in a deep valley covered with greenery and gardens, and the monastery is surrounded by walls and towers with a five-headed church, reminding me of the surroundings of Moscow; I had forgotten how far away I was from it. Here they showed me letters from our Emperors from Peter the Great onward, state gifts in rich revetments, vessels, and an image of the Mother of God bestowed by Catherine the Great, surrounded by pearls and diamonds of a tremendous cost.

I will not begin to explore the details of the Montenegrins' hospitality; it must surprise a Russian, but I will say it made the greatest impression on me. I saw a Sparta embodying the full sense of the word 'republic,' a fatherland of equality and true freedom, where customs replace law, courage stands watch over liberty and injustice is restrained by the sword of vengeance. I marvelled at the heights of the spirit, pride and bravery of that people whose name terrifies all their neighbours. The image of their lives, the immaculateness of their morals and their exclusion from all luxury are truly worthy of praise. For the three days I spent with them, I was transported to a new world and became acquainted with my predecessors of the 9th and 10th centuries, witnessing the simplicity of the patriarchal era, conversed with Ilya Muromets, Dobrynya and other heroes of our antiquity. The wildness of their character and cruelty against their enemies prompts them to renew a continuous war against all of their neighbours, for they are content with their own works and have no need to utilize trade. This custom, resulting from ignorance, is outweighed by the purity of morals, filial piety and familial happiness. Having collected detailed information about Montenegro and the Bay of Cattaro, I will try to accurately depict the properties of the people, who are so close to us in their origins and religion but by their devotion, love and zeal for Russia are all the more worthy of my compatriots' attention, and yet this country has not yet been described by any traveler.

Instead of spending a night at Stanjevići, I was released from Cetinje much later in the afternoon on the next day, after a lunch. As a dark night fell, I stopped to lodge in the small village Bjeloši without reaching the first monastery and on the fifth day, after riding for more than 70 *verstas* [74.68 km], I returned through Stanjevići, Budva, Rose and then on to Castelnuovo where my trabaccolo rested. That was the manner by which I toured the Cattaro province and in the course of time gathered enough information for an accurate description of it. Even still, it would be imperfect and superficial if I did not try to believe the testimony of many knowledgeable persons and I am most indebted to K.V.R. who delivered to me the most detailed description of one Austrian engineer and drafted a map.[10] But as this officer was carried away by the spirit of Catholicism and represented the character of the people in a completely distorted form, I borrowed from him only statistical and partial historical descriptions.

10    See the map in the next chapter.

I cannot keep silent about two cases that can demonstrate to what extent the Montenegrins are devout and devoted to our sovereign. In Bjeloši, the parish priest was bearing the Scriptures and I asked if they were prints from Kiev. I opened a book and began to read. All those who were in the house stood up and when I stopped, they asked me to read a few more prayers. And then I turned to the icons and everyone began to pray. A silence fell and the sighs of the people which previously touched me now moved me to tears. At the end of the reading, every face was quite moved and the conversation ended in the regret that they lived so far from Russia and could not see the splendour of our churches or pray in them to God. Another event gave me great pleasure: to my first guide I presented a portrait of the Emperor. When he learned whose image he held in his hands, he fluttered with joy, embraced me, kissed my hands, thanked me in frantic, jumbled words, pressed it to his chest and then crossed himself, kissed it reverentially and gave it to his household to show everyone and finally placed it in the corner among the icons.

# 28

# Description of the Bay of Cattaro[1]

The province was previously a part of Venetian Dalmatia and lies around a bay which in antiquity was known as Sinus Rhyzonicus. Now it is called Boka Kotorska, or the Mouth or Bay of Cattaro, from which the inhabitants are known as the Bokez. The bay extends from west to east across 40 *versta*s [42.67 km.][2] Its mouth is formed by the cape of Ostro from the north and Žanjic from the south and close to the southern cape are the bare islands of Mamula and Gospa. These two islands create three entrances between the capes. Ships must remain closer to Ostro and sail straight to Castelnuovo and drop anchor at a depth of 15 to 18 *sazhen*s [32 to 38.4 m] where the floor is mud. Merchant vessels are held in quarantine at a depth of 7 or 8 *sazhen*s [14.94 or 17.07 m] at Rose which is across the bay, opposite the town. The depth throughout the entire bay is sufficient for warships. Up to the very walls of Cattaro the water reaches 7 *sazhen*s and the floor is mud throughout. The latitude of Castelnuovo is 42° 27' north.

## Area, Population and Frontiers

The province lies around the bay and has the appearance of a triangle with its longest side 70 *versta*s [74.68 km] long and its shortest 30 *versta*s [32 km] tall. Its population is believed to be between 40 and 60,000. It is bordered on the north by Herzegovina, Montenegro and Albania in the east, and the Adriatic Sea to

---

1    Bronevskiy's note: 'Some call it 'Venetian Albania' and under that name are understood to be the Slavs of the Greek confession; but it is not correct, because the Albanians are Greeks'. Translator's note: The Albanian language is neither Slavic nor Hellenic but occupies an isolated branch of Indo-European and is believed to have evolved from one or several antique Balkan languages predating the Slavic migration. There were and still are Greek communities in Albania however. Robert Elsie, *Historical Dictionary of Albania*, 2nd ed. (Landham, Maryland: Scarecrow Press, 2010), p.265.
2    This is nearly twice the real width of the bay at its most generous diagonal measurement.

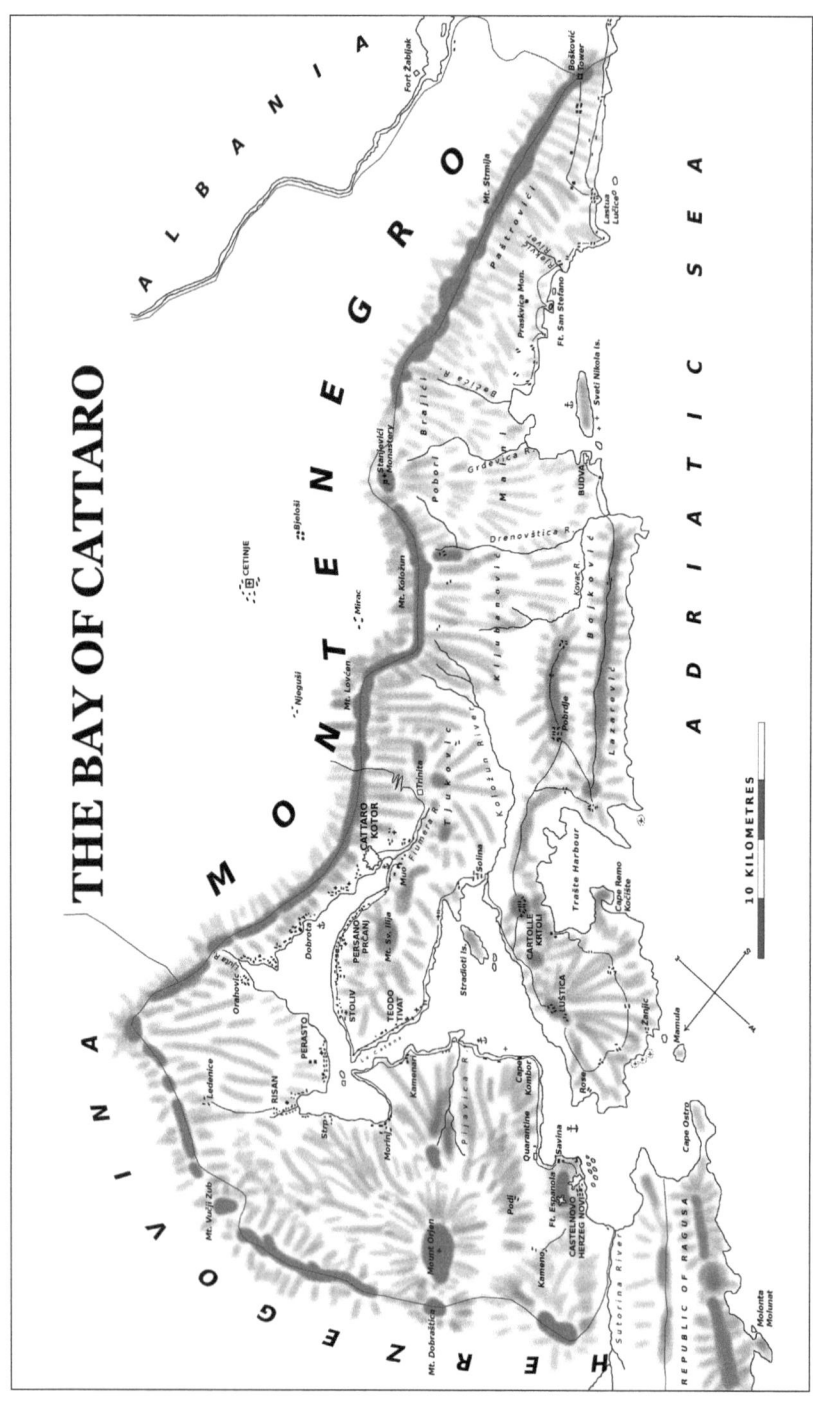

THE BAY OF CATTARO

the south and west. The Republic of Ragusa, fearing the Venetians more than the Turks, bought from the former a strip of land several miles wide, in order to secure their borders from Cattaro and Dalmatia.

## Internal Division

The province is divided into several communities or districts: 1) Castelnuovo, 2) Cattaro, to which belong Persano, Stoliv and Teodo; 3) Dobrota, 4) Perasto, 5) Risan, 6) Cartolle (Krtoli) and Luštica, 7) Župa, 8) and the three districts of the Paštrovići mountains. The first four of these do not have a large population. Catholic and Orthodox Slavs live there. The latter districts are much more populous than the former and its residents are more predominantly of the Greek faith.

## Castelnuovo

Several partially dilapidated homes comprise the structures in Castelnuovo; there is not a single shop and besides one poor tavern with a tattered billiards table, there is no entertainment for officers. Catholic churches and a monastery of the Capuchin Order serve over 400 urban residents. For the Slavs of the Greek confession, who comprise the greater part of the population in this district, there are not far from the town the monasteries of Savina and Topla. The suburbs have the best buildings. The surroundings, especially the Kuti valley, present many picturesque locales. The residents of Castelnuovo engage in significant trade.

King Tvrtko of Bosnia built this town in 1373 and from that time it preserved its name as a new fortress. It suffered many misfortunes from sieges and earthquakes. The Spanish with the aid of the Venetians took this town in 1538. The next year, as soon as the Spanish finished the fortress of Espanola, the glorious Turkish admiral Hayreddin Barbarossa arrived with 200 galleys and an army of 30,000, seizing the town by storm. Unsuccessful attempts were made to recover the town for Venice, but the fortress remained in Turkish possession for 148 years. Finally in 1687, the Venetians united with the Knights of Malta and under the leadership of General Jeronim Korner forced a capitulation from its defenders.

The fortress was an irregular quadrangle with tall towers at its corners. The upper section, called the terrestrial castle (*castel di terra*), lies on a hill and has a circular tower named Santa Chiara with two storeys of guns and casemates safe from bombs, and the walls between the towers serving primarily against musketry are so tall that an approaching enemy cannot assail them. The lower section, called the maritime castle (*castel di mare*) was almost completely destroyed by an earthquake. Underground passages running along the walls and connecting the casemates have for the most part collapsed.

The fortress of Espanola lying on its height dominates the surrounding area and is the best defensive position in Castelnuovo. Espanola is a square fortification with four towers at its corners, a ditch and a lunette on its northern side only. Each side is 30 *sazhens* [64 m] long; the walls are very thin, only suited to stopping musketry and their height is 23 feet [7.01 m]. Only one of the towers is armed with cannons on two levels; the casemates in them are safe from bombs. Inside the fortress are powder magazines, a cistern and a collapsed chapel. Due to the difficulty of the roads which make it nearly impossible to deliver artillery, a siege of Castelnuovo will prove unsuccessful unless the enemy has control of the bay. Admiral Senyavin reinforced Espanola in the greatest fashion.

From Castelnuovo to Cattaro, the bay is referred to as a channel. Leaving the broad anchorage at Castelnuovo and rounding the cape of Kumbor, one sees across the vast stretch Teodo, whose left bank is decorated with beautiful homes, gardens of varying fruitfulness and vineyards, and whose right bank is low and dotted with a few country houses. To the north rises a steep bank with bare cliffs. Far on the southern side of the stretch, on the small island of Stradioti, can be seen the old Gothic church of St. Mark surrounded by half-ruined walls. Further in the bay is a narrow channel of water called La Catena[3] which has a width in places of no more than a *versta* [1.07 km]; the mountains standing on either side seem to converge and represent a massive gate. The current from the east here is very strong. Passing through the channel, the boat seems guided by heaven. From this point the bay turns south and at the very end is seen the town of Cattaro. I have yet to see a more terrible or more charming place. Huge, stony reddish mountains are piled on one another haphazardly; Lovćen, being one of the tallest, conceals and reveals its snowy peak from behind the clouds. The elongated gulf resembles a lake lying at the bottom of a deep and shaded ravine whose banks are almost entirely covered with fortresses, towns and villages. Beautiful buildings, numerous ships and green, bountiful gardens hidden in narrow valleys decorate a truly romantic location and constitute an enchanting contradiction with the dull appearance of the barren mountains.

## Cattaro

Not seeing yet the fortifications, one glance at Cattaro inspires fear. A high precarious rock surrounded by stone walls along ravines whose terrible steepness gives the impression of everything being hewn into the rock. The fort seems to have been lowered into a cauldron over which the bare mountains stand bent over.

---

3    Bronevskiy's note: "'Verige" in Slavonian, meaning "chain" and so named because it was once locked with a chain'.

At the top is a castle which flew the Emperor's flag under the clouds and there the rays of the sun played on Russian bayonets.

The town was built at the foot of a mountain and on the sea; two narrow streets and a small square make up the best of it. Fine, massive buildings stand here. The homes are very dark because they are obscured on one side by the mountain and on the other by the high walls of the fortifications. Other homes scattered along the slope stand over one another. To move from house to house, one needs to climb up and down poor staircases carved into the rock. Some houses are nearly leaning against the slope, while others stand such that the upper streets have one storey and the lower have three or four. During rainy weather, it is dangerous to traverse for the water flows down these stairs quickly, but this inconvenience brings the benefit that the yards and streets are washed clean after a storm and mud is never found in the town. In Cattaro there are three nunneries, one Franciscan monastery and one hospice, 17 churches in all and one Greek church in the name of Saint Lucas the Evangelist. In the Catholic cathedral of Saint Tryphon are kept many pieces of relics. On that saint's day, the Venetian government, in memory of the courageous protection of the town by its citizens, would treat them to a public feast and handed them the keys to the town with its fortress guards at their disposal.[4] The residents, most of whom are settled Italian families, number up to 4,000. Although the women are embarrassed to take a *cavalier sirvente*,[5] the Slavs' strict morality had already deteriorated much; however it was still far from the debauchery of larger cities. The nobility are polite and hospitable, and in the coffee houses which they call casinos, one can find the best company. There are balls here, but they are of course organized by Russian officers; the Bokez do not like to dance and even less so to spend money. They prefer recreational trips by boat to Dobrota, Muo and Persano. In general, life here is boring, except for walking on the ramparts and the old *scalares* that climb up into the beautiful valley. In the summer at noon, the stones are so hot that the heat in the city becomes unbearable, while in the winter, due to the height of the mountains the sun is only visible for a few hours; up high it will still be day, while down in the town it is already evening. Every Saturday and Sunday at the Fiumera Gates gather crowds of Montenegrins for a bazaar. It is strange to wonder what heavy burdens are carried over the terrible mountains by poor women, and even more strange that their stout and burly men follow behind them with only a musket on their shoulder.

---

4    In the Roman Catholic Church, Tryphon was venerated on the 29th of October [10th of November], while the Eastern Orthodox venerated him on the 1st [13th] of February. *Menologium with a List of Ranking Individuals in 1806*, vol. 1, p.iv.; *Calendarium Romanum Generale* (Vatican City: Typis Polyglottis Vaticanis, 1969), p.145. [*The General Roman Calendar* (Vatican City: Vatican Polyglot Press, 1969), p.145.]

5    A married woman's public companion and often her lover. Also known as a cicisbeo.

To escape the heat, I went before dawn up into the hills where the castle of San Giovani (Sveti Jovan) is located. The road carved in ledges had the steepest turns. This rock is even steeper than Gibraltar. I counted more than a thousand steps before I became tired and bored yet I was not even half way up the mountain. My efforts to reach the summit before sunrise exhausted me so much that I would have been in dire straits were it not for the reviving effect of an ice-cold glass of water offered to me by a non-commissioned officer on guard. The spring beating under the rock from the very top is the greatest comfort for the fortress lying under the clouds. The fortifications here are amazing and are built over 600 feet [182.88 m] above sea level. Between the castle and the fortress, according to the lay of the mountain, the walls or breastworks are made in such a fashion that, while protecting one another, they also separate the town from the castle. Behind these works, the two objects of 'the Casemate' and Saranzo are built to mutually cover each other and contribute to the coverage of the lower town's fortifications. Each contains a cistern and space enough for 8 guns and a hundred soldiers. From here large stones can be rolled into the town. The castle at the top however can contribute very little to the fortresses below. Its walls are thin and have held surprisingly together over the ravines and pitfalls; in them are made compartments for musketry and cannons which are for the most part bronze, long-barrelled and small in calibre. Some of them are mounted on swivels along the battlements like small naval guns while down below are fashioned large rectangular embrasures. Here are found several guns which were used since the very beginning of firearms and forged from iron rods. Large guns of 48 *funt*s [23.6 kg] and mortars are arranged on the walls facing Dobrota, where they stand much thicker. It is a wonder what strength the Venetians must have exerted to haul them up here. The powder chamber and arsenal are covered with a thick vault which is safe from bombardment. In the latter, they showed me long muskets or blunderbusses on swivels called wall guns; which are loaded with a one *funt* [491.4 g] ball and are very useful for galleys or ships during boarding actions. Over the southern side of the castle towers a steep rock on which only Montenegrins can climb. Sometimes they amused themselves by shooting down at Austrian sentries, but shots from such an extreme height are never accurate. If the town is taken, the castle cannot be forced to surrender by any other means but starvation.

Leaning against the wall on one side and holding on to a low railing, I ascended the narrow and steep stairs to the uppermost section of the castle and upon the last step, I involuntarily closed my eyes. Imagine yourself at such an altitude that no snake would dare to slither and only the eagle can perch and directly above a precipice so deep the sun never graces its depths, at the bottom of which roars a river (named Fiumera) eroding the bottom of the mountain and flowing down the northern side of the town into the sea. Overhead, another rock rises so high that you cannot see its apex without losing your hat as you throw back your neck. The barren mountains scattered in disorder, one on top of another, and the turbulent din of the river represent nature in all its savagery and horror, but when you lower your gaze to see it in all its glory; the trees, gardens, buildings and ships appearing in the recesses between the mountains and in the inlets of the bay, enlivening the dreary site, will make you marvel at how fertility and sterility reside so close together. The town under my feet appeared to have no streets but be simply a dense jumble of houses. Cattaro's bay at the farthest edge was like a dish filled with water in which small boats were arranged for the entertainment of children. The frigate *Mikhail*, next to the fortress, looked like a model which one could hold in one hand; the merchant vessels anchored far away were hardly black spots and boats gliding under sail were like flies buzzing over the surface of the water. A cold wind, despite the heat of the sun, forced me to leave the castle and descend and go bounding down the steps so quickly that I reached the bottom in half an hour while climbing to the top had taken two.

The unapproachable position and beautiful spring water compelled man to build a city here, and the castle was its first fortification; when the town spread, then it was surrounded with breastworks and conjoined with the castle by walls which formed a triangle. In 1667, after a powerful earthquake, the Venetians fortified the town with seven bastions with curtain walls between them, thin and lined with embrasures for muskets; their height is between 25 and 28 feet [7.62-8.53 m] and their thickness is 5 to 6 feet [1.52-1.83 m]. Nature has done more here than man's artifice; the fort can only be attacked from the north but that direction is guarded by two walls with earthen ramparts surrounded by a moat while before them flows a river which has a depth of 6 feet in the winter. In the summer it dries out but the bed is 60 *sazhen*s [128 m] wide and prevents entrenchments as the water is always a foot or two deep. The heights above the village of Dobrota present an opportunity to construct opposing batteries though it would be necessary for the enemy to control the sea, otherwise they would not be able to bring in their artillery. The cut stones are so skilfully laid that although in some places the walls are cracked from the earthquake, the special strength of the mortar holds them together and they certainly shall continue to stand for several centuries. At the southern gate, which is protected by a tower and wall behind it, under the arches of its drawbridge, rages the great vent of a spring which is powerful enough to turn a mill's wheel. The water is colder in the summer than in the winter. Was it not Moses himself who, with the strike of a rod, unleashed water from a stone?[6]

Cattaro, before building its present fortifications, was several times besieged. A united attack in 1301 by Turks, Venetians, Ragusans and Croats was not successful.

6    Exodus 17:1-6.

Even before the proliferation of gunpowder, in 1378, the Venetian Admiral Vettor Pisani took the town in an assault and sacked the publicly revered relics of St. Tryphon. The present robbers of Europe, seizing Rome and Loreto, took only gold and silver – how our values change! In 1420, with the help of the local Paštrović clan, the Holy Roman Emperor Sigismund took Cattaro. In 1539, the Turkish admiral Barbarossa seized Castelnuovo and twice assaulted the fortress with great losses which ultimately forced him to withdraw. In 1563, an earthquake destroyed nearly the entire town and two thirds of the population died in the ruins. In 1570, the Turkish admiral Pertau proceeded to the fortress with a large fleet and after considerable losses, and fearing the arrival of the Venetian fleet which could blockade the narrow mouth of the bay, hastily set sail to escape without landing any soldiers ashore. In 1571, the Turks, having occupied Montenegro, laid siege to Cattaro on land and built a fort in the channel with 18 guns, the remains of which are still visible, but the Venetian admiral arriving from Corfu with 25 galleys took this fort and forced the Turks to quit their siege. In 1657, 20,000 Turks besieged the fortress for two months, but as there was a small flotilla ferrying provisions to the garrison, they bravely defended themselves even despite a breech on the side facing Dobrota. The Turkish assaults were repelled with great losses. In 1667, another earthquake buried more than half of the residents. After that, they were never so powerful and every two years or so minor quakes would do no damage and become a mundane occurrence for the population. The plague also visited the town on two occasions, being brought in on vessels from the Levant. On land, the town was generally protected by the surrounding Montenegrins who had no allegiance to the Ottoman Turks.

Persano, Stoliv and Teodo make up the district of Cattaro, otherwise named after the Miočević clan. It is inhabited mostly with Italian people and is very well kept: houses built by the sea have a beautiful appearance; the mountains up to two thirds at Persano are fruitfully cultivated; and the county of Teodo lying in a valley presents the most picturesque sight. The affluent citizens of Cattaro live here in the summer in their country manors. All kinds of fruits grow here in abundance and sweet wines and liqueurs are produced which are nigh equal with Spain's. The fortress, or rather the tower, of Santa Trinita with four small cannons protects the road from Cattaro to Budva and stands at the entrance in a treacherous gorge known as the *scala sancta*.

## Dobrota

Dobrota lies at the foot of a steep chain of Montenegrin mountains and extends from the Ljuta river to the walls of Cattaro, nearly 6 to 7 Italian miles [11.16-13.02 km] long, but has a width of no more than half a *versta* [533.4 m]. Although nature does not provide the people of this land much benefit, their diligence and industry have made them the richest of the Bokez. The people of Dobrota and Persano have the largest number of vessels. The homes are of a fine architecture and built almost entirely on the very edge of the shore, the gardens appearing as if on bare stone surround this oblong village and the many boats anchored outside their windows create a pleasing sight. These citizens, with a modest education, enterprising in trade, courageous in battle, and honest in conduct, deservingly hold the respect of the Montenegrins with whom they primarily trade and by which they profit. Dobrota has 1,700 residents and three churches, of which Saint Eustace, the newest, most handsome and affluent of the three could adorn a great capital. The people of Dobrota are hospitable, but jealous in the extreme: their wives and daughters are always shut away and not even shown to friends. The other Bokez who generally adhere to this Turkish custom seldom agree to give their daughters for marriage with the people of Dobrota, as even nuns have more freedom. The people of Dobrota are the most zealous Catholics; under the previous government, they did not allow Orthodox Slavs to stay in their village for more than 24 hours and no labourer, no matter how skilled and faithful, could serve the same household for more than three years.

## Perasto

The village occupies a narrow, barren strip of land along the shore. The people of Perasto are quite enlightened, rich in maritime trade and for the most part wear French fashions. The village of 1,800 residents has constructed an amphitheatre and from a distance at sea it appears more romantic than it really is. Above the town on the mountain, more than 200 feet [60.96 m] above sea level, the people built a citadel which serves only to protect them from raids by the Montenegrins. Opposite the village, in the direction of Risan, there are two islands: on one is the Madona d'Agosto or del Scalpello, a fairly opulent church with a miraculous icon of the Mother of God. On the 3rd [15th] of August, the Day of the Assumption, many worshipers gather there and perform a so-called circle dance.

Russians in Perasto must by all means visit the home belonging to Martinović, here you will see the traces of the patronage of Peter the Great. The sovereign who founded the Navy sent the petty boyars to many far-flung places for the sake of establishing a seafaring tradition, including sixteen people who were sent to Perasto and received by the learned gentlemen Marko Martinović. In his home is kept a picture, which Mister Mažarović, a native of Perasto, describes as follows: Martinović is seen behind a table on which maps and mathematical instruments are laid. Gentlemen in rich boyar clothing stand around the table and listen to their teacher with attention. At the bottom of the image are the following names: Boris Ivanovich Kurakin; Yakov Ivanovich Lobanov; the Princes Pyotr, Dmitriy and Fyodor Golitsyn; Grigoriy and Mikhail Khilkov; Ivan Danilovich;

Andrey Ivanovich Repnin; Abram Fyodorovich Lopukhin (brother of the Tsaritsa Evdokiya Fyodorovna); Vladimir Sheremetyev (brother of the field marshal Boris Petrovich); Ivan Rzhevskiy; Mikhail Rtishchev; Nikita Lanovich; Grigoriy Buturlin; and Mikhail Matyushkin.

A ship was armed for these nobles, on which they cruised the Adriatic Sea in order to study together both the theory and practice of navigation. Martinović wrote a kind of poem which describes the events encountered during these voyages and jokingly tells how some of them were frightened and others captivated by all that they saw and learned. This creation is printed in the Slavonian language in Venice.

The aforementioned three communities produce significant trade, their inhabitants are Catholic and a portion of them follow Italian customs.

## Risan

This ancient town was built by the exiled Queen Teuta of Illyria. It must be assumed that there was once a rather important dock, for the whole bay was named Sinus Rhyzonicus after it. Risan was built on the shore and as the only road from Herzegovina to Cattaro passes through it, the 1,800 inhabitants generate considerable trade in horned livestock, sheep, wool and wax. Risan's district contains a number of Orthodox communities, who are considered the best and most educated, as the locals have trading vessels, but their wealth is inferior to the inhabitants of the aforementioned Catholic districts. Conversely, they are braver: during the rule of the Venetians and Austrians, they together with the Paštrovići better resisted the Montenegrin raids than any other community. During our stay here, the people of Risan and generally the Slavs of the four Orthodox communities have shown an excellent and diligent bravery to us. When General Auguste de Marmont attacked Castelnuovo, they volunteered to defend the defiles and roads throughout the district of Cattaro without the aid of our forces. By their devotion to Russia, which they honour as the mother of their fatherland, many have distinguished themselves in our military service, one such family being the Counts Ivelić. The first count, Marko, now a lieutenant-general and senator, held important assignments for the affairs of the region on three occasions; to the second count, Petar Ivanovich, a major-general who served with distinction in the 1808-1809 war with Sweden and the following Patriotic War of 1812, I owe much for the information here which he provided for me.

The people of Risan believe they are descended from the Romans. A few similarities in costume, the remains of a bridge and part of a mosaic floor seen in the vicinity lend credence to their assertion. The village of Carine, not far from Risan, preserves its name as the abode of Queen Teuta; here were her palace and castle, of which only a few walls can still be seen. Six pillars remain of the bridge and the mosaic floor covers only three feet [91.44 cm] of ground. The mountain on which Carine sits has a massive grotto or a long underground cave called Špila which deserves special attention from any lover of natural wonders. The mouth of the cave has a width of 20 *sazhen*s [42.67 m] and a height of 8 [17.07 m], and under its enormous vaults which are not supported by anything, angular heavy stones hang. The passage to the interior of the mountain extends for 400 *sazhen*s [853.44 m], at which a surprising lagoon filled with water appears, having a depth of 4 *sazhen*s [8.53 m] and an unknown length. The arch of the cave here becomes so low that no one has dared to measure how far it extends, but this body of water probably signifies a vast void within the mountain. Villagers from Carine take water from here by the light of torches. During the summer it is as cool as ice while in winter it is warm. The floor of the cave from the mouth to the lagoon is so smooth and level one would think it were carved out by human hands. During heatwaves the people of Risan and nearby villages like to visit the many small caves dug out by the water, and some serve as cellars in the summer. On the left side of the lagoon, a part of the wall is smoothed out and covered with the names of travellers. At the end of autumn, the cave is filled with vapours which condense and drip down from above such that the water becomes inaccessible. This subterranean rain is a rare and frightening sight. Water pours forth through the full width of the passage with enough force that everything turns to foam. Like a great river which has no waterfall, the water flows into the sea for a *versta* and a half [1.6 km] from the mouth of Špila with a strong enough current that no boat with a dropped anchor can resist it. A collapsed castle lying on the mountain above the cave complements the view from afar: vapours rising from the water immerse the walls of this fort in a light mist that conceals the summit of the rock; clouds during rainy weather descend from the crenellations of the towers and create the impression that the castle is ascending to heaven through a wavering passage of fog and cloud. The noise of the water is repeated in echoes which seem to vibrate the base of the mountain around Špila.

Opposite Risan, across the small gulf by the village of Vitoglav, another cave named Sopot is an even more formidable and magnificent sight. The water bursts out of a hewn rock at an altitude of about 400 feet [121.92 m] through a narrow hole like a typhonic column which disintegrates into a broad dome of foam and falls straight into the sea like a waterfall. Some people believe that the waters of these caves are connected underground with those under Cattaro. Frequent earthquakes here, and the great collection of waters in the womb of the granite mountains, are an object worthy of close examination by naturalists.

The remaining three Orthodox communities occupy the southern side of the bay. In Kartoli and Luštica there is a handsome forest. The residents do not have boats but their valleys are rich with grain and some are engaged in gardening.

Župa has great advantages. This district is divided into four counties: Lazarević, Bojković, Kljubanović and Tjuković. This stems from the Venetian government bestowing the title of count on to some Bokez instead of the indigenous use of prince. In the Kljubanović county is the monastery of Lastva, surrounded by a stone parapet which can withstand attack from a regular army.

Budva is an ancient town. Pliny called it Balua and Butua. A fortress built on the peninsula lying on the steep rocky slopes is mostly collapsed. The harbour is protected by the island of Sveti Nikola with an anchorage open to southerly winds. In the town there is one Orthodox and one Catholic church. In 1697, Suleyman Pasha Scutari besieged Budva with 10,000 men, but General Korner came to their relief with the aid of citizens from the surrounding countryside. After this, the fortress was taken several times by Turks and Greeks and their ruins are still visible. In 1797, at the request of the locals, the Metropolitan Petar Petrović took Budva, but when the Austrian Emperor offered to restore to the Bokez their previous rights, they reverted their allegiance and the Metropolitan left the town.

The inhabitants of the three districts Pobori, Brajići and Maini, during the slightest disruption of their privileges, often rebelled against the Venetians along with the other Orthodox Slavs, and especially against the Austrians who fortified the monastery of Santa Maria di Maini. They presented the Metropolitan of Montenegro with ecclesiastical authority in the province in order to keep the people obedient.

The Paštrović district is on the farthest frontier of the Bay of Cattaro. The residents there waged a continuous war with the Montenegrins and Turkish Albanians before the arrival of Russian forces in Cattaro. Their bravery is exemplary and they often defeated the Montenegrins. They are especially attached to their laws and ancient customs. The frequent raids by Turks and Montenegrins had completely ruined them, but now when the Montenegrins have befriended them, our commanding admiral, through polite intercourse with the Pasha of Scutari,[7] knew strict measures would compel them to show respect to subjects of the Russian Emperor. The predatory Albanians did not dare to attack them thereafter. Thus, with the advent of the Russians, the misfortunes of this courageous people suffering under the scourge of war even in times of peace came to an end. Justice must be given to the Paštrovići as they are every bit as grateful as is commensurate to the mercy and protection provided by of our government. They and the people of Risan were first on the field, fought in the front lines and distinguished themselves in all of our engagements with the French. The Holy Roman Emperor Sigismund, during

---

7    Ibrahim Bushati governed the Pashalik of Scutari (Shkroda) from 1796 to 1809. Robert Elsie, *A Biographical Dictionary of Albanian History* (New York: I. B. Tauris, 2012), s.v. 'Bushatlliu, Ibrahim Pasha (-1809)'.

the conquest of Cattaro, received help from them for which many were elevated to noble dignities, and for this reason their ancestors were faithful to Austrian rule. The name of Paštrović is unfairly by some said to be derived from *pastori-vecchi*, meaning 'the old shepherds'. This is one of many mistakes that foreign writers make without knowing the Slavonian or Russian language and basing their conjectures on the apparent similarity of words.[8] Their true name in the Slavonian tongue means 'on the side' or 'living along the frontier,' since their land is on the extreme border separating the Slavs from the Albanians.

The fortress of San Stefano, in the Paštrović County, lies on a rocky peninsula that connects with the mainland by a low sandy isthmus. From the sea, it could once protect the entrance of the bay but, apart from the surviving powder magazine, its walls have completely collapsed. The locals generate unremarkable trade. Opposite the town, on a height, stands the Greek monastery of Praskvica under the governance of an archimandrite.

## Produced Goods

The high, barren mountains surrounding the bay attest to the poverty of this country. Only near the coasts are there gardens and plantations and while they decorate the savage landscape, they do not supply enough food for subsistence. Further inland between the mountains, the valleys provide more convenient land for agriculture; however endless wars between these inhabitants and the Montenegrins and a lack of available labour prevent the full utilization of these places. Small fields worked with a pickaxe scarcely give grain for three months, and are supplemented by potatoes. Along the shores are grown in open air grapes, olives, figs, and the odd orange and lemon tree, as in Italy. Stoney soil and intense

---

8    Bronevskiy's note: 'For example, one French traveler claimed that Aleksey is a diminutive of Aleksandr, and that *imene* is the name of a favourite drink among Russians. Someone with him once asked for a glass of kvass and others added on with one voice: "*i mne, i mne!*" [And for me, and for me!] This ingenious Frenchman founded his conclusion on this experience. In the English geographical dictionary edited by Gordon, an article on rarities in Russia contains the following nonsense: "As one of the chief rarities of the country, we may reckon that strange sort of melon found in or near to Astrakhan, Kazan and Samara. Some of the natives term it *baranets* (little lamb), others *zoophyton* (the animal plant). The first name would seem most proper as in figure it resembles a lamb and such is its vegetable heat that according to the vulgar expression, it consumes and eats all of the grass within reach. As the fruit ripens, the stalk is covered with a substance exactly like short and curly wool. A part of the skin of this remarkable plant is to be seen in the King of Denmark's public repository of natural rarities at Copenhagen and no man can distinguish between it and the ordinary lamb. Many Muscovites use the skin of this rare vegetable instead of furs for lining their vests." – Indeed they are truly warm!' Gordon, *Geography Anatomized*, pp.76-77.

heat accelerate maturation and therefore the climate resembles the African; after the torrid heat, the winter contributes rain for sometimes six weeks in a row. For a lack of meadows, cattle are not at all bred here. Beekeeping could bring great benefits if they could harvest honey without endangering their bees. The silk produced in small quantities by their women has a special beauty. Thick wool, linen and multicoloured ticking are produced but only for their own domestic needs. The meagreness of their terrestrial products is compensated by an abundance of fish and the Bokez hunt them very skilfully with harpoons. The homes of the inhabitants close to the shores, especially among the Catholic population, are calm, clean and handsome in appearance. Further into the mountains however they are covered with tiles and have hearths without chimneys. Along the rough roads there are no carts and loads are carried on pack donkeys.

## Trade

The Bokez generate significant trade in the Adriatic, Levant and Black Sea. Their growing prosperity can be estimated by the number of their ships, which in recent years has increased substantially. In 1798, they possessed 264 vessels; in 1806, 381 vessels; and in 1807 their number reached 500. Except for the smallest, they are all armed with between 6 and 28 guns. On these ships, up to 7,000 very fine sailors are employed. Their skippers are ignorant of the science of navigation and manage their ships according to habit and familiarity with the waters they sail. The Bokez, rivals to the Ragusans, like them carry foreign products and provide for their families with this trade, sparing them from the unhappiest life expected of their desolate land. Without trade, they could not exist. Of their own goods they export yearly: 4,000 barrels of crude olive oil, 12,500 *pud*s [204.76 t] of wine berries, an equal weight in wax candles, 125 *pud*s [2.05 t] of silk and 175 *pud*s [2.87 t] of honey. From Montenegro and Herzegovina are yearly imported roughly 110,000 sheep and goats and 15,000 cows and pigs, whose smoked and salted meat is sent from Cattaro on to Venice and Trieste. Sheepskins and oxhides are exported in an unprocessed condition. From Montenegro, they import 15,000 *pud*s [245.71 t] of cheese and just as much from Herzegovina by the road through Risan, which is then shipped to Italy and the Levant along with 150,000 *pud*s [2,457.11 t] from Morea. The Bokez are equal in works to our industrialists in alacrity and ingenuity.

## Religion

Under the rule of the Venetians and Austrians, the Greek faith was extremely oppressed. The intolerance of the Roman Catholics reached the point that not only did they not allow the people of the Orthodox confession to worship freely, they even prohibited the import of liturgical books from Russia. Although these books have been published in recent years in Vienna and Budapest, the Slavs did not have any confidence in them and preferred to secretly acquire their Bibles, prayer books and so forth from Kiev and Moscow printing houses. Persecution seemingly from the superstitions of the 11th and 12th centuries did little to convince Slavs to convert and instead sewed a mutual hatred between the Catholics and Orthodox. Bloodshed between them did not justify these policies in our enlightened age, especially because the inhabitants of the Orthodox confession are much more numerous here than the Catholics; the latter hardly constitute a quarter of the population. Should it then be astonishing with what enthusiasm the Slavs embraced the Russians when we entered their province and established Orthodoxy as the primary faith; when they could freely celebrate their holidays and import sacred books so rare to them; when they were united with the Montenegrins as a single people after such long and continuous warfare and finally saw an end to their misfortunes and a beginning for their prosperity? When the Russians arrived, a golden age began for the Bokez; liberation from all their obligations, peace with the Montenegrins and trade with Herzegovina and the other Turkish regions promised them great benefits. The humility and true Christian tolerance of the Russian monarch, allowing the free worship of the Catholics, shut the mouths of the proud clergy whose ambition was the cause of many evils. This measure put an end to the enmities which had separated for so many centuries a people of one origin. The churches, monasteries and clergy are maintained by the parishioners. Each family delivers bread, oil, wine, candles and all other necessities at appointed times. In this fashion, the local priests who subsist on these donations perform prayer services, baptize children, marry couples and practice all the other rites without any need for bribery. Being so deprived of self-interest, they retain the importance and dignity of their office and live in the true spirit of Christ.

## Customs and Attire

The Bokez of the Catholic faith are not as strict in their lifestyle as their fellow countrymen of the Orthodox faith. Although both have some education from dealing with foreigners, they are extremely attached to their ancient customs and their character has not changed much; it is nearly identical to that of the Montenegrins, for which reason a description of the customs typical of the latter must be understood to apply to all the maritime people as well, especially those of the Orthodox confession. On the other hand, the Bokez are discontent like the Swiss with their homeland. Public entertainment is unknown to them, and only occasionally do troupes of wandering actors visit Cattaro. Sometimes they invite guests but since women are not allowed into such communities, these visits are quite boring. The veil worn by their wives outside the home, an invention of jealous husbands, has changed very little from a nearly opaque silk to muslin, then from muslin to fleece and finally they are worn now only for appearances and taken off when in the company of their kin. The women of the higher class are stately and elegant; the peasant women are healthy but cannot boast of their beauty. The character of the Bokez bears importance like that of all trading peoples. Their hospitality is tinged with thrift, but never to the point of avarice. Their music and dances are exactly the same as those of the Montenegrins. The latter amusement is not consistent with their extreme jealousy of the Bokez and their rude dealing with women, whom they treat like their slaves. In military tactics, they are similar to the Montenegrins and although they cannot equal them in the art of marksmanship, the Bokez – especially the Orthodox portion – are just as brave and fight even with greater order and better demonstrate subordination. In diet, they most commonly eat polenta (cornmeal porridge), fish and meat.

A resident of the Bay of Cattaro.
Illustration from original publication.

The Italians settled in the region wear their own attire. The Bokez dress differently from all the other Illyrian Slavs. Wide, baggy Greek trousers that reach down to the mid-calf; jackets with convex silver buttons and lined with braid and lace;

sandals when travelling and half-boots at home; round hats, under which the Catholics have a black velvet cap while the Orthodox wear one in red. Their jackets are decorated with copper and silver plates (called *toke* in Slavonian), which are worn on their chest and legs instead of armour. The residents of Župa dress like Montenegrins. To both costumes belong the triangular dagger called a *khanjar,* the sickle-shaped *yataghan* sword, a pair of pistols, a long musket, an antique Slavic sword or Turkish sabre on a silver chain and a cartridge pouch in the style worn by the Albanians. The poorest have weapons decorated with fine carvings, mother of pearl and stones in an Asian taste, while the rich have raspberry or black velvet jackets lined with metal embroidery which, like the buttons and plates, are all in silver. The women's attire is singular: a short white dress with full sleeves, girded with a wide belt, embroidered at the hem and on the sleeves with beautiful patterns, over which a Turkish tunic is worn; on their feet are worn sandals tied with coloured ribbons; and the head is bound with a kerchief. Their girls and maidens dress in a very similar manner to our national costume. Necklaces of coins or corral are the finest of their decorations. Blue and red are the predominant colours used. All of their clothing is made at home and besides their ribbons and scarves, nothing is imported. The Bokez are very skilful in embroidery and especially in dyeing cloth. Illnesses stemming from a luxurious life are unknown to the Bokez, even by name; they are so healthy that in Cattaro there is only one apothecary and one doctor. Another doctor, living in Castelnuovo, emigrated for fear he would starve from lack of business.

## Education, Language and Craftsmanship

The Orthodox clergy present lead the most rigorous life and are greatly enlightened. The majority of the clergy can speak Italian and are avid scholars. Having a great influence on the common people, they prevent all violence between them and execute the government's directives. In each church is a school where boys study religion and learn to read Slavonian. Every holiday, during services, these children stand in two rows on either side before the royal doors [of the iconostasis]; four in white robes serve at the altar and two stand in the wings and read very loudly what is then sung by the deacon. After the liturgy, the priest testes the children in the catechism and then after announcing to them what holiday will follow the next day or at what hour their class will resume, he blesses them and dismisses them to their homes. Most of the Bokez however, especially those who do not live on the coast but further up the mountains, are deprived of this upbringing by a shortage of priests. The affluent among the Catholics send their children to Italian universities. Some of the nobility occupy positions as lawyers but do not study law as in other places and can singlehandedly confound cases at personal profit. The Bokez speak the Slavonian language mixed with Italian words. The Catholics write in the Latin alphabet, while the Orthodox – those few who are literate – can write in the church alphabet.[9] The coastal and urban residents speak Italian in the Venetian dialect. Besides metal working, making muskets, a single dyeworks in Cattaro and soap and coarse twine produced in Perasto, there are no other manufactories.

## The Aristocracy

In former times, when this land was a republic, the chiefs of the districts were elected by their people and while they occupied public office, they were called princes. After that, under the Venetians, they were renamed counts for a time and as they were approved for this title or position, they would pay 25 thalers and secure the title for their children. In the same way, those occupying lower civil positions called themselves nobles, but neither the former nor the latter were recognized in Venice as such. Real nobles holding letters patent, in which there are no glorious titles, are considered the oldest, for the comtal dignities were given to the Bokez by the Venetians in recent times. The family of Medin, the Counts Ivelić and Counts Vojnović are the most honourable of their nobility. However these ranks do not give any advantages: the very lowest of the mob has exactly the same rights as the foremost of the nobles. Here, true dignity is based on the command of general respect rather than nobility. The selection of the people's leaders usually falls to the best and most prominent families, however even the most simple villager who has earned the respect of his fellows can be selected as the captain of his community, although with very limited power.

## History

In the archives of Cattaro resides a letter given by Alexander the Great of Macedon recognizing the bravery they demonstrated in the many wars of that great conqueror, giving them eternal and hereditary possession of a portion of land from Aquilon to the south of Italy, and granting that the indigenous people of those territories be their slaves.[10] Although scholars cannot agree on the ancient events of this country, it most likely seems that Queen Teuta, expelled from Illyria with

---

9    Whereas Peter the Great reformed the Russian alphabet in 1708 for civil administration and secular publications, the church retained the old script in addition to the liturgical language of Church Slavonic. The older variants of Cyrillic used in Cattaro and Montenegro would therefore resemble the 'church script' to a Russian observer. Andreyevskiy et al., *Brockhaus and Efron Dictionary*, s.v. 'Гражданский шрифт'. [Andreyevskiy et al., *Brockhaus and Efron Dictionary*, s.v. 'Civil script'.]

10  Bronevskiy's note: 'I had the opportunity to read this ancient privilege of the Slavs written in the certificates and diplomas of the Counts Ivelić'.

A Bokez or Bocchesi girl.
Illustration from original
publication

many retainers, first chose to reside at the very site on which Risan now stands, and soon after wished to retire from the dangerous frontier by consolidating herself in Cattaro, which Pliny references as the Roman colony of Ascrivium. As these are not very reliable, we will cover only the latest events. In Risan and Cattaro lived maritime robbers or pirates who reigned over the sea and terrified the inhabitants of the shorelines. In 866 AD, Budva, Risan and Rose were razed to the foundations by the Aghlabids, a nation residing in the vicinity of Carthage. After the departure of these barbarians, the remaining inhabitants united with the Bosnians expelled from their lands by the Hungarians to build Cattaro and found a republic. In 1115, King George of Duklja presented the republic with the island of Privlaka which is now known as Stradioti and the places now known as Luština, Kartoli and the valley of Župa. In 1250, King Radoslav,[11] for their loyalty to his

11    Stefan Radovoslav of Serbia died in 1233 in exile. 1250 falls within the reign of Uroš I the
      Great. Sima Ćirković (ed.), *Istorija Srpskog Naroda*, vol. 1 (Belgrade: Српска Књижевна
      Задруга, 1981), pp.308-314. [Sima Ćirković (ed.), *History of the Serbian People*, vol. 1
      (Belgrade: Serbian Literary Society, 1981), pp.308-314.]

father, Stefan the First-Crowned, and son, Simon Nemanjić, strengthened these locations with men from Cattaro. Under King Uroš and Queen Helen d'Anjou, the residents of Cattaro were given the Upper and Lower Župa (called in Slavonian *Grbalj*, meaning 'plains'), Lozica, Dobrota, Ledenice, Bijela and the Kruševica to the Fiumera (rivers by the walls of Cattaro). In 1361, the Tsar of Serbia Stefan Uroš V reconfirmed and strengthened the right of ownership to all the aforementioned locations given. In 1368, when Serbia was divided into four parts, the republic, being under the auspices of that kingdom, concluded an alliance with Louis I, King of Hungary and Croatia; ten years later, Venice, being at war with Hungary, took Cattaro, plundered it and then withdrew. In 1382, Louis's daughter Maria gave the republic to Tvrtko, King of Bosnia; but after a two-year war, the brave Cattarians regained their freedom. After this, they fought with the Albanians and Ragusans. In 1391, Cattaro concluded an alliance with Ragusa, Dulcigno and Antivari; the inhabitants of the latter two were infamous pirates.

At the beginning of the 15th century, when the Turks overran all the border provinces, the Cattarians, fearing them, voluntarily surrendered to the sovereignty of the Republic of Venice on the following conditions: 1) that their faith and laws would remain inviolable; 2) that money levied from the regions would be used on the construction of public works and salaries for civil officials; 3) that the Republic of Venice could not hand them over to another power, and if they were unable to defend them, then the people would again remain independent and have the prerogative to elect other patrons. The Venetians fulfilled those requirements exactly and the Bokez lived happily under their rule, always remaining their faithful subjects. The Venetians, controlling Cattaro, at various times conquered Castelnuovo and its three districts, but Risan and the Paštrovići voluntarily subjected themselves to the protection of Venice with their privileges retained. With the destruction of the Venetian Republic in 1797 by the Treaty of Campo Formio, the Bay of Cattaro was ceded to the Holy Roman Emperor but the courageous Slavs opposed this and sent representatives to Vienna. The Viennese cabinet recognized all of their privileges and General Matija Rukovina took the region from the people's deputies on the same terms as it had belonged to Venice. In 1804, the French government, planning to occupy Montenegro, assigned an 18,000-strong corps which was intended to go ashore near Budva. French agents, seeking to preclude resistance from the inhabitants who were dissatisfied with the Austrians, assured them that it was the will of the Emperor of Russia; but when the Slavs learned from the dispatches entrusted to Lieutenant-General Count Ivelić that our Emperor did not give such consent, they armed themselves and the French were compelled to abandon their treacherous enterprise. By the Treaty of Pressburg, this region was again unjustly given to the Kingdom of Italy, or really to France; the people took up arms and as described before certainly swore themselves to the Russian Emperor. In 1807, by the Treaty of Tilsit, the region was surrendered to French forces. In August of 1812, the people of the Bay of Cattaro, learning of the French invasion of Russia, so readily and unexpectedly attacked the French force that the latter could not unify or coordinate, were partly beaten and forced to lay down their arms. By the request of the people of every district, the Russian Imperial flag was raised over their fortresses. Finally, in accordance with the decisions made at the Congress of Vienna, the province was given back to Austria.

## Military Survey of the Bay of Cattaro

The fate of Cattaro depends on who controls the sea; without a fleet it can neither be taken nor kept. I have said already what an excellent military position this province provides in relation to political blocs; now I will explain what forces are necessary to protect it and what forces are necessary to take it.

The quantity that we deployed there, 2,500 soldiers, is not enough; but 6,000 Jägers who are trained in mountainous warfare, with the aid of the Montenegrins and Bokez, who could muster 20,000 men in times of crisis, should be able to repel a strong enemy such that the most skilful and decisive general with 30,000 men of the best regular army will not be able to accomplish anything here. Let us now consider the possibility of an attack from the frontiers of Ragusa and the Ottoman Empire, believing the French and the Turks to be enemies who cannot exert naval power in the bay.

From the side of the republic, Castelnuovo is the weakest point; the enemy must clear the way from Ragusa and lay artillery on the heights of San Carlo and Santa Anna to drive the fleet away from the fortress, after which it will not be difficult to take. Two roads run from Castelnuovo to Cattaro: the first follows the coast which can be approached and fired on with canister and grape by ships, therefore no invading army can march here; the other, passing through the valley of Kameno, the villages of Morinj, Krivošije, exiting on the left of Ledenice and then to Velince, is a route that only mules can take and is laid from mountain to mountain, cliff to cliff and at heights of 50 *sazhen*s [106.68 m] above treacherous abysses, where not only will artillery be impeded, but even infantry will require bridges to be erected. From to Velince to Cattaro there remain two roads: the first follows the shore by Dobrota, where columns can still be harassed by naval fire and it is obviously impossible to transport artillery trains under grapeshot; the latter road passes through the high mountains belonging to Montenegro and covering a distance of 50 *versta*s [53.34 km] and presents no small difficulties crossing the Devil's Bridge: here it is necessary to lift one's cannons by pulleys and then, when reaching the summit of the mountain beside Cattaro, descend into the village of Škaljari along a ramp within 40 *sazhen*s [85.34 m] of the defending fortress's fire. Assuming that the enemy is already before Cattaro, which can be attacked only from the side of Dobrota (the north); but with the mountains standing close along the shore, exposing any army and its trenches to naval bombardment, it is therefore clear that a siege of this fortress, when defended by a fleet, is as attainable as the chimera. It must be said however that nothing is impossible and one turns to the example of Napoleon conducting an army with artillery through the Alps by the Simplon and Mont Cenis passes.[12] I would agree, but he accomplished what he set out to do without harassment from the enemy; here at every step, he would have to fight with the inhabitants, who are much better shots than his voltigeurs. The ground does not allow you to execute any skilful manoeuvres or bring the full power of an army to bear. There is no water along the whole road, there are no means for living at the expense of the civil population as they barely possess food for 4 or 5 months, and the transportation of provisions and ammunition for an army of 30,000 would require 12- or 13,000 mules and horses; and how will they be fed? Even the most ambitious commander would not undertake such a campaign, as the conquest of this province would require far too much sacrifice for too little benefit. I will not begin to say what the Turks can accomplish, for after a while they became very sensible and if they wished still to conquer this province, then it is safe to say that 50,000 janissaries would lose their heads here.

An enemy who controls the sea, landing armies in the port of Trieste and hastening to occupy the channel of La Catena, can bypass the difficult defile at Scala Santa, besiege Cattaro and cut off her communication with Castelnuovo. In a word, it is easier to conquer Cattaro from the sea than from the land because of a belligerent population who will side with whoever has a fleet that can protect their trade and will resist whoever does not.

---

12    When Napoleon crossed the Alps in 1800, the majority of the Army of Reserve used the Great St. Bernard Pass and only made feints through the other passes with small detachments. Ward et al., *Cambridge Modern History*, vol. 9, pp.59-61.

# 29

# Description of Montenegro

The Montenegrins, waging unceasing war against their neighbours, do not allow a single foreigner to enter their land. The traveller who wishes to be taken to this locale would be in danger of losing his life; they would pursue him as a spy for some other state intending to conquer them. For that reason, of the many travellers in Europe, not one has ever visited Montenegro and no log describes its wonders, its government, the people's customs or their way of life.

By occupying the province of Cattaro with our forces, the Bokez and Montenegrins merged into one people and their previous hostilities were ceased. One doctor from the coast, a very educated individual, was summoned to the interior lands for the benefit of the sick and rendered some service to the governor of Montenegro and to the Metropolitan himself, and did not pass up the opportunity to take advantage of the authority entrusted to his title and command of languages. Becoming acquainted with him was useful for me, as he willingly shared his observations. The trust the Montenegrins have for Russians, my journey to the mountains and the interactions with them during the fleet's stay in the Adriatic also provided opportunities to gather information on their character and governance. Having collated the doctor's observations with my own, I believed my notes on the spot and took advantage of the testimony of Archimandrite Vukotić, one born Montenegrin and a few other well-versed Bokez who had connections, so that I especially could consider myself obliged to present a report on Montenegro, equal to the one on Cattaro, to Count P.I. Ivelić. With such help and being able to compile an accurate and thorough description, I dare to offer it here. Its merit lies in the novelty of its information, rather than its eloquence. The land of the Montenegrins presents neither inscriptions nor ruins; news of its inhabitants does not contain such curiosities which readers find in the descriptions of ancient Greece; but often the wild flower is just as fragrant as and even more colourful than those grown in the garden.

## Frontiers, Area and Population

The very name Montenegro indicates a mountainous land. The whole province is covered with mountains and protected by chains of high rocks, which, being covered with forests of spruce, give them a black appearance from which the name Black Mountain (Montenegro; Crna Gora) came. It lies between and adjoins Herzegovina and Albania and its exact number of inhabitants cannot be correctly determined, but it can be said approximately that it has a circumference of about 300 *verstas* [320 km], a length of 90 *verstas* [96.01 km], a width of 50 [53.34 km], and contains 500 square miles [1729.8 km²] of land. It is divided into the following five districts, referred to as a '*nahija*' by the inhabitants: 1) Katunska; 2) Lješanska; 3) Pješinčka; 4) Riječka; 5) Crmnička; and 6) the region of Brda, annexed in 1796 by the Metropolitan after defeating Mahmud Pasha Scutari. The Berdan or Highland people successfully engage in agriculture, do not resort to robbery and defended the borders of their fatherland with courage, which earned them the respect of the Montenegrins. In this region there is the large village of Bjelopavlići, where trading is conducted every week.

Montenegro is the only land in Europe which has no cities. In the whole region there are 116 villages, the largest of which does not have more than a thousand souls to its name. The population of each village is protected by the number of people able to bear arms: thus in all of Montenegro, 15,000 warriors can take the field and as they lead a life perfectly suited to warfare and carry arms from 16 until advanced old age, then the number of warriors is multiplied by four to estimate the total population as being roughly 60,000 people. They themselves assure that in their country they can produce 30,000 armed men. Villages are built in valleys and near rivers in which the water is excellent; houses are a single floor and divided into two parts: in one half are placed domesticated cattle and the other, with a hearth but not a chimney, serves as the living space for the family. The walls are built by simply stacking stones on top of one another; only for a small number of two-storey homes and monasteries are lime mortar and tile roofs used. The rest are covered with straw and resemble poor huts, in which the best furniture is made up of the skulls and captured weapons of enemies, intended to remind the youth of the glory of their forefathers.

The monastery of Cetinje, the main seat of the Metropolitan, is surrounded by walls with embrasures and several small cannons. The national assembly gathers there. It is also the place where they keep the documents given to the Montenegrin people upon our every Emperor's accession to the throne.

The monastery of Stanjevići, donated by the Venetians, is located in the region of Pobori on the Montenegrin frontier; it is also fortified with stone walls with a parapet and covered with cannons. Its natural location is unassailable. The chapel, built by the Venetians, is decorated with the many gifts bestowed by Russia's monarchs.

## Climate

The severity of the weather, extreme hots and colds, do not disturb the people much. The air is fresh and healthy. It is very dry in the winter which helps with the flexibility of the body and strengthens it so that the Montenegrins are capable of bearing their immeasurable burdens, while in the summer the heat is tempered by easterly winds beginning at noon which cool and refresh the inhabitants. The Montenegrins reach an old age: I saw 70-year-olds at the siege of Ragusa and have been assured that many of them even live to a hundred.

## Illnesses

Diseases are very rare among Montenegrins, which they owe to their temperance, the purity of the air and especially the decency of their lives. They do not dance at nightly balls until exhaustion, their passions are not aroused by theatrical performances and they do not know any of our whimsical fashions; from this, many diseases are unknown to them even by name. The treatment of headaches, fever, lacerations and other injuries that occur during their travels from the heat of the sun or the cooling wind that stops suddenly, they leave to nature or make use of herbs and roots. Experience teaches simple means to cure serious conditions and this knowledge is passed down from father to son. Among them are skilled bonesetters. Their treatment of wounds demands special attention. To light wounds they apply spider webs, moss and tinder fungus and to more heavy cuts they apply ivy leaves or a garlic skin. For severe wounds they make a poultice from grass known to us by the name Ivan-and-Maria (melampyrum nemorosum) crushed between two stones, some people add salt, and from this simple remedy wounds are closed in 15 days. They do not know about the use of lancets, but they perform bloodletting behind their ears as done to horses and on the calf of the leg with a razor. When their heads ache from the sun, they let blood from the nose, pulling their heads back tightly with a cord, and pushing into the nose a folded piece of paper or grass. Despite crude foods, constant war, and the deprivations suffered on frequent journeys, they live until death without hardly any attacks or outbreaks. A simple life foreign to vanities and tensions of the mind preserves their health.

Enlightened or worldly men more quickly become victims of passions harmful and contrary to nature. Customs of service, sitting for long periods, rare ventures outdoors, excessive use of fatty and delicious foods, extravagant entertainment, whimsicalness, softness, vanity, shame, envy and many other passions take hold stronger and little by little exhaust the bodily forces. Even the highest virtues of sensitivity, compassion and love for one's children become harmful when, during relaxation, they strongly upset the soul. But the Montenegrin, limited in his desires and easily satisfied, lives happily and fairly. When his fatherland is in danger and its precious independence is threatened with slavery, he quickly but without haste takes up his musket, fights, frees himself and thereby ends his anxieties. His soul, although moved by passions and subject to virtues and vices, does not have the same degree of sensitivity: he helps his neighbour but does not suffer from his sufferings; when he dies for his fatherland he falls in battle, not from the discouragement or heartbreak of his misfortunes; the death of a friend, the loss of a wife or his only son, although causing him great grief, does not deprive him of all his spiritual strength and weaken his health, making him a victim of tender feeling. In short, his upbringing draws him closer to nature, such that as a simple child he is relieved of the multitude of diseases to which our way of life and sensitivities subject us.

## Produced Goods

Despite frequent raids on their neighbours distracting them from agriculture and the barrenness of the mountains, several valleys satisfy the needs of the population by producing grain, grapes and wine berries, pears, apples, excellent plums, beef, cheese, leather, wool, flax, honey, etc. The current Metropolitan also taught them how to cultivate potatoes and introduced them into general use.

## Agriculture

Agriculture is limited to simple methods approved by experience and without improvement, and by that singular habit their arable lands and gardens are reasonably maintained. Where there are no roads and the land is very mountainous, the work must be difficult. Fields of grain are cultivated by pickaxe and produce is transported on donkeys. Horses and oxen are rare. Sheep and especially goats, kept in large numbers, constitute their most important source of wealth. By the lack of meadows and shortages of fodder, they are forced in winter to sell a part of their herds and flocks in Cattaro; but in the spring, by raiding the flocks of their neighbours, they always recoup the loss. From the quantities and affordability of domestic birds brought to market in Cattaro, it must be concluded that they have a great many of them. Montenegrin dogs are highly respected in Italy and throughout the Levant; they have heads like a calf's, are quick, vicious and so clever that in the darkest night, they can smell a stranger from beyond earshot and give terrible grief to anyone wishing to pass through the village quietly in the night. During the day, they guard the flocks and are so fierce and strong that they themselves can attack predatory animals. At night, they guard the village from surprise attack.

## Trade

The degree of enlightenment of a people is measured by their successes in agriculture and trade. These two arts mutually assist one another, and one of them is the strength and welfare of kingdoms; but what kind of trade can be generated by the Montenegrins, who do not tolerate communication with the affluent and plentiful regions surrounding them and whose farming is still in its infancy? They engage only with Cattaro and theirs in the only market where they sell their products; and even then, their sales are small and purchases even smaller. Beyond fruit, grain and oil, they bring to the Bokez wool, silk in bundles, wood, coals and much salted and smoked mutton and cheese that go to Trieste. The moderate Montenegrins retain most of these products for their own needs. In exchange, they receive muskets, pistols, lead, powder, knives and swords, tiles for roofing, iron tools, writing paper, salt, clay pottery, simple glassware, and further still they buy motley scraps of chintz or silk scarves, red caps, Venetian beads for their women and other petty things. That is the extent of their trade, to which the benefits are always in their favour and have been constantly so for the longest time. From this we can conclude that gold accumulates from day to day in their land and that the ones whose dress is poor has a small treasure that is never spent and lies in the corner of his home. Trade is made by exchange or by cash, the method most simple and reliable; because they are afraid of deceit, they never make contracts with people they poorly know. The people of Dobrota serve as their executors, taking money or goods from them in advance and delivering to them in good time bread, fish or other supplies and faithfully keep their word. Typically they have such intercourse with godfathers and godbrothers;[1] this distant kinship makes their pacts sacred and inviolable. Besides small Turkish coins, Venetian gold ducats and Austrian silver thalers, they do not accept any other currency.

## Education, Craftsmanship and Language

The Montenegrins are perfectly ignorant. Those who know how to read and write are honoured among their kind as learned men of science. The higher clergy and the nobility who have served in the Russian Army are quite well versed. Besides

---

1    Bronevskiy's note: 'As a pledge of friendship, they trade crosses with each other and call each other *pobratim*, that is "cross brother" or "godbrother", and are revered no less than brothers of blood'.

the sacred books printed in Kiev, they do not read any others. Free crafts or cottage industry, excluding those necessary to life, are also completely unknown to them, since luxury goods become unnecessary in the rough way of life that they lead, as with the least educated of people. In each household a thick and sturdy cloth is spun from their own wool and flax. Their clothes are not subject to the variability of fashions; they are always simple and identical, so other products are largely unnecessary for them. Having those necessary skills, such as the basics of forging and locksmithing which serve the repair of their muskets, they otherwise live in perfect ignorance of the arts and craftsmanship. Their women are their best artisans. The Montenegrins, having retained their liberty and having little communication with foreigners, have preserved their Slavic language in complete purity. Their pronunciation is softer and more pleasant than the Serbs', the Croats' or the Dalmatians', since the first mix their Slavic words with Turkish, the second with German and the third with Italian. They write with church Cyrillic.

## Governance

Montenegro is a republic[2] in which equality is supported by poverty, liberty by courage, and the law is replaced by established custom. This small region is an image of government without printed laws. Montenegrins, paying no taxes and collecting no public treasury, are governed by themselves and live peacefully and happily. The government of Montenegro can be called popular and elective. The assembly of the chieftains (*Skupština*) is the most precious pledge of their independence; it is where war and peace are decided by a majority of voices, including the Metropolitan himself, the *guvernadur* or governor and four *serdars* or military commanders.[3] The procedure is that when they gather on the vast meadow by the monastery of Cetinje, the Metropolitan sets out a need to wage war, conclude peace or make some decision, and asks if they agree or not; the priests and chiefs dispersed among the crowd repeat his speech word for word; a cacophony breaks out and the people discuss, interpret and argue, but it does not transpire like among the representatives of other nations, for these men cut ears and noses; until the toll of a bell signals them to be quiet and no matter how strong a dispute may be, the people will be fall silent. The Metropolitan again asks them what they have decided and whether they agree with the proposal. The usual

---

2    Montenegro under the leadership of the prince-bishop may also be called an ecclesiocracy.
3    Montenegro's governor was Vukolaj Radonjić from 1804 until 1832, when the pro-Austrian faction led by the governor was purged, Radonjić and his allies were executed, and the office of the governorship was abolished. Tomica Nikčević, 'Guvernadurstvo kao Politička Struja Crne Gore,' *Matica* 43 (Autumn 2010), pp.191-210. [Tomica Nikčević, 'Governorship as a Political Force in Montenegro,' *Matica* 43 (Autumn 2010), pp.191-210.]

answer is: 'We're for yours, *Vladika!*' (which is what they call the Metropolitan). The dignity of the *vladika* and governor became hereditary due to the respect they enjoy, the numbers of their well-wishers, and partly the petitions by which they express their desire to pass the office to their child or relative. Thus in the families of Petrović and Radonjić these titles have already been established for a long time. The *serdar*s are elected for life and are highly respected for the fact that they assume a courage and deftness proven by the experience of many battles. This rank cannot be hereditary for every Montenegrin who boasts of being brave seeks to attain them. The *knjaz*s or village chieftains are elected by the elders of their households; sometimes they also keep the title for their children and if they are worthy, they will be elected. These princes are no different from our elected village elders. The governors and *serdar*s have neither honours nor marks of diligence or reward and very little influence on government; they are invited by mediators in minor quarrels and participate in the assembly; because without their consent as representatives of the people, it is not possible to reach any kind of resolution. The supreme, spiritual and civil power rests in the hands of the Metropolitan, but only by the fact that he deserves it with his enlightenment and moreover with courage and decisiveness; otherwise the people, being displeased, would not obey him and his power would have been rendered miniscule. From this it must be concluded that the rule of the present *vladika* is just and humble. Their model of internal, civil government resembles that of the ancient patriarchs: the elder or father of the family has complete power over his household. There is no hereditary nobility here, everyone has equal rights and privileges and even the very last Montenegrin may be for a time a *knjaz, serdar* or governor. However those of them who received nobility from the kings of Serbia for their service or occupied a post as a representative of the people, though they have no diplomas or letters patent, should in fairness be recognized and given the dignity of nobility everywhere.

## Laws

By the word 'laws' I refer rather to what takes their place.[4] Here there are no judges, no prosecutors, no advocates and, perhaps to the surprise of many, no legal suits. Property passes to children by male inheritance: the elder receives the house and institution while the young chooses the best part of the land; they never sell it, usually live together and share a common economy; established custom replaces written wills and each reverentially respects his father's property. Surrounded by

---

4    A formal legal code was first drafted in Montenegro in 1796 and approved by the national assembly in 1798, then reaffirmed with amendments in 1803. Frilley and Vlahović, *Contemporary Montenegro*, pp.57-58.

enemies, they know that their strength is in their harmony and accord, which is why they rarely quarrel with each other. Raiding their enemies is glorious, but theft on their land is considered dishonest and crimes of this kind almost never occur. In cases of theft, they resort to a priest who, after mass, lights a candle of black wax and demands the return of the stolen goods and threatens the thief with a curse. The faith of these uncorrupted people is so strong that by the third proclamation, most of the perpetrators fall on their knees and confess. Besides public repentance, no punishment is imposed on them; but he is deprived of public respect by word of mouth and even in his household he loses authority. A criminal who has lost his honour falls into despair and usually kills himself or leaves his home and fatherland.

The Montenegrins, like the Bokez, are very sensitive to honour to the point of being spiteful and vindictive. Their bragging is not inferior to the self-praise of the French. Any quarrel begins with cursing but ends with someone being shot with a musket or cut down with a sabre. Those among the Bokez who are more enlightened will warn their opponent that they seek a deadly duel. In the case of the Montenegrins, if one is killed or wounded, his relative will avenge him in what they call 'blood for blood'. If they cannot kill openly, then in the guise of friendship all cunning tricks will be employed to achieve their goal. The widow of a murdered man keeps the bloody shirt so that her son, when he comes of age, will take revenge and if the murderer should fleet the country, then the son will take revenge on his neighbour. This innocent victim then finds new avengers; then whole villages have taken up arms and neither the governor nor the *Vladika* himself can end the bloodshed. These customs are reminiscent of those barbaric times of the 11th and 12th centuries when brutal strength was justice and not criminal and when people who criticized this custom were shown contempt.

Such bloodsheds are not too frequent however. They are dissuaded in the following way, which also serves in various other disputes: both sides send negotiators to establish a court, which they call *poslati na vjeru* – sent on faith. Agreeing to a peace, the mediators are elected equally on both sides, a number of volunteers that can extend from 10 to 40 persons. These judges unite to listen to the plaintiff and defendant, inquire in detail about the case and consider a musket shot or sabre blow not by its harm caused but by what it could have done and a solemn pronouncement is made according to the sound judgements and proceedings. Once made, it cannot be appealed. The perpetrator is condemned to pay a fine: for one wound he will pay 10 gold coins, for two wounds 20, but for murder he will pay 120. If the offender cannot pay such a sum, then he will pay only what it costs to treat the wounds and for murder, gifts are presented to the offended party consisting of weapons or fine clothing. To receive greater satisfaction in the case of a murder, the offender is humiliated and forced to publicly beg for forgiveness. The judges and parties form a large circle with the condemned man in the middle, having a musket, sabre or dagger on his neck, who is then made to crawl on his knees to the feet of the offended party. The latter takes off his weapons and embraces his attacker, saying 'God will forgive you!' The circle shouts with joy and congratulate the reconciled parties and the enmity is sincerely forgotten. After reconciliation, the guilty treats all of the judges and bears the costs of this magnificent holiday. It should be noted that such judgements (which they call a bloody circle or bloody court) have no partiality: here money cannot influence a sentence, for the fear of revenge will keep them impartial, no matter how beloved a man may be.

A husband who kills a criminal wife, just like a caught thief, is subject to legal punishment; if, after investigation among their relatives, she turns out to have been innocent, he pays blood for blood to the father or brother, or they kill him. For the murder of a woman, after reconciliation and humiliation, no bloody tribute is paid. A girl who gives birth before marriage is stoned to death with the father or brother throwing the first stone, while the seducer is shot to death by his neighbours. In a case where 12 witnesses are required and such a number cannot be attained, the accused must undergo a trial by ordeal or concede guilt. Such an ordeal is conducted by throwing a red-hot piece of iron into a bucket of boiling water and forcing the person to pick it out with their bare hands.

Emperor Paul I ordered the establishment of a permanent court under the name of *Kuluk*, consisting of 60 elected elders, and endeavoured to pay them a yearly subsidy of 2,000 *chervontsy*.[5] These honourable judges had to deal with all civil and criminal cases but as these judges on the one hand are the envy of others due to their salaries and honours, resulting in disorder and unrest, and the defendants, who were previously accustomed to choosing their own judges, did not agree to be judged by the *Kuluk*, this supreme court, by the Emperor's own order, was abolished the following year.

## Religion

The Montenegrins are deeply pious. Their faith is simple and sincere; they do not miss a holiday and when they are not in their church, the do not do anything without making the sign of the cross. Although few can read the Lord's Prayer, they blindly fulfil their Christian duties. Prayer, alms and reconciliation with their

---

5    A '*chervonets*' referred to a coin minted in gold, which encompassed Russia's five- and ten-ruble coins, the latter also being known as an 'imperial,' giving a nominal value to the subsidy of 10-20,000 silver rubles. *Complete Collection of Laws*, collection 1, vol. 16, pp.691-692. No. 12,116; Ibid., col. 1, vol. 24, p.298. No. 17,748; Ibid., col. 1, vol. 24, pp.758-759. No. 18,178.

enemies before Holy Communion are the virtues which have already softened their wild nature. They strictly observe the fasts, which is not difficult with their already moderate lifestyle. The rites of their Orthodox faith are the same as ours, but they do not revere the icons painted on canvas and walls, which seems to only be because such were used by the Catholic oppression of the Orthodox in Cattaro and perhaps (though hardly likely) due to the actions of the Catholics who, in Ragusa a hundred years ago, set fire to an Orthodox Church during Easter and everyone attending matins that night perished.

## Christmas

Of the number of church celebrations which are greatly similar to ours, the rite that they hold on the Nativity is derived from and it seems has survived from the earliest Christian era. On the eve, each family at sunset prepares a *badnjak*, a thick oak log split in places and decorated with laurel branches. The elder with his family lays the log on the hearth and when it lights up, pours oil and wine and throws a handful of salt onto the fire, and then he lights candles and a lamp before the icons and prays for the welfare of his family and all Christians. He takes a cup of wine, tastes it a little, and gives it to his eldest son, who in turn passes it on. The goblet is passed around the whole family regardless of sex – a special circumstance as women are excluded from the community of men in all but church rites. This patriarchal prayer shows their faith in heavenly providence and the expectation of an abundance in earthly fruits. At the end of this, the men step out onto the heights, shoot off their muskets and loudly announce the beginning of the celebrations. At this time, the spectator will be amazed by the sound of gunshots and screams of 'Christ is born!' In every village throughout Montenegro, shooting erupts at the same time. They sit down to a well-laden table in the midst of which three loaves are placed in the form of a sugar loaf and surmounted by a green laurel branch stuck through an orange or apple. In front of each man is placed a bow and arrow made or cut from bread, depicted as ready to be loosed. The elders give this a different meaning, but it is likely that the bow represents the exploits of their ancestors and the laurel of the glory they achieved. The holiday lasts eight days, during which, like with Easter, the piled straw on the table is not removed and meals are ready for receiving any visitor, pilgrim or poor person. The Montenegrin during these days abandons restraint, does not think of the future and forgets the present; he forgets even himself and consumes as much as would have lasted him for many months. Marriages and christenings do not illicit such magnificent feasts as Christmas and the poorest families, to pay for their appetite, will sell off something of theirs; even those in mourning are not free from the celebrations, the only difference being that the bereaved do not fire their muskets or go out to visit their neighbours and friends.

## The Clergy

Monks in Montenegro are very few. They lead a strict and completely reclusive life. To their ranks are admitted dedicated people from among the most prominent citizens who engage in study and teaching, are reasonably enlightened, and hope to achieve the dignity of the Metropolitan See and participate in the assembly during the election of the *Vladika*. They are divided among four monasteries located in Cetinje, Stanjevići, Brčeli and on the bank of the Crnica river. The secular clergy barely know how to read and perform their services and their attire does not differ from the common people. The priest, entering the church, will take off his weapons at the entrance and is the first to take them up during a cry of 'who is a warrior?' They are distinguished by bravery, and therefore most of them, by the election of their parishioners, will command war parties. The priests are highly respected regardless of the dignity of their post and do not have any additional income, but are content with their property and never part from their family.

## The Diocese

Credible writers believe the foundation of the local archdiocese to lie in the 14th century. Some attribute this to the Tsar Stefan of the House Nemanjić, others to King Stefan of Serbia, who established the archdiocese of Peć with Metropolitan rank in order to broaden the adherents in the country, dependant on the Patriarchate of Constantinople. Roman writers claim that Makedonios, one of the Orthodox bishops, in 1640 wrote a humble letter to Pope Urban VIII but it is not clear if he or his successors simply wanted to fabricate a connection with the Western Church. On the contrary, the independence of the Montenegrin Metropolitans is also evident from the fact that in 1720, during a consecration, the Ottoman Sultan sent his *chaush* or messenger to convey his respect and assure them of his benevolent disposition. The present Metropolitan, Petar I, was patronized by Empress Catherine II to assert spiritual independence. Petar receives from our court considerable assistance; his other income consists of donations and fees from his own property, which can reach 40 to 50,000 rubles.

## The Present Metropolitan

The influence of the Metropolitan of Montenegro on the Slavic peoples of Serbia, Bosnia, Herzegovina and Dalmatia, and his assistance to our forces in the war against the French, will perhaps make details about him entertaining.

Petar Petrović was born in 1753 in the village of Njeguši, near Cattaro.[6] Appointed since childhood to be the head of the republic, he was educated in St. Petersburg in the St. Alexander Nevskiy Monastery; this education combined with his natural talents made him worthy of this dignity. Passing through all the ecclesiastical ranks, in 1777 in Vienna, he was received favourably by the Emperor Joseph II and in that same year was initiated as the Metropolitan at Karlovci.[7] Departing from Vienna to St. Petersburg, although he was assisted by the Abbot Dolci and the Ragusan Count Zanović, his proposals were unsuccessful. On the other hand, at the court of Catherine the Great he was received with great attention. During his second return from St. Petersburg, at the time of the Russo-Turkish War of 1787, he created a diversion in Bosnia and Herzegovina and in 1788, influenced and discouraged the soldiers of the Pasha of Scutari from participating in the war against Russia.[8] This devotion won him the grace of the Empress. The glorious defeat of the pasha made him even more renowned.[9] Emperor Paul I also bestowed his grace and decorated the Metropolitan with the Order of Saint Alexander Nevskiy. In 1806 he was most obliged to take the citizens of Cattaro under his dominion. Emperor Alexander I, in addition to many generous gifts, awarded him an opulently decorated Metropolitan's *klobuk* for his excellent courage displayed in the protection of the Bay of Cattaro.[10]

Petar Petrović is fairly tall, has a slender build, a ruddy face, a handsome appearance, with lively and attentive eyes. I had the occasion to see him during the arrival in Cattaro when he was in the church, at the changing of the guard, during the inspection of the fortifications and in the home of the governor, General Musin-Pushkin; I saw him fulfil the roles of high priest, sovereign prince, general, engineer, and graceful courtier and I can say that he does not resemble Peter the Hermit who assembled an army of crusader knights; he is solely in the

---

6    Other sources attest that Petar I was born in 1748. Jacques L. C. Vialla de Sommières, *Voyage Historique et Politique au Montenegro*, vol. 1 (Paris: Alexis Eymery, 1820), p.368. [Jacques L. C. Vialla de Sommières, *Historical and Political Voyage to Montenegro*, vol. 1 (Patris: Alexis Eymery, 1820), p.368.]

7    Petar was consecrated as the metropolitan bishop in 1784, two years after his predecessor and great-uncle Sava died. William Denton, *Montenegro: Its People and their History* (London: Daldy, Isbister and Co., 1877), p.248-249.

8    Kara Mahmud Bushati governed the Pashalik of Scutari (Shkroda) from at least 1778 to 1796. Elsie, *Biographical Dictionary of Albanian History*, s.v. 'Bushatlliu, Kara Mahmud Pasha (1749-22.09.1796)'.

9    Kara Mahmud invaded Montenegro with 30,000 men in 1796 and was defeated by Petar at the Krusi Pass, the Pasha himself being among the Ottoman casualties. Denton, *Montenegro: Its People and their History*, p.255-256.

10   A *klobuk* is an item of clerical attire, comprising a tall cylindrical hat with an attached veil. Andreyevskiy et al., *Brockhaus and Efron Dictionary*, s.v. 'Клобук'. [Andreyevskiy et al., *Brockhaus and Efron Dictionary*, s.v. 'Klobuk'.]

figure of a bishop, reconciling in himself those qualities which are so contrary to the crozier. In the church when he with great import took up the throne, he was a tsar. In the home of the general, with his black velvet coat, girded with an opulent cummerbund on which hung a sabre adorned with precious stones, a round hat and sash of the Order of Saint Alexander Nevskiy over his shoulder, he looked more like a general than a bishop and in fact he commanded with greater dexterity than the regular officers in front of the lines on parade and during the inspection of the fortifications.

Metropolitan Bishop Petar I Petrović-Njegoš of Montenegro (reigned 1784-1830). Vialla de Sommières, *Historical and Political Voyage to Montenegro*, vol. 1, plate between pages 368 and 369.

He always surrounds himself with a numerous retinue; his guard of warriors are real giants, of which the shortest member is no less than 2 *arshin*s and 12 *vershok*s [195.58 cm] and in front of them always walked a man a whole 3 *arshin*s [213.36 cm] tall. Their weapons shine in gold with engravings, mother of pearl and coral and their clothing is all trimmed with gold and silver embroidery.

Petar speaks Italian, French and Russian just as well as his native Slavonian language but in his policy he believes it is prudent to employ interpreters in public negotiations with the former two. He is a stranger to prejudice and superstition, loves education, enjoys conversing with foreigners and closely observes the course of political events in Europe, knowing how to exploit various circumstances and skilfully turn difficult scenarios. His travels, education and natural acuity give his conversations clarity and geniality, and his disposition has the most keen politeness and grace. His mind is occupied without interruption and ambition governs all of his thoughts and actions. It generally seems that he is firmly disposed to conquest. His political and military talents and the spirit of his people could be encouraged in success if he would be able to accustom the Montenegrins to subordination, without which their courage is fruitless. With his sublime intellect, courage and resolution, he became the reigning autocratic *vladika*. His will is considered law and the Montenegrins obey him blindly; they are afraid of his gaze and when they fulfil his command they say '*tako vladika zapovijeda*'.[11] Thus combining temporal and spiritual power in himself, he has done much good for his country in stopping its frequent killings and unrest. However, his power is mild: he employs anathema against the disobedient and if at this time someone dies suddenly, the naive people say: 'the wrath of God has struck him, so of course he was guilty!'

The Venetians and Austrians do not recognize him as the *Vladika* of Cetinje, Skadar and the Maritimes, or in other words the Metropolitan of Montenegro, Albania and the Bay of Cattaro, possibly due to the fact that the latter two regions were not under his control; but through his spiritual influence he was able to arouse their alarm and compel them to respect his dignity and seek his friendship and good favour. During war he personally leads his forces and is reputed to be as skilful a general as he is a politician.

## The Montenegrin Manner of Warfare and Their Tactics

The Montenegrin is always armed: in the most peaceful activities he has a musket, pistols, sword and cartridge pouch. Wearing weapons in the east is revered as a sign of distinction and independence. In their free time, the Montenegrins practice target shooting and are accustomed to it since childhood. Even in their games and amusements, you can find a military spirit. Undoubtedly they are recognized as the most skilful sharpshooters of them all. Accustomed to labour and difficulties, they perform Suvorovian marches with merriment and without fatigue; using the butt of their long muskets, they vault over wide ditches and cross such abysses where our soldiers would need to build a bridge; they climb to unapproachable rocks with ease and they patiently endure hunger, thirst and all other deprivations. When the enemy is defeated and retires, they overtake him so quickly that they could replace cavalry, which cannot be deployed in their native mountains.

Like the Knights of Malta, they are constantly at war with the Turks. Dwelling in mountains where at every step in their difficult defiles a handful of brave man

---

11    Serbo-Croatian for 'thus the bishop commands'.

can stop an entire army, they are not afraid of any unexpected attack, for they are always on guard on their borders and within 24 hours their warriors can be gathered at any point being threatened. If the enemy is strong, they burn their villages, raze the fields and entice him into the mountains, where, surrounded, they attack with desperate courage. The Montenegrins forget themselves and their private quarrels and concerns when their fatherland is imperilled. They obey their leaders and as courageous republicans they consider it a blessing – divine mercy – to die in battle. Here are true warriors who are like wild barbarians out of their country, subjecting all to fire and sword. Their concept of war completely differs from the rules adopted by enlightened peoples. They cut off the heads of their enemies who fall into their hands while armed and give mercy only to those who voluntarily surrender before battle. Seized property is considered rightfully theirs and the fair reward of courage. They themselves fight, in the fullest sense, to the last drop of blood. The Montenegrin never begs for mercy; if he is seriously wounded and cannot be saved from the hands of the enemy, his comrades will cut off his head. During the attack on Klobuk in Herzegovina, a small detachment of ours was forced to retreat. One of the officers, overweight and advanced in years, fell to the ground in exhaustion. That very moment, a Montenegrin rushed to him and drew his sword, saying 'you're very brave and must wish that I take your head. Say a prayer and cross yourself…' Struck with surprise and horror, the officer gathered his strength and, with the aid of that very same Montenegrin, he caught up again with his men. All prisoners are believed to be better off killed. The wounded otherwise are carried out of battle on their shoulders and to the credit of the Montenegrins it should be said that they have saved our officers and soldiers in that fashion. Like the Circassians, they make constant raids in small parties solely for seizing cattle and revere it with youthful bravado. In these fights and skirmishes, none of their neighbours can compare with them. Being safe in their homes where no one has dared to disturb them for a long time already, they continue to plunder with impunity and disregard the threats of the Turkish Porte and the hatred of their neighbours – in short, the name of the Montenegrin is terrifying.

Their weapons, some bread, cheese, garlic, a little vodka, old clothes and two pairs of rawhide sandals comprise the whole baggage of the Montenegrins. On campaign, they do not look for protection from either the sun or cold. In the rain, the Montenegrin, wrapping his head in a cloth shawl, will curl up in a ball on the spot where he stood, his musket under himself, and sleep very peacefully. Three or four hours are enough for him to regain his vigour; the rest of his time is spent on incessant night and day attacks. They can never be kept in reserve, for it seems they cannot tolerate the sight of the enemy. When their cartridges are all spent, then they humbly ask for more from any officer nearby, and having received them and cursing Bonaparte, they run headlong into the frontline. If the enemy is not visible, then they sing and dance or engage in robbery in which (credit where it is due) they are very adept, although they do not know the more elegant names for it: contributions, requisitions, borrowing by force and so on. Robbery is simply robbery to them and they do not at all deny it.

Вуко Юро
Славнѣйшій стрѣлокъ Черногорскій.

Vuko Juro, renowned Montenegrin marksman. Illustration from original publication.

This is how these irregular armies fight: being in an excellent number, they do not openly reveal their strength before an attack as they employ cunning. They hide in ravines and send out only a small number of shooters who fall back and lead the enemy into ambushes where they will be surrounded, preferring bladed weapons since their strength and bravery lend them a greater success. If they are weaker, they choose advantageous positions on the high rocks from which, uttering all kinds of curses, they call for a battle. The greater part of them attack at night for their method is surprise. However, no matter how few they are, they try to tire the enemy with an endless battle. The reader will learn later that the best French voltigeurs, always at the forward posts, were annihilated and the enemy generals found it most convenient to stand under the protection of their artillery, which the Montenegrins would not approach. Soon they became accustomed to them however, and with the reinforcement of our Jägers, they boldly assailed the batteries. The tactics of the Montenegrins are limited to sharpshooting. A small rock, a depression, or a tree hides them from the enemy. Shooting for the most part from the prone, they guard themselves and by their accurate and fast shooting, they bring death to the closed ranks of regular forces. They are also distinguished for having a good eye and are able to exploit the features of a location. As they fought in feigned retreats, the French, regarding this as cowardice, were always deceived and ambushed. On the contrary, they are cautious enough that they are never deceived by the most cunning manoeuvres. They can hear or seemingly smell the enemy and reckon him when it is hardly possible to see his movement through a telescope. Their extraordinary audacity triumphed over the art of the experienced French soldiers. Attacking the enemy columns from the flanks and front while dispersed and demonstrating personal courage, they were not afraid of the terrible, continuous fire of the French infantry. General Jacques Law de Lauriston wanted two Montenegrins captured and sent to Paris to be exhibited, but one of them broke his own head against a wall and the other starved himself to death.

From this it is possible to conclude that the Montenegrins, outside of their mountains, cannot stand alone against regular forces because once they have spent all of their fire, they cannot remain for long on the field. Their courage in assisting our forces and the fruits of victory were squandered due to their disorder. During the siege of Ragusa, it was impossible to find out how many of them were under arms as they would constantly retire individually to their homes with loot while others returned and after several days of tireless labour with minor profit, they would again quit to their mountains. One cannot conduct a long campaign with them and therefore nothing important can be accomplished. However, in terms of their ability in mountainous warfare, without any knowledge in tactics, they largely have an advantage over regular forces. Firstly, they dress lightly, are exceptional shooters and charge their muskets much faster than soldiers armed with muskets with straight stocks, and who do not always know how to hit a target. The Montenegrins in the heat of battle, lying prone and scattered, fire as a unified front. That is why in a party of 100 or 150 men, they will intrepidly attack a column of a thousand. In proper battle, one banner can be used to judge their movements. They shout coordinating orders at one another to suddenly focus an attack on a side found to be weak. From the main banner carried beside the Metropolitan, they are told by voice what must be done. Then suddenly they rush forward and boldly penetrate into an enemy square and almost always cause it to dissolve in disorder. Imagine a wild howl encouraging the Montenegrins and terrifying the French, and add to that the severed heads hanging from the warriors' necks and behind their shoulders! All of this should produce, I believe, a terrible effect. In the skirmishes of the vanguard, in the destruction of pickets, and best of all in exterminating enemy reserves, the Montenegrins can serve with the army to great benefit; and if we subordinate them to military order, which is not impossible, then with 100,000 such soldiers, we could give a good lesson to the best regular armies.

## Way of Life and Customs

The life of the Montenegrin is uniform. He wakes at dawn and retires at sunset; when the nights are long, he will spend a few hours with his family at the hearth where the burning spruce wood provides light in lieu of a candle. War is their primary passion. Their activity, enterprise and courage inspire terror, but in equal measure to how cruel they are against their enemy, they are meek and peaceful in their homes. Among his labours and when alone, the Montenegrin looks sullen, while in company he is always cheerful and wilfully gives in to joy. They have much wine, but they drink it moderately and never get drunk enough to dull their feelings. When speaking with notable foreigners, they are neither base nor insolent, and what is most surprising is that with such ignorance, they are very witty and speak with dexterity. The Montenegrins have no concept of the inequality of ranks and classes and therefore, without excluding their commanders, who they are obliged to obey only in battle, they treat others very freely and bow with a small nod of the head and a movement of the hand which is graceful enough to have been taught by a dancing instructor.

Hospitality, the sacred virtue of all nations, stemming from their Slavic roots, is considered a duty by the Montenegrins. The traveller who is caught on the road in a storm demands it from the first house and if he does not know anyone in the village, then he usually goes to the home of the *knjaz*. Without asking for his name, his destination or the purpose of his journey, the owner sets his wife or youngest daughter-in-law to wash his feet and with both hands on his shoulders, they await his order and wait on him like a maid. Upon departure, the grateful guest slaps the owner on the shoulder and says: 'thank you, compatriot, you truly have a kind wife'. The Montenegrin cannot refuse hospitality to a deadly enemy, even the murderer of his son, and pays him the attention he is due. Like the knights of old, they are bound to their word of honour, and keep a secret entrusted to them from a friend or an enemy with equal perfection.

Elders are shown the greatest respect. The chief of the village is generally the oldest person. A young man stands up for the entrance of his elders and kisses their hands respectfully; women kiss the hands of men, but the forehead, right shoulder and hand of the elders. The feelings of filial love oblige even further this reverence – an excellent custom which strengthens the bonds of their community and bestrews the road to the grave with flowers. This custom along with their courage against the enemy reminds one of the happy days of Sparta.

To the shame of enlightened people, the Montenegrin has respect for his neighbour's wife. Josephs are not uncommon among them, but women like the wife of Potiphar are completely unknown.[12] Women are considered the lowest creature. The Apostolic words 'the wife shall fear her husband'[13] are in full effect here. The Montenegrin requires his wife to be obedient without complaint and to slavishly serve him. However, they do indulge their wives and admit them to the table when they are not entertaining guests. Women are free enough that they are not hidden away from men like the Bokez do; only the girls are kept at home except for church services and grand holidays. The wife takes the surname of her husband and is called by his name like a patronym. Their campaigns, trips to Cattaro and frequent absences of their husbands favour infidelity, but their women are chaste, possibly in part out of necessity for a sure death threatens them and their lovers if they are caught. However, the Montenegrins have such respect for the fairer sex that it is a great dishonour and cruelty to offend a woman and therefore they are employed as couriers and often spies. A beautiful woman in the Montenegrin camp can be as calm and safe as under the supervision of her mother; it would have been a terrible dishonour for whoever falls in love with her. On campaign, the wife bears the provisions of her husband and having a dagger and a pistol, she can defend them if need be. The mother, even in the gloom of mourning, will boast of her son's wounds and although she is more a mother than a republican, she most closely resembles in that case the women of Sparta.

In summary, the Montenegrin, being sober, hospitable, a respectful son, a tender father, a kind brother, a spouse of authority but a slave to his word, has so many virtues that his brutality to others is outweighed by the happiness of his domestic life, which reminds us of the golden age of our forefathers. Although he loves his wife and children, he leaves them with the utmost sorrow, for he loves his fatherland even more. He parts with them with the determination that his country shall prosper on his return. Admiral Senyavin in a short time acquired from them unlimited authority; he was not only able to stop the decapitation of prisoners and had them brought in alive, but beyond all expectations he persuaded them, with the help of the Metropolitan, to undergo a journey by sea, something they had never done before. A company of Montenegrins boarded the 74-gun *Moskva*. With great difficulty, they were persuaded to stow their weapons in chests and even

---

12    Joseph in the book of Genesis was a Hebrew slave who at one point is brought into an Egyptian noble's home and becomes his trusted steward, but the master's wife attempts to seduce him and when he refuses her, she accuses him of rape, using his discarded clothes as evidence. Despite his chastity and loyalty to his master, he is imprisoned on the charges of rape and seduction of a married woman. Bronevskiy means to say that both the men and women of Montenegro are chaste and monogamous. Genesis 39:1-20.

13    Ephesians 5:33.

though they were treated with affection and indulgence, they caused considerable anxiety. When the captain invited their chieftains to breakfast, the whole troop entered the cabin without invitation. Noticing that the officers were served more than the sailors, they wished to be given the same. Upon the capture of the fortress of Curzola, Christmas was approaching; they did not give their captain any peace and asked him to take them to Cattaro as soon as possible. When he explained to them that the ship could not sail opposite the wind, they fell into despair and sat hanging their heads. When the ship approached the entrance of the bay and they recognized their black mountains, they cried out with joy and began to sing and dance again. Saying goodbye, they embraced the captain and other officers with gratitude and invited everyone they found agreeable to visit them; when the sailors told them that they could not leave the vessel without the captain's permission, they said with surprise: 'if you wish it, then who has the right to forbid you?'

The Montenegrins believe in visions, prophesy and witchcraft. If a wife sees in a dream that her husband will be exposed to any kind of danger, then he belays his future plans. In this way, a woman replaces her freedom with cunning, and meekly commands her proud man who considers it lowly to kiss a beautiful woman's hand. Spilling oil at the table is considered a bad omen, which is averted by the recitation of mysterious words by the old sorceresses on the full moon. Talismans are worn around the neck to guard against evil spirits and divert enemy bullets.

Montenegrin women are extremely hardworking, sharing in the fieldwork during the summer among the men and weaving fabrics in the winter to make study cloth, dressing themselves and their husbands, and are quite adept in all simple handicrafts. They are so healthy that they do not suffer bouts of illness at all and continue to work on the very day of childbirth. Children guard their herds and when they come of age, they join their parents in their labours and march to war at the age of 16.

## Appearance and Apparel

The very sight of the Montenegrin displays manly courage. They are generally tall with broad shoulders, lean, and have an especially graceful proportion to their whole body. Black hair, a swarthy face and moustache gives them a warlike appearance and a most masculine handsomeness. Male attire consists of a white, course cloth coat like ours and called *belača*; in the summer, they wear linen underneath like our peasants wear, blue, and in the winter they wear broadcloth. A shirt like the Russians' covers them to the knees; in winter, it is lined with hide. On the head or crown of the head is worn a red cap with a black silken tassel. A shawl, which they call a *struka*, or a long rag of thick cloth serves instead of blankets and bedding and keeps them from the rain, heat and cold. They do not wear camisoles over their shirts. A piece of rawhide leather tied to the soles of the foot serves as a kind of ancient sandalwood, which they call *opanci*; in the summer their legs are bare while in the winter they wrap themselves up with cloth. The coat is tightly girded with an Albanian belt with pouches. Tucked into that belt are worn a pair of pistols, a *yataghan* sword, dagger and knife. A sabre is tied on the back horizontally. A leather cover is attached to the musket to guard its lock from the rain. Even their poorest have weapons decorated with pearl, silver and coral; they represent all of their wealth and bravado. The Montenegrin will not leave his home before testing his weapons and ensuring that the hammers drop correctly, the flints are sparking and the pans are primed with powder. However they worry little about their appearance and their breath smells a little of garlic and lard. Covered in mud and blood, as I saw them in camp at the siege of Ragusa, they are terrifying to behold.

A Montenegrin girl. Illustration from original publication.

The women are short but very beautiful. They dress almost the same as the men except in the summer they wear less – only a shirt that covers the bosom over which is a multicoloured *panjava* or apron, decorated with long cords and tassels. Girls braid their hair and decorate their red caps around its edges with coins; that or a beaded necklace is the best and beloved of their costume. Their coats are sleeveless like a Turkish tunic while the shirt underneath has wide sleeves embroidered with beautiful patterns. The nobles and common people, rich and poor, have the same dress with the only difference being that some wear silver buttons and plates on their legs and married women wear kerchiefs over their caps.

## Marriages

That passion which enhances pleasures and grants a person new existence, love, does not precede or accompany marriage; instead they depend on the will of the parents. The ceremony of matchmaking is similar to ours; the only difference is that the groom, having gathered his family and heading for the home of his bride, attacks it in mock battle while the brother of the bride demands a token, typically in the form of women's clothing. After the crowning, the bride is accompanied with music and shooting to the husband's home, from which she flees to her parents in the third day, and then her husband purchases her with only 10 cartridges. During a second marriage, the widow-bride does not wear a crown and instead of music, she is accompanied by the banging of bowls and pans. Daughters do not inherit their father's estate but brothers are so generously rewarded when they surrender their sisters that they, along with the gifts that their relatives and even neighbours bring them on the first day, having already a small flock and their property, are quite comfortable in their means. No matter how much the husband loves his wife, he is ashamed of this feeling and caresses her only in private; love after marriage is a secret mystery and therefore in one house the men and women live separately. Shyness and chastity are the values of both sexes equally.

## Funerals

The wife and children of the deceased call on their relatives, cry, and claw at their own faces until they draw blood. The women cut off their hair and lay it on the grave. The funeral is simple; a plate or stone planted vertically in the earth marks the tomb of both the rich and the poor; thus equality is preserved even beyond the limits of life. If the father of a family dies, they make a doll dressed in the best martial garb and place it on the table surrounded by weapons and trophies taken from the enemy. This doll, for commemoration, remains on the table for 40 days.

## Games and Amusements

The Montenegrins absolutely love music, singing and dancing. Returning from the field, from travel or even while in view of the enemy in battle, they sing and dance almost without interruption. Wooden flutes, a kind of *gudok* which they call a *gusle*,[14] and zithers comprise their musical instruments. The blind play the zither artfully. Singing their favourite national songs, they delight in their listening and pay for it generously, because here they are better able to reward people for pleasure rather than for service.

Their songs are borrowed from the epic poem *Osman* by Ivan Gundulić and several Ragusan poets. They glorify the exploits of the Slavonian people. Prince Marko and Jure Kastriotić (the glorious Skanderbeg) are the most frequent subjects. Romances expressing the sweetness and torment of love, I never heard; they are replaced by melancholy songs depicting the loss of a father, wife or mother or longing to return to their native land. Each verse ends in a repetition which is continued by a roll until their voice gives out. In their martial songs, pictures of battles and bloodshed preserve the memory of their national heroes and ignite their hearts with the fire of courage; these replace a formal history. Other songs performed with harmonious sounds send the people into a fine reverie.

Dancing is the favourite pastime of the Montenegrins. Hand in hand and forming a circle or pairing one against another, under great strain of the muscles, arms waving and jumping from one foot to the other, or pressing both tight together and leaping forward, quickly spinning and stomping hard with their feet, they shout: '*skoči gore!*' – jump higher!

They play at spar fighting, target shooting, running in races, games with balls and throwing stones called discuses, like our game of *gorodki* – in short, all the games which resemble the trials of war. Women play rarely: only on the great holidays and then only the very old are admitted into the company of the men, while the young women visit one another and converse among themselves. The Montenegrins do not gamble and their conversations are generally about family and national interests. Instead of going for a stroll, the Montenegrins climb to the summits and precipices of cliffs and stretch out on the ground to spend a few hours contemplating the stormy sea and coastal villages in view.

## Hunting and Fishing

In two large forests there are bears, wolves and foxes. Furs are readily bought in Cattaro. The shooting of boars, rabbits and hares is considered a pleasant pastime. Eagles, falcons and other birds of prey are very common. In the winter are caught many quails, partridges, larks, ducks, snipes, thrushes, finches etc., which are

---

14   A *gudok* is a three-stringed musical instrument played upright in the lap with a bow. The typical *gusle* of the Balkans has only one string, however. Andreyevskiy et al., *Brockhaus and Efron Dictionary*, s.v. 'Гудок, музыкальный инструмент'; ibid., s.v. 'Гусли, музыкальный инструмент'. [Andreyevskiy et al., *Brockhaus and Efron Dictionary*, s.v. 'Gudok, musical instrument'; Ibid., s.v. 'Gusli, musical instrument'.]

rarely eaten because hunting, taking on the image of war, is conducted for practice and pleasure rather than with the object of capturing the quarry.

Small rivers flowing into the Bojana, which runs along the border, and into the large Lake of Skadar, especially the rivers of Crnojevića and Sitnica, as well as the lake itself, which they call the Zenta, are very abundant with fish. Small sardines and carp belong to these rivers and in Italy are revered as a rare delicacy. In the lake and rivers are caught unusually sized trout which can reach a weight of 40 *funts* [16.38 kg]. In addition to their consumption by the locals, five or six large vessels with salted fish are sent from Cattaro to Trieste and Messina every year. Their better catches are in April and May. I was assured that during this period, typically, many gulls nest there presumably to feed on the fish. Killing them is considered a sin, as when they appear in Montenegro the fishermen from all the villagers gather and perform a petitioning prayer and lay relics in the water before throwing rye bread as bait, and as soon as a fish appears on the surface, the screaming gulls descend on them. The fish are driven by the thousands into the nets and the fishermen show their gratitude by feeding the birds with some of the catch. While the fishing continues, the birds become accustomed to people and cooperate with them and do not leave the banks of the rivers and lakes until the work is done.

## Diet

The main diet of the Montenegrins consists of wheat bread mixed with maize for the affluent, rye for the poor, onion and garlic. They rarely eat meat but when they do, typically a whole ram or pig is roasted on a spit. They often have green vegetables, but in moderation, and selling a large portion of their yield. Coffee and other luxuries are completely unknown to them. They eat so little that their bodily strength is really quite surprising.

## Antiquities

Rectangular tombs built of pillars with arches are made of brick and so firmly that many are still preserved. In the interior of the country can be found lamps and bracelets of green copper, which were worn on the right hand of the deceased. Some of these tombs contain medals of Phillip and Alexander of Macedon, and many more coins of the Eastern Empire. The Montenegrins do not respect these rarities and in Cattaro they trade or sell them off for a pittance. By the mouth of the Crnica river, on the island of Vranjina, the ruins of an ancient structure can be seen which is regarded by the inhabitants as the palace of Skanderbeg and a part of the land around it is still called Skanderija.

## History

Titus Livius and Pliny called the original inhabitants of this country the Labeatae (the blessed), whose origin is unknown.[15] Also unknown is the origin of the people who replaced them: some think that they came from the shores of the Sea of Azov and settled on the eastern side of the Venetian Gulf, while others believe that the inhabitants of Illyricum were descendants of the Celts who served in the armies of Alexander the Great and long defended their liberty against the Romans as independent powers. Finally their last king, Gentius, being defeated by Praetor Lucius Anicius, lost a portion of Dalmatia from the Titus River, now the Krka, to the Drina with the nearby islands, stretching east to the peaks of the mountain range called the Scardus in the Geography of Ptolemy. Montenegro belonged to the Illyrian Kingdom, whose kings reigned from Scodra, which is now Scutari. After the partitioning of the Roman Empire, the land from Cattaro to the Drina was a part of the province of Praevalitana in the Eastern Empire.

At the beginning of the sixth century, a then virtually unknown people appeared under the name of the Slavs, signifying a brave people,[16] sacked the empire, humiliating the Goths, and came to occupy a large portion of Europe from the Baltic Sea to the river Elbe, Tisza and the Black Sea. The language and customs of the Montenegrins and the other Slavs of Dalmatia, Croatia, Bosnia and Serbia leave no doubt that they share the same Slavonic root as us. At the beginning of the seventh century, the Slavs, concluding an alliance with the Greek Emperor after the invasion of the Hungarians, entered Illyria and expelled the Avars and established new regions under the names of Croatia, Slavonia, Bosnia and Dalmatia. All of these regions were united under the Kingdom of Serbia but this strong power collapsed from internal disorder. The thefts and provocative wars of the weak independent princes were stifled by the people. In the 15th

---

15   Several Illyrian and Celtic tribes were attested to live in the vicinity of the Bay of Kotor and Lake Skadar, not to mention the inland further north and east. Pliny the Elder names the Autariatae, Cerauni, Daorizi, Daesitiates, Docleatae, Deretini, Deremistae, Dindari, Glinditiones, Melcomani, Naresii, Scirtarii, Siculotae and Vardaei as tribes or states in the region, and the Lebeatae, Enderini, Sasaei and Grabaei as former inhabitants. John Bostock and H. T. Riley (eds.), *The Natural History of Pliny*, vol. 1 (London: George Bell and Sons, 1893), pp.259-262.

16   Bronevskiy is presenting that hypothesis that '*slavyanin*' is derived from '*slava*' (fame or glory), but even in his day there was an alternative etymology from '*slovo*' (word), meaning that the Slavs were 'those who speak' or 'those who are intelligible,' the opposite of the '*nemets*' who is mute or unintelligible, which came to refer to foreigners but especially Germans and is an association that still exists in almost every Slavic language today. Иван Штриттер, *История Российского Государства*, vol. 1 (St. Petersburg: Федор Брунков, 1800), pp.5-6. [Johann Stritter, *History of the Russian State*, vol. 1 (St. Petersburg: Fyodor Brunkov, 1800), pp.5-6.]

century, George, subduing all other rulers, restored the Serbian Kingdom and his descendants under the name of Crnojević preserved it until 1480,[17] at which time the [Southern] Slavs, weak from internal war, almost everywhere lost their independence; some to the Ottomans and others surrendered to foreign rulers [like Venice and Hungary] and even converted their faith and forgot their native tongue.

From that time onward, Montenegro was regarded as belonging to the Sanjak of Scutari, but as the Turks could never establish themselves in it due to frequent resistance, the Montenegrins occasionally payed the *kharaj* (tribute), sometimes they gave nothing, and always considered themselves to be independent. In 1571 and 1657, the Turks conquered Cattaro and Montenegro, but after two years of efforts, the Montenegrins broke free again. Since 1656, from the time of the Vladika Danilo [Šćepčević] Petrović,[18] it must be understood that Montenegro did not at all belong to Turkey. Over the course of two centuries, the Porte sought ways to subjugate this province. Even when the Turks were the terror of the Christian states, they were still convinced that all their attempts on Montenegro were in vain. After the death of the glorious Skanderbeg, the brave Albanians were compelled to yield to force, yet the Montenegrins remained free. The ruins of Krujë, Skanderbeg's capital stained with Muslim blood, stand on the site where the Sultan Murad II with 150,000 men was beaten by just a handful of people, including Montenegrins, and are visible by the border beyond the Drin River. In 1612, Mehmet Pasha invaded with an army of 30,000 but the Montenegrins defeated him; the pasha, with great loss of life, razed a village in the district of the Bjelopavlići. The next year, Arsolan Pasha wished to redress the shame of his predecessor and entered Montenegro with 60,000 men; circumstances were favourable as the districts of Montenegro were hostile to one another and divided. The pasha reached the villages of the Kelmendi and Bjelopavlići without resistance. This misfortune quickly reunited the Montenegrins and they attacked the pasha with courage at a tract of forested road called Husev Lug. Most of the enemy army fell on the site and the victors made off with a rich booty, while the pasha barely escaped with his life in the company of a cavalry detachment. This glorious victory guaranteed their liberty and tranquillity. The Montenegrins from then on became

17    A partially unified Serbian Despotate was first ruled by Stafan Lazarević in 1402 and was succeeded by the Branković dynasty in 1427. The Crnojevići established themselves in the breakaway state of Zeta (roughly corresponding to Montenegro) under Stafan I in 1451 and did not fall to the Ottomans until 1498. Ćirković, *History of the Serbian People*, vol. 2, pp.64-70; Ibid., pp.218-230; ibid., pp.266-8; ibid., pp.535-40.

18    Danilo I was not elected until 1697 and consecrated in 1700. Denton, *Montenegro: Its People and their History*, pp.225-227.

terrible to their neighbours and sought to reaffirm their glory. Military exercises became their passion and hatred for the Turks became hereditary.

The consequence of this situation was that they offered their services to all the powers fighting with the Ottoman Empire. The glory of Peter the Great aroused in them a desire to seek connections with Russia. In 1712, by their own volition and without any external assistance, they sent deputies to offer their allegiance and Peter the Great accepted Montenegro under his protection. Since that time, the nation had become the shield of Christians oppressed by the Turks, who found in them a friendly hospitality and safe haven. These so-called *uskok*s or emigrants, receiving the rights of citizens and being accepted as brothers by blood, are still now distinguished by courage and loyalty to their adopted fatherland. Since Peter the Great, our sovereigns have not ceased to care about the welfare of the Montenegrins, paying special attention to the means that might protect them from an external attack, disrupt the insidious designs of the neighbouring powers and end the internal enmities which weaken them. When Venice declared war on the Ottomans in 1716, the Montenegrins armed themselves for the protection of the republic and its subjects, but after the conclusion of peace [at Passarowitz in 1718], their alleged titles and promises were abolished, and so they declared themselves as subjects of Russia, for which our monarchs, excluding good deeds and prayers, did not demand anything from them. The Empress Elizabeth, during a famine, sent great sums for the preservation of the people. Paul I decorated their churches with generous alms and established the supreme court of the *Kuluk*. Alexander I founded schools and determined a sufficient sum to maintain them. The people, feeling this investment, did not remain ungrateful; in all the wars of Russia with the Ottomans, they did not flee from the field and died with courage and unshakeable fidelity. In the war of 1768, the Montenegrins took the city of Podgorica and the fortress of Žabljak, sacked the surroundings, kept Bosnia and Albania in check with unchallenged terror, and occupied the numerous soldiers of the Pasha of Scutari and other neighbouring forces, thus constituting an important diversion serving in Russia's favour. In all of Catherine the Great's wars with the Sultan, they played an active role. In 1785, Mahmud Bushati, Pasha of Scutari, sought to tame this province; he gathered a terrible army and penetrated deep into the country, but the Montenegrins stood firmly in the tight passages and the pasha, having razed the villages in his path, was compelled to withdraw with great losses. Since then, the Montenegrins have been harbouring a desire for revenge. In 1789, they found an opportunity to satiate themselves: by uniting with the Austrian corps under the command of Major Josef Philipp Vukasović, they routed the pasha, penetrated into Albania and burned many villages, returning to their homes with a rich plunder.

At the behest of our court, Lieutenant-Colonel Count Marko Ivelić recruited a corps of 5,000 volunteers in Herzegovina and the province of Cattaro. The Metropolitan of Montenegro, leading a significant force divided into several detachments, conducted light skirmishes and raids and kept the neighbouring pasha at bay across the border, providing a significant diversion for our forces fighting on the Danube.

The peace concluded at Sistova in 1791 did not confirm their independence. The Sultan demanded a small tribute in accordance with their subjection. The Montenegrins refused and rejected even the slightest form of dependence. The Porte tried to persuade them to negotiate, but every persuasive effort was in vain and the Turks again resorted to force of arms.

In 1796, the same Mahmud Pasha of Scutari received a decree which ordered the merging of forces with the neighbouring pasha and to subjugate or exterminate in any way that rebellious tribe of Slavs. The pasha thus attacked with an excellent force consisting of the bravest Albanians and janissaries. The Metropolitan Petar Petrović, commanding the meager numbers of his people, met the enemy near the town of Krusi, near Podgorica on the border of Montenegro and announced that there they must either triumph or die. Deciding to end the bloodshed in a single battle, he came into view of the enemy on the heights, made a feinted attack on the Turkish camp and then, having fallen back, instructed 5,000 selected warriors to defend the defiles; ordered to place their red caps on the rocks and making a long march at night, they took up positions in the enemy rear to cut off their retreat. In the morning, the Turks were deceived by the fires and red caps left behind, approached the defile and the 5,000 Montenegrins, like the Spartans at Thermopylae, fought desperately and did not give up a single step, maintaining the hopes of the whole army for several hours. At noon, the Metropolitan passed through the impassable mountains and appeared in the rear to descend and strike with all his might into the amazed enemy. The Turks fought furiously. The Montenegrins, defending their fatherland, neglected their own safety and cut into the crowds; the fighting lasted for three days. The enemy died in the thousands, as they could not break through to escape and were crushed. 30,000 were left fallen on the battlefield.[19] The pasha himself was killed, while his baggage train and rich camp fell to the victors. The head of the pasha, as the most glorious trophy, was kept in the monastery of Cetinje along with numerous standards and banners. This tremendous defeat terrified the Turks and safeguarded the independence of the Montenegrins, while the idea of the latter's invincibility further strengthened

---

19    30,000 is the number typically given to Mahmud Pasha's whole army. Denton, *Montenegro: Its People and their History*, p.255-256.

their bravery. The result of the battle was the absorption of the border territories of Brda, Kuči and Piperi by Montenegro.

In 1803, Bonaparte turned his gaze toward Montenegro and sought to establish himself there, hold the Ottomans in fear and in time cut off its most valuable territories from it or otherwise deliver an irreparable blow. As the Montenegrins have so far offered their services to anyone who promised them assistance against the Turks, Count Ivelić, then a lieutenant-general, seeking to guard against the bondage of Bonaparte disguised as aid, was sent as an ambassador to expose this deceit to the people and take the necessary precautionary measures, which had complete success. After the occupation of the province of Cattaro, Montenegro along with it became a significant possession of Russia. The commander-in-chief of both regions, Admiral Senyavin, being so far from the fatherland and with very little money but with the general, sincere devotion of all the Slavs, was able to overthrow the insidious plans of all the hostile powers poised against him. This devotion and admirable confidence in their courage was affirmed even more by the victory at Old Ragusa, the rout of General Lauriston, the taking of the heights of Bergatto (Brgat) and the fortified batteries thought to be an impregnable position, and finally the defeat of General Marmont, who, despite having an excellent force, was compelled to retreat from Castelnuovo and think about his own safety after being refused his conquest.

## Conclusion

This nation which is so close to us is so poorly known, despite speaking one language with us, having the same faith, descending from the same blood, and while we, their brothers, stand on the highest tier of enlightened nations, they lead a savage life among barbarians and keep the same customs as our ancestors during the time of brave Prince Svyatoslav.[20]

Switzerland, a land of similar features to Montenegro, delivered herself into a state of happy contentment from the deepest depths of infertility and desolation. Holland, covered with swamps, threatened by the sea and without any good piers, transformed itself into a centre of global trade. Siberia, under our paternal rule, bears rich harvests from the frozen earth. Dalmatia, though unfavoured by nature, was able to transform itself by the zeal and genius of Enrico Dandolo. The Bokez

---

20   Svyatoslav the Brave was Grand Prince of Kiev from 942 to 972 AD, but did not come of age until 964, before which his mother Olga ruled as regent. His short rule was spent in almost constant warfare in a series of campaigns against the Khazars, Circassians, Bulgarians, Byzantine Greeks and Pechenegs. Andreyevskiy et al., *Brockhaus and Efron Dictionary*, s.v. 'Святослав Игоревич'. [Andreyevskiy et al., *Brockhaus and Efron Dictionary*, s.v. 'Syatoslav Igorevich'.]

acquire their provisions by sea while their neighbouring kin in Herzegovina, the Bosniaks and Serbs, under the yoke of oppression and bondage, extract from agriculture and trade all the fruit they can manage under the careless eyes of their tyrants. Yet the Montenegrins, being free and independent and always standing watch over their liberty, do not know the benefits of the wisdom of law and the subordination to monarchs, and so make no effort and show no desire to overcome their ignorance. The working of the land for the Montenegrin is nothing but an extraneous pursuit for which he applies only his physical strength; there is no form, no improvement, and everything is limited in simple ways which, established as tradition, become sacred. The passion for war extinguishes in him the desire to accumulate wealth and he is content with meagre sums, holding public posts free of charge, neglecting excess, and leading a worriless life of voluntary poverty. Trade is also unknown to him except for the unsubstantial exchanges in Cattaro; raids and looting are the extent of his interactions with the affluent provinces surrounding him. This alienation does not come from the fact that his spiritual abilities are limited; on the contrary, he has good common sense and surprising intelligence, proven by the examples of those who serve in the Russian Army and elsewhere abroad. They have the ability to study languages and sciences but are more inclined toward handicrafts and in a short time assimilate into other peoples, but their success abroad does not benefit their fatherland as those who leave rarely return. By their carelessness, this people, incessantly relying on the blessing of Providence for doing evil, do not comprehend the natural inclinations of their minds, even without a trade, to separate them from the stubborn ignorance of their native upbringing.

The dreams of philosophers on independence can find in the domestic life of the Montenegrins a model of happy freedom, but a friend of mankind will always discover in it the disorder of personal whim, where the right of the strong and inexorable vengeance replaces all law; one wishes in his heart that they free themselves from the countless calamities of war, being equally destructive to both them and their neighbours, and abandon that life that is contrary to the dignity of man. Under the rule of wise laws, the powerful hands of the Montenegrin might turn from looting to the cultivation of the land, their harvests would be more abundant, the wild forests and bare mountain peaks could by their labours become host to numerous herds and flocks. To plant apples, pears, pomegranates, almonds, figs and other fruit trees, on these lands hitherto unused, could be of great benefit to them. Finally grapes planted on the stony soil, covering the gaps between their rocks, would increase their quality of life.

It is known that in the 12th century all the wool of Bosnia and Serbia was brought through Montenegro to the Bay of Cattaro, whence it was shipped to Venice. In less than a century, Bosnia and Herzegovina had a permanent connection with

Castelnuovo through Risan. Albania, in order to avoid the dangers of maritime navigation in winter and wartime, often attempted to transport its goods through the lands of Montenegro; the route would be shortened and the caravans would be freed from attacks and harassment, but fearing the authority of the Turks, all such proposals were rejected. Ragusa and Cattaro, the two closest harbours and placed nearly in the middle of the Adriatic, served as a refuge in the stormy sea and became the focus of trade for the Turkish regions with Italy. By letting goods through their territory, they could restore the lost trade of antiquity. In this fashion, by adopting more peaceable rules and tempering their obstinate character, the Montenegrin would see agriculture and commerce flourish in a short time and would learn all the arts that derive from those two sources of general welfare. Harnessing them would both improve his existence and expand his imagination and enlightenment. In short, bringing them closer to a sedentary life, it would be possible to turn the nation's minds to other subjects, give them a new direction, inspire new thoughts and thereby give them new considerations to enable the path to prosperity.

No other people have such a need to transform their government and customs, but how will this remedial change be effected? Can one hope that, convinced by the well-being of other enlightened peoples, they will seek glory in imitating them? Their eyes are closed to the light, like a dying man whose severity of illness makes him numb to his own suffering, and so they cannot ignite the noble competition which devises grand works. The current Metropolitan has all the prowess and ability to instil in them such excellent determination, but he reigns over a people immersed in the darkness of ignorance, which his elevated knowledge and assertive power does not seem able to overcome and most likely he does not have the strength to undertake such an important transformation. It can only be the work of that Lord alone whose name is in the greatest esteem to this proud, arrogant people; He, whose celebrated feats are the singular benevolence to His subjects, and the happiness of His dominion!

# 30

# Sailing to Trieste – the Blockade of Venice

On the 15th [27th] of April, after the return of the frigate from Corfu, we left Castelnuovo for Trieste to transport Court Councillor Skripitsyn with dispatches for Russia. With a clear sky and a quiet wind, we floated carelessly near the shore of Ragusa. By evening, the coast wind began to fill the upper sails and though the frigate was not too shaken, it quickly gained speed. From the islands which we passed, the cool breeze bought to bear the scents of flowering trees and many birds could be heard singing on the yards; the youths bravely climbed the masts and caught them to feed them and set them free again. Many porpoises played around the frigate, rising out of the water and diving again very smoothly and without haste, seemingly wanting to entertain us. Orcas, distinguished from dolphins whom they more or less accompany by the sickle-shaped fin that stands up like a plume of feathers on their back, are found in all seas and like to approach ships to amuse themselves by racing against them and quickly overtaking them. They typically swim toward that direction from which a new wind should be expected. On the 16th [28th], despite a dark night and foul wind, we passed the Curzola channel very closely and dangerously. Captain Baillie, who took the island of Curzola, stood aboard his ship [the *Aziya*] anchored while the *Letun* and *Ekspeditsion* cruised about the island of Lesina (Hvar).

Having passed Isola Lunga (Dugi Otok), we saw a trabaccolo heading to Zara (Zadar) and fired a shot to demand an inspection, but the boat did not raise a flag and started to flee to a line of small islands surrounded by rocky shallows hoping to hide amongst them. Assuming the boat must be hostile, we gave chase and after a very narrow strait between two submerged rocks, we stopped it with several cannon shots by the island of Unie; the crew fled and the trabaccolo was seized with its cargo of maize and vegetable oil.

On the 20th of April [10th of May], when we approached Trieste, a French gunboat from Capodistria (Koper) dared to attack us during a period of still air. The first of our shots fell very close due to damp powder, which gave the enemy the impression that our guns were all of a small calibre. They approached us closer but several well-aimed shots forced them to immediately retreat and as one ball struck below the waterline and another hit a gun carriage, the boat immediately pulled to shore after entering the harbour. Our losses consisted of some damaged and destroyed rigging. On the next day, we read in the Trieste papers with laughter about the lavish news of a brutal and bloody battle in which the sailors and marines covered themselves with glory. 'The enemy frigate *La Belle Venus* lost 200 men killed and wounded, while our losses were also quite significant: 12 brave men and one lieutenant'.

I cannot say anything about the beautiful town of Trieste, as I was occupied with the duties of my post and had no time to tour anywhere, visiting only the theatre and taking a walk through the public garden. In the opera of Merope, the glorious Imperatrice Sessi delighted the audience with her incredible voice; she was not feeling well and her leg ached, so the audience demanded she be given a chair. She was worthy of this respect, singing so admirably that no one in either the parterre or boxes dared to move. God save those who needed to cough or sneeze. The park consisted of a sparse oak grove without a shadow and there I saw many Italians and Germans together, who could quickly be differentiated at a glance. The German men sat in groups on the grass, drinking and eating with a mug of beer in hand and a pipe between the lips; round, ruddy women bustled around them and smeared butter on bread for everyone. The Italians, on the contrary, made great theatrical strides, whistling the aria sung by Lady Sessi *'cari miei figli venite!'* – 'come my dear children,' while they gazed into the eyes of women who, with a beautiful figure, pale face and an ardently tender glance, willingly accepted the courtesies of these knights, which seemed indecent to us. When the evening grew dark and the moon had yet to appear, the quiet whispers and rustling of feet gave way to the rumbling of carriages pulling up and speeding away. In the grove were left only those who hoped to enjoy greater pleasures than to recite the incomparable Sessi, the foremost singer in Europe then. Only the cicisbei remained, to whom the husbands entrusted their authority, but to what end? The question is unanswerable! Our term 'household friend' is somewhat close to the concept of a cicisbeo but is to the better benefit of the husband and in the capitals [St. Petersburg and Moscow] there is not even the shadow of *cicisbeismo*.

On the third day of our stay in Trieste, we were informed that Russian and British warships were prohibited entrance to Austrian ports, precisely in response to our occupation of the Bay of Cattaro and the failure to return that province. For that reason, the *Svyataya Yelena* and our frigate were forced to withdraw from the town with a cannon shot. However, the friendship and alliance of both empires did not diminish at all from these circumstances. It is easy to guess that the Austrian court was forced to take such a policy by Bonaparte, though they assured us that they had the consent of our own court. Then Napoleon thought to remove our ships from Venice, but this proved to be a mistake and he soon saw that he had lost the remainder of petty trade in that port. Before that decision, we could not seize the vessels leaving Venice and sailing close to the coast in shallow waters past our ships anchored in Trieste; they entered the harbour according to the rules of neutrality without detainment. Now, our frigate departed from the city for three *verstas* [3.2 km] and began stopping and inspecting every vessel that could no longer pass or evade it. Every night, when the wind blew from the direction of Venice, an armed launch returned with several prizes, loaded for the most part with provisions. After several days, more than 100,000 rubles worth of prizes were taken. The people of Trieste foresaw trouble and cut off their relations with Italy by sea, but it was too late to benefit anyone. One suspicious passenger was detailed and brought to the frigate, but the captain ordered his release, as he claimed to be an Austrian merchant and presented his passport. That passenger was the French general Gabriel Jean Joseph Molitor, who complained to the governor of Trieste that they allowed us to inspect vessels so close they were nearly in the harbour and made a lot of noise about it, so we then became more cautious and inspected all passengers strictly (and Austrian passports were no longer believed so readily).

On the 4th [16th] of May, during the blockade of Venice and while being near to Istria, we inspected two Austrian trabaccolos found to be loaded with money, but from the papers and the testimony of the skippers it was clear that they had left Venice and so they were seized as prizes. The captain of an Austrian military brig at a great distance from us sent an officer to our frigate to say that these ships were under his escort, but as the skipper and his passengers during interrogation assured us that the money belonged to the Bank of France, which had an order to exchange Austrian copper coins in Trieste for silver, our captain replied that not only could he not return the two captured trabaccolos, but he would inform the authorities that they were in violation of the rights of neutrality by being escorted by Austrian warships. Our captain intended to detain the Austrian brig, but the dead calm of the wind prevented it and the brig returned on its oars to Trieste, where we also returned Consul Pellegrini,[1] who came aboard thinking we had captured the brig and congratulated us for two million florins good plunder. The next day, unloading the trabaccolos, 35,000 guilders were discovered; the boats and crews were released. Most of the money, along with three French generals, was aboard the military brig and on the other Austrian vessels which still remained in Venice.

---

1     Caesar Pellegrini was Russia's consul general in Trieste from 1806 to 1816. *The Foreign Policy of Russia of the 19th and 20th Centuries*, series 1, vol. 4, p.719.

After the Treaty of Pressburg, Napoleon's true character and politics were revealed. Lucky and extraordinary impudence placed him above all laws. Charmed by his victories, he no longer knew any limit to his ambitions: disturbing the peace of Europe, he no longer sought plausible reasons for the oppression of any state, and especially enjoyed making the most impudent demands to humiliate the dignity of the Austrian Empire. Exchanging Hanover and Lauenburg for the Upper Palatinate and the Principality of Neuchatel, Napoleon managed to embroil war with Prussia against Britain and Sweden. Seeking to pit Russia and Austria against each other, he thought Cattaro would prove an effective lever. For this, occupying Braunau, Napoleon announced that when Cattaro was handed over to his troops, Braunau would be returned to Austria and to sweeten the bait, he promised then that the French armies would withdraw from Germany. Prince Karl Phillip zu Schwarzenberg was sent to St. Petersburg to solicit as ambassador and by the time he arrived, Napoleon demanded in writing from the Viennese court free passage for a force of 40,000 men through the Austrian possessions to reach Dalmatia. When these forces were near Trieste, the Austrians were compelled to close their ports to the Russian and British ships and finally to allow French garrisons in Trieste and Fiume. One can say they ordered Russian merchant vessels to be detained in the harbour of the former. On the 6th [18th] of May, the governor of Trieste, Count Pompeo de Brigido, declared to the Russian skippers that if they did not leave port in six days, they would be detained there, but as they could not prepare in such a short time, it seemed they would violate the ultimatum; for that reason, on the 7th [19th], having received dispatches for the admiral from the Russian ambassador to Vienna, Count Razumovskiy,[2] by way of a courier from Naples named Luciano Spiridaro, we relinquished our post to the *Svyataya Yelena* and returned to Cattaro with nine Bokez vessels to deliver all of this information to the commander-in-chief.

---

2   Count, later Prince, Andrey Kirillovich Razumovskiy served as Russia's minister plenipotentiary to Austria from 1790 to 1799 and again from 1801 to 1807. Andreyevskiy et al., *Brockhaus and Efron Dictionary*, s.v. 'Разумовский, Андрей Кириллович'. [Andreyevskiy et al., *Brockhaus and Efron Dictionary*, s.v. 'Razumovskiy, Andrey Kirillovich'.]

# 31

# Return to Cattaro – Ball Lightning

Quiet and varying winds allowed us to maintain a launch armed with two cannons which entered the shallow harbours of the Dalmatian islands where small vessels could hide without slowing down our frigate's course. A few more vessels were taken in this fashion. Passing Istria, all sails were set and soon the nine merchant boats disappeared when until now we were sailing together.

A high wind blowing evenly across the sea was very beneficial to us during the day. The sun, whose last rays enflamed the west, slowly sank into the sea and the most beautiful evening replaced the day, prompting the wind to die down until the sea became still. All around us was so quiet that as I walked along the frigate from end to end with a megaphone in my hand, I looked with anxious anticipation at the sky where not a single cloud disturbed its stunning azure. I then turned my bored eye to the calm mirror of the water which shone in the clear light of the moon like an immeasurable field strewn with diamonds. The perfect quiet did not last long and a light wind began to blow again; with joy I looked over the stern to admire the long fiery devil which seemed to be tied to the helm, dragging behind the frigate and tracing our course. We already began to anticipate our arrival at Castelnuovo but the wind proved unstable and hummed only for a moment before dying out again. When a fresh breeze picked up again, it brought with it thick and darkening clouds and as it grew stronger, we were forced to stay under easy sail. The frigate glided along the smooth surface of the sea which offered little resistance to her bow.

Around midnight, when the darkness was impenetrable, the eastern horizon suddenly blazed with brilliant fire. A small fireball slowly floated by the shore to port and increased in speed and grew in size until it equalled the moon. A tail hung behind it like a comet and its course was like the fall of a wandering star. In the middle of its flight, the ball spat sparkles so bright that the night turned to day for a few seconds, and when the ball collapsed with a great crash, its visible diameter seemed to be around 50 *sazhen*s [106.68 m]. This phenomenon, originating from terrestrial gasses and electrical forces, was called by others a flying serpent of fire, and here the common people believe that it loves beautiful women and when it enters a house, it will bring wealth and good fortune to the family.

The latter came true for us in fact: we quickly raced past Lesina where over the fortifications the French tricolour was hoisted with a gunshot, and then two hours later we passed Curzola where the Russian flag flew and the *Aziya* and *Letun* were anchored; that same evening, when the *Svyatoy Mikhail* stood in the Calamotta, the fortifications at Ragusa saluted us from 11 guns and on the 12th [24th] of May, under all sails in a fresh wind, when the frigate was nearly blown onto its side, and under the very stern of the admiral's ship, we saluted him with 9 shots and nimbly doused the sails to come into Castelnuovo and drop anchor.

The Castelnuovo anchorage, so isolated and empty, now formed a pretty picture in the span of six *versta*s [6.4 km]. To see vast ships of the line, little light brigs and a multitude of merchant boats of various type, all under the Russian flag, at such a far distance from their fatherland made the Russian heart swell with pride. There came the sudden shouts of sailors hauling the ships' cargo and the piercing sound of the whistle called the men to receive their ration of wine and food; then came the sweet sounds of a huge booming orchestra merging with the merry songs of sailors audible in the distance: all of these alluring sounds together comforted the spirit. Everywhere there was traffic and activity. A dense smoke swirled up into the clouds from a ship which was rolled onto its side and slathered in burning pitch.[1] Several painted dinghies chequered the sea and dazzled in the eye. It seemed that two under sail were poised to collide and the men would perish, but with one small movement of the rudder, they passed by clear yet so closely that the sailors could shake hands from boat to boat. Another craft carrying large sails lay nearly on its side with the waves spilling over its edges, but such risks become habit and call for no special courage; they are in fact amusing to young officers who revel in such seemingly dangerous conditions.

1    Bronevskiy's note: 'For caulking the draught of the hull, the old coat of pitch [and accumulated filth] was typically burned away [in a process known as breaming]'.

# 32

# The Liberation of the Detained Ships in Trieste – 21st of May [2nd of June]

After the arrival of the frigate in Castelnuovo, on the next day, the 13th [25th] of May, the vice-admiral departed for Trieste with the *Selafail*, the *Svyatoy Pyotr*, the *Moskva* and the *Venus*, both to free the ships detained by the Austrians and to convey them past Istria and those ports where the French had reinforced their flotilla of galleys. On the 14th [26th], at the island of Meleda, they met with the *Svyataya Yelena* and seven corsairs under military flags, which were accompanied by 38 Bokez vessels. The *Svyataya Yelena* saluted the admiral with 9 shots and sailed abaft to have a dialogue. Then the *Selafail* raised the signal to set every possible sail, but on the 15th [27th], the wind by the island of Lissa (Vis) changed direction and became foul. We met 5 British transports with land forces aboard, who attempted without success to take the island of Tremiti. Quiet, alternating winds kept the squadron at sea until the 20th of May [1st of June]; that same today, at noon, a strong squall with rain appeared. The ships flew on the wind and soon passed Istria with cannon shots, raised signals and ready for battle, standing on anchors with springs.[1] As soon as our ships spotted Trieste, the squadron fell into combat order under the very batteries of the town. Soon the military commandant of Trieste, Lieutenant-Field-Marshal Anton von Zach,[2] sent his adjutant to congratulate

---

1    Bronevskiy's note: 'To attach a rope to the anchor line a fair distance from the hull so that by pulling in or releasing the spring line from the opposite end of the ship, the craft can be made to rotate in all directions on its anchor'.

2    The Austrian rank of lieutenant-field-marshal (*Feldmarschall-Lieutenant*) was equivalent to lieutenant-general and stood between major-general and the ranks of full general, rather than directly below field-marshal as its name might imply. *Dienst-Reglement für die Kaiserliche Königliche Infanterie*, vol. 1 (Vienna: K.-K. Hof- und Staats-Druckerei, 1807), p.243.; Ibid., vol. 2, pp.89-99. [*Service Regulations for the Imperial-Royal Infantry*, vol. 1 (Vienna: I.-R. Court and State Press, 1807), p.243.; Ibid., vol. 2, pp.89-99.]

us on our arrival and ask that the squadron, by the authority of the Emperor's command, give a customary shot by cannon. The vice-admiral replied: 'shoot! I will see where your shots fall and know where I should be positioned'. The adjutant did not expect such an answer, gave a bow and departed. All night long, the decks of the ships were illuminated with lanterns, people stood by their cannons with lit match cord and armed boats sailed around the harbour. The detention of our ships and the formidable position of our squadron gave a just cause for the citizens of the city to fear a terrible resolution. They awaited the morning in bewilderment and we too wished to know how this unpleasant circumstance would end.

During the night, Zach delivered the Austrian Emperor's order to close its ports to Russian and British ships. The commander-in-chief replied on the morning of the 21st of May [2nd of June] with these brief words: 'your proclamation has been received and I will leave the port as soon as I mend some of the damage to my ships'. After this, negotiations began and officials proceeded without interruption back and forth between the *Selafail* and Trieste. The persistent Austrian diplomats tried to convince the vice-admiral that the decision to ban us was followed at Napoleon's insistence, who otherwise would seize Trieste and Fiume, the only harbours left in Austrian possession; we were assured that a 20,000-man strong French corps was nearby and already two generals had arrived in the city with the intention of monitoring the Russian squadron and moving their forces in should we not retire by morning. Then, referring to the sincere friendship and firm alliance between our courts, they asked and hoped that the Russian admiral would certainly not dare without specific orders from our Emperor to act like the French generals, who carried out their demands with the bayonet during times of peace. 'Your situation is difficult,' answered Senyavin, 'and mine does not leave me the slightest reason to hesitate in my choice. Your policy seems to me, as an officer and not a politician, to be incongruent with the friendship and alliance of which you assure me. In accordance with my duty and with my force that you see here it is not appropriate of me to allow you to humiliate the flag for which I am greatly responsible; this is a matter of honour and respect due to my fatherland'.

During these conversations, the frigate *Avtroil* arrived around noon at the anchorage with news that the French had occupied Old and New Ragusa and were threatening to attack Cattaro. This new violation of the rights of the people prompted the vice-admiral to take a decisive action. The *Svyatoy Pyotr* and *Venus* received orders, delivered alongside supplies for the sake of secrecy, that the former was to attack the batteries at the Lazaretto Nuovo and the latter those on San Carlo, so that the ship and frigate, entering the harbour itself, would be in the rear of the main and strongest battery on the side of the quarantine, to which the admiral's ship and the *Moskva* were close enough for pistol shots. In the last note to Lieutenant-Field-Marshal Zach, which the commander-in-chief gave to the Austrian officials, he answered:

> To Lieutenant-General Zach,
> Military Commandant of Trieste,
> Your Excellency!
> In response to your letter earlier today, I ordered one of my ships, which may have moved closer to within cannon range, to retreat – and you see it. The ship on which I stand, although I do not think it is within a shot's reach, will also withdraw if the wind and cruel squalls should allow me. However, as you assure me, Lieutenant-General, of the constant friendship of our most prestigious courts and the confirmation to forbid the entry of Russian ships to your ports; although I do not have orders from my Emperor on this matter, for my own part I wish to avoid ill-will so I have forbidden my officers to go ashore and you will know that this is done. After an hour, I hope to depart from here on a long voyage to the complete satisfaction of both yours and mine.
>
> D. Senyavin
> 21st of May [2nd of June], 1806
> Aboard the ship *Selafail*.

Leaving the Austrian officials, the admiral said to them: 'now there is no time to continue these fruitless negotiations. You must choose one of the two: either act on the instigation of the French generals or maintain the true meaning of the right of neutrality. My choice is made, so here is my final demand: if after one hour you have not returned those vessels you have detained, then I will take by force not only mine but your vessels as well, both in the harbour and at sea. I assure you that the 20,000 Frenchmen will not defend Trieste. I hope however that in an hour we will be friends and I only ask that there is not the slightest insult to the honour of the Russian flag and truly wish for your own well-being. Tell General Zach that it now depends on him to keep the friendship of our august monarchs which has been so helpful to you on many occasions and can continue to be beneficial. Assure him that in one hour, I will begin the action'.

It proved to be the terrifying movements of the squadron despite the threats of the French generals rather than a diplomatic conviction that forced General Zach and the governor of Trieste, Count Brigido, to fully satisfy Admiral Senyavin's demands. When everything was ready and we were waiting, I confess, with great impatience for the first shot of the admiral's ship as our signal to begin the battle, the harbour suddenly erupted with shouting proclamations of '*vivat!*' and we were pleased to see Russian flags hoisted again on the detained vessels. At the same time, the *Selafail* and *Svyatoy Pyotr* set sail. The captain of the *Moskva*, Hetzen, received an order in anticipation of the arrival of a courier from Trieste to blockade Venice and to conduct the liberated vessels past Istria, which would be further escorted to Cattaro by the *Venus* and the *Avtroil*. The departure of our admiral was given a farewell with cannon and musketry and cries of '*ura!*' and the *Selafail* replied with music from its band, whose agreeable sounds were audible at great distance due to the softness of the wind. At this time a flag was hoisted over Trieste's citadel, and a rumour spread in the town that the Russian admiral would meet the governor in person, which saw the embankments covered with gawking crowds.

Thus Senyavin took the first step into the field of diplomacy and we can say that he was the first of the military officers of the lawful powers to demonstrate the means by which one can deny the unbelievably arrogant demands of the French generals and agents, who seek to trample on the dignity of those they frighten with threats both in wartime and in peace. With one decisive act, Senyavin cut through the Gordian knot which had been tied by the hand of Napoleon and thereby stopped and reversed that disturbance which could not only sour relations but even unleash a war. They considered the matter guaranteed, but they made a mistake. Senyavin, with his firmness, managed to maintain our alliance with Austria and left not the slightest reason for further voluminous diplomatic correspondence.

At night, due to a dead wind, the *Selafail* and *Svyatoy Pyotr* approached the fort of Capodistria on the current. Two gunboats came out from that port and fired several shots in the air from an inoffensive distance. Our ships did not respond, since their balls did not reach far. The next day, our consul, Pellegrini, sent the following quote from the *Moniteur*: 'the brave flotilla of the Kingdom of Italy courageously attacked the massive Russian ships and with sure gunnery forced them to retreat further into the sea. The battle took place near Capodistria. The enemy losses must be considerable, and we learned that by a single shot fired from the boat *Battaglia di Marengo*, the admiral Senyavin was killed'.[3]

On the departure of the commander-in-chief, in order to satisfy the urgent demands of the French generals on one hand and to prevent us from going ashore for any plausible reason on the other hand, we were ordered to the quarantine and so stayed anchored in the harbour and were delivered all of our necessities by the fire watch. After two days, and probably after the departure of the French generals, our officers were permitted to enter the city but only in undress frocks. At the

---

3    *Le Moniteur Universel* did publish a story of a naval engagement between an Italian and Russian force and attributed it to the 2nd of June, but places the location as the island of Hvar and gives the Russian squadron as consisting of only a brig, galiot, xebec and trabaccolo. It also does not name any commanding officer killed. Perhaps Bronevskiy attributed the quote to the wrong journal or confused it with another incident. *Gazette Nationale ou le Moniteur Universel* 164 (13 June 1806), p.1. [*National Gazette or the Universal Monitor* 164 (13 June 1806), p.1.

theatre, we were given seats gratis. The merchants, who constitute the greater part of Trieste's population, extolled the deed of our vice-admiral with praise; for to lose trade would be painful not only for their town but for all of Austria and of course for that very reason, the singular message we left throughout Trieste was that Russia was a free power.

# 33

# En route from Trieste to Cattaro – The Cyclone

On the 25th of May [6th of June], while on the anchorage of Trieste and seeing that a gunboat had left Capodistria, we weighed anchor and were quickly prepared a tow line during the period of calm wind, but when the boat saw our movements, it turned back. On the 26th [7th], when all 17 vessels due to be escorted were made ready, the captain of the *Moskva* who came from sea made the signal to weigh anchor. Departing Trieste during a continued calm period, we were forced to drop anchor twice, but a small passing wind blew which we exploited under sail just enough to clear Istria; the enemy flotilla did not leave their fortresses. On the 29th of May [10th of June], the *Moskva*, leaving the convoy, returned to their prior duty in besieging Venice. On the next day, we heard fire from that direction and later discovered the cause. On the 30th [11th], exploiting the calm air, a large convoy of small merchant ships under the guise of several French gunboats left Venice intending to reach Istria. The *Moskva* caught a small wind and began to manoeuvre, fired on the closest craft, and forced the enemy convoy to return and take cover in the shallows.

The ships of our convoy were varied specimens of old and new shipbuilding: tartanes with sails sloped forward; the beautiful appearance of polaccas with masts made entirely from whole trees; and xebecs with a myriad of triangular sails. Moreover, the unhurried, cheerful and melancholy songs of the Slavs recalled the age of Igor and Oleg and their raids on Tsargrad[1]. We travelled very slowly and exactly as you would while in a harbour, accepting visits and guests

---

1   Tsargrad is an archaic Slavic name and poetic appellation for Constantinople. Grand Prince Oleg of Kiev and his son Igor besieged Constantinople in 907, 941 and 944 AD. Andreyevskiy et al., *Brockhaus and Efron Dictionary*, s.v. 'Олег'; Ibid., s.v. 'Игорь Рюрикович'. [Andreyevskiy et al., *Brockhaus and Efron Dictionary*, s.v. 'Oleg'; Ibid., 'Igor Ryurikovich'.]

aboard who often stayed to dine with us. On Sunday, almost all the skippers came to attend mass.

The days were very hot, and those light winds blowing from the sea typically at noon and from the shore around midnight were our great relief. The night winds brought warm, stifling vapours from the land such that at midnight one suffered just as much from the heat as at noon. In the afternoon of the 30th of May [11th of June], on the peak of the island of Lagosta, with a fresh northerly wind, the air was filled with a thin fog and soon in the distance, about four *versta*s away [4.27 km], the sea began to broil noisily and spray up to the sky, while clouds descended in long sheets like loose sleeves. The water swirled around with incredible speed and scattered a great rain, generating a noise like the bubbling of molten metal. Finally the sea joined the clouds with a multitude of cones, whose sharp peaks touched the heavens and with a terrible din they began to spin, thicken and move. Eleven huge vortexes quickly sped towards us, and the convoy scattered in all directions to escape them, but as some of the ships without guns were in peril for the want of them, we set all sails and ran downwind like Don Quixote charging at a windmill, being forced to give battle to the columns of water.[2] A volley from starboard tore into two of the cyclones and a few shots from port dispelled another, which seemingly took out another with it as it collapsed. Admiring the destruction of these giants, we saw one straight ahead of the bow and another was already even closer; in the moment, the frigate could not turn, a whole volley flew past, and there was nothing to do but to lie to and bring the frigate to a halt. It was already so close it was frightening, but luckily one sure shot from the bow knocked down this colossus too, and the waves that crashed over the bow proved harmless. Our convoy vessels also successfully fought with these cyclones, which seemed as if to purposely come at us from three sides, and as they fell one by one, another rose in its place. One of the vortices fell near the *Svyatoy Pyotr* and, touching it with only its splashes, tore off all the sails and broke the lower yards of the masts. One can imagine how much harm could be done if such a column of water fell directly onto a ship.

A cyclone, or otherwise a waterspout, draws to itself circular vapours and the flow of air towards them is so strong that birds flying nearby are carried away by the water into the clouds; even fish which cannot swim away are lifted into the sky. When the sun is seen behind one, the whole column is lit with multicoloured light, the water seems to shimmer inside and bubbles away just as in a waterfall.

---

2    It was a common belief in the 18th and 19th centuries that waterspouts could be dispelled by cannon fire, if not by the ball itself then by the concussive force of the charges being set off. 'The Nature of Water-Spouts,' *The Universal Magazine of Knowledge and Pleasure* 7 (July 1750): p.154.; Hans Christian Oersted, 'On Water-Spouts,' *The American Journal of Science and Arts* 36 (July 1839), p.266.

One should imagine a large river quickly flowing from the sea to the heavens and showering all around a pearly rain.

The creation of typhoons and tornadoes is attributed by physicists to electrical forces. They say that when there is a strong electrified cloud at a fair distance from the sea, then between that cloud and the water two opposite currents of electrical matter begin, the cloud's flowing downward and the sea's upward. If the first current is stronger than the second, then the particles of vapour of which the cloud is composed are entrained by the matter flow and form a column of water or cyclone. If, however, the current flowing from the water up to the clouds is stronger than the opposite, the water is entrained up out of the sea and rises to the clouds in a reversed funnel.[3] Ultimately a column is formed, which is called a tornado. After the formation of the column, not only the upper cloud nor sea but the entire cyclone gains the power to attract other neighbouring vapours and water, hence the powerful currents of air. Quickly the whole column begins to spin around and draw the water upward to the clouds with a centripetal force. Seafarers call water columns of both kinds by the name 'typhoon';[4] tornadoes also refer to rapid whirlwinds which turn the water up to a dangerous height but by the force of wind alone, taking a circular course, they lift up the sails without causing further damage. Typhoons typically follow periods of heat and are especially characteristic of hot climates, by the fact that they are rarely seen in the northern seas. Tornadoes usually occur before or after turbulent weather. A whirlwind raising dust on land is also a tornado.

Passing the islands outside Old Ragusa, the *Uriil* and two corsairs fired along the shore where it must have been believed a battle was unfolding. The 31st of May [12th of June], toward evening, the convoy entered the Bay of Cattaro, in which stood the *Selafail*, the *Svyataya Paraskeva* under the flag of Rear-Admiral Sorokin, the *Svyatoy Pyotr* and the *Svyataya Yelena*. Still in Trieste, a Lieutenant N. who distributed signal books to the skippers suspected a passenger on one of the vessels who had papers for a captain in Russian service. The lieutenant, speaking to him in Italian, noticed something unusual in him and ordered the skipper to

---

3    Cyclones are created by cool storms passing over warm, moist surface air. Updrafts of warm air collide with powerful, shifting winds above which create rotations of air along an axis – a vortex. As the vortex gains speed and broadens, it also extends further down toward the ground or sea. Waterspouts however can begin on the surface and extend upward, compelled to spin by winds below the clouds. Electrical activity does not drive convection. Rather, strong convective cycles can generate electrostatic charges that result in lightning strikes. Thomas Malone (ed.), *Compendium of Meteorology* (Boston: American Meteorological Society, 1951), pp.676-679.

4    In modern terminology, both English and Russian, 'typhoon' refers only to cyclones in the northwest Pacific Ocean. Tropical cyclones in the Mediterranean are called 'hurricanes' or 'medicanes'.

observe his behaviour. When the frigate came before the entrance of the bay, in order to let the convoy pass ahead, the skipper fetched several letters entrusted to this passenger for delivery to Perasto, Cattaro and other Catholic communities. The skipper also announced that his passenger had a great deal of money with him and spent all night locked in his cabin writing, for which Lieutenant N. departed with the skipper and discovered that he was a spy sent by the enemy. The admiral ordered that same hour that he be taken to Espanola Fortress.

I took several papers to the *Selafail* and the admiral invited me to dine with him. This was the first time I met my commander and I confess I considered myself fortunate that I had several minutes in his company. Receiving my affection and encouraging me, his manners were so simple and noble that he suddenly, if I may say, gave credence to his fame. At the table, Dmitriy Nikolayevich [Senyavin] seemed to be surrounded by his own family. His conversation was diverse and pleasing to everyone who participated because he seemed to forget himself and thought of only others when conversing with them, and even though I was the last of his guests, I was not ignored. He recognized the experience of a person who saw much, read much, and often reflected on the benefits, weaknesses, passions and shortcomings of the human heart. When one of the guests turned the conversation over to prior political events, he presented his opinions with such modesty, no matter how passionately he believed them. When the conversation turned to Russia, his eyes lit up and everyone listened to him with attention and only in these cases did it seem dangerous to contradict his opinion.

## 34

# A Look at the Montenegrins' Preparations for War

On the 1st [13th] of June, the whole fleet sent out rowing boats for the transportation of the Montenegrins from Cattaro to Castelnuovo. The streets were filled with crowds. On the square near the main guard house, the Montenegrins of the first division were given small ensigns which the people preferred to real [army] banners because they had the Cross of St. Andrew. Each village constituted a party or a company according to its population, their numbers being unequal. Each district was a corps under the command of a *serdar*. All the Bokez and Montenegrin warriors were led by the Metropolitan himself. Such an order of battle, it seems to me, encourages competition and asserts concord; because in a given company all of the warriors are mostly relatives. The companies and corps belonging to different villages, towns or districts compete with one another to excel and in battle, any that stay behind would be shamed. The election of the chiefs of the companies deserves attention. The warriors of a single village, forming circles, elect candidates among themselves; these according to their seniority take turns recounting their exploits and battles fought, proven by their wounds, and they also dispute one another and argue, creating a loud commotion. After a general agreement, they finally elect the most worthy and brave and take off his weapons and administer to him an oath to obey, where he will lie down and put his own head to the ground. After this, this chief takes the flag, goes to the church with everyone and leads a prayer for supplication, administers an oath and returns to the town square to stand in the circles; they draw their swords and all shake them in the air, suddenly shouting: 'for the cross, for the faith, for the Holy Mother of God, for the White Tsar and the Fatherland, we swear by the bones of our ancestors, by their glory, to serve to the last drop of blood and never beg for nor give any mercy, to die or be victorious!' Such preparations shake the soul. But the heralds arouse the fury of this semi-savage people even further, shouting ceaselessly until their voices are tired and hoarse: 'to arms, brave Slavs! The old betrayers of Ragusa have deceived us, given their fortresses to the French, and as they once burned the churches of Christians, they now hope for aid from the godless, threaten to raze our lands and destroy us with fire and sword! The blood of our burned brothers screams out! Go forth, take revenge on those murderers, traitors – your enemies!' These words inspire malicious curses: the Montenegrins wave their daggers in the air and shout 'to the blackened foul Dubrovnik, off with the heads of the fallen faith', which would refer to the Ragusans and the French. I could not seat the Montenegrins on my boat, as one would climb into it and another would watch, then he would climb in while the first got out again; this was not a force that could be subordinated. They obey us – and then, not all of them – only when they see the enemy before them.

# 35

# Sending the *Letun* to Preveza

Upon receiving notification from the minister to the Ionian Republic, Count Giorgio Mozzenigo, Vice-Admiral Senyavin instructed the commander of the brig *Letun* to capture a French corsair which had seized a Russian vessel in Preveza. The commander of the brig, Lieutenant Ivan Butakov, arrived at the entrance to the bay of Preveza on the 8th [20th] of February and demanded that the Russian vessel be returned. The corsair, at the insistence of the government, released the Russian vessel and moved to the opposite bay, and on the following day attacked the brig; the battle lasted for an hour and a half and the shots from the corsair did some damage to the town. Although the French xebec was stronger than our brig, it exploited a moment of calm to row to the inside of the lip of the harbour where it unloaded one side of its guns and, arranging them in two batteries, stood between them in the shallows. Upon the return of the *Letun* to Corfu with the liberated Russian boat, the commander of the *Feniks*, Captain-Lieutenant Ivan Sulmenev, together with Butakov were ordered to destroy the French corsair. Both brigs set out on the 13th [25th] of February. On their arrival at the harbour, a Turkish brig of 16 guns came out to meet them and followed behind. The enemy corsair stood by the village of Salagora, at the mouth of the river Louros where it was still defended by two aforementioned batteries. The brigs could not reach an effective proximity in the shallows and their shots could barely reach the enemy, so they aborted their attack and the corsair fled further up the river. During this engagement, the Turkish brig was a quiet spectator. The vice-admiral informed the Turkish authorities that if an enemy corsair is allowed to build a battery on their shore, allowed to detain ships laden with provisions for the Russian squadron, and if the necessary measures are not taken to restrain the initiative of enemy vessels, then he will be forced to take a series of measures which could stop such abuses of authority. In this incident the intrigues of the enemy are plainly visible, but Ali Pasha, who was already acquainted with the vice-admiral by personal experience, learning that it would not be profitable for him to make such trouble, took advantage of the first chance to convince Senyavin of his friendly disposition. The pasha, according to Turkish custom, sent several gifts to the admiral, for which, it must be believed, he received something quite significant, because despite the intentions of the enemy, who disrupted the supply of provisions in order to harm us in Corfu, Ali Pasha had always been a good neighbour and a good friend of the admiral.

# 36

# The Action of Captain Baillie's Squadron

The vice-admiral arrived in Cattaro on the 15th [27th] of March and personally ascertained the devotion of the Bokez to our Sovereign Emperor, receiving though their deputies declarations of a readiness to sacrifice not only their property but also their lives. Respecting such a sincere devotion in the people, in which there was no doubt, he endeavoured to protect and help them as much as possible. Having established a police and convoys to Trieste and Constantinople, and having sent 30 vessels variously armed with 8 to 20 guns for the blockade of enemy ports in the Adriatic sea, he then ordered Captain Baillie to attempt to take possession of the islands along the Dalmatian coast with the ships of the line: the *Aziya*, the *Svyataya Yelena* and the *Yaroslav*; the frigates *Venus* and *Mikhail*; the brig *Letun*, the xebec *Azard* and the schooner *Ekspeditsion*.

As a result of this order, Captain Baillie left the Bay of Cattaro on the 29th of March [10th of April] with the *Aziya*, *Yaroslav*, *Svyataya Yelena* and 9 trading vessels. In the channel of Calamotta, he united with the *Ekspeditsion* and *Azard*, and at noon on the 30th [11th], the *Yaroslav*, *Ekspeditsion*, *Letun* and *Azard*, having anchored off of the port of Curzola, opened a heavy fire on the fortifications upon the signal of a pistol shot. In less than half an hour, the guns on the walls were wrecked and the enemy defended himself with only musketry. When the *Aziya* dropped anchor, a shore party consisting of two companies of a naval regiment and several sailors rowed on boats directly to the fort. The enemy commandant, seeing himself attacked from sea and land and believing that the *Svyataya Yelena* with its nine merchant vessels were drawing closer to the fort with their own landing parties, which in fact was not the case,[1] hauled down the flag and departed with the garrison, laid down their arms and surrendered unconditionally. Taken prisoner

---

1     Bronevskiy's note: 'These vessels were intended to travel to Trieste and were with the squadron solely to deceive the enemy'.

were: 1 lieutenant-colonel, 2 captains, 5 junior officers, 20 non-commissioned officers, 5 drummers and 227 privates; 85 men were killed. In the fortress were taken 12 bronze cannons of various calibre, and a proportionate stockpile of ammunition and supplies in its magazine. Nine vessels were taken as prizes.

After the capture of the island of Curzola, Captain Baillie learned that there were several French soldiers on the island of Lissa and sent the *Ekspeditsion* and *Azard* immediately to capture them. The commander of the schooner, who was opposite the port of Luka and spotted a three-masted vessel under sails, caught up with it and captured upon it 39 French soldiers and an officer along with all the military supplies they were carrying. Lieutenant Sytin, commander of the xebec, captured a few more men and seven guns in the fortress of Lissa, and on the 5th [17th] of April, he took two 12-pounders [5.87 kg][2] and one 8-pound [3.92 kg] gun from the fortress of Camisso at the port of San Giorgio (Viška), also on the island of Lissa. After this, our cruisers continued their search for the enemy, intercepted several more soldiers, took a considerable amount of ammunition and provisions, and thereby were compelled to leave in our control all the islands, which were quite far from the Dalmatian shore. With the small vessels in Ballie's squadron, 14 vessels were captured by just the 9th [21th] of April.

On the 17th [29th] of April, Baillie arrived at the fortress of Lesina and on the 19th [1st of May], on a dark night, he established a battery on the small island lying opposite the mouth of the harbour. As soon as the enemy noticed that the islet was occupied, they directed strong fire against it with small arms, but an armed trabaccolo under the command of Midshipman Kharlamov, the xebec *Azard*, a Bokez corsair under Lazar Žuanović, a launch with 24-*funt* [11.8 kg] carronades and two cutters with swivel guns quickly drove them off with canister fire. Despite the firefight, which lasted all night, on the 20th of April [2nd of May] at 5 in the morning, the sailors under the command of Midshipman Milon and Second Lieutenant of the Artillery Demetrios Palaiologos constructed a battery of two 12-*funt* [5.9 kg] and one 6-*funt* [2.95 kg] gun and began to open fire. The enemy's sporadic fire quickly fell silent. At half-past seven, a landing party of 100 soldiers under the command of Staff-Captain Skorobogatov[3] and 42 sailors under Midshipman Bashutskiy went ashore under the cover of the ships, charged with bayonets and quickly occupied the grounds of a Catholic monastery, but the French garrison sallied from the fortifications in excellent strength and repelled our forces from the walls and drove them back to their vessels. Our losses consisted of 11 killed, 33 wounded and the following captured: Staff-Captain Skorobogatov, one

2    Assuming old French pounds or *livres* (489.51 g). François Cardarelli, *Encyclopedia of Scientific Units, Weights and Measures,* trans. M. J. Shields (London: Springer, 2004), p.82.
3    Nikita Skorobogatov of the 4th Naval Regiment. *The Complete Naval Roster of 1806*, p.145.

*garde de marine*, and 32 enlisted men who were covering the retreat and became stranded on the shore. The enemy must have taken significant losses, for until the French troops collided with ours, they were under fire for two hours from all the vessels with both solid shot and grape. On the 25th of April [7th of May], Captain Baillie observed that the enemy had become very numerous with personnel and, having placed large guns in advantageous positions, began to damage our ships, so he decided to leave his enterprise at the fortress of Lesina and to continue to search in other places where he could expect success from the poor strength of the enemy.

The commander-in-chief, having given the necessary instructions in Corfu for the protection of the republic against the enemy and having assured Ali Pasha that it would be more profitable for him to remain with us in good conscience than to help Napoleon, arrived in Cattaro with the greater part of his fleet on the 19th of April [1st of May] and, having received a report on the successful actions of Baillie's squadron, made for the island of Curzola with the *Selafail*, *Svyatoy Pyotr*, and the *Avtroil*. On the 27th of April [9th of May], the admiral was surprised not to see any flag flying above the fortress when he arrived. Soon a few French sentries appeared, upon which he ordered the ships to drop anchor. A very fresh wind prevented landing a party ashore at that time. By evening, the admiral learned that seven French vessels carrying around 350 men arrived from Makarska during the night of the 26th [8th], unexpectedly attacked the small detachment of soldiers under Second Lieutenant Voyeykov[4] left by Captain Baillie, captured them and then occupied the fort. Of those seven vessels, two turned back before the arrival of the squadron, but the other five were seized by the *Avtroil*, including two 18-pound [8.81 kg] guns. The wind ceased by evening, the rowing vessels were sent on patrol around the fortress, and a landing was made before the break of day, but the French also left the fortress in the night and fled the island from different places on resident boats to reach the Ragusan shore, from which the neutral authorities of Ragusa returned them to Dalmatia without resistance. The rowing vessels were only able to intercept one boat with 16 French soldiers aboard. In addition to the seven fortress guns, a fair quantity of provisions and ammunition was taken. Our soldiers taken prisoner, with the exception of the second lieutenant, were returned.

On the 29th of April [11th of May], leaving the *Avtroil* at Curzola, the admiral sailed to Lesina. Around noon, between the islands of Lesina and Lissa, the *Aziya* united with the squadron. Having received a report from Captain Baillie on the presence of the enemy in the fortress of Lesina, the admiral saw that with his meagre forces, under the present circumstances, it was difficult to keep the island secure, since the French could pass through Austrian territory from Italy to Dalmatia without hindrance and nearly every day could reinforce their strength.

---

4    Aleksey Voyeykov of the 2nd Naval Regiment. *The Complete Naval Roster of 1806*, p.135.

Consequently, taking possession of it, he would need a large number of military ships and a strong garrison to protect it, and the enemy could always attack the fortress with a strong force via the island's proximity to Spalatro (Split). For this reason, the admiral returned with the squadron to Curzola where he left for its defence the *Aziya*, the *Azard* and three gunboats converted from prize vessels, and sailed to Ragusa. At the behest of the inhabitants of Curzola, having approved Count Grisogono as civil governor of the island, who had governed the island during the Austrian administration, the admiral not only never levied any taxes from the inhabitants, but all income provided was to their own benefit.

# 37

# General Lauriston's Occupation of Ragusa and Abolition of the Republic

The Senate of Ragusa, upon learning of the arrival of our commander-in-chief in Cattaro, sent Senator Vladislav Sorgo to pay respect and ask for his benevolent protection for the republic. The admiral on his return voyage from Curzola to Castelnuovo was received in Ragusa on the 6th [18th] of May with great honours and festivity. He was hopeful for protecting the republic from the catastrophe which loomed daily by the malicious orders of the enemy, always searching for some opportunity to oppress those independent regions that, in their individual weakness, could not offer any resistance. The violation of neutrality was not only revealed by the free passage through their territories of the fleeing garrison from Curzola, but Consul Fonton was ordered to give up a claim to the prize of a French corsair seized in the port of Ragusa and furthermore by their deigning to grant the senate's request to allow 10 republican vessels to enter the blockaded ports of Puglia to purchase wheat and oils there. The senate accepted this gesture of generosity with gratitude but afterward, in the port of Zuliano, an enemy corsair seized a Bokez trabaccolo and as the French general, with deliberate insult, did not even reply to the letter sent by the rector requesting its release, it was necessary to think that the enemy did not intend to spare the republic, despite it being under the protection of the Ottoman Porte just as much as ours. For this reason, the commander-in-chief was compelled to order all French vessels be seized, not only along the coasts but also in the very port of Ragusa. According to this measure, all enemy corsairs were either captured or destroyed and the people of Ragusa remained calm.

During his visit to Ragusa, the admiral made the following condition to the senate: upon the first reception of news about the entry of French forces on the republic's land, the main city and fortress of Ragusa would admit a Russian garrison and the government would arm its citizens in order to act in concert with

Jacques Alexandre Law, Marquis de Lauriston. François Gérard, 1824, oil on canvas, Palace of Versailles.

our forces. For that purpose, the *Svyatoy Mikhail* was positioned in the channel of Calamotta. After such an agreement, it could be expected that the Rector and senators, seeing the difference in actions between the Russian and French generals and not being able to maintain neutrality, would need to accept Russia's side as soon as possible; were they to side with the French who had inadequate force at sea, they would jeopardize their trade, without which they cannot exist. Additionally, knowing what kind of mercy was shown to the Bokez and even the inhabitants of Curzola conquered by force of arms, contrary to what could be expected from French rule, they should not violate these terms, but two or three senators were seduced by the promises of the French agents and believed that France had greater means to protect them from their enemies than the Russian navy and army in the Mediterranean Sea. Despite objections, they betrayed the republic to the French. The policy of obediently accepting the demands of a strong power, which had preserved the existence of Ragusa until the present, had now failed and the republic perished. On the 14th [26th] of May, at the same time that the admiral departed to Trieste, General Jacques Law de Lauriston crossed the Turkish frontier with a corps of 3,000 men and arrived in Slano to then occupy the city of Ragusa on the 15th [27th]. On the 16th [28th], the French general announced in Napoleon's name that the independence of the Ragusan Republic would not be recognized until Russian ground forces withdrew from Cattaro, Corfu and all other previously Venetian possessions and the squadron withdrew from the shores of Dalmatia. Since our Russian admiral had no intention of obliging the enemy, the republic was annexed by France. Although the senators soon saw their error, the people had already lost their freedom, trade and prosperity.

# 38

# The Capture of Old Ragusa – The Battle in the Mountains – Lauriston's Defeat – The Siege of New Ragusa

Learning of the occupation of Ragusa by the armies of France, the Metropolitan Petar Petrović with his force of Montenegrins and Bokez, along with two companies of the Vitebsk Musketeers and one company of the 13th Jägers under the command of Major Zvyagin, marched to meet the enemy. On the 21st of May [2nd of June], the French along with the citizens of Ragusa met our forces 5 *verstas* [5.33 km] from Old Ragusa and a battle began. Forward positions were immediately captured. The enemy, formed in a line of battle, could not withstand the rapid attacks of our irregular forces, were disordered and withdrew to Old Ragusa. In this action, our side lost one Jäger killed, 5 wounded and 9 Montenegrins and Bokez killed, 7 wounded; while the French and Ragusans lost up to 250 men. One French officer fled into the sea and drowned. On the 22nd of May [3rd of June], Major Zabelin[1] with four companies of the Vitebsk Musketeers and four of the [13th] Jägers joined the Metropolitan and the French withdrew from Old Ragusa in the night with four spiked guns. Our forces immediately took their positions and on the 23rd, 24th and 25th [4th to 6th of June], the Montenegrins and Bokez along with the reinforcements of our soldiers fought unceasingly with the enemy, always driving them back, and occupying all the area between Old and New Ragusa. As

---

1   Kirill Vasilyevich Zabelin was the commander of the 13th Jaeger Regiment from 1805 to 1808. Александр Подмазо, '13-й Егерский Полк,' *Шефы и Командиры Регулярных Полков Русской Армии (1796-1825)*, http://www.museum.ru/1812/library/podmazo/shefcom_e.html, last modified 18 December, 2006. [Aleksandr Podmazo, '13th Jäger Regiment,' *Chiefs and Commanders of the Regular Regiments of the Russian Army (1796-1825)*, http://www.museum.ru/1812/library/podmazo/shefcom_e.html, last modified 18 December, 2006.]

these battles took place along the shore, the *Uriil*, a Bokez corsair, gunboats and an armed rowing vessel arranged by Rear-Admiral Sorokin provided supporting fire to the Montenegrins with canister and grape. In this battle, the Montenegrins lost 13 men killed and wounded, while the enemy lost 8 officers and up to 300 soldiers. On the 25th of May [6th of June], the Montenegrins seized a banner, a drum and 150 muskets from the French. After this, the French generals were frightened by the courageous confrontation by our forces, especially the daring of the Montenegrins, whose determination increased with each success and who did not show any mercy or take any prisoners. They constructed fortifications in nearly inaccessible places on Mount Bergatto before Ragusa and did not advance closer than those. Despite the courage of the French voltigeurs, the enemy's forward posts were always beaten by the Montenegrins.

The commander-in-chief learned of the French occupation of Ragusa while in Trieste and arrived in Cattaro on the 27th of May [8th of June], reaching Old Ragusa on the 28th [9th]. On receiving a complete assessment of the situation from the Metropolitan, he endeavoured to deepen the enemy's defeat. Making the necessary arrangements in Cattaro on the 31st [12th], the whole fleet and the armed vessels of the Bokez arrived at Ragusa on the 1st [13th] of June. On the 2nd [14th], the admiral, in agreement with the Metropolitan, decided to take two points from the enemy, Bergatto and San Marco (Lokrum), and if the opportunity presented itself and our forces were evenly matched with the forces and positions of the enemy, then the fortifications of Ragusa itself would be taken. As a result, the Metropolitan, leading the Montenegrin and Bokez forces with Major Zabelin's detachment, set out for Ragusa. Reaching the forward posts, they drove the French from the place and killed 80 men, forcing them to flee to the fortifications. By the 4th [16th], Major-General Prince Vasiliy Vasilyevich Vyazemskiy, chief of the 13th Jäger Regiment, arrived with his eponymous battalion from Corfu and, along with the irregulars from Cattaro, were transported by galleys from Old Ragusa to the encampment before New Ragusa, where he took command of the regular forces. On the 4th, Admiral Senyavin, the Metropolitan and Prince Vyazemskiy inspected the positions of the enemy both from sea and on land.

On the 5th [17th] of June, the weather was clear all day and the wind was very quiet at 4 in the morning when the signal was made to begin towing toward Ragusa the *Selafail*, *Svyataya Paraskeva*, *Svyatoy Pyotr*, *Svyataya Yelena*, the frigate *Venus*, the xebec *Azard* and five gunboats rowing on oars. To find the strengths and weaknesses on the island of San Marco and in the fortress, Rear-Admiral Sorokin opened an exchange of cannon fire with his detachment and dropped anchor opposite the heights where our soldiers stood. That same day, our fleet proved vital and glorious for our brave armies in the battle. Despite the scorching heat of the sun and the unequal strength and unapproachable position chosen by the enemy, this battle can justly be likened to the Saint Gotthard Pass, as there one had to fight with nature itself to overcome the steep, bare cliffs which protected the enemy's guns.

The enemy dug in on inaccessible rocky heights above Ragusa, built batteries there in advantageous locations and were ready to receive an attack. They occupied a line from the sea to the Turkish border, which was not a very extensive distance, and thus even stronger. Their labour perfected what nature already excellently provided for them. Their right wing was covered by the sea and a steep slope, the left by the Turkish frontier where there was no need to defend. Ahead of its front were steep high cliffs and they occupied four key points which were covered one by another and connected such that each could support the others. The enemy's numbers reached 3,000 regulars and up to 4,000 fit and well-armed Ragusan shooters. Our regular forces consisted of 1,200 men and up to 3,500 Montenegrins and Bokez. With such numbers it was very difficult to attack the enemy's front, as it is known how well the French can strengthen positions and lay their batteries in the most advantageous configurations; yet the commander-in-chief ordered an attack to be made and early in the morning of the 5th [17th] of June, the Metropolitan sent a portion of his Montenegrins to skirmish in order to seize the forward posts of the French. The Montenegrins rushed ahead bravely and before the strongest point, on the most treacherous peak, they immediately took one forward post, were bolstered by their success, and impetuously attacked the next. Prince Vyazemskiy, noticing that the enemy was trying to lure the Montenegrins on, ordered three companies of Jägers under the command of a Captain Babichev to reinforce them, and they scaled the heights with great haste although the steepness hindered them. The enemy tried to drive off the Montenegrins, but Babichev's arrival thwarted their aspirations. The Montenegrins and the Jägers united and bravely carried on. The employment of these three companies and the detachment of Montenegrins was dangerous, as they stood on the precipice of the abyss.

At this time, Prince Vyazemskiy, in accordance with his orders to definitively master the heights, began to execute on them in earnest together with the Metropolitan. The attack was hastened all the more by news from the neighbouring Turkish pasha that enemy reinforcements were approaching. The Metropolitan with his irregulars immediately proceeded to the captured height. The amazed enemy, not expecting an attack from that side and regarding it as an impossibility, very desperately defended the position and attacked in earnest Captain Babichev and his detachment, yet his three companies and the Montenegrins were encouraged by the personal presence of the Metropolitan and did not yield one step to the enemy. While the Metropolitan fought on the edge of the cliff against excellent forces bearing down on him, Prince Vyazemskiy divided his small detachment into two columns and, sending ahead a party of volunteers under the command of the brave officers Krasovskiy, Klichko, Rennenkampf and Michaud, marched on the fortified batteries on an impregnable height with the determination characteristic of a hero possible only for a Russian warrior. Lauriston noticed this general movement and with all his strength hindered our volunteers and struck at the Metropolitan, whose person was put in great danger; the columns overcame the steep ground and had already come close to the peak. Retreat was not possible in this scenario, one step backward would spell doom. We watched on from our ships, the site of the battle being visible from the harbour, and did not dare to lower our eyes, expecting in anxious agony to witness a disaster. Finally our banners appeared at the top of the mountain, the shouts of '*ura!*' echoed and our army moved forward to disappear from our sight into the gorges.

The enemy, being pushed out from behind the rocks, stopped between their batteries. Both of our columns united with the Metropolitan's force and after a small firefight, charged with bayonets and swords. The French defended themselves stubbornly, but were compelled to withdraw. The Metropolitan and Prince Vyazemskiy attacked relentlessly and gave the enemy no time to recover. Our officers who were always ahead of their men exerted themselves in a manner worthy of the disciples of Suvorov[2] while the Montenegrins competed with our soldiers and stormed the first fortification with such fervour that the redoubt with 10 guns was immediately taken by sheer force. Being protected by the natural cover and disregarding the canister fire which ardently aimed at repelling those brave attackers, they took the three French lines and batteries one after another. The generals then tried to demonstrate their craft by encircling our flanks, but it did not help them any and they were repelled everywhere and everywhere the Russian bayonet and the impudence of the Montenegrins was triumphant. The French, being pursued on their heels, managed to stop behind their fourth position along the crest of the height above Ragusa, but even there they could not restrain themselves for ten minutes before frantically breaking and running. The Montenegrins, Bokez and all the volunteers hastened to cut them off from the city but their fear gave them an incredible speed and their retreat was successfully covered by the darkness and walls of the fortifications. At this time, enemy reinforcements arriving sought to halt the victors but withdrew after the first onslaught. The agile Montenegrins ran ahead and lay down along both sides of the road, hitting the enemy rearguard even on the very bridge while under canister fire from the city walls. Besides the exchanges of fire from the irregular forces that began in the morning, the battle during the scorching heat of the day lasted from 2 in the afternoon until 7, and the last shots fell silent at 8 pm. And so, with the

2    Bronevskiy's note: '[The regiments of] the 15th Division, stationed in the Mediterranean, had served under the command of Suvorov in Wallachia, Poland and Italy'.

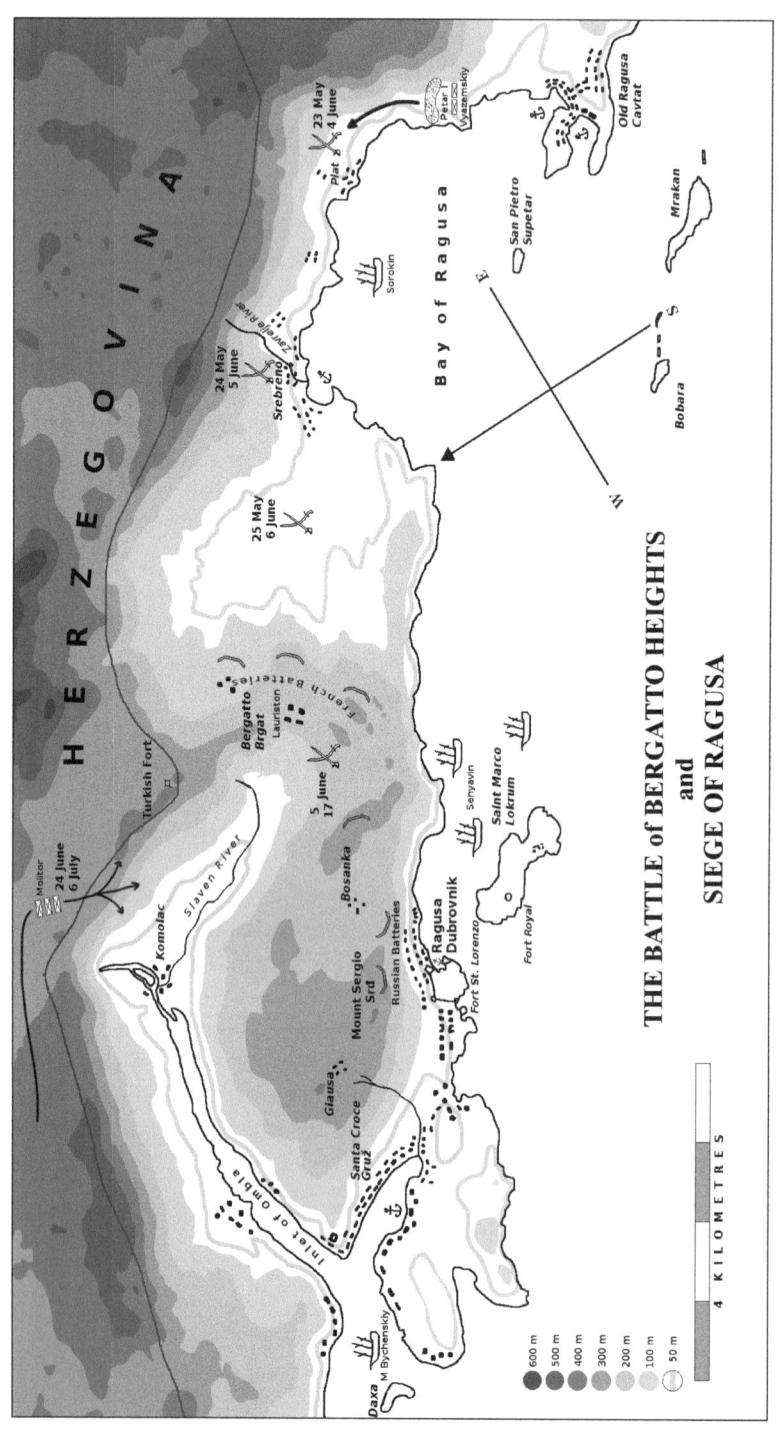

THE BATTLE of BERGATTO HEIGHTS
and
SIEGE OF RAGUSA

aid of the Almighty, a handful of men won a glorious victory over a superb enemy which had been led by the skillful General Lauriston and occupied the strong and inaccessible Bergatto heights above Ragusa.

In that battle were taken 19 guns of various calibre; General François-Joseph Delegorgue was killed along with 18 other field and company officers, among whom was the colonel who was aide-de-camp to General Lauriston, and up to 400 privates, with 23 taken prisoner; on the next day were taken another 68 men who were hiding in the caves and gorges. The Ragusans lost up to 400 men combined dead and wounded. From our side, one *portepee*-ensign[3] and 16 privates were killed; 3 officers and 30 soldiers were wounded; and one man was missing in action. The Montenegrins and Bokez lost roughly 100 men killed and wounded.

The prisoners were saved by our soldiers. Despite the fact that the admiral promised them a *chervonets* for every prisoner safely delivered, the Montenegrins were so bitter that they did not show any mercy to the French and immediately cut off their heads, including even General Delegorgue. However they must be given credit for their rare bravery and those who distinguished themselves, recommended by the Metropolitan, should be mentioned: the Metropolitan's brother Sava Petrović, his secretary Vladević, the Montenegrin governor Vukolaj Radonjić, the archpriest Jovan Proroković, the priest Lazarević, and the Montenegrins Vuko Juro and Milo.

At first light on the 6th [18th], a landing party was dispatched to the island of San Marco comprised of up to 600 naval soldiers and sailors with a company of Jägers, placed under the command of the 2nd Naval Regiment's Colonel Philippe Boissel. The *Svyataya Paraskeva*, the *Svyatoy Pyotr*, the *Venus*, the *Azard* and 5 gunboats approached the island from a fair distance and bolstered the landing party with their cannons. The party, fully assembled, divided into three columns and marched at the quick step[4] to the foot of a very stony, overgrown patch of

---

3    The Russian Army borrowed the old Prussian method of producing officers by having candidates from the nobility serve as non-commissioned officers for a period before promotion, the 1796 regulations requiring at least three years. These men were known as sub-ensigns and could be further distinguished for meritorious service as *portepee-* or swordbelt-ensigns with the right to carry an officer's sword and knot. Their typical role in the battalion line was as a colour-bearer. *Его Императорского Величества Воинский Устав о Полевой Пехотной Службе* (Smolensk: Типография Губернского Правления, 1797), p.2. [*His Imperial Majesty's Military Regulations on the Field Infantry Service* (Smolensk: Provincial Government Press, 1797), p.2.]; ibid., p.201; *Complete Collection of Laws*, col. 1, vol. 25, p.39. No. 18,328; Ibid., col. 1, vol. 43, part 2 (1801-1812), p.279-282. No. 20,252.

4    The quick step was defined as 120 paces per minute. The military pace had a length of one *arshin* [71.12 cm]. The slow or ordinary step was 75 paces per minute. Д. А. Скалон and Н. П. Михневич (eds.), *Столетие Военного Министерства 1802-1902*, Part 4, Section 1, Book 2, Vol. 3 (St. Petersburg: Тип. 'Бережливость', 1903), p.185. [D.A. Skalon and N.P.

shrubbery on a high mound, at the top of which stood a fortification surrounded by fairly high stone walls and protected by five large guns. The enemy opened up at the columns with three of the guns, first with solid shot and then with canister, and finally when our forces deployed and surrounded the fortress, a heavy fusillade began. The Jägers and sailors rushed up before the walls and, hiding themselves behind the stones and bushes, inflicted considerable damage on the enemy. Our men began to storm the fortification with great courage, but the location was very advantageous for the enemy and the steep parapets and deeply dug moat stopped them. The admiral, intending only to make a reconnaissance and seeing the impossibility without a loss of strength to take this redoubt (as the island did not represent a convenient place for building batteries against the city, requiring balls to be fired in high plunging arcs, and the French here could freely receive aid from the city), hurried to the island and ordered a retreat. The soldiers, all in fine order and without the enemy's pursuit, boarded the row boats and returned to the fleet. In order to better harass the city with the positions already occupied, the detachment of Prince Vyazemskiy was reinforced with four companies of naval infantry. During the attack on San Marco, we lost 13 men killed and 57 wounded.

That same day, Prince Vyazemskiy cut off the supply of water to Ragusa, within which, besides the cistern, there was none. In order to protect our right flank against surprise attacks and to open communications with the naval detachment in the port of Santa Croce, it was necessary to take one height from the enemy. On the 6th [18th] of June, Major Zabelin was sent with two companies and a portion of the Montenegrins for that purpose. They approached the height and struck at the enemy with bayonets, forcing them to retreat to the very gates of the fortress and killing nearly 80 men in the action. At the same time, Captain Second Rank Mikhail Bychenskiy immediately removed from the shore all the vessels standing in port and with great haste prevented the enemy's intention to burn them. Besides 69 guns, 20 large merchant vessels were taken fully armed along with a wharf and naval arsenal with a notable quantity of supplies of every kind. Additionally, a multitude of trabaccolos and smaller naval vessels were taken.

Thus closing off the enemy in Ragusa alone, encircling the city from the sea with ships and from the shore with infantry, depriving him of water and provisions, the admiral examined the positions around the walls on the 7th [19th] and ordered that two batteries be built in the centre of the height occupied by our forces. Two 48-*funt* [23.6 kg] guns and two 24-*funt* [9.83 kg] carronades were delivered up from the ships with extreme difficulty. 500 sailors dragged them over 10 *verstas* [10.67 km] over rocks and into the steep mountains. The first battery was finished

Mikhnevich (eds.), *Centenary of the War Ministry 1802-1902*, Part 4, Section 1, Book 2, Vol. 3 (St. Petersburg: 'Prudence' Press, 1903), p.185.]

on the 10th [22nd] and the second on the 12th [24th], from which point they began to operate well enough that each shot inflicted damage on the enemy; the city lay at the foot of the mountain below a steep incline from which it was quite convenient to shoot. These batteries were soon reinforced with an additional three mortars.

The batteries operated incessantly in excellent order. The most skilful Montenegrin sharpshooters, setting themselves up in the ruins of houses under the walls, inflicted the greatest harm on the enemy, who sent out small detachments to repel them from the fortifications. From the first days of the siege, the inhabitants began to suffer from deprivation. The Ragusans had never been punished so cruelly for a political mistake or, better said, a miscalculation. The Montenegrins and Bokez, by their customs and laws of war, seized everything that the Ragusans had not managed to evacuate or destroy. Neither the convictions of the Metropolitan nor the authority of the commander-in-chief could save those who fought against them with the French. The brave but insubordinate Montenegrins had a terrible and inexorable vengeance. After the battle on the 5th [17th] of June, the residents who fled behind the walls found new oppression from their allies, with whom they had hoped to easily conquer the Bay of Cattaro and devastate the Montenegrins. Deprived of trade and liberty, they were forced to pay contributions and hand over to the French the republic's rich treasury. General Lauriston, following the laudable habit of his government of living on someone else's toil, did not bring any provisions, which is why at the beginning of the siege, the garrison was forced to confiscate as much grain as could be found from the residents and requisitioned the cistern solely for themselves. Thus they were oppressed by the vengeful hand of their ancient foe and rival and in those they called friends they did not find a good defender; their rulers proved to be cruel and mercenary and the too unfortunate Ragusans died by sword, fire, hunger and thirst. Only those who fortunately did not flee into the city found a benevolent, truly Christian patronage from their enemies. As it was impossible to save the rest of the republic from the raids of the Montenegrins, the admiral invited the inhabitants to retire to the Ragusan islands, to which the ship captains would not permit access to the Bokez and Montenegrins, and declared them to be under the protection of the Emperor of All Russia. The Ragusans who later repented wished to swear an oath of loyalty, but the admiral rejected their request in order to shield them from French persecution, though he allowed them to trade and, to their amazement, especially for the French, he did not demand any contributions or levy any tariffs from them.

## 39

# Sailing to the Shores of Dalmatia

The captain of the *Venus* was instructed to sail along the coasts of Ragusa to search for the enemy, for which on the 17th [29th] of June we moved to Calamotta and on the next day, together with the *Azard*, sailed through that channel close to the shore and then joined the *Avtroil* by Stagno. Her captain, Backman, had on the previous day for reconnaissance landed several sailors who encountered the French by Slano, approximately 500 men coming from Stagno, and had a brief exchange of fire without losses and withdrew. On the same day, a detachment of Montenegrins also fought that same French group, which, according to the assurances of the locals, had retreated to Stagno where it was believed they united with a large force intended for the relief of the besieged Ragusa.

On the evening of the 18th [30th], our detachment passed a very narrow strait between two high islands, the steep banks of which nearly converged and appeared like a ruined gateway. The day was sweltering and by evening the wind became calm. The pale blue clouds that adorned the sky were seen on the bright mirror of the water, so motionless was the sea. The sun on the clear horizon, which can never be seen on land, created a magnificent panorama as it set. Long beams showered the border where the vault of the sky met the sea and ignited the clouds close to the horizon, the sea burned with purple fire, the massive golden ball gradually dropped down at last into the water and the scarlet colour of the sky little by little faded until extinguished. The night came and the sky changed its décor; the moon came out of the high mountains and countless millions of bright stars blazed on the calm, slightly wavering surface of the sea. On the 19th of June [1st of July], with a quiet breeze, our detachment crawled slowly forward before exploiting a fresh wind by midnight and we finally dropped anchor by Curzola on the 20th [2nd].

# 40

# The Island of Curzola

---

Entering the strait, we saw on the Ragusan shore several soldiers. We drummed an alarm, loaded the guns with canister, and were ready to give a full volley when the captain ordered the drummers to beat a retreat; the soldiers were Austrians. The commandant of Curzola sent word to us that 3,000 soldiers under the command of Lieutenant-Field-Marshal Count Heinrich von Bellegarde, by the consent of our Sovereign Emperor, were going to assume control of Cattaro to deliver the province to the French. 23 vessels under the escort of two military brigs lay in the port of Rosato. Count Bellegarde soon sent us his adjutant to ask whether we had any papers for him from the admiral. Due to the illness of the captain, Lieutenant Matvey Nasekin visited the Austrian general in his stead and announced that there had been no command from our commander-in-chief and therefore the convoy could not continue on its route. Since Ragusa was under siege and all the ports of the republic were blockaded, the Austrians were compelled to agree to wait for the admiral's orders.

The island of Curzola in antiquity was known as Black Korkyra. It stands separated from the Sabioncello (Pelješac) peninsula belonging to the Republic of Ragusa by a strait of the same name. Its length is four *versta*s [4.27 km] and its width is no more than one [1.07 km]. In the winter, despite the *bora*s that blow through here, the floor is entirely mud so the anchorage is quite convenient for large ships. The island is comprised of small mountains covered with oak forests and shrubs. The island produces a notable quantity of fine red wine, but anchovies and sardines are the majority of their exports. Besides those, the island produces firewood and its inhabitants are engaged in the construction of small seagoing vessels. The fortress of Curzola, four poor walls in a square containing several houses, lies on a cape at the base of an elevation which towers over the site. The town is believed to be built by Diocletian. Its position near the enemy ports and the possibility of being defended by a single company of soldiers made it a very important point for us, since ships there had shelter, received wine and firewood not found in Cattaro, and could at any time block the ports of Dalmatia. The whole island's population was 6,000 people.

The level coast of Sabioncello where the town of Oneum stood in antiquity is shaded by high barren rocks, though beautiful gardens lie at their feet and the coolness of the evening prompted us to visit ashore. Do not be surprised that we went so boldly into enemy territory. The Slavs and generally the other resident subjects of France regarded us as their friends due to the mercy of the Russian monarch. No matter how much the French tried to shake their confidence in the Russians or assure them that they belonged to a great and enlightened nation, they retained respect for us and feared the French like the plague. As soon as we went ashore, the owner of the first garden we passed invited us into his home. It stood on the slope of a green hill in the midst of several trees planted in widely spaced rows. On one side, ivy and myrtle covered the walls of the house and on the other, grape vines covered the entrance and lined the paths to the sea and into the village. Not far from the home, a small brook murmured its way between almond, fig, carob and silk trees, appearing and disappearing in the thick shadows. The cosy house represented all the pleasant simplicity of rural life. The furniture was of pear wood in an English style, in one corner stood a hand mill and in another a girl gently unwound silk at a spinning wheel. Rosina, as she was called, went out on her father's orders and soon brought us coffee and handed out everyone a tobacco pipe, and then offered us liqueur and fresh fruit just picked from the tree. The girl was quite beautiful and so we did not want her to be our servant. The quick-witted Ragusan adapted to our customs and ordered her to sing us something. Lowering her eyes and trembling, she began to sing in a very gentle voice an Italian romance ('*Vieni, o Nice, amato bene*' – 'Come, o Nice, sweet beloved') and accompanied herself on a guitar. You might think that her father was rich but besides his garden, his only possessions were a few birds and goats leaping about the rocks. At the same time, it can be rightly noted that many Ragusans have surpassed their fellow Slavic neighbours in education. Although the sky was covered with clouds, the pleasant location and fresh air encouraged us to climb the mountain. The old monastery of Saint Francis, surrounded by walls and sad cypress trees, rather crowned the barren and savage rock. It became very dark and lightning flashed in the distance, so we did not try for the summit and turned back. In our descent, our mountain which was lower than the others seemed to be their equal. Is it not so that in the world, the insignificant and immoral seem equal to a virtuous man? Is it not so that the insolent flatterer and ignoramus overshadow the virtues of the modest, unassuming man?

# 41

# Cruising along the Dalmatian coast – The Return to Cattaro

After returning to our frigate, the Ragusan shepherds following us announced that they had seen before sunset several French military vessels stopping in the bay on the northern side of Sabioncello. Because of the dark night and torrential rain, two officers sent on armed boats to inspect the enemy's position returned without success. The commandant of Curzola sent confirmation of the first news, for which the detachment weighed anchor at dawn on the 21st of June [3rd of July]. We safely manoeuvred through the strait and spotted 11 French xebecs and gunboats by the sandy shallows of Cape Gomena (Lovište) at 10 o'clock.

The enemy set out of the channel rowing on oars against the wind and circled the long peninsula, unfurled his sails and set a course for Spalatro. While we were then forced to perform small revolutions slightly into the wind to bypass the shallows, the flotilla, which was already sailing on the wind, was able to evade us to a comfortable distance. Entering the great stretch between the shore of Ragusa, Dalmatia and the island of Lesina, called the 'small sea,' the frigates began to overtake the enemy flotilla. In that very moment, the *Venus* was not much farther than a cannon shot when the wind suddenly stopped and we could only look on the enemy powerlessly from afar. The French furled their sails and again set out on oars and soon completely disappeared. The calm lasted until evening.

By night, following the enemy's route by compass and making use of a light wind, the *Avtroil* was successful in locating one xebec, which had fallen behind due to the difficulty of its course. At dawn on the 22nd of June [4th of July], the flotilla was discovered again at the shore by the village of Podgora between Makarska and the Narenta River. A fresh wind filled the sails that morning and the frigates took flight; in no more than half an hour, the *Avtroil* opened fire. The *Venus* joined the battle soon after. The enemy dispersed in all directions; three gunboats closest to us ran to shore. Chasing the other two, one was sunk and the second ran aground.

We approached the shore and were forced to drop anchor as the wind died out. The enemy vessels, taking advantage of this period to flee on oars, went one to Spalatro and the others into the mouth of the Narenta. The *Avtroil* also dropped anchor and both frigates sent out boats to seize the vessels abandoned by the enemy. A xebec named *Henri* with 14 bronze cannons was taken by the *Avtroil*, while the *Venus* captured a demi-xebec named *Tremenda*[1] with two bronze guns.

Inspecting the boat sunk by the *Venus*, it was found that although it was not suitable for continued service, it was possible to salvage its guns. The captain asked me to haul them out. Shortly after our divers managed to recover a few muskets and other small arms, the boatswain set out to haul the cannons. Suddenly the enemy fired several shots at us from a house and garden wall nearby ashore and we replied with grapeshot from the boat. Soon the French who had fled from the ships we captured were attacking us in earnest, but we continued our labour and had one gun out of the water while still returning fire. During heavy fire from both sides, a settler came out to the embankment and boldly passed through the crossfire to the boats. Our men, seeing that he was unarmed and incessantly making the sign of the cross over himself, missed him safely with all of their fire. The French turned all of their shots at the old man and he dove into the water and began to drown, but was close enough to the sunken boat that our men at work saved him and brought him before me. I asked him what prompted him to take such a risk. 'Sir!' answered the Slav, 'I am not afraid of death, and I must ask you to spare my home; everything I own is inside. It doesn't matter, but the Dalmatians expect to be saved by you, yet is it not your first step to oppress those people who are brothers to you in blood, faith and ancestry? We're already suffering enough!' He then burst into tears. Although he was very plainly dressed, his use of Italian compelled me to ask who he was. 'I am Count Ivičević and the civil governor of this district,' he answered, pointing at the mountains.

'Go quickly to the frigate,' I told him, 'the captain will naturally order me to retreat. We have an order to spare the Dalmatians in all cases; rest assured that your house will be intact'. Half an hour later, as the count went to the frigate, I heard gunfire from behind the gardens. The French were beginning to retire yet the captain at the same time sent word that I was not to pursue them but to deliver the guns to the frigate promptly.

As soon as the French left the garden and house, a crowd of people came to the shore. The count offered me aid in raising the sunken boat, and the action suddenly changed. We were surrounded by kind villagers who wore their sincere joy on their faces. In a few minutes we had their complete trust and even their women and children mingled with our sailors without timidity. Hearing foreigners speak

---

1    Italian for 'Tremendous'.

in their language so clearly for the first time, they smiled with admiration. The old women standing in the distance said a prayer; the men looked at us curiously from head to toe, clapped their hands and said with delight 'here are our Christian brothers'. Meanwhile as the work continued, the hospitable Slavs brought wine, bread and fruit and set up small fires on the beach so that we were treated to the best that they could offer. With heartfelt pleasure I saw how kindly our people treated the inhabitants and we can say that not a single battle, not a single famous victory, had ever ended in a finer or more pleasant feast. Should it not be regretted that a people so devoted and akin to us obey a foreign ruler?

In the evening, those Dalmatians who attacked the French returned and announced that they had managed to burn another boat, which was also damaged and lying on the rocks. The crew who had fled that craft, so they assured us, along with those who fled the boats we captured were now all beaten. When the guns and various ammunitions were salvaged from the sunken boat named *Battaglia di Marengo*,[2] the craft was donated to the local inhabitants. The detachment weighed anchor and on the 23rd of June [5th of July], Lieutenant Nasekin, named the commander of the xebec *Henri*, seized a battery of two bronze guns and a boat loaded with wine at the village of Sveti Juraj on the island of Lesina.

Arriving in Stagno on the 24th of June [6th of July], the detachment was arranged such that the enemy did not dare to transport its forces from Dalmatia to Ragusa, but was compelled to march along the shore and over the covered mountains where no roads ran, relying on donkeys to carry their provisions. From Stagno we moved to the Narenta River, where we managed to intercept several vessels with provisions. On the 29th [11th], having received news of the siege of Ragusa being lifted, we arrived at Curzola with a fresh wind and from there went on to Castelnuovo on the 3rd [15th] of July. The captured xebecs, flying the Russian flag above the French, saluted the admiral with nine shots each. After they were examined, the admiral renamed the *Henri* to the *Zabiyaka* and the *Tremenda* to the *Uzhasnaya*.

---

2    Italian for 'Battle of Marengo'. The original publication gives its name in Latin characters and it is likewise written in Latin in Veselago's *List of Russian Military Vessels from 1668 to 1860*, page 755.

# 42

# Lifting the Siege of New Ragusa

When the Highest order was received on the 4th [16th] of June to hand over the Bay of Cattaro to the Austrians, then for as long as it was possible to keep it a secret, the Montenegrin and Bokez forces were very friendly and bravely supported our own forces; but after, when State Councillor Sankovskiy, as a trusted official from the court, began to prepare the people to obediently accept His Imperial Majesty's decision, they became utterly despondent and did not show any more of their fervent zeal. When they learned that the Austrians had to surrender them to the French, they lost all of their cheer. In this state, it was expected that a regular army alone was absolutely incapable of undertaking an assault on Ragusa, a fortress quite strong and with an excellent garrison of the French alone, besides the residents who were also well armed and ready to defend themselves to the last of their strength. For this reason, the only feasible course was a siege in which the enemy would not surrender unless his provisions and water were exhausted. It is necessary to give due credit to our tireless soldiers, who, being always in the open air and almost unceasingly under arms, could stand so long in perfect vigil with a patience worthy of true heroes.

The line occupied by the regular forces was reinforced by another battalion of the 13th Jäger Regiment, delivered from Corfu. This line was very long for the 2,300 men occupying it, of which the whole detachment was comprised, yet the only fear was that the Turks might let the enemy pass through their lands, exposing our soldiers to fire from two directions, but they assured us that they would not pass without a bloody fight. Every ball and bomb from our batteries caused some damage in the city. The enemy, having directed all of his guns at them, only damaged one of the 48-*funt* [23.6 kg] guns, striking the centre of the barrel with a shot, and killed one naval cannoneer and two Montenegrins. In respect to the unfortunate situation of the city's population who, because the French had seized their bread and water, were exhausted from hunger and thirst and then had their homes damaged by bombardment, the Admiral Senyavin offered the French capitulation and twice entered negotiations. Lauriston, having no lack of food and awaiting his relief hour by hour, had no desire to surrender but was inclined to negotiate for the Bay of Cattaro to be left in our possession in exchange for France holding the Republic of Ragusa.

The French made sorties on the 16th [28th] and 21th of June [3rd of July]. In the first sortie, at midnight, up to 350 men attacked us on our right flank but were immediately repelled with 10 killed and 23 wounded taken prisoner. On the latter date before evening, the Metropolitan sent a detachment of his Montenegrins to set fire to the houses in the suburbs closest to the fortress walls from which the French had been skirmishing and harassing them, and the French responded with a sortie of up to 400 men under the cover of canister fire from the fortifications. In this action, according to the number of muskets captured by the Montenegrins, it is possible to estimate that the enemy losses reached 100 men, while ours in both incidents consisted of only 3 privates of a naval regiment and 8 Montenegrins. After these unsuccessful attempts, the French did not leave the walls and the siege continued in such a state until the 24th of June [6th of July].

On the night of the 23rd and 24th of June [5th and 6th of July], 250 Montenegrins sent to reconnoitre the enemy's position met with the French approximately 8 *verstas* [8.53 km] from Ragusa. Despite strong numbers, the Montenegrins attacked the French and retreated under an exchange of musketry. At 4 in the morning on the 24th, the news arrived that an enemy relief of around 500 men was coming to Ragusa from Stagno. The Metropolitan sent some men to the river to occupy the enemy in a firefight, while Prince Vyazemskiy sent a half-company of musketeers to the redoubt to observe the enemy's movements. The Montenegrins only just reached the river when the enemy, marching in three columns of nearly 3,000 men under the command of General Molitor, appeared on the heights belonging to the Ottoman Porte. They marched close to their fort, which then raised a Turkish flag, and straight toward the rear of our line. The commander-in-chief, seeing a strong enemy in the rear of our detachment, issued an order to the Metropolitan and Prince Vyazemskiy to retreat to Old Ragusa. The Montenegrins and Bokez, as many as those that could be assembled, with two companies of the 13th Jägers under the command of Captain Babichev were sent to intercept the advancing enemy, repelled the forward screen of enemy voltigeurs and halted the first column. Molitor was surprised by the bravery of this small force and directed all of his strength against them. The Montenegrins and Bokez, as stated previously, did not have the same courage as they once had and began to retreat to Old Ragusa. There remained only a small portion of the men from Risan with Count Ivelić and several Montenegrins with Governor Radonjić. This detachment, reinforced by Captain Babichev at a favourable location, bravely resisted to their last cartridges and then withdrew in good order to Old Ragusa. The brave Captain

Babichev, covering the withdrawal, managed to take another 30 men prisoner. Meanwhile, Prince Vyazemskiy left a few sentries along the ridge of the mountain by the batteries to conceal his movements from Lauriston, united with the force on the left in two columns on the slope, and then, discovering that Molitor had cut off his retreat to Old Ragusa, Vyazemskiy took the suggestion of the Metropolitan to make a glorious manoeuvre which saved our soldiers from a clear and imminent disaster. In order to convince Molitor that he had committed to the retreat to Old Ragusa and give that impression to the garrison in the city, he left a battalion of Jägers on the height under the command of Major Velizaryev to screen the retreat from Lauriston who emerged from the southern gates of the city; his other force, having made a counter-march, passed northward through the defiles hidden from the enemy to the port of Santa Croce. The French generals, believing they were attacking our army from three sides, left the fortress on the right and came upon the left flank and rear, were deceived by the aforementioned manoeuvre, and awaited our force from the side of Old Ragusa which did not come. Vyazemskiy reached Santa Croce and did not see any opposition, so he began to board his men on vessels sent by the fleet. In this fashion, our forces boarded vessels two *verstas* [2.13 km] from the enemy fortress and in view of the enemy from all sides. The enemy's advanced party attacked Major Velizaryev when our forces were already aboard, but this brave officer repelled them by bayonet and proceeded onto the boats as well, under the covering fire of gunboats and armed rowing vessels. When the Metropolitan and Prince Vyazemskiy had already left the shore to a thunderous cheer of '*ura!*', Molitor and Lauriston approached the pier from both sides and were met by a volley of grape and canister from Captain Mikhail Bychenskiy, who commanded the transportation of the ground forces.

During this glorious withdrawal, our losses were one man wounded and 10 Jägers left behind at the batteries on sentry. In order to prevent losses in larger numbers and to grind the retreat to a stand-still, the four guns – one of which was already damaged and the others exhausted of ammunition – and three mortars were left behind with spiked vents. This victory was costly to the enemy; his losses in the continuation of the siege from the 5th [17th] to the 24th of June [6th of July] and on that final day, including the Ragusans and according to the testimony of the prisoners captured, reached up to 2,000 men, but it is probable that he lost more than 3,000, as the inhabitants were dying of disease and fatigue.

# 43

# The Good Intentions of the Bokez

On the 25th of June [7th of July], the commander-in-chief sent Rear-Admiral Sorokin with three ships to the port of Santa Croce for the orderly deployment of our forces and aboard the *Selafail* he personally went directly to Cattaro to organize and give warning of every danger reported to him by the locals, first of the Austrians and then of the French. Upon his arrival in Castelnuovo, the deputies from the eight districts submitted a letter containing the following:

Your High Excellency!
Our honoured chief and patron!
Hearing that the Emperor wishes to give our province to the French, we, in the name of the whole nation, declare: without wishing to defy the will of our Monarch, we are unanimously agreed to leave the fatherland and follow your fleet wherever and brave any and every fire. Let only a barren, ash-covered tract remain to sate the greed of Bonaparte. Let him know that the brave Slav would rather have no country and wander the earth than to be his slave. You know our love and devolution to our Monarch, you saw that we spared neither life nor property for the glory of Russia; to you, our great and benign *admirant* (as they spelled 'admiral'), in the name of the elders, our wives and children do we petition and ask to intercede at the throne of the merciful and compassionate Monarch. Turn him to our prayers, that he not reject a people loyal to him, a people whose every citizen has sacrificed property and fatherland for a small corner of earth in his vast Empire. There, under his authority in a peaceful and safe refuge, we could be sure that the sacrilegious hand of the robbers of Europe could not touch the dust of our bones and there we would consecrate ourselves to the service of a homeland new yet still native to us, take comfort, forget our loss, and forever bless his name. If, contrary to our expectations and hopes, we must obey our worst enemies, the enemies

of faith and humanity; if you cannot allow us to follow you, then remain a passive spectator to our fate. We choose to defend our independence with weapons in our hands and we are all ready to lay our heads down[1] for your fatherland likewise. In defending it, let our blood flow like a river, let the crosses on our graves testify to future generations that we preferred a glorious death over a shameful servitude and would submit to no other sovereign but the Russian.

Many households had already relocated to Corfu, others were loading their effects onto boats and preparing to set fire to their old properties; several corsairs suggested attacking the 3,000 Austrians in Curzola, which was defended by only two military brigs. A terrible vengeance would have possessed them in some way. It was naturally impossible to look on such a rare determination indifferently. From here the screams of women and children could be heard; the Bokez looked dejectedly at the admiral's ship, which they thought came to bid them a final farewell, and the fleet loaded with soldiers sailed straight for Corfu. The commander-in-chief was in a most difficult situation. On the one hand, in a matter of great importance which attracted the attention of many powers, his own security required that the orders be immediately executed; but on the other, such a decisive desperation and destruction of a whole people so devoted to Russia imposed upon him the duty of mankind and love for the glory of the fatherland to not act on such orders without first receiving a new report on the transpiring circumstances. Senyavin faced the dilemma with nobility and did not hesitate in making his decision. The deputies, having submitted their missive, stood before him in tears and, while sobbing unceasingly, asked him to be their intercessor before the Sovereign. After a brief reflection, the admiral said to them: 'we will send to the Emperor those selected from among the most notable citizens and hope together for His Majesty's mercy or for a change in the enemy's position in these political affairs.[2] For so long as I can, I will not leave you brave and generous people. I will accept all responsibility and I am ready to protect you with all my power and will. Calm yourselves and do not give in to despair'. This feat brought Senyavin out of the midst of ordinary men. Since that time, his name has become better known throughout Europe than in his own country because modesty, alien to self-promotion, has always been the virtue of great men who are consoled by the righteousness of their deeds and do not care whether they are famous or obscure.

---

1    Meaning 'to be decapitated by our enemies'.
2    Bronevskiy's note: 'The Archimandrite Vukotić and three deputies were graciously and favourably received by the Emperor'.

On the 28th of June [10th of July], Rear-Admiral Sorokin arrived on the roadstead with the fleet and as the ships dropped anchor, the ground forces immediately occupied the fortifications of Castelnuovo and Espanola. On the next day, the commander-in-chief himself made dispositions and appointed several labour-details in order to restore Castelnuovo to a proper defensible condition. In Cattaro and Risan were only 3 companies, as the inhabitants themselves volunteered to protect them. The forces were arranged such that they could sally out and meet the enemy if necessary, and the fleet on the same day again departed to repel the enemy from the seas. The people, seeing from us such activity and commitment to their defence and realizing that the Russians would not abandon them, recovered their former vivacity. All the roads ahead of our posts were occupied by the best detachments of the Bokez and Montenegrins, whose parties again appeared before the walls of Ragusa. The gratitude and diligence of the Bokez people were unparalleled: the entire region resembled a military camp and everywhere were heard 'love live Senyavin!' Wherever he appeared, large crowds accompanied him with reverence, bowed to the ground and kissed the dust on his boots. The Montenegrins fired celebratory shots ceaselessly and no matter how often we persuaded them to save their cartridges for the French, they good-naturedly replied: 'our good father Sovereign has more *chervontsy* than cartridges'. Dmitriy Nikolayevich, in the spirit of modesty, shied away from honours and from all the expressions of love and gratitude which the people showered on him. His subordinates who experienced his personal courage and impartial justice could not help but marvel at his noble determination and I dare to say that this period in the admiral's life represents the true expression of his civil and military virtues.

Lauriston and Molitor, although they also received reinforcements that brought the number of their forces up to 8,000, did not dare to step out onto the field and still sat locked up in their fortifications. The more zealous among the Ragusans could not even boast of the French occupation, for they were deprived of their commerce and had nothing to support themselves, were forced to pay unending contributions and nearly gave the clothes off their backs to dress their naked guests. They drank deep from the cup of sorrow. Most of their vessels, which were in the ports of Russia and Britain, were detained, others were taken into the hands of their cruisers. The Bokez corsairs enriched themselves at the expense of those who sought their ruin. On the other hand, the French took everything they could. Learning from such a sad experience, many of the capitalists fled their homeland and only their enemies found peace and protection.

## 44

# Cruising the Small Sea – The Sirocco Winds

Under the new orders, instructing us to intercept the communications of enemy forces from Dalmatia to Ragusa, the *Yaroslav, Venus* and *Zabiyaka* set out on the 5th [17th] of July to cruise the small sea or otherwise the bay of the Narenta river. The weather was now becoming hot, though it certainly did not surpass the scorching heat of Africa. The dew and gentle breeze did not at all temper the air at night and the humidity was replaced by the fiery rays of the midday sun. After a windless period, a rather fresh southeasterly wind blew which soon filled the air with moisture. The shores were shrouded in haze. The rays of the sun, penetrating and refracting through the misty clouds, gilded their edges. The whole atmosphere seemed to be aflame and seemed to our wide eyes like a great furnace full of flickering coals, as the dark clouds stood silhouetted against the light of the sun and burning along their edges. A strong wind, known by the Italian name of 'sirocco' quickly turned into a heavy, suffocating breath. The heat became so strong that the painted walls of the frigate and the cast-iron cannons could not be touched, and pitch began to drip down from the rigging as it softened. The *simoom*,[1] as it is known by seafarers, has its effect two feet from land, its breeze is similar to the noise of a flame emanating from a closed vent; this wind does not last more than ten minutes. A man killed by this fiery vortex appears to lie down and rest as if in a sweet dream. Since Arabia, where the *simoom* rages, lies to the southeast and south-southwest[2] of Italy, naturally the wind passes through a great expanse of sea and becomes saturated with vapours, thereby losing its mortal danger. Despite this coolness, the sirocco, spawn of the *simoom*, causes great harm in Sicily, Malta and Corfu. Fortunately it does not occur every year and typically lasts no more

---

1    Arabic for 'to poison'.
2    Bronevskiy's note: 'In Sicily and Italy, the sirocco blows from the latter direction and directly from the Gulf of Sidra, behind which lie the sandy steppes [of the Sahara]'.

than two hours, but if it continues for a day, which sometimes happens, then the fields wither, leaves and fruits on the trees fade, turn yellow and fall, the walls of stone houses crumble, small springs dry out and everywhere the water became warm. Animals can predict the approach of the sirocco and run to take shelter in the shade of forests where they immediately lie down or stand with their heads hanging. When the first signs of the wind appear, the townsfolk hurry to lock their doors and shutters and hide in their cellars or whichever is their coolest chamber. Dust is picked up in the streets and works its way into the smallest cracks, and, in a few minutes, meat, vegetables, bread and everything else edible are spoiled. The sirocco can produce painful seizures in people, especially those who are overweight and sanguine, with abundant perspiration, fever, dizziness, reddening of the eyes and an irresistible call to slumber.[3] An unconscious victim will sweat profusely, sleep restlessly and wake up feeling weak as if after a fever. While at sea, the sirocco has less power and does not harass a healthy man so much, but it is extremely necessary to overcome sleep, avoid great movement and exertions, and it is strictly forbidden for men to sleep on the decks uncovered, as the abundant moisture falling at night produces a dangerous cold.

The sirocco continued for a little more than an hour and then the sky cleared, the wind stopped and by evening the air had become cool. At Meleda, we found the xebec *Azard*. This island was covered in woods and rich with vineyards. The Abbott Jean-Baptiste Ladvocat believed that it was here, and not on Malta, that the Apostle Paul survived a shipwreck, but this is not correct; the Apostle, having built a new ship, sailed for Rome and along the way passed Syracuse and Messina, which proves Ladvocat's mistake, which of course stems from the fact that Malta and Meleda in antiquity were both called 'Melita'. On the 8th [20th] of July, we stayed at Curzola, where the *Svyatoy Pyotr* and 23 other vessels stood with 3,000 Austrian soldiers. On the 9th [21st], we arrived at the appointed post in the small sea.

The detachment was located such that communications between Ragusa and Dalmatia and the adjoining islands could be completely halted. The ship, frigate and xebecs alternated in their cruising. In the first few days, several vessels were intercepted, but eventually traffic died out and even the fishermen, with whom we did not interfere, stopped appearing. French forces occupied the surrounding shore and marched incessantly back and forth, oppressing the inhabitants loyal to us on the slightest suspicion. One day, the *Zabiyaka* passed near the Monastery of Zaostrog and was attacked by the French who occupied the gardens. The *Venus*

---

3     These are essentially the symptoms of what is now termed 'heat exhaustion' and the more severe 'heatstroke'. Rodney Rhoades and David Bell (eds.), *Medical Physiology: Principles for Clinical Medicine*, 3rd ed. (Philadelphia: Lippincott Williams & Wilkins, 2009), pp.564-565.

Auguste-Frederic-Louis de Marmont, Duke of Ragusa. Jean-Baptiste Guérin, 1837, oil on canvas, Palace of Versailles.

came to her aid and fired a volley of grape, and for recompense, the French levied contributions from the monks! An army of 20,000 men assembled and located in the small region, constantly under arms for fear of landing parties and rebellions from the local population, suffered extreme difficulties in barren Dalmatia, which subsisted only by trade and was now deprived of it. The French levied contributions so long as there was still anything to take. From heat and fatigue, over the course of the summer, the inhabitants assured us that up to 8,000 soldiers perished; a tight blockade therefore cost the enemy much more than in battles and our meagre forces held the advantage over the superior numbers of the French. Bonaparte, for whom nothing is impossible, ordered the chain of supply to beat a track through the inhospitable mountains in order to supply those forces on the shore. The unfortunate residents, regardless of condition, were assembled and made to work like slaves until nightfall, under guard by soldiers, to establish that road which came to be known as 'Napoleon's Road'. This unpaid labour, along with heavy taxes, conscription and all manner of oppression drove the poor Dalmatians into a dire condition. Resentment became universal and in some places the people took up arms, villages were burned, and the provocateurs, whom the French would have once called true sons of their fatherland, were executed by firing squad. These events forced General Marmont to declare martial law in Dalmatia, which only deepened the calamities of the people.

The water began to spoil in the heat and this stinking water was rationed out to the sailors and officers at one glass a day. In all our voyages in the Mediterranean Sea, only now did we feel the extreme dangers of it. Discovering a source in an unoccupied locale, a rowing vessel loaded with barrels was sent under the cover of the xebecs; the enemy arrived to head them off, but a Lieutenant Vecheslov[4] with 80 naval soldiers occupying an advantageous height did not allow them to harm the workers who then returned to the frigate with their load of water without a single loss. On the 31st of July [12th of August], the French informed us of the peace concluded between Russia and France and on the 1st [13th] of August, we received the order to cease hostilities. As a result, the detachment arrived at Curzola on the 2nd [14th], where they united with the *Svyatoy Pyotr* and, evacuating the garrison there, set sail for Cattaro on the 5th [17th] of August to arrive on the 11th [23rd] and unite with the whole fleet assembled there.

---

4    Lieutenant Zakhar Vecheslov was enrolled in the First Naval Regiment. *The Complete Naval Roster of 1806*, p.135.

## 45

# Negotiations for the Transfer of the Bay of Cattaro

---

On the 4th [16th] of June, Lieutenant-Field-Marshal Count Bellegarde and Colonel Count Joseph l'Espine, the plenipotentiary Austrian Commissars, delivered to Admiral Senyavin the command of the Sovereign Emperor to relinquish Cattaro to the Austrians for its peaceful transfer to the French. The commander-in-chief, reasoning that the Emperor had not yet received notification of the seizure of the Ragusan Republic, which had been under the auspices of Turkey, Russia's ally, declared to both the Austrian counts that: 'until Ragusa was abandoned by French forces and the independence of the republic was protected by a guarantee, Cattaro will not be surrendered to Austria'. As a consequence of this, Count l'Espine tried to persuade General Lauriston to quit Ragusa, but he rejected this and made the counter-offer that he should occupy Cattaro and leave Ragusa to the Russians. The Bokez however, swearing among themselves to resist being given to either the Austrians or the French, sent a petition to our court on the matter. The admiral then found a new reason to give no decisive answer to the Austrian representatives until he received a second order.

On the 19th [31st] of July, Count l'Espine, describing the restrained position of his government with the French retention of the Braunau fortress and the threats to occupy Trieste and Fiume, suggested that the French retreat to Stagno and let the Austrians occupy Ragusa, thus becoming a buffer between the French and Russians and allowing us the opportunity to safely evacuate the Bay of Cattaro, after which the French would assume control of the province from the Austrians. The admiral, seeking to gain time and knowing that this proposal could not be fulfilled, agreed only for appearances. During these events, the French Captain Techtermann arrived from Ancona with a letter from the State Councillor Pierre d'Oubril containing an extract from the peace treaty between Russia and France, which he signed on the 8th [20th] of July in Paris.[1] As this officer never met Mr d'Oubril and hastened to return to Ancona in an unusual fashion and, once dismissed, took advantage of the still winds to travel to Ragusa on his trabaccolo, the admiral became suspicious about the reliability of the papers brought to him and was compelled to respond to Count l'Espine that before receiving new orders from the Emperor, Cattaro could not be surrendered. The Austrians, frustrated by the unsuccessful negotiations, announced that they had the power to occupy Cattaro by force, complained about the deliberate delays, were upset that our rowing vessels were patrolling around the Austrian shores and concluded their missive by not entering into any further discussion. Due to these threats, Captain Baillie was ordered to hinder the landing of Austrian ground forces and observe them like an enemy. As there were several coerced Bokez among the number of vessels brought from Trieste to serve as transports, General Bellegarde could not exert any sort of force while the negotiations continued.

On the 27th of July [8th of August], Artillery Staff-Captain Magdenko, who had been taken prisoner, arrived from Lunéville with a duplicate of the treaty and a verbal confirmation from d'Oubril to hasten the surrender of Cattaro. In his company also came a French captain with a letter for the admiral from the Viceroy of Italy,[2] then another letter from him arrived the next day with his aide-de-camp Colonel Sorbier, and a third dispatch from Mr d'Oubril confirming the signed treaty. Unaware of the authority invested in this minister, the admiral, though he could no longer doubt the accuracy of the treaty, nevertheless sought to wait until he received word from the Emperor and delay the surrender until precisely instructed by the Russian court. He ordered military actions be ceased with the sole intention of ensuring the possibility of a retreat in any event and be ready with a greater force against whatever offensive the French would predictably conduct despite the peace. The Austrians renewed their demand, on the occasion of peace with France, arguing that there was no obstacle to proceeding with the surrender of the province to them, but the admiral replied that such a transfer was halted by the treaty and did not mention anything that should be given to the French; they

1    Pierre or Pyotr Yakovlevich d'Oubril served briefly as Russia's minister plenipotentiary to France from April to July of 1806 to negotiate a peace treaty and guarantee the safety of prisoners of war, but the agreed-upon articles of the treaty were rejected by Emperor Alexander as dishonourable and contrary to Russia's interests. Александр Михайловский-Данилевский, *Описание Второй Войны Императора Александра с Наполеоном в 1806 и 1807 годах* (St. Petersburg: Штаб Отдельного Корпуса Внутренних Стражи, 1846), pp.1-6. [Aleksandr Mikhaylovskiy-Danilevskiy, *Description of the Second War between Emperor Alexander and Napoleon in 1806 and 1807* (St. Petersburg: Staff of the Independent Corps of the Interior Guard, 1846), pp.1-6.]

2    Eugène de Beauharnais served as Viceroy of Italy (under Napoleon as King) from 1805 to 1814.

Pierre d'Oubril. Krüger, 1905, print reproduction in *Издание Великого Князя Николая Михаиловича Русские Портреты XVIII и XIX Столетии,* vol. 1, part 1 (St. Petersburg: Экспедиция Заготовления Государственных Бумаг, 1905), plate 24. [*Grand Prince Nicholas Mikhailovich's Edition of Russian Portraits of the 18th and 19th Centuries,* vol. 1, part 1 (St. Petersburg: Expedition for the Preservation of State Papers, 1905), plate 24.]

were alarmed and confused and demanded an explanation. The admiral referred them to Mr Sankovskiy, who was given the order to surrender Cattaro to the Austrians through the civil government, but Sankovskiy had fallen ill and did not wish to enter the negotiations.

On the 30th of July [11th of August], General Lauriston arrived in Castelnuovo with instructions from the French commander-in-chief General Marmont for the evacuation of the province. After the usual greetings, negotiations began. Lauriston asked that the Bokez people be assured that Napoleon promised to excuse their past hostility. The admiral replied that the best way to reassure the populace would be to solemnly promise that they would not be burdened with taxes, contributions, road-building, fortification maintenance without pay, and be made exempt from conscription; in a word, that they would enjoy the same peace and prosperity as they had under Russian occupation. Lauriston replied that that certainly could not be fulfilled, as his government adopted a system to maintain its soldiers at the expense of the people. He also demanded that all the Ragusan ships be returned, since the republic had always been neutral; the admiral replied that he himself had issued a proclamation that the Emperor of France annexing the republic to his lands did not first recognize its neutrality and furthermore, the French government not long before considered the vessels of the Ionian Republic fair prizes precisely because of the Russian forces occupying Corfu. As a result of these many and repetitive discussions, the admiral set a deadline for the surrender at the 15th [27th] of August, hoping to obtain confirmation of instructions by Count Razumovskiy from Vienna, and outwardly made preparations for evacuating the province. He announced to the Austrians that in fulfillment of the articles of the treaty, Cattaro would be handed over directly to the French and not to them. Alarmed by this announcement, they sent a letter on the 31st of July [12th of August], protesting with strong and fair arguments against the immediate surrender of the Bay of Cattaro to the French. Shortly after, they arrived in person aboard the admiral's ship, turning away from their former threats to soft persuasion and frankly admitting that the reason for which they so strongly insisted on the surrender was that Marmont and Lauriston assured them and vowed on their honour that Admiral Senyavin had supposedly invited the British to occupy Cattaro.

The admiral, now having received the protest so necessary to him, announced to Lauriston and Mr Sankovskiy that before receiving the Highest order from the Emperor, he would never consider proceeding with evacuating the province, especially since there was no historical precedent of a treaty's articles ever being fulfilled before its ratification. Lauriston was surprised by this sudden change and broke off negotiations, and, testifying to his personal respect for the admiral, regretted the time wasted and bid farewell in the custom of the French diplomats, saying that he was afraid this stalling would have terrible consequences for Europe and that the admiral was greatly troubling his Sovereign and his fatherland with his inaction.

The Austrians thanked the admiral for his part in relieving them of their difficult position. However, on the 13th [25th] of August, a courier from Count Razumovskiy bearing dispatches from the Ministry of the Naval Forces arrived, which confirmed the will of the Emperor concerning the surrender of the Bay of Cattaro to the Austrians; but since this dispatch was sent before the receipt of the report on d'Oubril's conclusion of peace with the French, the admiral replied that he had decided to wait for the Emperor to issue new orders and would not surrender Cattaro to either the French or the Austrians until such orders were received.

The Metropolitan, known for his subtlety in the political affairs of the time, proved an important figure and did not allow himself to be deceived by either flattery or generous promises. The French used every sort of intrigue in addition to open negotiation. The Metropolitan learned their methods by necessity, both to retain the obedience of the Bokez people and for future developments in Herzegovina and Albania where he wielded considerable power through his spiritual office. He slyly learned of the intentions of the French government and helped to open the eyes of the neighbouring pashas so that the significant gifts bestowed on the Pashas of Scutari and Trebinje by the French government would not accomplish anything. As soon as the admiral addressed the people of Herzegovina, their deputies came with offers of service, and the pashas – especially the Albanian Ali Pasha – remained good friends to us and nothing the French did could persuade them to betray us.

After Lauriston's departure, the Austrian dignitaries again submitted several notes, asked, urged, pleaded and again lost their moderate composure and succumbed to indecent measures; the admiral found it prudent not to include them in any further explanations of his policy. Finally on the 26th of August [7th of September], a courier from the court brought an Imperial order from the 31st of July [12th of August] for the resumption of hostilities and stipulating that if Cattaro had been surrendered, to retake it and all previous positions that had been occupied by the land and naval forces before the treaty signed by d'Oubril but never ratified by the Emperor.[3] It must be imagined how delighted the admiral was by such a command which vindicated his caution and all the orders he gave at his own discretion. In order to have time to assemble the irregular forces, the admiral invited the Metropolitan and all the various chiefs to announce to them the will of the Emperor and on the next day, a part of the fleet and all the corsairs set sail with orders to seize enemy vessels in all the remote corners of the Ragusan territories.

Thus, d'Oubril's prompts in triplicate, the flattering persuasions of Eugene, the Viceroy of Italy, the insistence of Lauriston, Bellegarde and l'Espine; none could shake Senyavin's resolution and proved moreover the importance Bonaparte attributed to our removal from Dalmatia and the occupation of Cattaro by his forces. His goal in concluding peace naturally was only to deceive Senyavin's vigilance, to occupy Cattaro and reinforce other points that would bring him closer to Herzegovina and Albania. He would then flood Dalmatia with soldiers to clear the path to the possessions of the Ottoman Porte and either seize them or compel that state to join him in malice against Russia; yet the admiral's cautious and prudent behaviour set an immovable obstacle before all of his plans. The French efforts to announce as soon as possible the treaty concluded between Russia and France brought them certain benefits. The Neapolitan court considered itself

---

3    Bronevskiy's note: 'The Sovereign Emperor, not approving of this peace, ordered negotiations to be reopened with the French government on new terms, including the exclusion of Dalmatia and the Bay of Cattaro from French possession'.

completely abandoned by Russia and the British, believing the same, left Calabria, which suffered the vengeance of the French, and this peace had the very opposite effect on the unfortunate Calabrians from those emotions which Senyavin could illicit from the Bokez people. Napoleon, having learned of an attack on his forces, was indignant and furious, and the lie in the *Moniteur* which exposed his failure,[4] something he was not used to bearing, served as the best praise and reward for Admiral Senyavin. In vain, the mercenary journalists tried to assure everyone that Cattaro had been taken, which was announced in Venice at the theatre with a drumbeat, but on the contrary, soon everyone knew that Senyavin, not allowing himself to be deceived with negotiations, defeated their generals and remained the peaceful possessor of the province of Cattaro.

---

4    On 27 July, *Le Moniteur Universel* reported that the Russians defeated at Ragusa had withdrawn to Corfu and the town of Cattaro had fallen to a Catholic uprising loyal to France, who then defended the city against the Orthodox Bokez and Montenegrins. *Moniteur Universel* 208 (27 July 1806), p.2.

# 46

# Continuation of Military Actions from the 2nd [14th] to the 23rd of September [5th of October] – The Battle of Castelnuovo

After the conclusion of the treaty, as early as the middle of August, the French began building batteries at the very mouth of the Bay of Cattaro on the cape of Ostro. On receiving orders to continue military operations, the admiral, seeking to gather more irregulars and make his necessary preparations in secret, waited for the batteries to be finished so that they could be captured in a complete state without needing to use his own men to labour over them. The French generals, despite the peace, continued to reinforce the entrance to Cattaro and dared to bring their forward posts to the very edges of our frontier. The admiral asked General Marmont to position his forces back to where they stood when the announcement of peace was first heard, and if he were to refuse, Senyavin said in his letter: 'I will be forced to use other means'. Marmont replied exactly as Senyavin hoped he would, saying caustically that nothing could frighten him and his forces would not yield a single step. On the Emperor's name day,[1] which was marked by joy, the

---

1    Alexander I celebrated his name day on 30 August [11 of September], the date that Saint Alexander Nevskiy's remains were moved to St. Petersburg in 1721. *Слово на день Святого Благоверного и Великого Князя Александра Невского, на Тезоименитство Благочестивейшого Государя Императора Александра Павловича, Благоверного Государя Великого Князя Александра Николаевича, и на Рождение Благоверной Государыни Великой Княжны Ольги Николаевны* (St. Petersburg: Типография Медицинского Департамента Министерства Внутренних Дел, 1825), pp.1-15. [*Speech on the day of the Holy, Blessed and Grand Prince Alexander Nevskiy on the Name-Day of the Pious Sovereign Emperor Alexander Pavlovich, Blessed Sovereign Grand Prince Alexander Nikolayevich, and on the Birthday of the Blessed Sovereign Grand Princess Olga Nikolayevna* (St. Petersburg: Press of the Department of Medicine of the Ministry of Internal Affairs, 1825), pp.1-15.]

whole fleet save the admiral's ship left the bay and the beginning of new hostilities was announced. Rear-Admiral Sorokin with four ships and a frigate was ordered to blockade the ports of Ragusa. The *Venus* assumed her post covering the coast from Budva to Molonta (Molunat). At the same time, on the 2nd [14th] of September, the irregular forces under the command of Count Vojnović and Vuko Juro attacked the French column and drove it away with great losses from the border. Marmont, surprised by this attack, changed his former tone and announced in another letter to Senyavin that he had decided to leave the fortifications and wished to withdraw to the positions of the 2nd [14th] of August; but it was already too late and hostilities had begun. On the 7th [19th] of September, the *Svyatoy Pyotr* and *Venus* knocked out a 10-gun battery on the lowlands of the Cape of Ostro and from then until the 13th [25th], the ship of the line lying anchored at the tip of the cape, the frigate under sails, and several gunboats on the side of the bay constantly harassed the enemy with solid shot and grape and prevented them from continuing their labours in their earthworks, killing several men.

On the 9th [21st] of September, Captain Baillie captured two trabaccolos in the Bay of Ragusa, taking prisoner 17 officers and 46 privates and seizing a fine quantity of ammunition and entrenching tools. On the 12th [24th], the *Venus* intercepted two other enemy ships laden with provisions intended for Ostro and drove them to the port of Molonta, where three armed rowing vessels with an officer were dispatched to capture them. As they came into the shallows, a heavy firefight broke out with the French sharpshooters, whom the officer dispelled with cannon shots before retreating without losses.

On the 13th [25th] of September, when a satisfactory number of Montenegrins and Bokez had been assembled under the leadership of the Metropolitan, our regular forces marched out of Castelnuovo and at the same time the batteries on the cape of Ostro were strongly attacked by our vessels; as soon as our soldiers appeared, the French hastily abandoned all their works and regrouped in a line between Debeli Brijeg and the port of Molonta, and by evening that same day, after a brief defensive action, they abandoned the entrenchments which they dug anew in that port. In both fortifications were taken 38 guns, including 5 mortars and charges in proportionate quantity, while in the port of Molonta 10 vessels with provisions were taken.

On the 14th [26th] September, the enemy continued to withdraw over the heights of Vitaljina along the channel to Old Ragusa. The Metropolitan pursued them impetuously and occupied the whole Debeli Brijeg. On the 15th [27th], the battle carried on without a minute's quiet just as during the previous two days. The French retreated step by step. On that day, an enemy flotilla consisting of 10 boats and a brig, standing in the port of Old Ragusa and sending ahead a large trabaccolo carrying 180 badly wounded men under a flag of parlay, set sail to attempt to break out for New Ragusa; but when our frigate, the *Venus*, set out on Captain Baillie's signal, the flotilla returned and the trabaccolo was captured.

On the 16th [28th], the Bokez and Montenegrins, having a platoon of Jägers with each detachment, displayed a rare fearlessness in the presence of the commander-in-chief and, inspiring one another, forced the French to quit their fortified camp at Vitaljina. Count Sava Ivelić especially distinguished himself on that day, attacking with his men from Risan and seizing the natural barrier called 'Wolf's Tooth' (Vučji Zub). After this, the enemy retreated to his main camp at Old Ragusa. To everyone's dismay, the brave Montenegrin *vojvoda* Uskoković died;[2] our losses overall were minimal however, while the enemy suffered some 340 men killed. The enemy flotilla again tried to reach Ragusa, but the *Venus* sailed into the entrance of Old Ragusa and blocked them in. Due to the dead wind, it was not possible to launch an attack and the frigate engaged in an exchange of fire with the boats and coastal batteries without losses and retired in the night to a single cannon shot.

As the arrival of forces from Corfu was expected on the 20th of September [2nd of October] and it was expected that many Montenegrins would have assembled by then, the admiral planned on launching a decisive attack on that day from both land and sea, but on the 17th [29th], Major-General Emanuil Grigoryevich Papadopoulos [of the Greco-Albanian Legion] discovered through several small skirmishes that the enemy was very strong; prisoners told that on the previous day two enemy regiments arrived from Dalmatia and the whole force had been assembled in one place. Marmont appraised our small detachments and sought to cut them off from the fortresses and destroy them on the field. At dawn on the 18th [30th], he precluded our attack with his own offensive, united the forward posts and attacked the headquarters of the Metropolitan on the River Ljuta, conquering it. His Holiness was in grave danger and retreated in a bloody but glorious battle to the tracts of Mojdež, Kameno and Mokrine. Even before the battle, one French general and his two adjutants encountered a party of Risan under Count Ivelić and were killed.[3] After the Metropolitan's retreat, General Papadopoulos, seeing seven

---

2 *Vojvoda* is Serbo-Croatian for 'duke' or 'military commander'.

3 Only one French general died during their Dalmatian campaign, the aforementioned Delegorgue. Perhaps Ivelić's men encountered a field-grade officer and mistook him for a general. In the town of Castelnuovo (Herceg Novi) there was once a mausoleum referred to as 'The Tomb of the French General', but was later found to actually contain the remains of a Turk killed at Sutorina. One French officer of note killed on the 18th [30th] was Captain Gayet, aide de camp to Marmont. Paul Pisani, *La Dalmatie de 1797 à 1815* (Paris: Alphonse Picard et Fils, 1893), p.261.; Noel Charavay, *Les Généraux Morts pour la Patrie*, vol. 2 (Paris: Noel Charavay, 1908), pp.4-10.; Auguste Viesse de Marmont, *Mémoires du Maréchal Duc de Raguse de 1792 à 1832*, vol. 3 (Paris: Perrotin, 1857), p.14. [Paul Pisani, *Dalmatia from 1797 to 1815* (Paris: Alphone Picard and Sons, 1893), p.261.; Noel Charavay, *The*

enemy columns, each twice as strong as him and rushing toward our forces on three sides, and occupying a disadvantageous position, retreated to Mojdež in the night and took advantage of his position on the border of the Bay of Cattaro. The Metropolitan stood with most of his force in the other passages leading to Cattaro. At the same time, two battalions of the Kolyvan and Kozlov and four companies of the Vitebsk regiments from Corfu were replaced in the fortresses by sailors and naval infantry and joined the detachment of General Papadopoulos. The admiral arrived in camp before sunrise, arranged the soldiers for the best possible defence, and verified the reported superiority of the enemy, from which he concluded that he would lure the enemy to the fortifications and wage a decisive battle there; for that, he ordered Papadopoulos to hold his position as long as his strength held out, and then retreat. The admiral assembled his whole force at Castelnuovo, positioned two ships of the line on either side of the fortress and placed the other vessels along the shore. Then by telegraph he notified the residents of the movements of the enemy. All night and day, the sailors brought in from the fleet prepared the fortress for a defence and dug batteries in hidden positions. The people, encouraged by such activity, did not lose heart and prepared to desperately protect their homes.

The nation's history will mark among the examples of heroic exploits the battle of the 19th of September [1st of October] which was fought in the vicinity of Castelnuovo, wherein 3,500 of our soldiers with 2,000 residents stood against 20,000 Frenchmen led by one of their best generals.[4] The brilliant courage of this small detachment acquired a new laurel crown for our invincible infantry.

At dawn, the enemy attacked our forward posts at all points and soon a general battle began. General Lauriston made the first attack but he could not resist our fire and was repelled; another strong column met the same fate. Marmont, reforming the repelled columns behind his line, unceasingly introduced fresh detachments into our fire; our forces repulsed them with strong musketry and canister fired from elevated batteries, and drove them to flight with bayonets before turning to their positions; thus, for seven consecutive hours, every brave effort by the French was foiled. When the day faded into evening, the courageous General Papadopoulos withdrew in good order to the next position assigned to him, with the 13th Jägers screening him. The enemy attacked here on our left flank, though it held with absolute firmness, and as that place would allow the enemy to surround

---

*Generals who Died for the Fatherland*, vol. 2 (Paris: Noel Charavay, 1908), pp.4-10.; Auguste Viesse de Marmont, *Memoirs of the Marshal Duke of Ragusa from 1792 to 1832*, vol. 3 (Paris: Perrotin, 1857), p.14]

4    Marmont in his memoirs estimated his force as being 5,900 strong and was comprised of the 5th, 11th, 23rd, and 79th regiments of the line and the 18th light infantry regiment, along with a contingent of the Italian Guard. Marmont, *Memoirs of 1792-1832*, vol. 3, pp.13-18.

our detachment and was nearly out-manoeuvred, General Papadopoulos retreated little by little and protected himself with alternating counterattacks between manoeuvres. Marmont praised the courage and steadfastness of our infantry in his report on this case; here one of our companies would fight against a battalion, and one Jäger battalion repelled a whole regiment. For all that, the enemy pursued our troops very closely and hoped to break into the fortification on his heels, but as soon as they approached the shore by the Sutorina river, a volley of grape from the gunboats and launches halted them. Under such cover, our people calmly entered the town and the French stopped at our previous positions.

On the 20th of September [2nd of October], the commander-in-chief agreed with the Metropolitan to admit the enemy, even to encourage them to assault the fortifications. Meanwhile, in order to cut off his convoys, strong detachments of Montenegrins were sent to the road to Old Ragusa and every other warrior capable of bearing arms were sent to Castelnuovo and entrusted to Mr Sankovskiy. The people were not discouraged, not a woman or child was crying, and every man was armed from young to old.

That same day, Marmont, not seeing any obstacle from our side, changed his position and from a distance of three *verstas* [3.2 km] he immediately sent out two strong columns: one followed the shore while the other headed to Kameno and Mokrine. The first appeared to attempt an attack, the second appeared to intend to break into the province's interior through Risan; but both of these appearances were deceptions, as the French knew that without artillery they could not effect anything against the fortresses though they could face the garrison in the field, and also that they could not enter Risan in such numbers. Their aim was to appraise the strength of our fortifications, to lure out the regular forces and, if possible, to cut them off and destroy them. The first enemy column set fire to the suburban homes of the Bokez and one Turkish home on the border that rose no arms against us. This cruelty was punished and cost them a terrible loss. When the first column approached our fortresses, they and the *Yaroslav* formed a crossfire of canister and grape which broke them and very few remnants managed to unite with the second column. The thunder of the cannons signalled a general offensive. It was not possible to hold back the Montenegrins and Bokez in their places at the sight of these burning homes. With a frightening cry, they poured out of their hidden positions and ran down the hillsides to attack the column from all sides so successfully that they alone immediately drove it back to the enemy camp. Marmont sent another to reinforce them, manoeuvred about and employed every technique of the art of war, but nothing helped him. The Bokez and Montenegrins were encouraged by the presence of the admiral and Metropolitan and used every feature of the ground to their advantage, successfully striking the enemy with heavy and accurate musket fire. The battle opened up into a general engagement, with brave men flocking from all sides and lit up with extraordinary sparks of courage. Our forces supported them only in necessary cases. From noon until 5 in the evening, the battle continued with extreme cruelty on all sides. After then, Marmont withdrew to their camp but even there he was not left in peace and the firefights crackled all night. Parties of the Montenegrins and Bokez again arrived and entered the firefight, spurred on by a jealousy of the battle-weary of the previous day, which forced the enemy to stand all night under arms.

On the 21st of September [3rd of October], Marmont had the false hope that the Bokez would appraise his army as too strong to continue attacking; having learned from experience that without strong artillery, he could not be safe in his camp from the continuing harassment of our irregular warriors; having received news that the Herzegovinians, in revenge for the burning of their villages, had united with the detachment of Milo, a Montenegrin *serdar*, and took Vitaljina, butchered our prisoners and destroyed two baggage trains; and moreover hearing that the admiral had met with these large numbers of armed locals and now had the strength to annihilate his army on the spot; he concluded that nothing could be done but to retreat and left the camp so hastily with seven guns that they salvaged from the ruined homes and cast off all of their burdens and 25 of our wounded as prisoners, that only the Metropolitan and his light forces could pursue the French to Old Ragusa, where the enemy stopped in a fortified encampment.

On the 22nd and 23rd of September [4th and 5th of October], large parties of Montenegrins passed through the fortifications and put everything around Old and even New Ragusa to the sword and returned to their homes rich with plunder, not having experienced any resistance from the French. On the 24th [6th], our forces returned to their quarters. The brave soldiers, exhausted in the course of ten days of incessant fighting and marching, were awarded with the rare attention of the commander-in-chief. For all the men present, a full feast was prepared with two rounds of grape wine.

Our losses on the 19th of September [1st of October] alone were painful: 175 were killed or missing, with 12 officers and 276 privates wounded. The Montenegrins and Bokez throughout the continuation of military actions lost up to 800 men killed and wounded. The enemy also suffered significant losses: one general [sic – see note above] and 18 officers killed; General Molitor and 37 officers were wounded; 47 officers and 1,300 privates were taken prisoner, the latter were intercepted by our cruisers and Bokez corsairs. The officers were engineers and artillerists sent to Bosnia and Albania to fortify some of the positions there. Napoleon's evil intentions against Russia were uncovered in the plans and papers confiscated from these prisoners. The total enemy losses consisted of 50 guns and

3,000 men killed and wounded.[5] Moreover, in this short time, the fleet seized more than a million rubles worth in prizes, military equipment and provisions.

The local population, for all of their savvy in mountainous warfare, are not capable of conducting either long-range or long-term campaigns, and for that reason, their bravery and enthusiasm to cooperate with us did not completely achieve the desired results. At times, they put our regular forces in jeopardy when they returned to their homes for economical obligations. Our 3,000 regulars were rather few to defend the province and the slightest losses further imposed on them, so far from Russia, could not be replenished. Therefore, the admiral, presumably to compensate for the Montenegrins' propensity to leave our service and to excite their jealousy, brought in the Albanian Legion from Corfu. No matter how hard this development was for the Montenegrin people, who by custom were wholly intolerant of subordination, their unlimited respect and trust in the admiral and the encouragement from the Metropolitan to accept Imperial service soon saw 2,000 Montenegrins and 1,000 Bokez assembled in a manner like regular soldiers and training in several Jäger manoeuvres[6]. With these numbers and the special propensity of the people to wage a partisan war, the admiral sent strong detachments against all the enemy's lines of communications while conserving his regular infantry. Ruining baggage, attacking convoys and forward posts, these brave warriors unceasingly brought their spoils to the camp at the Savina Monastery (where, to our surprise, they did not build tents but lived in the open air), and almost every day they brought us prisoners. The French locked themselves in the walls of Ragusa and were deprived by our fleet of all communication by sea. No aid came to them from their fatherland. And as they are not accustomed to be content with their own and already completely deprived the inhabitants with their taxation, they proceeded to the last resort and robbed the churches, seized all the gold and silver they could from the citizens who had any left and melted them down for minting coins which they thought could buy them access through the Ottoman territories, but Senyavin drew the pashas' attention to the burnt homes of the Porte's subjects and opened their eyes to Napoleon's intentions so that, despite all the intrigues of French agents, the self-intrusted pashas were inclined to take our side. Senyavin's proclamation to the Slavs of Herzegovina, with the aid of their bishop Arsenije, was received with enthusiasm and this people sent deputies to show their favourable intention to unite their arms with ours; but despite this fortunate development, the admiral did not sway from his intent to

---

5   Marmont gave a different set of figures, nearly the inverse of Bronevskiy's: 350 Russians killed, 6-700 wounded and 211 captured. 400 Bokez and Montenegrins killed and 800 wounded. 25 French killed and 150 wounded. Marmont, *Memoirs of 1792-1832*, vol. 3, pp.18-19.

6   Bronevskiy's note: 'This number grew to 5,000 soon after'.

deprive the French of provisions through Herzegovina and found it much more convenient to wear them out with hunger and partisan bands, and moreover wished for the enemy to sally out again. In attacking them in the field with the help of the Herzegovinians, he could cut them off from Ragusa, which would then surely be easier to assault in such a scenario. Thus, by very limited means, Senyavin became the powerful defender of the region and defeated the French generals and diplomats using both sword and pen with equal success.

The proclamation to the Bokez and Montenegrins, testifying to their merits in relation to their own circumstances, deserves to be placed here:

> To the Noble and Honourable Gentleman Knjazs, Serdars, and all the People,
> In the continuation of military actions, I had the pleasure of witnessing feats of the people's zeal in the engagement with the enemy alongside the army entrusted to me, from a singular desire for glory and a boundless devotion to His Majesty the Sovereign Emperor Alexander Pavlovich, Autocrat of All Russia, the true benefactor and defender of all faithful sons of the Holy Church.
>
> Warriors! You have shown great bravery, manliness and diligence with perfectly orderly conduct. The impudence of the enemy who has dared to set foot on your land has been punished. The enemy is surprised by your firmness and has lost so many men that he will not soon be able to gather new strength and again offend you. Congratulating you on your victory, I thank you for the good treatment of prisoners and wish in every way that humanity will not be tarnished in the future.
>
> Such good deeds which I have reported to my Sovereign Emperor are to your credit, honourable gentlemen and people! With my deepest gratitude, I hope that your true dedication and courage shall remain forever inextinguishable. By your laudable drive to virtuous feats pleasing to God, I will keep you in my reverence and benevolence forever.
>
> Aboard the *Selafail* in the Bay of Cattaro
> 24th of September [6th October], 1806
> Dmitriy Senyavin.

**47**

# Sailing along the Coast of Epirus to Corfu

On the 25th of September [7th of October], our frigate left her post at Old Ragusa and returned to Castelnuovo. I hurried ashore to review the battlefield. The sight was terrible! The bodies of the dead were scattered about the various positions; some lay face-down, others turned their pale faces to the sun. Here, enemy lay upon enemy, and the Montenegrin and Frenchman sat peacefully like friends. Women, looking for the bodies of their spouses with grieving wails and dishevelled hair, wandered around the former camp of the enemy and around the burnt-out houses. The thunder of battle died down, replaced by the voices of prayer and humility, and my attention was drawn by the dull ring of a bell toward the church where I saw a funeral: a quiet procession carried five coffins and sadly sang them to their eternal rest. Empathy was worn on the faces of the soldiers who bowed their weapons to the earth and were torn by the sorrows of the mother who, with hesitation and an unsteady pace, walked to the grave of her only son. Such a sight would touch even that hardhearted tyrant who never ceases to pour out the blood of his fellow man for his own personal gain and exaltation.

On the 30th of September [12th of October], the captain received orders to sail to Sicily, Malta and Sardinia to procure powder for Cattaro. The wind was very fresh and the frigate spread its sails like wings and soared like a swan between the many vessels lying on the roadstead. Rolling to one side and passing very closely astern of the *Selafail*, we saluted the admiral and by the time the echoes of the final cannon shots off the mountains faded away, the frigate was on the open sea. All the bustle of the crowded anchorage was replaced by the whistle of the wind and the crashing of the waves on the wild rocks which now stood between us and the towns and ships of the bay. Passing Budva, where the Russian flag flew, we kept close to the shore, and the many towns, rivers, villages and fortresses with ships floating calmly along their docks, formidable rocky cliffs and lovely green valleys moved behind one another and passed by like some mechanical phantasmagoria. On the shores of Epirus, a site of historical interest stood at every step. Durazzo

(Durrës), ancient Dyrrachium, built by the Corinthians, stood on a low peninsula; this was where Cicero spent his time in exile. Krujë and the Drin River to the north, the glorious country of Skanderbeg, scourge of the Ottomans and restorer of the Kingdom of Epirus, now constitute only ruins. Valona, haven of pirates, is known for the fact that Caesar and Pompey both came here overland, the first to conquer and the second to defend his country. Beyond Valona stand the mountains of Keravnia, now known as Chimera. Their terrible appearance and frightening height certainly gives them their name. Then stood Dodona, made glorious by its divinations, and from there flowed the legendary rivers of the underworld, Acheron and Cocytus. The inaccessibility of the mountains has preserved the remnants of independence for the brave Albanians and generations of Souliotes, who, like the Montenegrins, were a terror to the cruel overlords of their country. The battles and skirmishes in which these brave warriors held off against Ali Pasha would not bring any shame to Lacedaemon himself.[1] Their women did not concede the virtue of bravery to the men. In one intense battle, the young leader of the Souliotes fell and his death shook his warriors, who forgot the fight and gathered around his body to howl with grief. Then came the mother of the slain man who covered his face with an apron and took up his weapons to stand in his place and drive off the enemy alongside his comrades. When they were victorious, she returned to her son and uncovered his face, kissed him and said with great sorrow: 'I have avenged your death'. Santiquaranta (Sarandë) and Butrint once belonged to the Venetians, the latter of which was home to the palace of Pyrrhus, son and heir of Achilles. The fortified town of Parga, one of the Venetian possessions on the shores of Albania, then belonged to the Ionian Republic. The women of this city are famous for their beauty. The Albanians, or Arnauts as the Turks call them, are renowned for their extraordinary courage and comprise the best infantry of the Ottoman Empire, serving as the bodyguards of every pasha. Unfortunately, their cruel bravery is employed to oppress their own nation.

---

1    Lacedaemon was the mythological founder of Sparta and attributed namesake of Laconia. Smith, *A New Classical Dictionary*, s.v. 'Lacedaemon'.

# A Word on Ali Pasha of Yanina

Ali Pasha became independent with the aid of the Albanians; he obeys the Sultan only when he wants and even killed several good *chaushs*, which brought him the golden snare of 'commander of the faithful'. His great-grandfather was a Greek who fell from the faith. His grandfather and father devastated Epirus at the head of numerous gangs of robbers. His father was murdered by Ikhlaus, a Greek chieftain. Ali had many courageous experiences, gained the favour of the Epirean *proestoi*, or elders, and through their representation at the Sublime Porte, he became the *debenci agha* or guardian of all the inroads to Greece, killed his father's murderer, and through intrigues acquired the Pashalik of Delvina, followed by Trikala and Yanina. From 1787 he began to rule Greece independently. Since that time, Ali has tried to please the Greeks, allowing them to build new churches, ruining the wealthy Turks, and at the same time getting rid of his most dangerous rivals, bound the people to him, who, in lieu of brighter prospects, came to prefer their indulgent lord over the oppression of other tyrants. He decorated Yanina with four magnificent palaces designed in the European manner, fortified it with a citadel and stocked it with three years' worth of military supplies and provisions. In the event of a disgrace, he had a sure and impregnable refuge. On an island in the middle of a lake, he had a castle built by French engineers, and even though its position made it unassailable, it was defended further by a flotilla of galleys.[1] In this castle are all of his treasures which are quite significant. He receives annually up to four million piastres, and his two sons have two million each. The size of his army ready at any time reaches 16,000 men and in wartime, it can swell to 30,000.

---

1 Ali Pasha's refuge was on Ioannina Island in the lake of Pamvotis, but the extensive fortifications constructed during his reign were in the city of Ioannina itself, on the western bank of the lake, and not on the island. When the Porte finally sought to curtail his power in 1820, he would fight a two-year siege in the city's citadel before surrendering and settling briefly in exile on the island before his execution. Elsie, *Biographical Dictionary of Albanian History*, s.v. 'Ali Pasha Tepelena (1744-05.02.1822)'.

# Corfu – 2nd [14th] of October

The strong tailwind betrayed us at Strada Bianca and we entered a seemingly enchanted region where the winds were equal parts quiet and strong from all directions. The four ships inadvertently split in disparate directions and somehow each was running windward. Escaping this zone, we reached the northern strait where we spent a night in still calm. On the morning of the 2nd [14th] of October, 30 hours after our departure from Cattaro, we dropped anchor in Corfu.

View of the Citadel in Corfu. Illustration from original publication.

In my previous brief stay in Corfu, I could not view anything, but now I will give an account of my observations collected at various points in time. The town is not large and its streets are narrow and crooked; the best of them, Calle d'Acqua, during the heat of summer is covered with canvas stretched from roof to roof and on the ground floors are found galleries supported by plain columns which give her an appearance resembling Saint Mark's Square in Venice. Officers and the best society were always gathered in the casino (coffee house) under the pavilion. In the evening, the square and spianata was filled with people taking walks and from there they attend the theatre. One part of the city was very unclean and in a minute it could be guessed that it was home to the Jewish community, who, like everywhere else, comprise the class of the richest merchants here.

The Church of Saint Spyridon, in which the relics of that saint lie, deserves special attention. The iconostasis is decorated with ancient, very poorly made images. The plafond was also fixed in rich gold frames, with carvings in poor taste. In the middle of the church hangs a golden chandelier, and on the sides huge silver ones, the latter two having been donated from the Venetian Republic and the army under the command of Count Johann Matthias von der Schulenburg which repelled a strong attack by the Turks on Corfu in 1716. On the other side of the church a sort of high chair was made, in which you cannot sit but against which you can very comfortably lean. In Greece and all the Slavic lands, they prefer to yield to the elders. The Church of Saint Spyridon is revered as the richest in the east, as not only the Greeks but also the Catholics sent contributions to it; no sailor, nor even a man of the land, goes out to sea or undergoes any endeavour without first praying before the relics and bringing something as a gift. The 12th [24th] of December is the feast day of Saint Spyridon, the patron of Corfu, and is marked by a great celebration. The uncovered relics set upright in a golden case are paraded around the city to the thunder of guns from the fortress and the ships in the harbour. A certain monk named Kalochairetis transported these relics from Cyprus to Corfu in 1489, and in 1512 gave them as a dowry to his niece;[1] and by testament, both the church and the relics are bequeathed to the descendants of her husband Stamatello Bulgari (or Stamatios Voulgaris), either male or female, for all eternity. As a result, the archpriests of this church are always assigned from among the family of the Counts Bulgari, as well as several priests whose dignity is venerated as honourable but also very profitable. The revenues of the church are under the control of a special committee in which one of the counts is always present; a portion of these is used for the decoration and maintenance of the temple, and the rest is used for

---

1    Bronevskiy's note: 'In the wedding contract between Assemine and Bulgari, among other things, it says: "*Parimente gli da in Dote, e in nome di dote (ardisco dir con divota Circospezione) l'onorabile e santa Reliquia del Miracoloso S. Spiridion tutto come si trova* – I also give her a dowry and in the title of dowry (with due respect I dare say) the honest, holy and miraculous relics of St. Spyridon exactly as they are". This custom is sanctified by time and habit and has been in use up to the present day. These details are provided by Count I.N. Bulgari'.

those lands purchased for the church. Consequently, they are held by the counts in private ownership. At the request of this family, the church and relics of St. Spyridon were taken under the protection of Russia in 1801, which was signified by the instalment of the Imperial coat of arms over the western gates, the same place where the victorious Admiral Ushakov knelt. A lamp is kept burning at all times there. In that gesture, the counts, both out of devotion to Russia and for the self-interest of their country, were motivated to preserve the influence of Russia not only on the Ionian Islands but throughout all of Greece forever, no matter the political turn of events. In that they were naturally not mistaken, for faith has always been and will be the strongest link between peoples and no force of events or circumstances can weaken it. In another church, the relics of Saint Theodora are preserved, though she does not have a head.

## Fortifications

Corfu is revered as one of the most fortified places in the world and consists of five fortresses, three of which face the sea and two face inland. They are placed such that if the enemy takes possession of one, all the others can turn their guns against it. The main fort, containing the town, has two ramparts and a dry moat from shore to shore, while behind the town a channel of water forms a cape on which stands the citadel like an island. This cape is very high and steep; its peak is divided into two round hills, one with a battery and another with a semaphore station. The fortress is entered over a drawbridge. Directly opposite the gate, on the square, is the home of the commandant, which has the most magnificent appearance. Nearby is a marble monument to the Count von Schulenburg, who freed Corfu from the Turks. The statue takes the form of a Roman warrior. Through a beautiful foyer, I entered a narrow and dark corridor which led me to a small square, and there, over the bridge to the aforementioned gate was written 'Citadel of Sant'Angelo'. It occupied the top of the hill and served as the last and most reliable refuge for the garrison. Several collapsed houses could be seen, destroyed in the capture of Corfu [in 1799] by Russian bombs. I climbed the hill to the telegraph and from there I saw the entire layout of the fortress as if on a map. I climbed back down that narrow and dark corridor to the part of the fortress where the barracks and other buildings were raised. Powder cellars and magazines are carved into the interior of the hill. A large corridor, crossing the barracks completely through the foot of the hill, was amazing; this serves for the descent into the harbour and the docks called Mandraki. The old fort was the first fortification of Corfu, built by the Genoese, and to this day the coat of arms of that republic is still visible, embedded in the wall, worn with time and covered with moss.

The new fort was built on the other side of the town: to imagine it, one must think of a deep dungeon, high walls and finally a steep mountain lined with thick stones from which huge vaults are excavated within the fortress. From the town, one passed through the subterranean works to a small space where there are several private residences. Then follows a staircase that leads to a nunnery, then another stair against the wall which is so steep one cannot look at the top without losing his hat, to terminate at the platform on which the guns were distributed. Only the breastworks toward the city were recently repaired. A few cisterns were built there. Through another underground passage, one arrives as if on a balcony and again down a narrow and steep stair to the 'new square,' furnished with cannons, barracks and magazines. On that square, the ground had holes drilled through to illuminate and ventilate the underground vaults below. The town appeared from here to be on a slope, the streets were not clearly visible and the houses all seemed very small. I ascended to the very top of the wall and the suburban fortresses looked like mounds. There was nothing pleasant in the view of the surroundings of Corfu: desolation and ruins stood everywhere. The anchorage with its many ships looked very crowded and the snowy peaks of the Albanian mountains seemed quite close. From the new square, underground passages led out into the countryside and into the suburban forts. The wonderful though fruitlessly fantastic construction of the fortress should surprise everyone. I could not understand with what force the Venetian authorities hoisted these huge guns up to such heights and I did not want to believe my eyes in how human industry and nature supported one another here. The establishment of the fortress was estimated to be at the end of the 13th century.

The island of Vido, lying near the city within a cannon shot, at first glance promises the convenience of being the first step in capturing Corfu, but its batteries are all below the parapets of the three forts and do not grant an enemy in possession of it much benefit. Admiral Ushakov surrounded the island with ships, knocked out all of the batteries which peppered him for no more than half an hour, and took the island with such bravery that the garrison was frightened and soon laid down their arms before a handful of soldiers and sailors. Corfu, having a garrison from 10 to 15,000 strong, could not be taken in any way but by hunger and thirst, for the main inconvenience is that the food is mostly obtained from the Albanian coast and water collected from rain or imported and stored in the cisterns is not always sufficient.

## Gouvia

Gouvia, where there was a Venetian shipyard responsible for constructing their ships of the line, was razed to the ground by the French; only three sheds remain where the scaffolding was kept. The other structures are survived by just one wall, on which many inscriptions are found; one of which testifies that the shipyards were founded in 1734. The beautiful, peaceful bay surrounded by ruins, with the gothic architecture of monasteries and the newer styles of small manors visible in the distance, and the wide road paved with slabs of stone and lined with trees leading back to Corfu created a secluded and charming locale. It is impossible not to be surprised by the skill of the French in destroying everything, and it is impossible not to wish that these structures, possibly costing millions, were restored.

## The Ruins of Ancient Corcyra

At the gates of the fortress where the cape on which the town of Corfu stands begin the outer fortifications, a large portion of which were built by our engineers. From here, along the valley leading through the villages, at a distance of three *verstas* [3.2 km], one comes to the ruins of houses, a monument to the merciful French. In one desolate monastery, a monk with a bowl in one hand and the other pressed to his heart met us with a low bow and when we gave him two or three coins, he did not fail to say a few abusive words about the gentlemen of France. He volunteered to show us the ruins of ancient Corfu but apart from some tall grass and large heaps of stones, I did not see anything. Yet when I looked around, I fell in love with that place. On one side stood a huge church with five domes, surrounded by marble columns and shaded by old oak trees, while on the other was laid out the camp of the Kura Regiment in the shade of orange, lemon and olive trees. This sight forced me to remember where I stood, see what was under my feet, and recall the glory of the Greeks, convincing me of the terrible injustice that is the impermanence of kingdoms and nations. The monk assured us that the church we saw was built by the Apostle Peter himself and that he once preached the faith within. Wandering through the ruins, I saw two rarities: a palm tree and a tree over a hundred years old, the leaves of the latter were about three feet [91.44 cm] long and two inches [2.54 cm] wide. The inhabitants cook them for food and they taste like the flesh of a gourd.

On that part of the island, Odysseus, rescued from a shipwreck, was met by the beautiful Nausicaa and was received amicably by King Alcinous. Homer added much wonderful and poetic detail in his song of the gardens of Alcinous, though we cannot hope to find the palace of the King of Scheria, the bronze walls surrounding them, the golden doors and dogs made by the hands of Hephaestus; but the learned Italian Carlo Giuseppe Botta, with the *Odyssey* in his hands, believed the items therein and found a perfect similarity in the locations. He says that time, destroying the works of human hands, has spared the creations of Nature, and describing the traces of the ancient building and coins found there, he concludes quite plausibly that the Messongi river is the source where the princess Nausicaa washed her dress and met the nude Odysseus, and the oak grove existent in the present is the same where Odysseus disappeared in anticipation of her return.

## Benizze

Whoever visits in Corfu and does not visit Benizze (Mpenitses) should regret that he did not have the free time or failed to make use of it. Hearing its many praises, I was looking for an opportunity to see this place and the case soon introduced itself. Our acquaintances, the army officers who served on our frigate, were offered to sail to Benizze, and so the eight of us boarded a boat and took off from the frigate. Circling around the rocky cape of the old fort, we started along the shore. From the side, the island of Corfu displayed nature and human works in all their splendour and in their best form. The greenery was much fresher and more delicate and the homes were of a simple and pleasant architecture. Kardaki, where the fleet procured its water, is situated on a rocky hill on top of which stood a regimental tent and at its foot a tower over the sea. Beyond that ran a small river with a camp stretching along one side. All of this together attracted our attention and we ordered the sailors to briefly stop rowing so that we might take a longer look at this beautiful sight. Finally, after 17 *verstas* [18.14 km], we landed at Benizze and went straight to the house of a wealthy noble in Corfu, Andreas Kalogeros. Although the road was difficult and the heat of the sun was unbearable (in October), we crossed five *verstas* [5.33 km] without fatigue between the gardens and Kalogeros's house, which supposedly had the best garden in Corfu. The road took us between two high walls covered with grape vines. In the courtyard of the manor there were many buildings. Having risen on a stone staircase separate from the house, we found ourselves on a small terrace narrow enough to be practically a column; a drawbridge fell before us and we entered the upper floor of the house where the owner, a wise man of about sixty, received us affectionately. The upper dwelling consisted of one room partitioned into three areas, whose walls were adorned with muskets, daggers and sabres of an extravagant value; in the columns between the windows, loopholes were cut for mounting a defence with musketry. The combination of such a strange entrance to the home, the large arsenal of weapons and the courtesy of the merry elder gave us an excuse to ask what the cause was for such strict security. 'Once,' replied the host, 'I was afraid of the Algerians, then of the French. Now I'm only afraid of reptiles, but I can't shed the old habit'. He showed us his garden in which the best feature was the inclusion of a bathing pool with a convenient means of adjusting the water level; it had a ceiling made of the intertwining branches from the bountiful trees, such that one could pick fresh fruit off the limbs while swimming. The hospitality of this Greek dreamer was greatly appreciated, and knowing our customs, he forgot his own and offered us one thing or another without any reluctance. We did not stay for dinner though, thanked him, said goodbye and returned to Benizze. There on the coast, in the thick shade of the trees, we dined gaily on a lawn and waited for the heat to subside; by nightfall we were already back aboard the frigate. The air, water, land

and fruits in Benizze are considered to be the best on the island. The beautiful location attracts rich landowners and their manor houses across the area present a pleasing variety of architecture.

## Various Comments

The mild climate, lemon and orange tree orchards, flowering meadows, olive groves and vineyards where spring reigns eternal make Corfu one of the finest places in all the Mediterranean. Fruit trees of all kinds grow in the open air, and flower in a variety of cycles so that one can have mature vegetables and young greens at any time of the year. The wine berries here are considered the best in the Levant. There is little grain grown on the island, as oil, from olives in particular, is imported from the island of Paxos and wine, salt and fruits prove more profitable. Free trade and the expense of approximately 12,000,000 rubles in Corfu for the maintenance of the army and navy has enriched the inhabitants, but they seem outwardly impoverished either by a habit of moderation or a deliberate pretence. Russian generosity has not changed them much and no matter how much the government has tried to reduce poverty, it seems unaffected. To mention the heat here would be to reiterate what has been said by many others, so I will only add that the heat is always tempered by the breezes off the sea. In September and October, the venom of scorpions and centipedes is deadly: a wounded man can die within a day. However, the danger from them is not as great as one typically thinks: if anointed quickly with an oil in which a scorpion is drowned, then the injury is rendered harmless.[2] The winter months bring tedious weather with a light rain falling almost uninterrupted for several consecutive days, punctuated with heavy deluges. Northwesterly winds bring clouds and terrible thunderstorms, sometimes in conjunction with an earthquake. One never gets used to the thunderous booms and brilliance of the lightning; they shake even the firmest soul. After these terrible phenomena, in deep winter, the weather becomes pleasant and even hot. The air is refreshing and the land, scorched by the hot sun, again blooms with greenery. Therefore, the climate of Corfu is very healthy and our soldiers were not especially subjected to disease.

Here is one example of local justice that can happen whenever the law lies only on the table and not in the conscience of the judges and where crimes are ignored. One rich noble, a secretary of the senate, decided to seize the profitable garden of his neighbour, a peasant with a comfortable estate and known for his honesty and

---

2    Scorpion oils and other folk remedies which seek to extract an antivenin from the creature itself are either completely ineffective or harmful to the wound and were debunked by experimentation as early as 1731. Charles Alston, *Lectures on the Materia Medica*, vol. 2 (London: Edward and Charles Dilly, 1770), pp.510-513.

love for the republic. He hired a poet on the peasant's behalf to write a libellous lampoon against the senate, and then he himself made the denunciation against his victim. The peasant was arrested and sentenced to be shot. The verdict was announced in town on the eve of the execution and someone out of compassion stood up for the condemned man and clearly proved that he did not know how to write. Luckily the true writer was discovered and he apologized and gave up the name of the secretary. Do you believe that was the end of the case? The poet was shot and the peasant was released, but his estate was awarded to the secretary by the court!

The republic is governed by an aristocratic council or senate. The chairman of this body is called the *principe* (prince). Its laws are borrowed from the legislation of Venice. The senate consists of 140 members and deputies elected from the nobility, merchants, artisans and common people.[3] The seven islands that comprise the republic are Corfu, Cephalonia, Santa Maura (Lefkada), Ithaca, Zante (Zakynthos), Paxos and Cerigo (Kythira), and their deputies are succeeded every three years.[4] The power of the senate in such a weak republic is not significant; as for the [aristocratic] citizens, they have their personal privileges and the condition of their poor does not concern them. They do not think of the future, are cold-blooded about the present and are satisfied only with the memories of their past.

The nobility rent out their property and incessantly grumble about the laziness and negligence of the peasantry and their own inability to compel them, as the peasants remain complete masters of their abodes until the expiration of their terms and do not pay their duties. The landlords and their tenants have long been enemies. The French were received at Corfu with joy when they reassured the nobility that they would instil obedience in the people, but they effected little except to award the best land to those who assisted them more, having confiscated it by right of conquest from the less cooperative. As a result of these events, several noblemen left for Russia and asked for amnesty. When we captured Corfu, the devotees of the French then fled their homeland in turn. In that fashion, there remained among the nobility a seed of enmity which cannot soon be removed and everyone wishes to find their party of choice in control of Corfu; but it must be said that our faction is larger, finer and nobler. Despite the fact that the tenants were brought to heel and that one evil was cured, the people are loyal only to the Russians, as our influence is impartial and does not depend on particular cases.

3    The 1803 constitution of the republic described a bicameral body consisting of a Legislative Assembly with 40 members, and an executive Senate of 17 members. *The Three Constitutions of the Seven Ionian Islands*, p.47. Article 32.

4    Members of both bodies were elected for only two years. *The Three Constitutions of the Seven Ionian Islands*, pp.50-60. Articles 43 and 96.

On all of the republic's islands, the number of inhabitants reaches 300,000 people of the Greek confession. A portion of the nobility belongs to the Catholic Church, and all faiths are tolerated. The languages of Greek and Italian are in equal use. Turkish silver and Venetian gold are in circulation but all other coins are accepted in exchange.

## History

Corfu was known as Corcyra, Scheria, Phaeacia and Kassopaia in antiquity. The revolts of the island against its metropolises and masters, according to the description of Thucydides, were known in even the remotest history. In exile on Corfu, Aristotle paid for a passion which philosophy cannot always keep in check.[5] Simonides and Polykleitos, citizens of this island, attained immortality: the former in poetry and the latter in sculpture. In the golden age of Greece, the island fought against Corinth, Sicilia, Athens and Syracuse before finally being disgraced by the Romans. The Corcyreans distinguished themselves in the Roman legions and took the side of first one triumvir and then another, and the island was the meeting place of Cicero and Cato after the Battle of Pharsalus. The former could not tolerate an unfavourable blow of fate and killed himself in Utica; the latter took command of the remaining legions of the republic, lost heart and surrendered power to Caesar before losing his own life. With the deaths of these great men, the Romans lost their freedom forever. Soon after, Mark Antony and Octavius celebrated an unholy marriage which cost the whole world many tears and scarcely fifty years later, Agrippina arrived on Corcyra before the funeral of Germanicus. One church on the island remarkably escaped the persecutions of Diocletian.

In the middle ages, the Corcyreans belonged to the Eastern Empire and served in the armies of Constantine the Great, Constantina and the other Greek emperors. They defended Rome from the Goths under the leadership of Belisarius, and later Constantinople from the Turks. Crusading knights assembled on Corfu to sail for the conquest of the Holy Sepulchre. The bishops of Corfu, Apollodorus and Saint Arsenius, are known for their teachings and participation in the ecumenical

---

5    Some biographies of Aristotle asserted that he was exiled from Athens for including the name of a supposed lover Ermia among the goddesses. This may be derived inadvertently from Hermias, his father-in-law, for whom Aristotle wrote a hymn after his death. Whether his passion was romantic or filial, the charge laid against him was *asebeia*, a lack of piety or respect. Likewise, his refuge has been asserted to be either Corfu or Chalcis. George Wright, *The Shores and Islands of the Mediterranean* (London: Fisher, Son and Co., 1840), p.44.; William K. C. Guthrie, *A History of Greek Philosophy*, vol. 4 (Cambridge: University of Cambridge, 1981), pp.44-45.

councils. When Roger founded the Kingdom of Sicily, Corfu and Epirus united into a duchy and were given to Michael Komenos, bastard son of the brother of Alexios III. At this time, the Genovese had by treaty a trading post on Corfu and constructed the old fortress. Afterward, the duchy was conquered by Charles of Sicily but this yoke was soon thrown off. The Corfiots, weakened by this effort and threatened by the encroachments of the Genovese without the means to further defend themselves, decided to solicit a patron in quite a strange way. They laid down a challenge that the first party to meet their deputies on the Adriatic Sea would be proclaimed their masters. A Venetian galley met them first and its captain was declared their master but he instead handed control to the republic, which paid a small sum to the Sicilian court to assuage them of their dispossession. The Venetians built a new fortress and all the other fortified sites except for the Genovese citadel. The Turks, besieging Corfu several times, never captured it and its walls were the limit of their conquest. The siege of 1716 under the leadership of Soliman was the most glorious. The Turks had already taken the city and the army and people were trapped in the old fortress when Count von Schulenburg marched out with a small force and drove the enemy away. Such an unexpected deliverance is attributed by the Corfiots to Saint Spyridon, and they assure us that the Turks now believe in him and send gifts to his reliquary.

In 1797, by the Treaty of Campo Formio which abolished the Republic of Venice and divided its territory between Austria and France, Corfu and the other six Ionian Islands came into the possession of the latter. The importance of this acquisition for France was soon overshadowed by the attack on Egypt and the destruction of the fleet at Aboukir. In 1799, while Suvorov liberated Italy, Admiral Ushakov conquered the hitherto unconquerable Corfu at the head of a combined Russian and Turkish fleet. Vice-Admiral Senyavin, who served then as a captain, especially distinguished himself in the taking of the fortress of Santa Maura. The Treaty of Amiens on the 13th [25th] of March, 1802, recognized the independence of an Ionian Republic under the protection of Russia and Turkey. Every three years hence it would pay 750,000 piastres to enjoy independence from Turkey yet with all of the benefits of her subjects. Recently, with all of the islands but Corfu occupied by the British, the Ionian Republic was recognized as under British protection by the Congress of Vienna.

# 50

# Sailing from Corfu to Syracuse

Taking on provisions and fresh water, we left Corfu on the 4th [16th] of October. The wind was strong and blew against us during the entire journey. The sky was overcast and by nightfall a thunderstorm began when the wind subsided slightly. In the pouring rain, we were occupied constantly by damage to the sails and rigging and there was much commotion. A new challenge was then added: the current and winds together sent us adrift from the coast of Italy at an incalculable speed, making the charting of our course difficult, and all the worse for the gloom of the storm blotted out the sun and stars. For several days we wandered like a traveller lost in a dark and endless forest. We took on water constantly from the rolling and pitching of the vessel. The captain was so concerned that the officers had to be on deck continuously. No one had time to change out of their wet clothes and the decks dried out from the heat. On the orlop deck,[1] the piercing creeks of the bulkheads, the action of the pumps and the hammering of the caulkers reverberated like in an empty barrel and did not give a moment's rest. To our passengers who were unaccustomed to this sort of deluge, it seemed that the frigate was close to flooding. When someone was relieved from watch and retired to his cabin, they pestered him with ridiculous questions and wanted to understand everything happening around them.

Finally the sun broke and the wind eased down somewhat. We spotted Catanzaro, over which flew the flag of King Ferdinand,[2] as the Calabrians stood bravely for his rights like a new Vendée. Gaeta, under the shield of the heroic Ludwig, Landgrave

---

1   Bronevskiy's note: 'The section under the lower deck where the provisions and cabins for [some] officers are located'.
2   Ferdinand III and IV reigned as King of Naples and Sicily from 1767 to 1805, when he was deposed by the French in Naples and replaced by Joseph Bonaparte and then by Joachim Murat in 1808. He continued to control Sicily under British protection and would be restored in Naples in 1815, finally reigning as Ferdinand I of the Two Sicilies until his

of Hesse-Philippsthal, defended itself stubbornly. André Masséna, the child of victory, a worthy champion of Napoleon, lost 20,000 men at Gaeta and did not manage to subdue Calabria. The head of the patriots, Michele Pezza, nicknamed Fra Diavolo (brother of the devil) and rightly deserving of it, fighting a war with scattered bands, little by little broke nearly his whole army. The English general John Stuart, landing with 5,000 men in the Gulf of Sant'Eufemia, defeated General Jean Reynier's 7,000-strong corps. The conclusion of d'Oubril's treaty prompted the British to return to Messina and the marauders of Europe were free to pursue new projects, whereby the rage and grief of the inhabitants reached its zenith. The French burned towns and villages, shot those they captured, and branded the sons of the fatherland as rebels. Fra Diavolo in turn burned and hanged the French and called them bandits. Neither side showed any mercy. Fertile Calabria became coated in ashes and ruins.

Manoeuvring near the coast, the wind grew stronger the closer we approached Messina. In the strait itself, it nearly died out and although the frigate made good progress on the first day, the second brought a storm and the captain was compelled to turn downwind and head out to the open sea. Without sails, by the current and wind against the hull alone, the frigate flew like an arrow from a bow. Away from land, the wind intensified again and the pitching of the frigate began so strong that without grasping the rigging and ropes deliberately laid out as handholds, one could not stay planted on his feet. The shrouds and stays weakened and we were afraid of losing the masts. Water poured in from all sides, the frigate dove deep and buried itself in the waves, and the whole vessel trembled from the crashing and turbulence at the rudder. The scattered clouds soon converged and the sun vanished. The wind raged with a violence I had never seen before. We began taking on water faster and it became dangerous to stay out at sea. The captain, having invited the officers to a council, decided to sail to Syracuse, as during a northerly wind, it was not possible to reach the port in Malta during the great tumult.

Passing Catania, we witnessed an accident. A merchant brig coming from Messina intended to head into port for the same reasons as we did, but on a beam reach they set staysails, and as both of their masts fell, the boat rolled onto its side. In a minute, the craft was flooded and swallowed by the waves with barely even its debris remained on the surface. Our passengers covered their eyes with their hands at such a terrible spectacle and one of the most devout among them wished to confess and receive communion. Our good-natured monk approached me to ask if he could perform the service to a Catholic.

death in 1825. Ward et al., *Cambridge Modern History*, vol. 9, pp.262-267.; Ibid., pp.381-382.; Ibid., p.661.

On the 14th [26th] of October, approaching Syracuse, we prepared to set the foresail and two reefed topsails; the officers with megaphones in their hands directed the men to their places and explained their tasks. The captain, with his experienced eye, estimated the distance at which we would come into a perpendicular wind and ordered the sails to be set. When the lieutenant asked 'ready?' and then shouted 'heave! Haul the sheets! Left rudder!' it can be confessed that the hearts of even the most experienced sailors would begin to pound. The frigate rolled over, scooping up water, the foresail tore, and the masts stooped over. As the frigate flew toward the entrance, there came a dangerous and decisive moment. The entrance to Syracuse, no wider than two and a half *verstas* [2.67 km] and crowded on either side by ridges of rocks, presents a path so narrow as to say that the slightest deviation in course, hesitation, lethargy or error could crash us on one or the other cape. Anyone could imagine with what expectation and with what eyes we gazed at the approaching town. Terrible breakers crashed on the right and left, lapping up on the walls and high tower of the fortress, which we passed from no more than 60 *sazhen*s [128 m] away. Onlookers certainly could not remain indifferent as they watched the frigate passing between the stones, nearly on its side, especially when it escaped the violence of the waves only to head seemingly straight at the tower. Conversely, it is impossible to describe the joy felt when the frigate passed the reefs and entered the harbour where ships lie as calmly and safely as on a river. The sea, which a minute ago had been carved down to the abyss and stirred up as if by some supernatural force, became in the bay absolutely flat and quiet. We furled the sails, cast anchor and believed that the danger had passed. Although the waves by the town were not violent, the wind howled thunderously above between the masts and rigging. Two anchors could not hold us; the frigate dragged them off to the stone-studded south side of the harbour and while we managed to let down the topmasts and yards, cast a third anchor and prepared a fourth, the frigate came within less than a hundred *sazhen*s [213.36 m] of the shore. It was necessary to reduce the height of the masts to lighten the force of the wind, but in that miserable moment, as the anchors were sliding along the sea floor, we suddenly came to a stop and the waves rebounding from the shore pushed us back on the lines so that amidst the frightening breakers we found our salvation from the rocks which were so dangerously close. The storm continued steadily all night and if we did not have time to enter Syracuse before sunset, then in all likelihood we would have capsized in the sea during the night; as besides other damage to the hull and masts, the frigate was struck by shot below the waterline and was leaking.

# 51

# Syracuse

The port of Syracuse, as if deliberately built by man, has an almost circular basin with a reliable muddy floor and possesses a depth between 5 and 11 *sazhen* [10.67-23.47 m] uniformly across its space. Entering between two capes, only a portion of the bay is exposed to easterly winds and so the harbour is tranquil and safe. On the shores of the surrounding bay, one cannot see any remains of ancient Syracuse, but beyond there rise the mountains gradually in a beautiful panorama. Between them, Mount Etna looms up to the clouds and on dark nights illuminates the tranquil waters of the harbour with an incomparable light. There is a small port where small boats dock which has long been named Marmora, for in the past the whole was covered with marble, and some of its slabs are still visible even today.

By noon on the 15th [27th] of October, the storm ceased and the frigate sent parties to the town for provisions and proceeded to repair its damage. The quarantine officer made several inquiries such as where we came from and if we had any dangerously ill people onboard before announcing our freedom and congratulating us on behalf of the governor for our arrival. The captains of the British warships and the colonel of a Scottish Highland regiment paid us a visit and the colonel was invited again for lunch the next day.[1] The governor of Syracuse kept us in his company for dinner. His grey hair completely contradicted his agile movements and a quick glance revealed the passion of youth, courage, and a firmness of spirit. A great company was gathered at the table. The governor appeared as the most notable personage in floral brocade, silk, and with large rhinestone buttons on his jacket. They all had the magnificent titles of dukes, princes and marquises with many Spanish adjectives, even the names of saints such as Don Francesco, Conte de San Giovanni. The meal

---

1    The British Highlanders garrisoned in Syracuse in October 1806 were the second battalion of the 78th Regiment of Foot, accompanied by the regimental colonel, Major-General Alexander Mackenzie Fraser. John Keltie (ed.), *History of the Scottish Highlands: Highland Clans and Regiments* (Edinburgh: Grange Publishing Works, 1887), pp.684-691.

was the most luxurious and suited the Italian taste; spicy root vegetables and fine aromas were ubiquitous, meat was scarce, most dishes consisted of greens, fish, fruit, cakes and iced treats. Each dish was introduced by the host with a great multisyllabic title signifying its quality and dignity: *Boeuf à la Mode, Bombe de Sardanapale, La Pietanza di Frederico Grande*, et cetera. He advised to eat one with old men, another with young ladies and girls. A Malvasia di Lipari, Lacryma Christi, a Syracuse and a Marsala all stood untouched: they consumed very little wine and even then watered it down half-and-half, but gaiety and merriment were plainly visible on every face. The flexible and sweet-sounding language, spoken intricately and sharply with a rare talent, makes Italian conversations (whenever a foreign language is not employed) generally fun and amusing. Although jokes made were frequently risqué and sometimes provocative, the men and women were able to parry and riposte with the same arms. The conversation quickly moved from topic to topic: jokes, amorous adventures, scholarly debates, impromptu verse, European politics and news from around the world. Every word invited a witticism and every speech turned to laughter. Sarcastic epigrams composed on the fly mocked the tawdry King Joseph Bonaparte and they were apparently not upset at the loss of their country.

After dinner, the governor showed us his grenadier regiment which was garrisoned there. Major-General Aleksey Nikolayevich Bakhmetev instructed the Neapolitan Army in the Russian exercises as he could remember it and combined Russian words of command with Italian. In manoeuvres, every soldier clearly demonstrated that he understood as well as his colonel for what purpose each movement was typical and in which case each should be preferred over another; in short, the Italian soldier, while not having a particularly warlike appearance, seemed to understand his craft better than he cares for appearances.

The town of Syracuse is not large, standing on a peninsula whose isthmus has a canal dug through it, and is surrounded by a stone parapet; this fine external fortification gives it the best defence against an attack over land. From the sea, it is enclosed by a wall and by the lighthouse are placed heavy cannons. The tower on the cape serves as the lighthouse. The tall antique architecture of the homes, a square decorated with a pond, and streets which are just wide enough and paved with cobblestones and marble sidewalks give Syracuse a very handsome appearance. The theatre is not great and its actors are even less deserving of attention. The best buildings are the monasteries and churches, and there are so many monks and beggars in the town that out of 15,000 inhabitants, it seemed by their attire that one could hardly see any respectable burghers, although the impression is not strictly true. The cathedral (il Duomo) was decorated with a colonnade, whose beautiful columns face in to one another. I entered the temple during Mass and the bishop's ministry, opera music and choirs did not attract my attention so much as the elegant architecture of the architrave and balconies. 34 columns in the Doric order, embedded in the walls, were revered as the remains of an ancient temple to Minerva. Among the treasures kept is a relic with three skilfully-carved busts of Roman soldiers: one white, the second scarlet and the third painted with a natural skin colour. In another home there are four columns, which it is said are the remains of a temple to Diana.

On the next day of our stay in Syracuse, we observed the training of a Scottish regiment; the attire of these warriors resembled the Romans, preserved from antiquity, and the strange appearance of their colourful skirts especially drew the eyes of their spectators. The soldiers were all very young, blond, fresh-faced and I could say fine lads. Lord Douglas, a perfectly handsome young man at 18, a captain and an heir of great wealth, was the subject of many a conversation among the local ladies. His gilded sword, diamond-studded brooch fixing his plaid, his neck as white as snow and his kilt, which revealed the whole of his legs as he ran before the formation, likened him to Mars or Adonis. Their training surprised me. The manual exercise was very simple and brief and the men performed their movements without the guide of a fugleman. The soldiers played with their muskets like children but shot quickly and aimed quite accurately. The colonel wanted to hear the opinion of our army officer, and he said to him: 'their musketry is quite fine, but the front is poorly aligned, they wheel around crookedly and hold their muskets sloped too far backward'. The last complaint was addressed by the colonel by saying that the musket stocks were angled, but conceded that the first complaint was true. After the manoeuvres, a special kind of training began: the muskets were laid on rests like a sawhorse and reed canes were distributed, which the soldiers wielded like swords. They scattered about the square, caught one another, chased, dodged, thrashed, and made all manner of acrobatic feats. After this, they fell back into line and made left- and right-face turns, accompanying each movement with a call and clapping their hands in time with the foot.

At six, we retired to the dining table. The food was good and the drink even better: dishes were not served in order but each man took what he pleased; those who were shyer than others and did not know this custom were forced to start with cake and then eat a beef steak, confections, radishes, pudding and turtle soup. When the toasts started, musicians appeared. The drum major, a bronze-coloured American in rich attire and crowned with feathers, walked around the table with a bagpiper in tow who blew into his pipes as hard as he could with every toast. The musicians played a medley of Scottish folk songs which contained something of the melancholic, akin to all northern peoples; their simple tones touched the soul. The English custom of sitting at the table for a great deal of time is shared by the Scottish. After dinner, the servant put out cheese, pickles, devilled eggs – so named for their use of the pungent cayenne pepper – nuts, and finally to quench everyone's thirst, two bottles per man were placed on the table and a third was kept in reserve on the floor. He bowed, stepped out and locked the door; then we began to drink without witnesses. 'Sir! To your health!' was repeated on all sides, glasses were emptied, and the conversation became animated. Bonaparte took the stage and the man who had previously been deeply quiet threw his head up and shouted with all the others: 'goddamn him!' Finally they stood up for two whole hours and marched about with a surprisingly firm step. I had to agree with my neighbour Pickney that it was possible to make a habit of drinking deeply without ever becoming drunk.

Lord Douglas invited us to tea. Pickney, the regimental quartermaster, a peculiar man in his late 40s and still a lieutenant, accompanied us. Walking down the street, I asked him: 'why is it your colonel and captains are so young while the subalterns are so old?' He explained that in his army, ranks can be purchased and that the lord has ten Arabian horses in his stable while he only has just one mule. 'What an abuse,' I said, 'what an injustice'.

'Not as much as you think,' Pickney said. 'It is easier for the government when the children of the nobility raise their own regiments on its behalf. You would agree that a rich man has better means of serving as a colonel than a poor man with no prior education. As it happens, our formation drill is simple, never changes, and you can learn it in a few weeks'.

'How do you distinguish bravery?' I asked.

'We don't!' said Pickney. 'Every man should serve without the goal of accolades. We don't award orders and ranks for that, and after a war when the soldiers are dispersed to their homes, they have no particular advantage. The wounded and the poor are taken in by hostels, but according to their needs and not their rank'. I did not contradict him but I could not agree that the sale of ranks without merit could have a benefit. The conversation then turned to the composition of the officers. Pickney assured me that the army officers, like their naval counterparts, shared a communal table. An excellent institution! The young man is always under the supervision then of his commander and does not need to worry about what he will eat tomorrow and does not have an excess of personal effects, with which our infantry officers are necessarily encumbered.

The handsome captain entertained us like a rich man. His tutor, an educated doctor, joined us and treated the lord like a friend and peer. A beautiful Englishwoman in a red spencer also joined us for tea. She bowed deeply to us, fluttered her blue eyes fashionably, and suddenly blushed and sat down in modest confusion. 'Who is this?' I asked Pickney. 'His wife or sister?'

'Neither,' said Pickney playfully in a quiet voice.

Returning to the frigate, the quiet, cool evening prompted us to take a stroll down the street. Multicoloured lanterns illuminated the vestibules of the houses from which the sounds of guitars and singing could be heard. These serenades and the slightly twinkling stars and twilight of the evening created a siren's call too dangerous for the seafarers. Their long strides diminished and grew softer and quieter, then one departed on the right, another meandered about and ducked out on the left, and when I came to the pier I had only one fellow left in my company.

In reciprocation, we invited guests to breakfast and the day was beautiful. Under a pavilion made of British, Neapolitan and Russian flags we set a table on the quarterdeck. Three chefs were at hand to prepare dishes according to each guest's tastes, but they all requested Russian cuisine. The Scottish found them delicious but the Italians claimed that our cabbage soup and buckwheat porridge will cause indigestion. There was no shortage of wine and quickly sincere customs without any pretension brought the guests of such different nations and characters closer together. Heads became heated and the army officers began to wage a conversational war with all manner of shot, canister, bomb and bullet flying, while the naval men flew over the company with a howling tempest and all sails set and flapping in the air. The theatres of war in Egypt, the Caribbean, East Indies, America and Europe collapsed into that small space on the deck between two masts. The noise and shouting gradually increased and those who did not know foreign languages spoke incessantly; the Italians explained themselves better than others while the English and Russians all talked over each other without regard for the finer details. After dinner, they requested that we have the sailors sing. Twenty of the best singers were selected and accompanied by a clarinet, horn, tambourine and drum. They began to sing joyful and cheery songs. The Scottish were pleased and the Italians fell silent. I asked one of the nobles beside me how he liked our music. 'A hearty people!' he said and clasped his hands. But when they began to sing slow, lingering songs and the peasants on the field appeared before us; when they began to dance, all the guests were surprised, closed in together, and enjoyed it so much – especially the Italians – that the dancers were asked to continue until they collapsed.

### The Ruins of Syracuse

Ancient Syracuse consists of four parts: Arcadina, Tica, Neapolis and Ortygia, which were separated by three walls and defended by three forts. The town had a circumference of 20 miles [37 km] and its citizens were so affluent that it passed into proverbs with the phrase 'as rich as a Syracusan'. Its construction is credited to Archias of Corinth in 734 BC. Under the rule of Dionysius the Elder, the Carthaginians besieged the town without success and their commander, Hamilcar, was killed. Later, an Athenian fleet was also destroyed and their whole army was taken prisoner. In 211 BC, Syracuse fell to the Romans under the command of

Marcellus, who plundered the inventions of Archimedes. The present town stands on the site of Ortygia, while the other sections are barely visible ruins.

Past the draw bridge over the channel through the isthmus and several paces from the glacis stood a well which had the appearance of a cellar with a descending flight of stairs. Inside, there are six marble pillars. From there begins the magnificent aqueduct which runs from the Anapo River where it flows into the sea between two marshes. It has the appearance of an arcade which stretches out of sight. This arcade or bridge is 14 miles [25.98 km] long and supported by thick pillars and arches, gradually dropping from the mountains to deposit a whole river into the well and then throughout the city via a subterranean plumbing system.

Beyond the gardens and plots near the aqueduct two *versta*s [2.14 km] from the city stands a steep cliff, the foot of which is inundated with caves and grottos. One such grotto was known as the Ear of Dionysus (Orecchio di Dionisio). It was carved very smoothly into the strong rock of the mountain. The grotto opening or entrance, around 80 feet [24.35 m] tall and extending to a width of 30 feet [9.14 m] at the ground appears like two letter S's conjoined at their upper ends. The length of the floor also proceeds into the mountain in an S-shape for a length of 250 paces. The gradual parabolic curvature of the walls as they twist and diverge toward the opening is akin to an ear trumpet which fed into a chamber. On the walls are visible the remains of rings and chains where prisoners were once bound. The trumpet is now partly broken and the chamber itself has been destroyed but some of the properties are still preserved; if you tear a small piece of paper in the grotto, it reverberates very loudly. Two men standing 50 paces apart and speaking in a low whisper can understand each other quite clearly. Ordinary conversation becomes loud and every utterance is echoed several times. A pistol shot becomes a boom of thunder which will roll and oscillate through the whole interior of the mountain for nearly five minutes. Standing outside the ear, the shot resembled the broadside volley of a hundred-gun ship of the line which petered out into an exchange of musketry. It would be interesting to hear music in this place. Considering the formation of the ear, it must be assumed that the amplification comes from the great height and width as well as its resemblance to the human ear. The slightest movement in this kind of structure shocks the air. The Palace of Dionysus was on the mountain directly above the prison. In order to see the chamber where the tyrant would listen to the condemned, we had to hoist ourselves up with a rope and pulley, rising to a height of 200 feet [60.96 m]. A cross wind passing through a window showered a mist throughout the passage, which accounts for why words in the chamber are harder to hear than in the prison. They assured us that when the ear was whole, the main advantage was that words did not echo in the prison but were only audible in the hearing room of the tyrant.

Beside the Ear of Dionysius is an enormous cave supported by thick pillars. Stones for building houses are quarried from here. In the age of the tyrants, these deep caves served to imprison criminals but now they ferment nitrates in them. The cliff seems to have been deliberately hewn for the addition of homes and the remains of walls visibly remain in some places in the stone and lime.

On the left side of the cave lies an amphitheatre. Even at first glance, one cannot be surprised by the courage and strength of the structures of the ancient architects. Imagine a whole mountain in the form of a semi-circle and divided into three terraces or galleries joined by several hundred steps. On both sides of the theatre, there are the remains of eight entrance stairways which had balustrades of marble. We were shown the remnants of the inscriptions, whose letters were so effaced that nothing could be parsed, but the learned Count Gaetano, a native of Syracuse, discovered by long research that the letters on one side read 'Basilissas Philistidos' denoting that the theatre was built under the patronage of Queen Philistis, and the other reads 'Aglisos,' which he considers to be the architect's name. On the upper and central terrace, two mills are visible, standing one above the other and driven by a channel of water flowing down step by step. The view from the mills is incomparable: the port of Syracuse was a vast and calm lake with the town standing on the narrow peninsula draped in a light fog which gave it the impression that it was floating. Arethusa, the glorious source in ancient myth which flowed in the middle of the antique city, now meandered along a short distance from the amphitheatre. Remembering the adventure of Actaeon and Alpheus,[2] though we were sure that the present nymphs passing this river to wash their dresses would not be so cruel to us, we did not go to look at its clean waters and ordered our guide to take us to the ruins of the town.

Where Syracuse once towered there is now a vast field with a space of three miles [5.56 km] that appears to be nothing but heaps of stones. All of this space is occupied with columns, capitals and marble slabs with inscriptions, broke and lying about in disorder where gardens and orchards once stood. Here are the sad remnants of one of the best cities of antiquity. In the place of the palace, considering several fragments from the wings and cornices already overgrown in the ground, we were indignant at seeing that robbers were allowed to abscond with many rare marbles and precious monuments. With a heartfelt sorrow, we passed this desert

---

2    Actaeon was a mythological hunter who accidentally spied the goddess Artemis and her nymphs bathing and was punished by being transformed into a stag and then killed by his own dogs. Alpheus was a river-god who fell in love with the nymph Arethusa and pursued her to Sicily where Artemis transformed her into a spring in order to keep her chaste underground, yet Alpheus was successful in catching his love and anything dropped in the river supposedly would wash up in the spring. Smith, *A New Classical Dictionary*, s.v. 'Actaeon'; Ibid., s.v. 'Alpheus'.

from end to end and were overjoyed if we saw under the thorns or the root of a fig tree a portion of a wall bearing the stamp of all-destructive time. Is it not inevitable that the glory of the conqueror, of the barbarian who has exterminated entire nations, to fall? Do not all the newest monuments erected in vanity crumble and disappear like magnificent Syracuse?

Approaching the sea, we saw the remains of the loopholes from which Archimedes threw stones down on the Roman navy. The foundations of the battlements were built of heavy stones which were very tightly laid without any clay, lime or cement. These were significantly better preserved than the other ruins in Syracuse, as the raiders did not know how to tear up the stones that Archimedes had set there.

Leaving the ruins and descending from the platform to the plain, the guides led us to a monastery. The Capuchins showed us their church in which there was nothing remarkable. Stepping outside, we lit a few torches, opened a great door and stepped down a narrow staircase a few steps to find ourselves in a dungeon which had no end, so a guide assured us. It is impossible not to be surprised to see in the womb of the earth streets, housing, chapels, a whole town and it is impossible to calculate how many hours were spent and how many thousands of hands toiled to carve out the stone into that immense subterranean building. On either side of the galleries or streets were chambers packed tightly one beside another. The intermediate walls serve as the supports for the vaults. In every room or niche stood a table in the middle and a hearth in the corner. Around the three walls there was a wide bench with small indentations serving instead of beds. Even these items are carved from the same soft and smooth stone. After passing a certain distance, there are several pillars supporting the circular structure of the church, which has three entrances. The remnants of the throne, cross and images all carved into the stone were still remarkable in places. In the centre of the vault of each church, to convey the light and air of the sky, a large hole is punched through to the surface and the same is done along the arches of the galleries at equal intervals. In these churches, the pure prayers of the first Christians ascended to the throne of the Heavenly King and God granted them the patience and courage to suffer their torments during a cruel persecution. Praying for their torturers and dying under the executioner's axe, these Christians in their piety parted with life indifferently. Even mothers did not sob or complain but poured out their sorrow in earnest prayer and abstinence. A monk showed us that one of the lords of Syracuse, a vicious persecutor of the Christians, ordered his soldiers to set fire to the underground buildings and a few thousand who were taking refuge were asphyxiated by the smoke. The catacombs, as the Capuchins assured us, extend as far as Catania over 30 miles [55.56 km] but that no explorer has ever studied where they end. The third entrance of the churches is located opposite the altar and its corridor leads to the catacombs. The sight of tombs and bones lying in these dark passages lifts one's thoughts to God, to Whose breast we shall all return sooner or later. The pious, who honour these remains as the bodies of the martyrs, collected the ashes of those who suffered for their faith so that some part of them might be buried. Coming to the first shaft whereby one can access the surface, the whole underground was identical except that the main corridor proceeded straight and turned off to the left and right for the churches. Reaching the second shaft, no farther than three *verstas* [3.2 km] from the first, the guide warned us that here the vaults are weak and often collapse; several coins persuaded him to continue on, but the torches burned down and forced us to return quickly up through the second shaft and its dilapidated stairs to emerge in the open air again. We were again in the middle of the ruins and decided to settled down to rest for a while. One of us sat on a large broken foot while the others sat on the steps of a collapsed porch. The bright night sky full of stars, the quiet and cool air, the azure waves of the sea lapping around the shore, the tunnels, churches, catacombs and innumerable bones all terrified the imagination and set the soul away from worldly cares toward contemplations on the next life.

## Touring the Countryside

Pickney was obliged by his duties to travel to Catania and suggested that I visit Mount Etna with him, with a doctor and a captain volunteering to accompany us, but as the frigate was made ready, I was only at liberty to accompany them for a few miles. We sat in a carriage with two servants following in a cabriolet. Crossing the plain, we turned into the small foothills and saw cultivated fields and gardens everywhere with small streams and diverting canals flowing in all directions. The poor stone houses of the villagers under the shadows of chestnut and mulberry trees and surrounded by vegetable gardens are not proportionate to the abundance of the land. A manor house on the mountain in a superb location aroused our curiosity and, leaving the carriage on the road, we climbed toward it on foot. The path led us through Indian figs, rose bushes and myrtle from ledge to ledge and finally through a grotto laced with ivy before reaching a vast terrace in the centre of which was the summer house surrounded with a neat garden. The gardener told us that the owner was in town and the house was locked up. By its large glass panes, bronze frames and brocaded curtains, one could imagine the splendour of the interior. The paths delineated with ropes, trees trimmed in fashion, flowers planted in patterns, and fountains that spit water into the air to form monograms were all amazing at first glance for their unexpected appearance, but the singular exclusivity of the contrivance, without the choice of natural beauty, quickly tired the observer regardless of its intricacies and fine craftsmanship.

Returning to the vehicles, we crossed a river's ford, rode through a meadow and spotted crowds of villagers harvesting fruits and singing merry songs. A steep slope covered in forest came up and the road became difficult, so we proceeded again on foot. The intertwining canopies of the trees sometimes formed a covered alley which sheltered us from the sun yet still let the cooling breeze slip through. After emerging from the woods, there were spread out around us groves of oak, cypress, poplar, fig and almond, complete with wild grape vines, and nearly every plant bore fruit. Descending the opposite slope, we passed an orange grove whose trees on the banks of a small stream rolling down the hill were beginning to flower and gave off an enchanting fragrance. The imagination was transported to the golden age of Arcadia, where nature demonstrated abundance and luxury at every step and poured euphoria into the soul.

Before evening, we stopped in the small village of Melilli which lay not far from the coast. I was not successful in seeing the sugar plantation present there. While I was preparing the supper, my companions admired the location from the balcony. 'Look', said the doctor to me, 'how beautifully the sun sets. See how its rays play off Mount Etna's snow'. I had not seen snow in a long time and looked on its whiteness with great pleasure. The pines and cedars growing near the peak and swaying in the wind reminded me of our northern fatherland. Immersed in a sweet reverie, we gazed at the volcano's summit in deep silence. The gloom of the night deepened with the smoke which built more and more, swirled into a vortex and swelled into a thick pillar of unimaginable height. Behind Etna, the setting sun and its last vanishing beams dimly illuminated the slope and the long amphitheatre of mountains lying in the interior of the island, after which everything before us was blanketed in twilight. Meanwhile in the east, where the sea stretched out endlessly, the moon rose in the clouds and the silence of the evening was soon broken by wind and rain.

The dirtiness of the hotel forced the Englishmen to move out to the stables where they settled down in the hay and I thanked them for the fine company, wrapped myself up in a greatcoat and sat in the cabriolet. The rain and cold wind forced me to ride faster. The Italian drove the horse into a gallop, bored me with his conversations and when I closed my eyes and pretended to be tired, he began to sing theatrical arias before soon telling me: 'here is Syracuse'. The frigate weighed anchor and I hired a skiff, catching up with her as she was already leaving the bay.

**52**

# Sailing from Syracuse to Palermo

---

At midnight on the 19th and 20th of October [31st of October and 1st of November], we crawled out of Syracuse on a quiet breeze. At dawn, Etna emerged as a giant before our eyes and the wind picked up. When we were opposite Augusta, we saw several small vessels in its harbour. From there to the north and south were various bays, harbours and capes. Catania, lying at the base of Etna is famous for the beauty of its women, who they say are as dangerous as its eruptions. Taking advantage of the opportunity, I measured the height of the volcano with the aid of an octane and found it to be 3 *versta*s 65 *sazhen*s [3.34 km] tall. The circumference of its base is 315 *versta*s [336.04 km]: on its fertile ashes at its base grow sugarcane and all kinds of grains. Higher up its slopes are vineyards, olive groves and other fruiting trees. Next higher are the apple and pear trees, and then to the peak lies the eternal snow.

A terrible eruption made it famous. In 1669, Catania was destroyed, 18,000 residents were killed, and many of its streets were covered in lava. An earthquake in 1783 affecting Sicily and Calabria killed 40,000 people in just a few hours. Since then, there have been no powerful eruptions from Etna, however it constantly smoulders and threatens the island. If Italy did not have Vesuvius, Etna and Stromboli, those vents of the terrestrial womb burning beneath her, then the land would either be deprived of its fertility or perish entirely. Descriptions are filled with the destruction caused by the earthquake. New mountains are thrown up, old ones are shifted or toppled, whole cities are swallowed up, new islands emerge in the sea and rivers are diverted. In 1538, a new mountain (Monte Nuovo) arose from the flat earth in Naples to a height of 67 *sazhen*s [142.95 m]. In 1707, the island of Nea Kameni emerged from the waves in the Santorini Archipelago. Many of the Aeolian Islands have risen and fallen. Sicily, according to Pliny, Virgil and Ovid, was once connected to Calabria but broken off by an earthquake at some unknown time. It is also likely that the Straits of Gibraltar and Dover were once isthmuses. This devastating natural phenomenon comes from combustible substances which ignite when mixed together.[1] This fire is irritated by air and intensified even more by water. The strength of the fire is so great and the eruptions so devastating that they cause earthquakes. Hard metals are converted by this heat into liquids called lava, which boils up and swells until it spills out of the muzzle of the mountain and from there flows down the slopes in fiery rivers, destroying everything in its path. Superstition ascribes to these natural events a fabulous origin: the Sicilians consider the mouth of Mount Etna to be the gates of hell, and whose subterranean rumbling and bubbling they attribute to the wails of the damned.

Before reaching Messina, the location of the small town of Scaletta is amazing. A rock having the form of a sugarloaf was covered in homes from top to bottom, divided by three walls, and appeared like a monumental cone deliberately set on the shore of the sea. Here is where the great oil is produced from the fat of the small whitethroat birds and others. On the 21st of October [2nd of November], we passed the Punta del Faro and with moderate alternating winds, holding between Sicily and the Lipari Islands, we entered the harbour of Palermo at sunset on the 23rd [4th], dropping anchor beside the British ship *Pompee* which flew the flag of the glorious Rear-Admiral Sidney Smith.

---

1    Volcanos are generally understood today to be a product of tectonic forces where plates diverge or converge which force up molten rock from the mantle toward the crust of the Earth to escape through a vent, sometimes violently if the passage is obstructed and pressure builds. The majority of volcanoes therefore coincide with inter-plate fault lines and eruptions can overlap with earthquakes, although the two are separate phenomena. The explosion of a volcanic eruption is not the result of a chemical reaction. John Rafferty (ed.), *Plate Tectonics, Volcanoes and Earthquakes* (New York: Britannica Educational Publishing, 2011), pp.82-91.

# 53

# Palermo

---

Despite a light rain, the officers went ashore within an hour of dropping anchor. Lanterns illuminated the main street, open shops and coffee houses and the clatter of carriages and coaches rushing through the crowds of pedestrians with coloured lamps and torches in hand[1] turned the night into day and made for a dazzling spectacle. From the sound of music and singing, one can immediately guess that one stands in an Italian city. As soon as we set out a few steps along the embankment, a crowd of half-naked boys surrounded us. They offered us rather unexpected services for their age. Day and night they give foreigners no peace and share their most insolent proposals with the same calm spirit as the merchants in our hotel courtyard who ask as you pass: 'wouldn't you like some sugar or coffee, sir?'

The position of Palermo provides the most picturesque view. It lies on a low, flat valley bordered in the distance by hills and mountains covered with evergreens. At the top of one mountain can be seen the old town of Monreale, while on another, in the clouds, stand country houses with gazebos and belvederes, from which the rich and noble could enjoy the panorama of valleys, towns, harbours, ships and the open sea.

Toledo and Maqueda, the two main streets intersecting at right angles, split Palermo into four quarters. The first begins at the seaside promenade and stretches from east to west to end at the Royal Palace with a Gothic gate and a tall tower above it, which appears like a toy model of a Chinese house when seen from the quay. Should anyone need an idea of the most beautiful street in the world, they must visit Toledo in Palermo. On two broad lines intersected by a ridge with an Arabian reservoir, paved with marble, all the houses are of equal height and

---

1    Bronevskiy's note: 'After 9 o'clock at night, by order of the Palermo police, residents cannot leave their homes without a lantern or torch'.

are all enriched with terraces, statues and flower vases. Their open-air gardens on the roofs, along with the porticoes and porphyritic colonnades, form such a striking complex that their façades alone are amazing. Unfortunately, the porches, entrances and vestibules are filled with crowds of ugly beggars. With plaintive moans, they pursue everyone and their slovenliness, only parts of their body being covered with the rags they wear, create a strong disgust which runs contrary to the pleasant first impression.

Would you like an idea about the interior decoration of these palazzos? Come with me to the home of the Princess di Butiro, the richest person in Palermo. The arch of its gate is lined with pearl shells and mirrors; at night, when a large chandelier is lit, the reflected flames illuminate the entrance with the brightest light. A fountain, decorated with statues of naiads, sirens and tritons in the centre of the courtyard paved with white marble, frames the view of a grand staircase behind it. On one side are several figures atop the columns of the balustrade and on the other are marble vases in which water cascades down like parabolas of crystal. Then the eye is drawn to the portico which stands on four columns of black marble with golden veins. Through a huge door one enters the central floor where large Tuscan mosaics decorate the walls, floor and ceiling of a vast hall. The second chamber is decorated with yellow satin. Light blue velvet with silver fringe and tassels demarcate a reception area. A rotunda follows. In the middle of a porphyritic platform is a pool with a small staircase surrounded by silver grating and surrounded by walls covered with crimson velvet. A beautiful collection of fountains sculpted as Venus with cupids and nymphs poured coolness into the room. The ceiling in the dining hall depicts an assembly of the gods of Olympus and is alone worth around 40,000 rubles. Stucco work and paintings, rich furniture, abundant bronze, porcelain and silver halt the visitor at every step.[2] Finally to reach the façade on the opposite side of the house, one must cross a long gallery of mirrors to a small circular room occupying the space between the first and second courtyards of the home. From the end of the gallery, this room takes the form of a temple, whose mirror ceiling, large circular window and additional large mirror framed between two azure columns, silk carpets and several steps for a dais were paralyzing in their splendour. Into this latter refuge of taste and luxury I was led by my hostess, a woman of about thirty. They say her beauty is still as fine today as it was then. I was seated on a brocade stool between her and a dressing table, on which, along with a prayer book, lay the operas of Metastasio,

2    Bronevskiy's note: 'It is worth noting that in Italy the floors are made from a composition which can contain all manner of colour if desired and which becomes as hard as flint when coated with polish. The construction of their homes contains almost no wood at all: the floors and stairs are marble, and most of the framing is in bronze'.

Boccaccio, *The Maid of Orleans* and many other such works. Relics and a mosaic crucifix also rested humbly between pomade, perfume and other cosmetic items. Arabian incense smouldered in Etruscan vases. She had a lofty Arab and three beautiful handmaidens as her attendants. There was also the handsome baron, who was recommended to me for a private companion. He, not paying attention to our conversation, whistled the famous aria: '*Se tu m'abbandoni, mio dolce amore!*'[3] I drank a cup of chocolate served on a golden tray and in Japanese porcelain, bowed and left, yet my imagination has remained in those halls of the sun whose magnificence could rival even the rich palaces of the orient.

## Fountains

In the centre of the city lies a beautiful fountain, preserved since the reign of the Saracens, which features eighty figurines constantly cascading water. We cannot but regret that the square in the middle of the city is very small and the fountain is placed in its corner. The fountain in the Royal Square also has the finest group of marble sculptures in the latest style. Each square is decorated with a pond and in every house and on every floor, the murmuring of waterfalls is incessant. Palermo does not have a river;[4] whence then does the water come? 25 *verstas* [26.67 km] from the city, the Saracens excavated a vast reservoir in the mountains, which is kept almost always full with a few springs and rains in the winter. From here, with the use of plumbing, the water is brought under the earth and chilled and then reportedly enters the city by canal. According to the laws of hydraulics (that the angle of incidence be equal to the angle of reflection), the water can rush from the fountains up to even the terraces. The perpetual motion of water pouring from the mouths of animals, fish and monsters into silvery overflows shaped like sheaves and pyramids was a pleasure in the hot climate, especially under the midday sun. On a clear day, the sun casts rainbows through the shimmering crystal streams. At night, coloured lamps are placed behind them and fill the squares with dazzling spectacles.

## Churches

On every street there is a monastery or a church, but not one of them is in the middle of a square where one might see their entire beauty. Most are built in the Gothic style and inside, the most elegant taste is combined with an amazing

---

3     Italian: 'If you abandon me, my sweet love!'
4     Bronevskiy's note: 'The Oreto River, flowing south of the town, has a dry bed for most of the year'.

splendour. The portico of the cathedral is decorated with a colonnade and statues of the Four Evangelists. In the narthex, water gurgles ceaselessly from two pristine pools. Entering the nave, one will be surprised at first glance by the wealth on display. Uncovered altars with silver and bronze columns, vast vaults and choruses supported by pillars of granite, porphyritic tombs containing kings and viceroys, the most beautiful painted images, and all manner of enamel, gold and marble constitute a wondrous fortune. The eye wanders and the soul takes a sacred delight in such a temple. Gagini, revered as the Michelangelo of Sicily, adorned the choirs of the cathedral with the most exquisite statues whose only defect is that they are placed so high they appear miniscule. The relics of Saint Rosalia residing in a golden ark along with the bones of Saint Peter and the hand of Saint John the Baptist are kept here on the main altar, which is adorned with two columns 15 feet [4.57 m] high of pure lapis lazuli. Among the treasures in the temple is displayed the cross donated to Saint Rosalia along with one from a Spanish king which is studded with diamonds, five of which are extraordinary.

After the cathedral, the second according to its riches and ornaments is the Church of San Filippo. The music hall attracts attention. It has a special entrance and occupies the entire length of the church on the right-hand side. The gallery around the hall is supported by rose-coloured columns. The choir, like a round temple, stands especially at the end of the hall; its half-cupola rests on a wide cornice standing on two rows of columns. The vault of the choir depicts an azure sky. The Mother of God in the clouds is represented in such a way that her hand reaching down seems to descend from the sky toward the observer. The Eye of Providence, surrounded by golden rays, is placed in the opposite direction from the choir. A large magnifying glass, facing east and located behind the Eye, receives the rays of the sun and sends it to mirrors embedded in the vault to spread a dazzling glitter throughout the hall. The optical effect of glass, azure and gold is so extraordinary that the Mother of God with the angels hovering around her takes on a truly heavenly radiance. At night, lamps are placed by the magnifying glass and the hall is illuminated even more spectacularly than in the day. The artist, with an intricate contrivance, hid the musicians behind the cornice of the choir and connected the halls such that the echo off the vault reaches the listeners below with such an amazing concord that the music sounds as though it were coming down from heaven.

'How I would have liked to hear music in that beautiful room', I said as I left. The courteous, stout and perfumed prelate gave me a ticket for an oratorio depicting the Nativity. It began with a thundering symphony which gradually softened and when it almost subsided entirely, a distant voice sang out, accompanied by oboes and flutes. I searched with my eyes for whence it came and as it grew closer I could clearly hear 'Glory to God in Highest Heaven'. Hearing this choir of angels,

I turned my eyes to the sky and saw the angels there on the cupola without any surprise and rejoiced that the powers of heaven were so close to me. The wondrous choral singing of the magi's 'Come and Worship' did not produce almost any kind of reaction after the effect I felt from the angels. They fell silent and one gentle, sweet voice delighted my heart again; I did not dare move or even draw a breath – I turned again to heaven and listened but did not comprehend how a mortal could connect such harmonious verbiage with such inexplicable expressiveness and tenderness. I cannot forget to say something about the unique voice of a young nun who, despite the recent and profound impression made by the angelic songs, delighted all listeners with new and touching sounds. All the heads turned reflexively to the choir but she then finished. When the whole performance was over, I left the hall filled with feelings of reverence and said to myself: 'Praise the Lord with timpani, strings and organs',[5] as nothing exalts the soul so much as music and song.

Not only the best churches, but the smaller chapels too are decorated with works from the most skilled artists. Raphael, Michelangelo, Correggio, even as copies, represent the extraordinary creations of the visual arts. Having examined a copy of the Nativity closely, where Correggio surrounded the infant Jesus with incomparable light, I then stopped in amazement at the image of the descent from the cross. Some unknown copyist so successfully duplicated this image from the original that the most learned experts cannot distinguish copies from the originals. The body of Jesus, as a man, illustrates true death. The Virgin Mary, on whose knees the Saviour is laid, tilts her head down to him and stretches out her hands in despair; this pose alone shocks the soul. Intense sorrow is depicted on the weary face of the Mother of God, who dries her tears and does not let them spill from her half-closed eyes. 'Like a giant', says Mercier-Dupaty, 'who cannot take small steps, likewise it was impossible for Michelangelo to choose anything mediocre for a subject'. He imagined the Mother of God at the very moment when, seeing the scourges and death covering her son's body, she cried out with a rending heart: 'woe is me, my light and my joy are bound for the grave. My child and my God! Mark my words, I will be buried with him'.[6] Her face in this image says more than any words could. Two angels kneeling weep and their tears roll down like pearls. Any viewer is inevitably moved to tears themselves by the sight of these figures – the sorrow of the Virgin and the death of the Saviour. Even if Michelangelo had only crafted this one piece, his name would still be remembered for generations.

5    A paraphrase of Psalm 150.
6    Bronevskiy's note: 'See the canon "Lament of the Blessed Mother of God" [by Symeon the Logothete]'.

In the Carmelite monastery, an image covered by a curtain aroused my curiosity. Having pulled back the veil, I looked and was surprised, asking 'what is it?' A monk smiled and said it was Saint Genevieve. 'It's well to cover it,' I said as I replaced the curtain. The liberties of the Italian artists, it seems, already cross the line of decency and due respect for the icons of saints. In the Catholic churches there are many such paintings, from which the devout look away while others examine them at length and with great pleasure. Mary of Egypt, the Mother of God nursing the baby Jesus, Saint Theresa and the angels are copies of the Greek and Roman Venus and cupids. However, I saw in the image of the Annunciation a truly divine beauty and integrity in Mary. In the fresco of the Assumption painted on the dome of the church of the monastery of Saint Cecilia, one can see true angels. All of them are generally charming and among them are many small works which alternate with the larger pieces in a complimentary fashion. The only shame is that some of them are set so high that they are hiding in the clouds.

In the Church of Saint Francis, a painting of a guardian angel by the immortal brush of Raphael is displayed for its rarity. The angel's attire is white with snow and the surrounding light cannot be imitated; his eyes seem to glow with life and in all his features one can see the deity.

## Monks

In Italy, foreigners are surprised by the great number of monks. Especially in Messina, there are so many that in the streets, gardens and on the promenades one needs to look in earnest to find the secular folk. Their large numbers are the result of state decrees. In as much as the education of children of both sexes is granted to the clergy, and since their pupils usually wear black cassocks, the apparent number of monks and nuns increases. The advantages enjoyed by the clergy are excessive. In Sicily, the court and criminal law are mostly in the hands of the abbots. Rich monastic estates do not pay any taxes. The monks are not only personally exempt, but even their relatives – that is to say, their whole families – enjoy the same privilege. Noble families which have no members dedicated to the service of the church buy their privileges from monks who have no next of kin. Some parishes and even private households have the right of sanctuary, according to which a murderer with fresh blood on his hands hiding in such a church or home can avoid punishment by the civil authorities. These monks, having great wealth and all the means to lead a quiet and luxurious life, withdrawing from the public in their youth, being celibate and as is customary, taken into every home favourably, often cause turmoil in the families where they very soon learn how to make themselves necessary. Every decent household has its own confessor and abbot-tutor, who are included in all household arrangements and decisions; the will of the head of the household is largely in their hands. Their generous donations to the poor, instead of good, produce the greatest evil and by excess serve to expand that class of misfortunate idlers.

## Beggars

Those ugly half-humans – the beggars – wander and crawl about here in such crowds that one inevitably asks the question: what is the cause of their great numbers? The devotion of the local Catholics who consider it the chief virtue to give alms to those begging has made begging a lucrative craft. Generally, a large part of the people, according to the Italian expression '*il dolce far niente*' (sweet it is to do nothing) work no more or less than necessary to avoid starvation, which is little indeed with the availability of cheap and abundant food. If they could do no work at all and produce nothing, the Italian rabble would consider it fortunate, and beggars intending to agitate wounds on their body rejoice when they become incurable, in which case the situation of a beggar becomes undoubtedly more comfortable than that of a hardworking day labourer. It is all the more unpleasant to see them on the embankments of the harbour where the best society goes out for walks in the evening: here the beggars discover old wounds, the more depraved among them eat insects, mud and all manner of filth and put on displays of anguish and suffering until they are given their alms. The lower floors of large houses, out of philanthropy, are left for the refuge of these paupers, yet at night and even in poor weather, they lie in the streets and take shelter under the porticos and awnings. Once, when I went to the theatre, I gave a half-thaler to a beggar and the English officer accompanying me said to me: 'naturally you wouldn't know that these miserable creatures have no need for alms. I assure you I know this from experience. One man seemed to me to be completely dying, and taking out a Spanish doubloon (32 thalers), I asked him: 'if you have change, here is your thaler'. It seemed as if he could hardly speak before but he quite clearly asked me to accompany him to his dwelling and when I agreed, he set out briskly before me, despite his legs appearing crippled a minute ago. I was even more surprised when this beggar brought out from his cellar four rather large bags full of gold coins. There are some who amass ten thousand or more and one such figure recently before his death refused his daughter 10,000 thalers but donated 5,000 to the decoration of his parish church'.

## Criminals

Almost every day there is discovered a murder victim and a killer. Theft is conceded to the mob and murders are perpetrated by decent people. Scoundrels from the poor make up another class of beggar. They can be divided into rogues, murderers and so-called judicious thieves. The first, under the names of barons without baronies, are always well dressed. In the coffee and gambling houses, theatres and everywhere else, they banter and mock each other and if one manages to lift the pocket watch off a foreigner, he will boast as if it were a good deed. Their audacity is improbable. Once, when I went to dine with the minister, such a baron met me mounted on a beautiful horse, saying that he had not eaten in three days, and asked me for chocolate. I invited him to come to my quarters where I could not only feed him but hoped to render him some assistance. I could see that one of his arms was wounded and as I began to dress it, he hugged me firmly as if as a token of gratitude and began to search my pockets. He pulled out a thaler, gave the horse his spurs and rode off.

A beggar with a hardened heart and a fit body, having no time to steal stealthily in the middle of the day, will often kill a man without even finding a kopeck in his pockets. The daggers of these murderers can be employed as secret vengeance for a modest fee. One must be very wary of them and for protection many citizens carry pistols and walking canes with hidden blades, even with the permission of the government. The local mob reveres thievery done with agility and strangers never interfere if they witness a robbery; this agility cost the life of one of our best sailors. A thief yanked a handkerchief out of his pocket and ran down the street, while another waiting around the corner of a building struck the sailor in the heart with a dagger. The killer took refuge in a monastery with the right of sanctuary. The chief of police could not do anything but, at the request of our minister, the king ordered the extradition of the murderer. The monks released him in secret and effected his escape, for which they were deprived of that right. This unusual severity surprised the clergy. The royal guard, after a battle with the bandits, brought in the whole gang of them along with their leader.

The last class, the prudent robbers, constitute a large body. Scattered throughout the island, they obey a boss; the current leader, going under the name of a count, with swift and unrelenting vengeance has brought everyone to trepidation. He had previously divided his power and sold letters of protection to those who were already safe in town, on the roads and in the fortresses. Those robbed of justice by the courts, having then proven to him the truth of their cases, received satisfaction. The judges were killed on the street or sent to prison; in the former case, a note was usually left on the victim in his coat pocket with the most laconic message: 'for the bribes!' – in short, the excessive power of the nobility, the unrestraint of their crimes, and the limitations and difficulty of the justice system all were checked by the punitive dagger of this boss. The government is too weak and mild and seems to lack the strength or desire to destroy such a deeply rooted evil. Although in every district there are a sufficient number of *sbirri*, as they call their police investigators, they can be summarized with three words: rich, fat and lazy.

## Gardens

La Flora, the public garden, constitutes the finest decoration in Palermo. Two avenues divide it into four beds. One resembles several islands with gazebos and various models of Chinese bridges. Another is modelled after an English garden, where oaks, cypresses, plane trees and combinations of fruit trees are interspersed with fragrant bushes of rose, lavender, lily and jasmine. The third is planted with rare trees from distant lands around the world. The final bed was not yet finished and intended for ruins and follies. Eight paths emerge from the centre and at the end of each stands a gazebo or some other building; along their sides they are covered with rows of citrus trees and flowers which fill the air with perfume. In the centre on an octagonal clearing, arranged with cages of songbirds and fine statues, stands a beautiful statue with gold fish swimming in its marble basin. Another fountain at the end of the alley represents Panormus (the ancient name for Palermo) in the form of a crowned woman with an eagle (an emblem of Sicily) and the symbol of fidelity under foot;[7] a group of excellent ancient works.

On the queen's birthday, the garden and city are illuminated. The orange tree avenues appear as dark green walls strewn with shining stars between which, after a certain distance, pyramids of white fire are set. Covered alleys hung with colourful lanterns take on the appearance of decorated arcades. In the pure crystal of the fountain water dazzle pink, blue and violet lights. The orchestra in the distance heard on the wind, a nearby melancholy harmonica, ladies in white dresses and evocative shadows of the Champs-Élysées produced a delightful variety and the Flora took on that sort of decoration which poetry attributes to the magic gardens of myth and legend. On the embankment, crowds were surging like waves on the sea. The coaches and carriages circled around and could hardly move together with the throngs of pedestrians and all the homes along the water were lit with one unbroken pool of light. Toledo was decorated with transparent paintings. Palermo, enveloped in flame, seemed to perish. At every step, one's gaze was arrested, but the viewer, by will or compulsion, had to continue onward. Haberdasheries, fashionable shops and coffee houses on the lower floors were so diversely illuminated that Toledo attained its most brilliant form. Lamps, chandeliers of faceted crystal, mirrored candles and balls of water throwing

---

7    This sounds like a description of the Genius of Palermo, which is in the centre of the city's botanical garden, depicting a crowned figure sitting on a rock with a sceptre, eagle, snake and dog and rests his foot on a lictor's fasces, but he is a bearded old man and not a woman. A ruined tablet below reads '*prima sedes, corona regis et regni caput*' to proclaim that Palermo was the first seat, capital and site for coronation of the medieval Kingdom of Sicily. Jeremy Dummett, *Palermo, City of Kings: The Heart of Sicily* (London: I. B. Tauris, 2015), pp.212-213.

light upon bronze, silver, artfully hung fabrics, and along with the multicoloured lanterns hung on the arches and columns of porches and awnings, splitting, refracting, and casting innumerable rays, spread the brilliance like a million stars brought down by sorcery from the heavenly vault.

The Royal Botanical Garden, situated behind the Flora, is not extensive, but all of the medicinal products from the four corners of the world are grown there.

Palermo is famous for its gardens and is surrounded by them; no capital can boast to have better. Those belonging to the nobility do not yield to the magnificence of the crown's. They are all regular, trimmed, filled with statues and water fountains and generally present more magnificence than charm. The home of the Prince Belmonte, which occupies the wild cliffs at the foot of Mount Pellegrino by the sea, was soon cultivated with a garden in the English mode that robs the glory of other superfluous gardens.

## Bagheria

Bagheria, famous for its gardens, lies 12 *versta*s [12.8 km] from Palermo and occupies the whole length of the Cape of Zafferano which forms the east of the Bay of Palermo. This is the home of the richest nobility and is adorned with a wonderful collection of palaces, old castles, triumphal gates, mausoleums, arboretums and houses of every sort of architecture, laid out as if by a general plan. In a comfortable climate and under a clear sky, the gardens of Bagheria are always green and bountiful with flowers and fruits. The beauty of nature, revealed by the hand of taste and artfulness, is presented here in full splendour.

The Monastery of Silence, which is always shown first, deserves special attention. It is surrounded by a wall with four towers at its corners. Banging on the knocker, a porter appeared with a heavy ring of keys and silently unlocked the door. The gate creaked open and after we passed into the courtyard, we went up the landing to the cells. In the corridor, a barefoot monk wearing a worn cassock girded by a woollen belt grasped the rope of the bell to call our arrival, but was stopped by our appearance and turned his head to look at us with curiosity. At the other end of the corridor a servant in secular clothes was sweeping the floor, but when he saw us, he lifted his head and leaned on his brush, also seemingly surprised by our attire. The first cell was opened. A young monk sitting at a table with a glass of wine and a cheerful smile seemed to be regaling and offering us to join him. I wished to take a glass but his hand did not relinquish it; it was as cold as ice – the charm vanished and I saw before me a wax statue. Sliced oranges, pomegranates and dates whetted our appetites but they too were only wax in my hand. In the second cell, an old monk was reclined reading. At our entrance, he slowly lowered the book from his eyes and began to sit up; but as if we had said not to worry and being so confined, he remained in his present posture. In the third cell, Héloise sat at a writing table in deep and sweet meditation with pen in hand. Her pose and charming, touching facial features conveyed her unhappy passion. In the fourth cell was the dying Abélard.[8] His pale face and languid eyes betray a man with one foot already in the grave. His pained love, it seemed, had not yet died out. His right hand was clutching his heart. These wax statues have been so excellently constructed that it is impossible not to mistake them for the living. The mechanism that put them into motion and thereby made the deception even more convincing, unfortunately, was mostly deteriorated.

The home of Duchess Patorno has a majestic appearance. It contains a fine and even rare illustration. In the first room there are portraits of sovereigns who had patronized the sciences and arts. Scanning over their eyes, my gaze stopped on the face of the greatest of Tsars. 'Here is our Peter!' I reflexively exclaimed, and all the Russians – however many of us were there – crowded around the portrait and looked on him gratefully. They viewed no other portrait in that room. In the next room, three paintings in the full height and length of the walls portray the battles of Granicus, Issus and Gaugamela. Several full-sized figures bear a marvellous liveliness. Alexander the Great could be recognized by his light helmet. His horse was leaping lively with tail and mane flying in the air. You cannot look without shuddering as the Scythian cavalry cuts into the Greek ranks and as the Macedonian phalanx repels the Persian infantry. The terrible bloodletting is depicted with astonishing accuracy. It will take several days to view all the images with the necessary attention. I will mention only the best examples: 1) Venus and Mars depicted when Vulcan intends to catch them with his net. It cannot be expressed with what colours the artist has depicted the charms of the goddess of love. Her scarlet lips seemed to be roses. The mixture of modesty and passion can be seen in all the features of her face and she weakly pushed away the hand of Mars. He, the most beautiful of men, stands before Venus on one knee and stooping over. The helmet, dropped in haste, still rolls across the grass. It is impossible not to envy this happy god. Cupid leans against a tree with his right hand on his knee, wearing a sly smile and pointing to the corner of the painting where the head of jealous Vulcan appears in the shadow. The expected end of this confrontation is writ boldly. 2) Armida resting with Rinaldo under the shade of a tree. On a hot day, you would want to be in that beautiful grove and on the shore of that stream. 3) A sleeping beauty, carelessly uncovered, will always attract the gaze

---

8    Heloise was a 12th Century French noblewoman who had a love affair and surviving correspondence with her tutor, the philosopher and theologian Peter Abélard, before becoming a nun and abbess. The salient feature of her letters was the unapologetic rejection of political marriage – likened to prostitution – in favour of romantic love. Peter Abélard and Héloïse, *Letters of Abelard and Heloise with a Particular Account of their Lives, Amours and Misfortunes* (Chiswick: Whittingham, 1824), pp.1-43.

and perhaps even the hands of spectators. 4) In a Claude Joseph Vernet painting, the sea is agitated and the clouds are flying but the ships are almost motionless. 5) Virgil strains the last of his strength and writes his own epitaph. 6) The capture of Messina; a grand canvas. A storm and the drowning and burning ships below are presented so naturally that it feels as though you are in danger when you look upon them. 7) Masaniello in his red cap, a simple fisherman turned leader of the discontented, is different from the other rebels. The expression in his eyes and the dagger in his hand foreshadow what can be expected from him.

Near the home of Patorno we saw the wonderful building – practically a castle – belonging to the Duke Palagonia surrounded by moderate walls on which ugly statues are placed. It is not possible to pass them without laughing: a horse with a bovine head; a donkey with the head of a turkey; a harlequin, a Quaker and a Frenchman in fashionable clothes; King Midas with donkey ears; and finally a human figure with a wolf's snout, wearing a uniform coat and cocked hat so evocative[9] that one cannot mistake whose likeness he is meant to bear. The gate of the palazzo and the courtyard in front of the house are set with ugly images of all kinds of animals not found in nature. The flight of stairs of the finest Sicilian marble leading into the front of the house is decorated with family busts. In the first chamber, the ceiling is comprised of four large mirrors joined at their corners such that when five people enter, twenty are seen above. All the doors in the home are lined with broken mirrors mixed with crystal and all the glass was in various colours: blue, green, red, yellow and purple. The next room featured Chinese columns of porcelain; some of which are made from broken kettles, coffee pots, cups and even vases. The marble tables are embedded with glass, tortoiseshell, nacre and expensive stones. The whole house is filled with reptiles, demons, ugly dolls made of porcelain and variously coloured marble. In summary, this magic castle represents not only the Ovidian metamorphic and romantic adventures of the pagan gods, but also the wondrous dreams of a frustrated imagination; the most ridiculous of which is a man with a large head on a skinny body, riding a crocodile, sailing across a strait to an island, and dragging behind himself on ropes a flotilla of hideous boats! What surprised me more however, was the chapel of this eccentric host. The first thing that will amaze a visitor on entering is the representation of hell, where mutilated fools lie about frying in fire or hanging by their ribs. In the depiction of heaven, Saint Rosalia is the central figure, who is flanked by Christ and the Virgin Mary, and above are half-angels and half-demons. In the middle of the chapel are four winged animals, which I was told represent the Four Evangelists. On the plafond, Saint Francis is lashed with ropes

9    Bronevskiy's note: 'That wolf in particular, with his fierce and bold predation, once inspired fear and horror to many nations but now has been caught and deprived of his means'.

to a wooden cross while at his feet hangs a large chandelier. It is not clear how such liberties, especially among Catholics, are tolerated by the government.

Leaving the house of oddities, the garden which we entered begins with an alley covered with grape vines where one becomes accustomed with the famous Greeks, Romans, popes and kings through their busts. The vast garden is a wonder of luxury, splendour and order. Every lane is straight. Pavilions made from cypress trees, summer houses, artificial ruins, grottos and cellars all stand in careful symmetry. Patterned flower gardens with fountains and topiaries cut into spheres, cones and pyramids exhaust the eyes. Alleys of trellises are broken up with garlands. The uniformity and artificial appearance in every object means that in a regimented garden such as this, one only needs to view a portion to have seen the whole. Only a few paces are necessary to tour the whole grounds. There is no pleasure in strolling through such a garden, for the refined craftsmanship which disfigures nature cannot strike the imagination.

The gate, the arch of which was beginning to deteriorate, attracts attention with its antiquity. Two lions of black marble lie on either side of the gate and heavy streams of water flow from their open mouths. Through the gate we entered an English garden. A myriad of paths strewn with sand and rambling through the grass in all directions, crossing and merging with one another, take one through the valleys and hills. Flowering trees, untouched by shears and interspersed with oaks and poplars, seemed to us northerners such a spectacle that we esteemed ourselves transported to a land of enchantment. Lemon and orange waft through the air, fig and almond trees are laden with fruits. Passing a stream barely trickling through the sand, we saw a noisy spring that gurgles determinately from under the root of a stump. In this garden, it seems, nothing is artificial; nature in her full majesty, generously offers her gifts and the soul, lost in pleasure, meets every object with new amazement. At every step, you think to stop and it continues to unfold further and further ahead.

Ascending a hill covered with oaks, cedars and hazel trees, we saw a gardener and behind him ran a straight avenue of orange trees which ended with a small house with a green roof, appearing like the projection from a magic lantern. We descended and ran down the line. The house was bright, clean and standing on a platform dotted with flowers. Before its modest façade, a fountain threw up water in a circle of arcs like a sheaf. Several paths from the house, as from the centre of the garden, lead in all different directions. We chose a path lined with jasmine and came to a marble basin. Four nude nymphs, noticing a satyr lurking behind a rose bush, plunge into the water, but in timid confusion, they stand up again one by one knowing that the clear water cannot conceal them, and turn their backs to the satyr, thus all the more exposed from the front. This charming confusion is portrayed so well that it seems the marble itself is blushing. In another basin, a beautiful Bacchante serves a seashell to a monster so that it might drink. The whole garden is filled with fountains in which many have no water but the most excellent statues hold attention. The whole mythology of gods and goddesses is there; from their multitude, the vegetation and the flow of water, they seem animated. Here, the tritons, sirens and naiads splash about; there, Pan, nymphs and cupids rest in the shade or play on the young grass. Some of them would have done honour to the Greek chisel. I will mention only those that I liked the most. 1) Daphne, pursued by Apollo, runs between laurel and myrtle bushes, becomes snagged, and falls. Apollo rushes ahead and will soon overtake her. Poor Daphne! By her face one can see her fear, vexation, and the pain of the branches scratching her legs and tearing her clothes. 2) A girl in a short and light dress dancing with a tambourine in her hands is frozen in the best posture. This marble seems almost translucent. The folds in the fabric are so well hung that they reveal the whole figure of the torso and illustrate all the flexibility of the body. 3) Leda and the swan. An absolutely extraordinary work of art! Observing Leda, one wants to become the swan.

Following the sound of water, we came to a splendid waterfall. It shoots out from a natural rock on which could be seen the occasional curving tree. Falling with a terrible yearning, it crashes into a spray, boiling and rushing on as only foam, but reforms and flows further to roll on as a quietly murmuring stream. Climbing along the shore of that stream, at every step we met new items. On one side, a half-withered olive tree stood over ruins that had sunk into the ground; on the other, Neptune floated in his shell; and on the hill, a broad ring of trees concealed a tomb, showered with flowers by a weeping genius.

The sun was already setting and we did not get to examine the third garden before being forced to return. We boarded the carriages, passed a sugar plantation and a field of cotton, crossed the Chinese bridge which connects to artificial hills with one arch and finally looked on the temple of glory standing on the steep rock of the Cape of Zafferano where the sea crashes.

## 54

# Sailing from Palermo to Malta

---

On the 6th [18th] of November, not without regret, we left that capital where wealth, luxury, idleness and poverty come together in a strange combination. Variable and gentle winds favoured our voyage. In the evening of the 7th [19th], we reached the strait between the Aegadian Islands and Sicily. The island of Marettimo, with a castle serving as a prison, recalls the punishment of the most terrible and fierce criminals. One of our Neapolitan pilots assured us that some of the condemned are made to sit on logs over the water, others are sent down into the dungeon, and others still are marked to starve to death while chained to the wall. Patricides in particular are thrown in the sea to be torn apart by sharks. The smoke of the French Revolution, which wafted over the Neapolitans, filled the castle of Marettimo with whole families of Jacobins, most of whom perished and not many were ever returned to the light. The anguishes of torture, quartering, breaking on the wheel and dismemberment by horses did not reduce criminal activities. The judgements from the Criminal Court of the Kingdom of Naples constitute atrocities of immeasurable magnitude. One woman from Palermo, known as the Infernal Witch, derived a poison from whitewash which left no sign on the body. She sold it for 40 years before her crimes were finally exposed. A wife, wishing to dispose of her husband, put the poison in his pasta and retired to another room, saying she already ate. Left alone, she became horrified by her crime and wished to forewarn her victim, but when she ran back into the room, she saw that her only son, a 10-year-old child, had eaten half the plate. She clutched the child and fainted, waking up to find her son now in agonizing convulsions and dying in her arms. The unfortunate mother recognized her atrocity and demanded death for herself. The old woman who provided her the poison gave up in court a list of over 5,000 such clients.[1]

---

1    Bronevskiy is likely referring to Giulia Tofana, a Palermo poisoner with a predominantly married, female clientele. A solution of lead and arsenic is attributed to her with the name

The town of Trapani, where Aeneas lost his father Anchises, stands on a low peninsula, beyond which are Marsala and Mazara surrounded by green mountains and a sea abounding with corals and pearls. These make for a pleasing view where the rare abundance of the land is met in equal measure by the marvelous wealth of the sea. On the 9th [21st] of November, strong winds from the southeast forced us to tack about and be wary of the dangerous submerged rocks called the Skerki lying in the middle of the sea between Sicily and Africa and not precisely located on the maps. Over the stones there are 11 feet [3.35 m] of depth and small ships pass through them without any harm during calm weather. On the 11th [23rd], the western horizon was covered with clouds which were rolling towards us and two strong winds fought each other. We reduced our sails in anticipation. Soon the wind with rain and thunder prevailed and a storm descended on us. As we were already close to Malta, we lay to for the night. At dawn on the 12th [24th], when we had no hope of entering the harbour, the wind unexpectedly softened and we were able to reach Malta under all sails. As soon as we dropped anchor and tethered ourselves to the walls of Valletta, the wind resumed its cruelty. If we did not reach the harbour in time, we would have been compelled to endure a storm on the sea that would last two days.

View of Malta. Illustration from original publication.

'Aqua Tofana,' which she sold for 50 years. One of her own customers reported her to the Papal authorities and she confessed under torture at least 600 names of clients and victims. She was executed in Rome in 1659. A. Wallace Hayes (ed.), *Hayes' Principles and Methods of Toxicology*, 6th ed. (Roca Raton, Florida: CRC Press, 2014), p.15.

# 55

# Malta

## Port and Fortifications

The Maltese port consists of two bays. The first to the east of the town of Valletta is divided into many small bays where ships stand over a depth of 6 to 12 *sazhen*s [12.8-25.6 m], safe from all winds except those vessels close to Valletta, as they were subjected to exciting northerly winds and violent waves from the west. The second bay to the west, called Marsamuscetto, has in its centre Fort Manoel which serves as the quarantine for goods imported from contaminated locales. In this bay, the ships are completely separated from each other in quarantine. At the entrance to Malta, vessels should adhere to the right-hand side because the cape on the left has a small stony reef. The width of the entrance is not more than 125 *sazhen*s [266.7 m].

Malta is revered as one of the strongest fortresses in the world. It consists of the following nine fortifications surrounding the gulf: 1) Valletta, named after the Grandmaster Jean de Valette who founded it in 1566; 2) Fort Saint Elmo on the tip of Valletta's peninsula which protects the entrance to the harbour; 3) Floriana, behind the town on the same peninsula; 4) Vittoriosa, meaning 'the victorious', is so named in commemoration of a stubborn battle against the Turks. It was formerly called Birgu; 5) The Citadel of Sant'Angelo, which protects the entrance to the port with a three-tiered artillery battery; 6) Fort Santa Margherita; 7) The town of Senglea; 8) Fort Cottonera, whose walls protect the land routes of the previous five forts; and 9) Fort Ricasoli, which lies on the eastern side of the entrance to the harbour, opposite several strong batteries. The walls of hewn stone and all the fortifications are in the best possible condition. At the entrance of the harbour, the sight of such a multitude of forts will surprise every traveller, but judging by the nearly 40,000-man garrison that would be necessary for defending it, all the towers and bastions seem almost useless and the whole island is not worth the costs of maintaining its garrison and repairing its walls and other structures. The

Master Alof de Wignacourt laid irrigation from Citta Vecchia (the old city) and this glorious aqueduct has existed since 1616. Malta cannot be surmounted; it can only be conquered by the one who takes London. Without a strong fleet, it is not possible to besiege the island. By its advantageous position, in the hands of the English, Malta became a focus of Mediterranean trade. Having in it a safe haven, the British fleet sent out squadrons into the Strait of Messina and the island of Favignana to disrupt communications between the French and Spanish ports with the Levant. In Valletta, for the conservation of grain, vast underground magazines were built in the soft stone of the mountain and ventilation pipes ensure that the stores are safe from moisture. The government purchases all the grain coming from Sicily and Russia and shipments from Spain already arrive on neutral vessels.

## Valletta

The town of Valletta, or as it is typically known, Malta, has a view distinguished from all that I had seen before. There are no streets save for only one running from the square to the mountain ridge, all the other paths are staircases carved out of the stone of the steep slopes. The houses are high without roofs and generally of old Italian architecture, all the windows have balconies and wooden frames painted red. The walls are built very thick, due to the limestone being soft enough to be quarried from the mountain with axes and only hardening up when exposed to the air. Shops are filled with colonial goods and the town is so clean that it is easy to guess that the English are governing here.

As soon as we dropped anchor, the captain of the port with the adjutant to Admiral Alexander John Ball congratulated us on our arrival and the latter invited our captain and the other officers to dinner on the behalf of his admiral and the commandant of Malta. We really did not really wish to attend, as it required powdering our hair, wearing dress shoes and riding off to endure tedious compulsions. Beyond expectations, we did not sit very long at the table, however this was only in order to escort the ladies into another hall and when the gentlemen returned, the servants departed and we began to drink. If the English exclude their women from their company when they intend to get drunk, then naturally they save them from their most unpleasant pastime. Rising from the table, the ladies occupied special chambers where the gentlemen only entered when requested. They brought me into one of them and introduced me to a Lady Elliot who wished for me to converse with her daughter in Russian. When I turned and saw her, I became mixed up and forgot my mother tongue. She blushed and darted her eyes away and back as if to say 'please start speaking'. Finally a few words fairly well pronounced by her satisfied the mother and others. Our conversation was interrupted by an invitation to the theatre. The ladies stood up, left behind the needlework they were engaged in, and went to the theatre together, which was small for the present audience but very clean for Italy. The music was excellent and the ballet was elegant. In the opera buffa, the truly buffoonish fool, actresses and dancers compelled applause from the parterre by their beauty rather than their artfulness.

First thing the next day, we set out to see the Church of Saint John. Its appearance was Gothic and had nothing attractive about its exterior, but its interior has such artful architecture and tastefully rich ornamentation that justice must be given. The mosaic floor deserves special attention and is considered to be the richest in the world. It portrays tombstones with inscriptions and images depicting the feats of the deceased Knights of Malta. Precious porphyritic stone, marble, lapis lazuli, agate, jasper and other expensive materials comprise portions of the mosaic, which certainly must have cost a great sum. One portrays a naval battle, another a broken pyramid, and a third bears coats of arms and trophies; in summary, the whole breadth of mosaics which number at least two thousand is difficult to express. Along the sides of the church were eight altars decorated with monuments to the grandmasters of the order. I will note the best of them: on the annex of Saint George are two Moors holding up a white marble tomb on which a bust is placed, although I cannot remember which master it portrayed; the purity of the marble and the shape of this monument is excellent in all respects. Saint Catherine's featured a mosaic portrait of a grandmaster which was indistinguishable from the painted copy and the tints and shades of all its stones were chosen with the utmost craftsmanship. From the church, we descended into the catacombs where the bones of the grandmasters who distinguished themselves with peaceful exploits are buried. A small hall receives light from above with tombs on either side. On the cover of the first is carved a statue in monastic robes from a single piece of marble. This monument was dedicated to Fillippe de l'Isle-Adam, the founder of the Order of the Knights of Saint John of Jerusalem.[1] The tomb of Jean de Valette was moulded out of copper and was portrayed in a knight's panoply with his hands folded over the cross, which trembles if you touch it. Jean de la Cassière in a cardinal's cassock is sculpted in clay on his tomb's lid. The former, as it is known, founded the city, and the latter commissioned this church. The other grandmasters

---

1    Fillippe de l'Isle-Adam was not the founder of the order; he was the 42nd Grandmaster. During his tenure, he secured the Island of Malta as the order's new permanent residence in 1530 after they lost the Island of Rhodes to the Ottoman Empire in 1522. The original order began as the hospital at the Church of the Holy Sepulchre in Jerusalem under the rector Peter Gerald which was converted into a monastic order in 1099 after the First Crusade captured the city and was recognized by Papal Bull in 1113. The order was militarized under his successor, Raymond du Puy in 1118, known variously thereafter as the Knights Hospitaller, Knights of St. John, Knights of Rhodes and Knights of Malta. Whitworth Porter, *A History of the Knights of Malta* (revised ed.) (London: Longmans, Green and Co., 1883), pp.9-20.; Ibid., pp.375-386.; Ibid., pp.695-696.

have busts with inscriptions. From the catacombs, we were brought into the church proper of Saint John the Baptist. It consists of a hall with windows overhead. Great paintings representing the exceptional deeds of the knights decorate its walls; the best of the images in my opinion is of the beheading of Saint John. The cruelty of Herodias and the horror of the servant holding the plate with the served head are depicted with extraordinary skill. The most opulent of all is the annex of Mary Magdalene which is adorned with silver lattice exceeding a man's height and a massive chandelier. Three other gilded images and all the utensils of gold or silver were sent to France by the ever-pious Frenchmen during their occupation of the island. That great nation leaves everywhere a similar monument to itself. In the same annex, we were shown examples of Byzantine painting of a very poor quality and their only dignity is the claim that they were painted 300 to 500 years ago.

By evening, we went out into the newly planted garden. It was small and consisted of two paths and three beds and seemed to be intended only for flowers. A strong wind and heavy clouds forced us to hurry back. As soon as we entered the street, rain began to pour down with such volume and force that benches were carried down the path and trays and tables full of produce in the market were knocked over. We ducked into an English tavern, lit the fireplace and asked for coffee and pipes, laughing at the adventure of a companion who slipped on the pavement and fell into a puddle. The doors opened and with the same sort of laughter entered several English naval officers. In a minute we were all acquainted. We invited them to dry themselves by the fire, tea was served followed by punch, and we conversed unceasingly. The wind howled outside and the rain beat against the windows. We endeavoured to pass the time together but disputed over who was hosting whom until the matter was settled by every man paying his own way. Some went to the theatre while the others stayed to cook a fine supper. When the theatre finished and the inn was filled with visitors, our fellows returned and we went out into the hall where the table was especially covered and set for us. To our surprise, it was occupied. A king of the stage in a crown and mantle with Diana and nymphs at his side loudly called for a servant to wait on him. The owner stepped in and announced to them that the table was reserved and the actors stood up and apologized, but we decided to invite them to join us. The agility and learned expressiveness of the actors knew how to quickly revitalize the conversation. The modesty of the actresses soon relaxed into a casual gaiety. Music was struck up as the theatre owner wanted to compensate us for our courtesy and surprise us with an unexpected treat. After the meal, the actors offered their crafts. The dancers were as light as zephyrs and as slender as the graces when performing their tarantellas, all'espagnolas and other national dances. The singers delighted us with some of the best arias. Meanwhile, glasses rang, wine was pouring and many hung heads were lost in pensive thought; finally, those who were not passed out already wished to retire for the evening. Another dispute arose over who would occupy the room and lots were cast without satisfaction. The decision defaulted to the host, who assigned a bedroom to each man, but still we squabbled. Ultimately, the best chambers were taken by those who could reach them first. I received the beautiful hem of a parka, a satin blanket, a mirror over a bed, and a poor cupid mercilessly nailed to the ceiling by his puffed out cheeks. A silk curtain hung over the window. I threw myself into the bed but I had slept enough already that night and rose again after an hour.

## Citta Vecchia

At the invitation of our Consul, Antonio Regnaud Carcas, having dined at his country home, we visited Citta Vecchia (Mdina), 10 *verstas* [10.67 km] from Velletta. We did not ride so much as roll along that fine road hewn into the stone, covered by walls on both sides. By the lay of the island, sloping from the centre to the shore, the walls towering one behind another give Malta the appearance of a heap of white stones when viewed from the sea. In fact, the ground consists of thin stone in many places covered with earth no thicker than two *vershoks* [8.89 cm]. The diligence of the 100,000 inhabitants, an excessive number for the given area, has transformed an island seemingly condemned to eternal desolation into a vast garden. The cultivation of this land requires extraordinary labour. The stone is first broken into small pieces and then driven into the earth and interspersed with it and special pits are needed for planting trees. The Maltese stone contains such moisture that despite the great heat, all the plants thrive better here than on Sicily. For the processing of cotton, growing here in abundance, factories have been established. Besides oranges,[2] preferred by the Portuguese, melons transported from Sicily on beds of earth and other fruits are grown to be the most delicious. The inhabitants of Malta receive most of their food from Sicily. Passing several suburban houses built in the English style, of which there ought to have been more here, we saw Citta Vecchia standing on the mountain, which was not especially high but was very steep. The town is encircled by walls which are completely neglected and greatly deteriorated. Over the gate, we were shown an Arabic inscription and, in the town, A Punic inscription is preserved on a building named the Palazzo dei Giurati, but no one could interpret it for me. The town was

---

2   Bronevskiy's note: 'Here, oranges are grafted to a pomegranate tree, from which they acquire a red-coloured flesh'. Translator's note: Blood oranges, which Bronevskiy alludes to, are a natural mutation and cannot be produced by grafting together orange and pomegranate trees, though it was once a widely-believed myth. 'On Budding and Grafting or the Influence of the Stock Upon the Scion and Vice Versa,' *Journal of Horticulture, Cottage Gardener and Home Farmer*, vol. 5, series 3 (1883): pp.173-174.

called Medina under Arab rule and when the Knights acquired it, it was made the capital and named Citta Notabile. It was quiet in the town, the streets were overgrown with grass, we did not meet a single pedestrian and the houses seemed to be empty. We were brought to the Cathedral of Saint Paul, where ancient vessels and clothes were preserved. Unfortunately, the caretaker was not home and we had to satisfy our curiosity with the church alone. The gate is cast from copper and its poorly-made images from Scripture indicate that they were made in the Middle Ages during the decline of the arts and sciences. The cathedral is massive, in two storeys, with walls covered by already quite old brocade. The altars decorated with crooked columns and two ancient Greek images attract attention.

The abbot of the monastery volunteered to show us the cave of the Apostle Paul. A *versta* [1.07 km] from the town stood a chapel in the centre of the cloister and enclosing its entrance. Descending a few steps, we entered the holy dwelling. It consists of three chambers, one of which has a crucifix carved on the wall, the second shows the semblances of a bed, and the third was unfinished and seemed to serve as a kitchen, as one wall was black with soot. The Apostle Paul, having suffered a shipwreck on the island of Malta, walked to the docks and while taking shelter in a cave, was bit by a serpent and shook it off into the fire, blessed the earth and smeared some of it over his wound. For that reason, the monk assured us, there are no snakes on the island and the soil has the ability to cure poisonous bites and stings. Both are true, for indeed on Malta there are no reptiles and the Maltese soil, soft and yellow like chalk and sticking to the fingers, produces sweat and strengthens the stomach. The grotto on the eastern side of the island, which is called Calypso's, we did not have time to inspect. And so the cave of the Apostle Paul and the Grotto of Calypso, according to experts who have probably determined the positions of places with the descriptions of the ancients, are on the Island of Malta and not the Adriatic islands of Meleda or Fano as others believe.

## History of Malta

In remote antiquity, Malta was ruled by the African King Battus. Homer mentions this island under the name of Hyperia and says that it was inhabited by the Phaeacians. The Phoenicians then established a colony on it, called Ogygia. The Greeks took possession of the island in 736 BC and gave it the name of Melite, either because they discovered honey there or in honour of the nymph. From the Greeks, the island passed over to the Carthaginians and the Knights of Rhodes have found many inscriptions there in the Punic language. During the war for Sicily, the Romans drove out Carthage and placed Malta under the jurisdiction of the Praetor of Sicily. After the fall of the Roman Empire in the first half of the 5th century AD, it was controlled by the Goths and then the Vandals. At the end of the 9th century, the Arabs became its proprietors. The 11th century saw the coming of the Normans under Count Roger who expelled the Saracens and from 1190, Malta belonged to Sicily. Charles d'Anjou, brother of Saint Louis, annexed it to his possessions. It is believed that John of Procida was exiled to the island for his conspiracy which resulted in the Sicilian Vespers. After this, Malta fell to the Kings of Castile and Aragon and Charles V, King of Spain, in 1530 bestowed it on the Knights of Saint John of Jerusalem exiled from Rhodes. With the help of other Christian powers, the knights were strengthened and bravely defended against the Turks; later their fleet successfully defended trade from the predation of the Barbary pirates. In 1798, General Bonaparte, on his way to Egypt, landed a portion of his army by some likely secret compact, and after several shots, the island, for all the strength of its fortifications, was surrendered to the French. British and Russian squadrons blockaded Malta for two years.[3] Over the course of the blockade, the knights sent deputies to St. Petersburg, wishing to gain their lost independence. The Emperor Paul I, accepting the title of grandmaster at their request, had good intentions in mind. The Royalists expelled from France among the ranks of the order had found a refuge on Malta and thus hoped to resist the ambitious designs of the revolutionary government. The vow of the knights to patronize the seafaring Christian powers in any conflict against the Turks would likely have changed their objectives. The introduction of the Greek language would have restored the decadent knights, as Greece and Slavonia, having received a strong promotion in European politics, naturally soon emerged from insignificance. A strong Russian fleet would make Malta an irresistible stronghold, the freedom of Italy would always have readers of truth and law at its disposal, and if the foresighted monarch's wishes were accomplished, it would be possible to say with certainty that Europe would have been saved from many of the disasters that plague her today. As it is known, Malta ran out of provisions and was forced to surrender to the British before the deputies could notify them of the high and reliable patronage they had won. The Order of Saint John enjoyed its advantages for a short time, then it was abolished and now, although it still retains a grandmaster, he has only titular powers and resides in Palermo as a private citizen. The Maltese are distinguished by their customs and habits, which neither time nor circumstances have altered; they are brave, hardworking and work patiently, though with displeasure, at loosening their bondage. Their lifestyle and attitude toward foreigners is similar to that of the Sicilians. The common people speak a corrupted Arabic, while the nobility use Italian. The air which is cooled by the winds is healthy, but in the summer the city becomes excessively hot.

---

3     Ushakov's squadron aborted their effort to help blockade Malta in order to besiege and capture Corfu. Britain was assisted however by Portuguese and Neapolitan forces. Ward et al., *Cambridge Modern History*, vol. 8, pp.629-646.

## Russian Prisoners

No small number of our prisoners and deserters, for the most part coerced to serve, can be found in almost every state, especially in Austria. Despite the agreements for releasing prisoners of war, a great number still remain in captivity – Bonaparte forced them into his Polish Legions, the Austrians pressed them into the Croatian regiments, the English sent them to their colonies, as did the Swedes and Danes, and it can be said that these unfortunates are scattered all over the globe. The English in particular use every means to retain the Russians in their service; but who does not love their fatherland? At the first convenient opportunity, they flee in disgust as soon as a Russian military ship arrives in port. The Russians are relieved from guard detail and never return to their barracks. On our arrival it was evident that they did not have time to take the necessary precautions and eight such men appeared on our frigate. The next day, the adjutant to the governor asked, without any further inconvenience or searching, that we return their runaway soldiers. On the instructions of the captain, I answered that we did not have the habit of accepting foreigners and we could vouch that there was not a single Englishman aboard our frigate. 'Perhaps it would be found', answered the adjutant, 'that you presently have a larger number of souls aboard than you announced to the fire watch upon your arrival'.

'Were that so, do you keep Russians in your regiments?'

'Of course not', said the adjutant dismissively and then left and did not say another word about it.

In the same way, we took on several men in Messina. It is impossible to remain silent here on the point that our ambassadors, by virtue of the treaties and the powers instilled in them, being citizens of those foreign cities where they solely represent our government, not knowing the language, and most importantly not being Russians themselves, solicit far too weakly, it seems, on the behalf of our prisoners of war, who are moved from country to country and service to service and are detained everywhere without proper protection. On the contrary, where the consuls are Russian, or at least assigned from those foreigners who did not own property at their posts, we usually received our men released legally and generally such towns and cities had no prisoners. In 1807, as everyone knows, a regiment was assembled in Malta from Russians, Slavonians, Poles and Greeks who rebelled when they were to be sent to the East Indies, locked themselves in a fortress and, after a brave defence, set fire to a powder magazine; together with them, several inhabitants and one ship were blown into the air.[4]

---

4    The Froberg Regiment which mutinied on 23 March [4 April], 1807 also contained
     Albanians, Serbians, Greeks and Bulgarians, mostly all recruited from the Ottoman

Empire, and had predominantly German officers overseeing their training. Feeling tricked by their recruiters and mistreated by their officers, they barricaded themselves in Fort Ricasoli and hoisted the Russian naval ensign in place of the British colours, demanding a discharge and safe conduct to Russia. They threatened not only to kill their hostages, but to fire the fort's guns on the city if their demands were refused. Many of the men defected back to the British side when provisions ran low, but a minority retreated into the powder store and set fire to it. They escaped before the explosion and were not captured and hanged until 13 [25] April. Whitworth Porter, *Malta and Its Knights* (London: Pardon and Son, 1871), pp.351-354.; J. Aikin (ed.), 'Narrative of the Late Mutiny at Malta,' *The Athenaeum* 2 (1807): pp.343-347.; Albert Ganado, 'The Froberg Mutiny at Fort Ricasoli in 1807,' *Times of Malta*, last modified October 16, 2016. https://www.timesofmalta.com/articles/view/20161016/life-features/The-Froberg-mutiny-at-Fort-Ricasoli-in-1807.628162.

**56**

# Sailing to Cagliari

We departed from Malta on the 19th [31st] of November. At the narrowest point of the entrance, the wind changed and the frigate was nearly cast ashore. After two careful rotations, we reached open water. The winds were strong and foul and did not let up for the entire voyage to Cagliari. Following the Sicilian coast to the west, we slowly proceeded but had the pleasure of overtaking an American military brig, which was famous for its ease of movement. In Malta, I made a point of visiting them. In Messina, I saw a schooner. Not only the appearance of the American warships, but also the comfortable design, the mechanism of their rigging, their strength and even cleanliness prevail a great deal over the English vessels. It seemed not long ago that the great rulers of the sea found a dangerous rival in the United States. The green banks of Sicily presented beautiful locales at every stretch. Girgenti, standing on the site of ancient Agrigentum, now serves as a hub of trade in bread and salt. On the hill in front of the town, one can see several poor huts, among which stands a ruined wall from a temple to Zeus. After passing the barren and uninhabited island of Pantalleria in the middle of the sea between Sicily and Africa, before the dangerous Skerki reefs, the wind intensified on the evening of the 22nd of November [3rd of December], black clouds swept overhead at an extreme speed, the sun sank into the sea with a purple glow and the night became oppressively dark. Light strobed in the distant clouds and at 9 o'clock, when the wind was very strong with rain pouring in from the opposite direction, the sails lay against the masts, the frigate rolled onto one side and then swung back and capsized to the other. A thunderstorm began, lightning crashed down one after another all across the sea, and electric sparks scattered over the decks. The whole crew was called above deck and mustered all of their strength to brace about the yards.[1] A strong stench of sulphur indicated that the frigate had caught

---

1    Bronevskiy's note: 'To rotate them to the opposite side of the mast'.

fire somewhere and the danger was heightened by the fact that we had taken on 200 *pud*s [3.28 t] of gunpowder in Malta which lay in the hold, being unable to all fit in the powder magazine. The captain and officers with lanterns in their hands ran about and looked everywhere and fortunately found no signs of fire. The storm passed but the sky still flickered with lightning beneath the impenetrable gloom ahead while the vault of the sky burned behind us. The sea boiled as in a cauldron and the white rim of the horizon glowing brighter than the crests of the waves seemed to spill over with a heavenly fire. An hour later, the torrential rain extinguished this majestic fire and the horrible darkness faded. The frigate began to fly in a reaching wind at 17 *verstas* [18.14 km] an hour, but as the Skerki was close on the map, we lay to until dawn, thereby wasting a good deal of time as in the morning the winds again turned foul.

Finally on the 26th of November [7th of December], before the sun rose, the thick, dark canopy of clouds which loomed over us for so many days finally withdrew with a northwesterly wind and we quickly rushed to meet the sun, shining its penetrating rays through the gloom and banishing it over the horizon behind us. When the sun rose in its full glory, the coast of Sicily glimmered on the starboard side. The high mountains appeared as small blue hills which vanished and reappeared behind the rolling waves. The wind began to slow, shifted to an easterly direction and fell quiet. The sea calmed down and everyone took on a merry appearance after an hour, the day became beautiful and by evening Sardinia appeared. We arrived in Cagliari on the 27th of November [8th of December].

# 57

# The Adventures of a Captured Russian Officer

As soon as we dropped anchor under the walls of Cagliari, a figure came to the shore screaming, dressed like some poor beggar, and climbed up to the quarterdeck, glanced about joyfully and crossed himself, saying in a poor Russian accent: 'Glory to God! My misfortunes have finally ended'. He then asked for the captain and handed him a piece of paper. Our minister[1] proposed that one Lieutenant Stepan Yashimov of the Saint-Petersburg Dragoon Regiment be admitted to the frigate from captivity so that he could be delivered to the admiral. I brought him into the wardroom and introduced him to the officers there. Being from Kizlyar by birth, he forgot his mother tongue and had a great difficulty in explaining himself in Russian, interspersing his speech with Turkish, French and Italian. We tried to accommodate him and supplied him with all of his necessities. Yashimov soon became acquainted with us and with this new chapter in his life; in a short time, with his keen sharpness of mind and cheerful disposition, he earned the love and respect of us all. Serving in the headquarters of Prince Repnin, then Potyomkin, and being patronized by Count Orlov, although he had a poor education, his particular skill in etiquette made him a pleasant conversationalist. His prolonged misfortune did not dampen his courtesy and the experience of a 50-year-old man generally garnered respect. He told us with all candour of his adventure abroad for seven years, which, although having nothing to call its kin, was certainly not a fictional invention and therefore I will recount it as I heard it from him.

---

1   Yakim Grigoryevich Lizakevich served as Russia's ambassador to the Kingdom of Sardinia from 1802 to 1809. *The Foreign Policy of Russia of the 19th and 20th Centuries*, series 1, vol. 1, p.738.

Yashimov served in the First Confederation War,[2] in both Turkish wars[3] and the last Polish war,[4] and finally on the 10th [21st] of September, 1799, by Zürich, he received two wounds and was captured by the enemy, who took him to Marseilles. I will not repeat what he suffered on the road; anyone who had the misfortune of being in the hands of the French knows how they treat prisoners. A certain General D. arrived in Marseilles to replenish his Polish Legion and used Russian soldiers.[5] They were not given a proper ration of bread and were not permitted to leave their barracks – better called a prison. All manner of persuasion, threats and promises were employed, and ultimately starvation coerced them to accept their new service. The disobedient were sent as slaves to Spain. Even officers were not spared and so Yashimov was also invited to join the Polish Legion. He sought an opportunity to meet General D. and complain about their mistreatment, boldly telling him the truth, and, being upset with the general's answers, he called him a traitor to the fatherland. Yashimov was imprisoned and handed over to a court martial. Not expecting the consequences of his imprudence and inappropriate behaviour, he decided to flee. He asked the 30 Austrian soldiers and one Russian in prison with him to join in and everyone gladly agreed. Yashimov managed to convince the prison guard who, out of a singular compassion, not only gave them a clear passage to escape, but prepared a boat for them at the pier. Unfortunately, it was pouring rain that night and the men on the fishing boat had no idea where they were going at sea.

Afraid of pursuit, they rowed hard all night long and when day broke, Marseilles could not be seen. They then began to wonder where to steer themselves. Having no knowledge of navigation or even an understanding of the geography surrounding the south of France, they argued for a long time before giving in to Yashimov's will, choosing a direction that would take them directly as far from France as possible. Some of the men aboard were so ignorant that they thought that where the sky touched the sea was truly the end of the world. In the control of the boat they found many difficulties; however, like Robinson Crusoe, our floaters adrift soon learned how to turn the rudder and keep the sail inflated with the wind. Without any visible landmarks around them, they could not know in which direction the wind was changing and therefore were always at its mercy. Fortunately, in the Mediterranean it blows constantly from the north in the summer and is almost always gentle. One day the wind intensified, the boat began

---

2    The War of the Bar Confederation, 1768-1772.
3    The Russo-Turkish Wars of 1768-1774 and 1787-1792.
4    The Kościuszko Uprising of 1794.
5    Likely Jan Henryk Dabrowski. Eugène Fieffé, *Histoire des Troupes Étrangères au Service de France*, vol. 2 (Paris: Librairie Militaire, 1854), pp.44-45. [Eugène Fieffé, *History of Foreign Troops in the Service of France*, vol. 2 (Paris: Military Library, 1854), pp.44-45.]

to roll and the inexperienced sailors removed the sail and began rowing but the oars were knocked out of their locks. The boat tipped even further and began to draw water. Yashimov, no more versed than the others but more daring, raised the sail against their protests and the boat began to fly fast enough that it righted its list. The unchanging appearance of the sky and sea, the uncertainty and insecurity in oneself little by little led even the most vigorous into a state of depression.

On the fourth day, they ran out of water and their small reserve of bread, which the kind jailer did not forget to place in the boat. Something white suddenly appeared in the distance and as they watched it intensely, it transformed into a ship with all sails set. Shouting with joy, they took up their oars and vigorously tried to catch up with the vessel, shouting in a chorus with all their might and waving their hats and handkerchiefs, but it was all in vain. The ship's crew did not notice them and passed them by to disappear over the horizon. Everyone wanted to continue chasing the ship, but Yashimov alone thought it would be more prudent to keep to their old course. The men argued and under some threat or menace, Yashimov convinced them to keep the boat on its old bearing. Hunger, thirst and exhaustion led everyone to despair. Only Yashimov had hope and encouraged the others to continue manning the boat without quitting. On the seventh day after leaving Marseilles, to the inexpressible joy of all, a shore appeared and God led his ignorant pilgrims to the wharf of salvation with His invisible hand. They were met by a grand city, a towering fortress and over its walls fluttered a bloody flag depicting an arm gripping a sword. The weary sailors stepped ashore and wanted to kiss the ground, but they were approached by bearded men in long robes and turbans. They asked one another where they had landed and Yashimov answered 'In Africa! Algeria!' Stunned with fear, they cast their eyes down. They were outnumbered by the crowd of armed locals who were curious as to whence they had come and how Yashimov, who was a Kizlyar Tatar and knew several words in Turkish, came to be responsible for the others. The Berbers, who are described to us only in the very darkest of shades, upon hearing that the unfortunate foreigners had not eaten or drank for three days, took out some money or gave bread and fruits for their aid; some even argued over who would have the honour of inviting them into his home. The fear that they had fallen into the hands of bandits soon passed and each man enjoyed the hospitality of their hosts.

On the third day, Yashimov was presented before the janissary *agha* and then before the *dey* himself.[6] Afraid to say 'Russian,' he called himself a Tatar and as

---

6    Mustafa bin Ibrahim was the Pasha-Dey of Algeria from 1799 to 1806. Louis de Mas Latrie, *Trésor de Chronologie, d'Histoire et de Géographie*, vol. 2 (Paris: Librairie Victor Palmé, 1889), p.1840. [Louis de Mas Latrie, *Treasure of Chronology, History and Geography*, vol. 2 (Paris: Library of Victor Palmé, 1889), p.1840.]

a consequence of this deception, he was forced to join the janissaries of the *dey's* guard and quickly made a *chaush* with a small fort not far from Algiers under his command. His subordinates, having their own xebec, captured a Christian brigantine belonging to Dalmatians. Yashimov, hearing a language intelligible to him among the prisoners, was overjoyed but feigned ignorance, and endeavoured to free them and himself. The brigantine close to the shore was guarded by just one sentry. The Russian soldier who shared Yashimov's misfortunes from Marseilles persuaded the skipper and his men to join in and at night, when he himself stood watch, unseen by anyone, he let them out of prison and guided them to the craft. The sentry was seized, bound and thrown into the hold. When the brigantine set sail, the fortress was alerted and as the wind was soft, the Algerians were able to overtake it with two boats and intended on boarding her. Yashimov encouraged the Slavonians and rushed to the front to confront the attackers and drive them back off the ship. The Algerians were repelled but his fellow soldier and another man were killed in this skirmish and Yashimov received a light wound for his efforts. The others became timid at the sight of several other vessels off the coast and did not listen to Yashimov, abandoning the brigantine in a launch, but fortunately they left behind a small skiff. He climbed in the little boat, dropped himself into the water, unfurled the sail and exited the bay, keeping close to the coast. Once the Turks regained the brigantine, they did not bother to pursue the fleeing boats. The next day, when the wind turned foul for him, he ducked into the one clear place and left his boat to look for a while and wait for evening. He did not stray far from the shore and entered the first house, using his wound as an excuse and was received with compassion. He would visit nearby Tunisia, inquired about which road to take, purchased a horse there and departed early in the morning. On the fourth day, he reached the Tunisian frontier without harassment from anyone.

In Tunisia, no one asked who he was or whether he had a passport. He enjoyed his freedom and lived from *han* to *han*.[7] Yashimov soon had to sell his horse. The money that he managed to collect when he was a *chaush* eventually ran out and he had to think about his meals on a daily basis again. Finding no opportunity to board a Christian merchant vessel, he was forced to labour for his daily bread, fell ill and was brought to humiliation by needing to ask for alms from the compassionate folk. He was eventually offered to enlist as a sailor on a xebec of 16 guns and set out to sea. Against his own desire, unfavourable circumstances forced him to become a pirate and, fearing more than anything to spill the blood of Christians, the pious Yashimov secretly prayed to God from the deepest depths of his soul to relieve his conscience of that foul necessity. His prayer was heard; the corsairs cruised for a whole month without seeing a single vessel and finally took

---

7    Bronevskiy's note: 'What the Turkish call guesthouses'.

shelter on an island. Horrified by the prospect of raiding and unable to reconcile himself, Yashimov sought and found an opportunity to go ashore at night, avoiding his fellow crewmen and started inland along the road. He soon saw a light and stepped into the hut where it burned, frightening everyone inside with his Turkish attire. Yashimov tried to assure them by handing over his weapons and asked to be taken into town. He then learned that he had landed on the island of Corsica.

A few days later, Yashimov was presented to the commandant of the fortress of Bonifacio, who questioned him and, despite declaring himself to be a Russian officer, ordered him to be put in a [French] soldier's uniform. A year later, General D. arrived on Corsica to inspect the regiments there. Fearful of this news and the chance of being recognized, Yashimov disguised himself in a peasant's costume, hired a boat, and sailed over the strait to Sardinia. There they also did not believe that he was a Russian officer and they too threw him into the ranks of a garrison regiment which was employed in searching for raiders. Twenty times Yashimov fought with those desperate thugs until his luck finally turned and his regiment was ordered to relocate to Cagliari. He immediately appeared before our Minister Lizakevich and after seven years, the disasters, deprivations and misfortunes of Yashimov came to an end.

His misfortunes ended, but an unrelenting fate prevented the old man from dying in his fatherland. Yashimov was received favourably by the commander-in-chief. When the fleet sailed for the Aegean Archipelago, he was meant to remain on Corfu so that he could ride for Russia at the first opportunity. Being outside himself with joy, he was however moved by a noble sentiment and decided to refuse the admiral's charity and asked to be taken to the archipelago with the fleet so that he might earn his attention and affection. During the capture of Tenedos (Bozcaada), the battle in the Dardanelles and the defence of the Tenedos citadel, Yashimov demonstrated outstanding courage and activity and one may say that he sought death. He always remained on our frigate and suffered the same fates with us from Lisbon to Palermo and finally from Trieste, he accompanied us on the overland journey back to Russia. In Lemberg (Lviv), when the column was supposed to depart, Yashimov was not found in his quarters, and searching all over town, there was no sign of him. The owner of the house in which he was quartered said that he only spent the night with him and in the morning asked to repair his pistols as quickly as possible. He collected them at noon and never returned. In town there was a rumour that a Russian officer quarrelled in a tavern with two Polish uhlan officers on leave from Warsaw. It is very likely that poor Yashimov was killed in a duel. A short distance from Radzivilov,[8] in the village of Kolek,

8    A small town or village in the Governorate of Volhynia which lay on the border with the Austrian Empire and served as a designated port of entry. Today, it is known in Ukrainian

the Saint-Petersburg Dragoon Regiment was quartered and I was curious to know whether he truly served in that regiment. I found one trooper who remembered him well and attested that Yashimov had served in his squadron for five years.[9]

as Radyvyliv and belongs to the Rivne Oblast. Евдоким Зябловский, *Новейшее Землеописание Российской Империи*, vol. 2 (St. Petersburg: Типография И. Глазунова, 1807), p.223. [Yevdokim Zyablovskiy, *The Latest Geographical Description of the Russian Empire*, vol. 2 (St. Petersburg: I. Glazunov's Printing House, 1807), p.223.]

9    In Major-General Kamenskiy's 1900 history of the St. Petersburg Dragoons, a Lieutenant Stepan Yeshimov [sic] is listed as entering the regiment in 1791 but departing in 1798, rather than being captured in 1799. Евгений Каменский, *История 2-го Драгунского С.-Петербургского Генерал Фельдмаршала Князя Меншикова Полка 1707-1898 гг.*, vol. 2 (Moscow: Типография Вильде, 1900), appendix IV, p.30. [Evgeniy Kamenskiy, *History of the 2nd St. Petersburg Dragoon Regiment of Field-Marshal Menshikov 1707-1898*, vol. 2 (Moscow: Wilde's Press, 1900), appendix IV, p.30.]

# 58

# Cagliari

---

The ambassador Lizakevich visited the frigate and afterwards introduced the captain and officers to the King of Sardinia. His Majesty wore the Order of Saint Andrew the First-Called for our reception and, upon his entrance, he removed his hat at the table and took several steps to meet us, very graciously giving each of us a few words. On his orders, 500 *pud*s [8.19 t] of powder were allotted to the frigate and as it was better quality than the British, by the captain's request, it was exchanged for the powder taken on in Malta. The powder was brought to us secretly at night. This caution delayed us in the boring capital for more than two weeks. Besides the boulevard, which runs for a hundred paces and is surrounded by stakes, and a very small theatre where the soot of its oil lamps conceals the poor actors and leave the audiences with headaches, there were no other items worthy of curiosity.

## 59

# Returning to Palermo

---

Taking as much powder as we could, we left Cagliari on the 13th [25th] December. The wind was calm and the weather was beautiful. As soon as we reached open water, the wind freshened somewhat. Sardinia retreated and Sicily emerged out of the sea. It is falsely held that voyages at sea are fraught with disasters and can only plunge the curious traveller into the mire of boredom and fatigue. Anyone wishing to behold majestic, pleasing, terrible and frightening phenomena must cross the ocean to see them in their full brilliance and splendour. If the storm causes trepidation, then a light, moderate wind and clear weather paint the most charming vistas in equal measure. As the ship cuts through the waves, they animate with millions of fish and countless birds soar through the air. After a long, uneventful voyage without seeing land for several days and months, what can be compared with the enthusiasm of a sailor during its sudden appearance, presenting him with different sights and locales as if for his amusement. How slowly the ship seems to float then, the mountains and valleys hardly moving, and impatience inspires new thoughts and increases so greatly the pleasures enjoyed of those things that he so rarely and briefly sees. During a slow circumvention of several high capes, several voices cried out: 'there's Palermo!' The lovely capital, in its cosy position surrounded by gardens, appeared before us. Forgetting our labours or concern for service, every man hurried to ponder and plan their adventures and went to change clothes, ready to go ashore before we even dropped anchor.

## The Rescue of an American Ship

On the 21st of December [2nd of January, 1807], a previously clear sky was suddenly disturbed by a squall from the north; in half an hour, the waves became violent enough that the frigate began to pitch and roll much further than at sea. During the night, the wind became a storm and by dawn, an American three-masted vessel which had come from Brazil with a rich cargo, losing three anchors several *sazhen*s from the shore, ran aground. The Americans fired gun after gun asking for help and waved their hats and hands in the air, but it seemed impossible to save them. People crowded along the harbour and the police were already preparing to rescue the men aboard. From our frigate, we launched a boat with an anchor. Boatswain Vasilyev with 20 of the best sailors, holding on to the frigate's astern tow line, dropped anchor ahead of the American vessel's bow and passed them the line at great personal risk. The Americans could not pull it up and our people, due to the choppy waves striking the side of the boat, could not hold themselves steady. The experienced boatswain prepared a solution. Hauling themselves down the tow line as closely as possible to the bow of the vessel, the boatswain requested a thin rope to tie around himself and then, giving signs so that it was understood what he intended to do, he bravely dove into the water. The Americans hazarded a guess and pulled, and in this fashion our people were hoisted up onto the ship one by one. The skipper was in town then, so Vasilyev took on the role of commander. He tied the tow line around a spike and fastened it to a mast and despite the terrible wind and waves, they managed to take down the topmasts and yards.

The storm ceased on the third day and the skipper hurried back to his ship. He shook hands with the sailors and gave the boatswain a large purse of gold pieces but to Vasilyev's honour, he replied that he could no receive such an award without his commander's permission. The skipper, together with our men, came aboard the frigate, thanked the captain and offered twice the sum for their rescue, in accordance with their law. The captain assured him that we do not have such a law and that nothing is demanded for giving aid to a crew in distress. The skipper was surprised, touched and pleaded for us but when he was sure we would not take a reward, he went down onto the deck, saw the icon and priest administering services, quietly waited for him to finish and then approached, knelt down, and poured 600 gold pieces into the church box. The boatswain and sailors, with the captain's permission, were personally awarded generously and were granted leave from the frigate for three days. Then the skipper invited the captain and officers to dine with him. Upon our arrival, Russian flags were hoisted up on the masts and all the American vessels in the harbour fired salutes from their guns. With some sort of ritual by the skipper, their sailors nailed a golden inscription to the stern reading: 'The *Triton* was rescued by Russians on January 2, 1807'.

## The Shipwreck of the British 80-gun ship *William Tell*

As seafarers need to take every precaution, they do not rely on luck and cannot trust the most accurate calculations, as the misfortune of the *William Tell* proves.[1] The captain of that ship, renowned in the British Navy for his knowledge and bravery, personally confirmed the positions of the submerged rocks of the Skerki reefs and for the past month, with a strong western wind, heading to Malta, he could not determine his position along the Sicilian coast through the fog and relied on the fidelity of his maps. Thinking he was 20 miles [37.2 km] from the Skerki and on a dark night, while travelling 10 knots, he crashed onto the hazards and was wrecked; only two officers and 137 sailors were saved. While dining with Admiral Sidney Smith, I met the doctor who miraculously survived the wreck. At 9 o'clock, he went to his cabin on the orlop deck and lay down to sleep when suddenly he was thrown out of his cot and felt the rushing of water around him. He grabbed something floating nearby and found himself on the wreckage of the poop deck which washed up the next day on Sicily close to Marsala, along with the other survivors. It must be noted that several of those who slept in the lower decks and on the orlop were rescued, and yet those who were up above managing the sails all drowned.

## Theatre

There are four theatres in Palermo. It is known that the Neapolitan court had the best actors in Europe, but here there is neither the glorious enormity of the San Carlo nor the quality of its singers, but the opera buffa and harlequin are excellent, the ballet is fine as well, but on their tragedies – especially tragic operas – nothing can be said. At the royal theatre named San Ferdinando, I saw the great Metastasio's *Didone Abbandonata* (*Dido Abandoned*). The actress played poorly in the first acts but in the later few she surpassed herself. She so strikingly embodied the despair left by Aeneas on the Queen of Carthage that all the audience shared her suffering. She especially delivered with great expression and ardour the last

---

1    The French 80-gun *Guillaume Tell*, renamed the HMS *Malta* by the Royal Navy after its capture, was never shipwrecked in the Mediterranean. The British ship that did crash on the Skerki Reef was the 64-gun *Athenienne*, wrecked on 16 October, 1806. 350 souls onboard perished, including the commander Captain Raynsford, while 143 survived. True to Bronevskiy's retelling, the poop deck served as a raft for a handful of survivors, but the other rafts were tangled in the rigging and failed to save their passengers. William O.S. Gilly, *Narratives of Shipwrecks of the Royal Navy between 1793 and 1857*, 3rd ed. (London: Longman, Green, Longman, Roberts and Green, 1864), pp.100-106.

monologue when Dido exclaims 'che dei?' (what gods?) and then, reproaching herself for her blasphemy, she continued:

*Ah che dissi, infelice! A qual eccesso*
*Mi trasse il mio furore?*
*Oh Dio, cresce l'orrore! Ovunque io miro,*
*Mi vien la morte, e lo spavento in faccia:*
*Trema la reggia, e di sader minaccia.*
*Selene, Osmida! Ah, tutti,*
*Tutti cedeste alla mia sorte infida:*
*Non v'è chi mi soccorra, o chi m'uccida.*
 *Vado… ma dove? Oh dio!*
 *Resto… ma poi… che fo?*
 *Dunque morir dovrò*
 *Senza trovar pietà?*
*E v'è tanta viltà nel eptto mio?*
*No no, si mora; e l'infedele Enea*
*Abbia nel mio destino*
*Un augurio funesto al suo cammino.*
*Precipiti Cartago,*
*Arda la reggia, e sia*
*Il cenere di lei la tomba mia.*[2]

Having said this, she runs into the burning halls and collapses to disappear behind the sparks, flames and smoke. The scenery was generally excellent, but the later acts were especially amazing. The frightening movement and noise of the waves, the whitening of their crests, the blazes, thunder and lightning, and the brutal effect of the water and fire combined were so lifelike that it seemed I was actually witnessing them there on the stage. Finally, the booming orchestra transitioned into something softer and Neptune appeared in a brilliant chariot, surrounded by floating sirens and tritons before the curtain fell. When I left the theatre, I saw the

---

2 Bronevskiy's note: 'Here is a weak translation: "Ah, what I said was unhappy! To what excess / Has my anger driven me? / Oh God, the horrors grow! Wherever I go / Death comes to me, and fear is before me: / The palace trembles and threatens to fall. / Selene, Osmida! Ah! everyone, / Everyone, yield to my treacherous fate: / There is no one who would save me or kill me. / I go… but where? Oh God! / I rest… but then… what will I do? / So I will die / Without finding pity? / Is there so much cowardice in my breast? / No, no, I will die; and the unfaithful Aeneas / Has in my destiny / A fatal curse for his journey. / Raze Carthage, burn the palace, and let / her ashes be my tomb"'.

scenery from the production represented in nature. The rain, wind, lightning, and ships shaken in the port all re-enacted the opera I had just seen.

## The Improvisator

A young, poor man educated in the Academy of Music became famous here for the extraordinary ability to speak in verse without preparation. I had an occasion to hear it. He was asked if, following the social attitudes, women should cast aside modesty and shyness and seek love among men. He took up a guitar and played a loud symphony, sang a verse about the creation of Adam and Eve and then continued to play, and these interludes gave him time to compose his thoughts, a fact that was clearly betrayed on his face. Like Pythia, he entered an apparent ecstasy and his poems with musical accompaniment only just composed changed from tone to tone. Sometimes his expressions were folksy like a natural poet without formal training, and sometimes they were strong and smart, and finally he ended each medley with funny verses; for the Italians, humour is as necessary as air. He sang for half an hour and his audience were in admiration. At the dinner table, the improvisator addressed each guest with a greeting which they called *brindisi* or toasts. Hearing my name, he grimaced and said that it smelled of the north, however he composed three verses, with which he was not pleased. Finally he volunteered to praise the name of our Emperor Alexander. Comparing the sovereign with Titus and Alexander of Macedon, he performed such an ode that the listeners were beside themselves. They asked him to repeat it and this wonderful poet said something quite different, with a new measure and it proved to be even better than the first. They wanted to submit it to the press and, to my great surprise, he could not remember the couplets of the first verses and continued to speak in verse even as he apologized for his memory.

From the improvisators one should not demand high sentiment, especially because many of them have no education; but the average and even the celebrated among them, such as Corinne crowned in Rome,[3] cannot be expected to reach the same artfulness in any other language. By their ability, naturally they imbue their language with such a mellifluous lyricism that even the most decrepit dialects such as the Venetian, Milanese and Neapolitan become soft and pliable. The Sicilian dialect, interspersed with Arabic and Greek, received the special ability of rapid or extemporary composition of poetry and therefore Sicily has more improvisators than the whole of Italy.

---

3    The eponymous character in Anne Germaine de Staël-Holstein's 1807 novel *Corinne, ou l'Italie*. A fictional improvisatrix who was crowned a poet laureate in Rome and falls in love with a Scottish lord at the close of the 18th century.

Tasso, Ariosti, Petrarch and Metastasio, knowing the Italian language, elevated it and through every kind of verse made it flexible, pleasant and sonorous. The Italian writers are condemned for excessive affectation, but Petrarch, the sweetest singer, was able to combine tenderness with strength and brevity. The operas of Metastasio are revered as among all the best – *Themistocles, Rogero, Dido Abandoned* and *The Clemency of Tito* have made his glory immortal. In them he combined the beauty of high tragic composition with heroic emotion. Many of his small poems and especially the arias in his operas breathe the delicacy of Anacreon. In the poem *Jerusalem Delivered*, the undying Tasso, in his supposedly saccharine tongue, was able to equal and surpass many of the epic poets; even Milton. The description of hell is certainly an immense creation. Voltaire was justly surprised, for example, that in the tender Italian language so many thunderous and harsh words could be found to describe it. Armida's garden, the enchanted forest, Tancredi fighting with Argante, the death of Clorinda, the love of Erminia, Solyman's attack and many other episodes are examples of his inimitable creation. Lastly, *The Furious Orlando*, so critical and so exalted, shall also remain unrepeatable though in a different fashion. Ariosto depicts alternately the sounds of weapons, the fragrance of meadows and groves, Alcina's magnificent chambers, and in even the most terrible and dreadful he presents a natural charm. Everything lives and breathes under his pen; everywhere in his fiction can be seen his talent and eye for beauty. The reader follows the magician without any effort, wanders with him from land to land, rises into the air, and fights on the back of a winged monster. It is doubtful that in any other language, the author of *Orlando* could produce something like that.

## Common Games

Bullfighting is one of the favourite pastimes of the people. For this spectacle, the mob assembles in the square. I passed by once and stopped to observe one but could not stand the sight of the poor animal's painful death and never again walked near that square where bulls were killed for amusement. Instead of this disgusting pleasure, there is also the noblest of dances. In Palermo, music can be heard from morning until evening. There are many packed dance halls here which serve breakfast and wine and have ample volunteers ready to dance. In addition to the national dances, they also perform quadrilles in which the steps are absolutely theatrical. For the common folk, there are many.

Puppet comedies, Chinese shadows, harlequins and clowns are very typical. Besides the aforementioned, narrators amuse people with short stories which are often intricate. A square is formed out of benches and the listeners sit down while the narrator stands in the centre and begins in a loud voice, accompanying each word with gestures and actions. For example, if he says that a man fell in the mud, he himself falls down. If he needs to narrate a fight, then he fights with a clown, his usual assistant. On holidays, his story begins with the life of a saint and ends with laughter. In the last week of Lent, the Passion of Christ is accurately portrayed and the narrators speak with such great fervour that they weep, receiving large sums of money, as the people do not understand the Latin spoken in their churches and are eager to hear these performances in the common tongue.

Among the carnival performers belong horse racers of a special kind. Once while approaching Toledo, I saw a throng of people in the street, windows were covered with carpets and cuts of silk and the balconies and terraces were occupied by ladies and gentlemen looking on at the events below. I heard a drum, a shot from a cannon and eight horses with high, carved saddles covered with rich cloths, manes and tails intertwined with ribbons, rushing spiritedly down the street – without riders.

## Statistics of Sicily

Sicily, by virtue of its fruitfulness, was considered the breadbasket of Italy in antiquity. The land's fertility is still amazing today. Grain scattered over barely cultivated land springs forth a hundredfold. Its mountains rising like an amphitheatre are covered with a fertile forest from their peaks to their bases and contain within them silver, gold, the most beautiful marble, agate, jasper and lapis lazuli. Vesuvius [and Etna], fertilizing the earth with its ashes, moreover produces a great deal of sulphur, pumice and lava. The valleys of the whole island are never depleted and yield four harvests a year. An eternal summer promotes the growth of delicious fruits; even the rarest crops typical to countries below the equator can grow here in the open air with certain care. The abundance of springs, small rivers and water in general over the whole island is astonishing and the rivers and surrounding sea are abounding with all kinds of fish. The sea, in addition to its many safe harbours, delivers another kind of wealth as if in competition with the land in corral and pearls. The air, water, earth and subterranea fill the bosom of this blessed island with all the necessities of life, Proserpina could still pick the beautiful flowers here and Pindar and Theocritus could still sing to the herds grazing in the rich meadows of Sicily. The bees on Mount Vesuvius still drink the nectar from the savoury flowers which give their honey a pleasant smell.

During the reign of the Romans over Sicily, science and art flourished. The Arabs adorned it with glorious aqueducts. Everywhere, the prosperity and splendour of its ancient history can be seen in its remaining monuments. This land, with its small population, has since suffered under the rule of the viceroys who allowed pirates to harass its coastal villages unimpeded. The king's stay and the resettlement of wealthy nobles awakened a dormant industry and her strength began to develop again. Last year, Sicily's products sold twice as much as when the court was in

Naples. On the southern shores are grown sugar cane and coffee. There is no doubt that within 10 years, these cash crops will not be necessary, as the revitalization of their agriculture and commerce will make the Sicilians abundant in all of their products and able to rival England in trade with their substantial fleet of merchant vessels.

In the interior, the island is excessively hot while the same air, cooled by sea winds, is healthy on the coasts. Besides the heat in June, July and August, endless spring reigns over the rest of the year and the stifled plants bloom green again. The sky is always clear in the summer months, the wind blows stronger in the winter, and there are often rains and thunderstorms but always briefly and at high noon it becomes so hot one must always find shade. It snows in the mountains, rarely but for several hours. Despite their wealth, the people are slovenly, live in poor stone houses, work very little and eat fruits and vegetables for the most part. Fish and shellfish are preferred over meat, which is not consumed in the extreme heat.

## History

For the triangular shape of Sicily, Thucydides named it Trinacria. The name of Sicily comes from the Siculi, the nation that migrated to the island from Italy. At various times, it was occupied by the Greeks from Naxos, Colchis, Corinth and other states. Most of the island belonged to the Carthaginians while the rest belonged to independent kings. The Romans were called in by the Mamertines against King Hiero of Syracuse and his allies the Carthaginians and by defeating them, conquered the whole island. During the fall of the Roman Empire, Genseric, King of the Vandals, sacked the island. Belisarius, commander of Justinian's army, recovered the territory for the Eastern Empire in 535 AD. In the 9th century, Sicily fell prey to the Saracens, whose Emirs reigned in Palermo until 1071. The Normans expelled the Arabs from Calabria with the help of the Greeks and then from Sicily. Roger II founded a new Kingdom of Sicily in 1139, which became the source of several prolonged wars. Constance, daughter of Roger, married the future Emperor Henry VI in 1186 and delivered both Sicilies to the House [of Hohenstaufen] of Schwabia. Later, Manfred, the illegitimate brother of Conrad IV, was recognized as the heir, but the Count of Anjou devastated the kingdom in 1266 with the blessing of Pope Innocent IV and killed Manfred. Peter III, King of Aragon, married to the daughter of Manfred's daughter, pressed her claim and became King of Sicily and in 1282, on Easter day at the first strike of the bell, the mass murder of the French began. This terrible crime, referred to as the Sicilian Vespers, was the cause of a war which ended in the expulsion of the French from Sicily.

Modern history contains the tragic ends of two queens: Joanna the First and the Second. The former killed her husband Andrew II [of Hungary] on the eve of his coronation. Her youth, beauty and the policy of the Pope acquitted her, but her reign was plagued by misfortunes and she was felled with her crown by the dagger of vengeance. The latter met the same fate as Queen Elizabeth of England.[4]

In 1713, according to the Treaty of Utrecht, the Kingdom of Sicily was given to the Duke of Savoy. In 1718, Phillip V, King of Spain, sent a fleet and army to seize the island, but the British Admiral George Byng broke them and forced the Spanish to return unsuccessful. The Treaty of the Hague gave Sicily to the Holy Roman Emperor Charles VI and the Duke of Savoy was compensated with the island of Sardinia. In 1735, the Spanish and French together retook Sicily and at the conclusion of peace, Sicily and Naples were given to Don Carlos, the eldest son of Phillip V, King of Spain. When Don Carlos ascended to the Spanish throne by inheritance, then to his son Ferdinand he abdicated the crowns of Sicily and Naples. Engrossed by the extraordinary events of our times, Ferdinand twice lost Naples and twice recovered it with the generous support of the Russian Emperor. Due to the terrain of the island, Ferdinand was not afraid of the formidable forces of Napoleon. No matter what scheme Napoleon might undertake, it could be said that the island, even without a navy, would be protected by the king and the ancient hatred of his people for the French would prove to be a heavy stumbling block. The ties between the Sicilians and Neapolitans could not quell their animosity and they always remained alien to one another, which is another reason why Napoleon would meet strong resistance. Since neither Naples nor Malta can be occupied without holding Sicily, where they procure their grain, Sicily's relations are more threatening to Naples than Naples is to that island, whose independence is a necessity for the British; as without Sicily, they cannot rule the Mediterranean.

---

4    Both Joanna II of Naples and Elizabeth I of England died without children and left their titles to other houses. Joanna was the last monarch of the House of Capet in Naples, falling to René I of the Valois in 1435, and Elizabeth was the last reigning Tudor in England, falling to James I of the Stuarts in 1603. Margaret Kekewich, *The Good King: King René and Fifteenth Century Europe* (Basingstoke, UK: Palgrave MacMillan, 2008), pp.47-55.; George Palmer, *A History of England* (Boston: Robert S. Davis and Co., 1861), p.20.

**60**

# Sailing from Palermo to Messina

On the night of the 6th [18th] of January 1807, we left Palermo and under all sails on a mild wind we headed into the dawn. A fog lay over the capital but when the sun began to rise, the haze thinned and Palermo could be seen on the horizon as if half submerged into the sea. The light of the east and the twilight of the west produced surprising changes in the shadows. The night had been dark with the moon concealed behind the clouds and no stars shone, but when the rays of the sun approached the edge of the horizon, they separated the waves from the heavens and illuminated one side of the Sicilian amphitheatre; the east glowed with a purple gleam, while the west slumbered still in darkness and gradually gave way to the coming light until the sudden emergence of the sun.

A strong northerly wind contributed to our voyage and gave us the pleasure of approaching the shore. The Aeolian Islands and Sicily, between which we adhered, presented new sights. The wind blowing from the islands brought to us the smell of oranges and lemons, but toward evening, the wind intensified somewhat and forced us to manoeuvre. At midnight, when we approached the Milazzo, the wind suddenly died down and the frigate would not turn due to the force of the waves, coasting downwind and passing only a few *sazhen*s from the shore. The people who came out onto the embankment with lanterns were close enough to be discerned by face. Before daybreak, the fire of Stromboli appeared. We were now 30 miles [55.6 km] away from it and could hear its underground, unintelligible rumbling.

On the 7th [19th] of January, we safely passed Scylla and Charybdis and dropped anchor in Messina. The frequent wrecking of ships built poorly and piloted even worse gave these hazards an exaggerated strength far exceeding the lofty allegories of the imaginative Greeks. Homer and Virgil eloquently described them under the guise of two cruel nymphs. Scylla, daughter of Phorcys (son of Neptune), was said to be the love of Glaucus. Circe, another nymph, seeing that his love was unrequited and having her own petitions met with scorn, employed poisonous herbs in the spring where Scylla frequently bathed. When she emerged from the water, she became so ugly that her reflection frightened herself and she threw herself into the sea. The gods turned her to stone and struck an abyss in the sea with her name. The noise of the water is attributed in poetry to the barking of dogs and howling of wolves, which surround Scylla in the sea.

# 61

# Messina

According to Strabo, Messina was known in antiquity as Zancle. Expelled from Peloponnesus, the Greeks of Messene gave it its present name. The Carthaginians' siege, together with King Hiero of Syracuse, was unsuccessful but Pyrrhus succeeded in taking the city and razed it to its foundations. The Romans, who were called in to help against the Carthaginians, held Messina in their possession, which was the source of the Punic Wars.

Two days before our arrival, several sharks appeared in port. One of them grabbed a boy whose feet were dangling off the embankment and a few seconds later, a boy missing a foot emerged near an English frigate. They sent out a boat to save him, but as they began to pull him out of the water, a shark jumped out of the water furiously and instantly snatched him down and swallowed him. In the town, they displayed one of the sharks they caught not long ago. The length of this monster was slighter more than six *sazhen*s [12.8 m], propped up by his crimson jaws with at least 200 very strong and sharp teeth in six series. The last four series are bent back like the prickles of an artichoke and the teeth of the upper jaw fit between the gaps of the lower. The throat was so vast that there was no doubt that it was this sort of shark and not a whale – whose throat is narrow – that swallowed the Prophet Jonah. In the stomach of a shark caught in Marseilles was found a whole man in full panoply, which is why the French call the animal *le requin*.[1] The sharks often chase ships and grab anything jettisoned into the water, being capable of swallowing a whole cadaver in an instant. They pursue fish without rest, are gluttonous like a hyena and as bold and brave as a tiger. Sharks would have depleted the ocean if their vision were not compromised by a membrane covering the eyes and its upper jaw being longer than its lower giving it an overbite, though

---

1   Bronevskiy is referencing a folk etymology that ties the French name for the great white shark with 'requiem'.

it can still grab its prey. Its shortcomings are compensated by acute hearing and agility.

For catching a shark, a thick iron hook with a chain three *arshin*s [2.13 m] long is used. The chain is attached to a reliable rope tied to the stern of the boat. A piece of corned beef is fixed to the hook along with a floater which prevents the chain from sinking completely to the floor when they are thrown into the water. When dropped in the water, the shark responds to the sound and greedily eats the bait and jerks the rope. When it feels the resistance of the boat holding the line, it flies into a frenzy, gnaws on the chain and rushes all around, jumping out of the water, spinning and rolling about and throwing up everything it had inside. The fishermen wait until the shark is exhausted and bled out before pulling it into the boat; as when it is still lively, it can bite off limbs or kill a man with a blow from its tail. Their meat tastes disgusting and is difficult to cook, however the Italians eat it virtually rotten. The hard skin is used for cleaning furniture and the fat is prepared as an inferior blubber.

When a shark appears, the residents flee the water and scatter in all directions. The sharksucker, referred to as a remora here, is the only thing not afraid of the sharks and can always be found preceding their arrival. The length of the remora is no more than an *arshin* [71.12 cm] and it has spikes on its head pointed toward its tail which somehow embed themselves into larger fish[2]; it is even able to feed on sharks and cling to large rocks. Based on this ability, ancient writers thought that Mark Atony's galley was retarded by them at the battle of Actium. Equally so, a ship of Periander of Corinth sent to Cnidus to retrieve 300 young men destined to be made eunuchs could not progress despite a favourable wind, which is why in the Temple of Aphrodite in Cnidus, the remora (which they called ship-stallers) were honoured for being miracle-workers. The property of the suckerfish to pursue any fish and dig into it has given cause to use it for catching other fish, a skill known to the ancients and, I have been assured, still in use today in the Greek archipelago. They attach themselves so strongly that even larger fish cannot escape from its grasp and exhaust themselves enough to be hauled up by the fishermen.

---

2    The remora or suckerfish has a flattened dorsal fin resembling a plate within which are a series of slats which can produce a strong vacuum. This suction cup is the primary method of attaching itself to other animals, ships, rocks etc., and its fine spikes or needles only provide additional friction but do not pierce the flesh of its hosts. William Perrin, Bernd Würsig and J. G. M. Thewissen (eds.), *Encyclopedia of Marine Mammals*, 2nd ed. (Burlington, Massachusetts: Academic Press, 2009), s.v. 'Remoras'.

# 62

# Sailing from Messina to Castelnuovo

---

Receiving lead and paper for cartridges from the consul, we departed Messina on the 11th [23rd] of January. At the Cape of Spartivento, the British frigate *Seahorse* was waiting for us. We overtook her when the wind was calm and when it was refreshed, we lost sight of her completely. On the 13th [25th], we approached the southern strait of Corfu with a strong northwesterly wind and were already prepared to see our friends and acquaintances again in an hour or two; but here we learned that one cannot conquer the sea and instead of Corfu, against our will and intentions, we were diverted to Castelnuovo. The setting of the sun foreshadowed a storm, black clouds were rolling in from all directions, the moon disappeared behind them and not a single star twinkled. Suddenly, a strong squall from the southeast forced us to reef our sails and tack, becoming gloomy and terrible by midnight. At dawn, all sails were knocked out and we could not enter the strait of Corfu, neither from the north nor south, and were forced to follow the wind into the Adriatic.

The sky cleared with the rising of the sun, the sea was as white as snow and a blue mist was seen streaming over the Albanian mountains, whose snow stood above the clouds. With only the course sail of the foremast, the frigate travelled at 22 *versta*s [23.47 km] an hour and from such a speed, appeared to be drowning in the waves. The merchant ships travelling with us in the same direction held themselves back as one should, while we shot past them like an arrow shouting 'bon voyage' as we left them behind. Nothing can compare with the thrill of a speedy flight, objects whizzing past and sinking into the sea as quickly as they appeared ahead and each is instantly replaced by something new. Passing Valona, a northeasterly wind turned southeasterly and blew with cruel gusts. At Durazzo, on a beam reach, we quickly passed our fleet in the night and learned from the number of lanterns[1] that the admiral's ship was present, but as the powder was meant to be delivered to Cattaro, we maintained our course. Despite the *bora*, darkness and rocks, we tacked under reefed topsails and came to drop anchor at Castelnuovo on the night of the 15th [27th] of January. There we found the ships *Svyatoy Pyotr*, *Moskva*, and *Svyataya Paraskeva* with three smaller vessels under the command of Captain First Rank Baratynskiy, who was charged with defending Cattaro. A squadron consisting of five ships under the command of Captain-Commodore Ivan Ignatyev arrived early that month from Kronstadt and was sailing for Corfu together with Admiral Senyavin. This endeavour by the fleet, continuing the desire of the Emperor to protect this region in every possible way, was very encouraging to the people and affirmed their unshakable zeal and devotion to Russia.

---

1    Bronevskiy's note: 'Flagships at night are illuminated by a prescribed number of lanterns, from which one can always determine which ship the admiral is aboard'. Translator's note: According to Russian naval regulations, a rear-admiral in command would display two lanterns at the stern and one in the topsails. *Book of Naval Regulations*, pp.38-39.

# 63

# The Capture of the islands Curzola and Brazza

---

The enemy, after their unsuccessful attempt to take Castelnuovo, remained inactive at Old Ragusa. During an onset of inclement weather, the admiral retained 2,300 irregulars and dispersed the rest, but in the event that they would be needed again, they could be rallied by telegraph and assemble within 24 hours. The Montenegrins and Bokez remained in service, with each *bajrak* (banner) retaining an officer and several privates for guiding their movements. On the 4th [16th] of October [1806], in order to assess the strength of the enemy and if the rumours that they retreated proved to be true, to occupy Ragusa, the Metropolitan marched on Old Ragusa with the 13th Jäger Regiment and his irregulars. The admiral arrived there with four ships, but the French forces were occupying their fortified camp in the same numbers as earlier, for which the Metropolitan engaged in a few light firefights and returned to Castelnuovo with several prisoners and no losses. Due to the enemy's proximity however, the skirmishes were frequent and the forces were exercised endlessly, a state in which our men had an advantage and brought in captives every day. The small size of our forces and the remoteness of the territory from our fatherland, from which there was no hope of receiving aid quickly, did not allow us to seize anything important; it was impossible to consider acquisitions when the conservation of force was the best course of action for the defence of the province. As in Dalmatia, the spark of dissent was smouldering under the ashes and the French also feared an attack from us, and as the war in Prussia had already begun, both armies remained inactive, waiting for the fate of the south to be decided in the north.

The French ambassador to the Sublime Porte, General Horace François Sébastiani, managed to take advantage of d'Oubril's treaty, convincing the Ottoman government to replace the Hospodars of Moldavia and Wallachia in violation of their treaty with Russia; this could become the cause of a new war and the position of our forces in Cattaro was made all the more difficult. However, when the Sovereign refused to ratify d'Oubril's treaty and Senyavin defeated

Marmont's offensive, the Porte satisfied the just demands of our court and for some time remained in alliance with Russia and Britain. The admiral relied on this alliance, reinforcing the garrisons of the Cattaro region with six companies of the 14th Jäger Regiment, and proposed to mount an expedition to see if it were not possible to take the islands of Curzola, Lesina and Brazza (Brač) and establish a post there so that the inhabitants of Dalmatia who wished to become subjects of the Russian Emperor would not fall into the wrong hands, in the event that the French were defeated in Prussia and would need to abandon Dalmatia.

In consequence of this, on the 26th of November [8th of December], the commander-in-chief deployed the ships of the line *Selafail*, *Svyataya Yelena* and *Yaroslav*; the frigate *Kildyuin*; two transports and five Bokez corsairs; and two battalions of Jägers with 150 of the best Montenegrin and Bokez sharpshooters to capture the island of Curzola. To prevent damage done to the homes and the deaths of innocent residents, the admiral ordered the flotilla to hold fire until the enemy fired first when approaching the fortress. As soon as the first ship came into line with the fort on the 27th of November [9th of December], the French began the action. Each ship passed in front of the fort and fired two or three charges per gun. After this barrage, the squadron dropped anchor. The next day, surrender was proposed but the French commandant refused it and said that the inhabitants were not his and we should not endeavour to harm them.

At dawn on the 29th [11th of December], a force numbering 1,019 men landed 4 *versta*s [4.27 km] from the fort. Forming three columns under the command of Colonels Boissel and Boboyedov and Lieutenant-Colonel Ivan Velizaryev and the overall command of the admiral, the force attacked the redoubt by the monastery of Saint Biagio which covers the main fortifications. This redoubt was defended on one side by two guns and from the other by the main fortress's batteries. The French, sallying from the redoubt for 300 paces, took cover behind stones; the Montenegrins crawled up to them and were the first to open fire before immediately withdrawing as usual. The French gave chase but when they noticed our Jägers were manoeuvring to attack them on the flanks, they halted, fell into close order and bravely rushed at the first column. The courageous Colonel Boboyedov, receiving them with strong fire, counterattacked with bayonets and, being reinforced with naval infantry at that same moment, sent the enemy to flight. In this action, Boboyedov, the staff-captain of his company[1] and a lieutenant were wounded; as his company was rather disrupted by these

---

1    Field-grade officers (major to colonel) in the regular army and naval infantry regiments were also the nominal commanders of companies, which were effectively commanded by staff-captains in their stead, similar to how the regiment itself had both a chief (usually a general) and a commander (usually a colonel). The remaining companies were led by full captains. *Military Regulations of 1796*, pp.4-8.

losses, the French running to shelter in the redoubt were able to recompose themselves and rushed back out. The Metropolitan's brother, Sava Petrović, with his Montenegrins, Bokez and several Jägers bravely and quickly struck the enemy in the left flank and cut them off in the redoubt. The French defended themselves inside with strong musketry and canister fire. Sailors pulled two mountain guns onto the height and knocked out the redoubt's two guns with several successful shots. A company from Colonel Boissel's naval infantry regiment, which had just lost its captain, rushed furiously at the redoubt and all the other men with them broke through the gate with some effort and ended the action. The French fled back to the main fortress. The first man to enter the redoubt was Sergeant-Major Kharitonov of that naval infantry company.

On the 30th of November [12th of December], the *Yaroslav* and several armed rowboats opened fire on the fortress in coordination with an attack on land by our forces. The French answered with cannon and musket shots but after a few minutes, they fell silent, hauled down their flag and raised a white one. All fire ceased upon a signal. The French garrison exited, laid down their arms, and were in our custody. Our forces ceremonially entered the fortress and raised the Imperial Russian flag.[2] Taken prisoner were Colonel Orfengo,[3] 13 officers and 389 private soldiers of the 81st Regiment of the Line, with 6 officers and 150 soldiers killed and 3 officers and 45 men wounded; a total force of 606 men. The losses on our side were 3 officers and 21 soldiers and Montenegrins killed; 9 officers and 66 privates wounded. Fourteen guns were laid in the fortress with a sufficient stock of powder and ammunition. In order to avoid the difficulties of keeping the prisoners, they were released on their word of honour not to serve until an exchange is made with France, rank for rank; the healthy were sent to Ancona and the wounded to Spalatro.

On the 2nd [14th] of December, the *Moskva* transported another 100 Montenegrins. The admiral left two companies in the fortress and the *Svyataya Yelena* to cover it, and loaded the rest onto ships which set sail with a fair wind on the 8th [20th] for the island of Lesina, dropping anchor between it and Brazza on the 10th [22nd]. The ships passed a battery built on the peninsula opposite the island of Solta and fired several shots. 400 Jägers were immediately landed, under the command of Captain Romanovich of the 14th Jäger Regiment. The Montenegrins and Bokez were commanded by Midshipman Faddey [or Thaddeus] von Tiesenhausen. The French occupied two high hills near the battery. Captain

2    Bronevskiy's note: 'The Sovereign Emperor deigned to reward each man of the lower ranks who participated in the capture of Curzola with one ruble'.
3    Marmont's memoirs refer to him as a *chef de bataillon*, equivalent to major. Marmont, *Memoirs*, vol. 3, pp.30-31.

Romanovich divided his detachment into four parts and attacked the enemy so quickly and broadly that the French, seeing themselves cut off, surrendered after a brief firefight. The action was decided without any losses on our side. 4 officers, 79 soldiers and 18 four-pound [1.96 kg] guns were captured. It should be noted that the Montenegrins distinguished themselves here not only by their courage, but by their obedience and mercy. They were foremost in their swift approaches against the French and although they lacked strength, they dared to open fire; in the matter of the laws of war, the Montenegrins could have treated them quite cruelly, but instead they showed a surprising grace and took several prisoners, including the commander of the detachment, Captain Buret, without killing or offending a single man. This campaign became legendary among the Montenegrins, who hitherto had never seen more water than the Lake of Skadar yet willingly boarded our ships and travelled on the sea. These men returned home and told miraculous tales to their friends and word of the admiral's affection toward them bound them all the more to his authority. Their poets composed a song for this occasion, in which the name of Senyavin and other brave commanders are committed to posterity and the tongues of Russian and Slavonian are united in the recitation.

The occupation of the island of Lesina, strongly reinforced and with a sufficient garrison, would have cost us a greater sacrifice, but when the admiral was preparing to proceed with an attack on Lesina, the brig *Bonasorte* dispatched by Count Mozzenigo brought notice that Ali Pasha took Preveza, summoned the squadron of Sheremet Bey and positioned his army to threaten Corfu. After the revelation of such events, the admiral was forced to abandon his intentions and consolidate his forces for the defence of the Ionian Republic, returning to Curzola on the 11th [23rd] of December after the destruction of the battery on Brazza and the establishment of a naval post there, close to Spalatro.

# 64

# The Action between the Brig *Aleksandr* and a French Flotilla

The *Aleksandr* was left at the island of Brazza for observing the enemy and to cut off communications between Spalatro and the island of Lesina. General Marmont, learning that one brig armed with twelve 4-*funt* [1.96 kg] guns and crewed of 75 men was occupying such an important position, dispatched from Spalatro three gunboats, one trabaccolo and a tartane named *Napoleon* carrying as many soldiers onboard as would fit. The gunboats were armed with two 18-pound [8.81 kg] guns and several swivel guns; the *Napoleon* alone was stronger than the *Aleksandr*, having two 18-pounders at the bow and six 12-pounders [5.87 kg] broadside.

On the 12th [24th] of December, the residents who were well-disposed to us, learned of the enemy's intention and warned the commander of the brig, Lieutenant Ivan Semyonovich Skalovskiy, and promised to light beacons on the shore of the island of Solta, one for every boat in the enemy flotilla. To that end, they left two of their comrades in the town of Spalatro. When the lieutenant heard this, he prepared the brig to receive the enemy, especially for a boarding action. Around midnight, a *garde de marine* who made a tour reported that several ships were coming from the direction of Spalatro and that he witnessed five fires on the shore. To prevent a surprise attack from the enemy, the brig set sail. The night was beautiful, with a clear sky and a moon shining in all of its glory. Unfortunately, the wind was very calm and our brig did not have time to circle the western extremity of Brazza before meeting the enemy flotilla. Skalovskiy ordered to keep as close to it as possible and turned to his men to say: 'there's a boat among them named the *Napoleon*, boys! Remember that you have to honour to defend the name of *Aleksandr*! If I'm killed, do not surrender so long as you have your heads! God be with you!' Skalovskiy opened a full volley across the oncoming boats and then ordered a cease fire; the enemy was encouraged by this and came on furiously on oars and under sail to the sides of the brig and immediately attempted a boarding action under a new hail of fierce musketry and cannon fire. He allowed them to approach into his grapeshot and kept up a continuous fire. The enemy boats quickly aborted and tried to stay astern of the brig, but it turned about and fired on them with both port and starboard. The French boats, crowded together and harassed by grape and musket fire, became confused. After an hour, the wind became rather quiet. The brig could not manoeuvre and the boats, by virtue of their oars, were able to attack from astern where only two swivel guns and a few sharpshooters provided the weakest resistance. This unfavourable situation could not shake the courageous Skalovskiy; he ordered Midshipman Luka Melnikov to set out in a launch and tow the brig so it could redirect its side toward the enemy. Under grape and bullets, over the course of two hours, Melnikov performed his dangerous and daring mission with precision. The boats, being so close, several times attempted to tether to the sides of the brig but were repulsed and continued to fight at close proximity.

Finally, after three hours of persistent battle, the *Napoleon* lost her mainmast, another boat sank, and the others were damaged enough to begin withdrawing. The brig gave chase with the help of its tug until the enemy escaped out of range on their oars. Were it not for the dead calm, the enemy flotilla would certainly have been destroyed or captured. The brave Skalovskiy, all of his officers and crew received an exceptional reward from the Sovereign. On the brig, 5 men were killed and 7 were wounded; its hull and rigging were perforated like a sieve. The enemy, according to accurate information, lost 217 men killed, wounded and drowned. The remaining four boats, especially the *Napoleon*, were so damaged that if rowing vessels were not sent out from Spalatro to intercept them, they would not have reached port.

Marmont was so confident of victory that he warned the ladies attending his ball that they would not be surprised by gunfire and boasted that he would tomorrow bring them the impromptu gift of the Russian brig *Aleksandr*. All of his guests drank a toast to the health of the French forces. But at dawn, his unfortunate *Napoleon* and three boats came into harbour all beaten and swamped. He was so distressed by this failure that the commander of the flotilla and all the officers were arrested, held in the fortress and court martialled.

From the crew of the brig, the sailors Ustin Fyodorov and Ivley Afanasyev especially distinguished themselves. The former was wounded by a bullet in the leg but refused to leave his post for the doctor and bandaged himself with a handkerchief to continue firing until a second bullet struck his left arm. 'It's nothing', Fyodorov said, 'I still have my right hand'. Dressing his new wound, he went abovedeck, took up a sabre, and greatly desired the French to dare boarding the brig. Afanasyev was wounded by grape in the leg and when he dressed his wound, though he was weak from loss of blood, he returned to his gun and told his astonished comrades that 'it's shameful to sit down below. Remember what Ivan Semyonovich said: "don't give up until you lose your head" and I'm still in one piece, thank God'. But with those words, he was struck in the head with a splinter and fell unconscious. A cabin boy (whose name unfortunately was not given to me), a youth of 12 years, loaded his gun through the whole battle and stood behind the bulwarks completely exposed with such a cheerfulness as could be found in a mere student. The skipper took notice and praised his courage after the battle, asking if he was already unafraid of everything. 'What's there to be afraid of, Your Nobleness',[1] answered the youth, 'you can't die twice, and you can't escape the first. If the French didn't flee, I wouldn't be able to save myself'.

---

1    'Ваше Благородие' (Vashe Blagorodiye), literally 'Your Nobleness,' was the formal address for the lowest ranking nobility, grades XIV to IX (encompassing midshipmen and lieutenants in the navy). Леонид Шепелёв, *Титулы, Мундиры и Ордена Российской Империи* (Moscow: Центрполиграф, 2005), pp.pp.28-29. [Leonid Shepelyov, *Titles, Uniforms and Orders of the Russian Empire* (Moscow: Tsentrpoligraf, 2005), pp.28-29.]; Ibid., pp.138-140.

# 65

# Anecdotes and War Stories

The generosity and exemplary honesty of Private Ivan Yefimov of Captain Tovbichev's company, 13th Jäger Regiment, garnered the attention of an enemy commander. In the battle of the 5th [17th] of June, 1806, at Ragusa, a French soldier captured by our Jägers was taken by some Montenegrins who, as usual, wanted to behead him. The Jäger scolded them, begged them and finally conceded the prisoner to them to get them to relent with the assurance that the prisoner would be exchanged at headquarters for a *chervonets* in accordance with the admiral's promise. It was all in vain as they tore off the Frenchman's necktie and a naked sabre shone over the unfortunate prisoner's head. The merciful Yefimov, seeing that he alone could not save the man, took off his cross and brandished his money, saying: 'here is everything I have, but if any of you dare to slaughter my prisoner, I will stick the first of you with my bayonet and you'll need to kill me after him. Think of what a sin it is to kill your brother – the Metropolitan will curse you!' The devout Montenegrins shuttered at these last words, took his money and handed over the Frenchman to the Jägers at headquarters while petrified with fear. This prisoner was kept aboard the *Svyatoy Pyotr*. After some time, Yefimov came aboard the ship to visit his guest. The Frenchman recognized him and rushed to embrace him, called him his deliverer and then left him to run below deck and return in a minute. He urged the Russian to take two thalers that he had earned on the ship as a token of his gratitude. The Jäger did not accept them and could not understand the prisoner, nor could anyone else. Finally a *garde de marine* who spoke French was summoned and he explained the whole matter. The Jäger, without arguing or denying that he personally paid to spare the Frenchman's life, said only: 'maybe he's mistaken'. The Frenchman swore that he could pick him out of a crowd of 40 million Russians; that the face of his saviour was as memorable as the face of his mistress. Then the Jäger said with modesty: 'If I saved him from death and paid my own money for it, it wasn't under the belief that he would pay me back; and now that he's a prisoner, he's got much more need of his money than I do. I'm glad that he remembers me – when he takes a man prisoner, let him do what a Russian did for him'.

After the exchange of prisoners, the French soldier who was rescued by the Jäger, seeing that the Russians were kept no better than criminals, approached Marmont and said: 'General! I was a prisoner of the Russians and can assure you that they kept us just like their own men or even better. We were permitted visitors and furthermore, one Russian soldier rescued me from death, paid off the Montenegrins with all of his money and asked for nothing in return'. Marmont, wishing to encourage and continue such conduct, sent for 100 *Napoleons d'Or* to be delivered to the Jäger. In an order to the army, it was announced that if someone paid to spare a prisoner from his personal cash, then, with sufficient evidence, he would be compensated. Two months passed before finally someone came aboard the *Svyatoy Pyotr*, found the Jäger and presented him to the admiral. Senyavin asked: 'why did you not come sooner?'

The Jäger replied 'I had no proof. When I gave my money, there were no witnesses besides God, but I was sure that Your Excellency would find me'.

The admiral praised his conduct, gave him the package of a hundred gold coins and said: 'the French General sends this to you as a reward'. The Jäger opened it and asked the adjutant who delivered it how many of the coins were worth one *chervonets*. The exchange was two French gold pieces for one Russian.

The Jäger asked for the sum of 13 *chervontsy* from the packet, turning to the admiral and saying: 'I'll take only what I originally paid but I don't need the rest'.

The admiral was touched by such honesty and nobility of spirit, exchanged the Napoleons for *chervontsy* with extra and said 'accept them, not from a French general but from me. You have brought honour to the Russian nation. You are worthy of this reward and moreover, I am promoting you to corporal'.

***

On the 19th [31st] of September, during the retreat to Castelnuovo, Second Lieutenant Arbenyev of the Vitebsk Regiment was taken prisoner by a French officer who drove him away from the fighting. Along the road, in the bushes, lay a wounded grenadier from the Kolyvan Regiment. The French officer asked Arbenyev to order the man to drop his musket, but the soldier instead took aim and shot the enemy in reply. At that time, the Jäger regiment covering the retreat halted; Arbenyev had a moment and wanted to take the grenadier to a safe place. 'Don't worry, sir!' said the grenadier. 'I'm badly wounded and I feel like I'm going to die. Don't tarry for nothing. The enemy's close; save yourself and hold a service for my soul'. Arbenyev rushed back, gathered several men from his regiment, luckily met a doctor, and came back with them to find his rescuer in the same place but now delirious from blood loss. The doctor bandaged his wound and Arbenyev laid the man on a greatcoat and ordered him be carried to his quarters so that he would look after him from then on. The admiral, having learned of this, awarded Arbenyev with a personal visit and put the soldier in the care of the finest doctor. He recuperated despite two serious wounds.

\*\*\*

Lieutenant Nikolay V. Korobka, sent from Capo Cesto (Primošten) on a prize trabaccolo to Cattaro, met with two French corsairs near the chain of islands that compose the Calamotta Channel on the 16th [28th] of November, 1806. Neither escape nor defence was possible. The cargo of the boat was worth 80,000 rubles and therefore it was expected that the owner would not miss such a convenient opportunity for his liberation. The lieutenant believed that his prisoners were loyal to the enemy and was about to prepare his six sailors to submit to their fate. The skipper of the boat, Paolo, noticing his confusion and listening to the advice of his friend Natale Calligaris, went to Korobka and said: 'return my papers and hide yourself and your people in the hold. I'll handle everything'. Meanwhile, a corsair approached and fired a shot. Paolo went aboard the French vessel and handed over the passport to the commander, who advised Paolo to beware of Russians before dismissing him. The corsairs returned to the shore and Paolo entered the cabin where the lieutenant was seated, embraced him, and kissed his hand, saying 'I was more worried about you than my own affairs. Thank God you are now free and I am again your prisoner'. He turned his papers back over to the lieutenant.

'I would better prefer depending on the generosity of your commander than to be freed from a French corsair,' said Korobka.

Senyavin, who knows how to appreciate noble and magnanimous deeds, received a report on this incident and immediately wrote on the reverse of the page: 'Return the trabaccolo and its cargo to the skipper – release him to the port of his choice that would be most profitable for him – for the liberation of an officer and his men, award him 200 *chervontsy* and give him a free pass to all blockaded harbours, no matter where the skipper should wish to go'.

\*\*\*

This act by the admiral soon became famous throughout Italy. One Ragusan vessel returning from Smyrna met with an Austrian one. When the skipper of the latter was notified that the city of Ragusa was besieged by our forces, he advised the Ragusans to surrender to their enemies the Russians rather than take shelter among the French. The Ragusans sailed straight to Castelnuovo, struck their colours and proved correct in their estimation. The admiral freed him and his vessel, with its cargo worth 300,000 rubles, and ordered his free passage to his family who were withdrawn to an island.

\*\*\*

When the island of Curzola was taken, the corvette *Dnyepr* under the command of Lieutenant Dmitriy Balzam was sent to Spalatro for transporting the wounded French with an order from the admiral that under various pretexts it would remain in the harbour and, if possible, take on Slavonians dedicated to Russia. Upon his arrival, the corvette's commander turned over the prisoners and asked permission to procure fresh water and provisions for the crew. The provisions were supplied in the evening and the water was promised on the next day. In the morning, our fleet appeared at the island of Brazza and Marmont dispatched his chief of staff to summon Balzam that he might personally ask him: 'what are these vessels and what is their intention?' On the answer that it was the Russian fleet, Marmont angrily announced that he would make the lieutenant a prisoner of war for Senyavin attacking the very place where negotiations were transpiring. The magnanimous French general offered however to release Balzam if Senyavin returned to him the cannons and Frenchmen he had captured at Brazza, which he ordered Balzam to express to the admiral in writing. Balzam answered that he could not make offers of that kind to his commander-in-chief. Marmont was unsatisfied with the lieutenant's reply and told him that he would order a senior officer to bring the corvette into the harbour. Balzam instead informed Midshipman Kovanko aboard the boat that he was being detained and ordered him to leave port quickly and at any cost.

Kovanko assured the captain of the port in Spalatro by various pretexts that he could not enter the harbour and when a slight breeze blew which would benefit a French flotilla in attacking him should he linger any longer, he sent a letter to Marmont containing the following: 'General, if you will not respect common law with respect to the flag of parlay, and if my commander will not be set free, then I will hamper you here and can set fire to anything standing in the port. I will only await your response for half an hour' and so on. Marmont, believing that the midshipman had received instructions contrary to his order, was angry and offended, but Balzam calmly explained that a French general could not give orders to a Russian officer and that Kovanko was doing what every officer committed to his sovereign would do and what even he, Marmont, would have done were he in the same situation. With this, it seemed that Marmont relented and invited the lieutenant to dinner, during which he asked him about the number and rank of our ships and was surprised that in such a late month Senyavin was not afraid of the Adriatic *bora*. Finally he released Balzam on his word of honour that he would return the next day for breakfast.

Balzam, seeing what sort of general he was dealing with, considered himself in the right to violate this promise and upon returning to the corvette, made every preparation for weighing anchor, which was to be done after the setting of the moon around midnight. A powerful contrary wind prevented them from leaving however and upon a second invitation from Marmont, he returned to shore, lawfully handing over the corvette to Midshipman Kovanko with the order to haul anchor at the first sign of a favourable wind and try to reunite with the fleet. After breakfast, Balzam complained to Marmont that he was being detained against all military law and asked permission to withdraw with the corvette. Finally, after the many obstacles and threats, and it must be thought, after the advice of other generals, Marmont released the lieutenant and the corvette was able to re-join the fleet at Curzola.

***

How greatly the character of the French, renowned with a particular courtesy for their enlightenment and education before the revolution, had changed was demonstrated in a certain fashion by their actions with prisoners. Our soldiers returning from Dalmatia told us the following: they were kept as criminals in a prison, starved, deprived of what generous individuals had brought them, and compelled to join their army by such means of coercion. The officers were not treated better. Midshipman Nikolay Galich and *Garde de Marine* Kozyrskiy, despite the tender age of the latter, were deprived of shoes and partly of their clothes, were marched through the whole of Dalmatia barefoot and tolerated unprecedented arrogance from their captors. In order to assure the inhabitants that our army was defeated and Cattaro was captured, the same sixty prisoners were taken out of the prison secretly in the night and driven through the city again in the day by the beat of the drum for all to see. I will not describe other actions, as they are all unforgiveable, especially since they did not at all resemble the indulgences granted to their men when captured. It can be said with all certainty that the rights of prisoners of war do not exist with the French today.

## Excerpts from Correspondence

From the correspondence of the admiral with the generals of France, I intend to inform the reader of only two letters which clearly reveal the actions and spirit of the followers of Napoleon. Lauriston, defeated and besieged in Ragusa, complained to Senyavin about the cruelty of our soldiers and suggested that he order the Montenegrins and Bokez to return across their borders. Here is the response to that ridiculous proposal:

> Sir, General Lauriston!
> In your letter from the 27th of May [8th of June], you complain of the cruelty of my soldiers, consequently the Russians. You are so mistaken, general, that I consider it rather superfluous to refute what you wrote but I will make only the remark that both you and I hold prisoners. Your

officers and soldiers can testify to the sort of humanity with which we treat them; on the contrary, our people who are sometimes unfortunate to be taken as your prisoners are stripped of their clothes and even their boots. Several of my soldiers liberated during the second capture of Curzola could convince you of this truth and I myself was a witness to it.

Regarding the Montenegrins and Bokez, I consider it necessary to give you a better idea. These warlike nations are very little at all enlightened; however they never attack friendly and neutral lands, especially those without power. But when they saw that the enemy was approaching their borders with the intention of setting fire and sword upon their hitherto peaceful hamlets, their just indignation and bitterness reached a point that neither my authority nor the pleas of the Metropolitan himself could restrain them from their Asiatic custom: they expect and give no mercy and behead any man taken prisoner. According to their laws of war, they preserve the lives only of those who voluntarily surrender without fighting, and many of your men taken alive by them can attest to that fact. The people of Ragusa under your command, moreover, act just like the Montenegrins.

I admit, sir, I do not see the end of the misfortunes that you inflicted on the province of Ragusa and moreover you are forcing the inhabitants to fight against us, exposing them to twice the calamities … one way to avert these misfortunes is to leave the fortress, free the people, who before your arrival enjoyed neutrality and peace, and only then can you suggest that the Montenegrins should return to their homes, et cetera.

D. Senyavin.

When, during small exchanges, the safe-keeping of a considerable number of French prisoners became difficult, the admiral wrote to General Marmont for making an exchange, and since fewer of our soldiers were in their captivity than we had of the French, the admiral agreed to disclose the roster so that the exact number of our captive comrades, rank for rank, would be released in France. The proposal was accepted but not fulfilled: many of our men in captivity, under coercion, were pressed into the French regiments stationed in Dalmatia. Marmont, refusing to return these at Senyavin's request, referred to these Russian prisoners as Poles who voluntarily entered French service and concluded his letter with a pontification on the enlightenment of the French nation. Here is the reply to that letter:

Sir, General Marmont,
The explanations in your reply to me from the 7th [19th] of December concerning the enlightenment of the French nation are absolutely

necessary for me. It is not about enlightening your compatriots but about how you, sir, treat Russian prisoners of war. Your recent conduct with the commander of the corvette which I dispatched to Spalatro can serve as proof that the consequences of enlightenment and education are sometimes completely contrary to what should really be expected from them. I shall only tell you, sir, that of the thirty soldiers dubbed by you to be Poles, four came to me and they were all natural Russians. Let Bonaparte fill his legions; I do not request anything else from you but the return of my soldiers, and if you do not do this, I will find myself compelled to interrupt your present communications with all the enlightened, belligerent nations.

D. Senyavin.
Vice-Admiral of the Red Flag,
Commander-in-Chief of the Naval and Ground Forces in the
Mediterranean Sea.
10 [22] December, 1806.

## A Military Banquet

After the expulsion of Marmont from Castelnuovo, the admiral hosted a magnificent military banquet for the encouragement and reward of the soldiers, which deserves special attention. After a thanksgiving service to honour God for the victory He gave us against an excellent enemy force, the army smartly passed in review through the square in the fortress. There, the brave soldiers awaited the hearty meal prepared by the commander; each man received a portion of vodka and a bottle of grape wine. In the centre of the tents and between the tables set, the admiral's table was distinguished by a flag raised over it and regimental guns placed before it. Orchestras of musicians stood on the sides. The commander-in-chief did not invite men to his table according to rank or seniority; only officers distinguished for their bravery and exceptional feats were granted this honour. The health of the Jäger Yefimov was the first to be toasted, during which there were five shots, and his comrades shook him in their arms as the assembly shouted 'ura!' In that same fashion, all the guests were awarded the special honour of a personal toast to their health. The participants of this festival could not speak without emotion; all the soldiers at the table felt their extraordinary honour and sincerely and continuously exclaimed: 'God preserve our father-commander!' At the end of the banquet, the father superior of the Savina Monastery, an 80-year-old elder, entered the admiral's tent and greeted him with a true, faithful expression of the universally held feelings of love and gratitude. The last words of his speech were 'long live Senyavin!' and these words were repeated by the army and local people assembled with a choir more powerful than the thunder of cannons. The admiral rejected all of the honours offered to him. To fully know the value of good leaders and to be grateful of them for all their care and attention has always been and will continue to be the core virtue of the Russian soldier.

Here are the means and reason Senyavin acquired an unlimited authority from generally all of his subordinates, both officers and soldiers. Everyone was sure of his attention and was happy or eager to seek danger in battle. Senyavin himself, who was modest and moderate in temperament but strict and demanding in service, was loved like a father and respected as a just and righteous leader. He fully grasped the vital art of commanding admiration and used it solely for the common good. Is it any wonder then that under his command the soldiers and sailors did not desert and there were no such crimes that deserved special punishment? The commission of court martial had almost no business to conduct and the men admitted into the hospitals made quick recoveries.

**66**

# The Flood in Cattaro

---

On the 23rd of January [4th of February], shortly after noon, black clouds converged and closed off the sky at the peaks of the mountains. The sun glowed through the thick haze like a ball of heated shot and was only rarely directly visible. The clouds descended even further and the day turned to night with the disappearance of the sun. A strong wind with rain and thunder quickly approached. Lightning struck the peaks of the mountains, one after another, dazzling the sky with a frenzied fire, and the echoes of the thunder were so strong that the air was howling. In the impenetrable darkness where one fumbled down the path by the brief strobes of lightning, the rocks surrounding Castelnuovo could be seen spilling over with rushing streams of water. The sight was both terrible and majestic. A few minutes later, the storm reached us and the clouds seemed to unleash upon us like a second sea in the sky. The shower was more than half an hour with incessant lightning splitting the sea and shaking the air. Fire, air, water and earth mixed together and no single thing could be seen. When the thunderstorm passed and the sky began to clear, the massive streams opened to form wide, foaming waterfalls. The slopes of the rocks and mountains roared with the racing water. This flood caused significant damage. The vineyards were washed away for the most part, sand, mud and stones were brought down, countless cattle perished under the water, a mill was torn off its foundations and the trees in the gardens were pulled out by their roots.

# 67

# Remarks on the Flow of Winds in the Adriatic Sea

The direction of the winds in the Adriatic and the Mediterranean throughout summer follow the course of the sun; in the morning, it starts to blow northeasterly, then easterly, and little by little passes to southerly, from which toward evening it becomes a westerly wind. At night it shifts from northwesterly to northerly and then swings back to northeasterly by morning. The reason for this is obvious: the sun during its course successively warms all the points of the horizon, reduces the air[1] and drives it along in an order of directions reflecting its own movement. The midday heat is generally cooled by the northerly and northwesterly winds and the daily winds typically blow from the sea; at night they come from the shore with warm vapours which are dispelled by the sun in the morning. These vapours condense in the sea's moist air and produce dew which falls in large drops that are conducive to growth and refresh the air for sailors. An hour after sunrise, the air is clean and cool. During the heat of summer, the sky is always a clear and beautiful azure without rain; instead, rain is replaced by whirlwinds and the sirocco, a product of the noxious *simoom*.

Near the autumn equinox, the bright azure of the sky begins to darken and the strong *bora* begins to blow, which is the primary enemy of the seafarer in the Adriatic and much of the Mediterranean, especially off the coast of France and on the western side of Italy. Soon after the winds, at the onset of November, sometimes before or after, there are thunderstorms and *bora* gales with torrential rains regularly and a finer rain every day. The thunder claps in the mountains

---

1    Where warm air expands and rises, a low-pressure zone is created, resulting in cooler air from higher pressure zones rushing in to equalize. The sinking and blowing of cooler air also creates low-pressure zones which are filled by the warmer air, which gradually cools at higher altitudes and falls in turn, resulting in cycles called cells. The directions of these cells are affected by latitude, humidity, terrain and the rotation of the earth. K. Bharatdwaj, *Physical Geography: Atmosphere* (New Delhi: Discovery Publishing, 2009), pp.79-106.

are so strong that one cannot acclimate to them and even the most daring person is involuntarily frightened and startled. From September to March, the Adriatic blows with northwesterly and southwesterly winds for several days straight, which, together with the prolonged *bora*, create great difficulties at sea. On the contrary, the sea and coastal winds in the summer are favourable.

# 68

# Sailing to Corfu

---

Upon receiving news that was still untrue about the breach of peace with the Turks, on the 29th of January [10th of February], we left Castelnuovo with two prize vessels and the military transports *Diomid* and *Kherson*. The wind was quiet and foul but became strong and fair on the 31st [12th] and we arrived in Corfu where we found the admiral and a squadron which had arrived from Kronstadt. This squadron consisted of the following ships:

1. the 74-gun *Silnyy* under Captain-Commodore Ivan Ignatyev;
2. the 84-gun *Rafail* under Captain Dmitriy Lukin;
3. the 74-gun *Moshchnyy* under Captain William Crowe;
4. the 84-gun *Tvyordyy* under Captain Daniil Maleyev;
5. the 66-gun *Skoryy* under Captain Reinhold (Roman) van Scheltinga;
6. the 44-gun frigate *Lyogkiy* under Captain Aleksandr Povalishin;
7. the 32-gun sloop *Shpitsbergen* under Captain-Lieutenant Aleksandr Malygin;
8. the 24-gun corvette *Flora* under Captain-Lieutenant Vsevolod Kologrivov;
9. and the 18-gun cutter *Strela* under Lieutenant Ivan Gamaleya.

The frigate, corvette and cutter would be left in the Adriatic.

The beautiful corvette *Flora* was wrecked off the coast of Albania. Sailing from Curzola to Corfu on the night of the 26th of January [7th of February], a fierce squall with lightning stripped her of her bowsprit and foremast, the collapse of the latter damaging the main topmast; in this condition she was carried ashore where the anchors were dropped between Dulcigno (Ulcinj) and Antivari. The next day, with a favourable wind and choppy waves, Captain Kologrivov weighed anchor and proceeded south, but unfortunately the wind again turned him to the shore. Under his damaged rigging he could not manoeuvre as necessary and on the night of the 27th [8th], the corvette crashed on a shoal and lost its rudder. Despite the masts being taken down and the jettisoning of the carronades and all the burdens to alleviate the corvette at this time, it became clear by the next day that there were no means of saving the vessel and the captain, who had not yet known about the war with the Turks, evacuated his men to the shore. The Albanians seized their weapons and took everything they fancied and escorted them to Berat where Ibrahim Pasha declared them to be prisoners and sent them to Constantinople on the 8th [20th] of February. Both the crew and officers were chained and kept in a gloomy prison for two years.

Before the commander-in-chief's departure from Cattaro, a rumour spread that the French intended to evacuate Dalmatia in order to reinforce their army in Prussia, for which everyone's orders were being made with the belief that occupying the province was no longer required. Residents were already expressing their long yearning for the protection of our Sovereign Emperor, and the Austrian army (which grew by an additional 3,000 men) still waiting for us to surrender the Bay of Cattaro could not avert us. Captain First Rank Baratynskiy, left as commander of a squadron consisting of three ships, 8 small vessels and all the corsairs, was instructed not to admit them and to strictly observe that General Bellegarde has not moved from Giuppana to the neighbouring islands of Dalmatia. Later however, the French withdrew only their superfluous forces and detachments from the islands and reinforced their garrisons in the fortresses. Besides the frequent skirmishes with the irregular forces near Old Ragusa and the tight blockade, military operations continued as before. Colonel Knieper commanding the land forces received the order to defend Cattaro to the last of his ability,[1] in conjunction with Captain Baratynskiy. In the event of a probable war with the Turks, the admiral suggested to Mr Sankovskiy that he take advantage of the Herzegovinians' loyalty and for that reason, before his departure to Corfu, he left a proclamation which was accepted with lively enthusiasm that the security of Cattaro was ensured, and the French generals, not seeking the aid of the Turkish pashas, could not deprive Cattaro of provisions by blockade or dare to take the city itself.

---

1    Fyodor Evstafyevich Knieper (Kniper) was the commander of the 14th Jäger Regiment from 1804 to 1810. Виктор Безотосный (ed.), Энциклопедия 'Отечественная Война 1812 года' (Moscow: Российская Политическая Энциклопедия, 2004), s.v. 'Книппер'. [Viktor Bezotosnyy (ed.), The 'Patriotic War of 1812' Encyclopedia (Moscow: Russian Political Encyclopedia, 2004), sv. 'Knieper'.]

# 69

# The Senate of the Ionian Republic presents a Sword with Diamonds to the Admiral – News on the War with the Ottoman Empire

On the 31st of January [12th of February], the *Venus* arrived in Corfu. We found there the admiral with 8 ships, 6 frigates and the other small vessels. The Mediterranean Sea had naturally not yet seen such a large and magnificent Russian Fleet. The addition of our naval forces to our ground forces here greatly benefited trade. The greater part of the merchant vessels, be they Greek, Slavic or Italian, were under our flag. Onto five of the ships and three other vessels came 4,360 men to serve, which swelled our fleet to 12,268 men.

Corfu was rightly revered as the capital of our acquisitions in the Mediterranean. It was more like a Russian colony than a Greek city; everywhere you could see and meet Russian people. The residents adapted to our customs and many learned to speak Russian; even their children sang Russian songs. In Corfu, we enjoyed rest and entertainment. The strict morality of the Slavs who did not know public amusements made staying with them boring, and so when arriving in Corfu, everyone rushed to the spianata, the theatre and the masquerade. From the long Venetian domination here, the Greeks adopted some Italian customs, namely that when they sit down to dinner, they close their shutters and lock the door. Only the rich receive guests and then very rarely. Despite the fact that some of our officers were married here, the Greeks rarely appeared in the company of our ladies, but the carnival holidays running from Christmas to Easter enabled the mingling of these beautiful hermits, who appeared in the finest dresses and masks as they walked along the spianata and Calle d'Acqua. These holy days are the time of lovers' affairs and no matter how jealous the husbands are, the Greek women are able to deceive and evade their vigilance.

After the arrival in Corfu of the fleet from Cattaro, on the 17th [29th] of January, news came that our army had occupied several fortresses in Moldavia, but as the Minister of Foreign Affairs informed us: 'so that our forces in this region be not considered a hostile act, do not begin military operations before receiving reliable information and orders from the Imperial Court', the admiral was in a position of great difficulty and remained in prolonged uncertainty. Meanwhile, Ali Pasha assembled an army, built fortifications, occupied Preveza, and detained our consuls and the Ionian vessels laden with provisions intended for Corfu. The commander-in-chief was forced to take appropriate measures and this pasha came to understand so briefly the admiral's zeal that after a short negotiation, fearing the dissent or uprising of his Greek subjects and fearing we sought to agitate among the Moreans, satisfied all of our requests and ultimately declared the desire to remain a neutral and friendly neighbour of the republic. The admiral then declared that 'the Pashas of Albania and Scutari do not intend to participate in our war with Turkey, so their vessels shall be considered free so long as they deliver all necessities to Corfu and Cattaro', with which the British admirals subsequently agreed. This decree provided for the maintenance of our forces and wholly benefited the republic.

The representatives of the people, feeling to the fullest extent that the commander-in-chief always and constantly strove to protect their peace and prosperity, approved by the supreme legislative body a motion to grant a solemn testimonial token of their gratitude and acknowledgement which came in the form of a gilded sword studded with diamonds and a baton decorated likewise, both of which were presented to the admiral on the behalf of the republic. As a result, the President Savio Anino[1] issued a decree on the 4th [16th] of February to the Republic's minister to the Russian court to request from His Imperial Majesty to consent to such a motion.

On the 24th of January [5th of February], the British government, through our chargé d'affaires in London and one of Tatishchev's couriers,[2] expressed the wish that four ships under the command of Rear-Admiral Greig would unite with the English squadron in the Greek Archipelago in the capacity of auxiliaries and two more would be sent to protect Sicily. The admiral was unwilling to split his force however, and responded that upon receiving accurate news on the break with the Turks, he himself would proceed to the Dardanelles with 10 ships and decide with the commander of the British squadron how to deploy or otherwise

---

1    Count Savio Anino served as President of the Ionian Republic from December 1806 to August 1807, when César Berthier's expedition occupied the islands and annexed them to France. The senate was greatly reduced and the functions of the president fell to Berthier as governor general. *Three Constitutions of the Seven Ionian Islands*, pp.113-127.

2    Dmitriy Pavlovich Tatishchev was Russia's ambassador to Naples and Sicily from 1805 to 1808. Andreyevskiy et al., *Brockhaus and Efron Dictionary*, sv. 'Татищевы'. [Andreyevskiy et al., *Brockhaus and Efron Dictionary*, s.v. 'The Tatishchevs'.]

act in accordance with how the Royal and Imperial Courts themselves would instruct him.

Finally the quandary over which side the Turkish government would favour was resolved. The corvette *Pavel*, sent to the Black Sea, on reaching the island of Chios, learned from our consul there that the Porte had already begun hostile actions. On the way back, the corvette came to the island of Milos and met with an English frigate, on which the ambassador, Mr Italinskiy, was aboard.[3] The war with the Ottoman Empire was confirmed by the fact that the brig *Sfinks*, coming from the Black Sea, had been taken captive in Constantinople and the crew, at the request of our agents who had not yet left the Turkish capital, were dismissed and departing for Corfu. After these concrete proofs, the commander-in-chief made the following orders: the main command in Cattaro was entrusted to Captain First Rank Baratynskiy, as mentioned earlier; and Major-General Nazimov[4] was left for the protection of the Ionian Republic with two ships and 9 smaller vessels under the command of Captain First Rank Lelli. The fortress on Santa Maura, being the most threatened by Ali Pasha, was entrusted to Major-General Steder.[5] To Count Mozzenigo, as head of the civil department, the admiral suggested taking advantage of the support of the Albanians and Moreans and enrolling them in our service with salaries as warriors in the Light Infantry Legion, with our officers attached to oversee them. Since the defence of the republic fell to a severely limited force which was now being divided between two points, their service to bear was far heavier. To that end, the admiral ordered that the soldiers be given half a *funt* [205 g] of meat per day and a bottle of wine on holidays. By these means we could hold the Bay of Cattaro and the Ionian Republic with very little force. The courage of the soldiery, the diligence of the officers, the respect of the generals, the confidence of the people and most of all, the rare unanimity of the army and navy commanders, helped Senyavin fulfil and justify the choice of the Emperor in appointing him as commander-in-chief in the Mediterranean.

3    Andrey Yakovlevich Italinskiy would return in 1812 to help negotiate and sign the Treaty of Bucharest, which ended the Russo-Turkish War of 1806-1812. *Complete Collection of Laws*, col. 1, vol. 32, pp.316-322. No. 25,110.

4    Fyodor Viktorovich Nazimov was the chief of the Kura Musketeer Regiment from 1805 to 1814. Bezotosnyy, *The 'Patriotric War of 1812' Encyclopedia*, s.v. 'Назимов'. [Bezotosnyy, *The 'Patriotric War of 1812' Encyclopedia*, s.v. 'Nazimov'.]

5    Ivan Ivanovich Steder (Shteder) was the chief of the 14th Jäger Regiment from 1800 to 1812. Podmazo, *Chiefs and Commanders of the Regular Regiments*, http://www.museum. ru/1812/library/podmazo/shefcom_e.html, last modified 18 December, 2006.

# 70

# The Departure of the Fleet for the Archipelago

After a long period of foul winds and cloudy weather, a tailwind began to blow on the 10th [22nd] of February and the squadron consisting of: the *Tvyordyy* under Vice-Admiral Senyavin's flag; the *Retvizan* under Rear-Admiral Greig; the *Silnyy*; the *Rafail*; the *Moshchnyy*; the *Skoryy*; the *Selafail*; the *Yaroslav*; the frigate *Venus* and sloop *Shpitsbergen* set sail. Boarded on the vessels were two battalions of the Kozlov Regiment constituting 950 soldiers under arms; 36 artillerists; and 270 men of the [Greco-Albanian] Light Infantry Legion.

Due to the strong wind, the ships were arranged in column one behind another and then lay to when they entered the channel; when the last vessel came under sail, the *Tvyordyy* raised a signal: to ploy into sailing order and set every possible sail. The topgallants were hoisted and the vessels stretched out into a line, quickly passing Corfu and Paxos for the open sea. The next day, the wind abated somewhat but was fresh enough to satisfy the typical impatience of the sailors. The squadron split into two columns and our frigate remained windward of the *Tvyordyy* for repeating the admiral's signals.

At dawn on the 11th [23rd], the rock of Lefkada, famous for the death of the immortal Sappho, fell below the waves. The green Zante, rightly called the golden island and the flower of the Levant, rose up to meet us and behind it, as if to create a striking contrast, stood the barren islands of Strofadia, abode of the fabled harpies. The Peloponnese peninsula then unfurled. I looked on all the sites we passed with extreme curiosity, for each one was marked by some famous episode. At Navarino, the ancient Pylos, the Athenians won a victory over the Spartans in 425 BC and at Methoni, screened from the sea by the islands of Schiza and Sapienza, for which the surrounding water was known as the 'sea of wisdom', was now unfortunately dangerous for merchant vessels to approach due to piracy. From here, the Morean coast seemed dull and infertile. At a certain distance inland, the white bare mountains called the Taygetus reveal a desolate view. Living on their slopes were the Maniots, descendants of the Spartans, who retained their independence. They are just as severe, love liberty, respect their elders, sing songs almost exclusively about war, and have no fear of danger or death. Most importantly to note was that Mehmed II, the fortuitous conqueror of Constantinople, did not dare to test his luck against these brave republicans. They watched our ships float past them from the tops of their cliffs and eagerly awaited the appearance of our soldiers in order to receive them as brothers and lay their liberty at the feet of the Russian monarch.

On the 12th [24th] of February, when we reached Cape Matapan, the wind died down briefly only to pick up again. The two currents from the Dardanelles and Adriatic met there and their competing influences alternated very strongly. At the same time, the winds from the west and east, flowing over the vast expanse of sea and discharging through the mountains, were intensifying, which often precede a storm. According to the Greek poets who invented such beautiful fantasy, the Cape Matapan or Tainaron was the birthplace of Hercules and these currents were imagined as terrible depths leading to the gates of Hades, which the hero used to capture the hound of Cerberus.

I expected the island of Cythera, where Venus emerged from the sea and the enchanting Helen of Troy was born, to be the most beautiful, decorated by nature with the most splendid flora and fauna – a romantic paradise – but instead the modern Cerigo was nothing but a heap of lifeless rock. If we assume that its appearance has remained unchanged since the dawn of time, then the goddess of love had good reason to move to Cyprus, but if the ancient poets believed that beauty lies more with an inner superiority of the spirit, then they rightly honoured Cerigo as the birthplace of the goddess of joy. In fact, the island is only ugly in appearance from afar, as its interior, sheltered by its bare mountains, is filled with fertile valleys and pleasant locales. Its olive and citrus groves, fragrant flowers and vineyards all irrigated with clear streams are worthy of being the birthplace of that goddess and the mortal Helen, whose beauty spelled the ruin of the city of Troy.

The wind completely abated as we came to Cerigo and the ships were dispersed by the currents. We passed through what seemed like a magical barrier within which the wind dazzled the sea and toyed with our ships from all different directions, but once we crossed the line, they suddenly stopped and we began to drift on the current again. To prevent the rumour of our fleet's arrival in the archipelago from spreading before our flag could appear before Constantinople, all the merchant vessels we encountered were detained with the fleet.

Finally in the evening of the 12th [24th] of February, a faint wind blew and we came to the fortress lying on the rocky shore of Cerigo with a few houses and towers. Passing another fortification at San Nicolo (Avlemonas), we saw a multitude of islands and entered the archipelago. The sun set on the horizon ahead and the dusk burned crimson across the clear sky. When it faded into night, the gently rolling sea was illuminated by the brilliance of the moon and stars. The first night spent under a Grecian sky was charming. The celestial vault visible on the water seemed to float on its surface, disrupted only occasionally by a gentle wind which stretched and compressed the constellations.

At dawn on the 13th [25th], we were on the eastern side of Morea by the Cape of Malea. To our starboard stretched the long chain of the Cycladic islands, of which Milos, like the coasts of Morea, showed a bright green façade; the others were nothing but barren rocks. On Candia (Crete), the conical peak of Mount Ida covered with snow, exceeding the ceiling of the clouds, could certainly be imagined as the birthplace of Jupiter. The gloomy appearance of the mountains that cover the island correspond with the morals of its inhabitants. The Turks of Crete are revered as the bravest and most daring sailors; they engage in piracy and attack ships by boarding action like the filibusters of the Caribbean.

On the 14th [26th] of February, the flowering shores of Attica appeared, where liberty, science and the arts had once flourished under a bright sky, but now everything was in ruin – glorious monuments to the Greeks who astonished the world with Solon, Lycurgus, Pericles and Leonidas; those today who live in mournful humiliation and slavery bear little resemblance.

On the 15th [27th] of February, the *Tvyordyy* raised the signal to prepare to drop anchor. Thoughts of where we will be sent and when hostilities will begin occupied each of us while we waited. Having rounded the eastern tip of the island of Hydra, we quite peacefully dropped anchor between that island and the hard shore.

# 71

# The Island of Hydra

The island of Hydra is nothing more than a long bare stone without a single tree in sight lying around 8 *verstas* [8.53 km] from the mainland. The town of the same name is built on a steep rock. From the edge of the shore where a small harbour can be seen to the top of the mountain, there are tiers of buildings scattered all across its slope like an amphitheatre. Clean white houses, two-storey and covered with red tiled roofs, ascend along the ledges higher and higher as if tethering the sea to the sky when seen from afar. A great many windmills surround the town and frame it like a fine picture hung in a sparse and tidy abode, as this great collection of beautiful buildings make a striking contrast with the bare and dull landscape surrounding them. The residents of the island, the Hydriots, deserve to bear the honour of being the most agile and brave sailors. Dwelling on desolate land, they spend their whole lives at sea selling other people's wares and are very fond of transporting contraband. Their boats are built according to their singular skill, are surprisingly light on the move and seem to be designed exclusively for smuggling. Despite the science of European shipbuilding, hardly any master can construct a boat similar to the Hydriot vessels. Greek vessels generally have a very acute draft, can bear little cargo and are so thin and weakly fastened that on long and turbulent voyages, they are altogether inappropriate – all the qualities of a seaworthy vessel are sacrificed in favour of manoeuvrability, but with moderate winds and especially when close hauled, they are unrivalled.

The contentment and abundance of the Hydriots does not show any signs of an oppressive Turkish despotism which all travellers instantly scold and curse. On all the islands of the archipelago where the Turks do not live, the inhabitants are self-governing and having paid their very moderate yearly tribute, they take advantage of every possible freedom. It can be safely said that they would not fare so well under any other gentle government. It is remarkable that in Hydriot laws of trade, every sailor and even every boy serves without pay but instead receives a portion of the cargo or prize money; sometimes the sailors pool their money, build a boat, elect a captain and then purchase their cargo all on their collective capital. Thus staking their property in the ship or its cargo, and being for the most part all close family, each man takes an equal role in the profits and losses and man their posts with great zeal. Their vessels are armed with cannons and the Berbers never dare to attack them.

News of the arrival of the Russian fleet in the archipelago spread quickly. The chiefs of the islands of Hydra, Spetses and other nearby places offered their services to us with enthusiasm and a rare preparedness.[1] After the capture of Tenedos, the other islanders, the independent Maniots, Souliotes and later the Moreans offered to assemble a corps. Nearly the whole of Greece arose and was ready to be freed from the yoke of occupation with our help, but the admiral, acting cautiously, declined their enthusiasm for a time and even the Turks who were trapped in the archipelago, who could not harm the Greeks with their small numbers, left the peaceful alone and even saved Christians from the terrible vengeance of their cruel rulers. In a proclamation issued in Hydra, the inhabitants of the archipelago were declared to be accepted under the special auspices of the All-Russian Emperor while the ports on the mainland and the islands of Candia, Negroponte (Euboea), Mytilene (Lesbos), Chios, Lemnos, Rhodes and Cyprus occupied with Turkish garrisons were recognized as hostile. To distinguish the Christian vessels from those of the Turks, it was determined to issue new patents on the flag of Jerusalem[2], under which – in agreement with the English government – they could trade with the allied powers. That way the Greeks would be free from all culpability except those that, on their own volition and maintained at their own expense, joined our fleet with 20 excellent vessels armed with 10 to 26 guns and fulfilled military service with fervour and a competitive jealousy. The Greek archipelago thus became the domain of Russia and our flag was met by the inhabitants not with bloodshed and death but with jubilation and gratitude. Many corsairs set out under her for cruising and the Russian flag fluttered not just in the archipelago but throughout the vast space from Egypt to Venice. The Berbers, having learned of such formidable armament, renounced their alliance with the Ottomans and respected our merchant's ensign on the Mediterranean without exacting any shameful tribute or plunder.

1    Bronevskiy's note: 'On the third day after our arrival, five vessels from the islands of Hydra and Spetses armed with between 18 to 26 guns joined our fleet'.

2    A flag featuring the cross of Jerusalem, which consisted of a large cross potent or a Latin cross with four smaller crosses in the quadrants formed by its elbows, all either gold or red on a white field. It had long been established as a flag of neutrality and convenience for merchant vessels. Travers Twiss, *The Laws of Nations considered as Independent Political Communities* (London: Oxford University Press, 1892), pp.330-332.; *Les Pavillons ou Banniéres que la Plûpart des Nations Arborent en Mer* (Amsterdam: David Mortier, 1718), p.18 and plate 63. [*The Flags or Banners which most Nations Have at Sea* (Amsterdam: David Mortier, 1718), p.18 and plate 63.]

# 72

# Rendezvous with the British Fleet

A strong, foul wind lasting four days held up the squadron at Hydra, during which time the ships took on fresh water from the Athenian shore. Finally, on the 21st of February [5th of March], we weighed anchor on a weak but fair wind. The night was quiet, the sails were barely filled and the ships were subjected to the strong current of the abyss of Euripus, but when light broke and the squadron passed the island of Andros, the wind was refreshed. The dawn was rehearsing on our starboard side and to port, south of Negroponte, stretched a long chain of islands whose sunken peaks drowned in the sea and flashed in and out of view behind the waves. At noon, the wind stopped but picked up again in the evening and we were pleased with the prospect of soon reaching those places where we would raise a new trumpet to the mouth of glory to announce our new deeds. Cannon shots ripping through the air ushered in the admiral's order to close the line and set all possible sails. Along the whole line, as if by mutual agreement, there came sounds of music and merry songs with tambourines and drums. In the night, we covered a longer distance and in the morning of the 23rd of February [7th of March], the observational ship *Selafail* sent ahead to uncover the enemy notified us by signal that she spotted a fleet of 12 ships. To the question of what nationality they were, the *Selafail* answered: 'unknown; they fly no colours'. Then the *Tvyordyy* raised the signal to form the order of battle, for the rear to set sails, and to prepare for an engagement. Approaching the island of Tenedos (Bozcaada), we spotted a warship and then the whole fleet closer to the Dardanelles.

Upon a signal to identify itself, the ship responded by raising the English flag, then weighed anchor and approached us. When the fortress of Tenedos was visible, the admiral's ship gave a signal to prepare for an assault by landing party. The admiral led the fleet past the fortress on a shot of grape with a furled-up signal 'start the battle' visible on the topmasts of his ship. We watched intensely and impatiently for it to be deployed, but in vain. Admiral Senyavin continued past the fortress, not considering it apt to kill several people without a purpose and was waiting for the first shot from the fortress. The Turkish commandant, despite the desire of his janissaries, also did not want to be the first to instigate the battle and to our surprise, our whole fleet passed by peacefully. The merciful Turk did not fire a single shot even at the last ship of our line when we could not reasonably harm the fortress. Our squadron anchored near the British, who consisted of 2 three-deckers, 5 two-deckers, 4 frigates, 2 bomb vessels and a brig, under the command of Vice-Admiral John Duckworth.

We learned of an action the British squadron conducted against Constantinople. On the 7th [19th] of February, after waiting for a strong tailwind, Duckworth set off for the Dardanelles with 7 ships, 2 frigates and 2 bomb vessels. The Turks were not yet ready and although they fired from several batteries, they did not inflict any damage on the British. At the cape of Pesquies or Nagara Burnu, the last battery on the Asian side, stood a Turkish squadron consisting of one 64-gun ship, four frigates, four corvettes and three gunboats. The British took one corvette and a gunboat without resistance, while the Turks themselves set fire to their ship, and the other vessels fled to Constantinople. On the 9th [21st] of February, Duckworth reached the capital and then suffered from a dead calm or a weak and foul wind which lasted for nine days. Meanwhile, Constantinople and the Dardanelles were greatly reinforced. The embankment was armed with more than 200 guns, ships and frigates near the shore were set so that at any point the attacking British ships would be exposed to fire from three sides. Bombardment could not frighten the Sultan either, as the inhabitants of Constantinople were so used to fires that they would not be coerced to beg for peace even if 10,000 houses were razed to the ground. It is known that in the capital the houses are built from thin wood and decorated with inexpensive furniture as at any time of the year it is possible to live in the open air and in the event of a house fire, the Turks endure their hardship with their money, a heavy coat and a carpet – which is all the luxury in the world to them – and do not think of saving their home. For these reasons, the British admiral could not enter negotiations and accepted that the best course of action was to retire from Constantinople without having done anything.

On the 19th of February [3rd of March], passing the Dardanelles, the Turks opened fire from all their batteries. The balls, especially those hewn from marble, were a whole *arshin* [71.12 cm] in diameter and could pierce a ship's hull straight through both sides. One such shot smashed through more than three-quarters of the diameter of the mainmast on the HMS *Windsor Castle* and snapped it off. The *Pompee* under the flag of Sidney Smith was struck by a stone shot on a fender which punched such an extraordinary hole, greatly moving and disheartening the crew, that the ship would inevitably sink if it were hit again just a foot lower. Arthur Legge, captain of the *Repulse*, visiting Constantinople two months earlier and inspecting the Tophane Arsenal in the company of the *kapudan-pasha* (their

View of the Dardanelles from the Archipelago. Illustration from original publication.

grand admiral), was surprised at the size of their marble shots and told the pasha that he thought such balls were only suitable for decorating city gates. Seydi Ali rebutted: 'I hope we should never have a quarrel with you. If that should happen, you will see what harm they can cause'. Upon returning back through the Dardanelles, a stone shot crashed into the captain's cabin of the *Repulse*, pierced both sides and made such a breach that two cabin boys side by side could climb through it. The two frigates were so chewed up in the hull that they could no longer take to the open sea. The casualties suffered were also significant, reaching 600 dead and wounded. With this fruitless expedition, the British seemingly sought to warn the Turks about us and opened their eyes to the truth that the Dardanelles were not impassable.

Despite all of these impossibilities, Vice-Admiral Senyavin, following the Sovereign Emperor's exact orders, sailed for Constantinople with the greater part of his fleet and on receiving assistance from the British in order to force the Porte to sign a peace treaty, he suggested to Duckworth another attack be made against the capital with their joint forces; but the English admiral imagined that it would hardly succeed even with 50 ships. Senyavin beseeched him with all of his ability for two days. The glorious Sidney Smith and his brave British captains, whom he called the 'fire-eaters', finally agreed to try again, but Duckworth resolutely and in writing refused. We first wondered what compelled that admiral, without waiting for our squadron, to sail on the enemy capital with his small force but our perplexity increased even more when, upon Senyavin's presentation, Duckworth announced on the 1st [13th] of March that he had another appointment and left us alone with just two ships and two bomb vessels to reinforce our fleet.

After this, the admiral invited the captains to a council and after considering the circumstances, endeavoured to capture the island of Tenedos and strangle Constantinople with a tight blockade. With God's aid, we succeeded in every task but the British, instead of accompanying us in the Dardanelles or freeing the Prussian Danzig from siege,[1] drove their soldiers away and like in Buenos Aires and in Egypt were beaten and had no success.[2]

---

1    Danzig (Gdansk) was besieged by the French Marshal François Lefebvre in March and fell on 12 [24] May, 1807. Ward et al., *Cambridge Modern History*, vol. 9, p.289.
2    The Alexandrian Expedition and the Second Invasion of the River Plate as a part of the ongoing Anglo-Spanish War were both conducted in 1807 and resulted in defeats for Britain against Egypt in the former and Spain in the latter. Admiral Duckworth commanded the Royal Navy's contingent in the Alexandrian Expedition. Ward et al., *Cambridge Modern History*, vol. 9, p.235.; Ibid., p.753.

# 73

# The Capture of Tenedos

On the same day that the British squadron left us, Rear-Admiral Greig was dispatched with the ships *Retvizan* and *Rafail* and the frigate *Venus* to the island of Tenedos with a proposal for the Turkish commander to surrender his fortress. After courteous relations on the 3rd [15th] of March, the pasha replied that he would defend himself until exhaustion. On the 4th and 5th [16th and 17th], a strong wind blew and on the 6th [18th], the admiral left the *Skoryy* and *Selafail* at the mouth of the Dardanelles to observe enemy movements and then brought the rest of his force to Tenedos. On the 7th [19th], a landing party was organized and the ships took their assigned places on the 8th [20th]. At dawn, the *Moshchnyy*, *Venus* and a corsair began the action with a bombardment of the Turkish pickets who fled the beach. The fortress opened fire on the *Rafail* and the ship responded with perfect diligence such that the fort was supressed and the rare shots fired off did no damage. The party landed immediately: 160 Albanians and several Hydriots from the corsair knocked out the Turkish forward posts and thereby cleared an area for the regular forces who came ashore in good order, assembled and split into two columns to march onward. The first column, consisting of 900 men from the Kozlov Regiment and four field guns under the command of Colonel Fyodor Padeyskiy,[1] marched to the left into the hills while the second, 600 soldiers from the 2nd Naval Regiment with four cannons and six light pieces under the command of Colonel Boissel, marched to the right along the sea shore. Rear-Admiral Greig accompanied the first column while Senyavin organized all the movements from the second column. The Albanian sharpshooters with

---

1 Padeyskiy was the commander of the Kozlov Musketeer Regiment from 1802 until 16 [28] March 1807; thereafter he became the regimental chief until 1814. Bezotosnyy, *The 'Patriotric War of 1812' Encyclopedia*, s.v. 'Падейский'. [Bezotosnyy, *The 'Patriotric War of 1812' Encyclopedia*, s.v. 'Padeyskiy'.]

skirmishers from the regular forces and sailors advanced and fought ahead of the columns and the Turks withdrew as the offensive began.

Boissel's column, reaching an outwork, attacked the Turks there with his skirmishers and the light guns commanded by naval officers bravely brought up canister fire with an exceptionally lucky effect against the enemy. Major Gedeonov, detached from the first column, drove the Turks from the heights dominating the northern side of the town. Colonel Padeyskiy, having formed up his men under hostile fire from the fortress, broke straight into the suburbs with bayonets and a cry of 'ura!' The second column at that same time attacked the entrenchments and seized it despite stubborn resistance, capturing five banners from the enemy. The Turks rushed into the fortress. The first column, having driven the enemy from the town, met the enemies now fleeing from the trenches with a volley. Two guns were brought up and the Turks caught on the square and on the bridge took cover in the ditch; soldiers of both columns struck with bayonets and drove the enemy from the square to the very gates of the fortress. Meanwhile, a detachment from the second column captured the redoubt by storm and took seven guns. Midshipman Pyotr Salmoran raised the Imperial flag over its walls. The main fortification was fired upon by the field guns and the redoubt and the battle ended, though an exchange between the fortress and suburbs continued. The Turks defended themselves in the houses tenaciously. The Greeks disappeared with their families from that part of the town and were escorted to a safe place. Soon the Turks demanded mercy and we gave them every possible aid. The Greek women were provided tents and sentries to keep out the curious. Three Turkish women captured were taken to the admiral's ship and this fact, we would see later, compelled the Turks to capitulate sooner.

On the same day, we began to build four batteries, each of four guns, so that they could attack the fortress along with the two ships. By evening, the fortress almost completely ceased firing and our forces settled in around the town, which the Turks ignited in an attempt to clear out the grounds around the walls and rid themselves of our skirmishers' fire. On the 9th [21st], the admiral offered safe passage to the Anatolian coast along with their personal property in exchange for the surrender of the fort, to which the enemy agreed. One of the captured Turkish women was used as the courier for the letter.

On the 10th [22nd] of March, the garrison consisting of 1,200 men and up to 400 women and children were immediately transported to the coast and our soldiers raised the Russian flag over the fortress. The Greeks began to extinguish the fires and suffered this misfortune with great indifference, being pleased that they were rid of the Turks whose intact homes and stores of provisions were then given to the inhabitants made victim by this destruction.

In this action, two Albanians were killed and six of our officers and 73 soldiers and sailors were wounded. On board the *Rafail*, two sailors were killed and one *garde de marine* and six sailors were wounded. In total, our side suffered four killed and 86 wounded. The Turks lost around 400 men killed and wounded. In both fortifications were taken 79 guns, including 48 bronze barrels, and additionally three mortars and an ample store of ammunition.

The acquisition of the island of Tenedos relieved the squadron of its general need for fresh water and provided it with a convenient shelter within 25 *verstas* [26.67 km] of the Dardanelles, making it possible to observe the strait and to deprive Constantinople of its communication with the Aegean Sea.

# 74

# Description of the Island of Tenedos

This island was an assembly area for the Greeks besieging Troy and as Virgil tells us, the place to which the Greeks retired in order to trick the Trojans into a false sense of security. Part of the gate, several protruding columns and a tall heap of stones visible from our ships are the sad remains of the city of Ilium. Naturally these ruins do not belong to the ancient Troy or to the Troas, which Alexander the Great built upon the tomb of Achilles, but likely the remnants of Troy were restored already in later times. A few travellers however with the help of their imaginations have found here parts of the palace of King Priam and three nearby burial mounds called the tombs of Achilles, Patroclus and Ajax. Due to the fact a Turkish corps of 20,000 men was encamped near the ruins, it was not possible to tour them, but I often and with pleasure admired the beautiful site where they stood. The vast plain, riddled with many villages, was carefully cultivated and lay adjacent to the green ridges of Mount Ida with a glorious Olympus above all in their centre.

The island of Tenedos has a length of 12 *verstas* [12.8 km] and a width of 8 [8.53 km], with an almost round shape. Besides the three mountains lying in the north, the rest of the land is flat. Having ascended Toro (Göztepe), the peak higher than the others where the telegraph was established, the entire island with the town, fortress and harbour was visible all around like a drawing. In addition to a small oak and fruit-bearing forest in the southeast and several meadows and tilled fields on the western and northern sides, the whole island is covered with vineyards, which produce a celebrated Tenedosian wine, the flavour and strength of which is comparable with the greatest port wines.

The town is not large. Its streets are narrow and crooked. In three of its squares and several homes there are fountains with the most dazzling and clear water. The ponds in the town and the aqueducts demonstrate that the Turks are quite knowledgeable in these kinds of buildings. The Greek quarter in the north has bad stone houses with cellars for keeping wine. Looking around at the Greek monastery,

I confess I pitied the present Greeks, seeing all the terrible events, poverty and humiliation which weighted down their spirits. I vainly indulged in magnificent fantasies about the glory of their ancestors. Looking at everything called Greek today, all the charms of memory disappear and the sorrowful truth clearly reveals the misfortune of those people who with pride once called everyone who were not Greek barbarians! The Turkish quarters of the town feature beautiful mosques and minarets decorated with gilded moons which cannot help but enchant those who see them for the first time. The mixture of Greek and Turkish architecture, twisted columns and a great deal of very imperfect fretwork are strange and incongruous but pleasantly striking to the eye. The Turkish homes have an upper storey made of thin boards with windows facing the courtyard and whole streets consist of only high fences. The local Greeks have lived with the Turks for so long that they have accepted their customs, wear turbans and seem to think like the Muslims. Since the beginning of our stay, the Greek women did not appear in the streets; their only pleasure was to step out onto the terraces of their houses in the evening and tighten their shawls so that no one could see their faces, but gradually they softened to our customs. At first they smothered themselves with cloth but left their eyes open; then they went for strolls; then they sat on their terraces and balconies with their whole faces uncovered; then when they learned that it pleased our officers or garnered praise for their beauty, began to practice needlework at open windows without any shyness; and finally they cast off their veils, put on their fineries and went out on the town, animating the whole locale with their presence.

The cemeteries of the Turks and Christians present a stark contrast. The former is covered with cypresses and cooled by a murmuring pond, decorated with monuments in the form of tombs, pyramids and a great many feature marble pillars crowned with roughly hewn turbans on which those who died a violent death bore the inscription 'executed by order of the Sultan'. Turks killed on the command of the monarch are not considered criminals – they are credited with some kind of dishonour to their children, but they are memorialized like martyrs! Yet in the Christian cemetery, instead of tombstones, the ground is littered with dried bones and skulls between the tuffs of wild grass. There is nothing sadder than the comparison of these two cemeteries where, even in the equality of death, there is a distinction between the ruler and the slave.

The Turkish bath which survived the fire deserves special attention. It warms from below so that the heat can be varied from room to room as the furnace feeds separate shafts. Every five halls are covered with a glass dome and there is not a single window along its walls. The inside of the floor and walls are lined with white marble. In the first hall and in a few special small alcoves, the patrons undress. In the second, there is a pool of cold water in the centre. In the third, pure cold water streams into vases but comes out heated when one turns a tap. In the final halls where the floor is very hot and the air is quite hot still, low marble benches are constructed on which the Greeks wash themselves and have their bones set by harshly rubbing with a piece of canvas or some grass, no worse than our sauna attendants do. The Turks are legally obligated to wash themselves often and do not regret at all decorating the baths which have become for the women a theatre of luxury and flamboyance; this is the one pleasure afforded to them and they relish it fully. The Turkish women go to the bathhouses dressed as best they can and spend whole days in them, and these meetings between women deprived of most pleasures can of course be honoured with some joy, for only in the baths can they boast of their beauty, laugh, sing and play without prohibition, albeit in front of only their own sex.

The fortress of Tenedos was built by the Genoese. It has a rectangular shape, has a citadel with a tower, its walls are supported by a glacis, and it was separated from the town by a ditch or dry moat and a small square. The parapets were low, the walls were dilapidated, there were no casements to shelter against bombs and there were no structures inside for the garrison except a powder cellar. The fortress, being by the sea and under a mountain, cannot withstand a siege from land or sea for very long; plunging artillery fire from the heights, even musketry, can kill anyone inside and the fortress is completely open and defenceless from that direction. The guns are also defective; some fire marble shots like the Dardanelles guns or are loaded with bags of smaller stones as canister. A small redoubt protects the harbour from the south, which can fit up to 20 small vessels within. The strait between the island and the coast of Anatolia has a depth of 9 to 12 *sazhen*s [12.2 to 25.6 m], has a muddy floor throughout and makes for a decent anchorage, despite being open.

# 75

# Sailing to Salonica and Returning to Tenedos

After the capture of Tenedos, a Turkish squadron consisting of 8 ships, 6 frigates and 50 galleys and gunboats descended to the mouth of the Dardanelles. The commander-in-chief, wishing to reduce his force in order to lure the enemy out of his strong ambush, ordered Rear-Admiral Greig to sail to Salonica (Thessaloniki) with the *Retvizan*, *Venus* and one of the Hydriot corsairs and deprive that rich trading city of communication with the archipelago and if any target of opportunity should present itself, he would take advantage of the circumstances. On the 19th [31st] of March, the detachment left Tenedos. On the next day, we were held up by a perfect calm near Mount Athos. Its height of 2 *verstas* [2.13 km] seemed to shorten the distance we stood from it, and when the sun set, its long shadow stretched far beyond us to the east. During the solstice, the tip of the shadow reached Lemnos lying 100 *verstas* [106.68 km] away. Pliny wrote that the air on the summit is particularly healthy, for which its original inhabitants were once known as the *Macrobioi* – the long-lived. The excessive height of the mountain means that the sun cannot be seen while climbing its western slope until you reach the top. Philostratus, in the *Life of Appolonius of Tyana*, writes that many philosophers have retired to this mountain in order to better enjoy the spectacle of the heavens and so many settlements reside close to its peak and the pleasant surroundings that they are visible from a long distance.

In the remotest antiquity, Mount Athos was dedicated to Apollo, whose temple stood on that marble platform where the chapel of the Transfiguration of the Lord now stands. Even more so, it was known for the fact that Xerxes, although he could bypass it, wanted to carve out a canal through the peninsula for his armies; others assert that Alexander the Great intended to carve the mountain into a statue of a rider on horseback and to build a city on each hand. During the time of Christian persecutions, the hermits built monasteries there, of which there are now 20 and hence Athos has become known as 'the Holy Mountain'.

The monasteries are located along the slopes of the mountain one above another from the summit to the seashore, so that from a distance they appear like a great staircase leading up to heaven. The white walls which surround the monasteries like castles and the golden heads of the churches so astonish the eyes that I could not look away. I wished to bow to these sites and thought that, being so close, it would be unforgiveable for a Russian not to visit them. The sea was violent though, a breeze was picking up, and the lights flickering in the cells soon disappeared and died out. With a sunken heart, I had to part with these pious thoughts and sail on to where the wind took us.

The night was bright and the following day was clear with a mostly moderate wind. We sailed along the Macedonian shore and the closer we came to the Bay of Salonica, the more handsome the locales became. When we passed the town of Kassandreia surrounded by a chestnut forest, we discovered two completely different landscapes on either side of the bay. The eastern shore revealed a plain gradually sloping down from the horizon to the sea and covered with fields, meadows and small copses of fruit trees. Small streams flowing to the sea by curving courses draw patterns across the land further decorated by the many villages scattered about. The western side, the shore of Thessaly, is marked by high bare rocks cheerlessly bowing their heads to the sea. Not the slightest trace of habitation could be seen there, however the glorious Olympus rising majestically to the sky astonished us with its vastness. The sad pines growing on its heights, shaken by the wind, rocked precariously over the precipices surrounding them on all sides. In those dens covered with eternal snow settled a bellicose tribe of Epirotes who, like the Maniots, still retained their independence. 15,000 of these warriors annually descended into the valleys when the crops were ripe for the harvest and ravaged everything with fire and sword in order to deprive the Pashas of Salonica of their income and necessities, recoup their muskets and seize lead and powder for themselves. This handful of men, under the shield of the impenetrable mountains and a wild courage, did not fear punishment or revenge. Besides Olympus, the mountains of Ossa, Pelion and Pindus, the latter with a forked summit, glorified by the poetry of the ancients, as well as the Vale of Tempe, the greenhouses of Therma and the Peneios River lying about are all marked at every step by some famous deed or event.

On the 22nd of March [3rd of April], the ship and frigate dropped anchor not far from Salonica and the corsair went on further with the rear-admiral to inspect the fortifications to return in the night. The detachment dropped anchor on the 23rd [4th] within seven *verstas* [7.47 km] from the city, at a depth of 15 *sazhens* [32 m]. Several boats could be seen opposite us in the mouth of the river. Armed rowing vessels seized them and brought them to the admiral; from these craft, it was intended to bombard the city.

Salonica lies at the end of a bay between two rivers, surrounded by high four-cornered walls lined with loopholes whose circumference could apparently stretch for 20 to 30 *versta*s [21.35 to 32 km]. From the sea, the city is defended by only two towers armed with 19 large guns that fire marble shot. Their embrasures are very large and locked with iron gates. Between the towers, protruding somewhat forward, are 20 guns of ordinary calibres on a stretch of the wall; this was where merchant vessels stopped. From the overland route from the northeast, the city is protected by a castle called the Heptapyrgion or Seven Towers. It stands inside a glacis and is separated from the city by a large field. The anchorage of Salonica is surrounded by gradual terrain, the chain of the Thessaly Mountains is interrupted there, but in the distance another mountain range surrounds the plain. The land is irrigated by five rivers, of which the Vardar and Haliacmon are navigable and from these rivers, the water on the anchorage is fresh. The roadstead is protected by the Black Cape (Megalo Embolo) from the southern winds, has a general depth of 6 to 9 *sazhen*s [12.8 to 19.2 m], a floor of sand and mud and is generally convenient and safe. In the city there are 48 mosques, 30 Greek monasteries and 36 synagogues. The vast dome of the Cathedral of the Hagia Sophia, now a mosque, exceeds every other building. The Jews, richest of the inhabitants, generate considerable trade in bread and grain, lumber, cattle, wine and cotton.

On the 24th of March [5th of April], the launch from the rear-admiral's ship visited the city twice for negotiations: Rear-Admiral Greig demanded the extradition of French property, but since the governor of the city had 100,000 residents and was defended by 10,000 janissaries, he verbally refused. Our frigate weighed anchor in the afternoon in order to approach the fortress but was met by a cannon shot which struck the shallows and although it did us no harm after losing its force in the soft earth, our enterprise was arrested by it. A strong wind blew the next day, which forced the admiral to abandon his scheme. The detachment weighed anchor but stopped near the village of Epanomi without leaving the bay, due to a gloomy sky and strong wind. On the morning of the 26th of March [7th of April] when the wind eased down, the detachment again set sail. The corsair went to Skopelos to seize Turkish boats loaded with wheat, while the ship and frigate joined the fleet at Tenedos on the 30th of March [11th of April].

# 76

# On the Forward Post at the Dardanelles

On the 2nd [14th] of April, the *Moshchnyy* and *Venus* were assigned to the blockade and observation of enemy movements in the Dardanelles, relieving the *Rafail* and *Yaroslav*. The ships assigned to the vanguard typically held 8 *versta*s [8.53 km] away from the fortresses, standing by the island of Mavro (Tavsan Adasi) where freshwater was available. Since our vessels were close to the strait and always prepared to weigh anchor and give battle, not one vessel of any size dared to approach the Dardanelles since the arrival of our fleet in the archipelago. Trade completely ceased. The crowded capital, overwhelmed by their armies marching through for Bulgaria and burdened by the maintenance of another force assembled for the defence of the city and the Dardanelles, was soon depleted of its stores and magazines; a deficiency which was felt within a month.

The Dardanelles, known in antiquity as the Hellespont, received its name from King Dardanus who founded the city of the same name on its shores (now Çanakkale). It is impossible to believe that on such currents, which sometimes reach 6 Italian miles or 10½ *versta*s [11.2 km] per hour, Xerxes could approve the construction of a bridge across this strait, which makes the story of Hero and Leander even less likely.[1] The mouth of the strait between the European and Asian fortresses (Sedd-el Bahr and Kumkale) has a width of 10 *versta*s [10.67 km];[2] at the fortress of Sestos and the Cape Barbieri (Kepez) it narrows to 2½ *versta*s [2.67 km], then widens to 4¼ [4.53 km] from Abydos and Cape Pesquies (Nara Burnu)

---

1   Lovers named by Ovid and Virgil who were separated by the Dardanelles but would meet every night when Leander swam across the strait by the guiding light of Hero's lamp in her window. Although their love prospered for a time, eventually he was caught in a storm and drowned. Smith, *A New Classical Dictionary*, s.v.'Leander'.
2   The distance from cape to cape is closer to 3.6 km. The map included in the original Russian publication illustrates the shape and size of the Gallipoli Peninsula and Dardanelles very poorly.

to Gallipoli. The first fortifications were built by Mehmed II and refurbished by Mehmed IV, while the later forts were built in 1770 by François, Baron de Tott. Now they have laid new ricochet batteries virtually level with the sea (*à fleur d'eau*) so that a ship breaking through can be fired upon from both sides for the entire length of the channel, 63 *versta*s or 36 miles [67.21 km] and may suddenly be under fire from four fortifications simultaneously. Beyond all of these formidable defences, the winding course of the channel, the strong currents flowing from side to side, the shallows at the many peninsulas and finally the contrary currents at the mouth flowing both north and south to the opposing coasts make a passage through the Dardanelles very dangerous or even impossible.

77

# The Island of Imbros

On the night of the 3rd [15th] of April, three armed boats from the *Moshchnyy* and *Venus* with 120 soldiers, sailors and Albanians went to the island of Imbros (Gökçeada) to purchase provisions and invite the residents to transport them to Tenedos. At dawn, we landed on the southern side of the island. The local shepherds met us ashore without any reservations; then came the people of the nearby village who gladly offered, although not much, everything that they had and asked for no payment. Since we did not want to take anything for free, the Greeks quickly regained their wisdom and began to ask for a ruble where we first offered 10 kopecks. For all that we needed, these few houses could not supply us, so Lieutenant Grigoriy Ricord sent Midshipman Pozdeyev into town, which lies 20 *verstas* [21.34 km] from the shore. I remained with the boats.

Imbros is mountainous and fertile. The heights are covered with oak and elm forests. The valleys are irrigated by many small springs and are covered with fruit trees and vineyards; some produce wheat, barley and maize. Despite the wealth of nature, the inhabitants are poor. Their houses are made of stones without any mortar and their flat roofs are covered with slabs or thatching. The Turks require a gift from the elder of each village. For their freedom of worship, the governor of the island occasionally requires their arbitrary submission to him. If they do not immediately submit, he orders their churches be demolished.

This misfortune has occurred before and to the present residents. I do not know why the priest thought that I would have the authority to negotiate the reconstruction of their church. He gave a long speech expressing his petition. When the interpreter, who did not understand Italian very well, told me what he wanted of me, I was surprised, but remembering the words of the commander, 'indulge the Greeks as much as possible' and moreover believing that my refusal would not be comprehensible to them (for they esteemed not only officers but even common soldiers to be the loftiest of creatures), I gave my consent and was compelled to go along with the people wherever they would take me. We descended into a ravine closed on all sides by a continuous thicket of trees. Below the cliff, I saw with grief one of the walls of the chapel. The priest said a prayer and sprinkled holy water, while the parishioners began to vigorously straighten the walls, brought over a door and made a hasty roof of straw. Our men also helped them. I gave the priest a copper altarpiece and he was so pleased with this gift that he did not know how to thank me and took it around to show everyone.

When the repairs of the church were finished, suddenly a young man came running with a frightened face to warn us that the Turks attacked our men in the town and almost all of them were killed. I returned to the boats and gathered our men. Lieutenant Ricord ordered the detachment mount sentries on the heights and in order to wait for the best intelligence, he also sent the boats to a cape where it was more convenient to mount a defence. Meanwhile, men were returning from the town with provisions, saying that in the northern part of the island a detachment of Turks had assembled sailors for a fleet. The village elder sent a boat to Tenedos to notify the admiral about our situation. Around noon, Turks began to appear on the heights in the distance but disappeared behind the hills. Meanwhile, all of our men were gathered and at 6 in the evening, the boats were sent to Mavro.

The day was hot and the sea was calm, but the setting sun foreshadowed a storm. The sky was covered with darkness while the southern horizon pulsed with lightning and waves could be seen approaching from that direction. The boats were too heavily laden and began to take on water and though the wind had yet to reach us, the oars were knocked out of our sailors' hands with great force. Not having time to cast out the water, we were forced to jettison the purchased provisions, shot, powder and all other burdens. The wind blew after midnight but was foul and carried us toward the Dardanelles. The sailors had no rest the following day and rowed ceaselessly for 10 hours, straining to the last of their strength, but the boat moved very little forward against the waves. The wind freshened in the morning and at dawn the storm came, but fortunately I managed to bring us over the island of Mavro and could ride the full wind to reach the *Moshchnyy*. I was gravely anxious through that whole night, as without a compass I was not exactly sure whether we were holding to the correct course that would take us to Mavro. I could have been forced to seek salvation in the Dardanelles, which was the fate of the *Moshchnyy*'s other two boats. Fortunately, the *Skoryy* and the *Venus*, sent to Imbros by the admiral, saw them and rescued them. The *Venus* lost her topsails under the batteries of the European capes and could barely round Cape Greco (Helles) without extreme danger.

The *Skoryy* and the *Venus* arrived at the northern tip of Imbros and landed 300 soldiers and Albanians there, but the Turks were nowhere to be found; they had already departed by boat to the Gulf of Saros. The *Skoryy* returned to Tenedos and the *Venus* resumed its position in the vanguard. Onboard the frigate, I was met as if I returned from the dead, since the Greeks from Imbros assured them that we had all been killed.

On the 10th [22nd] of April, a Turkish squadron of 7 ships and 6 frigates came from the Sea of Marmara and stopped at the mouth of the Dardanelles near the Asian fortress, while two more ships stood by the European shore. That same day, four of our corsairs were sent to the west of Imbros.

The officers' stock had long been exhausted and the provisions issued to the sailors were also being rationed with a stingy hand. We had intended to replenish ourselves at Imbros, but I returned from there by the proverb: he who goes for anything returns with nothing. At midnight, on Easter,[1] we listened to the matins service and admired the salutes fired from the fleet and the fortress of Tenedos. We ourselves greeted one another like brothers during the thunder of the artillery and congratulated one another on that great holiday; we broke our fast with black biscuits softened by soaking. Being unaccustomed to such a strict fast on such a day, we cracked jokes about it but not for very long; soon everyone went to their cabins to philosophize, indulge in fantasies and sing melancholy songs. The sailors also came together, turned out on the quarterdeck in their new uniforms, and reminded themselves how everyone in Russia was rejoicing at that moment; they too joked among themselves to ease their grief. By evening, a launch was returning from the fleet and came along side us, filled with sheep, barrels of wine, baskets of eggs and assorted green vegetables. What a joy to behold! The admiral remembered us and set out a portion of his stock to break our fast. We were so delighted with the gift that we immediately lit a fire in the kitchen and pestered the cooks to hurry, finally sitting down to a dinner at midnight. At dawn, the sailors had a breakfast, games and songs began, everyone was elated, forgot the troubles of their past and enjoyed the present with great pleasure. The Turks in the Dardanelles were distracted and fussing over something and their ships moved from place to place without going anywhere. Perhaps they thought to take advantage of our holiday, but they would have been deceived; despite the great abundance of water received from Mavro, our wine barrels were tapped out.

On the 16th [28th] of April, the ships *Uriil* and *Skoryy* relieved us in the vanguard and we returned to Tenedos where our fleet had been reinforced with two ships arriving from the Adriatic and 20 corsairs, who received military flags to fly and were dispatched to cruise various places around the archipelago.

---

1    Easter in 1807 for the Orthodox Churches fell on the 14 [26] April. *Месяцослов с Росписью Чиновных Особ или Общий Штат Российской Империи, на Лето от Рождества Христова 1807*, vol. 1 (St. Petersburg: Императорская Академия Наук, 1807), p.vi. [*Menologium with a List of the Ranking Individuals or a General State of the Russian Empire in the Year of Our Lord 1807*, vol. 1 (St. Petersburg: Imperial Academy of Sciences, 1807), p.vi.]

# 78

# The Gulf of Saros

On the 21st of April [3rd of May], in order to sever communications across the Gulf of Saros which lies to the north of the Gallipoli peninsula and could convey provisions, the captain received orders to sail between Imbros and the coast of Rumelia. Rear-Admiral Greig at the same time took four ships to Smyrna where he cruised the entrance of that harbour between Chios and Mytilene. The commander-in-chief had the intention of blockading the richest trading towns, which would encourage the Turks to come out of the Dardanelles. We joined a Hydriot corsair, the *Kuryer Arkhipelazhskiy*, under Captain Ciriaco Scurti.

On the 22nd of April [4th of May], upon our arrival in the gulf, two ships were taken and proceeded to its very interior to drop anchor near the islets, one of which featured a fortified monastery. The Turks fired a few harmless shots at us. On the 23rd [5th], when returning, we spotted two vessels called sacolevas moored to the shore near Cape Paxi with a crowd of Turks ready to defend them. The manoeuvres that Captain Scurti undertook deserve a general commendation and would bring honour to even the best sailors. The wind was fresh, the corsair approached the shore under all sails and fired a volley and then continued with grapeshot as it sailed past, reduced its sails, held for a short period and stayed as close as possible to the sacolevas and sent a dinghy to secure a tow line and cut the mooring lines from the shore in an instant, hauling the craft away into the sea. Two prisoners taken on the sacoleva indicated that in the village there was an Ottoman magazine and ovens baking bread for their army. The frigate dropped anchor there and cleared the shore with several shots and all of our rowing craft were sent ashore. The Greeks did not hesitate when, after half an hour, enemy cavalry, artillery and infantry began to stumble down from the heights. They had time still to load up the other sacoleva with bread, flour and everything that could be carried under-arm and set fire to it all before withdrawing without a single casualty.

Our arrival in the Gulf of Saros caused the Turks a fair sum of trouble. Their large army, which was entrusted with the protection of the Dardanelles and the capital, united and occupied the coast surrounding the gulf, as they were expecting us to land ground forces there. The commander-in-chief found a means of communication with Constantinople and even with the army of General Ivan Michelson operating on the Danube, with the intention of circulating a rumour that a force of 100,000 Russian and British soldiers with Greek and Slav auxiliaries had landed in the gulf and was marching toward the Ottoman capital, a distance that would be only three days march. This rumour was believed so earnestly that 5,000 Albanians rebelled and spiked the guns in one of the Dardanelles batteries and after seeing their error, they fought a brutal battle and broke through into the mountains, putting all the Turkish villages in their way to the sword. This incident, along with the deprivation of bread which previously had been supplied by Egypt and the Greek archipelago, led to bloody events in Constantinople. Many pashas were executed and then the Sultan Selim himself was ousted from the throne.[1]

Completing a circuit of the Gulf of Saros and sending the prize vessels to Tenedos, we sailed west along the Rumelian coast. Past the cape and town of Aenos (Enez) could be seen 30 boats in the shallow mouth of the river beside a fortress. It was not possible for us to attack them, but our corsair sent their light craft in in the night and made off with two of the enemy's boats, and as we continued closely along the shore, we did not encounter a single vessel. We anchored in the open sea at a depth of 34 *sazhen*s [72.54 m] on the western side of Samothrace where the corsair re-joined us in the morning of the 24th of April [6th of May].

---

1    Selim III was deposed on 17 [29] May, 1807 and replaced by his cousin who reigned as Mustafa IV until 16 [28] July, 1808, when he too was deposed and replaced by his half-brother Mahmud II. Ward et al., *Cambridge Modern History*, vol. 9, pp.386-389.

# 79

# The Island of Samothrace

Samothrace has a circumference of 40 to 50 *versta*s [42.67 to 53.34 km] and lies on the western side of Imbros and opposite the coast of Rumelia. There is not a single wharf on the island, except an anchorage running along the western and southern sides of the islands. The view of the island from the west where we stood was of one of nature's finest prospects. The hills and mountains, each standing alone, densely fill all of the island's apparent space. The higher mountains have bare peaks and the occasional woods of shipbuilding species, the shorter form ledges, and the hills are covered with fertile groves with green valleys between. Lush meadows and huts are scattered along the shores of small springs like sparkling beacons standing out in their remote surroundings.

The Turks who were on the island fled to Rumelia. A new elder from the Greeks came to the frigate presenting gifts of fruits and wine and persistently asked the captain to send some soldiers to the town which lies about 5 *versta*s [5.33 km] from the shore in order to reassure the people and dissuade the Turks from returning to the island, should they learn of our frigate's departure. 40 soldiers and an equal number of Greeks from the corsair were sent ashore early in the morning, headed for the town inland by two roads. I was assigned to this detachment with instructions to invite the Greeks to convey provisions to Tenedos and if any Turks were encountered on the road or were bought to us by the locals, we were to take them prisoner.

We walked from hill to hill, mountain to mountain, everywhere meeting a breath-taking nature in full bloom, various and rich. Here we passed a forest of oak, walnut and chestnut trees; there we passed a patch of fig, almond and cherry groves, whose branches were interwoven with wild grape and jasmine vines. Descending from the mountains, we came into the beautiful valleys. A green carpet of meadows, vineyards and gardens dormant under the shade of the mountains, the fresh morning air and the magnificence of these wild places made every step a pleasant surprise. The appearance and songs of strange birds and the fragrances of unknown flowers made it feel as though we were transported to another world, where one's eye was constantly feeding the heart with new and animated impressions. Surely I was dreaming of wandering through the enchanted gardens of Armida. Sometimes our route took us over a narrow path carved into the side of a sheer cliff with rocks overhanging us and a yawning precipice underfoot, but after this precarious journey and having ascended a mountain, we came to a vista with a roaring sea open on one side and a quaint and quiet valley on the other. Homes were scattered about without any apparent order, nestled in the shade of pyramidal poplars. We could see vineyards and a large field of cotton separated by a vast flat meadow stretching out to a rock on which a poor church nearly half its height stood in stark isolation. Its adjacent cemetery was covered with cypresses. Below the church spilled out a waterfall from the rock, like a broken urn, and its bending stream appeared like a polished mirror from a distance. An abundant stream flowed through the valley, curving around the meadow like a brushstroke of light. Cattle quietly grazing on mulberry bushes, a herd of sheep wandering under the rock and resting around the waterfall and goats jumping over the cliffs completed the picture and solidified the cumulative charm of rural life.

Finally we passed through a tight gorge between two stone cliffs and on our right opened up the ruined walls of a fortress with a town behind it. In order to inform the inhabitants of our arrival, the mayor of the town who accompanied us asked us to fire a few shots into the air, after which we marched on with a drumbeat. Soon we saw a crowd of people who came out to greet us. A priest in a dilapidated cassock sprinkled us with holy water, handed me a cross of cypress wood and when he kissed me, he took the cross back and blessed the soldiers. He then said a short speech in which I and my interpreter understood only the name Alexander. Taking a bouquet from the boys of the village, he gave me and each of the soldiers a single flower and asked them to decorate their hats and shakos with them. After the ceremony, men who I took for civil officials, though their dress did not differ from the other inhabitants, brought me honeyed bread and salt. After the people loudly proclaimed 'long live Alexander!' we entered the town together and their faces clearly depicted their joy, interspersed with some sacred reverence. At the doors of each house, the owner stood with his hand on his chest and offered us bread and salt with a subtle bow. The women, with great curiosity – perhaps aroused by the drumming – tempered by modesty, looked down at us from the terraces.

The priest and elders led us out of town to a singular elevation where a small square space enclosed by a railing was covered with carpets. I was asked to enter and sit on a pillow, the soldiers began to line the edges, and a new ceremony began. The mayor with six others came into the square and sat at a respectful distance, kneeling before me. One of the elders delivered a lengthy speech with great ardour, but my interpreter, who had a poor grasp of Greek and even worse of Italian, said to me: 'they ask us to leave a few soldiers to protect them from the Turks and say that they are willing to care for them themselves and wish to swear an oath of loyalty'. To that I replied that the archipelago was already declared to be under the auspices of our emperor and that an oath was not necessary where there was no doubt as to the loyalty and devotion of the people. I directed their special requests to the commander-in-chief and explained that I only had authority to set the price of provisions and invite the residents to deliver them to Tenedos. The chiefs informed me that we could take as enemy property some of the provisions and cattle collected by the Turks for supplying their army in Rumelia. Moreover, wanting to prove their readiness, they promised to collect some more foodstuffs themselves by evening. Since they did not have suitable boats for transporting livestock to Tenedos, they would henceforth deliver as much firewood as they felt and as many provisions as they could at the price agreed upon and found most moderate. They kept their word: the elders in attendance told all the households what was required of them by evening and deliveries to the frigate began.

Just as on Imbros, I had to approve the restoration of a ruined church, but the priest here was more fortunate than the previous. The captain gave him a new cassock and a gilded icon of Saint Nicholas the Wonderworker. The mayor of the town invited me to dinner and afterward, like a priest during Holy Week, we had to go from house to house and certainly try something to eat with each host. The soldiers were also treated by the community with great care and generosity. In one house, I found a wounded Turk who had a bullet lodged in his leg. The local doctor lacked the necessary instruments, so I sent for our own doctor aboard the frigate who removed the bullet, gave instructions on how to dress the wound and provided the local healer with some medications.

I rather enjoyed the town. Three barren and rocky mountains, converging at their feet, formed an acute triangle, and from two corners quickly flowed a pair of springs that united and with one current drove several mill wheels and their small grindstones, which were simply built on the stream's bank without any structure housing them. Windmills were built on either side of the ridges, which also serve as a natural fortification, while a man-made fort stood on the third side of the triangle. Coming around the corner, you will immediately see the town, divided along the slopes into three settlements. At first glance, it appears like a wild, secluded position. The structures seem like a bunch of scattered huts and shacks with low and flat roofs. All of them are stone with no floors, have typically two small windows, and contain a single room with no plaster on its interior walls. The doctor's house, lauded as the finest, has a floor lined with carved cypress boards.

The fortress was built by the Genoese; along its walls there was only one round loophole and a collapsed building. Its cellar was used by the people for storing wheat. The corns blackened with time and could be separated by hand, but as soon as you squeezed them in your hand, they turned into dust. Yet wheat, as easily corruptible though it is, like a marble statue through the centuries has triumphed over time and shares in an eternal legacy.

Samothrace abounds in grain, fruits, livestock and tobacco. As the Turks who settled here constitute less than a quarter of the population, the Greeks have not yet lost their own customs. Dressing like the Turks, the women travel with an uncovered face; they are charming but not particularly beautiful, having instead meekness, chastity and a particular inclination towards peaceful family life which is common throughout the archipelago. All the bachelors who are rich, jealous and prudent seek their brides here. Samothrace was famous in antiquity for its shrines and temples, which were respected by at least the Eleusinians.

Having received more provisions on this small island than was expected, we weighed anchor on the 26th of April [8th of May] and made use of a quiet tailwind to sail close to the Rumelian shore. Near the village of Makri, we sunk three boats with several shots. A camp reinforced with earthworks lay there. The Turks fired at us from their muskets and even their pistols. Our corsair made off with one of their boats and set fire to another. The boats found close by the neighbouring towns were unloaded and towed back to shore. Thus we deprived the enemy of the last of their means of delivery between this shore and the archipelago. Rounding the Cape of Aenos, which stands on the left side of the mouth of the Gulf of Saros, and having passed another stone near the island of Imbros, we continued down to Tenedos and arrived there on the 28th of April [10th of May].

Rumelia is very well cultivated and the best smoking tobacco is grown there. The shore is inhabited by *askeri*,[1] or rather, military landlords. They pay no taxes and are only required in wartime to serve on horses which they personally maintain. Judging by the many settlements that are prominent by the shore, and especially by the large herds of horses, one must think that the *askeri* are prosperous. Their houses, having the appearance of a closed gazebo or pavilion, are typically built on the banks of a river and under the shadow of trees, have a handsome appearance and promise a cool and comfortable abode.

---

1   More specifically, those landholders or tax-farmers who controlled portions of land on the sultan's behalf and were expected to either personally serve as cavalry or raise and finance substitute riders in their stead were called *timarli* or timariots, and the cavalry so raised were *sipahi*. Tim Jacoby, *Social Power and the Turkish State* (London: Frank Cass Publishers, 2002), pp.31-41.

# 80

# The Island of Skyros

---

The captain of the frigate *Venus* with two corsairs, the aforementioned *Kuryer* and another named *Irida*, was instructed to head to the islands of Saint Eustratius (Agios Efstratios) and Skyros, where certain provisions and heads of cattle had been prepared for the fleet. On the 2nd [14th] of May, after taking 20 Albanians with an officer aboard the frigate, we weighed anchor and sailed for the island of St. Eustratius, where we lay to. The chief of the island came straight to the frigate, bringing a gift of several greens, fruits and wine. He promised to send 100 sheep to Tenedos on the next day and as much wine and vegetables as could be collected with the further addition of sending two boats laden with provisions each week to the fleet. At midnight on the 3rd [15th] we arrived at the harbour of San Giorgio, situated on the southern side of the island of Skyros. One of our corsairs proceeded to Negroponte and the other to Tinos, from which the latter sent us two cargo boats.

The harbour of San Giorgio is protected from western winds by the long island of Valaxa and by three small islands, which demarcate a large anchorage within the crescent of Skyros's shore, where on a depth of 10 to 30 [21.34 to 64 m], and then 40 *sazhens* [85.34 m], ships are safe from all wind. The best spot, where the soil is muddy, lies at a depth of 10 *sazhens* opposite one of the dilapidated structures ashore where a small patch of white sand all around it can be seen.

The morning was quiet and the day was the most beautiful, no settlement could be seen at all around us, but the meadows, fields and green forests growing on the small elevations beckoned us to go ashore. Sitting in the launch and approaching the shore, we noticed that the water at a depth of 6 *sazhens* [12.8 m] became as clear as glass. We saw below us thousands of polyps, urchins, starfish, sea horses and every kind of fish, so handsomely flecked, as might be impossible to imagine in our own climate. It seemed as though you could reach in and grab these plants and animals floating in the depths, but upon a more accurate study, they were actually lying on the floor. What really surprised me though were the schools of fish playing on the surface of the sea. Seven relatively large fish were chasing a school of smaller ones, which made various turns to evade, at times resembling the evolutions and manoeuvres of an army or navy.

As the chief of the island required two days before he could deliver livestock and provisions and while expecting the return of our corsairs, the captain ordered tents to be pitched on shore and half of the crew was permitted to bivouac there. An improvised sauna was immediately made from the ballast stones: the *banya* is a necessity for the Russian in any climate. Some of our men caught fish, others went into the woods with muskets, and both hunts were more than successful. The residents came to us bearing gifts and were so pleased by our arrival that they stayed in our tents until we took them down for our departure. They were all treated and embraced equally, as the chief could not be told apart from the farmhand.

Skyros has a circumference of approximately 150 *verstas* [160 km] and is covered with low mountains. The soil of the earth is stony and very fertile. Their grapes give a fine wine and fruit trees flourish in the woods without any cultivation. The inhabitants are employed in farming and the fields of grain provide them with abundant harvests. On the whole island, there are more than 400 households divided into three villages; the largest of them is called a town and lies to the north, approximately a mile [1.86 km] from the shore, and occupies such a height that the buildings seem to be hanging precariously over the water when seen from the sea. Curiosity prompted me and three comrades to walk to the town, but our guide showed us the ruins of ancient Skyros just five *verstas* [5.33 km] from the harbour and we aborted our journey, preferring the ancient town to the present one though we came to regret that preference in the end. Fragments of marble, deep pits indicating the former sites of buildings, thorny bushes and shards of crimson urns were all that remained of that magnificent capital where Pherecydes was born,[1] where Achilles in disguise was raised among the daughters of King Lycomedes and where ultimately Theseus died. The magnificent buildings, customs and even the appearance of the people are subject to change; everything has been extinguished by time and the barbarians in whose hands art, science and craftsmanship perish. Yet nature remains unchanged; we see it draped in the same veil as it was when the world was created.

Returning by another road, we entered a forest encumbered with fruits so rare that imagination carried me to the happy islands of the Pacific Ocean where men without science bask in the luxuries of an earthly paradise, secluded and unvisited. The sound of running water attracted our attention and we turned to see a beautiful waterfall. Dropping from a small height and breaking over mossy stones, the water

---

1     Pherecydes, the 6th Century philosopher, was born on Syros, not Skyros. Smith, *A New Classical Dictionary*, s.v. 'Pherecydes'.

turned to foam and then flowed quietly after, splitting into streams with an island between them. Gigantic trees whose roots were washed by the water below leaned over and conjoined their roots to form a living bridge. Further along the bank of the river it was not possible to pass: thorns, winding grape vines, rotting stumps and fallen trees forced us to take the shorter path. An open green meadow took us back to the camp.

On the 7th [19th] of May, after the arrival of the corsairs and taking on 70 heads of cattle and 400 sheep, we weighed anchor and tacked to the north with a weak and wavering wind. Around noon on the 8th [20th], cannon fire was heard and a few hours later a Greek boat which had departed from Tenedos informed us that the Turkish fleet had left the Dardanelles. Giving the corsairs a signal to stay united, we set all sails and early in the morning of the 9th [21st] of May, in the midst of a dense fog, we reunited with our fleet standing on the western shore of Tenedos and dropped anchor at our former position beside the fortifications. The force then consisted of 10 ships and 7 corsairs, with the addition of our frigate.

# 81

# The Landing of Turkish Forces on the Island of Tenedos

On the 7th [19th] of May, during sunset, the telegraph sent word that the Turkish squadron had weighed anchor and by noon it had come out of the strait to anchor off the coast of Anatolia opposite Mavro. It contained eight ships, of which one had 100 guns and three had 80 guns; six frigates of 50 guns; four sloops; one brig; and 50 gunboats and light craft. Their flag officers were the *Kapudan-Pasha* Seydi Ali, a *kapudan-bey* (admiral), *patrona-bey* (vice-admiral), and one admiral in command of the galley flotilla.

Confident that the Turks could not quickly seize the fortress of Tenedos even with their large force, the commander-in-chief set out with 10 ships in the evening of the same day during a northerly wind and circled around the south side of Tenedos to head for Imbros. With this manoeuvre, the admiral intended to bait the enemy into rushing the island and thereby luring him further from the strait. If the northerly wind continued for several days, as it was expected to do, our fleet could evade the enemy and cut it off from the strait to force it into a battle which they had carefully avoided; but on the 8th [20th], there was a dead calm and changing weak breezes from the north.

During the morning of the 9th [21st] of May, the wind was foul from the northeast, the sky was cloudy, and we witnessed a partial eclipse over a full moon, all of which promised a prolonged spell of inclement weather or a storm. In order to save the ships from an unfortunate voyage, the fleet returned to Tenedos at 9 o'clock in the morning and as soon as we dropped anchor again, we were hit by a squall from the north which blew with great force for half an hour before the gloom dispersed and the weather cleared. The wind stopped at midnight and to our annoyance, a light northeasterly resumed.

Meanwhile, on the 8th [20th] of May when our fleet was at Imbros, the Turks hastily landed a force 4 *verstas* [4.27 km] south of the fortress of Tenedos. Major

Gedeonov with two companies and two guns marched out and a short firefight drove the enemy's first detachment to retreat. The Turks withdrew to a small bare island within range of musketry from Tenedos and under the cover of strong canister fire, their flotilla of rowing vessels approached the shore again in greater force. The major, not allowing the shore party time to organize, immediately and fearlessly attacked the enemy on the shore itself in close combat. The Turks could not withstand such an onslaught and having no place to run, they threw themselves into the water and onto their boats; the next wave came ashore to replace them and suffered the same fate. French officers were among the landing party. Three times under the defence of their gunboats the Turks came ashore and despite their determination and courage, they finally retreated in great disorder and set sail for Anatolia. The residents of Tenedos and the Greeks of the other islands who happened to be in the town during this action demonstrated a laudable courage. 200 men were found among the Turks killed on the shore, 30 were drowned in the waves and moreover, two boats were sunk with all their souls aboard. Being struck with the canister fire of four guns during each retreat, their whole losses should be at least 300. On our side, with our advantageous positions that sheltered the men from the shot of the enemy's vessels, casualties were a mere 5 wounded soldiers and 4 Greeks.

82

# The Battle of the Dardanelles – 10th and 11th [22nd and 23rd] of May

On the 10th [22nd] of May, the northeasterly wind in the morning was quite convenient for the Turks, if they were to attack us, but the unsuccessful attempt on Tenedos softened their boldness and the two fleets stood in sight of one another in static preparedness. At noon, two vessels sailed toward our line. The *Venus* was signalled to set sail, but on closer inspection it was found that the vessels were Austrian; the skippers asked the admiral for permission to return to Trieste. Finally, at two in the afternoon, to the common joy of all, the wind shifted to a southwesterly, a rare thing there in the summer. No sooner did that wind blow than a cannon shot rang out from the *Tvyordyy* and a signal was given to weigh anchor. The hope of giving battle to the Turks was common through the whole fleet. We did not think about the dangers of the forthcoming action; our only fear was that the wind would turn or fall silent. In half an hour, all the ships were already under sail and arranged into the order of battle. We expected that the Turks, not daring to attack us, would receive our attack standing on anchor; but they quickly hauled anchor, then five of their ships close to the fortresses dropped anchor but cut their ropes again shortly after, and soon their whole fleet was under sails and heading toward the Dardanelles. The *Tvyordyy* raised the signal to set every possible sail and for each vessel to attack the enemy with all their ability. The lighter ships went ahead but the wind began to subside and finally changed to blow quite fresh from the west. The Turkish squadron hurried under all sails to enter the Dardanelles and had great aid from the wind. Although one cannot hope to master anyone in the narrow position of the strait, our brave admiral decided to deliver a sure blow to the gate of their fortress.

At 6 o'clock, as the day was already slipping away into evening, the *Venus*, in an advanced position, received a signal to attack a separated enemy vessel. We approached her astern and opened fire. Soon the *Selafail*, *Retvizan*, *Rafail* and the

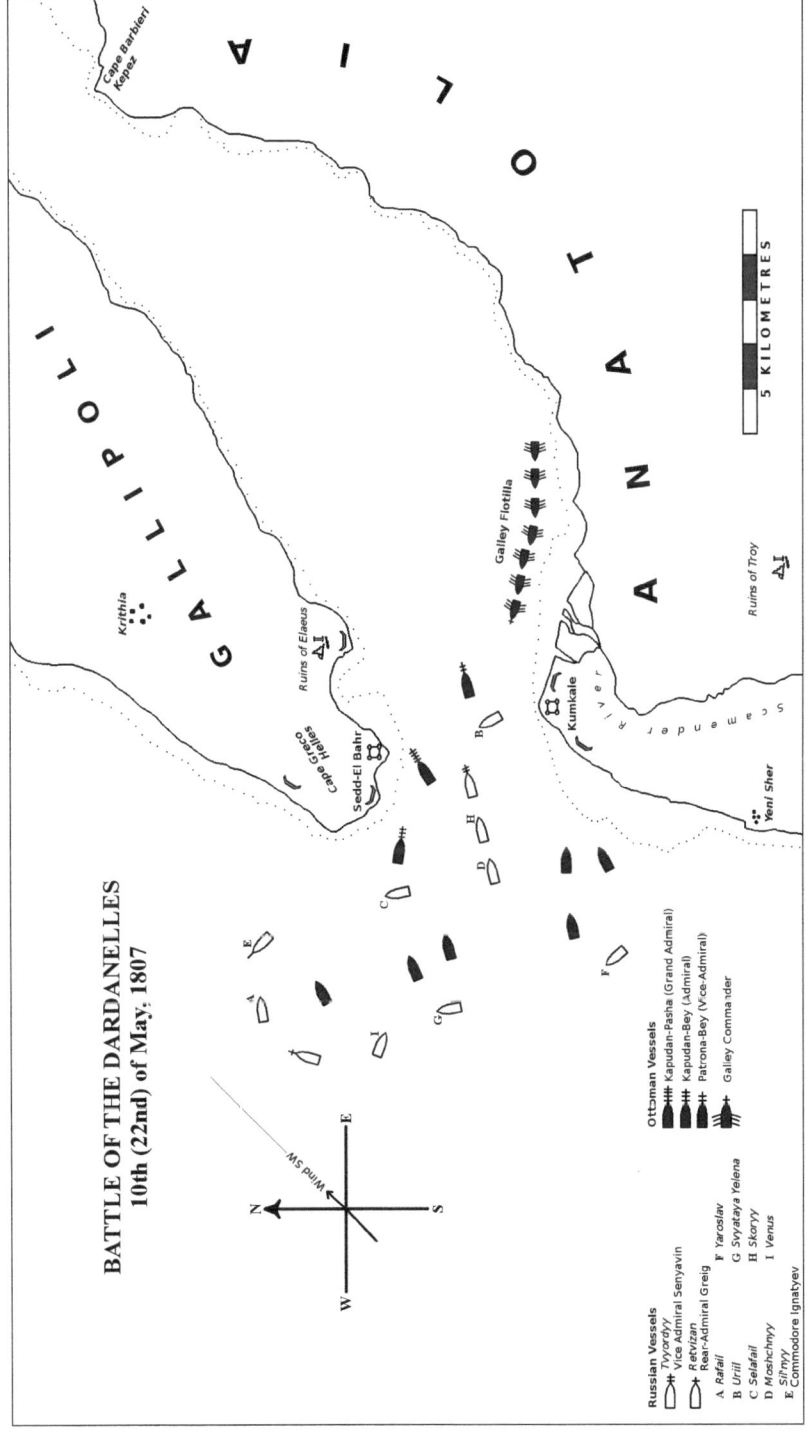

BATTLE OF THE DARDANELLES
10th (22nd) of May, 1807

**Russian Vessels**
*Tvyordyy*
Vice Admiral Senyavin
*Retvizan*
Rear-Admiral Greig

A *Rafail*        F *Yaroslav*
B *Uriil*         G *Svyataya Yelena*
C *Selafail*      H *Skoryy*
D *Moshchnyy*     I *Venus*
E *Silnyy*
Commodore Ignatyev

**Ottoman Vessels**
Kapudan-Pasha (Grand Admiral)
Kapudan-Bey (Admiral)
Patrona-Bey (Vice-Admiral)
Galley Commander

5 KILOMETRES

*Silnyy* engaged other ships and a battle began half an hour before nightfall. Our ships outran the enemy and passed between them, dodging their bows and sterns and temporarily fought them on both sides. The *Selafail*, the first to overtake the *kapudan-pasha*'s 100-gun ship, give a volley into her stern, and when she began to tack to starboard in order to avoid this fire, our ship kept herself astern of the enemy and again struck them in the rear. The *Uriil* passed the Turkish vice-admiral's ship so closely that the bowsprit damaged her rigging.

Senyavin strove to engage Seydi Ali and came astern of the ship of [the *kapudan-bey*] Bekir Bey, giving them battle on all sides; then he broke off and attacked the *kapudan-pasha* so closely that the yards of their masts nearly converged. Seydi Ali, showing at first a desire to fight, set off his guns very rarely and gained distance from the *Tvyordyy* under all sails in the direction of their fortifications. All the Turkish ships hastened to follow their admiral for the Dardanelles without another thought toward the battle; many among them who sailed alongside us did not defend themselves. On the contrary, our ships fell behind them, ran ahead of them, came alongside them, adding and removing sails to control their speeds, managed to pursue them and deliver broadsides against the majority of their vessels.

Darkness fell at 8 o'clock and the wind died down with both fleets entangled at the very mouth of the strait. From the duelling currents, some of our ships by the Asian coast were carried off from the Dardanelles and the others were drawn toward the European fortresses and carried into the strait. The marble shots from both shores struck friend and foe alike. To distinguish our vessels, three lanterns were raised on the masts, but the Turkish ships near us did the same; resulting in incoming fire by both our ships and their own forces ashore. To avoid damaging each other in the darkness, our ships began to withdraw from the strait and the battle ended at 9 o'clock, although some skirmishing continued until 11. The flight of the enemy fleet was so painfully hurried and disorderly that three ships ran aground near the Asian fortress. An hour after midnight, during a dead calm, our squadron was pulled out of the Dardanelles by the current and all the ships were signalled to drop anchor wherever they were.

During the battle, Senyavin's flagship, the *Tvyordyy*, came so close to the European fortress that the crew began to take casualties from musket fire. The admiral ordered the lanterns be covered and to begin towing the ship with its boats. Having lost sight of the lights that distinguished the ship of our commander-in-chief, the whole fleet became exceedingly worried and as we manoeuvred around the mouth of the strait and passed one another, we asked each other where the admiral was. Soon among the enemy's fleet however, a very proper running fire began and when the smoke cleared, three lanterns appeared. We shouted 'ura!' upon the revelation that it was Senyavin.

On the next day, when the *Silnyy* hauled down her broad pennant to half-mast, expressing the loss of her captain-commodore, we grieved the glorious death of this worthy commander who had promise to serve the fatherland as a fine admiral, and we were even more saddened when we failed to see the vice-admiral's flag on the mast of the *Tvyordyy*. I cannot describe the general confusion that was spread. Being present at the repetition of the signals, I was the first to notice the ship and looked on through a telescope, failing to see the flag on the mast, and imagined that it was wrapped around in the wind, or it seemed better to me. The captain, the lieutenant on watch and other officers who were on deck also watched the flagship and none of them could see the flag either. We turned pale. No one dared to ask each other if the admiral lived or died. The sailors one by one came onto the quarterdeck and they too were afraid to express their thoughts to one another. They found an excuse to retire in sad silence and bow before the icon. In this mood, we came astern of the *Tvyordyy*. Our captain, instead of the typical report, asked 'is the admiral well?'

'Thank God!' was the answer, but we were still doubtful. When finally Dmitriy Nikolayevich appeared in the gallery, a thunderous cheer of 'ura' resounded on our frigate! The admiral made a sign that he wanted to speak, but the sailors could not quickly be quieted and he departed with a bow.

In the morning of the 11th [23rd] of May, three Turkish ships had drifted far out to sea from the mouth of the Dardanelles. Two of them were being towed by a team of galleys. It was quiet until 10 o'clock when the wind began to blow and the squadron weighed anchor, reunited and by noon, when the wind freshened, it was signalled for Rear-Admiral Greig with the *Retvizan*, *Selafail*, *Skoryy*, *Yaroslav* and the *Venus* to try to cut off, capture or destroy the enemy ships. Meanwhile, the Turkish ships hurried toward the strait under all sails. Our detachment overtook them nearly at the fortresses but could not capture them, especially under their deadly fire which performed perfectly during the passage of their ships and galleys. After the first volley, the Turkish ships responded very weakly; the destruction of the sails, rigging and damage to the hulls could be plainly seen with the naked eye. The enemy benefited from a favourable wind which blew so strongly that they were propelled forward despite a contrary current; our detachment, turning our broadsides to the current in order to fire, were carried out of the strait, yet still we managed to thrice inflict great harm on the enemy. The galleys that defended an enemy ship standing aground by the Asian fortress turned and fled. Another ship, caught by the *Selafail* and then later by the *Retvizan*, ran aground under the cover of the European fortresses and their fleet. The *patrona-bey*'s ship, wishing to enter the strait by the Asian coast and being badly beaten, had at first dropped anchor but then hauled again and evaded the fire from our detachment only to run aground. The proximity of the Asian fortress prevented us from attacking it in earnest. The wind began to subside and the currents carried our ships away from the Turkish. The rear-admiral's detachment was signalled to rejoin the squadron. On the 12th [24th], our fleet stood at its previous position at Tenedos.

In this battle, 26 sailors died. Three fleet officers, one *garde de marine*, two Albanian officers and 50 enlisted men were wounded. The material damage was all repaired the next day. The Turkish fleet, regardless of their fortresses, the narrow passage, the cover of darkness and their attempts to avoid battle, was badly damaged. Three of their ships were unserviceable and they lost an estimated 2,000 men. The *kapudan-pasha* had his vice-admiral and two captains strangled on his ship. A few days after the battle, he accepted the vice-admiral very affectionately, but as soon as he stepped out of the cabin, he was assaulted and killed. This act at first seems cruel, but when examining the causes, it is apparently motivated by good intentions. The Turks think differently about death sentences than we do and they say that it is better to die suddenly and obliviously than to suffer for a time in anticipation of a certain execution. In Turkey, they do not inform criminals about their decided fate and when they take a man out of prison for his execution, they usually declare the Sultan's mercy and forgiveness. How many actually receive it? The condemned man, instead of having the fear of a most painful death, has hope until his escort takes his to the scaffold where, without any special preparation, he is suddenly killed and the demands of the law are fulfilled.

If, in a land battle, a man exerts all of his strength bravely, then at sea he must be completely fearless. Although in both cases he is guided by the Hand of God, in the latter case His Will is more evident. On land, a man fights and dies only by the hand of the enemy and we do not fear that the earth will part beneath our feet and swallow us, nor can we be thrown up into the air, and if we lose the battle on land, we retire into fortresses or find salvation in the prudent occupation of certain locations and the artfulness of one's commander. A seafarer however is separated from death by a single plank of wood and enclosed in a tight fortress floating on the water, in which there is no place to hide from the enemy; further, he must still contend with the wind and waves as much as the foe. Clinging too close to land or straying too far from it can be equally disastrous. Submerged rocks and shallows destroy his endeavours and whatever aids one scheme serves to hinder another. Advantage is only enjoyed by those who are favoured by the wind, or are said in nautical terms to be windward. Often even the most experienced and brave admiral, depending on the strength and course of the wind, cannot save his victorious fleet from a storm or take full advantage of a momentary victory. In a naval battle, death comes in all forms. In addition to cannon balls, grape, canister shot and bullets, men are struck by debris and splinters flying from the hull and masts. When a ship explodes or floods, nearly everyone dies and only the luckiest are spared. Boarding action surpasses the horror of a bloody assault on a fortress, because a desperate defender can set fire to his own ship and blow his victorious enemies into the sky.

On the 12th [24th] of May, while the body of Captain-Commodore Ignatyev was interred at the Tenedos monastery with military honours, our captain received an order to sail to the Dardanelles strait to observe the enemy's movements. The Turkish fleet was arranged in a line near Chanak Kolesi (Çanakkale), and one ship was being towed further into the strait by a team of gunboats for being more damaged than previously thought. On the 16th [28th], Rear-Admiral Greig took five ships toward the mouth of the strait to prevent any ship or even small boat from passing through. Thus relieved, our frigate and the *Moshchnyy* returned to Tenedos.

Captain-Commodore Ignatyev had been killed by a cannon ball to the head at the very moment he intended to descend upon an enemy ship. The fatherland lost in him an enlightened gentleman, a prudent seaman and a dauntless warrior. His ambition was truly dignified and with his extensive knowledge, his spirit was to strive for elegance and nobility in all things. Splendour in his domestic life and perfect selflessness in his naval service were the most distinctive features of his character. He was proud but preferred to pass on the distinctions of his subordinates and see them rewarded before him. He was unfortunately sometimes hot-tempered, but in this he sincerely repented. He never used his authority for evil and was afraid of being unjust.

# 83

# The Island of Psara

On the 21st of May [2nd of June], we received an order conveyed by the corsair *Irida* to search for a French corsair of 28 guns which had appeared in the archipelago and then to stand under Smyrna for some time to observe the ten merchant vessels preparing to depart from there. On the night of the 23rd [4th of June], the *Irida* held back behind us as we passed very close to the southern cape of the island of Psara and lay to. In the morning, while facing the port of San Nicolo, the captain ordered me to take two armed boats and examine the 18 craft in the harbour to ascertain if the French corsair was among them. The chief of the island, boarding the frigate, assured me that if the French dared to come, he would certainly have seized them. Despite his assurances, I examined all of the boats and, having found nothing suspicious, went ashore at the pier. The town of San Nicolo is built on the cape. Its streets are straight and in the centre lies a square with a beautiful church. The houses are of European architecture, of stone and with two storeys. The lower levels are used for crafts and peddling goods. The Psariots, just like the Hydriots, are revered as skilful shipwrights. Their island is fruitless and they live off of the sea, have many fine vessels and are well secure in their trade. Two of their corsairs served in our fleet at their own expense. The port was small, exposed only to southeasterly winds and at a depth of 5 to 9 *sazhen*s [10.67 to 19.2 m] over a muddy floor, vessels can find good shelter. Although it was very early in the morning, a crowd still formed around us. In order to see the town, I simply ran past them and after intense pursuit I was forced to enter one of the houses where I was served breakfast; the others asked to do them the same honour, but in a hurry to return to the frigate, I refused and headed back to the pier.

Leaving Psara, we sailed along the western side of the island of Chios, where a precipitous rocky cliff appeared before us, and turned east after passing Icaria. Beyond this island we came to Patmos, where Saint John in exile wrote the Book of Revelation. Both of these islands were covered with lush and vibrant greenery. Icaria received its name from Icarus, the daring son of Daedalus who flew too close to the sun and melted away his waxen wings and fell into the sea near the island that now bears his name. Although the day was very hot, our wings did not yet melt and we continued to sail along the northern side of Samos to anchor in the small crescent-shaped harbour called Vathy in the evening of the 24th of May [5th of June]. It is exposed to northerly and westerly winds and has a muddy floor at a depth of 22 *sazhen*s [46.94 m].

# 84

# The Island of Samos

---

As soon as we dropped anchor, two boats were sent from the town to congratulate us on our arrival and brought us a gift of vegetables, fruits, meat and wine. They petitioned us for their good Turkish governor, who left the town upon learning of our arrival and intended on leaving the island. The captain had it conveyed to him that if the Greeks on the island were satisfied with his governance, he would have nothing to fear from the Russians. To reliably find the location of the French corsair, messengers were sent to all the harbours of the island.

The day after our arrival in Samos was Sunday and we went ashore for mass. The town was constructed on a hill two *versta*s [2.13 km] from the harbour while all along the shore could be seen various shops and stores. The church had been recently rebuilt and had a pleasant exterior but inside, the paintings were so poor that the faces of the saints could only be recognized by their accompanying inscriptions. The iconostasis was painted in gold, blue, and red and decorated with sets of twisted columns standing one on top of another. For women, the choruses were closed by a curtain. For the elderly, the sides were lined with a sort of armchair which they did not sit in but could lean against. When the gospel was brought into the congregation, the name of our Sovereign was mentioned which spread silence through the church and all the listeners bowed with reverence. It is undoubtedly easy to imagine how content every Russian heart felt among that parish. The deacon, an old man of around 60 years, was famous for his singing. His voice was loud and clear and sang with such passion, power and exertion that it is difficult to do him justice. His ceaselessly turned his gaze to the sky, alternately placing his hands over his heart or extending them to the altar, and trembled all the time in complete ecstasy. There was something special in the nasal melody which brought all of its listeners into holy rapture.

The town named Chora does not lie properly; it has awkwardly fitting streets both curved and strait, wide and narrow. Every square has a fountain. The houses are in both Italian and Oriental styles and those who had a beautiful wife and were jealous would shroud their windows facing the courtyard with Turkish screens; those who were rarely at home screened all of their windows, balconies and terraces. One street was swept clean, another was littered with rubbish; a beautifully painted house was standing next to a ramshackle hut with only wooden slats in place of windows. The bazaar was shaded from the sun by a canvas. Goods were spread out on colourful silks over low benches in lieu of tables and the smell of a nearby butcher shop filled the air.

The archon, a glorious title held by the Greek mayors of the towns, invited us to his home. When we passed through the town, a crowd of people or rather the whole town followed us. In the square by the fountain, girls in braided ponytails left their water jugs to bring us bouquets of flowers, which we used to decorate our headgear. The archon was rich and his home was opulently decorated but without taste. The stone walls were covered with boards of carved cypress wood. The carvings were not much better than those our coachmen use to decorate their gates. We were led into a large room with windows on all sides which were round and multicoloured like the windows in mosques. The ceiling was busy with red, blue and gold stripes emanating from a circle from the centre of which hung a crystal chandelier. Fine carpets and florid silk divans on the floor in the Turkish style were of the best decoration in the Oriental taste, and the food and drink offered was also Asiatic. First coffee and pipes were handed out, then everyone was sprinkled with rose water, the room was filled with the smoke of burning mastic gum and frankincense, and then the hostess brought honey and almond pies, jam with black pepper, sherbet with ambergris, liqueurs and wines, also with aromatic additives, and finally dried pomegranate seeds. When we parted, each of us – even the interpreters – was gifted a lemon in which was sewn a pouch full of tobacco, a gilded pipe with engraved images of the reclusive monks of Athos and a cup made of blue glass.

The archon asked us to honour them with our presence during their festivities. We went to the pier and saw crowds of men and women on a meadow close to town. We were taken to the country home of the British consul and shown a balcony. The women's attire, which has preserved some features from antiquity, was even more pleasing for the fact that the youths are generally handsome and even among their elderly there is not a single ugly face. Their tunic reaches only to the knee and is held taut by a belt of brocaded white silk or silver. Their trousers of striped and translucent fabric are wide and voluminous and tied with pink ribbons to yellow and red Turkish shoes or slippers. The women wear small turbans and shawls with both ends of the turban cloth embroidered with silk or golden beads and are allowed to fall over the shoulders and rest on the open neck. Girls weave their hair into small braids and drape them over their shoulders. The neck and arms of everyone is exposed, and the breast is barely covered with a pink haze of fabric. Black hair against a white and fresh face, eyes full of fire and timidity, a majestic height, slender figure, eyebrows arched as if drawn on, their graceful harmony and well-formed faces gave their women such an extraordinary and charming appearance that despite their modesty, imagination finds in them similarity with those models by which the Greek sculptors and painters were unconsciously guided to create the most perfect works of beauty conceivable and attribute them to goddesses and nymphs. Their dances began and I could see in them the Olympic Games. A violin, a tympanum and bells accompanied by a dull and quiet singing provided their music. The dancers were joined hand in hand. A leader sang a verse and the crowd would repeat in unison only the last of his words. By his example they threw their hands up, smoothly stepped from foot to foot and swayed deeply from side to side, slowly walking in a circle. After this pantomime, also with a dull and somewhat quick music, came a circular dance in which the participants swirled in different turns, expanding and converging again in the centre. This dance was quite similar to ones that can be seen in Greek bas-reliefs and must be preserved from the establishment of the Olympics. Either due to its remote antiquity or for some special kind of pleasing quality, it produced a great effect on the audience; for even those who were not dancing, even the elderly, begin to imitate the movements of the dance in their seats or follow the steps with their feet and look on tenderly.

Samos lies opposite Ephesus and is separated from Asia Minor by the strait of Mykali. The island was once dedicated to Hera. In a magnificent temple was once held a yearly celebration marking the anniversary of her marriage to Zeus. At that time, the youths of all of Greece flocked to Samos. Mark Antony and Cleopatra, preparing a fleet against Octavius, lavished so many treasures, theatres and games in one such festival that the inhabitants, who were all too fond of games, asked each other: 'how will they celebrate if they win the battle?' Heaps of stone and marble are visible near the port of Vathy, as well as a marble wall collapsed into the sea, fragments of columns, capitals and an aqueduct which I have been assured are the remains of ancient Samos. Three *versta*s [3.2 km] from the town there stood only three Ionic columns remained from a temple of Hera; I did not see them and had no yearning to see them because a multitude of marble pillars remaining from temples and other buildings lay all about the harbour. Samos was also famous for being the birthplace of the philosopher Pythagoras, the zealous defender of the transmigration of the soul; the sibyl of Samos, who foretold the birth of Jesus Christ; and the tyrant Polycrates, who, after a fortuitous life, learned from experience that one should be perfectly content before death.

Samos is revered among the many islands of the archipelago. Its surface is covered with mountains and foothills called the Ampelos on which grow grapes that give a Muscat wine known to us by the name of Malvasia. The most delicious fruit ripen here twice a year. The scorching heat, refreshed by sea winds and nightly dews, constantly dampens the earth. Cotton, wool and oil deliver significant benefits for the inhabitants and moreover, silk and light fabrics worn by the Greeks and Turks are manufactured here. The Greeks strictly observe fasts, eat fish for most of the year and cook it with an excellent taste and are greatly skilful in catching it. They use round nets made of silk threads. In calm weather, young people walk along the shore and when they spot fish, they throw nets by hand and spread it over the water so expertly that as the weights descend and the drawstring is pulled, the net becomes a sack full of prey. Agility, dexterity and practice are necessary for catching fish in this fashion.

# 85

# Cruising between Chios, Chesme and Mytilene

On the arrival from Tenedos of the corsair *Panagiya* with orders from the commander-in-chief, we weighed anchor on the 29th of May [10th of June] and sailed east. Arriving in the Mykali Strait, we cruised those waters in anticipation of the French corsair, which had gone west around Samos. The winds were quiet and variable and the weather was tranquil. The coast of Asia Minor was low and completely covered in greenery and with many Turkish villages, which stand out with their fine minarets surmounted with gilded crescent moons. The fields that could be seen seemed very carefully cultivated. Looking at those memorable places of history, heaped with glory, turned one's thoughts to the ancient splendour of Greece; every step here is marked by a glorious event and a monument. Looking at them only from a distance, it was impossible not to regret passing them by. I was content with viewing them through a telescope and, remembering the stories and searching for ancient cities, I did not want to believe that a poor village like Ayasuluk stands on the site of beautiful Ephesus and its glorious temple to Artemis, revered among the Seven Wonders of the World. The construction of that building, decorated with 127 columns built by 127 kings, took the Ionians over 200 years. Herostratus, seeking immortal fame at any cost, burned down that temple on the same day Alexander the Great was born, and indeed his name is preserved in posterity along all the villains who have betrayed temples, nations and kings with fire and sword. In the Christian era, Ephesus was known for hosting the third ecumenical council [in 431 AD] which asserted against Nestorius that Christ had only one aspect. And there, where the Church condemned the veneration of icons, there is nothing visible but the broken images of pagan gods. Near Ephesus is a cave where it is said that seven children escaping persecution slept for 200 years before emerging. The pure waters of the Meander can still be seen, but without any swans swimming, just as there are no more poets in Greece. The fatherland of Herodotus, Hippocrates and Thales, the cities of Miletus, Halicarnassus and Cnidus, the Mausoleum and the temple to Aphrodite in Cnidus were all in the vicinity of Ephesus. The Apostle and Evangelist John attested that Paul wrote his letters to the people in Ephesus. Recollections of fabulous myth and idolatry did not so much occupy my imagination as the deeds of the apostles who preached the faith in these places. The coast from Ephesus to Chios was low, well populated and apparently well cultivated. A multitude of minarets in the form of columns and white obelisks, long and narrow like trumpets standing on their bells, loom over the land. The construction of their houses which is so different from ours, decorating their cheerful locale, gives even their small huts a charming appearance.

On the 31st of May [12th of June], having joined the *Panagiya* in the strait between Chios and Chesme, we seized two sacolevas carrying wheat. Here, the ancient heroes of Greece give way to the Russians. The names of Orlov, Spiridov and Ilyin shall forever remain in the annals of history in the era of Catherine the Great. I observed with particular curiosity the site of the battle where Admiral Grigoriy Andreyevich Spiridov defeated the Turkish fleet and was amazed at how 15 battleships and 25 other small craft could fit into the Bay of Chesme, the small size of which must surely have given the idea that it was feasible to burn them down and when the courageous Lieutenant Dmitriy Sergeyevich Ilyin introduced his fire ship, the Turkish fleet was completely devastated within five hours. Foreign writers, due to prejudice and bias, attribute the glory of the destruction of the Ottoman naval forces [in 1770] to their own countrymen. Count Aleksey Grigoryevich Orlov, awarded the victory title of *Chesmenskiy*, was said by Rear-Admiral John Elphinstone to be grounded or ashore; Ilyin's exploit is attributed to Robert Dugdale; and as there was apparently no one to replace Spiridov, they simply omit him entirely. In one English edition on the burning of the Turkish fleet, they wrote: 'Dugdale, a lieutenant in Russian service, during such a dangerous and courageous endeavour, withdrew his subordinates and alone guided the fire ship into the Turkish fleet'. By these false stories, when this action is still fresh in everyone's memory and when those who participated in the battle still live, they seek to rob the laurels from the brows of Russian commanders and moreover are not content with them, so they go on to slander the famous courage, obedience and subordination of the Russian warrior.

We spent two days between Chios and Chesme. Chios presents a vast garden stretching from the sea's edge to the slopes of the mountains, with bare summits in the north, west and south forming a range. Lemons, oranges, pomegranates and the best grapes spread out through the east like a natural and perfect orangery. In antiquity, Chios had 36 towns and was called the granary of the Roman people. Today, villages stand on the sites of the old towns but the grain of the arable land is so well cultivated that Chios is rightly considered the best and most fertile island in the archipelago. Silk, brocade and printed textiles are the island's products and they bring the residents profitable trade. Mastic, a kind of pleasantly scented resin which flows from the trunk and branches of the Lentiscus tree, is grown with great diligence on the island and constitutes the main source of revenue for the government. 2,500 *puds* [40.95 t] of the best selection of mastic go to the court. The serene beauties of the island chew it incessantly in order to freshen or perfume their breath and strengthen their gums and whiten their teeth as a result.

Chios is honoured as the birthplace of Homer. Some distance from the main town is shown a square house which the residents call the School of Homer. The reverence of the Greeks for all things to do with the great poet has seen to preserve this ancient monument. On this island, the ruins of one building are considered to have been a temple to Neptune close to a flowing stream whose water was said to cause madness among the ancients; the circumstances have now changed and the water does not harm anyone, though madness still abounds from the beautiful women that inhabit the area. The tragic poet Ion, the historian Theopompus and the philosopher Theocritus were all citizens of Chios.

The town of Chios is protected by a four-cornered fortress in which the Turks always station a garrison of 10,000 men. The buildings that occupy a fairly open and flat ground near the fortress around the harbour, both houses and churches, are in the latest European styles. The locals here are considered among all the Greeks of the archipelago to be the most enlightened and the greater portion of them speak Italian, are very courteous to foreigners and there is no place where one can live more freely, they assure us, than in Chios. For that reason and due to the low cost of living and the pleasant climate, many Italian and French families are settled here.

The girls of Chios are considered the finest decoration the sultans and nobles could possess. Their beauty is so glorious that some pay as much as 100,000 piastres for them. Such a high price, it seems to me, explains why the girls of Chios are so free and so incongruous with the jealousy of the Greeks; and moreover, they are better educated than the other women of Greece. The most inferior of society here can still speak Italian and learn to sing and dance. The avarice of their parents is certainly inexcusable, but the desire to have a strong patron in their son-in-law during the heavy bondage of Turkish rule somehow excuses them. Moreover, this is the custom here and like fashion, customs have their own laws.

On the 1st [13th] of June, we approached the mouth of the Bay of Chesme. The French corsair was disarmed and stood under the very walls of the town. On this evening, three sailors who had served on the corsair were captured on a boat travelling from Chios to Chesme and divulged to us that their captain, Nicolo Idrioti, learning that the frigate was searching for him, sold the corvette to the commandant of Chesme, disbanded his crew and left for Chios. A letter was sent to the commandant on the captured boat, but he responded with several cannon shots. Proceeding to Chios, we were met there in the Turkish fashion by three shots from the local fortifications at a great distance, and our corsair replied from its light gun. On the 2nd [14th], moving to Smyrna between the Spalmadore islands (Oinousses) and the Cape of Caleberno (Karaburun), we saw a brig armed for military service and fired a shot at her, raising a flag to signal that we demanded her to approach us. The brig did not raise a flag and set off in the wind with all sails set, aiming to take shelter in Chesme. We raised our topgallants and soon caught up. The brig hoisted an American flag and lay to; its name was *Hector* and its papers indicated that it came from Marseilles to Smyrna, both ports which belonged to our enemies and under blockade. Laden with sugar and coffee, the brig was detained and I was instructed to take her and another seized vessel to Tenedos to be handed over to the Court of Prizes.

The frigate remained at the entrance of Smyrna and intercepted two more vessels with cargo, on board one of which was captured the captain of the French corsair. On the 3rd [15th] of June, after a strong wind, the frigate took shelter in Skyros, whence they returned to Tenedos on the 7th [19th]. Manoeuvring to the north and around the western side of Mytilene, I admired its excellent position. This island is not inferior to Chios in fertility and is advantageous for its mountains are covered with forest suitable for shipbuilding and besides its safe harbour of Castro (Kalloni), it has three others at its disposal. Their wine berries are considered the best in all the Levant. Mytilene, called Lesbos in antiquity, was the fatherland of Sappho, Alcaeus, Pittacus and Theophrastus. Epicurus and Aristotle had their schools here. Terpander of Lesbos was the first to invent the seven-sting lyre and the Lesbians were famous not only for their skilled musicians, but also for the special depreciation of their morals.[1] For the honour of the women of Lesbos, it was necessary to at first treat her husband like a stranger and every visitor was obliged to take his wife, if even for a single night. Even the latest travellers write that this rite has changed only in that a priest seeks out the bride as the visitor,

---

1     The classicist Evelyn Abbott asserted that the unique parity between men and women in Aeolian society was a point of contention among the other Greek states, and the belligerent relationship between Lesbos and Athens undoubtedly contributed to their slanderous portrayal of Lesbian men and women as having lax morals. The poet Sappho, who surrounded herself with female peers and students and wrote affectionately about both sexes, became a focus for the accusation of sexual deviance in particular, though the Lesbians were accused of everything: sloth, drunkenness, blasphemy, etc. The word 'Lesbian' came to mean a debauched individual and 'Sapphic' in the late 19th century became a euphemism for female homosexuality. Bronevskiy seems to obligatorily report on this reputation but offers an alternative narrative by quoting his Greek pilot. Evelyn Abbott, *A History of Greece*, vol. 1 (New York: G. P. Putnam's Sons, 1888), pp.506-511.; Francis Lieber (ed.), *Encyclopaedia Americana* (Philadelphia: Lea and Blanchford, 1849), s.v. 'Sappho'.; James Sanxay (ed.), *Lexicon Aristophanicum, Graeco-Anglicum* (London: H. Woodfall, 1764), s.v. 'λεσβῐάζω'. [James Sanxay (ed.), *Aristophanic Lexicon, Greek-English* (London: H. Woodfall, 1764), s.v. 'Lesbiazo'.]

sometimes a rich man can choose but a poor man must suffer. The priest then blesses the couple, after which the newlyweds and relatives ease each other of their consciences. It seemed to me incredible that such a custom could be practiced among the Greeks of the present day. I inquired about this to our pilot, a Greek from Milos who was quite educated and could speak Italian and sing the poems of Homer. He said 'the truth is there are as few such girls on Mytilene as there are very many in Italy, but they cannot escape their rank; like everywhere, these unfortunate people support themselves at the cost of their health and virtues and always hide from the eyes of the world. You can conclude from this why they prefer foreigners and have frequent need of a priest'.

# 86

# Stationing in Tenedos

On the 4th [16th] of June, during a strong northerly wind, I manoeuvred into Tenedos aboard the *Hector*. The court considered the papers and recognized the boat and its cargo as legal prizes, due to Marseilles and Smyrna being enemy ports, and since three American vessels had been released on the basis that they inform their consuls that they were henceforth neutral vessels, one captured from Smyrna would be considered a fair prize. The skipper listened to the decision of the court with steadfastness, but his men, deprived of their deserved pay and at such a distance from their homeland, without any hope of obtaining aid anywhere, asked me to intercede on their behalf. The admiral saw their plight and ordered that their pay be compensated, to return a portion of their cargo which was then purchased for cash from the sailors, and to safely deliver them to Smyrna, Malta or a place of their choosing. The skipper, Luke Thorndike, and all of his men at first did not want to believe such charity and were so much delighted with the admiral's mercy that they wanted to thank him futilely, but Senyavin did not accept any gesture after learning their intentions. On parting, the skipper admitted that he considered himself too fortunate that he fell into our hands, as he had been thrice captured by the Spanish, French and British and was always released with nothing but the clothes on his back.[1] As the brig proved to be a very nimble craft and also capable of military service, the admiral ordered it brought back into the harbour, unloaded, repaired and armed with ten guns.

---

1   Israel Thorndike of Boston, owner of the ship and uncle of its skipper, petitioned the Russian government for the case to be re-examined and sought full compensation of the vessel, which did not occur until 1828 when Emperor Nicholas I examined several cases pertaining to captured American vessels and personally found in favour of the claimant. Thorndike was awarded 205,731 rubles, 28 kopecks in paper currency. 'Claims against Russia', *Nile's Weekly Register* 34 (March-September 1828), p.295.

The strict blockade of the Dardanelles produced in Constantinople a severe lack of provisions and provoked a riot; the Sultan Selim was overthrown by the janissaries and the new Sultan Mustafa decided to drive us away from the Dardanelles by seizing Tenedos. There were rumours that the *kapudan-pasha* would soon exit through the strait and in the event of a battle, the admiral chose a completely new battle plan and dispatched to the captains the following instructions:

> Circumstances oblige us to give a decisive battle, as so long as the flagships of the enemy are in fair condition, we must expect a very stubborn battle. Therefore the attack will be conducted as follows: according to the number of the enemy's admirals, each will be attacked with two ships – the *Rafail* paired with the *Silnyy*, the *Selafail* with the *Uriil*, and the *Moshchnyy* with the *Yaroslav*. On the raising of signal No. 3 with the French tricolour, these ships will immediately proceed toward the enemy flagships and attack them with all possible determination, as close as possible, without fear of the enemy setting fire to his own vessels. The previous battle on the 10th [22nd] of May demonstrated that the closer one keeps to him, the less danger he poses and therefore if one manages to board him, one can expect the greatest success. Upon receiving a shot of grape, open fire. If the enemy sets sail, destroy his masts; if he stands on anchor, destroy his hull. Attack with two from one side, but not from both sides; if it happens that a place is given to another ship, do not withdraw in any event further than the range of grapeshot. The enemy with whom you begin the battle is with whom you will end it by either sinking or capturing their ship.
>
> As for the multitude of unforeseeable consequences, it is not possible to provide every contextual instruction and I will not expound further. I hope that every son of the fatherland will honour his duty gloriously.
>
> The *Tvyordyy*
> Dmitriy Senyavin.

# 87

# The Landing on Lemnos

---

On the 23rd of May [4th of June], twenty janissaries were intercepted on a boat and explained that they had long gone without payment and suffered extreme deprivations. They deserted from the island of Lemnos with the intention of returning to their homes. The commander-in-chief dispatched Rear-Admiral Greig the next day with four ships to ascertain the condition of the fortress and garrison on Lemnos and if they are found to be weak, to ask for the commandant's surrender in the same fashion as Tenedos was offered mercy. The rear-admiral arrived at Lemnos, sent his offer and received the reply: 'as the elders and mayors are presently scattered across the island and cannot be quickly gathered, we ask that you petition us again later'. Meanwhile, on the 25th [6th], the commander-in-chief received news that several ships, frigates and other military vessels of various sizes had arrived in Gallipoli from Constantinople, so he sent the *Feniks* on to Greig's squadron to recall them to Tenedos.

The Turkish fleet was well reinforced and although the wind was beneficial to their exit from the strait, they remained behind their fortresses in the same position, prompting the commander-in-chief to again send Rear-Admiral Greig to Lemnos with five ships on the 1st [13th] of June so that by dividing our fleet, the Turks would be encouraged to leave the Dardanelles and once again try to fight us. On the 2nd [14th], the rear-admiral arrived at the port of San Antonio (Moudros) and sent a second offer of surrender to the *agha*, identical to the first. A full day and night passed without any reply and on the 3rd [15th], Captain First Rank Lukin with a detachment of 812 sailors and marines and 28 officers made landfall. That force crossed 40 *versta*s [42.67 km] in six hours, despite the difficult road, and came within sight of the fortress. Captain Lukin did not see or meet the enemy before occupying two heights and immediately sent ahead skirmishers who quickly discovered them, attacked and drove them into the suburbs. The Turks defended themselves there stubbornly. The battle, which lasted for two hours, was decided by the courageous exploits of the sailors who, having scaled the height on the flank of the enemy's line and fired down its length with heavy musketry and canister from a small gun they hauled up with them, forced the Turks to withdraw behind the walls of their fortress. Although the sun had set and the soldiers were exhausted from their rapid march, Captain Lukin maintained his aspiration and captured the advantageous heights in the night, a position from which it was equally convenient to defend or retreat to the ships. On the next day, when they were preparing to storm the fort itself, a command was received to forgo any undertaking that evening and to return to the ships in the Gulf of San Antonio. The commander-in-chief determined that the *kapudan-pasha* intended to come out and sent an order to Rear-Admiral Greig stipulating that if the Turks intend to defend themselves, to abandon the siege of the fortress and re-join the fleet at Tenedos. The retreat was orderly and without losses. To hold the enemy's attention, the *Svyataya Yelena* and the *Kildyuin* attacked the fortress from the north. The landing party withdrew from the heights at 10 o'clock at night and at the quick step arrived at the isthmus by early dawn, where armed rowing boats were arranged to cover their retreat, though the Turks made no pursuit. On the 5th [17th] of June, the party was taken aboard the ships and on the 6th [18th], the squadron reached Tenedos. Our losses in the battle outside the fortress were 14 killed and 6 wounded; the enemy lost an estimated 150 men killed and wounded and the squadron seized 7 vessels of various cargo.

The island of Lemnos lies between Tenedos and the Holy Mountain [of Athos]. The climate of the island is very healthy and never experiences terrible heat. For the wintering of a fleet, it possesses a very comfortable and safe harbour. Covered with hills and low mountains, the island at every step presents an image of rare fertility. Besides every kind of fruit, the land abounds with grain, vineyards, horned cattle and in particular a mineral soil known under the name of Lemnian earth or sealed earth (*terra sigillata*). It is revered as a medicine against pestilences, venomous snake bites and the common cold. To procure it, the chiefs of the island with a party of labourers ascend the mountain, which must have been volcanic at the dawn of time, for in its womb they find sulphur, alum, pumice and all the signs of an eruption. They dig deep and when they find a vein of the mineral soil, they excavate as much as they think will last them a year. Then they fill in their mine and do not allow anyone to harvest any until next time.

In the age of myth, when they had no understanding of fire-breathing mountains, they thought that Hephaestus, being cast down from the heavens by Zeus, crashed into this mountain and founded his first workshop below. One of the four glorious labyrinths was on this island. Emperor Gallienus expressly visited Lemnos to learn the properties of the mineral earth and when Philoctetes was wounded in the leg by a poisoned arrow, he was sent here to be cured.

# 88

# The Siege of Tenedos

In the morning of the 10th [22nd] of June, the telegraph informed us that that enemy's squadron had set sail. Between 8 and 10 o'clock, a Turkish squadron of 8 ships, 5 frigates, 2 sloops and 2 brigs exited the Dardanelles. The enemy manoeuvred all day in the mouth of the strait during a fresh northerly wind and anchored off of Imbros in the evening. The ships in our vanguard, the *Skoryy*, *Selafail* and one corsair, also dropped anchor leeward of them.

Tenedos. Illustration from the original publication.

On the 11th [23rd], our fleet weighed anchor at 5 o'clock but sooner after suffered a failing wind and could not move much farther than the islands of Mavro. Upon the departure of the fleet, the brig *Bogoyavlensk* came into harbour and took a position behind a line of rocks from which a good defence of the harbour's entrance could be given without obstructing the views of the fortress's guns.

On the 12th [24th], two Turkish ships and two frigates left the Dardanelles and united with their squadron. From the 11th to the 14th [23rd to 26th] of June, our fleet frequently attempted to approach the enemy and force him into a battle but the weak wind and strong current from the Dardanelles confounded the admiral's efforts. The Turkish fleet, following our movements, also manoeuvred away and maintained a distance so that in the event of a change of wind, they could retreat back into the strait.

During the evening of the 14th [26th], the wind turned slightly to our favour and our fleet formed two columns and sailed toward the five Turkish ships standing off of Imbros, but they followed suit and exploited the wind to join the others in the mouth of the Dardanelles. Learning that it was impossible to cut off the Turks from their fortresses in the event of a strong, foul and inconsistent wind and that the enemy demonstrated by their actions no intention of attacking us, it was decided to wait for the cover of darkness and move around the western side of Imbros where there is no strong current and thereby approach the enemy solely by the wind.

On the 15th [27th] of June, when our squadron was navigating between Imbros and Samothrace on a weak wind, the Turkish squadron tacked and shuffled about at the mouth of the strait several times, along with the galleys carrying their army, before sailing for Tenedos. At 3 in the afternoon, two enemy frigates in column from their vanguard attacked our corsair, which had been dispatched from our fleet and did not have time to reach the safety of the harbour and could not flee into the open sea for lack of wind. The captain of the corsair ran aground on a shoal and in that position, fought off his attackers with superb courage until he expended his last charge of powder. He then threw his guns into the water and evacuated his crew to shore. At 4 o'clock, a Turkish force of 10 ships, 9 frigates, a corvette, a brig and 70 galleys came within canister range and held under sail, opening heavy fire on the fortress, town, outworks and vessels in the harbour. Our side retaliated with excellent diligence, especially from the brig *Bogoyavlensk* which suffered a hit from every shot fired at it. During this action, which lasted until dusk, 30 boats approached the north side of the island and attempted a landing, but two companies and four guns dispatched from the town did not allow them. The enemy withdrew in confusion with losses. At 8 o'clock, the Turkish fleet dropped anchor between Tenedos and Anatolia, excluding one frigate and several smaller craft which purposely sought to sink the *Bogoyavlensk*. The Turkish frigate soon suffered a damaged rudder and lost its mizzen-topmast and her three row boats attempting to tow her to safety were sunk.[1] After this, the frigate rode the current and departed from the fortress to return to its fleet.

While that action was being fought, Colonel Padeyskiy, believing that the *Bogoyavlensk* could not withstand another cannonade and having need for more guns, sent me to the brig's commander, Lieutenant Pyotr Dodt, to request that he transfer his guns, ammunition and men in the night to the fortress, where the gunners were needed and the sailors would be put to better use.

On the 16th [28th] of June, the Turkish squadron was assembled along the coast of the island as close as the depth allowed. In 5 hours, two frigates and 10 smaller craft opened fire on our fortifications. Meanwhile, their galleys and sloops assembled on the Anatolian coast landed a force on the island. Major Gedeonov with 200 regular musketeers, 100 Albanians and one gun sortied from the redoubt in order to disrupt the landing as much as possible. On the arrival of this detachment to the landing area, more than a thousand Turks were already occupying the height and the other boats were ceaselessly landing additional troops in various places under the cover of canister fire from the ships and frigates.

Although preventing the landing of such superior forces under naval cover was not considered a real possibility, retreating without disrupting the enemy would be very dangerous, so for that reason the brave Major Gedeonov resolutely attacked the enemy's right flank and so quickly and fortuitously drove him from the height that the Turks rushed down to the shore in great disorder, where they faced bullets from their own men on one side and our bayonets on the other, and the widely dispersing balls of the naval grapeshot landing all about, they threw themselves into the sea in a panic and many drowned. Of the two boats that returned to rescue their people, one was sunk and the other lost its oars and mast on the shore. The Albanians rushed onto her and massacred everyone aboard.

The enemy's left flank, meanwhile, was greatly reinforced and encircled us from the right, took the heights and proceeded into the interior of the island, yet when they saw the fate of their right flank, they stopped and hesitated. Major Gedeonov, observing that he could not resist such a multitudinous enemy everywhere, and having lost 80 men killed and wounded, among them the courageous and experienced Captain Kutumov, he chose to exploit his initial good fortune and began to retreat. When the enemy ascertained how few his force was, they attacked swiftly, but a company of grenadiers sent to reinforce Gedeonov appeared from the right wing, fired a volley and charged with bayonets and the enemy collapsed on both sides. Another enemy detachment appeared on the heights on our right, but did not dare to descend from them, thereby denying a route of retreat. When

---

1    Bronevskiy's note: 'See the illustration of Tenedos'.

our three companies in column approached the redoubt, they had to pass under grapeshot from the two enemy frigates. They fired a volley but did not have time for a second as our people scattered out of formation and ran to safety without losses.

After uniting our forces in the redoubt defended by 14 light guns, we were suddenly attacked by a disproportionate number of Turks who, as it was accurately discovered, numbered approximately 10,000 men with several French officers among them. The enemy, having been repelled once, attacked five more times before retreating. Our shots of canister and musket fire left the redoubt surrounded by significant numbers of dead and wounded. When the Turks occupied the height which exposed our rear, Colonel Padeyskiy withdrew to the main fortress in such excellent order that not a single gun or man was lost. This action was accomplished by two of the companies withdrawing from the outworks charging with bayonets and when the large crowds were driven to flight, the field guns were sent ahead with the other men marching behind them into the fortress, all in good order. The small redoubt, subjected to every attack, could not have been defended and was abandoned. The enemy was so amazed by the courage of our forces and his own casualties that he did not even dare to pursue them and the two companies which had cleared the way for the withdrawal also entered the fortress walls without losses. As soon as the gate was closed, the Turks ran from all sides to the square and rushed the drawbridge; a volley of canister did not break their resolve, as the hindmost men in the crowd pushed the foremost from behind. When the area was covered with the dead and wounded, they retreated and occupied the heights, suburbs and the small redoubt, directing heavy fire against every side of the main fortress. In the evening, they received three large guns from the ships, a 9-*pud* [176.9 kg] mortar and a varied assortment of supplies and assault ladders. The enemy understood the weaknesses of the fortress and, believing they could easily gain access, immediately attempted an assault after our drummers struck the evening tattoo. The men carrying the ladders were killed in the attempt; the others ran up to the ditch in the dark and, being unable to find the ladders, tried to turn back but were restrained by the crowds following them and became jumbled together. They bravely stood under canister fire and became victims of their own rash confidence. After the considerable losses which are typical in unsuccessful assaults and escalades, they left us alone until morning.

The *kapudan-pasha*, knowing the lay of the fortress and that it could not withstand a serious attack from the sea, ordered the whole fleet to head toward it at the break of dawn on the 17th [29th], without sparing the ships. Meanwhile, gunboats were approaching the small redoubt and began to fire at our vessels standing in the harbour and the American prize vessel, the *Hector*, caught fire after the first shots. Lieutenant Dodt, who commanded the fortress artillery facing that direction, with his sailors manning the guns, succeeded in sinking two of them and three were repulsed with damaged masts, fleeing to the cape.

At 5 in the morning, a Turkish ship and frigate manoeuvred close to the fortress and incessantly fired on it; two others standing on anchor also opened up a fierce bombardment. All the other ships and frigates approached, but at 8 o'clock, the whole Turkish fleet suddenly ceased firing and withdrew with haste from the fortress, setting sail for open water.

After two days of continuous firing, the fortress had nearly exhausted its supply of powder, canisters and other munitions and most of the artillerists were wounded, so one can easily imagine the joy felt by the entire garrison when our fleet appeared, rushing under all sails from Imbros to Tenedos; this was the reason for the enemy's hasty retreat. On the 15th [27th] of June, as mentioned above, our fleet was manoeuvring through weak and contrary winds between Imbros and Samothrace; on the 16th [28th] when the wind picked up, they came in the night between Imbros and the European coast where they lay on anchor, leaving the *Venus* and *Shpitsbergen* under sail to observe the enemy's movements. On the 17th [29th], our fleet returned to Tenedos at dawn on a fresh and fair wind. The Turkish squadron ran on the wind as they approached Mavro and kept as close as possible to the southern side of Tenedos. Our squadron rushed to intercept the enemy but the Turkish fleet anticipated our intentions and made it clear by fleeing on the wind that they would avoid a battle and divert our squadron away from Tenedos if we pursued. The commander-in-chief, learning from the captain of the *Venus* who sent word ahead that the fortress was low on all supplies and could not stand for two days, ordered the entire Russian squadron to return to Tenedos and drop anchor in their previous positions. Three ships, a sloop and two corsairs set sail for observation of the Turkish squadron. At this time, the enemy fleet emerged behind Tenedos arranged in the line of battle and turned at the coast of Anatolia to tack again toward the west. After this, rowing vessels from all of the ships brought the fortress all of its necessary supplies under the cover of the *Venus* and *Shpitsbergen*. At 5 o'clock, launches armed with cannons, a sloop and the two corsairs attacked the enemy's galley flotilla standing by the mainland's shore. Two boats were captured, several were burned and sank, and the rest fled southward to Cape Baba; thereby depriving the Turks of the opportunity to land reinforcements on Tenedos. In the evening, after beating the tattoo, the Turks once again dared an assault, but the opening shots tempered their zeal and only the daredevils among them appeared on the square where they fell under the fire of our sharpshooters.

On the 18th [30th] of June, early in the morning, our squadron consisting of 10 ships set out to find the enemy. The *Venus*, *Shpitsbergen*, and two corsairs were left behind for the aid of the fortress[2] and the enemy engaged in brief exchanges of

---

2    Bronevskiy's note: 'The frigate *Kildyuin*, coming from Corfu with a British frigate, encountered the Turkish fleet on the evening of the 17th [29th] but managed to evade

heavy firing day and night from then until the 27th [9th of July], the day that our squadron returned to the island. The position of the fortress, standing on the most disadvantageous place between three nearby mountains from which it was entirely exposed, having no casemates, cellars or convenient places to protect people, made the whole grounds of the fort into a trap wherein cannon balls and bullets could freely choose their victims. The parapet was so low that it did not cover even half a man's height, but when the enemy began to lob their 9-*pud* [176.9 kg] bombs, destroying the rest of the structure, there was no longer any place to hide from their fire. Additionally, the Turks cut off the supply of water from the beginning of their siege and the extraordinary deprivation together with the scorching heat made the need for it all the most sensitive. The crying of women and children and the constant performances of services by the priests made the danger of our desperate situation inescapably acute. Yet all of this could not shake the resolution of our soldiers who had proven to be true heroes and the Albanians and residents of Tenedos competed with them for glory. Seeing the severed limbs of their wives and children, seeing their homes engulfed in flames, they condemned themselves to death and searched for it on the ramparts with a rare bravery. They did not want to hear mention of the surrender which the Turks twice demanded. The more we felt the oppression of the enemy, the closer we stood to death, the greater liveliness and resolution we found while manning the batteries for 12 straight days of continuous fire and the more courageously and willingly we took the places of the dead and wounded, and everything that the enemy could destroy during the day was repaired in the night.

The old soldiers admitted that in all their service, even under the command of Suvorov, who loved danger, they had never before been in such a dire situation. If the fleet did not return soon, then the commandant, in accordance with the general wishes of the officers, soldiers and residents, suggested taking the light artillery out of the fortress in a sortie and searching for death on the open field; even the Turks, especially their sharpshooters entrenched in the suburban houses which had been reduced to rubble, took high casualties and were beginning to suffer from the same lack of supply as we were. While we continued to fight on extremely bitterly, our fate depended on the result of the naval battle. Then when our disaster had reached its final degree, on the 25th of June [7th of July], to the indescribable joy of the garrison, the ship of the line *Skoryy* appeared and behind it followed our entire fleet. Loud cheers of '*ura!*' and a powerful salute of cannon fire let the Turks know that their fleet had been defeated and further proof came in the appearance of a Turkish admiral's flagship brought onto the roadstead.

them and arrived at Tenedos on 20 June [2 July]'.

# 89

# The Destruction of the Turkish Fleet at Mount Athos – The Surrender of the Besieging Forces on Tenedos

Upon the departure of our fleet from Tenedos, it was not known where to search for the enemy. Instead of going to Mytilene, which was generally thought to be abandoned by the Turks, the admiral led the squadron virtually in the opposite direction to Imbros and in the evening, the squadron lay to until midnight, 10 *versta*s [10.67 km] north of Lemnos. After midnight they proceeded to Lemnos under reduced sails. The admiral's presumption proved correct. At dawn on the 19th of June [1st of July], one Turkish ship appeared on the wind, quickly followed by 9 more ships, 5 frigates, 3 sloops and 2 brigs standing on anchor in a disordered formation below the fortress. The admiral gave a signal to set all sails and attack the enemy; the cannon shots were so welcomed by all that the officers congratulated each other on their good fortune to be able to fight the enemy; the sailors, who feared since the 9th [21st] that the Turks would succeed in evading us, prepared for the battle with high spirits. The Turks quickly and very adeptly formed the line of battle on a starboard tack. Their three flagships formed the centre and their large frigates also stood in another line. The enemy squadron consisted of the following ships:

1. *Mesudiye* (Majesty) of 120 guns under Kapudan-Pasha (Grand Admiral) Seydi Ali;
2. *Sedd-el Bahr* (Naval Bastion) of 84 guns under Kapudan-Bey (Admiral) Bekir Bey;
3. *Anka-yi Bahri* (Majesty of the Sea) of 84 guns under Patrona-Bey (Vice-Admiral) Sheremet Bey;
4. *Taus-i Bahri* (Sea Bird) of 84 guns under Commodore Huseyin Bey;
5. *Tevfik-Numa* (Sign of the True Path) of 84 guns;
6. *Sayyad-i Bahri* (Sea Fisherman) of 74 guns;

7. *Mal-beik Nusrat* (Prosperous) of 74 guns;
8. *Jebel-Andaz* (Dauntless) of 74 guns;
9. *Besharet* (The Annunciation) of 84 guns;
10. *Kilik-i Bahri* (Key to the Sea) of 84 guns under a commodore.

Frigates:
1. *Meskeni-Ghazi* (Camp of the Warriors) of 50 guns;
2. *Bedr-i Zafar* (Wholly Victorious) of 50 guns;
3. *Fakih-i Safar* (Lawful Traveller) of 50 guns;
4. *Nessim* (Breeze) of 50 guns;
5. *Iskenderiye* (Alexandria) of 44 guns.

Sloops:
1. *Metelin* (Lesbos) of 32 guns;
2. *Rehber-i Alam* (Leader of Knowledge) of 28 guns;
3. *Denuvet* (Warrior) of 32 guns.

Brigs:
1. *Alamit-i Nusrat* (Sign of Victory) of 18 guns.
2. *Melankai* of 18 guns.

On all of these vessels were a combined 1,158 guns, while our 10 ships had 754. Consequently, the enemy had an advantage of 404 guns over our ten ships of the line and their crews appeared to be double, judging by the men counted on the captured vessels.

In order to attack the enemy flagships two on one, our ships were grouped into the following pairs: the *Rafail* with the *Silnyy*, *Selafail* with the *Uriil* and the *Moshchnyy* with the *Yaroslav*. The Turks were downwind and opened fire from a long distance and kept up their barrage ceaselessly. The foremost ship, the *Rafail*, with great patience withstood the fire of the entire enemy line and did not retaliate with its own until it reached the very closest distance; this ship, having its after-sails badly beaten, could not retard itself in the wind and penetrated the enemy line between the ships of the *kapudan-pasha* and the *kapudan-bey*, fighting off the enemy on both sides before vanishing through the smoke. The other five of our ships, coming within pistol range, rounded to and tightened their line until the bowsprits were nearly touching the stern of the ship ahead and began to attack the three enemy flagships. When the battle began this way in the centre of the enemy line at 8 o'clock in the morning, the commander-in-chief [aboard the *Tvyordyy*] and the *Skoryy* proceeded to the ships and frigates of the Turkish vanguard and ordered Rear-Admiral Greig [aboard the *Retvizan*] and the *Svyataya Yelena* to follow him to the enemy's van. The *Tvyordyy* came ahead of the line, quickly knocked out a frigate and then attacked the ship behind her, forcing the ship to lie to and thereby halt the movement of the entire enemy line. The *Rafail* meanwhile appeared passing from the leeward side and despite many of its sails being tattered, was operating its artillery superbly. When the *Rafail* passed the foremost Turkish ship, being badly beaten, the latter started to turn toward the *Rafail* to engage it, but our admiral's position ahead of the enemy line prevented this movement and he began to deliver raking fire down the entire enemy line from his port side.

When the first two ships lying to began to manoeuvre, the ship of the *kapudan-bey* approached the *Tvyordyy*, bow to beam, and in a very short time was deprived of her remaining sails and yards. The *Skoryy*, following the ships beaten by the *Tvyordyy*, came between them and entered an unequal fight with three ships and a frigate, one of which attempted to board. The *Skoryy* defended itself with grape and musketry which killed so many men aboard the Turkish vessel that it abandoned the boarding action and fled to safety. The two ships and frigate of the Turkish rearguard then came around on the leeward side of the centre to assist the vanguard in their fight; our admiral immediately led his ship somewhat into the wind and attacked the first ship off the bow. He soon halted her and all the others vessels following. By the courageous exploits of the admiral's ship, the enemy became heavily crowded downwind of our other ships and began to flee from the battle at 10:30, heading directly for Mount Athos where they assumed they could burn their own ships and escape overland. At 10, the admiral signalled to the whole squadron to close with the enemy further and pursue them as tightly as possible. The *Rafail*, being in danger, withdrew to open water upwind when the Turkish line was halted in order to repair the worst of her damage.

Vice-Admiral Senyavin, bombarding and chasing the advance enemy ships, became deliberately downwind of both squadrons; the *Skoryy* and the *Moshchnyy* fought in the midst of the Turkish squadron, while the others formed a semi-circle, several replacing their sails as they became too heavily damaged.[1] The victory was undoubted. The entire Turkish fleet, despite a brave defence, would have been captured or destroyed were it not for the wind subsiding around noon. So that the beaten ships would not be subjected to an attack by superior forces and to prevent the repairing vessels from lagging outside the effective range of their shots, the admiral considered it prudent to halt the squadron in place, inspect themselves

---

1    Bronevskiy's note: 'Captain P. M. Rozhnov [of the *Selafail*], in the very heat of battle and under the hail of grapeshot, replaced his damaged yards; many other captains also repaired damage without disengaging from the battle. This action credited to the ship captains also demonstrates the great courage which animated our sailors'.

well, and then attack the enemy again. To that end, he ordered everyone to hold toward the wind.

The battle lasted four hours. Our squadron halted at the place of the battle and the Turkish reached a safe distance outside of range before also turning into the wind. Our ships suffered greatly in both sails and armament, especially the *Tvyordyy*, *Skoryy*, *Rafail* and *Moshchnyy*; the Turkish squadron was apparently equally injured, and all their masts except those on the ship of the second admiral stood like bare trees without their yards and sails. The admiral assembled his ships, ordered their damage be repaired as quickly as possible to be able to fight again on the same day, but the wind died out completely at noon and then changed to a weak breeze from the northwest, which the Turks turned toward and hauled as closely as possible in their tacking simply to avoid engaging us in battle again.

At 6 o'clock when the wind was refreshed, the ship of the first admiral [the *Sedd-el Bahr*] with one other ship and two frigates in fair condition began to lag behind their squadron. Senyavin ordered them to be cut off and by evening, when three of our ships approached close enough, the Turkish ship and two frigates abandoned their tow of the admiral's flagship and fled for themselves. The Turkish flagship was trapped and captured in the night by Captain Rozhnov with the *kapudan-bey* [Bekir Bey] still onboard.

On the morning of the 20th of June [2nd of July], the Turkish squadron was windward of ours and mostly held to the island of Thasos except the ship and two frigates who had been aiding the *kapudan-bey* and were now on the southern side of the peninsula of Mount Athos. Senyavin detached Rear-Admiral Greig with three ships to pursue them and cut them off. On the 21st [3rd], at 4 in the afternoon, the Turks managed to run all three of their vessels aground behind Ammouliani Island in the bay of Mount Athos during their flight and the crews set them alight when they abandoned them. The shocks of the explosions were strong enough that the ships 20 *verstas* [21.34 km] away could feel them. At dawn on the 22nd of June [4th of July], a voluminous smoke with two sources was spotted within the enemy fleet which was later confirmed to be the result of another ship and frigate being burned down.

After such a perfect victory, having destroyed two ships and three frigates and taking prisoner a full admiral, Senyavin faced a supremely difficult decision: whether to chase after the remnant of the enemy fleet or to return to Tenedos and rescue the garrison from an imminent and brutal captivity, which would require abandoning the rare opportunity of being the destroyer of the entire Turkish fleet. In this case, Senyavin did not hesitate to sacrifice his personal glory and ambition to save his brothers left behind and besieged by a grossly superior force, whose fate swayed his good heart. This choice surprised all those who could not be like Senyavin, moderate in their triumphs, modest in glory and jealous of true contributions to the fatherland. However, his decision can be explained with simple reasoning. After the battle, the wind was weak, variable and almost always foul when it blew at all between periods of dead calm every day. Consequently, after pursuing the enemy in such conditions, Tenedos would be lost and then the destruction of the enemy fleet would be less beneficial to us. Without a convenient port near the Dardanelles, there would be no means to replenish the men lost or to repair the damage suffered by the ships in the battle; we could only burn the Turkish ships and perhaps a few of our own and abandon the blockade of the strait or take up a new base at such a distance it would weaken our effectiveness and thereby compromise our primary objective: 'to deprive Constantinople of the supply of provisions by sea with a Russian fleet present in the archipelago'. The glory of destroying the Ottoman Empire's naval forces would only flatter the individual of the commander. Furthermore, the admiral hoped that by rescuing the fortress he could cut off the enemy's escape through the Dardanelles and then force them into a second engagement.

On the 23rd and 24th of June [5th and 6th of July], foul winds and calms prevented the squadron from advancing. On the 25th [7th] around noon, they arrived at Tenedos and stood on anchor along the channel. At the same time, the Turkish squadron stood on anchor between the island of Imbros and the Dardanelles. On the 26th [8th], the commander-in-chief delivered a proposal to Kadhim-Oglu, the commander of the Turkish forces, to abandon the island in exchange for safe passage to the Asian coast with all their property and weapons. In response, the Turkish pasha asked for permission to first communicate with the commander of the Anatolian camp, Serasker[2] Said Ismail Pasha, to whose authority he answered. By noon, the Turkish squadron of 7 ships, 3 frigates and 2 brigs weighed anchor on a fresh northerly wind and entered the Dardanelles.

On the 27th of June [9th of July], the senior commandant of the first four fortresses in the Dardanelles and the pasha's second in command, Haci Yussuf Agha, arrived on the admiral's ship with the consent to evacuate the island according to the previous proposal and on the 28th [10th], the 4,600 men of the Turkish force with all of their guns and ammunition were safely conveyed to the coast of Anatolia by our vessels.

The ship of the *kapudan-bey* captured, named the *Sedd-el Bahr* (Naval Bastion), had 84 guns, of 42-*funt*s [20.6 kg] on the lower deck, 22 [10.8 kg] on the central and 12 [5.9 kg] on the upper deck, all in bronze. This ship, although severely damaged in both its hull and rigging, could be repaired and continue service. 230

---

2    A commander of an independent corps otherwise holding the title of pasha of two or three tails. Andreyevskiy et al., *Brockhaus and Efron Dictionary*, s.v. 'Сераскир'. [Andreyevskiy et al., *Brockhaus and Efron Dictionary*, s.v. 'Serasker'.]

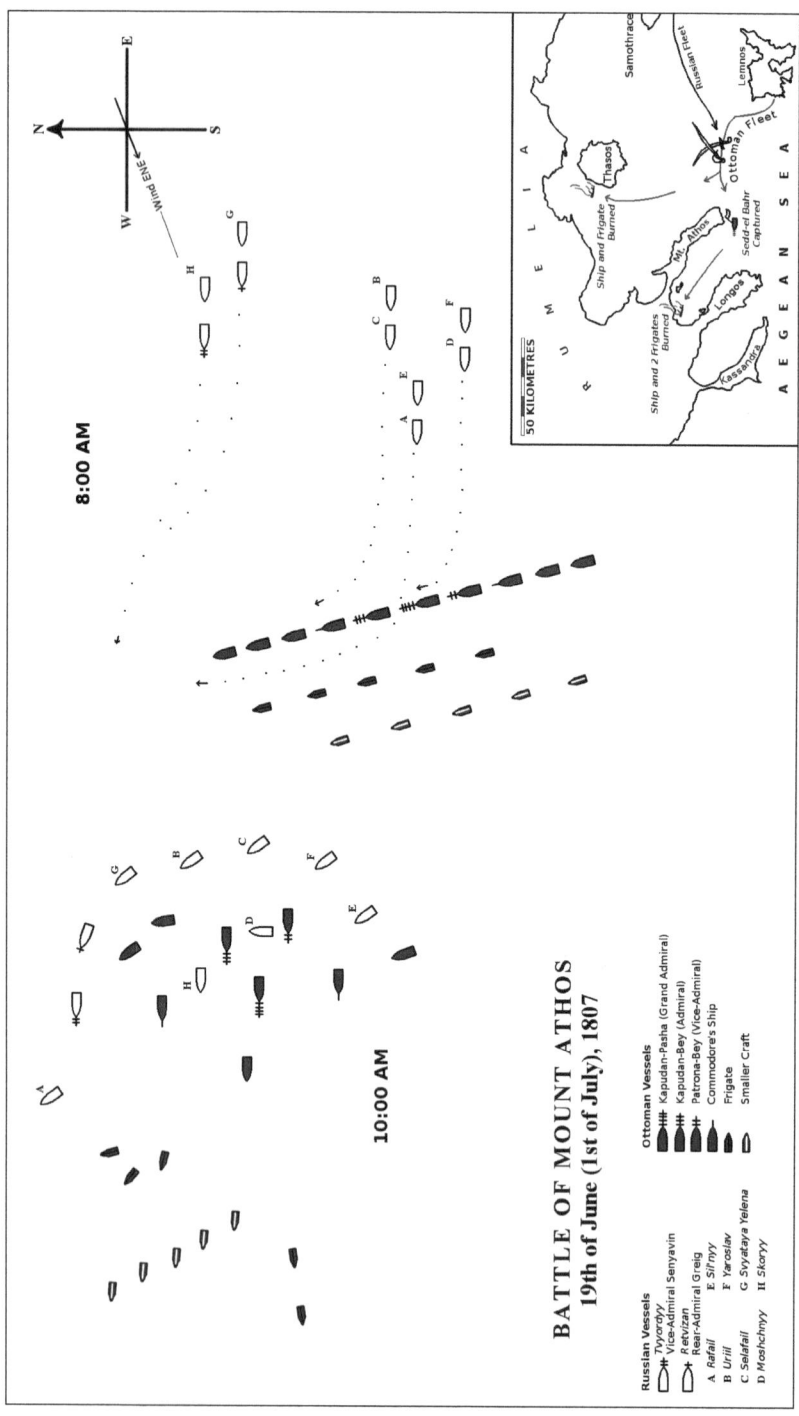

**BATTLE OF MOUNT ATHOS**
**19th of June (1st of July), 1807**

**Russian Vessels**

⚓ *Tvyordy*
Vice-Admiral Senyavin
✳ *Retvizan*
Rear-Admiral Greig

A *Rafail*    E *Sitnyy*
B *Uriil*    F *Yaroslav*
C *Selafail*    G *Svyataya Yelena*
D *Moshchnyy*    H *Skoryy*

**Ottoman Vessels**

⬤⫫ Kapudan-Pasha (Grand Admiral)
⬤⫫ Kapudan-Bey (Admiral)
⬤⫫ Patrona-Bey (Vice-Admiral)
⬤ Commodore's Ship
⬤ Frigate
⬤ Smaller Craft

8:00 AM

10:00 AM

50 KILOMETRES

Wind ENE

N / E / S / W

R U M E L I A

Samothrace

Lemnos

Russian Fleet

Ottoman Fleet

Ship and Frigate Burned

Ship and 2 Frigates Burned

Thasos

Mt. Athos

Longos

Kassandra

Sedd-el Bahr Captured

A E G E A N   S E A

dead were found onboard, as well as 160 wounded men, and the total number of prisoners taken counted 774; among them were 11 sailors that had been captured from the crew of the corvette *Flora*, and a midshipman and 5 sailors from Britain. The burned ship named *Besharet* (Annunciation), had 80 guns, and the frigates *Nessim* and *Metelin* were of 50 and 32 guns respectively. To this record of damage inflicted on the Turkish fleet must be added, according to reliable information, the burning of one ship and frigate by the island of Thasos and another two frigates were sunk by the island of Samothrace. This explains why from the 20 vessels that comprised the Turkish fleet at the beginning of the battle, only 12 returned through the Dardanelles. The *kapudan-pasha* had promised to bring Senyavin's head to the sultan, but instead he lost his hand. It must be said in all fairness that the Turks fought with desperate courage; on the flagship of Seydi Ali Pasha the killed and wounded reached 500 men, and not much fewer on the other ships. Such great losses in men very likely exceeded those suffered by the French at Trafalgar, despite them having 33 ships in their line there.

The casualties among the landing parties, both those counted by their own admission from the unsuccessful attacks and uninterrupted skirmishes over the course of 13 days and additionally counted among the bodies found on the island after the siege was lifted, reached 2,000 men killed and wounded.

The Russian Hercules, Captain First Rank Lukin, was killed in the Battle of Athos at the point in time when his ship [the *Rafail*] penetrated the enemy line and fought them on both sides. The glorious death of this worthy commander was a most sensitive loss for the fleet and the fatherland. Dmitriy Aleksandrovich Lukin was always an excellent naval officer; a brave, energetic and skillful warrior; and, moreover, a noble, compassionate, strict and just man who was beloved and respected by all of his subordinates. Although with an amazing bodily strength, he was gentle and patient, and even when he was angered, he never laid a hand on anyone. Demonstrations of his strength astonished everyone, though it was difficult to compel him to wield it unless in a merry hour and only among comfortable acquaintances would he sometimes give a show. For example, he could break horseshoes with little effort, hold a one-*pud* [19.66 kg] cannon ball with outstretched arms for half an hour; tilt up a quarter-deck gun with carriage, weighing 87 *pud*s [1.43 t], with one hand until it was practically vertical; or drive a nail into the ship's wall with one finger. With such an extraordinary strength, he was still deft and agile; anyone who would face him in a fist fight was in a dire predicament. Exploits of this kind made him most famous in England, where people sought his acquaintance with great effort, and in Russia, who does not know of Captain Lukin? Simply put, his name became renowned in all the navies of Europe and rare was the man who had never heard an anecdote about him.

Our losses in the Battle of Athos were as follows: 77 men in our fleet were killed, Lieutenant Mikhail Kubarskiy died from his wounds, and surviving wounded were 5 naval officers, two infantry officers and 182 enlisted men. The Tenedos garrison lost 3 officers and 52 enlisted men killed; 6 officers and 185 soldiers wounded. The resident population lost 160 killed and wounded. Our total casualties came to 674 men killed and wounded.

# 90

# Anecdotes

---

On the 9th [21st] March, during the occupation of the town of Tenedos by our forces and the confinement of the Turks in the fortress, the admiral wished to avoid unnecessary bloodshed and a prolonged siege by ordering the captive Turks to convey a letter to their commander offering clemency, but they refused on the grounds that they would put themselves at risk of execution for having surrendered the island, vowing to defend it to the last. When admiral's wish to grant mercy to the fortress became known among the captured women, one of them named Fatma announced to the interpreter that she wished to speak with the admiral and introduced herself with: 'generous Christian, your merciful protection and unexpected generosity to your captives has prompted me to offer my service to you and undertake the task of carrying your letter to the pasha. I wish to convince our adamant husbands that we have found in our enemies friends the likes of which are rare among our own faithful. I know that I am taking on a very difficult duty, I know that it is hardly possible to prove my testimony of you, the great commander of the Christians; but I do not waver about my assumptions and I hope to at least weaken the unjust prejudice against you. As a token of my gratitude for your mercy to your captives, for the sake of everyone else I condemn myself to certain death!' At this time, she took her son from her breast, kissed him fondly, fell to her knees and laid him at the feet of the admiral, continuing: 'I leave to you my child as a pledge most precious to a mother – if it is God's will to deprive me of life this day, then tutor and patronize him, teach him your faith, let him imitate you and be worthy of your care'. Fatma stood up and asked in a firm voice to be escorted to the fortress. The admiral, knowing that all Turks regarded women taken prisoner as dishonoured and typically put them to death, he was surprised by the determination of this woman. Being a father himself, he hesitated and wished to prevent this cruel sacrifice, but the heroine had already retired and descended into the boat with a rare firmness, not once addressing her son who called for her and stretched out his arms.

The admiral ordered a cease fire and had a trumpet signal for parlay. The Turks did not however respond to this challenge and when Fatma appeared on the square in front of the fort, several shots were fired from the nearby bastion. The heroine held up the missive and boldly approached the gate shouting that she had important news. After reading that Senyavin respected their customs and being touched by the leniency which the Turks did not expect from Christians, the commandant gathered his council and ascertained a general desire to accept the surrender on the proposed terms, determining to send an official out in response. The noble commandant himself escorted Fatma to the gate and when his subordinates demanded that she be put to death, he turned to them and said: 'I forbid it. She is not defiled, our enemies have respected her. What will the Christians think of us if we kill a poor woman? Fatma does not belong to us, she is their captive and must be returned'.

When Fatma boarded the ship again, the admiral personally gave her back her son and she threw herself on her knees, pressed him tightly to her chest and burst into tears, unable to speak a single word. She did not cry when she was parting with him toward a likely death, but now that she accomplished her feat, a mother's passion replaced all else in her heart. As she knelt and sobbed and showered her son in kisses, her veil slipped off but she did not seem to care or notice anyone else around her.

The Turkish official who witnessed this phenomenon, convinced of the truth of Fatma's testimony and seeing the admiral himself hand her the child with deep respect, approached the commander-in-chief and said: 'I thank the prophet – peace be upon him – that I might personally recognize your mercy. You wrote that you will convey us home with our property; we recognize ourselves defeated and by your magnanimity and strength, we cannot demand any more than what you have offered us. We confirm the conditions in your words alone and so the fortress is yours'. The whole affair was soon over and instead of a treaty on parchment with a wax seal we shook hands on it and settled the articles of peace with an honest word. One must imagine the Turks' surprise when the admiral ordered the interpreter to tell them that closed boats would be provided for evacuating the women, both of the fortress and those presently in captivity, and that the Turks might appoint their own people for transporting them to the Anatolian coast. The official admitted that he knew the rights of the victor and that it could not have been easy to give up so many beautiful women, and would not dare to intercede for their release. 'But now, when you yourself return them to us, believe that we know how to appreciate your mercy. We will strive to prove our gratitude to you in deeds'. Fatma, being the wife of a simple craftsman, was generously endowed by the admiral for such an unusual feat for a woman.

***

In the continuation of the siege, a resident of Tenedos, Jean Micantonio, captured a Turkish banner during their attack on the redoubt and afterwards burned down a coffee house standing by the leftmost face of the fortress, from which the enemy had been inflicting severe casualties on our artillerists. Micantonio, dressed like a Turk, crept up to the house at midnight, lit its flammable components and safely leapt into the ditch to return to the safety of the fortress. Another young Greek from Smyrna named Michel Krutitsa,[1] who escaped from a captured corsair with only the shirt on his back, did not lose heart and fought bravely in the most dangerous places and served as a courier to bring the admiral important messages, twice going aboard his flagship while under fire from canister and grapeshot. It was his bravery during the sinking of the burning brig *Hector*[2] however that brought him notoriety. His bold feats ensured that the nearby *Bogoyavlensk* was spared from catching fire and spreading to all the other vessels in the harbour.

*** 

The bombardment of Tenedos, a fortress with no casemates or cellars where one could at least lay the wounded, was our most terrible disaster. With the fall of each bomb, the cries of the women '*Panagia! Panagia!* – Mother of God!' would announce to us new victims. A 9-*pud* [176.9 kg] bomb destroyed half of the commandant's house. On the ground floor where the bomb exploded, one unfortunate woman lost her husband, brother, two adult children and an infant who was lying near her feet; in an instant she became a widow without support or comfort. I was so stricken by her loss that I tried to console her, but she could neither speak nor cry. She looked at us all with a dull glance as if she could not understand what had happened all around her; an indifference appearing like insanity. When the priest came to pay final respects, she began to pray diligently and asked him to give her communion. She gathered the pieces of her loved ones

---

1    Крутица – This is not a Greek name, but rather a Russian one which refers to a locale with steep cliffs or banks, such as the Krutinskoe Podvorye Monastery in Moscow, taking its name from the banks of the Moskva river.

2    Broncvskiy's note: 'It is worth noting that the two heroes Ajax and Hector killed during the siege of Troy have perished again at the present siege. When Duckworth's squadron awaited a fair wind at Mavro before making their attempt through the Dardanelles on Constantinople, a ship of the line named the HMS *Ajax* caught fire from a spark falling into her fodder and exploded not far from the port and fortress of Tenedos. Of the entire crew, save the captain and 13 sailors in a launch who were aboard the admiral's ship at the time, not a single soul was saved. The brig *Hector* under the Russian flag caught fire from an incendiary shell during the Turkish fleet's attack on Tenedos. Every man saved among the crew had injuries, including the captain, and the others burned to death. Thus two ships of two nations carrying the names of two Greek heroes died in the same fashion opposite Troy'. Translator's note: At least 300 men were rescued from the *Ajax* during the fire before she exploded. 250 perished. Gilly, *Narratives of Shipwrecks*, pp.121-136.

with the same indifference and with no sign of disgust, saying goodbye to them with some sort of joy and dropping them into the sea with her own hands (the dead were disposed of this way to avoid miasma). After such a deplorable rite was completed, she began to cry and speak again only to come to a stupor. Her sufferings did not last long; on the next day, under the pretense of watching over her relatives, she threw herself into the sea.

∗∗∗

On the same day, an Albanian who served in the Turkish army approached the ditch with a white flag and announced that he, on behalf of the pasha, had favourable conditions of surrender to offer to the commandant. This Albanian spoke with his compatriots on the walls as he awaited a response and discovered his brother among the garrison. Such an unexpected reunion overjoyed them but after questions about family and circumstances, reproaches began. The Ottoman Albanian apologized for his poverty, which compelled him into the Sultan's service. Ours said to him: 'look how God rewards a just cause; I was also poor but now I enjoy a surplus and I could help you. My conscious is clear, I serve an Orthodox sovereign, the only hope for restoring our degraded Greece. You serve our tyrants, the enemies of God and the church. I defend our fatherland while you oppress it. We are now enemies, it may happen that your hand will end my life or mine yours. What means can cleanse your soul? Our church will curse you yet pray for me. You have no hope in the future; I firmly hope for the mercy of my God'. This conversation was interrupted by the response of Colonel Padeyskiy, who ordered the pasha be told that he was mistaken to think he could offer us capitulation, rather the pasha will be asked about surrender soon.

The parting brothers would receive permission from the commandant to see each other again. The pasha also granted them permission but with an ulterior motive. His Albanian came to the ditch on the next day and told his brother that the sultan promised each loyal Greek 500 piastres and the residents of Tenedos in particular the freedom to have their houses rebuilt and all of their losses paid for if they agreed to surrender and force out the small number of our soldiers. 'You are not my brother, but my enemy', answered our Albanian in anger, leaving unhappily and never again left to meet his kin. In their ardent devotion to Russia, the Greeks again solemnly swore to shed their last drop of blood for us. Their hatred for the Turks was awakened in this case and they furiously crowded the house where the prisoners were being held, but the officer of the guard posted soldiers in front of the windows and prevented a massacre.

∗∗∗

The fate of the fortress of Tenedos and the Turks besieging it depended on the outcome of the naval battle. Although we did not fear a Turkish victory at sea, we worried that our admiral would not be so fortunate as to catch and destroy the Turkish fleet quickly and then be favoured by the wind so that he might immediately return to the island and liberate us. The position of our fortress and the dwindling supply of ammunition meant that we could not hold out for more than two weeks. In this mood, when everyone's thoughts wandered over the ocean of uncertainty, one of the Albanian leaders came to the commandant and asked to allow a solemn divination to satisfy the curiosity of his people. The commandant consented. The Albanian slaughtered a ram and examined its entrails according to the pagan rites and then roasted the pieces. He cut off the meat of the shoulder blade and held it up, turning it over and looking at all of its intricate details before clapping his hands and saying in a reassured voice: 'Thank God! The Turkish fleet is defeated; their ships have been taken by the air, water and fire'. When the officers asked him about our fleet, he answered: 'They are in the hands of God'. This rite was performed on the 20th of June [2nd of July] and the battle was fought on the 19th [1st]. The Albanian guessed correctly as near as possible. Let the reader now judge for himself whether the divinations of the Romans are based on what is probable or simply blind chance.

✳✳✳

During the battle of the 19th of June [1st of July] at Mount Athos, the admiral ordered Captain van Scheltinga of the *Skoryy* to stay close enough to his ship so that he could hear verbal commands over the thunder of the guns and the brave captain did just that. At the beginning of the battle, the brave and venerable Lieutenant Kubarskiy in control of the sails was seriously wounded and soon died and Lieutenant M.A. Denisyevskiy took his place. Suddenly fighting with three Turkish ships and a frigate within pistol range, one of the enemy ships approached close enough to lay its jibboom on the stern of the *Skoryy*. One daredevil tried to cut off our ensign but was killed and fell into the water. In such hot fire, the courageous Denisyevskiy lost a leg and discovered an unusual presence of spirit; standing in the open, he jokingly said 'a wicked power knocked me down'. He continued to give commands and would not allow himself to be taken below deck before the captain himself took command. Bleeding profusely and with his leg dangling from a single cord, in extreme pain, Denisyevskiy ordered a sailor to cut it off with a knife but the man supporting his leg replied: 'suffer just a little longer, Your Nobleness, the doctor will do it better'. When they carried him over the quarterdeck to the cabin, Denisyevskiy noticed a few men at the cannons and said to them: 'don't be shy, boys! Although you're few, make up for it with courage and work for the glory of Russia'.

A boatswain's mate on the same ship, Afanasyev, also distinguished himself with extraordinary bravery and contribution, peculiar only to those men who stand on the edge of the grave and are gifted with an unshakeable spirit and heart filled

'The Battle of Athos, 19th of June, 1807', Aleksey Bogolyubov, 1853, oil on canvas, St. Petersburg, Central Naval Museum.

with noble sentiments. Afanasyev lost his leg on the crow's nest and while being lowered down with a rope, he lost his voice from bleeding out. When the doctor was preparing to amputate his leg, he heard the name of Denisyevskiy repeated several times and raised his head to say to the doctor in a weak voice: 'leave me and help Matvey Andronikovich'.

'Thank you, brother', said Denisyevskiy as he outstretched his hand, 'but you know the law and I wouldn't want to take your turn or exploit your generosity'. These are the features worthy of heroes and worthy of the Russian heart.

\*\*\*

I will present one more example proving what a spirit animated our servicemen in this glorious battle. Afanasiy Solominin, a boatswain on the same ship, the *Skoryy*, was wounded by a bullet in the arm. He wanted to pull it out with his teeth but he could not, so he cut it out with a knife and dressed himself with a handkerchief and continued to man his post. His arm began to swell up badly but he did not go to change his dressing until after the battle and despite the doctor's decision for him to stay in the cabin and rest, the boatswain returned to duty immediately. Although being a veteran in his late 50s, like a young and agile man he ran about, screamed, took care of his duties, got angry and scolded his sailors in the typical boatswain's fashion.

## My Gratitude

In the battle of the 16th [28th] of June during the landing of the Turkish army on Tenedos, I was contused on my right side and later in the fortress, while commanding artillery in the citadel, I was severely wounded by a bullet that passed straight through the left shoulder. On the burnt brig *Hector*, which was under my command, I lost all that I had, and when I had to replace the first bandage, I had nothing to use for a second. In this state, the commandant, Colonel Padeyskiy, took me into his house and put me in the care of Doctor Bartolomeo Boliaco, a resident of Chios, whose skill and experience has treated many seriously wounded. I owe him my life. In the same room with me were placed the wounded women of the best families, including Maria, the daughter of our Consul Haliano. This beautiful 17-year-old was wounded and although it was not severe, it was in such a fashion that she needed to strip to her waist. Her face, neck and breast were coated in plaster from when a ceiling collapsed under falling cannon balls. The girl who suffered more from shame than pain eventually got used to my presence and took it upon herself to assist the doctor in changing my dressing. She did not leave me for a single minute during the siege.

When our squadron circled Imbros and returned to Tenedos, my cousin A.V. Levshin, learning that I was badly wounded, asked the captain for permission to take a boat ashore and visit me in the fortress.[3] He had to row through a crossfire of bullets and canister. A solid shot punched a hole through the boat though they arrived unharmed. My cousin's visit greatly surprised me and brought me so much joy. Not wanting him to continue to expose himself and his men to such danger however, I asked him not to try to visit me again in the future. As soon as he left, a bomb destroyed half of the house in which I was lying. Luckily the ceiling over my bed remained intact and I was unharmed among all the many killed and wounded in that building.

Upon the liberation of the fortress, I was transferred by a Captain A. of the Kozlov Regiment to his quarters from the powder cellar where I lay in the final days of the siege. The grenadier who followed me to my new quarters one day brought a bundle full of items with a note that read as follows: 'hearing that you

---

3    Aleksandr Vasilyevich Levshin served on the *Venus* from 1804 as a *garde de marine* and would have been with the fleet until the 17 [29] of June, while Bronevskiy was left on Tenedos after turning in the *Hector*. Levshin was promoted to midshipman on 12 [24] January, 1807 and stayed with the crew of the *Venus* until its departure from Trieste and return to Russia in 1810. *Complete Naval Roster*, vol.7, p. 402.

lost your property and were seriously wounded and knowing that you will not accept these things sent to you which you need and I do not, I would rather you do not know me. Do not seek me out; your effort will be in vain. Just know that I am your friend and want your recovery more than anything'. Having no way to guess the identity, let my unknown benefactor reading these lines accept my sincere gratitude.

When I returned to the *Venus*, one of the officers volunteered to share his cabin with me and during our first meeting, he treated me more kindly than the others. Our duties and the need to confide one's thoughts in another trusted person little by little fostered a mutual trust and friendship which did not resemble those relationships based on similar personalities or indulgence in one another's foibles which are more like a mutual agreement than friendship. On the contrary, in the disparity between our manners, we loved to be together and enjoyed sharing happiness and sorrow and were never apart during all of our service. We kept nothing secret from each other, frankly spoke the truth, sometimes quarrelled, and always saw the necessity in one another. In the present age when no one is loved by anyone but himself, when friends are rare, I found a friend in M.L.N. He was happier than I, having an opportunity to prove his position to me. As soon as the Turks were delivered to the Anatolian coast, he transported me to the frigate, helped the doctor to change my dressing, personally gave me medicines, lavished me with attention and followed me like a brother or father. The short experience of our vessel's doctor during the voyage from Tenedos to Corfu nearly opened the cover on my coffin, as he proposed amputating my arm and a portion of the shoulder, but N. argued against it. In Corfu, paying for an apartment for me, he found the glorious Caruso, a physician especially skilled at treating wounds, and after performing 18 operations and removing 23 bone fragments from my shoulder, he finally saved not only my life, but my arm as well.

To what extent Vice-Admiral Senyavin extended his care especially to the wounded, whom he treated with affection and indulgence, I submit myself as an example and note that all the wounded were met with attention according to their cases and needs. When the squadron returned from the archipelago to Corfu, while worrying about the surrender of the republic to the French, sending the army to Venice, preparing the fleet to return to Russia and labouring day and night, Dmitriy Nikolayevich still remembered me and sent an adjutant to ask about my health and when he might see me. The adjutant found me aboard the *Rafail*. Pleased with the flattering indulgence of the commander-in-chief, I accompanied the adjutant to the *Tvyordyy*. The admiral was standing on the quarterdeck when they informed him of my arrival. With such kindly attention he asked about my wounds and generously praised my service. He took me by the hand into the cabin and I was so amazed by this reception that I did not know how to show my gratitude. Nothing can be compared to my surprise when he put me in his office and said: 'I have found out that you are in need and to that end I wished to see you and ask how I might help you'. I requested that he pay for the doctor's work on my shoulder. Calling over the ship's captain Maleyev, Senyavin ordered that I be given 100 *chervontsy* in addition to the cost of my medicine and lodging. Doctor Caruso unexpectedly received a ring worth 2,000 rubles and since he had filed a request to be admitted into our service and given an oath of loyalty, he was appointed the general doctor for the 15th Division with a salary on the very next day. This worthy and highly skilled doctor was accepted as a collegiate assessor on the recommendation of the admiral and served afterwards as the head doctor of the Sevastopol Naval Hospital where he earned unquestionable fame and knowledge without peer.

By such means, Senyavin earned the love of his subordinates not easily acquired and despite the vicissitude of circumstances, his good works and renowned merits preserved his respect. The attention and aid he willingly paid to his subordinates and the sensitivity of his spirit will never be extinguished from the memory of all those who had the honour and good fortune to serve under his command.

## Various Comments

The beautiful climate, the bounty of resources, the favourable position for trade and the famous deeds of ancient Greece will always attract curious travellers to the islands of the Archipelago and garner the attention of politicians. The two chains of these islands, excluding the scattered ones, form an almost continuous line connecting Europe with Asia. These islands are of course the peaks of high mountains on the mainland which were cast off after many earthquakes and floods and the low valleys that divided them were swallowed by the sea until only the summits stood out as islands. The hard stone that comprises the peaks of the mainland and the soil of the islands alike is unquestionable proof of this.

The soil of the Aegean islands consists of a layer of fertile land on hard granite deep below. Not infrequently an entire island like Paros, Tinos and others has a stratum of the finest marble and precious jasper. This stone base locks in moisture useful for vegetation. All plants, although not growing as quickly as in our climate, bloom twice a year, yield fruits and never go dormant as in the winter. Where the forests have been cleared or wherever the land is not protected by the shadows of trees, the soil is deprived of its necessary moisture; indeed it is known that where there are no forests, the springs dry out and over several centuries, the land becomes fruitless. Except for several of the Cycladic islands which are merely rocks, most of the islands strike the eye with their greatness and variety of beautiful views. Nature here, for the most part, even in its uncultivated and wild state under a constantly clear sky gives man all that he needs in great abundance. Peach, apricot, almond and fig trees produce delicious fruits without any caretaking. The industrious Greeks produce mostly grapes, olives, silk and cotton.

The olive tree in particular is certainly the most useful product. They can regrow from their roots and are thus called eternal plants. They require no caretaking at all. Each tree produces around ten rubles a year income, so in Greece the dowry for brides and wealth in general is measured in quantities of olive trees. The olives sold to us in cans are not ripe; the oil squeezed out of the ripened olives and prepared without much skill or diligence we call 'wooden oil' (better for lamps than cuisine), in contrast to what we call 'Provence oil' (regardless of its origin) which is squeezed out of the same fruit with greater skill and care. The use of cheap oil in all of southern Europe is so great and ubiquitous that almost no butter fat is used at all in their kitchens. In all of Italy, the latter can barely been seen at all.

There is no country in the world that has undergone more changes than Greece. This famous homeland of the most elegant taste and the cradle of numerous arts and sciences now resembles a shadow of its former glory. Laws, science and warriors are equally glorified. Greece existed, so to speak, for a very short time, but that period, full of heroic exploits, is commemorated by the deeds of great men that will forever remain an invaluable pearl of their ancient history. The small, weak republics into which Greece was divided were carried away by the fates of the strongest among them, such as Sparta and Athens, both of which were sometimes enslaved and sometimes free and for a long time resisted the power of Persia; they would finally conquer that empire under the banners of Alexander, delivering the greater portion of Asia to his successors. But the glory of the Greeks was like the momentary glow of a lightning bolt, and dissention and feuds resulting from fragmentation into so many smaller republics made them all easy prey for any conqueror. The Romans conquered them one by one and left only the ghost of freedom, which too was soon exorcised and vanished.

The Egyptians were the first inventors of science and enlightenment. The Phoenicians practiced navigation and trade. The Greeks perfected the innovations of both. Elegance in sculpture, painting and other fine arts and an equal eloquence and precision in poetry are inventions that truly belong to the Greeks and to this day they serve as models for the artists of our enlightened age. With the decline of the sciences in the Middle Ages during the era of Gothic barbarism, some Greeks moved from Greece to Florence under the patronage of the Medici dynasty and gifted their preserved knowledge to us.

After the division of the Roman Empire into east and west and the awakening of the first bellicose hordes of unenlightened nations, the islands of the archipelago were taken from the Greeks one by one by the Venetians, Genoese, Catalans and other independent princes and dukes. During the crusades, they served as a haven for fleets carrying the crusading armies and pilgrims to Jerusalem and at the same time were a focus for trade between Europe and India through Egypt. Finally after the conquest of the Holy Sepulchre by the Saracens, the caliphs, and then the Turkish sultans who in 1453 also took Constantinople and the whole Greek archipelago. The Latin banners, persecuted from island to island, stopped at the stronghold of Corfu and kept it the only place wholly free from the power of the Ottomans.

# 91

# A Comparison of the Ancient and Present Greeks – Their Customs and Habits

The ancient Greeks were revered as a people who were flighty but brave, unjust but intelligent. Having a passionate mind, they artfully adapted to changing circumstances. They were so quick and adept in this performance that any desire became a possession and so arrogant that they esteemed what they conquered could not be taken away from them. The people were fearless and restless, their boldness surpassed strength, danger only heightened their courage and misfortunes deepened their hope. They chased disaster without thought and idleness was a terrible torment for them and an intolerable vice when found in others. Ceaselessly engaged in the future with no regard for the present, envying each other, waging civil war and shedding the blood of their fellow citizens, they could rarely agree on measures to defend their common fatherland and never united into a significant power. And if one can take pride in the glory of many great generals, lawmakers, philosophers and artists that emerged from this strife, one must also reproach themselves for the grave injustices done, as anyone who ever distinguished himself with famous deeds was almost always slandered, poisoned or exiled from his country.

This is how historians paint the Ancient Greeks. The present can be likened to the elder who has become weak and feeble in his advanced years and now blindly obeys his capricious servant without argument. However, for so many centuries the despotic rule of the Muhammedan rulers, despite the destruction of artistic and intellectual institutions, has not perfectly spoiled the spirit of the Greek people or completely changed their former character. Prolonged slavery and humiliation have inescapably weakened the virtues and strengthened the vices of the present Greeks. Based on this assertion in respect to the grievous yoke laid upon the people, the judgement of the benevolent will not be strict, for misfortune deserves leniency. It is difficult to accurately depict a character distorted by disasters and descended through misfortunes, so I will try to convey only its main properties. The Greeks are arrogant in good fortune and ingratiating in poor turns of fate; by a patient, evasive and amazingly slow pace, they almost always achieve their goals. Their love of liberty and equality has not yet faded away but mutual hostility rejects the alliances that could place them in the company of independent nations. They meet danger without hesitation and are eager to die nobly; there can be no doubt that they will sacrifice their lives for their liberation when the proper opportunity arrives. Their courage is not inferior to the stern Spartans, they are as brave in battle, as boastful and as dissatisfied when it ends, and no reward can satisfy them after even a small favour. For all their boasting, some travellers have questioned their bravery, but this is unfair and, in my opinion, comes from the troubled disposition and inclination to quarrels which plagued their ancestors. They are so shrewd and clever in industry and trade that they know how best to benefit themselves in far greater excesses, I believe, than their ancestors ever could, though they too loved and worshipped money.

In the fatherland of science and the arts, though there are several schools maintained by private individuals, there are no Apelles, Phidias and Praxiteles today; yet the sparks of that divine fire which their ancestors possessed are passed down to the present through a few remaining writings and by the oral tradition. Although having no education, many have fortunate talents which are palpable in the common villager. Politeness, dexterity, a special eloquence in expression and exposition of thoughts, witty and intricate wordplay, a sort of kindness, frankness and ingratiation that serves as a veil for cunning and often deception give the Greek an obvious advantage over other peoples in similar circumstances. This can be proved by the fact that very few students in foreign universities, at any time, succeed in all sciences, especially mathematics and all the most profound and abstract subjects. The Greeks of the archipelago engaged in seafaring speak Turkish and Italian but never learn their proper grammar. The new language, derived from the ancient but disrupted by Turkish loanwords nevertheless has a pleasing sound and measure. The ancient Greeks who wrote and captivated the hearts of their entire nation are not understood by the literate among the Greeks; they speak now only to the professors of European universities and the meagre lovers of literature. Those few educated Greeks rarely return to their fatherland and their newfound knowledge thus remains useless for their compatriots. The songs are Homer are sung with pleasure (though not everyone can understand them), proud of their glorious heroes, and they love the memory of the golden age of their unchallenged bliss. Passion for spectacles and amusements ease the painful captivity of the present Greeks. Like the ancients, as gullible as children, they vacillate from despair to joy with excessive speed. They sing and dance without fatigue during festivities, they sincerely love to drink moderately in company, and they can forget disasters after only a few minutes of nostalgic reminiscence and console one another with hopes for a better future and dreams of liberty. Their chief musical instrument is like a violin with three strings.

The taste of the Greeks in the decoration of their churches and homes and in their apparel has completely changed. Red and light blue are preferred over other colours and the mixing of these in their silks and painted interiors makes for an unpleasant motley. The carvings which decorate their churches and houses and the images they paint do not survive scrutiny either. They imitate the Turks in architecture and furniture, except for cleanliness and neatness. The mosques built by the Greeks at first glance elicit surprise and have much of the greatness and boldness in execution which was characteristic of their ancient constructions. In their way of life, they are moderate, temperate, strictly observe the fasts and do not know luxury. Those who are engaged in trade are extremely prudent in their disputes and in those who have little relations with foreigners one can still can find the hospitality and affability of their ancestors. They are not at all sensitive to the advantage of dignity. When meeting a foreigner, they call themselves by the titles of the oldest families, but these Palaeologues, Comneni, Lascarises and the various governors on the islands with titles like *archon, proestos* etc., have none of the rights and privileges particular to aristocracy and only command personal dignity. The very lowest of the labourers is treated as their equal and like him, they work in the field or in small shops selling their petty wares. What does distinguish such men is that the rich hire day labourers and leave only the easy tasks for themselves though they feel no shame in toil. This custom maintains and affirms the love of equality and it can also be explained that the wealthy live in moderation and conceal their affluence in order to avoid oppression by self-interested Turkish officials.

Trade from the vast territories of the Ottoman Empire all pass through the hands of Constantinople and the Greeks of the archipelago. During times of war, they serve in the navy; on the conclusion of peace, they travel around the Levant on their beautiful boats and visit the trading cities of the Mediterranean and Black Sea. They never travel further than Lisbon. Sacolevas used for small voyages close to shore have preserved the appearance of ancient vessels; they have a high bow and stern and are decorated with carvings and pendants. Vernet's painting of a ship on which the Saviour and His Apostles are caught in a storm is a close facsimile to these sacolevas. The Greeks of Asia Minor, as the latest travelers assure us, are successfully engaged in agriculture. The Moreans and the inhabitants of Attica live on the ashes and ruins of the woeful fatherland of Leonidas and Themistocles in extreme poverty. Internal war, looting by the Turks and the raids of the belligerent Albanians hinder their industry. The latter, under the rule of Ali Pasha, are accustomed to bloodletting and are considered a terrible scourge by both the Turks and their fellow citizens so they naturally conduct little in the way of working the soil. As trade, handicrafts and crop production, which comprise the wealth of all nations, in Turkey depend on the active industry of the Greeks, Sultan Selim II seems to have understood this subject of the state's economy and greatly facilitated those oppressions which, like in all despotic governments, were personally allowed by the civil governors who were given the authority to behead their own subordinates. Every subject Greek pays around 6½ piastres a year and if one adds gifts and other expenses to this sum, then in aggregate and comparison with the taxes collected in all the territories of the state, they comprise nearly a fifth of the annual levy of the subjects of the sultan. Many travellers indulging in dreams of ancient Greece and passing judgement on the cries of the present Greeks fall into the error of saying that the Greeks complain from a terrible, painful oppression. When the *agha* appears to collect the taxes (as a Turkish prisoner assured our admiral who was aboard the *Venus* for his transport from Tenedos to Corfu), the Greeks usually scatter and in every possible fashion evade paying not only bribes and gifts but also their legal taxes.

Mehmed II, having conquered Greece, granted the defeated people the right to freely practice their religion and his successors sold the higher dignities of the clergy, collecting considerable taxes for the permission to build churches and monasteries; although Christians were temporarily and individually oppressed, their church was never persecuted. The tolerance of the Muslims has always been greater than that of the Catholics in whose lands bonfires burned and so much blood has been shed for the faith and even now in their possessions, one cannot have the same freedoms – not even for money – as is granted by the Turks, those supposed enemies of Christendom. The Greek clergy are personally weakened by every duty. Their maintenance depends on the donations of their parishioners, so the parish clergy are very poor and are not much better off in terms of education, and do not enjoy the respect due from good morals and exemplary behaviour.

It would be unforgiveable to remain silent on the fairer sex: their beauty even now could serve as models for Hera, Diana and Aphrodite. In the large towns more frequented by foreigners, the Greek women like to dress up and show a desire to please; but only in a cautious and innocent fashion. Even a little coquetry needs to be hidden, that the purity of their morality not be besmirched by the shadow of debauchery. Living together with the Turks, they carefully avoid the society of men and like the Turkish women they spent their lives unseen: they rarely allow themselves to look through the bars on their windows at passersby on the street. On the islands where there are no Turks however, the women enjoy freedom. Their charms here could be made victim to a tempting philanderer, if their strict virtue did not protect them from it. Being without any education and consequently without the instructed manners and graces which elevate the natural talents to attract, they are replaced by modesty, simplicity, the subtlety of the natural mind and all the charming powers of innocence. It would be easy for them to seize authority which so much flatter a woman's pride, but to their credit, they do not extend themselves beyond handicrafts and the household. The position of the mother of the family and the duties of marriage (I will not say 'always' because there is no rule without exception) are executed with precision. The excessive jealousy of their husbands which comes from the custom of the land and might be a result of the climate, leads naturally to injustice and especially ungratefulness, which could be avenged in the typical fashion; but to the credit and glory of the Greek beauties, they prefer the good fortune, honour and vain renown of the family. In Constantinople and Smyrna, those unfortunates who are forced to make their living at the cost of their beauty and health hide in seclusion and dare not boast of their vice.

The torches lit at marriage ceremonies during the pagan era are still used today. It is carried before the youths in the bedroom and continues to burn until they rise out of bed. It would be a poor celebration if it were extinguished, so they care for it with all the diligence of the Vestals protecting the sacred fire. When a priest marries, as the holiness of a union requires that he does not fall in love with another and that the charms of his faithful wife keep him within the limits of the highest office, it is typical in the archipelago when a deacon is consecrated to the priesthood that he must choose a bride for himself from among the most beautiful but also virtuous and meek women so that he will be content and faithful. Is this not the reason that Greeks so eagerly seek initiation into the clerical ranks?

**92**

# A Word on the Turks

To give a fair idea of the Turks, a people alien to us in all respects, is almost impossible. Many travellers, not speaking the language and being prejudiced by fantasies of ancient Greece, condemn them in every aspect; they often wrongly judge their actions and motivations according to their own customs. Some of the information I have collected during my service in the Mediterranean and Black Sea, when they were both our friends and enemies, may also be insufficient, but prejudice and bias will not be found in these remarks.

Personal courage, generosity and steadfastness are the qualities of the Turks, by which they conquered many similarly warlike nations and in the better part of the world founded the powerful Ottoman Empire. A character quiet, brooding, noble and sometimes enflamed by passions make the Turk suspicious and cruel against his enemies. Despite that, they are not vindictive and quickly forget offences. Not because of the teachings of the Muslim faith but rather because of the evils of the Christians living among them, they are induced to despise all other peoples who will not follow their religious law which compels them to treat others with generosity, compassion and hospitality. They are good hosts; moderate, patient and pious. Miserliness and greed, making it necessary to employ every effort and caution to support oneself financially, is a vice only found among the nobility and bureaucracy. In general, the Turks are not selfish, indulgent to the destitute, keep their word, are especially grateful, and despite their almost complete lack of education, possess virtues equal to the most enlightened peoples. Fountains, bridges and the caravanserai (postal stations) arranged on the roads where a tired traveller can find rest and shade without pay are the monuments of their kindness worthy of imitation. Their conceptions are very simple and limited; they are fixated on the present, quickly forget the past and do not think about the future. The nobleman who has fallen on hard times endures it with firmness and does not show the slightest dejection; the commoner who has ascended to the supreme rank of the grand vizier holds his office with all the import and dignity expected. One says 'inşallah' (if God wills it) and the other replies 'allah kerim' (God is merciful) and both men are assuaged. Belief in predestination, an original dogma of their faith, makes them submissive to fate in all circumstances; for that reason, they spend most of their lives sitting on folded legs, drinking coffee and smoking tobacco with little interest for much else. Books, they believe, serve only as a reminder of humanity's foolishness and so, apart from the Quran, they read very few. Having no literacy, sciences or arts, they live very calmly and are cold towards all educated people. Knowledge necessary in their lives is passed from father to son and therefore their craftsmen, such as tailors, tanners, embroiderers and so on are exceptionally skilled.

On the other hand, the customs and properties of the Turks present an amazing contrast. They wash three times a day but are unclean because they rarely change their undergarments; they are both seductive and restrained; compassionate to animals and cruel to their enemies; they combine the austerity of the ancient Parthian with the decadence of other Orientals; they are slaves to conformity yet are personally free; unrestrained at home and immaculate in public; idle in leisure and lively in battle.

The honesty of the Turks deserves special attention and truly deserves our surprise. Merchants trust one another with millions without bills or receipts but on their sworn word alone and exchange payments with just a single witness. If someone cannot pay on time when no extension will be granted by a *qadi* (judge) or guarantors cannot be found, then the disputed property is given to the lender that same day and the guilty party loses his head. Turkish laws are very strict and precise; the proceedings, court decisions and executions are completed rapidly. As a result, lawsuits here do not drag on for a full century as elsewhere. The Turks themselves admit that with a hasty judgement, sometimes the innocent are put to death, but they justify themselves by saying: 'it is better to sacrifice ten sheep to kill one wolf, than to let him freely prey on a hundred or more'. Turkish justice is based on proving probability with reason and common sense. Their judges are renowned for their insight and honesty and are considered worthy of the dignity of their office and, to the surprise of many, I must say that the Turkish *qadi* regards the honour and esteem earned by his impartiality to be the greatest reward. In Turkey alone, a criminal with clean documents receives a proper punishment; an innocent man without such proofs can always rely on justice and the protection of the laws. The police are not visible in Constantinople. The Sultan himself, the grand vizier, or an official dressed up for it, walk around the city in disguise and strictly observe the sail of food, for example. If a *funt* [409.52 g] of bread after tax costs 2 *paras* or a twentieth of a piastre, then in all of Constantinople the Turkish bakers and grain merchants do not meet out their bread in exactly one-*funt* portions but always somewhat more, while the Greeks will often undercut the portion. For this offence, the guilty is nailed to a pillar through his ear. The Turks so much abhor a deception or forgery in trade that if you enter a Turkish shop, show no doubt about the quality or price of his goods; the Muslim will take extreme offence and often say: 'are you already taking me for a Christian?' This is their opinion of all Christians, which is in some respects fair. Here is an example of their honesty: one official from our diplomatic mission sent a child of 5 or 6 years to buy an *okka* [1.28 kg] of grapes. When the child produced his money, the merchant looked at him with a smile and asked: 'is your master's home far from here?' Determining how much the boy could eat along the way, he handed him an *okka* and a half [1.92 kg] of grapes for no extra cost and said: 'I wouldn't want your master to think that I deceived a child, but ask him to send a more loyal servant than you from now on'.

The foreigner living in Constantinople enjoys complete freedom. When a ship arrives in the harbour, the customs officer is the first to arrive. The skipper shows his passport and the Turk, not knowing what is written on it, looks at him and says '*peki*' (alright) and then asks the skipper where he came from, what is he carrying, and if he intends to stay in Constantinople or go farther. Regardless of the answers he receives, the official coldly repeats '*peki, peki*' to each; then he inquires if the skipper has anything more to declare and gives his typical answer again. He goes into the cabin where the skipper is obliged to serve him a cup of ground coffee without sugar and a pipe with a long stem and immediately lay before him on the table half a percent of what his cargo is worth. The Turk, keeping account with the fringe of his shawl in the same way we make calculations on accounts, he places the money in the sultan's bag and again repeats his '*peki*'. If he sees chests in the cabin or something similar to a bundle of goods not named by the skipper, he gives a reproachful look and asks 'but what is this?' and when told that they are the property of a passenger, he calms down again and repeats his reliable '*peki, peki*'. The skipper then gives him a gift commensurate with the size of his boat, somewhere between 10 and 50 *chervontsy*. With one last *peki*, the Turkish official declares that the skipper is free to go and departs, worrying a little that he might have been deceived in his investigation. The foreigner who has gone ashore will never be asked by anyone about his identity or where he is going, he will not be stopped anywhere and will not need to visit the police, because in all of Turkey there are no checkpoints. The time when the European was subjected to frequent insults in Constantinople has already elapsed and now, on the contrary, even the Greek insults the Turk. However, a foreigner of any rank would beware to insult a notable Turk, for at the slightest provocation he will shoot him dead and end the matter. The murderer will continue calmly along without fear of detention. The body remains in the street until someone else retrieves it. One official from our mission told me that when during a rebellion when the glorious Bayraktar [Mustafa] Pasha was killed, his body in its rich clothes lay in the street for a long time.[1] The cruel janissaries, noticing the covetous glances of the Jews who were looking at the attire of the murdered man, tore it off him and threw it in their faces but without touching anything else valuable. It is praiseworthy that looting which is so common among the throngs of all peoples are virtually unknown among the Turks.

The seclusion of their women is a consequence of polygamy and for how strange this seems to us, the Turks are likewise perplexed by how much freedom our women have. They think that a wife's liberty will necessarily lead her to debauchery and therefore believe that there is not one decent woman among Christians. Turkish women are even more surprised at this; they do not understand how it is possible to uncover one's face or body in the company of men after solemnly promising to only share one's charms with one's husband. If the Europeans say that holding a loved one in a cage and depriving them of the innocent pleasures of life is ingratitude, then the Asians reply that it is lowly to surrender the stewardship of their dominion granted by nature and the laws of God. If they are told that the abundance of women held in the seraglio is creating discord, they answer that ten obedient women are less disruptive than one disobedient. The Turks do not know the feeling of true love based on reverence and mutual trust. They do not know the flattering feeling of being chosen from many suitors and loved according to preference. They laugh at our torment over love and voluntary misery, they boast of their tranquility, enjoying pleasure without any addition of sorrow. They are not wrong in preferring to be ignorant of our feelings in that sense.

Turkish women are not so much slaves as is generally imagined; in their seclusion, they make use of that power which nature has afforded their sex to their favour. The high born can have visitors and take strolls and their husband cannot forbid it. Many wives do not allow their men to have concubines; in this case, the spouse keeps them in a separate house and just like we do, quietly visits them through the back door in the late night. This custom is now in vogue in Constantinople. During mutual visits, the guest leaves his shoes at the doors of the seraglio; the poor husband, no matter how tormented by curiosity or jealousy, does not dare to enter his wife's office. Here is the avenue for the tricks of love which the Turkish women use as skillfully as the Italians. The husband can only be confident when his wife is under the supervision of a eunuch or surrounded by her friends, and Mehmed the Conqueror, knowing this defect of theirs, not unfairly allowed the

---

1    The Grand Vizier Bayraktar (Alemdar) Mustafa Pasha was assaulted by the janissary rebels in his home on the 3 [15] November, 1808 and killed himself by igniting a powder magazine which destroyed his property, his bodyguards and several of his attackers. It is difficult to imagine that his body flew into the street intact. Andreyevskiy et al., *Brockhaus and Efron Dictionary*, s.v. 'Байрактар'. [Andreyevskiy et al., *Brockhaus and Efron Dictionary*, s.v. 'Bayraktar'.]

Turks to have many slaves. As the greater part of the people cannot keep more than one, and some of the nobles, following the newly adopted custom, are content with just one wife, polygamy seems to be in decline and the high walls and gates of the harems are no longer as strong as they once were.

Many regard the Turkish government as unlimited and autocratic, but could a nation exist at the height of glory and prosperity if it had no fundamental laws? Nowhere is the inviolable right of property so strictly observed as in Turkey. At the slightest violation of this, the sultans were deposed from the throne and viziers were put to death. Several civil decrees linking the sovereign to his subjects for the protection of persons and property deserve special attention. Let it suffice to say that Turkey is the only land where justice is observed with precision and impartiality. There is no list of estates in the treasury. The sultan takes the property of those who serve him on a salary only after they have been denounced for the theft of state property.

The geographical location of the Ottoman Empire and the bountiful provinces within provide countless benefits for trade although they enjoy almost no benefits, the total of exports exceeds the imports of all European nations. Trade does not meet any obstacles here and the enrichment of the people is of little benefit to the treasury. For navigation, especially along the coasts of the Mediterranean and Black Sea, the Turks have many more of their own ships than we do.

In conclusion, I will write a few words from Mr Eton about the reasons for the rapid rise and present sad state of the Turkish Empire.[2] The might of the Ottomans, in no way divorced from the state founded by the belligerent people, supported by military rule and fortunate conquests, was favoured by a confluence of unique circumstances. When the Greek Empire, with its weak rulers, corrupt mores, internal confusion and especially from the disputes between the western and eastern churches, began to decline, the Turks emerged from their countless Scythian dwellings, animated by courage and an irreconcilable hatred for the Christian, with a well-organized army under the leadership of a brave sultan. All of Europe was suffering under the scourge of its defective feudal system whereby the sovereigns themselves needed to ask for soldiers from their strong and autocratic subjects. The Turks meanwhile had a fine army which was accustomed to subordination, bloodshed and perseverance through deprivations. The Turks were our teachers in the art of attacking and defending fortifications, digging trenches and saps and destroying them, and especially the art of coordinating the wide movements of large forces. This excellent order, introduced in the Turkish army

---

2    William Eton, who wrote a general overview and history of the Ottoman Empire in 1798 and updated it with several subsequent editions. William Eton, *A Survey of the Turkish Empire*, 4th Ed. (London: T. Cadell and W. Davies, 1809), pp.i-xxiv.

before other nations, brought them victories and aroused in them a martial spirit. A victory over one foe taught them how to defeat the next and their conquests began to compound on one another. The fame of their victories preceded them and weakened the resolve of their enemies. In this fashion, the Turks spread their patrimony over Asia, Africa and Europe and Constantinople became the capital of an empire more vast and strong than any other state in Europe.

Before the reign of Ahmed III [who came to power in 1703], the sultans personally led their armies and their wars were continuously successful, but since the beginning of the 18th century, when they began to retire to their harems and leave their armies in the hands of the grand vizier, the successes of their conquests began to wane. Some of their supreme commanders however, gifted with martial prowess and daring and aided by the size of their armies, triumphed still over the armies which the Germans [of the Holy Roman Empire] could assemble. The Count Raimondo of Montecuccoli was the first to learn how to defeat these enemies, Prince Eugene of Savoy deprived them of their conquests and the Treaty of Passarowitz marked the end of Ottoman expansion. After the death of this great commander, all Turks were still terrors in the European imagination and constituted the strongest power, their warriors had not yet lost their courage and still regarded themselves as invincible and they did not soon approach their fall when meeting the brave ranks of the Russian armies. Rumyantsev-Zadunayskiy, Suvorov-Rymnikskiy and Orlov-Chesmenskiy[3] humiliated the pride of the Muslim, halted their rampage and avenged all of Christendom. The continuous series of victories which glorified the reign of Catherine the Great broke the arrogance of the Turks and their empire fell from the height of its military glory to become no longer dangerous for such a significant power.

What caused such a quick change in this state's structure and why, despite the Porte's weaknesses and inability to defend itself against attack, is it still counted among the major powers of Europe? On these two questions, Mr Eton, author of a history of Turkey, gives the following remarks:

A state which is governed by military laws and regulations, subject to an autocratic emperor and the governors he appoints and whose armies act solely to conquer new territories sows in itself the germ of its own decline. The loss of

---

3    These three Russian leaders all bear victory titles affixed to their surnames for battles against the Ottoman Empire: Orlov's for the battle of Chesme (1770), Rumyantsev's generally for crossing the Danube into Bulgaria in the later years of the 1768-1774 war, and Suvorov's for the battle of Rymnik (1789). Andreyevskiy et al., *Brockhaus and Efron Dictionary*, s.v. 'Орловы, графский род'; Ibid., s.v. 'Румянцев-Задунайский'; Ibid., s.v. 'Суворов, Александр Васильевич'. [Andreyevskiy et al., *Brockhaus and Efron Dictionary*, s.v. 'Orlovs, comtal family'; Ibid., s.v. 'Rumyantsev-Zadunayskiy'; Ibid., s.v. 'Suvorov, Aleksandr Vasilyevich'.]

a few battles and one unsuccessful campaign, depriving them of the advantages brought by being perfectly victorious, undermines the base of its power and so it is not surprising that such a powerful empire is soon weakened and is headed toward its destruction.[4] Another circumstance contributes to this. In the Turkish government there still remains a remnant of military pride and they still assume that their court is in the midst of an army camp with the sultan signing his orders: 'so given from Our Imperial Stirrups'. The distinction between victor and conquered continues still and in no greater contrast than today between the Turks and Greeks, who are not two parts of a single nation, and is the reason that the sultan, unsupported by the zeal and love of his slaves, cannot conceive of recovering his losses after failures and must always await the next outrage and disturbance to befall Turkey. Thus, the Turks who once frightened and threatened all of Europe with enslavement are now timid and weak, cautious in politics and seek their security by playing off the rivalry between foreign powers. They are protected in part by the belief that allowing the beautiful regions of Turkey to fall into the hands of other peoples, especially the Russians, might harm the benefits of all European trade.

No matter how weak the Ottoman Empire is now however, its subjugation is not as easy as we generally think it is. A courageous sultan, taking command of his army, could easily subordinate the rebellious pashas, who have become virtually independent, and abolish the *ulema*, as they call their spiritual council and the cause of many evils and unrest, and may suddenly restore power and grandeur to his empire just as quickly as it had declined. The line of fortresses along the Danube; the sparsely populated plains of Bulgaria bereft of water and provisions for a large army and especially having poor fodder for horses; and the narrow defiles in the Balkans where a regular army is deprived of its many advantages against the numerous Turkish infantry, utilizing some of the best sharpshooters, presents a difficult problem even for a brave and skillful general, especially against the strategy that the Turks found successful in the last war [of 1806-1812] of defending themselves in their fortresses and harassing with light detachments while avoiding a general battle. The shortest and most convenient route to capture Constantinople was shown to us by our ancient heroes Oleg and Igor – the fleet is in any case a necessity, as proved by the fortunate war of 1770.

4     Bronevskiy's note: 'The same reason saw the fall of Napoleon in France'.

# Notes on the Winds and Weather in the Archipelago

The archipelago, being in a temperate climate, has only two seasons, summer and autumn. In the course of summer, the sky is covered by a clear and beautiful azure. The northerly winds chill and temper the heat so well that the air is revered here as being the healthiest. As the heat increases, the constantly blowing northerly winds also increase, except that close to the shores around noon there are periods of calm. Coastal winds always blow at night. The reason for these changes is the following: after the sun has set, the air is filled with earthly vapours arisen by the day's heat and flows out to sea like its liquid counterpart, which produces a warm coastal wind and the condensation of dew. This wind begins around midnight and blows until the sea air, agitated by the sun's heat, returns to the land. In the Dardanelles, northerly winds blow almost without any change. The beginning of autumn in the archipelago is on par with our finest springs while in November and December, cold and strong alternating winds begin. The sky turns black with clouds and storms with terrible lightning excite the air. There are such heavy rains all the while that more water falls there in one week than we experience here in a year. The pouring rain, especially in the dark of night, is comparable in sound to a strongly falling hail. In these winter months, the clear after a storm brings the most pleasant cool weather and the sun at noon always has a gentle warmth. In the archipelago there are no long heatwaves or the pernicious sirocco that scorches the earth. All the vegetation is perpetually green and in the winter all of nature is in full splendour. Because of the many islands, rocks and underwear shoals, in rough waters, sailing through the archipelago becomes dangerous but its many convenient harbours compensate for this.

# The Return of the *Venus* to Corfu – Tinos Island

Having received the order to deliver the captive Turkish admiral and captain of his ship with their retinue to Corfu, as well as Lieutenant Karl Rosenberg and the Emperor's courier Fyodorov who was carrying a report for His Majesty, we weighed anchor on the 6th [18th] of July and halted at the island of Tinos on the 8th [20th] due to the wind. The town of San Nicolo or simply Tinos as others call it stands on the bank of a river and is protected by a citadel built by the Venetians on a prominent height. The anchorage is open to the northerly and westerly winds with a muddy floor and a depth between 12 and 17 *sazhens* [25.6 to 36.27 m], making standing on anchor unreliable. In antiquity, it was known as Hydroessa due to the abundant water on the island or Ophiussa for its abundance of snakes. The island featured then a glorious temple to Poseidon, the Cave of Aeolus and the tombs of Zetes and Calais, the sons of Boreas. The people of Tinos had participated in the battle of Plataea. Their island was the last to be taken by the Turks from the Venetians. It has a length of 25 *versta*s [26.67 km] and a width of 12 [12.8 km]. Its terrain is mountainous and fertile and bears much wine, oil and grain. Undyed silk stockings are produced here and their silvery whiteness is considered the finest. Well-cultivated fields and gardens around the town show that the people are hardworking. The residents have their own boats and engage in considerable trade.

Civil officials came aboard the frigate to pay honour to the captive admiral and offer him their services. As a sign of respect to their former commander, they brought to the frigate all the necessary provisions without payment. Bekir Bey, at first a corsair and then a pasha in Egypt, was considered to be a very brave and knowledgeable (despite being illiterate) admiral. The words he spoke when he surrendered his flag to our admiral and the conversation with the lieutenant who was sent to bring him to the *Selafail* prove his courage and deep sense of honour. When the *Selafail* approached, coming astern of the *Sedd-el Bahr*, she was prepared to deliver a volley; the Turks shouted '*aman!* – mercy!' and Lieutenant

Vasiliy N. Titov was sent over to bring the admiral and captain along with their flags to the *Selafail*. The pasha for a long time refused to give his flag to Captain Rozhnov, saying that he would not surrender to anyone except the admiral himself. After several false starts with the lieutenant, he finally summoned him for the last time and asked: 'why are the Russians so angry with me that all of your ships attacked me?'

'Your Excellency was braver and fought the hardest', replied Titov. This answer so pleased the pasha that he stroked his beard and immediately agreed to go aboard the *Selafail*.

Giving his flag to Dmitriy Nikolayevich Senyavin, he said with great import: 'If fate has forced me to lose my flag, then I have not been dishonoured and I hope that my victor will give me justice and testify that I defended it to the very last'. In Gibraltar I had seen four Spanish ships captured in the battle of Trafalgar which were badly beaten, but the *Sedd-el Bahr*, without yards or rigging, with holes punched in its hull and decks covered in chips, splinters, killed and wounded men, appeared to be in the most terrible state. Senyavin received the flag from Bekir Bey, returned to him his sabre and placed him in his cabin. He treated the Turkish admiral with such attention and sincerity that after the short time they spoke, they parted as dear friends. The pasha was very lively and witty: while the beaten Turkish fleet entered the Dardanelles and when asked why all of the Turkish ships had gilded lions for figureheads, he answered: 'good Muslims have the hearts of lions; it's just a pity we have the heads of donkeys'. When asked if his ship would sail well, he said with a smile: 'If she would not sail well, we would not have arrived here'. On reaching Corfu, Bekir Bey was put up in the home of the commander-in-chief.

General César Berthier, the new viceroy of the Ionian Republic, having made a visit to him under the guise of giving him a more comfortable and quiet home, transferred him to one in which not only did he have no rest, but he ever suffered from a lack of furniture. After making a house-warming visit as is typical of the French, Berthier found him a new beautiful dwelling even more respectable than the first. The surprised Bekir Bey did not say a word in reply, but when Berthier added with a grin: 'I regret it is not possible to deliver to you here such beautiful women as those with which your seraglio in Constantinople is surely decorated', he then replied with a biting scorn and condemnation for the Frenchman's ridicule.

At dawn on the 10th [22nd] of July, during a fresh northerly wind, we hauled anchor and left the harbour to be met by a British frigate that inquired about the location of our fleet. They announced later that they were carrying dispatches for Admiral Senyavin and stopped at our former place near San Nicolo. Passing through the channel between Andros and Tinos and then between Cerigo and Matapan the next day, we met with two British ships and a brig, one of which had a hundred guns and flew the flag of Rear-Admiral George Martin.[1] Coming astern of the hundred-gun ship, the rear-admiral congratulated us for three victories: the defeat of the Turkish fleet at Mount Athos, and the defeat of the French at Heilsberg and Guttstadt in Prussia. Senyavin's adjutant, Lieutenant Rosenberg, went to thank Sir Martin for his congratulations and learned from him that seven ships at the behest of their parliament had been sent to join our fleet at Senyavin's disposal and even Admiral Collingwood with 22 ships if necessary, to support our actions. The authority invested in the commander-in-chief certainly brought him honour, as to this day, not a single Russian admiral has ever commanded a British squadron. But the zealous disposition of the British government had already passed and was much too late as the Turkish fleet never again left the Dardanelles. On a weak and varying wind, we arrived in Corfu on the 18th [30th] of July.

---

1    HMS *Queen* of 98 guns. John Marshall, *Royal Naval Biography*, supplement to vol. 4 (London: Longman, Rees, Orme, Brown and Green, 1830) p.55.

# 95

# Peace Negotiations with the Ottomans – The Arrival of a British Squadron at Tenedos – The Return of the Fleet to Corfu

After the siege of Tenedos, the Turks left not a single good house standing in the surroundings; everything was knocked down or burnt and they even chopped down the fruit trees and tore up most of the vineyards. For this reason, the residents dispersed to the other islands where there were no Turks and some swore loyalty to us and sailed to Corfu in anticipation of an opportunity to move to Russia. As there was no need to keep the fortress and in order to enable a greater freedom of action against the enemy, the commander-in-chief placed the garrison aboard the ships, sent guns and ammunition to Corfu on the *Yaroslav* and *Sedd-el Bahr* and finally blew up [the town and fort of] Tenedos on the 24th of July [5th of August].

After the battle at the Dardanelles, Councillor Pozzo di Borgo joined the fleet under the direct command of Admiral Senyavin and began to negotiate peace with the Turks. The admiral wrote to the *kapudan-pasha* about the arrival of the minister plenipotentiary, but the pasha did not reply for a long time. In order to appease him, another letter was sent in the company of 20 freed prisoners of war. The pasha replied that he related the admiral's proposal to the Sublime Porte. Finally on the 27th of May [8th of June], after the ascension of Sultan Mustafa to the throne, Seydi Ali Pasha gave a response although it was merely courteous and said nothing decisive.

After the battle at Mount Athos, the commander-in-chief again queried about Pozzo di Borgo's petition for negotiations and the *kapudan-pasha* replied as before, that he would convey the proposal on to Constantinople. On the 15th [27th] of July, after a long wait, the *reis efendi* (the foreign minister) sent a reply to Pozzo di Borgo's letters.[1] In this too was nothing affirmative except notice from the *reis*

---

1    Mehmed Said Galip Pasha served as the *reis efendi* during the negotiations at Slobozia

that the grand vizier had received a letter from General Mikhail Andreyevich Miloradovich, commander-in-chief in Bucharest,[2] concerning an armistice that would be concluded between the land forces. The official who brought this letter on the behalf of the *kapudan-pasha* suggested verbally to Senyavin to assume a place at this conference. The admiral replied that the law strictly forbade him from leaving the fleet but could send a trusted person in his place.

On the 12th [24th] of July, Seydi Ali sent his flag captain with a letter with which he strangely sought to justify the defeat at Athos. The content is curious enough to be reproduced here word for word:

> To the Supreme, Most Honourable and Enlightened Admiral Dmitriy Senyavin
>
> Inquiring after the health of Your Excellency, we present friendship to you and naturally you know that in any faith it is forbidden to speak falsely. Your friend does not allow himself any deceit and does not abide by anyone who deceives. During the battle, you hoisted a signal to stop the battle, firing cannons with blank charges! After another signal, you told me to prepare again for battle. Your three ships answered that they were ready, but the others announced that they were not.[3] In all governments it is understood that after such a signal, the battle cannot commence for 24 hours, of which I know Your Excellency is also well aware. You told my messenger that they did not do this, but I know what I know. We hope that after you receive this letter, if God wills it, you will not hesitate to reply. Peace and health be upon you.
>
> Seydi Ali, Algerian Sea Captain.

Senyavin answered this absurdity by stating that according to European conventions, it is not only unusual but impermissible in the heat of battle to ask an enemy for a recess or cessation of hostilities, that he never thought of making

---

in 1807. Любомир Бескровный (ed.), *М. И. Кутузов: Сборник Документов*, vol. 3 (Moscow: Военное издательство Военного Министерства СССР, 1952), p.936. [Lyubomir Beskrovnyy (ed.), *M. I. Kutuzov: Collection of Documents*, vol. 3 (Moscow: Military Press of the War Ministry of the USSR, 1952), p.936.]

2    Although Miloradovich commanded the army at Obileşti on 2 [19] June 1807, a victory which compelled the grand vizier to retreat across the Danube and prompted the armistice negotiations, he was not the commander-in-chief of the Army of Moldavia. Overall command was held by Ivan Ivanovich Michelson. When he died on 5 [17] August, Emperor Alexander appointed Prince Aleksandr Aleksandrovich Prozorovskiy to assume command. Mikhaylovskiy-Danilevskiy, *Description of the Turkish War*, vol. 1, pp.51-71.

3    Bronevskiy's note: 'This was how the Turks understood our signals, if at all'.

such a signal and that he would never make such an excuse in the brave *kapudan-pasha*'s place to justify himself.

On the 29th of July [10th of August], the *kapudan-pasha* and the *serasker* in Anatolia notified Senyavin about the conclusion of an armistice at Izmail between the armies and demanded that, for his part, he also cease military action. The admiral replied that he would not cease military operations until Pozzo di Borgo was permitted to negotiate.

After an unsuccessful attempt on Egypt, with the change of ministries, the British government decided to finally entreaty with our court and assigned a squadron under Rear-Admiral Martin to support our fleet. On the 29th of July [10th of August], the *Kent* and a brig brought this pleasant news to us, after which arrived the *Repulse* and three frigates: the *Active*, *Apollo* and *Thetis*. The frigates immediately left to cruise around Salonica and Smyrna. Finally, on the 18th [30th] of July, Rear-Admiral Martin with the two ships *Queen* and *Montagu*, the former being of a hundred guns, arrived in Tenedos and saluted Senyavin with nine shots, which surprised everyone, as the British never offer salutes first. Senyavin ordered an equal number in reply and said at the same time: 'this is no empty gesture, it means something'. As soon as the British dropped anchor, Martin with all the captains of his squadron came aboard the *Tvyordyy* in full dress and placed themselves under Senyavin's command. No other Russian admiral has yet received such an honour. Sir Arthur Paget, who had been British minister plenipotentiary to Vienna, arrived with this squadron in order to engage the Turks in the negotiations of peace. The *Kent* was sent to the Dardanelles to announce his arrival, but the Turks in the previous fashion politely accepted the announcement without any decisive confirmation or rejection of the offer. Senyavin had a special gift, so to speak, to make people instantly love and respect him. He treated Martin to a fine dinner and Martin returned the courtesy; afterward, balls and feasts began to be held aboard the Russian and British ships marked by unconstrained gaiety and frankness. An amazing concord was established not only between officers, but also among the sailors.

On the 29th of July [10th of August], Vice-Admiral Collingwood, confidant and heir to Nelson's glory and hero of the battle of Trafalgar, joined our squadron aboard the 100-gun ship *Ocean* with the two 80-gun ships *Malta* and *Canopus*. Senyavin sent his flag captain Maleyev to congratulate him on his arrival. Collingwood arrived in the archipelago with a strong fleet in order to influence the negotiations with the Turks, dissuade them from heeding further council with the French ambassador Sébastiani, and hasten them to make peace. After mutual visits and greetings, Collingwood asked for the aid of two ships in order to determine if it were possible to attack the Turkish fleet in the Dardanelles Strait itself. Senyavin immediately replied that he was willing to assist him with all of his power and on the 1st [13th] of August, both squadrons departed and manoeuvred together to drop anchor again off of Imbros. The Turks were so concerned with our movement that they raised white flags on their ships the next day and our squadron proceeded cautiously into the strait to stand close to their fortresses. The vanguard of the combined fleets under the command of Rear-Admiral Greig stood in the mouth of the strait. The British ambassador led negotiations and the Turks informed us of the unfortunate news about military operations in the north. The wind was blowing constantly from the strait and nothing could be attempted. Competition between the two fleets was so great and confidence in the courage and determination of both admirals was so firm that there was no doubt about the success of any endeavour, but the circumstances suddenly, unexpectedly and completely changed. On the 12th [24th] of August, Baron Otto Dmitrovich Schöppingk arrived on the corvette *Kherson* with a letter from the Emperor and a copy of the Treaty of Tilsit, approved and ratified on the 25th of June [7th of July].

In consequence of one of the articles concerning the cessation of hostilities with Turkey, Senyavin notified Collingwood that he could no longer contribute his forces to a joint venture. The British admiral, expressing his sincere regret about such an unexpected turn of events, took it upon himself to deliver an open invitation to any of our vessels to return to Tenedos after the departure of our fleet, should they be able. The *reis efendi*, at the same time, notified Senyavin of the truce signed by Privy Councillor Sergey Lazarevich Lashkaryov, which demanded the surrender of Tenedos and the cessation of hostilities. The admiral asked to send an agent to make terms. On the 14th [26th] of August, the combined fleet was divided again with acute reluctance on both sides. The British remained at Imbros while the Russians sailed to Tenedos. The admiral and officers parted with expressions of sincere camaraderie and friendship. The departure was all the more regrettable because each man was aware of the consequences of the inevitable war.[4] Finally on the 23rd of August [4th of September], two couriers arrived from Tilsit, one by way of Trieste and Cattaro, the other by Naples and Otranto, both carrying an Imperial order dated from the 28th of July [9th of August] that required leaving the Greek archipelago, surrendering Cattaro and

---

4    The Treaty of Tilsit not only ended hostilities between Russia and France, but effectively bound them in an alliance and positioned Russia for a break with the United Kingdom, including joining the Continental System and cutting off all trade with Britain. When the British launched their pre-emptive strike on Copenhagen in September 1807 to prevent the Danish fleet from being captured by the French, this violation of Denmark's neutrality served as a convenient pretext for Russia to declare war. Ward et al., *Cambridge Modern History*, vol.9, pp.291-293.; 'Documents upon the Peace of Tilsit', *The Napoleon Series*, https://www.napoleon-series.org/research/government/diplomatic/c_tilsit.html, accessed 15 February, 2018.

the Ionian Republic to the French (of which a special directive had already been delivered to Commodore Baratynskiy[5] and General Nazimov), and for the fleet to return immediately to the Baltic and Black Sea ports.

In accordance with the Emperor's will, without waiting for the Turkish diplomats, the squadron left Tenedos on the 25th of August [6th of September] and arrived at Hydra on the 27th [7th], from which Admiral Greig was sent to Spezia with three ships to collect prize vessels belonging to the fleet and to conclude other matters. The admiral departed with the other six on the 28th of August [8th of September] and collected our small garrison from the island of Cerigo along the way. He arrived in Corfu on the 4th [16th] of September. The sloop *Shpitsbergen*, also on the way, was sent to retrieve the garrison from Santa Maura.

5    Ilya Andreyevich Baratynskiy was promoted to captain-commodore on the 15 [27] January, 1807. *Complete Naval Roster*, vol.3, p.115-116.

# 96

# Our Stay in Corfu – The Peace of Tilsit

After the arrival of the frigate *Venus* in Corfu, in the later days of July, we received word of the victories won at Heilsberg and Guttstadt and of the armistice soon after. All of us earnestly wished and hoped that the war would continue and promised ourselves undoubted successes; we awaited the future with agonizing expectation. Corfu was then like a swarming beehive; all the taverns and coffee houses were filled with politicians and bureaucrats of every rank and alive with discussion. Everywhere the people discussed military actions and poured over maps, doubting and speculating about every detail. The rumour of a peace treaty at Tilsit dampened these debates and the most gossipy were forced to remain silent or shrug their shoulders yet everyone still consoled himself with the faint spectre of hope. At last, a courier arrived with official news of the treaty and with the Highest orders, as mentioned above, for relinquishing Cattaro and the Ionian Republic to the French. Our army was to be transported to Italy and unite in Padua to await further orders. It is impossible describe the dejection which the Corfiots felt and they wore such grief on their faces. The expected termination of trade, oppression by military rule and fear of indemnities inspired them to mourn their fate in advance. The rich, merchants and capitalists, Englishmen and anyone who could hastily relocated themselves to Malta and Sicily, the last refuges free from the French yoke.

If the treaty of Tilsit is examined from the other side and not from the one with which we received it at the time, the impartial historian will discover in it the wise prudence of our monarch who prepared the salvation of Europe. For this, it is only necessary to pay attention to the noble purpose and selfless conduct with which the Empress Catherine and Emperors Paul and Alexander took part in the wars against France and then compare them with the actions of the allies Russia so diligently aided. I will not speak about the Revolutionary Wars in which the Empress did not consider it necessary to actively intervene, content only to send our fleet to Britain, but I will speak on the campaigns of 1799, 1805 and 1807. In the first, Suvorov liberated Italy and when he thought to shift the theatre of war into France proper, the Viennese cabinet sent him to Switzerland where, although Russian arms were crowned with unfading laurels, the hero of our age did not find promised aid and reinforcements and was forced to retreat to Bavaria. At the same time, Ancona was conquered by the Russian fleet and a landed army which raised the Austrian banner over its walls instead of the Papal standard. The British also attempted to raise their flag in Naples. Nelson contested the glory of the liberation of this capital by Admiral Ushakov and when our army marched from Naples to conquer Rome, a British captain cruising around Civitavecchia offered the French garrison to surrender and allowed the loading of several ships with the treasures of the Roman churches and the Vatican itself.[1] By these actions, the Emperor Paul rightly recalled his forces. In the war of 1805, the French forces marched unpunished through neutral territories and surrounded General Mack who, with 60,000 men, laid down his arms without a battle.[2] This glorious courtier field-marshal had distinguished himself in 1798 by a similar feat in the service of the King of Naples; he continued to avoid battle for several days, but by his beautifully worded actions on paper and in speech he destroyed an army of 80,000 – the same army that took him prisoner. The Prussian court hesitated for a long time and finally withdrew from the alliance. The fate of the war was then decided at Austerlitz. Prussia, having received Hanover and Lauenburg in exchange for Neuchatel and the Upper Palatinate, quarreled with Britain and Sweden, but they soon saw the net set for them and the need to act openly. Alexander, constant in his policy, with the same unselfishness, did not refuse to help Frederick[3] and reconciled him with Britain and Sweden, but the battle at Jena alone decided the fate of the Prussian war. The kingdom was conquered in six weeks, all the fortresses surrendered without resistance and barely 15,000 Prussians managed to unite with our army; Russian blood alone flowed on the banks of the Vistula for the salvation of our ally. The Austrian court maintained strict neutrality, following Berlin's example from the previous year. The British government, instead of promising to liberate Danzig from the French siege, sent an expedition to conquer

1    Captain Thomas Troubridge with the *HMS Culloden* and *Minotaur*, both of 74 guns. William James, *The Naval History of Great Britain*, vol. 2 (London: Conway Maritime Press, 2002), pp.281-283.
2    Karl, Baron Mack von Leiberich was effectively the commander-in-chief of the Austrian army marching through Bavaria, though it was nominally under the command of the Archduke Ferdinand Karl Joseph. He suffered numerous defeats and was surrounded in the town of Ulm where he surrendered on 7 [19] October, 1805, opening the way for the French to enter Vienna and leading to the battle of Austerlitz on 20 November [2 December]. Andreyevskiy et al., *Brockhaus and Efron Dictionary*, s.v. 'Макк'. [Andreyevskiy et al., *Brockhaus and Efron Dictionary*, s.v. 'Mack'.]
3    Frederick-William III was King of Prussia from 1797 to 1840.

Buenos Aires in South America and instead of acting in conjunction with our fleet against Constantinople, attempted to conquer Egypt. These events favoured Napoleon most of all and he became irresistible. The foreign war crawling toward the frontiers of our fatherland was stopped by the treaty of Tilsit, which should demonstrate the pernicious consequences of the disagreement and confusion between our courts that only served to prolong and expand the war. Europe was left to her fate so that in the meanwhile Russia could gather all of its forces and be ready to counter the powerful Napoleon.

In this situation, the Ionian Republic and Bay of Cattaro became unnecessary, as the maintenance of a fleet and army here depended on an ally who was now clearly acting only according to his own self-interest and could not contend with the superiority of the British Navy and the continuation of the war with the Ottoman Empire. Britain did not lose any of her subjects in battle and received a general profit from the war, inciting her enemies against France, promising them aid and always arriving too late with it, while all Europe mourned the deaths of a hundred thousand of their soldiers. The loss of the trade which typified Corfu in previous circumstances was also not so strongly felt; in spite of all its advantages, Russian merchants had little interest in the island. Our shipping is still to this day in the hands of foreigners, most of whom are present as visitors yet have their offices in our ports and even in the interior cities. Our merchant class comprehends the benefit of foreign trade, knows how to calculate its profit, are enterprising and of course willingly seek wealth beyond the seas, but Peter the Great's vision has still yet to become a reality.

# 97

# Relinquishing Corfu to the French – Evacuating the Army to Venice

---

On the 7th [19th] of August, the first French detachment with Brigadier-General Bernard Cardenau arrived onboard 30 vessels with no greeting or reception from the locals and on the next day, all the stores were locked up. Thereafter, the French brought over 200 or 300 men each day. The British cruisers managed to take advantage of such ferries and several boats were sunk with their passengers, a few were taken prisoner and their treasuries were seized. The remainder of their force arrived on the 12th [24th] along with Divisional General César Berthier (brother of the Prince Neuchatel) who was appointed commandant of the Ionian islands. On the 14th [26th], the French replaced our forces and began to appropriate the fortress artillery and magazines. From that day onward, all manner of public disturbances and oppressions began. Three levies were raised: the first for the maintenance of Berthier's extravagant court; the second required the citizens of the town to provide each soldier of the garrison daily with two *funts* [819.03 g] of bread and a bottle of wine, and for the barracks to be stocked with sufficient stores of firewood, candles, water and bedding; the third entailed the French with weapons in hand seizing all manner of cloth, canvas and cobbling materials and assembling all the craftsmen in the town to forcibly employ them in outfitting the soldiers of the garrison with a full and fine complement of uniforms in just a few days. Not the slightest subordination could be seen: soldiers and officers travelled together to the theatre, shops and taverns and were outrageous everywhere, beating the Greeks without mercy. Such actions disgusted us and gave the residents clear reason to prefer us over them. Berthier fruitlessly complained of our cold attitude toward his men but even the most passionate Francophile could not praise their conduct. Almost every day there were arguments and fights, even going so far as one coffee house refusing service to the French altogether.

In order to terrify honest citizens and so that they dare not praise only the Russians or cry over their misfortunes, Berthier enlisted a great number of spies: people raised according to the rules of the latest philosophy, atheists without faith or morals, citizens of the world who have no fatherland, the poor, the corrupted, those hoping to win the favour of their new government, card players, tavern brokers, and even public women; in a word, the people of the very lowest character rejected by society were eavesdropping everywhere, but in order to start a conversation and determine the opinion of another, they deliberately began by condemning the French. Such cunning tricks forced everyone to be cautious and these spies, being already well-known, were compelled to slander others in order to earn their salaries. First they condemned their benefactors, then acquaintances and finally all honest and virtuous citizens. When the government oppressed the best of its subjects by such purchased villains, what benefit could these informers possibly bring and what manner of abuse could their services prevent? I leave it to the reader to wonder how in our enlightened age, a nation boasting better education should suffer from such tyranny and, failing to understand the actions of their own Attila, they call him a great man – a genius!

On the 22nd of August [3rd of September], all hope was lost for the inhabitants. The tricolour was raised over the fortress and the republic was declared a territory of France. The senate was dissolved and the poor people did not even want to listen to the full proclamation, which had been read out at every intersection upon the beating of a drum. On Napoleon's birthday, 3rd [15th] of August, Berthier entered the church of St. Spyridon while surrounded by his brilliant staff with musicians and drummers, though when he saw the surprise written on our faces, he guessed at our displeasure and ordered the musicians to leave and for his grenadiers to remove their caps. In the evening, they entered homes with bayonets fixed to force the owners to light up their windows, although where they only had bowl oil lamps, the boys quietly blew them out. In the theatre, not one noble citizen was in attendance and soldiers in disguise planted in the boxes shouted in unison: '*vive Napoléon!*' On the contrary, our Emperor's name day was the most glorious celebration. In the morning, all the churches were filled with people and the bell-ringing continued all day, the theatre was full of spectators; when the illuminations were lit, the town and ships seemed to be aflame, every house and ship put up transparent illustrations and inscriptions in the windows with lamps behind them, and all throughout the streets one could hear constant shouts of 'long live Alexander!' and 'long live the Russians!'

On the 4th [16th] of September, the squadron dropped anchor as soon as it arrived from the archipelago and Berthier sent an official to congratulate them on their arrival and ask for a salute. Senyavin thanked him for the greetings but on the latter he answered that since we had not yet received a directive regarding salutes with France, he would not render honours to the fortress beforehand. With the arrival of the admiral, order was immediately restored. Guards from our men were mounted around the cities and the excesses of the French soldiery were curtailed and even Berthier refrained from dispensing military justice, especially in the homes where Russians were quartered. The Corfiots rested for a few days.

Senyavin had many things to do, most of them unpleasant. From morning to evening, senators and citizens came to express their gratitude and ask for protection from the French who treated Corfu like a conquered city; others came to bid farewell and weep. The French secretly did everything possible to retard the transfer of our soldiers to Italy and revealed that they intended for our army and navy to remain for the defense of Corfu, which worried us very much. The admiral resolved the whole matter in ten days. The docks and piers worked day and night to hire, repair and equip transport vessels for the crossing and everyone was dispatched in five days. We were sent every which way: Commodore Baratynskiy with his ships from the Baltic squadron was ordered to hasten to join the fleet in Corfu; Commodore Saltanov[1] received the Black Sea squadron for returning to the Black Sea and would take with them all the fortress supplies and personnel belonging to the 15th Division.

When the first detachment of soldiers gathered from the islands boarded ships headed for Manfredonia or Ancona, the heartfelt farewell which the inhabitants bid to our soldiers, a sincere testimony of the people's love for us, cannot be described by any pen. When the troops stopped at the Church of Saint Spyridon to receive a blessing for their journey, the clergy from all the churches came out in black vestments with crosses and holy water. The archpriest, giving bread and salt to General Nazimov, began to give a speech but burst into tears and could not continue. The drummers struck up a beat, the men departed and marched to the docks. Not only the streets and squares, but all the windows and balconies were filled with people looking on who, in the outpouring of their gratitude, forgot for a moment their grievances with their new rulers. Flowers rained down on the soldiers from the balconies and roofs, and frequently a voice of praise and thanks broke the mournful silence. When the soldiers boarded the rowing vessels, each said goodbye to an acquaintance and asked that they not forget each other, hugging one another and crying. For the first time, I saw and believed that the Corfiots had a reason to love the Russians; they were truly orphans without us. We can say that the people of Corfu and Cattaro were in turn loved by the children of Russia, who cherished and caressed them and left without any demand. The

---

1    Ivan Osipovich Saltanov was promoted to captain-commodore on 11 [23] January, 1807. *Complete Naval Roster*, vol.5, pp.16-17.

generosity and mercy of the Emperor Alexander should never be blotted out of the memory of these peoples.

The noble feat of the Souliotes serving in our Albanian Legion is worthy of mention. They did not at first agree to join Napoleon's service until they were absolutely convinced that they were no longer necessary to us and, even then, only on the condition that they should never be deployed against the Russians. When the French official who administered an oath to the Albanians informed them that such a proposal of conditions on their part was indecent and unnecessary, the Albanian chief boldly replied: 'on the contrary, it is necessary that you know in advance that if you are ever at war with the Russians, we will turn against you for their sake'.

We received news that Cattaro was handed over to the French. General Marmont, upon accepting this province, declared the past animosities forgotten and did not levy any indemnities from the people. He acted wisely, because the brave people of the bay, along with the Montenegrins, who rejected the generous promises and patronage of the great Napoleon, would certainly not tolerate the same oppression to which the Corfiots voluntarily surrendered. The captured Turks in our custody were released and transported to the Albanian coast. Admiral Bekir Bey, afraid that they would take his head like Sheremet Bey and others for not dying honourably in battle, remained in Corfu to await the mercy of the Sultan.

# 98

# Sailing across the Mediterranean Sea for Gibraltar

On the 14th [26th] of September, Rear-Admiral Greig arrived from the archipelago with three ships; he had been detained at Cerigo for a long time by calm winds. These ships were repaired in two days and the fleet was ready to depart on the first fair wind. For the absent Commodore Baratynskiy were orders to depart immediately for Russia with the ships *Svyatoy Pyotr*, *Moskva* and the *Sedd-el Bahr* and the frigates *Lyogkiy* and *Avtroil*, without entering any ports and even to avoid England. The same instruction was given to all captains. The small vessels of the Baltic squadron, due to their unreliability in sailing for such long periods of time, and so that they would not slow down the journey of the ships of the line, were transferred to the Black Sea squadron under Commodore Saltanov.

On the 19th of September [1st of October] during a calm wind, the squadron consisting of the same 10 ships that were in the archipelago along with the frigates *Venus*, *Kildyuin* and *Shpitsbergen* weighed anchor, left Corfu and bid farewell to her forever. The square and bastions of the fortress were covered with people and a multitude of skiffs surrounded the ships. The Corfiots said goodbye to their friends, some wished us a good journey and others wished for a storm to bring us back to them. The winds began to freshen and the ships took off. The skiffs lagged behind us and soon the whole of Corfu sank into the sea, grew dark and disappeared. All the hopes of the Corfiots passed and the ties of friendship between our hearts were severed.

After sunset, the wind grew very strong and foul, forcing us to beat windward for four days against choppy waves. The fast and frequent transition from pleasure to the various occupations and cares of service prompted outpourings of sadness in our company which was expressed by silences and dour faces. Our way of life contributed no small part to that. Everyone has his own duties on the ship and everything has its appointed times. At 7 o'clock after sunrise, everyone arises with the blow of the whistle; at 7:30, officers are served tea; at 9, everyone free from duties are called to prayer with the beat of a drum; at 10, vodka and hors d'oeuvres are served; at 11:30, we dine; at 5:30, we light the fireplace in the wardroom and sit down around the tea table, smoke pipes, drink tea or punch and converse as if we were family; at 7:30 in the evening, we take our supper and retire to bed. The distribution of watches is segregated so that each officer and sailor occupies a post from 10 to 14 hours a day. Arising at midnight, lying down at 4 am, never having a restful or uninterrupted sleep, one is already ready to go on deck and during storms, he might not retire to his cabin for several days, dozing for only a few minutes at a time while leaning against a gun. Here, disturbances and labours are our bivouacs which inconvenience us not only in sight of the enemy, but at all times.

On the night of the 23rd of September [5th of October], a foul, strong wind blew and the frigates seemed ready to break apart in the violent waves, but everyone was calm and besides the voice of the lieutenant on watch and the barks of the petty officers, no commotion or confusion could be heard. Suddenly a shot rang out followed a little while after by three more. The *Uriil* had given a signal in the night that she was in distress and the *Selafail* had lost her main course sail. The admiral answered by ordering them to stay in line until dawn. Toward morning, the wind somewhat abated and the squadron was ordered to lie to, the *Selafail* made its repairs and the admiral went aboard the *Uriil* to talk. The admiral crossed on a small skiff despite the choppy waves and to his great disappointment, he found that many of the beams on the deck were cracked, others were rotting and that the ship could not undergo a long journey at such a turbulent time of year. Therefore, Captain M.T. Bychenskiy was ordered to return to Corfu, to lay his artillery on the ships of Baratynskiy's squadron, and to repair his ship as quickly as possible and proceed with him or to turn to the Black Sea in the event of other severe damages.

On the 24th of September [6th of October], the wind began to wane as we approached Sicily, rounded the cape of Passero and came within sight of Malta. On either side we saw a beautiful collage of towns, harbours, villages, monasteries and a watchtower standing on a rock. As we coasted along, these sights were replaced by even finer ones as the bright night gave way to a clear day and all the objects around us were suddenly transformed. With such a safe voyage, we had already forgotten the anxiety and boredom of the past very days; we did not think that it could all change that very hour. Naval service, it is said, is very difficult, but for us there was always something interesting and greatly pleasing. Naturally in no other service is there so much inspiration for the imagination and soul as on the sea. Who among sailors has not sworn never to sail again and resign forever at harbour during a cruel storm, and who among them did not forget their oaths at the first favourable wind and when standing bored on dry land, did not gladly board his vessel again and start for the open water? Surrounded by disasters, even shipwrecked, though we talk of calms, we love only storms. Our thoughts are as fickle as our lives in this case; we are like the jealous wife who, caressing the first fruit of our love, tells her spouse not to be suspicious, but in turn begins to suspect the young maid and banishes her; when the husband becomes furious, she falls to her knees and begs forgiveness only to become more jealous and suspicious in the future.

On the 26th of September [8th of October], on approaching the western extremity of Sicily, the wind began to blow from the north and intensify; in order to haul as close to the wind as possible and move away from the African coast, the admiral led the squadron between Sicily and the Aegadian Islands. The night was dark and the strait contained submerged rocks. Without seeing any objects and guided by the map and compass, we groped dangerously through the darkness. During such passages which often happen at sea, vision and sense are in miserable numbness. With each ship in the column keeping an eye on the one ahead and every vessel carefully following the admiral's lead, the whole squadron fought all night against a foul wind. At sunrise, the wind subsided and turned to the east.

On our starboard side we could see the town of Trapani, off of port was Marettimo, Favignana and countless other islands. The Sicilian coast and the town were low with mountains visible at some distance, covered in greenery. One was surmounted by a monastery and another bore an ancient castle. Near the pier there were many boats with motley sails. These boats were used to obtain corals, the primary occupation of the inhabitants of Trapani. The corals come in various colours: red as blood, skin-coloured, yellow, white and marbled. The corals available in Trapani are of the finest grade. This marvelous product of the sea grows like the antlers of reindeer and is as dense and solid as stone. The trunk of the coral divides into branches and adheres itself to rocks. The bark covering it quickly vanishes when it is retrieved from the water and when it dries out, its surface is bumpy as if covered in grains and has many small apertures through which the coral receives its sustenance.[1] Naturalists believe that an animal-plant, called the sea nettle, is the basis of the coral. This plant is made up of a viscous substance that then hardens which mixes with limescale to become the coral. It is not without danger and difficulty that these corals are harvested from the seabed. The machine used for this is very simple and its recent invention has made coral fishing very profitable. In the centre of a wooden cross are attached heavy stones which can be immersed and hold the machine to the floor; to three ends of the

---

1    The skin or 'bark' of coral is the living organism, a colony of polyps, and the rest of the 'plant' is a deposit of calcium carbonate secreted by the polyps, slowly building up and out in layers. The bright colouration of coral reefs is created by symbiotic algae that live on the polyps and consume the coral's waste as sustenance. Sirindar Paracer and Vernon Ahmadjian, *Symbiosis: An Introduction to Biological Associations*, 2nd ed. (Oxford: Oxford University Press, 2000), pp.156-157.

cross are attached a tight rope net. On a sturdy line attached to the fourth end of the cross, the machine rushes through the water; the end of this rope is tied to the stern of a boat, which is towed by several other vessels all rowing or sailing together. The stones tied to the middle of the cross break off the corals which are then caught in the net and rise to the surface with it. The inhabitants of Trapani are considered to be the hardest working in Sicily; jewelry and haberdashery, cameos in particular, provide them with a considerable income. These cameos are carved out of solid shells and the best of the antiques are so similar to them that a real antique carved on onyx cannot be distinguished from the fakes on shell that have come into such popularity that a ring or bracelet is now sold for 2,000 rubles.

The squadron passed Marettimo and turned downwind. The sloop *Shpitsbergen* drifted under the wind, did not have time to round the western cape of Sicily and had fallen behind the squadron in the previous night. The weather was clear, the gentle, fair wind did not change and we uneventfully sailed over 200 to 300 *verstas* [213.36 to 320 km] in a day. When the wind intensified somewhat, the admiral did not delay the voyage forward and had us manoeuvre variously. The movements of the fleet would be perfectly enchanting if seen for the first time. When a ship is at anchor, it seems like a heavy, immovable hulk, but when one sail is unfurled, its appearance is transformed. When a second, a third and soon all of its sails are inflated by the blowing wind, the ship flies like a living creature. Her movements during attack and defence, when the fleet falls into columns out of disarray in a few minutes, evolutions from order to order, closing its gaps, spreading out, striking the enemy with the terrible thunder of her guns; all these present a spectacular, menacing and majestic sight. The ship can be likened to an animated body which takes off and slows itself and turns about in any direction with such accuracy and diligence that the large and complex structure seems like an intelligent creature. It is very likely that Peter the Great, observing the evolutions of the great British fleet for the first time, delighted in astonishment and said: 'Were I not Tsar of Russia, I would like to be an admiral'.

On the 30th of September [12th of October], after passing Sardinia, the admiral invited our captain aboard his flagship and ordered him to go to Gibraltar to procure pilots to guide us to Copenhagen and to ascertain our relationship with the British. Setting all sails, we quickly lost sight of the squadron behind us. On the 4th [16th] of October, we met the British frigate *Euryalus* which was blockading Carthage. They mistook us for the Spanish and were prepared to attack us, but as we approached and came astern, also ready for battle, they asked in one word which nation we sailed for. Friend or foe! Then the two captains had time to properly inspect one another and the circumstances. Coming close to the stern of the British frigate, we struck her with the jibboom and broke it off. An English lieutenant came to us with news for us and had questions of his own. Neither one nor the other was particularly pleasant. That same day, we reached Gibraltar.

As soon as we dropped our anchor, we immediately proceeded to address some of the damage to our vessel. The shrouds which had become slack were tightened and the sails were mended. The captain's care was not in vain, they were in anticipation of many of the troubles that awaited us in the Atlantic. In the greater number of adventures in which the sea serves as a stage, there are very few that can be truly considered unavoidable. If a ship leaving port is equipped and mended in every way necessary, then there is no reason to fear the ferocity of the elements. On the contrary, the dubious condition of a ship robs the captain of his confidence and the ship may perish despite his dextrous mastery, from even minor damages or deficiencies.

The next day, I and three companions went ashore with the intention of climbing to the summit of the Rock of Gibraltar to determine if our fleet could be seen and to admire the distant vistas. We were only in town for a minute to hire some donkeys and buy several British gazettes, which then were not afraid to rebuke Napoleon. The governor's garden did not seem very well decorated when I had previously seen it but now the grapes had begun to take hold and it seemed the trees were also flourishing, although none of them bore any fruit save the Indian figs. Our journey was not successful; the wind picked up around noon followed by rain and a thick fog fell over the mountain. Occasionally when the sun peered between the rushing clouds, the peaks of the Spanish and African mountains showed themselves. We reached the Cave of Saint Michael and my comrades descended with torches while I remained under the shelter of the rock. Under my feet across immeasurable space, the ocean was covered with white waves and an easterly wind blew from the peaks of the mountains with such force that they drove the visiting haze along the slope and down onto the surface of the water, giving the appearance that our frigate was floating in the clouds. My comrades from the cave desperately wanted to reach the summit but I was afraid that my wounds were not fully closed yet and remained waiting for them in the grotto, though they soon turned back anyway. Approaching the garden, the change in the warmth of the air was very acute. After a few minutes, we were transported from a cold climate to a temperate one and in the town it was even hot.

Here we received reliable news of the attack of Copenhagen by the British and of the movements of the French forces, which did not bode well for a prolonged peace. The friends of silence were deceived by the promises of Napoleon. Under the guise of restoring peace on the seas, without having a single boat in the water, the Emperor of the French apparently sought to conquer all of the continent's terra firma. One large army was assembled at the time at Bayonne; another, as if to deprive the British of the benefits of trade with Portugal, had already taken

Madrid. A British governmental gazette foreshadowed then that an important event was in store for Europe which should open the eyes of all reigning monarchs. At the same time as Napoleon plotted to dissolve the Spanish monarchy, twenty old Danish ships proved a stumbling block for the British government. The British fleet, without declaring war, suddenly entered the Sound, attacked and burned down the city of Copenhagen.

This unilateral policy was the cause of the displeasure not only of their allies, but even all the righteous among the British people. We learned here from the English that our Emperor was the first to express his displeasure, though the French *Moniteur* clearly and correctly stated that war between Russia and Britain was inevitable. We hoped that a war would not be declared before spring to spare such a significant portion of our naval forces, but, judging by their prior insincere actions, it seemed doubtful if the British wished to respect the flag of their dependable and ever-loyal ally and allow us to return to Russia. This news greatly saddened us and in this state of affairs, at such a late time of the year when there were no more than four weeks before the close of navigation in the Baltic Sea, we could hardly have any hope of returning to the fatherland.

# 99

# Sailing the Atlantic Ocean – A Storm

Our captain was received by the commandant of Gibraltar very politely,[1] although under a plausible pretext, the pilots were not granted an audience. We could not procure the necessary quantities of provisions and the prices were quite high. In a city that receives its grain from Russia, potatoes and corned beef from America, rice from China, and water and vegetables from Africa, such inflated prices are not surprising. On the 5th [17th] of October, at 8 in the morning, a perfectly illuminated floating street appeared. It was our fleet. On the admiral's ship a signal was raised to show its place and when we in turn lit a flare, we were ordered to stay united with the squadron and to weigh anchor if we were standing on one. The sky was overcast and the night became very dark. An easterly wind in the strait was quite fresh but at Gibraltar, where we stood, it was absolutely still. At the peak, the wind blew from different directions such that when we hauled anchor and ran downwind, suddenly all the sails were set on the masts and the frigate could not turn against the wind from the force of the waves. We were compelled to turn, coming so close to the shore that the waves thundering around us as they broke on the rocks brought us into awe: it would have been useless to drop an anchor on the rocky floor and we could not have been towed away with rowing teams; if the wind did not fortunately abate, then we would have been inevitably dashed on the shore. Over the course of four hours, the wind was at first reaching and then foul, strong and then quiet, as if crossing a magical line. Finally we escaped from the rocks, entered the strait and lay to, hauling up our boats with great difficulty. We set all sails and took off to catch up with the squadron, which we joined at dawn.

---

1    Sir Hew Dalrymple was Gibraltar's acting governor between November 1806 and August 1808. Hew Dalrymple, *Memoir written by General Sir Hew Dalrymple of his Proceedings as Connected with the Affairs of Spain and the Commencement of the Peninsular War* (London: Thomas and William Boone, 1830), pp.3-49.

A strong, prosperous wind gave us an indescribable joy: when we calculated the present course, each man determined a time and date when we would arrive in Reval (Kronstadt being likely covered over with ice by the time we returned). At that time, when we were revelling in our satisfaction and firmly believed that our journey would quickly and safely end, when we were already dreaming of setting foot in our homeland, at the same time we should have been fully calloused to the experience of being incorrect in our assumptions and having the most meticulous mathematical calculations foiled on the sea. At dawn on the 7th [19th] of October, all of our hopes and joys disappeared and everything around us changed. The easterly wind died down, gloomy clouds drifted from the north, a fog descended onto the surface of the ocean, and hurricanes and tornados appeared, the harbingers of stormy winds. We fought with them exactly as with our enemies, though as soon as we dispelled one with a cannon ball, another rose in its place. By evening, a strong squall from the north forced us to reef our sails and begin to beat to windward. Over 27 days, the opposing wind blew with constant cruelty. In the first ten days of tacking, we came close to the Cape of St. Vincent, swinging toward and away from the shore; the wind always swept in and drove us further and further toward crashing. The admiral led the squadron out onto the open ocean in the hopes of finding a different wind and breaking free of the strong current, but even at 700 *verstas* [746.76 km] from land, the same foul wind was blowing with equal force. If sometimes for a few hours the wind relented, then the terrible waves were even more monotonous for us and more harmful to the ships than the strongest wind.

Our ships, which were beaten everywhere during battle, had been in service for three to four years without major repair, sailing with depleted stockpiles and against strong winds for protracted lengths of time, were all generally in a poor state and some were even decrepit. The *Moshchnyy* signalled that her mizzen-mast had been damaged; the *Rafail* too had such damage as could not be repaired on the open water. One vessel after another incessantly tore their sails or snapped off a yard or topmast. After four weeks of violent and terrible rolling and pitching where for five or six days it was impossible to light a fire in the kitchen and therefore without warm meals or having any dry place to lay, the combination of thirst, hunger and cold began to pain our men living on the open deck. The captain and all the officers, not having any fresh food, sound sleep or peace, were more or less unhealthy. Everyone was exhausted to the extreme and lost patience; anger ran rampant. This state, dire though it was, pales in comparison to what we experienced on the night of the 27th of October [8th of November].

Locked up in a cabin below the waterline (on the orlop deck), wrapped up in my hammock, going several days without bandaging, my wounds were not yet closed and my health was distressed. All I could imagine were disasters. Unable to change my position and save myself from my dour dreams, I asked every hour where we were and poured over the map unfolded before me in the dim light of the dingy lamp. My boredom was broken or deepened by the doctor and another officer who was also laid up without a post to occupy him. They could not bear the terrible spectacle of the stormy sea and with every roll of the frigate, they saw the yawning of the grave. The shouts of the working sailors, the clapping of the sails and the squeaking of the hull drove them to despair. The fear increased in one of them to the point that our map was inaccurate and we were destined to crash on a stone or an island would rise out of the ocean and we would all perish on it in the dead of the night. Another man was afraid of whales and thought that this animal was so powerful that it could break and even capsize the frigate. My comrades, being idle and powerless witnesses to the means and efforts used for the keen navigation of the frigate, unaware of every effort being made around them and seeing danger in everything, passed only the most miserable judgements. Doubtful and concerned with everything outside of their knowledge and power, they were constantly trembling with fear of a premature death. Being dependent on the will of those who did not have the leisure to explain every movement and precaution was naturally very stressful.

On the 25th of October [6th of November], the northerly wind subsided, the clouds cleared and the waves quieted down. On the morning of the 26th [7th], the sun appeared and a southerly wind began to quietly blow, promising consistent fair weather. When we took observations at noon, we found ourselves at a latitude of 39 degrees, 27 minutes [North] and a distance of 154 *verstas* [164.29 km] from Cabo da Roca.[2] The passing wind gradually freshened and in the afternoon, the squadron proceeded under all sails along its present course at a speed of 18 *verstas* [19.2 km] per hour. Everything was now consigned to oblivion and the past seemed like a terrible dream as each man's soul rejoiced; boredom and uncertainty were replaced by hope and relief. As the period for reaching our home ports had already elapsed, and in order to avoid encounters with the British squadrons cruising the channel, the commander-in-chief decided to continue further from the coasts and bypass Britain along the western and northern sides to finally take shelter in the ports of Norway for the winter.

At 3 in the afternoon, the mercury in the barometer dropped unusually. The southerly wind grew so strong that the ships running downwind reefed their topsails. The clarity of the sky suddenly faded and gloomy clouds thickened and sank towards the sea. The sun glowed through the black clouds with a halo like a heated shot and foreshadowed a most terrible storm. At 4 o'clock, the admiral

---

2    This would produce a longitude of 11°11' W from the Greenwich Meridian or 13°21' from the Parisian Meridian.

signalled to spread out the line, prepare for a storm and carefully observe the movements of his ship during the night. The sun soon vanished and at 5 in the afternoon, it was as impenetrable as night. By 7, when the water became greatly agitated, a sudden southwesterly wind blew with a harsh squall. The sea began to boil with crossing waves and the whiteness of their crests was the only illumination to see in that terrible darkness. Sails were torn on every ship. Our frigate, heading on a broad reach was rolled over so far that her lower yards nearly touched the water and without sails but by the rigging alone, we flew so fast that the log broke off at 14 knots and we spanned over 25 *versta*s [26.67 km] in an hour. Despite the darkness, we suddenly saw a ship nearby. Turning the rudder to starboard, we came closer to them; turning to port, we nearly touched the admiral's flagship. The admiral's vessel burned several flares and the flashes of gun muzzles could be seen, though their thunder was inaudible. When the ship descended from the height of the waves' crests, it seemed to fall directly toward us – should they ever touch, in an instant, both vessels would be sent to the bottom of the sea. Our confusion at this time cannot be described. Finally, after overtaking the admiral's ship, we were free.

When the storm was in full force, as it was not possible to predict changes in the wind, around 9 o'clock the former northwesterly foul wind suddenly caught us with such a squall that the lower staysails were torn to pieces; the frigate thrown in such a rapid advance seemed to leave the stern behind, the masts creaked, several beams suddenly cracked, and a wave poured from the stern to the bow, spilling over the decks like a river. By special fortune, the frigate coasted with the wind without further damage. A new wind blew with such gusts that it was impossible to lift a single sail, new waves crashed into the previous ones which pitched our vessel so sharply it was impossible to walk without handholds. The frigate drew water on both sides, sometimes waves ran down the length from bow to stern, the walls separated from the decks and water passing through them to pool up in the hold and despite the fact that all the men were assigned to working the pumps, it did not decrease for some time. The frigate violently burrowed into the waves such that the lower gun ports were submerged and when rolling from side to side, the leeward chains were likewise plunged into the water. At 10 o'clock, the wind grew even stronger and the sky flashed with bolts of lightning but we could not hear the thunder over the roar of the wind. The power of heaven, the wind and the sea seemed united in our destruction. On one ship, a mast caught fire from a lightning strike and the sight of it will never fade from my memory: this minute seemed to be the last. Death in all its forms threatened us with either sinking or burning; the flaming ship soon disappeared in the darkness and its fate threatened to make us participants. The terrible pounding of the elements led us into a situation where there was no hope of salvation: the frigate was flooded by the waves, the men were knocked away from their labours and were all stricken with mortal fear, straining with their last desperate efforts while anticipating imminent death. But God in his wrath covered us with the shield of his mercy. The torrential rain extinguished the lightning and the wind softened such that at 1 in the morning we could already command the frigate under the lower staysails. If the storm – or better referred to as a hurricane – had lasted until dawn, then the whole squadron would certainly have been killed.

The coincidental circumstances of this storm are worthy of special comment. The 26th of October [7th of November] is the day of the Great Martyr Demetrius of Thessaloniki and the name day of our commander-in-chief Dmitriy Nikolayevich Senyavin. On that same day, in Saint Petersburg, it was announced that we officially broke relations with Great Britain and at the same time, perhaps the very same hour, the storm had begun which compelled us to seek refuge in the nearest port. This storm saved for Russia the better part of her fleet. According to the reports of the Lords Commissioners of the Admiralty in 1808, it was evident that in the month of October in Plymouth, a squadron of 14 ships was prepared which had the purpose of convincing or forcing our squadron to dock in England after passing the British blockade of Brest. If the foul wind lasted only a day, we would have had to fight against the 20 ships of the Brest squadron. If the foul wind kept us at sea for more than 3 days, then we could not enter Lisbon without a fight, as Sir Sidney Smith and his squadron would have planted their flag at the mouth of the Tagus for the blockade of that capital. Suppose that we, like the young David, would have succeeded in defeating the proud Goliath and beat the English; where would we find a place to winter? All the ports in the Atlantic and Mediterranean Sea were blocked by strong squadrons. Our situation was quite difficult and dangerous and what was it that saved us from inevitable death? The storm. Great is the Russian God and inscrutable are His judgements.

The foresight of the admiral saved us back in the archipelago. When Rear-Admiral Martin saluted him while standing on anchor at Tenedos, Senyavin thought that the British had some ulterior motive and when ship after ship formed a large squadron and finally Collingwood himself arrived, Senyavin became all the more cautious. As soon as word of the Treaty of Tilsit arrived, he immediately separated from the British under the convenient pretext of our relations with Turkey, rushed from Imbros to Tenedos and did not hesitate in returning to Corfu. If we delayed for several days, then the command of the British government to detain our fleet, despite the state of peace, would have been executed.

At dawn on the 27th of October [8th of November], not one ship was visible. The captain, believing that the squadron must have been under way on the wind, ordered us to turn to windward and within an hour we met the *Skoryy*, then another two ships and soon we were reunited with the admiral. The *Rafail* and *Svyataya*

The Fortress of São Julião at the Mouth of the Tagus. Illustration from the original publication. Despite the image's caption, it clearly depicts the Tower of Belém.

*Yelena* were missing. The mystery of their fate made us tremble for our comrades. Each ship approached the *Tvyordyy* and notified by signal what damages they had suffered. The *Yaroslav* signalled that she could not stay at sea and asked permission to shelter in the nearest port. The *Selafail*, despite the fact that the wind had quite subsided, indicated that she had a leak accruing 25 inches [63.5 cm] of water per hour. The *Retvizan* signalled that her rudder was damaged and could not follow the fleet. The *Silnyy* lost her main yard. All the other ships had severe damage and since the wind was foul and blew with strong gasps with no sign of changing, the admiral did not dare to defy fate any longer. To everyone's joy and relief, at noon he ordered the squadron to turn out of the wind and head to Lisbon.

On the 28th of October [9th of November], the wind subsided but continued to blow from the same direction and brought heavy cloud cover with it. At noon on the 29th [10th], sailing ahead of the fleet, we spotted the shore and informed the admiral. By evening, the Rock of Lisbon[3] appeared and we tacked in front of the entrance to the Tagus all night long under reefed staysails. On the 30th of October [11th of November], despite the strong wind and great agitation of the waves, a pilot arrived upon our signal and at 8 o'clock, the admiral led the squadron into the river. The local pilot craft have a strange appearance: they are covered with bulging decks with high bows and sterns, steep and curved in an arc. The bow is studded

---

3    Bronevskiy's note: 'The northern cape at the mouth of the Tagus River'.

with long nails, the stern is decorated with carvings representing a fish's tail and all their appearance is in some way like a flying fish. Their masts are low and hold triangular sails called lateens. Despite the repulsive appearance borrowed from Indian craft, they are not only easier under sails than the boats of the Dyle River and of Norway, but are safer and calmer on the waves than the English pilot boats.

# 100

# Lisbon

## Appearance and Advantages of the Port

The thick fog on the banks began to rise like a veil and as the squadron approached the mouth of the Tagus, objects were revealed to us, a multitude of fortresses and then the city itself rose out of the sea. As soon as we passed the first fort, São Julião, our ships finally stopped creaking and whining after some 40 days of continuous jostling on the sea. We stopped at the Tower of Belém. The *Rafail* and *Svyataya Yelena* had arrived there on the 28th of October [9th of November]. The former ship had its mizzen-mast burn down from the lightning strike, although the fire was extinguished, and some boards at the stern hung such that the ship took on water when it rolled. The upper deck had broken through from impacts and the ship was in serious danger. Despite the severe rolling, 18 guns were safely lowered from the upper deck into the hold. The skilful ship's carpenter, at the risk of his own life, managed to fix a sheath of planks to the transom and save the vessel. The *Svyataya Yelena*, also damaged, was accompanied to Lisbon upon signalling to the captain of the *Rafail* that he could not reach the port without escort. The squadron was assigned a six-day quarantine but the imposition was lifted the very same day on the admiral's testimony about the need to immediately repair damage to the *Rafail* and others.

The very next day, upon arrival in Lisbon, the admiral examined the ships and unfortunately saw that the entire squadron required vital repairs before they could sail on the open sea again. The Prince Regent[1] ordered that we acquire from the Lisbon dockyard everything necessary. The storm not only damaged the ships but deprived us of several men. On one ship, a sick officer was thrown out of his bed

---

1    The future King of Portugal, Brazil and Algarves, John VI, served as prince regiment from 1799 to 1816.

and killed; on another, two sailors were killed by lightning; on a third, a sailor was blown off a top-yard and fell into the water – a terrible death.

The mouth of the Tagus is disturbed by two shallows which form two fairways. By the latter, a citadel has been constructed to protect the entrance. Passing São Julião and keeping necessarily to the right, we came to the Belém on the left bank. Regular tides changing every six hours, depths between 10 and 25 *sazhen*s [21.34 to 53.34 m] and a muddy floor everywhere make the port of Lisbon one of the safest and best ports in the world. The ebb and flow make it possible at all times to enter and exit the river and also there is the convenience of the so-called six-hour docks to which a ship can be moored at low tide for a low price. In this respect, not even Constantinople can be compared with Lisbon. Looking on at such a majestic river, which from the mouth to the town has a distance of 13 *versta*s [13.87 km] and a width of 4 to 6 *versta*s [4.27 to 6.4 km], filled with ships of the line and a multitude of merchant vessels, it is impossible not to regret that our Neva, with all its beauty, does not have the same conveniences as the Tagus. The right bank of the river has a charming appearance. On that side can be seen two fortresses, many batteries, houses, gardens and monasteries. Behind Belém, on seven hills, a long amphitheatre of magnificent buildings appears before the eye and Lisbon is one of the capitals of Europe that can boast of having such an accommodating and beautiful position.

## Unpleasant Events

The hand of fate, having crushed Denmark, rushed to Portugal. Napoleon, who summoned to battle all the peoples of the continent against the arsonists of Copenhagen, decided at the same time to seize Portugal. The Prince Regent of Portugal did not secure anything by the concessions he made and having paid Napoleon 5,000,000 cruzados for his paternal patronage, he was then obligated to satisfy his every demand. On the 20th of October [1st of November], he declared himself to oppose England's war, yet Napoleon discovered a new cause for his scheme; his army crossed the Portuguese frontier on the pretext of rushing to Lisbon's defence against Britain. The Portuguese court quarrelled with Britain but could not defend itself against France with their aid and would not seek refuge in Brazil, which would have been easy prey for Britain at that time. The only course of action was to seek Britain's indulgence and George generously forgot his offence and lent aid to the royal family which had been so unusually deceived and oppressed. The court and many of the eminent families hurriedly prepared for departure, waiting hour by hour for Sidney Smith's squadron and the troop transports; but instead of the Royal Navy of Britain, they were met by a Russian squadron. The French spies who typically preceded their armies and the Englishmen remaining in Lisbon managed to spread foul rumours about our arrival. A new anxiety now gripped the court. On the 3rd [15th] of November, our admiral introduced himself to the Prince Regent and announced the reason for his arrival; all doubts were then dispelled and after an audience on the next day, the royal treasury was loaded onto a Portuguese squadron consisting of 7 ships, 3 frigates and 4 brigs.

## A Look at the City

As soon as we could go ashore, every ship's boats went into town with their officers. A crowd of curious people surrounded us on the embankment, with a surprising myriad of clothing and faces. Arabs, Negroes, Brazilians, Creoles, Mulattos and the residents of both West and East Indies in their costumes, along with the Portuguese in Spanish coats, tricorne hats and with their olive complexion represented a most unusual variety. The exterior of Lisbon promises more than it really contains. All the streets follow the slopes of the heights toward the embankment; some of them are wide, others are narrow and most of them are crooked. Between the hills, the streets are raised on arches so that when passing under them, the sound of the carriages can be heard overhead. Generally the city is not clean due to the fact that rubbish is never deliberately removed, since it is carried out to the river with the first rainfall. Traces of the terrible earthquake of 1755 can still be seen in certain quarters. The courage of these people is surprising when one considers how they erect massive, heavy buildings over the ruins and volcanic ash which ought to remind them of the burning earth beneath them and the splendour of the present is enough to erase the memories of their terrible past. Unfortunately, poor buildings with their rear sides facing the embankment detract from the view.

One market square (the *Praça do Comércio*) is built up with government offices of uniform design and a bronze monument to Joseph I has been placed in the centre, looking as if he is watching over the lovely river. The square always has a throng of people. From the square, to the right stands a ceremonial gate decorated with Doric columns. Among the public buildings and private houses, there are none who would draw special attention to their appearance; generally the structures have a heavy architecture with many balconies enclosed with tall iron bars. All the shops and magazines are filled with English goods which were being sold very cheaply in anticipation of the imminent arrival of their uninvited guests, the gentlemen of France. The British merchants and their offices could not save all of their property, as even a thousand ships would not be enough to evacuate all of their wares. They suffered a tremendous loss, as it can be said that until now, Portugal had been rented to Britain; not only essentials but also luxury items were delivered from Britain. For as many factories as there are in Portugal, almost all of them belong to the British, who have appropriated the domestic and foreign trade and all of the turnover, just as for us the Jews in Poland have become necessary for the people. It is possible then to judge how well the poor Portuguese should fare when the French arrive and expel the British.

The cathedral, for all of its vastness, survived the earthquake. It had a gothic appearance in which there is neither accuracy nor taste; yet this temple is considered the richest in Europe and its treasures are matched with El Escorial. I saw much gold, silver, precious stones and pearls, but in such a way that their values could not be appreciated. In ornamentation, there was neither anything legible nor artful and everything was covered with sacred dust, which it seems one dare not touch.

The Royal Basilica is considered the finest in Lisbon. The marble of this church was gathered in Rome and after being consecrated by the Pope, was broken and transported by ship to Lisbon. This church is built on an elevation open on all sides; the front faces the river and is decorated with 16 columns. The most beautiful dome and statues placed on the ends of the portico distinguish this church from all the other buildings of Lisbon and it will attract your eye no matter from which direction you enter the city. On entering, it is impossible not to praise both the elegance of the architecture and the position of the ornaments, though the abundance of silver columns, bronze and enamel decoration and gold encrusted with diamonds enclosing the paintings obscure the majestic and simple beauty of this temple. Removing the unnecessary flourishes and uncovering the painting and beautiful mosaic, this temple would have presented itself in the best possible form; for such a multitude of jewels conceal the best in it and produce exactly the impression that a young girl makes when instead of a simple white dress and one flower on his breast with simple diamond earrings, she would adore herself in a brocade robe with a large bouquet on both arms and weighted down her head, arms and neck with golden chains, diamonds, pearls and a centrepiece of coral or amber – wearing every heirloom her grandmother gave her.

There are 130 churches and monasteries in Lisbon, all of them generally in the Gothic style, with arches and very dark within as the windows are guarded with thick iron grating and set so high that the light barely reaches the floor. The monks enjoy great advantages, are very rich and live luxuriously. A convent sponsored by the piety of the present queen[2] is the only one that can be said to belong to the latest architecture. There is neither an excess nor a deficiency of rich ornamentations in it; a greater number of the images are well painted and the best of all is of Mary Magdalene. In it can be seen true repentance; her eyes are reddened from tears and all of her facial features so faithfully depict the feeling of the heart tempered for the Light and for zealous devotion to God that you doubt she had experienced the brutal trials of the Passion. The pious artist wished to portray a saint, not a

---

2    Carlota Joaquina was Queen Consort of Portugal from 1816 to 1826.

picture of a beautiful woman in grief and tears, where the delights of the lily white breast barely covered with her dishevelled hair and where the face, figure, hands and even the position on one knee would show only the cause of repentance and not the repentance itself. The Magdalenes I saw in Palermo and Malta, although considered miracles of art, I would place among drawings, but this work I would place among the icons and gladly light a candle before her. At the gate, I was shown a rare depiction of purgatory in fresco. In fact, the image of the flaming Gehenna, the multifarious tortures of the sinners, the terrible sight of the demons with sharp canine teeth, horns and tails, was amazingly terrifying. In eternal torment, where a special punishment was imposed on every sin, you look for your own fate among them and tremble.

## An Unexpected Outcome

Every day, I spent two hours to take a walk and learned so much of Lisbon that still today I would not get lost in it. On one quiet evening with two companions, we agreed to go to the theatre. The street we walked was illuminated; the doors and windows everywhere were open and at one house where we heard a soft music and a charming woman's voice, we stopped under a lantern and were spotted then by two ladies sitting on a balcony. One of them said something to us and made a sign for us to enter. Not wanting to understand such an invitation, we went away and barely took a few steps before a young man in a smart suit, holding his cloak in one hand to reveal that he was wearing a long sword, convincingly asked us to pay him a visit in a form of Italian barely understandable to us. Glancing at each other, we smiled, agreed and followed him. In the rather untidy anteroom, to which the staircase was very narrow and dirty, we were received by an old woman and two young brunettes. Then they led us into a large chamber decorated with silk wallpaper, fine furniture, and marble tables surmounted by vases of flowers, each with a mirror hanging above. The hostess put us on two sofas and the girls sat between us without any timidity. Satisfied with this reception, instead of going to the theatre, we decided to stay for two hours. But with much awkwardness and vexation, we could not understand each other. The gentleman spoke in some sort of Italian dialect into which he introduced several English half-words and chimeras which made him completely unintelligible; we began to speak in French, in English, in German; the ladies clapped their hands and answered in Portuguese or maybe in Chinese; from both sides we vainly laboured to make ourselves understood.

Finally the man spoke with the ladies, retrieved his hat and left. The old woman came out for something, the girls took us by the hand and led us to show their chambers and either sat down at the harpsichord or pointed to the river through the window. We were surprised and did not know what to think, reasoning among ourselves that it was well that they could not understand us. The young man soon returned with another, who could speak English. We then learned that we were in the home of a rich merchant who was trading in Brazilian diamonds, that the young man was a bachelor, the son of the woman and brother to the two girls. We were served cigars and cups of chocolate.

We were compelled to bow out for the sake of the theatre and confessed to the deceitfulness of our daydreaming. To our surprise, we learned that this act was not necessary any longer, as the women were curious to see the foreigners who were said to be respected and wanted to learn from them whether they really came to convince the Prince Regent to mount a defence against the French or not; whether we really brought an army of 100,000 men on just ten ships and so on.

Our arrival in Lisbon created a lot of commotion. The French agents tried their best to calm the people, to find sympathizers and boast about the close alliance of France with Russia, and dared to convince everyone that our admiral had been ordered to detain the Portuguese fleet. Minds were agitated, the news changed hourly, and the people, seeing the preparations for the departure of the royal family and feeling devotion to them, demanded arms. The government tried by every means to curtail this useless enthusiasm. The Regent was very active and often showed himself to the people and was received with shouts of joy. Crowds followed him everywhere and dropped to their knees or laid down flat in front of and behind his coach, frequently shouting: 'stay with us, do not leave us, we are ready to die for you and the fatherland'. The unfortunate prince, with a sad glance and mournful silence, sometimes turned his eyes to the sky. Once, despite the crowded street, I managed to see this touching spectacle. The Prince Regent rode across the square where soldiers were standing in parade and the soldiers ceaselessly shouted: 'long live the House of Braganza!' Sadly he did not stop and rode his carriage straight to the offices of the Supreme Council where he worked every day.

## The Theatre

The local theatre appeared very much like our Stone Theatre in St. Petersburg, but it seemed even more enormous. The boxes are separated from one another by partitions and decorated by extravagant luxury with mirrors, brocade and satin everywhere. The spectators that rent them are free to decorate them as they please, and this diversity of décor is more engrossing than pleasing to the eye. The Italian operas that are always here are produced by excellent talents; the ballet is also comprised of Italian dancers. I attended the national theatre, but as I did not understand anything, I would not comment on the amorous interlude where Harlequin and his constant companion Columbina of the Italian theatre, under different names and superb costumes here, play the first roles. The Portuguese music, with a harmony and simplicity resembling the Italian, and their dancing likewise displaying many bold – even indecent for the theatre – movements, show that the Portuguese share a lineage with the Italian people just as they share the same hot sky in the lands they populate. A folk dance called the *foffa* is very lively and full of voluptuous expressions, but without any tenderness or temptation, like, for example, a pantomime of our Russian dances or in the Italian *tarantella*. The Portuguese passionately love music and one can sail along the river every quiet evening and hear beautiful wind instruments and in the town, one often meets parties of young and noble people singing serenades beneath the windows of their beloved. Guitars, mandolins, flageolets or oboes combined in a trio are the most exquisite. This kind of courtship is very popular here; ladies listen with pleasure to these gentle songs that have long been composed for all kinds of love and are unashamed to throw a flower or two from their window or balcony in the fashion of Céladon.[3]

## The Aqueduct

The time was cloudy and rainy and having my health agitated by a prolonged, stormy voyage, I could not see all the sights of Lisbon, but after waiting for the first good day, I hired a wheeled sedan for four cruzados, drawn by an Italian, and ordered him to carry me to the aqueduct. Nothing can be more calm than this type of carriage, sitting in an armchair closed from the rain and dust and without the slightest sensation of jostling, crossing roughly six *verstas* [6.04 km] in an hour. The aqueduct is not far from the suburbs. As the Tagus River receives a large amount of water from the ocean at high tide, the supply tastes quite salty and is unfit to drink, which is the reason for the construction of a glorious aqueduct. Its strength, beauty and splendour are not inferior to those of the ancient Romans and Arabs. It was erected in 1748 during the reign of King John V by the famous architect Manuel de Maia; I say 'erected' because its height is quite excessive. Imagine a channel of water lying on an arcade with a height of 30 to 38 *sazhens* [64 to 81.08 m]. These arcades connect the hills and pass through the Alcântara valley, surrounded by carefully cultivated lemon and orange orchards and vineyards, in whose shade are scattered the handsome country houses of the affluent. One can reach the top of the arcades by scaling a staircase enclosed by beautiful iron fencing. On both sides of the channel are platforms of white marble. On good days, the residents of Lisbon come here for strolling; the sight of the surrounding

---

3    Céladon and Astrée are the central characters of the celebrated 17th century French novel *L'Astrée* by Honoré d'Urfé and Balthazar Baro. Despite many schemes and contrivances and the countless digressions of other characters who struggle with vices and dilemmas, their romance is expressed as an ideal, sublime and chaste love.

landscape, the vast city, the majestic river full of vessels coming and going to all the corners of the globe and lastly the view of the endless ocean produce such an image that one look at the panorama surprises the eye and imagination. I stayed in one place for a while and as I turned around I saw everywhere wonderful places, favoured by all the gifts of nature. The greenery was as tender as we have in May, sweet and bitter orange trees were blossoming and the rain that had fallen recently filled the air with fragrances.

## The Inquisition

Crossing through Rossio Square and seeing a massive Gothic building with small windows screened with iron bars, I asked: 'is this the city prison?'

'The Holy Inquisition', answered my guide.

'The Inquisition!' I repeated with horror, stopped and looked at the building. I silently argued with myself: how is this den of cruel fanaticism, this despicable hell contrary to the meekness of the Christian faith, humiliating to humanity, desecrating the Altar of the All-Merciful Creator, still tolerated in our enlightened age and the tears of the innocent still flow by their hands? Is it still now the ambition of those who should comfortably set an example of grace and patience, who vowed to be the mediators of our weaknesses and delusions, to instead demand bloody sacrifices and slaughter in the name of God? I shuddered. Here is the final monument in Europe to the savagery of barbaric superstition. Here is the only object in Lisbon worthy of being exterminated and the first reason why one could wish for the speedy arrival of the French here.

The verdicts of the Inquisitional court, on which the power of the clergy was based, are described by history with bloody strokes. We will open several pages of this superstitious period and despair over the millions of martyrs who died for their opinions not against the true faith, but only contrary to the ambition of the clergy. When the popes took advantage of the cases which superstition presented to them, they became powerful temporal monarchs; with the aid of a curse, war could be waged without an army and peace could be concluded; when absolving subjects of their oaths could deprive kings of their thrones and by their own will they could depose others of their property; then the clergy received great advantages, first of which being the court and its retributive verdicts, both civil and religious. The abuses of power soon became excessive. The popes, like the Tribe of Levi, charging a tenth of the incomes of the Christian states, easily amassed great riches. Every war in those times began with the blessing of the pope in Christ's name and therefore they were the most implacable and bloody. That was why Cortez and Pizarro, having conquered Mexico and Peru and exterminating millions of non-Catholics, could insult the mercy of the All-Benevolent and think to please God by burning and killing the Peruvians, attributing to their own honour what we now find terrifying. Finally the seductive conduct of the clergy, their cruelty and the just desire of the sovereigns to free themselves from the power of the pope precipitated the division and transformation of the western church. The invention of the printing press and the Reformation which broke out in 1517 [with the publication of Martin Luther's 95 Theses] were the most active means to weaken the power of the pope and the clergy. To maintain this wavering power, the Tribunal of the Inquisition had its inception.[4] The fires were stoked and in them thousands were killed according to spite and private revenge and by these horrors, the authority of the clergy was restored. In Portugal, this tribunal was established under John III in 1536.

After the completion of the Reformation and the prolonged wars of faith were lifted, Europe was driven into a new brutal and bloody struggle. The intolerance of the faith of the Catholics and Lutherans remained in equal force. In the Catholic lands, the persecution of other faiths was entrusted to the Inquisition and this persecution was terrible. According to a single opinion, sometimes based on the personal grudge of a priest with a citizen, one word on the subject of religion or especially criticism of the clergy spoken in the company of friends was enough to administer torture and painful death. This religious frenzy with a secret destructiveness had eagerly awaited the day that the Inquisition would be instituted on Portugal and Spain, that they might burn several Jews in revenge for the death of Jesus Christ. The affairs of the Inquisition were not subject to any authority and therefore not infrequently the kings themselves trembled before this secret tribunal. Today, the influence of the beneficial enlightenment has weakened the authority of the Inquisition and the Prince Regent had placed limits on it. This court now only cares about the preservation and integrity of the faith.

## Thoughts and Remarks

Sea voyages with many tribulations give a singular pleasure; one is virtually instantly conveyed from country to country and in a short time becomes acquainted with people living on opposite ends of the globe and in this travel, the martyrs of curiosity – so I might call every seafarer – find new fodder for their observations. How long were we in Greece, viewing its ruins, before suddenly finding ourselves in the capital of Portugal, where we never imagined ourselves setting foot. Everywhere we saw new customs, wholly distinct as much in nature itself as in clothing and manners, and in time they become ordinary; but nowhere

---

4    The institution of the Inquisition itself was established from 1229-33 by Pope Gregory IX and the Spanish Inquisition in particular was established in 1478 by papal bull at the request of Queen Isabella. Jean Antoine Llorente, *The History of the Inquisition of Spain* (London: G. B. Whittaker, 1826), pp.14-32.

were my gaze and thoughts as amazed by such variety as in Lisbon. It seemed to me that this place was populated by the inhabitants of some other part of the world. The reason for this is obvious: conducting trade with Brazil and India, Portugal adopted many Asian customs and mixed them with their own, thereby resembling very little the way of life of other Europeans. Here are some examples.

By virtue of the city's mountainous position, I saw few carriages but instead there were many sedans, very rich, gilded on their exterior and upholstered with velvet or brocade and trimmed with green curtains. The cry of the porters and the many servants surrounding the sedans create something extraordinary and evocative of Asia. The women here, despite their olive skin, are very pretty, slender, have beautiful black eyes, are lively, and a quick look reveals their great desire to please. Robes of black taffeta with many pleats, their usual and everyday attire, unfortunately deprive them of many charms, for which they compensate with many inappropriate precious stones, pearls and golden pendants. Their black curls lay loose on their shoulders interwoven with ribbons and flowers. When the ladies go for a walk, the black maidens dressed with the same exactness protect themselves from the sun by holding wondrous parasols above their heads. The ladies here are very devout and do not miss a single ceremony; not one mass or vespers. They spend their time going from church to church and so every day they take the opportunity to show off their splendid attire and boast of their numerous escorts. When they are not in church, they are sitting by the windows or on the balconies. Here, the fashion adorned by the Negress, with her curly woolen hair, shiny face and thick lips, is on par with any beauty. Creoles and Mulattas are very slender and always have an exposed and beautifully shaped neck and a gentle countenance, only occasionally surpassed by the Arab women. For this injustice, the poor women of Lisbon have every reason to complain; it would be unfair to reproach them for their free circulation and if during carnival holidays, they enjoy great liberties, then they are justified by the fact that their husbands have the most ruinous taste.

The theatre, masquerade, riding on boats up the river and strolling through the gardens near the city comprise the favourite pastimes of the whole world. The rich nobility live with extravagant luxury, and as everywhere else, they imitate other people's customs. The pride of the grandees, venerating titles and accidents of birth above all merits, is the source of many elegant qualities that make up true nobility. This pride makes them generous and virtuous. A nobleman, even a merchant, will never allow himself to commit a low act. A foreigner in other lands always has to be careful but here he can give his confidence to any man wearing a sword. The political weakness of the state, although making the Portuguese somewhat inactive and letting their enterprise and industry almost wholly fail, has not yet extinguished their spirit. They did not exhibit the sort of humiliation found in the last stage before annihilation; on the contrary, the Portuguese did not forget the glory of their ancestors whose bravery still smoulders like a spark under the ashes. And if that spark should be uncovered and fanned, the Bonapartists would not so easily smother that fire.

Here are some customs which are strange for a European: the women, instead of sitting comfortably on the back of a donkey, ride up closer to the neck. The tailor serves the same role as the shoemaker. The hairdresser covers his powdered hair with a hat, carries his sword in his hand, and wears two watches or perhaps he only has two chains. The commoners wear cloaks that give them a noble appearance and they are quite polite people. The Portuguese will not pass by a nobleman or foreigner without giving him his right hand as a sign of respect and to every acquaintance he meets on the street, he will not forget to remove his hat, bow and say: 'may God keep you for many years'. They sit with their legs crossed in the custom of the Moors. There are few beggars here and they are not as bothersome as in Italy; there are no murderers among them. The Portuguese only kill to avenge an insult. The day labourers and generally everyone working along Lisbon's riverfront are very poor in appearance and their only luxury is tobacco. A piece of bread, cod or herring and some green vegetables comprise their daily diet. This poverty or rather the appearance of poverty is voluntary. The people who live in hot climates where nature is generously abundant do not feel the sort of cold that would compel them to build warm houses and cover themselves with heavy clothing. They do not worry about their appearance and wear the same dress at all times of year. For the same reason, with little difficulty of procuring food, they have no fear of hunger for should their bread run out, fruits and nuts would replace it and the gifts of the forest are forever ready. There is never frost nor starvation here and the forest seems to be a bountiful resource for all the peoples living in the fertile lands of the south. The Portuguese regard their country as an earthly paradise and Lisbon as a miracle among cities, the greatest and richest in all the world.

## A Brief History of Portugal

Portugal in antiquity was known as Lusitania. Legend attributes this name to Lusus, son of Bacchus, who they say established a colony here. The modern name of Portugal comes from 'cale' or 'cala', meaning 'harbour' to the Celts due to the many good marinas located along the coast with the superfluous addition of 'porta'. Another theory is that Portugal is from 'Portus Gallorum' – the Port of the Gauls; as when Spain was controlled by the Moors, the Portuguese ports were then mostly visited by the Gauls. The origin of the name of Lisbon, some say, is derived from Ulysses, who founded the city on the Tagus estuary after the destruction of Troy and named it Olisippo. When Lusitania became a Roman province, they named the city Olisipo Felicitas Julia.

Portugal shared its fate with the Spanish provinces. Being a theatre of bloody battles between the Carthaginians and Romans and then passing from conqueror to conqueror after the fall of the empire, alternatively seeing the Suebi, Alans, Visigoths and finally the Moors as their rulers, it was freed from the latter's yoke by the sovereigns of Spain. Alfonso I, King of Asturias, in 745AD conquered what is now Portugal and then 300 years later Ferdinand the Great, wearing the crowns of both Leon and Castile, extended this conquest to the Mondego River. At the end of the 11th century, Alfonso VI gave Portugal with the rank of a county to Henry of Burgundy, a descendent of Hugh Capet. Since then, Spain was divided into two states and Portugal has hence remained foreign to her.

Count Henry, expanding the frontiers of his territory, managed to become independent. His son, Alfonso, in 1139 won a famous victory at Ourique with a small army against the numerous force of Mauritania (the Almoravids). He was proclaimed to be king by his soldiers on the battlefield and solemnly crowned at Lamego, and despite the obstruction from Castile to whom he still paid four ounces of gold yearly, the new king managed to persuade the pope to recognize him as an independent sovereign. The descendants of Alfonso, who reigned until 1383, guided the formation of the kingdom and already possessed a small navy. Among them, Denis I built many cities and elaborated on Lisbon, established the Military Order of Christ (to salvage the purged Knights Templar) and was successful in all his enterprises and was named Father of the Nation. After the death of Ferdinand I, the line of succession was broken and the King of Castile endeavoured to conquer Portugal but John I, Master of the Order of Aviz, defeated his army at Lisbon. On the battlefield, he received the sceptre and became the founder of a new dynasty.

John I, through victories and prudent rule, elevated Portugal to the highest degree of prosperity. Science and commerce flourished, he conquered Ceuta with his army and with his navy the islands of Madeira, the Azores and portions of the west coast of Africa. In 1478 during the reign of Alfonso V, Guinea was discovered and under his successor John II, the Cape of Good Hope was revealed. In the reign of Emmanuel the Fortunate, Vasco de Gama rounded the Cape of Good Hope and discovered the shortest route to East India while Juan Alvarez de Cabral, commander of another squadron, inadvertently found the coast of Brazil. These two discoveries brought to Portugal the treasures of world trade and so a small state rose to the degree of the foremost naval powers, instantly enriched, magnified and intensified. Under John III, the glorious general Albuquerque, by daring and successful conquests in the East Indies, brought honour to the arms of Portugal. In 1578, Sebastian embarked on a crusade against the Moors in Africa but was killed and the battle was lost. His great-uncle, the Cardinal Henry, reigned as King Henry II for just two years before dying with no heirs, bringing the second dynasty to a close.

By force and politics, Phillip II [of Spain] managed to subdue Portugal and for sixty years, the land was regarded as a province of Spain, though the Portuguese thought differently. At the time, the English and Dutch had conquered many of their possessions around the world. The cruel policies of the Spanish government aroused the ire of the Portuguese and after many efforts under the leadership of the Duke of Braganza, proclaimed King John IV, they secured their independence and restored much of their former possessions except for Ceuta. His son, Alfonso, having quarrelled with his wife and brother Peter, was forced to divorce his wife at the behest of the pope and then concede the crown to Peter. Joseph I was the most unfortunate and cruel of the kings of Portugal. During his reign, in 1755, a terrible earthquake devastated his whole kingdom. The Jesuits, suspected of plotting against his life, were expelled and their property was taken into the treasury. All the policies of this king hurried the decline of the realm, its power and productivity were at their lowest level, and the kingdom fell into dependency under Britain with a seemingly incurable damage. Fortunately for Portugal, the Marquis of Pombal in the post of prime minister received unlimited authority in his government. Pombal was the sort of great man that, as Schiller would say, challenged his century to a fight and using its own arms against it he was always triumphant. He rooted out the evil at its very source, restored the dignity of the throne, limited the power of the grandees and the clergy, weakened the influence of Britain, restored domestic industry and finally brought rational order to all the components of the realm. Yet the intrigues of the courtiers hindered the minister via outside forces and the difficult works he had begun remained imperfect and incomplete. In 1762, when the war between Spain and Britain broke out, the Kings of Spain and France proposed to the King of Portugal to join them and accept their garrisons in his seaside towns. Joseph declared war against them and the Spaniards crossed the border without resistance and being satisfied with their initial success, they continued to prosecute the war rather inactively. France did nothing but threaten invasion. The Count of Schaumburg-Lippe, commanding the Portuguese army and receiving several British battalions as reinforcements, halted the Spanish advances and drove them back to the frontier, saving Portugal.

Maria Isabel, the late queen and daughter of Joseph, assumed control of the government in 1777, immediately dismissed the famous Pombal and effectively reversed all the useful reforms that he introduced, restoring the mismanagement and inaction of former reigns and so confounding Portugal's foreign and domestic affairs. By excessive piety, the queen became a hypochondriac and was consigned to the Mafra Convent in 1792 after becoming incapable of ruling and gave herself over to devout pursuits.[5] Her son John from then on ruled the kingdom in his mother's name. With the onset of the revolution, the Prince Regent, allied with Britain, took little part in the war against France and later Spain. According to the Treaty of Badajoz [and Treaty of Madrid] signed in 1801, the fortress of Olivenza was ceded to Spain and a portion of Guiana to France. Now Portugal is preparing for the final blow and the court, in order to preserve its independence, has decided in desperation to carry out that advice which Pombal had given to King Joseph – to reside permanently in Brazil.

5    Maria resided in the Palace of Queluz during her incapability, not the convent or palace at Mafra. Neill Macaulay, *Dom Pedro: The Struggle for Liberty in Brazil and Portugal, 1798-1834* (Durham, North Carolina: Duke University Press, 1986), pp.2-3.

# 101

# The Actions of Commodore Baratynskiy's Squadron in 1807 before its Arrival in Portoferraio

Upon the departure of the commander-in-chief for the Greek archipelago, Captain-Commodore Ilya Andreyevich Baratynskiy, established four major positions for the blockade of Ragusa and Dalmatia: in the channel of Calamotta and by the islands of Curzola and Brazza and the peninsula of Cesto so that all communication by sea between the islands and shore were severed. In early January, the French landed 2,000 men on the island of Brazza, burned down several local homes and spread a rumour that Marmont intended on capturing the fortress of Curzola, but at the end of the month, they left the islands, began to withdraw their cannons to Zara and left only small garrisons in other fortresses; most of General Marmont's corps left Dalmatia by small detachments through the Austrian Littoral for Italy. A rumour quickly spread that under some secret treaty, the French would surrender Dalmatia to the Austrians who, in addition to the 3,000 men who were under the watch of our ships off the island of Giuppana, another 5,000 were preparing in Fiume, giving the commodore reason to take additional measures so that the Austrians might lose hope of exploiting the situation. After a long period of inactivity, they finally withdrew from Giuppana and returned to Trieste on the 4th [16th] of March. The people of Dalmatia asked for aid in the event that the French withdrew and at the same time announced that they would not accept any other army on their land but Russia's.

The commander of the frigate *Avtroil*, Captain-Lieutenant Dmitriy Bizyukin, in order to verify that the residents were correct in reporting that the French carried most of their guns from Spalatro to Zara, sailed along the coast on the 3rd [15th] of February as the wind permitted, approaching close enough to inspect all aspects of the fortifications. When the frigate approached the town, the wind suddenly died down and the waves brought the frigate within range. The enemy opened fire from two batteries built on the capes of the harbour with six large calibre guns as well as with two gunboats but the latter were quickly driven off. The cannonade on both sides lasted for an hour and 15 minutes before the frigate retreated on the refreshing wind and had no serious damage besides some broken rigging and holes in the sails and two men were injured by splinters. The residents who came from Spalatro would claim that the French suffered 5 killed and 4 wounded, as well as one of the battery guns being damaged.

The chieftains of Herzegovina, wishing to throw off the Turkish yoke, asked us for help. State Councillor Sankovskiy also insisted and strengthened his argument with the order from the Minister of Foreign Affairs Budberg to defend the Slavs from the Turks in any way possible.[1] Taking the orders of the commander-in-chief into consideration, the commodore did not undertake any expeditions against the Turks or French and tried only to take the best measures to defend Cattaro from two such powerful neighbours. He did not agree with the opinion of Sankovskiy nor with Colonel Knieper of the 14th Jägers who commanded the ground forces in Cattaro; but at a general council with the Metropolitan, Sankovskiy, Knieper and the commodore all present, it was decided to attack the Turks with two detachments. On the 2nd [14th] of April, a detachment of 1,000 regulars under the command of Lieutenant-Colonel Kirill Zabelin came from Risan to Nikšić, a town not far from the frontier. At the same time, the Montenegrins under the Metropolitan's command marched with them. A detachment of Bokez occupied the border settlement of Zubcov, while another with two companies of regulars marched from Castelnuovo to Trebinje and feigned an attack on Ragusa. The commodore also sailed to Ragusa with two ships in order to distract the attention of the French. This expedition ended without any apparent benefit. Despite the prohibition of the Metropolitan, the Montenegrins had only just entered Herzegovina when they began to drive off cattle, rob, and even disarm the inhabitants; for this reason, the locals retired to the fortress of Nikšić and were prepared to defend themselves against us. Lieutenant-Colonel Zabelin, encircling the fort, was ready to storm it but after Mr Sankovskiy's failure to provide provisions promised, going for three days without food and not seeing any possibility of restraining the Montenegrins despite all the Metropolitan's efforts, he decided to withdraw back to Montenegro, which proved fortunate as his detachment was forced to fight nigh constantly against a numerically superior Turkish force of infantry and cavalry with significant casualties. Despite all their courage, the Turkish mobs could not stop him. The detachment of Bokez reinforced by two companies of Jägers under the command of Lieutenant-Colonel Radulovich reached Trebinje and took

---

1    Baron Adreas Ebenhard (Andrey Yakovlevich) von Budberg served as Russia's Minister of Foreign Affairs from 1806 to 1808. Andreyevskiy et al., *Brockhaus and Efron Dictionary*, s.v. 'Будбергъ'. [Andreyevskiy et al., *Brockhaus and Efron Dictionary*, s.v. 'The Budbergs'.]

several Turkish banners in light skirmishes. The Bokez maintained good order, fought courageously and precisely obeyed the orders of our officers appointed to command them. Soon after the return to Cattaro, the chieftains of Herzegovina asked again through the mediation of Sankovskiy for assistance against the Turks, but it was no longer possible to attempt such an operation with a sufficient number of regulars without weakening the defence of Cattaro and the Montenegrins could not be relied on for assistance. At a second council, Sankovskiy failed to convince the others and taking into account a doubt that the Herzegovinians could levy enough warriors for the liberation of their country, the proposal of sending military aid was rejected.

At the same time, it is necessary to note that here, as in all the Slavonian lands, the number of warriors is counted according to the number of weapons that can be brought to bear, which is nearly the whole [male] population, for everyone from 16 to 60 years old will take the field when necessary. Paying due justice to the bravery, diligence and devotion to Russia among the Slavs, it is not imprudent to have caution just the same in order to not rely on their numbers or their promises which, although sincere, cannot be fulfilled by the manner in which they wage war. They never undertake long-distance campaigns and do not remain on the field for more than a week or ten days at most. Having given battle, defeated the enemy and subjected the local villages to the torch, they immediately return home with their loot. With regular armies, especially ours, their courage can be utilized but only for a single battle, as after that, each of them returns home for provisions or for personal economical concerns and rarely do they agree to follow an army for more than 50 *versta*s [53.34 km] from their home village. Therefore, in the company of a great multitude of these mobs who come and go of their own volition and who do not tolerate any subordination, a small regular force may suddenly find itself abandoned at the most critical moment and put in terrible danger. Even after a decisive victory procured in part by their courage, it is not possible to take any advantage from it.

The occupation of Dalmatia by the French will remain forever memorable for the unfortunate populace. Heavy taxes, conscription, a halt to trade and incredible harassment for the slightest suspicion of loyalty to the Russians could not humiliate the spirit of the brave people, despite all the horrors of military autocracy. Their patience reached its limit and the Slavonians vowed to either overthrow their oppressors or perish. The residents from Spalatro to the Narenta agreed to attack the French in coordination and sent trusted persons to Curzola to ask for assistance, assuring us of the sincere and common desire of the whole people to finally unite with the mother of their fatherland, Russia. Commodore Baratynskiy, unable to dispatch even a thousand men from Cattaro, did not dare to promise much. However, for taking proper measures in the area, he loaded six companies of Jägers aboard a ship and two transports and left Cattaro for Curzola on the 12th [24th] of May. Three days after the commodore's arrival on Curzola, the Hieromonk[2] Spyridon, who was in Dalmatia for communicating with the locals, informed Baratynskiy that an uprising had already begun. Preparations were made with such secrecy that the French did not suspect anything, but one event inadvertently ignited the rebellion before the assigned date. A courier sent from Zara to Spalatro was killed. The French shot several peasants and set fire to the village where the murder had occurred; the fire was a signal for a general uprising and alarms were sounded in the Principality of Poljica. After three days, the banner of rebellion flew in every locale from Poljica (Omiš) to the Narenta River. The patriots furiously attacked and the small, scattered detachments of the French were destroyed. These Slavs were prepared to die and showed no mercy, but since some regions were unprepared and others did not agree to join in, the lively General Marmont succeeded in gathering his forces in the greater fortresses and sallied out with the sword of vengeance, executing anyone taken prisoner and razing their villages. The patriots attacked day and night and did not think to save their lives or their property and neither their own deaths, nor the superior tactics or brutality of the French could discourage them. The fires and bloodshed were terrible. Commodore Baratynskiy was held up in Curzola by foul winds when he received news of the uprising. The crowds of the people, not having a mighty leader to guide them toward a certain goal, began to thin out and separate and the French soon occupied the whole seashore as before.

On the 22nd of May [3rd of June], Baratynskiy arrived with a landing force in Brazza, from which he took with him the frigate *Avtroil*, the corvette *Dyerzkiy*, the cutter *Strela* and the brigs *Aleksandr* and *Letun* and passed the town of Poljica lying several miles from Spalatro. The chieftains of this place immediately came aboard the commodore's ship and begged for our assistance against the enemy. The commodore, not having sufficient ground forces with him, asked them to be patient, but as it was no longer in their power to stop the uprising, he promised them possible aid and the patronage of our Sovereign Emperor. When the Russian vessels appeared, the patriots cheered, assembled and on the 25th of May [6th of June] launched a new courageous attack on the French. As the battle raged on the seashore, the squadron weighed anchor, approached closely and began to intensively fire grapeshot at the enemy, driving them back into the cover of their fortress. On the 26th [7th], five companies of soldiers and several sailors were landed not far from Spalatro. The French soon appeared on the heights on both

---

2    Both a monk and priest; either a monk that has been ordained or a priest that has taken the tonsure. Andreyevskiy et al., *Brockhaus and Efron Dictionary*, s.v. 'Иеромонах'. [Andreyevskiy et al., *Brockhaus and Efron Dictionary*, s.v. 'Hieromonk'.]

sides in such strong numbers that our forces, together with 1,500 Dalmatians, retreated back onto the vessels of the squadron. Although the enemy dispersed amongst the rocks and intended to discourage our return, they were amazed by our solid shot and grape fired from the frigates and armed launches and soon retreated with visible losses.

On the 27th of May [8th of June], when the *Moskva*, two corsairs and two transports with the remainder of the landing forces joined the squadron, the commodore, intending to worry the enemy and encourage the locals as much as possible, weighed anchor and moved south along the shore. The French were compelled to follow the ships along the shore down a difficult road and through stony mountains, in terrible heat and while being constantly harassed by the local patriots, in order to ensure that we did not land somewhere and capture a strong and critical position. The commodore, having halted the enemy marching behind him, approached the small ancient fortress of Almissa (Omiš) on the 28th of May [9th of June], landed 800 men and captured several Frenchmen within. On the 30th [11th], the enemy occupied the heights surrounding the fort, placed two guns in an ideal position and attacked it resolutely. The *Letun* entered the mouth of the Cetina River beside the fort with the aid of the gunboats and armed launches and fired her guns all day. Our soldiers confounded the enemy's every attempt with characteristic courage, though some 2,000 men had come to bolster their assault. Major Lazovitskiy, the commander of the detachment, being surrounded on all sides, received orders to leave the fortress in the night and fortunately deceived the vigilance of the French to return to our ships with only one dead and two wounded. The enemy only noticed our absence at dawn and rushed to the shore but were greeted with grapeshot and canister and retreated again. In this action, it is impossible not to pay notice to the brave deed of Midshipman Faddey von Tiesenhausen. He entered the town with one other sailor even before the capture of the fortress of Almissa and confronted a French picket. He resolutely approached the French sergeant and persuaded him and his twelve soldiers to be taken prisoner. During the withdrawal from the fortress, he succeeded in loading two guns onto the ships and spiked a third, so that it could not harm our vessels standing beside the fortress.

On the 31st of May [12th of June], immediately after the evacuation of the ground forces, the squadron weighed anchor and sailed along the coast on a fair wind, firing desperately, according to the French, at the heights behind them. On the next day, the commodore dropped anchor near the town of Makarska and when the enemy approached this position, he continued to the village of Drašnice on the 2nd [14th] of June. When the French followed him there, he returned to Makarska and, deploying his vessels, he met the French with grapeshot from one side and musketry from the other for two days. The rebels fought in the hills and mountains and sometimes brought prisoners down to the ships. The commodore saw the impossibility of opposing the superior forces of the enemy and tried to persuade the leaders of the rebellion to refrain from further actions before the political circumstances could change in their favour, but they replied that they swore to free themselves even without our aid and like the Bokez, to pledge their loyalty to the Emperor of Russia. On the 6th [18th] of June, the squadron departed from Makarska and while still fighting with the French ashore, they witnessed a violent clash between the French and the locals near the village of Tučepi and dropped anchor. All the ground forces were landed immediately and occupied the high ground to unite with the rebels. Together they drove the enemy out of the village and fought until dark from that advantageous position. The patriots harassed the enemy all night long. On the 7th [19th], the French received reinforcements and tried to surround and cut off our detachment from the shore with their superior numbers, but after a stubborn three-hour skirmish, our force retreated in good order and boarded the launches under the covering fire of the larger vessels. Despite all the courageous efforts and sound tactical art of the French, our losses consisted of 10 dead and 30 wounded, while they lost considerably more due to our naval forces. A thousand of the rebels and their families were evacuated by our squadron and transported to the island of Brazza.

Marmont finally exhausted his men with continuous marches and, seeing his strength reduced by half and fearing the arrival of a larger number of our forces, rescinded his orders and stopped shooting insurgents and burning down their homes. He abstained from taking further revenge and promised to forgive past aggressions by proclamation. The commodore, not seeing an opportunity to liberate Dalmatia with such a small force, also tried to calm the inhabitants. The mutual bloodletting then came to an end. Many parties of insurgents began to return to the towns and villages, though the more persistent of them moved to the islands we occupied. This ended the military action in Dalmatia. Although the intended objective was not achieved, from continuous battle over the course of six weeks, exhausting marches, scorching heat and lack of provisions, the enemy was inflicted such great losses that his superior force was no longer a looming threat to the province of Cattaro. The intention of the French to attack Serbia was also foiled thus. Moreover, the French received a useful lesson and since then become more lenient towards the people.

Marmont forgot his promise to the people when he received reinforcements from Italy; the best of the patriots were shot, their property was confiscated, and few escaped to our ships, ultimately accompanying us to St. Petersburg. The devotion of the Dalmatians deserves special praise. Despite being enemies of the Russians, they fell in love with us and their zeal, despite the unfavourable circumstances, was constant and unlimited. In this calamitous time for the people when the dreams of being Russian subjects were destroyed by destiny, the poets of abandoned Dalmatia praised the name of Alexander as a benefactor and patron; the memory of the Russians and the bitter sorrows they have endured will be dear to them and their descendants forever and our descendants will be pleased to learn that the Tsar was their adored enemy.

On the 4th [16th] of July, a strong detachment of French and Turkish troops appeared on the border by Castelnuovo. The commodore, having recently returned from Brazza with the squadron and ground forces, immediately delivered two ships and a corvette for the defence of the fortress and the enemy hastily retreated without attempting anything. This was how military operations ended. On the 14th [26th] of July, General Lauriston announced from Ragusa the conclusion of the Treaty of Tilsit. On the 23rd of July [4th of August], couriers from our court and the French arrived together with Highest orders from the Emperor to surrender the Bay of Cattaro to French administration and to withdraw our forces immediately to the Venetian region where in Treviso or Padua they would stay until arrangements could be made with the Viennese court to allow their transit through Austrian territory and then they would unify with General Michelson in Moldavia. In consequence of this, immediately after the arrival of General Lauriston with his forces, Castelnuovo was surrendered on the 29th of July [10th of August], while our forces in the surroundings became bivouacked. On the 31st [12th], all other fortresses were surrendered. On the 1st [13th] of August, a part of our ground forces were boarded onto the ships and transports. The slowness in the occupation of the fortresses, the difficulty in hiring private vessels, the apparent desire of the French authorities to delay our soldiers as long as possible and all the duties falling on the commodore could not be concluded any earlier than the 14th [26th] of August, which was the date when the whole squadron and ground forces were delivered to Venice. Under special provisions, our soldiers in Italy were supposed to be maintained by French subsidy, while our magazines, artillery and other supplies in the Cattaro fortresses were relinquished after an approximate inventory was drafted. Among the articles approved prior to the surrender of Cattaro by the commodore, Colonel Knieper, State Councillor Sankovskiy and General Lauriston, the Greek Orthodox faith was promised free practice and word was given that those who had sworn devotion to Russia would not be persecuted. By the intervention of Sankovskiy in particular, the Montenegrins, as subjects of Russia, were promised all the same privileges in their trade relations with French Cattaro as existed between Venice and the Austrian government.

Foul winds delayed the voyage of the squadron and inflicted damage on the transport vessels. The brig *Letun* was sent to Venice to fetch pilots and the commodore halted on the 23rd of August [4th of September] near Pirano in Istria in order to mend the damages and take on fresh water which was desperately needed on the hired private boats. The British frigate *Unité* soon arrived in Istria and her captain, Patrick Campbell, declared himself to be blockading Venice although he was powerless to do so. Baratynskiy's squadron nonetheless was permitted to enter, as otherwise Campbell would be regarded as committing a hostile act contrary to his own court and government. Commodore Baratynskiy, considering this announcement with the will of His Imperial Majesty that was for the transportation of our forces to Venice before receiving new instructions stating that 'under no circumstances shall action be taken against His Majesty the King of Great Britain', and not wishing to act solely on his own assessment, he invited Colonel Knieper and all the skippers of the military vessels to a council to consider the announcement of the British captain. According the unanimous opinion of the council, it was recognized that in these circumstances a forced entry into Venice might precipitate a diplomatic break with Britain. For that reason, Commodore Baratynskiy left the squadron for Trieste and from there sent a courier to Vienna to ask our Minister Plenipotentiary there, Prince Aleksandr Borisovich Kurakin,[3] how to act in such a difficult situation. After several days, the courier returned with the minister's permission to enter Venice despite any British naval presence and to fulfil the Emperor's orders as soon as possible. On the 9th [21st] of September, during a fair wind, the squadron arrived at the entrance to Venice and anchored in the shallow water 10 miles [18.6 km] away. The unreliable transports entered the interior of Venice along with the frigate *Avtroil* for repairs. Making use of a small number of rowing vessels sent from the French government, the ground forces were delivered over the course of three days. The commodore then awaited the return of the vessels being repaired in Venice and proceeded to Pirano where, on the next day, he received orders delivered by the brig *Bonasorte* from the commander-in-chief to immediately return to Corfu. As a precaution against the British and to accompany the transports returning from Venice to Corfu, the frigate *Lyogkiy* was left behind while the squadron of three ships and a brig set sail on the 16th [28th] of September, arriving safely in Corfu on the 19th [1st of October].

The commodore did not find the commander-in-chief in Corfu, but on his arrival he received the command to immediately follow for the Baltic Sea, to never enter any British port for any reason and to take refuge in French or other allied ports only in cases of extreme necessity. If he should be unable to reach Copenhagen in time, he would winter in one of Norway's ports. The vessels under the commodore's command could not mend their serious damage in such a

---

3    Prince Kurakin served as Russia's ambassador to Vienna from July of 1807 to September of 1808. Bezotosnyy (ed.), *The 'Patriotic War of 1812' Encyclopedia*, sv. 'Куракин'. [Bezotosnyy (ed.), *The 'Patriotic War of 1812' Encyclopedia*, sv. 'Kurakin'.]

short time, which is why the *Sedd-el Bahr*, the *Uriil* and the frigates *Lyogkiy* and *Avtroil* were to set sail under Captain First Rank Baillie and the remaining two vessels of the Baltic Squadron, the *Svyatoy Pyotr* and *Moskva*, did not leave Corfu until the 2nd [14th] of October. Passing Messina, the commander of the British forces stationed there, General John Moore,[4] sent an officer to warn Commodore Baratynskiy that he would not be admitted into Messina under any circumstances. The commodore had no need to stop there and rushed the English officer back to General Moore to say that if he wished to enter Messina, he certainly would not ask for the general's permission. On the 9th [21st] of October, between Sicily and Sardinia, a brutal foul wind lasting ten days forced the commodore to stay under furled sails. Finally a great gloom descended and a storm raged; both ships began to leak, several beams cracked, and the already damaged masts were for a long while unreliable. The commodore suffered the same fate as befell Senyavin's main squadron in the Atlantic Ocean and was forced against his will to take shelter in the nearest friendly port. On the 17th [29th] of October, arriving in the port of Ferraio on the island of Elba, the commodore inspected the vessels and found very critical damage which prevented a long voyage. He therefore decided to winter there in Ferraio. The Consul General to Livorno, Jean Calamai, with the utmost care successfully supplied the ships with provisions. The affectionate treatment and eager assistance of the island's commandant, General Pierre Durutte, made their stay on Elba a pleasant one. In December, Commodore Baratynskiy was instructed to give command to his senior captain and soon after returned through Italy and Austria to St. Petersburg.[5]

---

4     Bronevskiy's note: 'The very same who was killed in the Battle of Corunna, 1809'.
5     The command passed to Captain Yegor Pavlovich Hetzen (Gettsen) of the *Moskva*.

# 102

# Action of the Squadron of Captain First Rank Lelli in 1807

The commander-in-chief, before leaving for the Greek archipelago, entrusted the defence of the Ionian Republic to a military council composed of three individuals: Major-General Nazimov, commander of the ground forces; Captain First Rank Lelli, commander of a squadron comprised of two ships and nine smaller vessels; and the minister plenipotentiary to the republic, State Councillor Count Mozzenigo. All actions taken were according to the decisions of this council. Shortly after the admiral's departure, Ali Pasha gathered a force of 10,000 men and six armed vessels together with two French corsairs, and threatened to attack the fortresses of Lefkada and Parga. In response, two corvettes and a schooner were sent into the mouth of the Preveza Bay where the pasha's flotilla stood and a company of the Albanian light infantry were transported to Parga and a tender was sent for protecting it from the sea. Corsairs and small military vessels were temporarily sent to the other Ionian islands to cruise and maintain communications between the islands, depriving Ali Pasha of the opportunity to take any action against the republic; he could not even intercept shipments of food to Corfu. There was no danger from Italy as in all of Puglia, as the guards and garrisons there were occupied by the local population. Captain Baillie, cruising around Otranto, did not find one armed boat on that entire coast.

When new information was received that Ali Pasha had again gathered 20 vessels and 8,000 men in the Gulf of Corinth, likely to attack Zante or Santa Maura, Captain Baillie set out with the *Aziya* and the *Lyogkiy* to destroy that flotilla. Captain Baillie reached Zante on the 5th [17th] of May and procured the corsair *Akhill* there before continuing to Patras on the 9th [21st]. As the ship could not approach very closely in the shallow water, the frigate and corsair closed on the fortress and dropped anchor to open fire. Their bombardment lasted until evening and was quite effective, reducing the enemy to a weak force. On the 12th

[24th], the Turks brought up three large guns against our vessels, but the captain of the *Lyogkiy*, Povalishin, weighed anchor and pulled away with visible damage. There were no armed vessels in the bay except for one French corsair and three Polish, on which a crew from Ali Pasha were boarded for transportation to some probably near location; these vessels stood in a narrow bay reinforced by batteries on both sides. It was only possible to attack them on light rowing vessels and even then with extreme danger, as the enemy was perfectly protected and could kill an oncoming attacker with musketry from the high promontories. For that reason, Captain Baillie sent the *Lyogkiy* back to Corfu, requesting to send small vessels in its stead; but as it was not possible to collect them quickly from various places and as Baillie saw that the enemy disarmed its four boats and had no intention of harming us, he received a command to return his force to Corfu. From then until receiving word of the Treaty of Tilsit, Ali Pasha did not attempt any more offensives and feared a counter-attack from us, even forgoing an assault on Parga, which was one of the republic's possessions on the Albanian coast surrounded by his territory.

On the 19th of September [1st of October], Commodore Saltanov, in accordance with the order of the commander-in-chief, took command of the Black Sea squadron and assorted small vessels of the Baltic squadron. The commodore sent the remaining forces returning from the island of Zante to Venice with a reliable convoy escort on the 26th of September [8th of October] and then ordered all the vessels to gather at Corfu in order to be prepared for their voyage to the Black Sea. Political circumstances changed however, our forces still occupying Moldavia and Wallachia broke their armistice with the Ottoman Porte and on the 30th of November [12th of December], news was received of the break with Britain, along with an order to relocate the squadron to a less dangerous port. The commodore chose Trieste and Venice, both for protection and for more timely and accurate communication with Russia.

On the 12th [24th] of December, the squadron of 4 ships, 3 frigates, 4 corvettes and 4 brigs weighed anchor and the commodore saluted the fortresses with 7 guns, but one of the three French frigates which had arrived from Toulon assumed that the salute was intended for her and answered it in kind. The commodore sent an officer to General Berthier who at once replied with a salute of equal magnitude from the fortress guns. Due to the calm winds, the squadron anchored within sight of Corfu and then for celebrating Emperor Alexander's birthday, every ship was decorated with flags and set off 31 shots. At night, the city was magnificently illuminated. The *Svyatoy Mikhail*, *Grigoriy Velikoy Armenii*, 15 prize transports and all the old, incapable vessels were left in Corfu under the command of Captain First Rank Lelli. The condition of Commodore Saltanov's squadron, in the event of a battle with Britain, made everyone anxious; the ships were ragged and could not withstand a proper fight. Those proud rulers of the sea, however, had orders to evade battle with us. The two British frigates who met our squadron in the Adriatic Sea, after respectfully striking their colours, immediately retired to the opposite shore. The commodore lowered his flag in reply and continued on his course. The British, generally, especially those who served with us in the archipelago, were extremely dissatisfied with the latest policies of their ministers that deprived Britain of her most faithful and best ally. Parliamentary speeches were filled with reproaches on this subject. On the 28th of December [9th of January, 1808], a squadron consisting of the ships *Svyataya Paraskeva*, *Uriil*, *Sedd-el Bahr* and *Aziya*; the frigate *Lyogkiy*; and the corvette *Diomid* arrived safely in Trieste where the *Mikhail* already stood. Another force under the command of Captain-Lieutenant Konstantin Saltiy consisting of the frigate *Avtroil*; the corvettes *Dyerzkiy*, *Kherson* and *Dnyepr*; the cutter *Strela*; and the brigs *Letun*, *Feniks* and *Aleksandr* reached Venice.

# 103

# The Return of the *Venus* to the Mediterranean Sea

As the rumours of a war between Russia and Britain were more and more surely confirmed, and it became known that the Prince Regent decided to relocate to Brazil in the face of the impossibility of defending Portugal against the oncoming French forces, combined with the impossibility of reaching our Baltic ports before spring and the need to repair damages suffered by our ships, for which the regent granted all the required materials; the commander-in-chief ordered the squadron to spend the winter in Lisbon. Consequently, the captain of the frigate *Venus* received orders to return to the Mediterranean, locate the squadron of Captain-Commodore Baratynskiy and tell him where to reunite with the fleet, as well as to take dispatches to Palermo for Minister D.P. Tatishchev and instructions to Corfu. To the captain of the frigate *Speshnyy*, which was sent from Russia with a transport to deliver money and supplies to the fleet and stopped at Portsmouth to await the arrival of the fleet, instructions were given to immediately sail to Lisbon.

After a bout of illness, Captain-Lieutenant Yegor Fyodorivich Razvozov relinquished command of our frigate to Captain-Lieutenant Kondratiy Ivanovich Andreyanov. On the 9th [21st] of November, during a quiet wind, we weighed anchor. The current carried us on a crash course toward the *Retvizan* but we steered clear without any harm. Never with such reluctance did we ever leave the fleet as at that time; an accurate, secret foreboding brought everyone into a state of impatience and we thought that we would be separated from our comrades for a long time. Heading out to sea by the major thoroughfare, we saw in Cascais a British squadron of 7 ships standing on anchor, which had long been expected to facilitate the transfer of the Portuguese royal family to the Americas. A sloop belonging to that squadron approached us to ask in the name of their Rear-Admiral Sidney Smith where we were going and to inquire as to the health of our vice-admiral. When we gave our response, the British wished us a good journey and we set all sails. Under a moderate northerly wind, we soon lost sight of all coastal objects. Lisbon and the majestic Tagus with its countless ships remained only

View of Gibraltar from the Ocean. Illustration from original publication.

in the imagination; we saw nothing but sky and water and the play of lightning in the distance. We floated south into the vast expanse of the ocean alone like an orphan, all of our comrades left behind. At night, the lightning grew until the whole celestial vault was covered in flaming crimson like molten metal in a magnificent and quiet spectacle, but suddenly a storm from the northwest fell on us and the nocturnal fires were extinguished. The darkness became impenetrable, strong winds howled, and thunder pounded so strongly that it seemed the very firmament was shaking. As the din heightened around us, we took the precaution of removing our upper sails but we were deceived; instead of the expected wind, we were deluged with such a heavy rain that the storm expended itself and the sky began to clear. The stars shone and a silvery moon appeared in all its splendour.

On the 10th [22nd] of November, with a clear sky and moderate wind, we rounded the Cape of St. Vincent and met the sloop *Shpitsbergen*. Her commander, Captain-Lieutenant Aleksey Kachalov, was very pleased to hear that he should go to Lisbon and no further, as he did not at the time know where the fleet was. The sloop had difficulty evading the island of Marettimo during a close-hauled tack and while she spent no more than hour on this diversion, it resulted in her lagging behind the fleet for 45 days, during which time she fought against foul winds across the whole Mediterranean while we enjoyed fair ones. Here is an example of how precious time is for seafarers. The sloop pulled into Gibraltar for fresh water and procured provisions from British merchants who, despite the accurate rumours about a new war, did not hesitate to relinquish their goods on the captain's signature, knowing that the debt would be paid.

On the 11th [23rd] of November, as we approached closer to the Strait of Gibraltar, the wind freshened and the sky darkened over. The Rock of Gibraltar appeared to us from the ocean like an island; the other prominent stone on the African coast, Mons Abila or commonly called 'Monkey Mountain', also seemed to be an island from afar. In cloudy weather one should be very careful when exiting the Mediterranean not to mistake the low isthmus connecting Gibraltar with the rest of Spain to be the strait and run aground, and likewise to avoid the dangers surrounding Abila in the Bay of Tetouan. The anchorage at Gibraltar is very inconvenient and ships can stand on anchor at the New Mole on a depth of 10 *sazhen*s [21.34 m]. The sandy and shell-strewn floor can break anchor lines. During a westerly wind the heavy waves make it dangerous to stay on the roadstead, and during easterly ones there are such strong gusts that ships can be torn off their anchors. Only five ships can be accommodated at the New Mole while the Old can hold up to ten smaller vessels. With a lack of water and provisions, Gibraltar is altogether uncomfortable and dangerous.

We needed to send a report to the admiral, but the westerly wind was so strong that we could neither stand on anchor nor send a boat to the town. Fortunately, at the European cape, an American vessel on its way to Lisbon approached us and her skipper willingly took on the task of delivering our report to Senyavin. As soon as we entered the Mediterranean, the air and sky changed completely; in the ocean, the weather was already cloudy and severe, but now the most pleasant conditions surrounded us. Moderate winds astern did not bore us with slow sailing, the sky was clear, the air was warm and at noon, it even became hot. The day before, at the same latitude, it was cold on the open ocean and today it was as if we had inadvertently entered a wholly different climate. Our transit across the Mediterranean to Sardinia was safe and I was enthralled without interruption by the scrolling scenes before the Cape of Gata. Once in the night we came so close to the shore that the shrouding silence was broken by the splashing of waves on the flinty rocks, which suddenly stood before us threateningly. Beyond them, higher up, were several huts with lights flashing here and there in their windows. I listened with inexplicable pleasure to the ringing barks of the sentry dogs, imagining that I was travelling over land and, being tired from a long journey, I would hasten to a village for the night. Everything contrary to our chaotic life and connected with thoughts of rural life attracts the sailor, as even such ordinary objects are rarely presented to him; we still feel the great joy of those who move from the capital to the village for a short time each summer.

By Sardinia we were met with a foul wind and beat windward for five days, scarcely advancing a hundred *versta*s [106.68 km], though we still spent this boring time productively. According to our exact observations, we found that our maps and the British ones were incorrect and incongruent by several miles. On the 20th of November [1st of December], with a restless swell remaining from a strong wind, it was observed that the rudder head was rotten and cracked from above. After the calm continued until the 21st [2nd], a fresh and fair breeze blew, with which we quickly passed the space between Sardinia and Sicily. On the 22nd of November [3rd of December], the magnificent Palermo emerged out of the light fog and we dropped anchor between the Mole and a British squadron consisting of five ships and two frigates. The hundred-gun ship *Royal Sovereign* flew the flag of Vice-Admiral Thornbrough.

# 104

# Our Second Stay in Palermo

---

## Port and Fortifications

The vast bay is enclosed from the east by the peninsula of Zafferano and from the west by Mount Pellegrino. Being open to northerly winds, the port of Palermo is only convenient in the summer. Ships stop before the city at a depth of 18 to 20 *sazhen*s [38.4-42.67 m]. The floor is muddy with weeds. Northeasterly winds generate large waves, which require casting two anchors. On the mole, 200 *sazhen*s [426.72 m] in length and defended by two small forts, stands a lighthouse which shines out to sea every night. Three or four ships and an equal number of frigates can take shelter from every wind at a depth of 5 or 6 *sazhen*s [10.67 or 12.8 m]. The city is surrounded by a roughly square wall with towers and has four gates in each cardinal direction. There are no guns on the walls and neither the citadel itself which lies close to the northern wall nor the redoubt built on the end of the embankment can protect the city against an army, and only weakly against an attack by sea. In spite of the inconvenience of the port, the anchorage is already full of military and merchant vessels. Palermo is inferior to Messina in trade only by virtue of the fact that the latter's harbour is absolutely calm by the combination of its natural and cultivated shape. Palermo exports large quantities of grain, wine, oil, fruit, silk and various medicinal herbs.

## Two Acquaintances

Under all sails, we entered the harbour and approached the *Archimedes*, the last ship of the line remaining of the King of Naples. A crowd of curious people gathered on the mole. Several well-dressed gentlemen begged to come aboard the frigate and the captain admitted them, while four friends and I went ashore. The crossing was quick; a short push of the skiff brought us to the pier. At a brisk pace, we passed the arsenal, then a wide alley and through the main gate to step onto the street of Maqueda. As soon as we appeared, a crowd of peddlers offered their services to us. We could not drive them off and the evening favoured them. Where did one of our fellows go? 'Naturally no one is still in the gardens but it's early yet for the theatre', said one. 'I think I know what you mean', said another, 'let's go'. And off they went chasing after smoky-eyed cupids.

I remained alone and the messengers of the sirens circled around me, boasting and swearing; I laughed and walked on, when suddenly someone behind me said: 'if I may ask of course, are you a foreigner?' My first instinct was to grab my pockets but by the light of the lantern I saw an elegantly dressed young man with no malice in his face. Calming down, I answered that I was Russian. 'All the better', he continued, 'do not listen to this urban plague (*pesta de citta*), our sirens are very dangerous'. I thanked him for his good advice and asked this Baron N., as he called himself, for a cup of chocolate. The baron had been drinking already, did not refuse a glass of wine and finished a whole bottle. Words and complements flowed like a river. With the high title of *eccellenza* he praised my prudence and finally offered to take me to his box at the theatre which was fairly sized and gave me no excuse to think any differently about him than the most well-mannered person. Regarding myself as a knowledgeable physiognomist,[1] I put my trust in the baron yet I was cruelly deceived. We went hand-in-hand to the theatre and took up a box in the baignoire. The curtain had not yet risen though the theatre was full. Naturally, for something to do, I looked about to the left, to the right, and at the peep shows on the parterre. Noticing a beautiful face, I asked my friend (as he already called me) whether he knew this lady who was sitting in the box opposite us. 'Very well', he said, 'I once loved her. I'm retired now, so to speak, but I'm still listed on her long roster of friends'. His indiscreet response made me blush and I was vexed at Lavater,[2] however I could not believe that the lovely lady was so flighty. Not wishing too strongly that she be constant, I soon agreed to his suggestion to introduce me to her and assured me that I would be well received. After the first act, the baron brought me iced cream, liqueur and confectionaries; after the second, he went into the other box belonging to the lady. Soon after his departure, a servant asked me to pay a gold piece for the treats. I then understood what sort of man the baron was, reached into my pocket and could not find my handkerchief. The baron never returned.

---

1    Physiognomy is the pseudoscience of judging people's character by their facial features, body language etc.
2    Johann Kaspar Lavater was an 18th century Swiss poet, philosopher and theologian famous for his work in physiognomy. Bronevskiy means to say that he has incorrectly judged the character of his acquaintances. Andreyevskiy et al., *Brockhaus and Efron Dictionary*, s.v. 'Лафатер'. [Andreyevskiy et al., *Brockhaus and Efron Dictionary*, s.v. 'Lavater'.]

Two ladies sitting in the box beside mine lamented that they had so many rogues in the capital who were skilled in deceiving honest foreigners. Their regret was enough recompense for the two *chervontsy* and handkerchief I lost. We began a conversation, during the course of which I thought that the beautiful Lucretia (the name of the marchioness) should be like her Roman counterpart,[3] but soon I fell out with Lavater and my initial conclusion was wrong. The performance concluded, I gave my hand to the ladies, escorted them down the stairs and helped them into a carriage. They thanked me and reminded me that there would be a large festival in the Flora the next day. I slowly returned to the frigate and on the next day, I arrived very early in the garden. After three hours of boring search, I finally met the marchioness to find her with a handsome young gentleman! She recommended me to him but so coldly that when I bowed, I wanted to turn down a different avenue. Fortunately, her friend was alone and offered her hand. The marchioness occasionally turned to me with a word or two, and I soon corrected myself from my initial impression, seeing the wharf where I was to govern. The woman on my arm was a young widow and the sister to the marchioness. Her suitor, Don Rosario, was an affluent noble and a clever and amiable young man. He tried to gain my confidence and we became acquainted so quickly in a few minutes that, dining together at the lady's home, I was laughing with my two unexpected friends with all my heart.

## The Monastery of San Martino

We only intended to stay in Palermo for a few days but fate, never serving any interest but her own, kept us for months in the marbled capital of the Neapolitan king; marbled because here they use marble as ubiquitously as we use brick and field stones. During our five-month stay in Palermo, I had time to observe many curiosities. I will choose the best subjects to describe, starting with the monastery of San Martino, which deserves the special attention of every traveller.

This monastery, built in the mountains 12 *verstas* [12.8 km] from Palermo, is revered as the richest in Europe. My companions who had visited it said many good things but complained about a poor reception. There was a reason for it: they made the mistake in choosing a guide on par with my acquaintance the baron. The monastery's treasurer visited the frigate for several days and explained the cause of the cold reception to us. He asked that we honour them with a second visit,

3    Lucretia was a legendary Roman noblewoman who was raped by Sextus Tarquinius, son of the last King of Rome. She went before her father and husband and begged for vengeance before then killing herself with a dagger. On that same dagger, a band of men swore to defend their liberty against tyrants and overthrew the monarchy to establish the Roman Republic. Smith, *A New Classical Dictionary*, s.v. 'Lucretia'; Ibid., s.v. 'Tarquinius'.

scheduled a day and sent a member of his party, an intelligent and merry monk who spoke French and English, to accompany us. We travelled in four hired carriages which were very handsomely decorated. The road through the plains surrounding Palermo ran between gardens. Approaching the mountains, that majestic plain suddenly transformed completely. The winding and battered road led up a steep incline and became more frightening and difficult between the rocks; on one side was a high overhanging cliff and on the other opened an abyss. The horses often stopped and did not regain their strength during these respites. We walked on foot, taking off our coats, and were exhausted by the time the wondrous structure at last revealed itself in the distance. It soon disappeared again but the hard road smoothed out into a flat highway and we pleasantly rode down that wide avenue into the walls of the monastery.

A small bell rang, the thick iron gates swung open on heavy hinges, and a monk with a noble bearing and sprinkled with perfume greeted us with a bow and asked that we leave our swords with the porter. He assuaged us by saying that even the king disarms himself at the gate.[4] Entering the broad and sandy courtyard, we saw the long façade of the monastery whose pediment and portico gave it an appearance more like a royal palace than the modest dwelling of hermits. In the hall leading to the main staircase, a monument to Saint Martin of Tours can be seen. The equestrian statue adorned in Saracen armour set on a stone similar to the base of Peter the Great's statue in our capital depicts Saint Martin cutting his cloak to hand half to a beggar running beside him. The horse, saint and beggar are as cold as the marble from which they were carved; there is no art in the statue and the decoration is very mediocre. Such a large monument in the passage, drawing attention to itself, does not correspond with the beauty of the staircase. Several monks met us on the threshold. On the white marble stairs, touching the railings of agate with a hand, we walked through the large doors which opened before us and entered into a long and tall chamber. A marble parquet below, a painted plafond above, wide cornices and an extraordinary light reflecting off all the white marble walls give a grand impression of the monastery's wealth. Heading through a long hallway and then crossing into another where portraits of cardinals, holy men and past abbots of the monastery were exhibited, we trampled over several multicoloured mosaics and finally reached a reception room. What splendour! A parquetted floor made of cuts of green, grey and black marble, a fireplace of porphyry, white walls with pink borders, wide spaces between the windows decorated with grand mirrors, carved and gilded furniture; all of this cumulative brilliance amazed me and gave rise to the thought that all of this luxury was

---

4    Bronevskiy's note: 'Women of any title or rank were forbidden from entering the monastery but monks were not forbidden from seeing them outside the walls'.

excessive for a monk. What can I say about what I saw thereafter? I must agree that the monks utilized their annual income of 300,000 rubles well.

Before the couch on which I was seated, there suddenly opened a series of doors, one after another; a small monk came running into the reception room wearing a long silk robe and a four-cornered cap; behind him in the distance with a downcast gaze walked 30 fat and ruddy monks in pairs. The smaller monk was the prior. Not waiting for our greetings, he showered us with a thousand pardons, sat down, stood up again, talked to this man and then another, very vividly and dextrously animated his body, complained that the weather had been bad for three days and that he could not bear the cold, and posited that he would surely freeze in Russia with the first morning frost. Then he cursed and assured us that this was a rare fluke of Palermo's climate. Finally he changed his voice and spoke slowly and quietly: 'I am sure that the most respectable gentlemen of Russia would be honoured to share with us our meagre meal'. Thanking him for the invitation and in order to prevent him from starting a new conversation, one of us asked for permission to tour the church and other memorable sites around the compound. 'Whatever you like, ask it of me and it is my command. It would be my special pleasure to accompany you but I'm afraid my age and poor legs prevent it. Of course you may', he continued. 'First of all, visit our library – it has 40,000 books and many ancient manuscripts. I hope our museum will satisfy you; it was prepared for your arrival'. Here he entered into a learned expertise and began to liven up, speaking very eloquently and in intricate detail, revealing a mind enriched with great knowledge.

We were first taken to the great hall where they kept their library. A librarian with a proud demeanour brought us a catalogue and then, at our request, brought us classical books in all the branches of science and several manuscripts in Greek, Latin, Hebrew and Gothic; we looked through the pages of the former with a kind of scholarship, but only glanced at the latter. None of us, not even the monks, I think, could understand what was written in them. The most curious of the manuscripts was the Epistle to the Romans by the Apostle Paul which they assured us was written by the saint himself. Lastly, they showed us a Slavonic scroll in which, with the majority of the letters worn off the page, we could not make out a single word. We thought that this manuscript must have been Bulgarian or Serbian and written in the 12th or 13th century.

From the library we moved to the museum. Several halls were filled with all sorts of rarities. The consideration of each of them would take a collector of antiquities several days but we only looked at them briefly and continued through the halls. The first chamber was an arsenal filled with muskets, pistols, various coats of mail, helmets, swords, axes, berdiches and maces. The second was occupied by a collection of rare antiquities such as bowls, lachrymatories, fragments of the most ancient statues imported from Greece, among which were a torso of Zeus and several Egyptian idols and fragments from Greek temple cornices, reliefs and bas-reliefs. There was also a rare collection of metalwork from Syracuse and Carthage, and many Etruscan jars and vases. In this room on either side of the doors stood full-height statues of the Empress Catherine II and Maria Theresa of Austria. In the person of our great mother tsarina, unfortunately, there was no similarity. Her clothes consisted of a slender dress over a pannier and a corset made of shells like scales. The creation was unsuccessful and the monks promised us to change her hat and make the statue taller. The statue of Maria Theresa was even worse; if one glanced at it unintentionally, it might even frighten. The third room was filled with natural marvels of land and sea; among the former, they showed us a small piece of white marble which by marvelous happenstance resembled wood so exactly that one English traveller, wishing to be sure it was painted, bought a piece, broke it and brought it back. Among the minerals were some from Siberia. In the fourth and largest room, I saw ostriches, pelicans, tigers, crocodiles, hyenas, lions, Venus, maidens, old men and children. In the stuffed animals, statues and freaks preserved in jars of formaldehyde, I passed over so many items and became so tired of viewing that by the end I was barely paying attention to what was in front of me. Finally the monk who accompanied us took out a rich sheepskin case with a smile and placed it on the table. Out of it he took a black clay vessel and said with import: 'here is the cup from which Socrates drank his poison! Yes, good sirs, he drank from this!' As he said this, he rose a little and held the cup in both hands close to our eyes. His fellows smiled and so did we, but the guardian of the rarities did not change his expression. He showed one of us the inscription of *SOCRATUS* on the cup and said: 'Truly it is so, have no doubt!' So as not to give to this passionate lover of antiquities greater cause to try to convince us, we agreed with him and then proceeded to the last room which was occupied by the anatomical theatre, deserving of special attention. Waxen body parts were constructed, each separately, with such art and precision that they represented a perfect and judicious composition of the human interior.

From the museum, by dark passages, we were taken into the church. What gloom, vastness and splendour! These are the first words one will say upon entering. As soon as we stepped out into the centre of the temple, its echoing vaults stopped their thunderous marching and left me amazed. The splendid glitter of metals, precious stones and musical harmony which transitioned into a quiet hymn conveyed the presence of He who we could not comprehend but could be sensed in ourselves and in every object. The organs naturally were the work of a great master and could imitate a 40 piece orchestra. With the help of a mechanism driven by foot pedals, one could also play timpani drums and harmonicas of two kinds: one of metal bells and another of crystal glass. Only two people play these organs. The reverberatory effects are so strong that when they stopped playing, the sounds of their singing carried for a long moment. At the main annex of Saint Martin, a remarkably engraved silver platter resting on a raspberry velvet cloth and serving as a decoration for the altar was truly beautiful and masterfully crafted. Before the same altar were two large golden candlesticks which were so fine, they were worth 15,000 ounces (200,000 rubles at the present exchange rate). Of the monsters, paintings and statues which might surprise, three were especially memorable. 1) *The Sacrifice of Abraham*. This painting is amazing in the effect it produces. The patriarch is raising the sacrificial knife to slaughter his son with his face turned up to heaven and though he notices the angel hastily swooping down to stay his hand, when viewing the painting you fear that Abraham will soon complete his offering, as the angel is still far away and the patriarch seems poised to turn his head back down toward his son. 2) Jacob sitting on a bed accepts the bloody clothes of Joseph. The father's grief, his gray hair, the tattered clothes, one hand raised to his weeping eyes and the other dropping Joseph's coat, the feigned sorrow of some of the young men, the genuine sorrow of others, and the mutual reproaches depicted on the faces of the sons surround him have nothing like them for comparison. The skillful brush revived various feelings. Passing one's gaze from person to person, one cannot help but cry for one and then feel scornful prejudice for another, and the repentance of the third elicits an involuntary sigh. It cannot be said which is depicted better, the sorrow of the father or the tormented conscience of one of his sons. Even the most cruel and uncompassionate would say afterward: 'I forgive you'. 3) *The Statue of Saint Sebastian*, a reproduction of some other sculptor. The expression of faith and meekness in the eyes and the struggle of life with death here is surprising; his persecutors have pierced the beautiful body of the saint with an arrow and the cold marble suffers from the wound exactly like flesh. The saint's prayer for his tormentors depicted in his gaze is unmatched: one cannot see with what angelic gentleness and humility he anticipates his last breath, the moment when his soul will transition from the temporal to the eternal, without being moved. There are many excellent images and statues in the church but after those three, I closed my eyes so as not to spoil the first pleasing impression in my heart. I did not mention the appearance of the church itself; three words will suffice: marble, heaviness and disorder.

The monk who accompanied us asked if we would like to see their cemetery. My comrades agreed and went into the catacombs; I was afraid of the dampness and did not go there and mingled with three students along with the monks. Each of them was locked in a special cell and the key was held by a man on watch like a jailer. 'Have your pupils been forever condemned to such seclusion?' I asked the prior.

'Oh no! They are all allotted time every day, when the weather is fine, to walk in the garden and work there with their own hands; in poor weather, there is a hall for gymnastic exercises and there, under the supervision of a teacher, all sorts of amusements appropriate for their age are allowed. Only for three hours, when they must complete their lessons, are they separated and locked away'. The monastery educates, feeds and clothes 21 students, who are accepted for nine years and released at the age of 21. At the end of this period, each of them is free to choose their way of life. At their invitation, I visited the cells of the monks. Some occupied six chambers which were richly but tastelessly decorated. All the monks from the best noble families are very courteous, well-educated and a large part of them are academics who have devoted themselves to the sciences.

At four of clock we sat down not to an austere monastic meal but rather to a greatly luxurious dinner where such delicacies as *cassata, millefoglie, piatto di Priccia o di Premura* [sic], flavoured with lemon sugar, numerous vanilla and chocolate confectionaries, wines and fruits were all served one after another. The prior showed the sharpness of his mind, joking over Voltaire, heaping praise on the pope, regretting that he could not read Lomonosov or Derzhavin, making sly remarks at the expense of women, and lastly scolding Bonaparte. When we got up from the table, he ordered the students to sing the tender arias of Metastasio and then fell asleep on the couch. We quietly retired to the garden.

The plants in the botanical garden were planted according to the Linnaean taxonomic system. The monk laboured over it with importance as if from the pulpit and explained the properties of each flower and leaf. I preferred the cleaned forest more than the orderly garden which was still unfinished. Under a canopy of citrus trees and walking over a green carpet, in the centre of all the paths, swaying as if I had been pummelled, I stopped and with complete joy in my heart said to the monk who accompanied me: 'not even the enchanted garden of Armida could be greater than this'.

'I don't know when that garden came to be', answered the monk, 'but the one you see here is the fruit of a century of labours'. We entered an arbor cultivated on a hill from which the beautiful vistas around the monastery could be seen. On one side was a portion of a sandy alley cut by a river with many watermills, and on the other were green mountains covered in forest. Between them, in the distance, the silvery waves of the vast sea shone in the sunlight. Talking with the monk, I learned about the origin of their brotherhood. In the 4th century, in memory of the mercy of Saint Martin, which explains the statue set over the front entrance, their brotherhood was established. It is not known exactly when the poor monastery was built on the very site, but during Spanish rule it received rich estates and most of its marblework. There are now 80 monks in their community, though 30 live in Naples. They belong to the Benedictine Order. The prior has some significant authority at court.

The monks invited us to stay overnight but we had to return to the frigate, so we expressed our gratitude for the courtesy and hospitality and boarded our carriage again as it was just growing dark. The evening was quiet and pleasant, prompting us to walk a portion of the way. The cooks and servants of the monastery, on some pretense, came outside the walls and wished us a safe and comfortable journey and praised Russian generosity. I gladly gave one a piastra and to another who touchingly asked that we not forget them, I gave a few *grani*[5] but a third and fourth who I did not recognize stuck out their hands as well and without saying a word to them, I boarded the carriage. Our coachman drove the horses to the mountain so quickly that it was possible to guess that they had also been treated to the luxuries of a monastic meal. We did not need to intervene and although they could nearly break their necks at the frequent turns, they nonetheless took us quickly and safely through the city and down to the pier.

## Monreale

Acquaintances of ours among the officers of the royal guard, very well-educated young men, treated us to many pleasurable experiences which we would have missed without their guidance. The attention of our ambassador, D.P. Tatishchev, made them even more diverse. His High Excellency recommended us to many nobles and in the new year he introduced us to the king and queen at a royal gathering. Their Majesties were pleased to order us to open the doors at every important institution. We received tickets almost every day from the director of a theatre, a club, an association of nobles or from the monastery for a spiritual oratorio; we were never starved for pastimes.

One day, at the invitation of the guard officers, we dined in Monreale. This ancient town was built on a mountain seven *versta*s [7.47 km] from the capital. The road, carved into the side of the mountain, leads to the summit without difficulty; on one side are built stone handrails and on the other stand the occasional beautiful marble fountain interspersed with planted shrubs. Emerging from a steep, bare rock near the town, a rapid stream flows alongside the road before falling over a precipice into a vast pond overgrown with water lilies. At the top of the rock-spring was placed a statue of a young man severing a snake with an axe just before it could slither into the water; another is of a young man with a stone in his hand rushing to help the first; a third statue depicts a peasant woman hiding behind a pine tree stump in fear. This splendid road was built with the material

---

5    The *piastra* in Sicily and Naples was divided into 12 *tari*, each *tara* into 20 *grani*, and each *grano* into 6 *piccoli*. George Dennis and John Murray, *A Handbook for Travellers in Sicily* (London: Murray, 1864), pp.xxxix-xli.

support of the Archbishop of Monreale, Francesco Maria Teste, who used his great wealth for charitable institutions and the common good. The town standing under a canopy of rock is very small and poor, but the view of Palermo from Monreale is incomparable. The name of 'Royal Mountain' (which Monreale means in Italian) is justly given. There is no tavern in the town, so the visitor has to procure a dingy hut and send their cook to the market, but nothing could be procured there and we would have had to lodge without dining were it not for the mayor's personal visit and having everything we needed sent to us. We invited him to join us for our meal and while it was being prepared, we went to observe the ancient and once glorious cathedral which was hitherto revered as one of the richest dioceses in the Archdiocese of Sicily.

The Gothic temple is backed up from all sides by brick supports and stands in a conspicuous place on the very edge of a rock lapped by water so that it seemed ready to collapse. The partially open roof, the turrets thereon, the variety of narrow windows shaped like iron bars in which most of the glass has been knocked out, and moss and small plants that have penetrated and taken root in the cracks of the walls give the temple a look of deep and reverential antiquity. Two strong men could barely open the cast bronze gates on which the faces of saints were depicted. What a pity! The interior of the church was in ruin. Perhaps we were the last to see the remnants of the Gothic splendour of the ancient Greek churches, because this was one of the richest built by the Greeks who at the time already had their own churches and bishop in Palermo. They were Uniates who recognized the authority of the pope over them. The temple has the form of a basilica. The old mosaics on the walls are of particular interest. They consist of semi-precious and composite stones. The depictions of the saints are fully sized and set very high. The figures are all Greek and lack proportionality or taste; only the shadows were rendered with excellent skill. The real merit of this mosaic is in its gilding; all the space where there must be air, earth and sky are gold, which is spotless. The gold foil is laid over the stones and I was assured that this was a lost art, making the mosaic a rarity that travellers deliberately seek out and plunder by flecking off pieces as souvenirs. The bronze dais; the columns both twisted and straight, thick and thin, of granite, marble and copper; the adorned iconostasis; the carved frames from which the colours have already been worn away; all create something extraordinary and enchanting to the eye, despite the unrefined works. The visitor is suddenly transported back 800 years to when this building was erected. The Archdiocese of Monreale was founded in 1174.

Beyond expectations, we had a most delicious meal and after dining, the mayor treated us to coffee. In his home were a number of ladies from the province who were very affectionate to us and it was little wonder with dukes, princes and barons in our company. Their behaviour was calculated and hopeful; some did not dare to raise their eyes, others would briefly give a glimpse of tenderness or some meaningful glance; they watched, reflected and tried to appear cheerful one moment, but then blush for some reason the next; they moved from the harpsichord to the sofa, passing the mirror as if to casually adjust their shawl, and it seemed that the only regret they had was that they regretted nothing else. The good-natured older mothers, adjusting the curly locks or waistband of their lovely daughters, no matter how people talked about the prospect of matchmaking or how the conversation might begin, always managed to secure a betrothal and so on.

## The Belvedere

On one fine day, with three comrades, I visited the belvedere lying 15 *versta*s [16 km] from Palermo. In the gorges of the mountains, in a narrow defile surrounded by steeply standing bare rocks, lies a secluded retreat of a village in which a summer cottage was built on the edge of a mountain overlooking the city named the Royal Belvedere. Unfortunately, the groundskeeper of this palace was absent but we could force our way into the adjacent peasant's house where a free room could accommodate us. The palace servant whom we took to interpret the Sicilian language for us brought out some slaughtered game, a fine wine and fruits and prepared for us a decent meal.

Although the day was hot, we ascended to the top of the cliff immediately after eating and looked down on the collection of shacks, trees and the simple architecture of the belvedere. Further out, a lovely view amazed the eye with a single glance. It is not possible to choose a better position for the capital. Each subject was arresting: the vast array of magnificent buildings surrounded by the crenelated walls, the Flora garden, the waterfront and harbour, a fortress here, a prominent house with colonnades there, a Gothic monastery and rustic homes under the shade of their orchards of olive, palm, citrons and pistachio trees which were continuous with the surrounding greenery. Fountains shaped like pillars, pyramids and collapsed towers which appeared from a distance like obelisks gave excellent decoration to the panorama of the city. The scattered Aeolian Islands on the horizon emerged from the boundless expanse of the sea. A steady wind over the water carried away winged ships in every direction; some hurried to the pier and others departed. I scrutinized the line where the sea touched the mountains and valleys in low and high places, bending with the multifarious capes and bays. Enjoying the combination of disparate objects united by nature, science and deliberate style produced a seemingly miraculous splendour. My admiring senses became restless, greedily searching for new curiosities and one of them presented itself right under my feet. Near the road, carved into the mountain and leading to the belvedere, a rapid stream escaped from a rock and noisily fell and broke over strewn stones that impeded its course. Below in the terrible depths, a mill stood in a dangerous position; the rapids upstream poured directly onto the wheels below and crashed into foam which threatened to flood into the mill's broken roof.

The pleasant surroundings of Palermo inspired the Sicilian poets to call it the Conca d'Oro (Golden Conch), the Aurea Valle (Golden Valley), the Garden of Sicily and lastly Felice (the fortunate or happy). We left the belvedere at sunset and returned to the city by the light of the moon.

## The Cave of Saint Rosalia

The cave that houses the relics of Saint Rosalia is worthy of the reverence and attention of every Christian traveller. The saint, as some believe, was the niece of King William the Good, or remembered by others as the daughter of a Lord Sinibaldo of Quisquina. In the blossoming years of her youth, at the age of 15, she rejected the comforts of the world and in 1159 chose to live in the mountain of Peregrino where she subsisted on only roots. She spent the remainder of her life in solitude, prayer and fasting. After 500 years of oblivion, when the plague raged through Palermo in 1624, one devout man saw in a dream where the bones of the saint lay and saw that if they were toured around the city three times, the plague would be lifted. The revelation was not respected at first, but when the righteous managed to assure the clergy and the people, the government was then compelled to agree to its submission. The uncorrupted body of the saint was found, reverently paraded through the city and the infection indeed ceased. Since then, Saint Rosalia is recognized as the patroness of Palermo. In her name, they began to build churches and erect monuments. In remembrance of the city's survival of the plague, a celebration on the 8th [20th] of May was held named the Prayer of 40 Hours. The most magnificent holiday though is set on the 2nd [14th] of July in memory of the saint and lasts for five consecutive days. I was not in Palermo at that time, and so I will only describe the cave which has been transformed into a church.

The road to the cave, which lies 9 *verstas* [9.6 km] from the city, is very treacherous. The mountain is nearly perpendicular and is impossible for carriages to climb. We passed through a defile where footpaths have been rather comfortably built and with each step, the valley surrounding Palermo opened further with new sights. At the top of the mountain, the sea appeared but as soon as we entered the other side, everything vanished. We were, so it seemed, suddenly transferred into a wild, barren and uninhabited wasteland with only a few goats climbing from cliff to cliff. As we ascended, we became severely exhausted and stopped for a rest on a pile of stones that the Sicilian writers call the ruins of a fortress built after the deluge, still in the reign of Saturn, made glorious during the Punic Wars when Hamilcar Barca, the Carthaginian commander, defended himself for three years against 40,000 Romans. The remote ringing of a bell broke the silence around us and we arose, descended the slope and met with many pilgrims with staffs in their hands, most of whom were walking barefoot. We finally saw the church and a few nearby houses for sheltering the monks.

Entering through the doors to the cave, one cannot help but be in awe. In this temple there is no mosaic, no precious ornaments or any magnificence that should be expected from great donations and offerings. Imagine a massive and dark hall with a vault consisting of bare, protruding stones. The darkness, broken only by two lamps burning before the main altar, the quiet warmth of the prayers and finally the dismal anthem of the organs instill respect for the place and pour into the soul sweet feelings of faith. At the end of the liturgy, we approached one of the five altars surrounded by a silver-plated cage. This altar was decorated with four silver pillars which, like an icon, were covered with gold and silver foil on the depictions of hands, feet, eyes etc. We were given a wax candle and showed a white marble sculpture of Saint Rosalia which was placed under the altar. She is presented in the posture of resting in sweet slumber and holds a cross in one hand with her other pressed to her breast. A crozier lies beside her. She wears a dress of golden brocade studded with diamonds. The face is uncovered and beautiful. The monk assured us that all the traits of this work are very close to the real relics which were transferred to Palermo and stored in the cathedral. A guardian angel stands at the head of the tomb and stoops down to hold a branch of myrtle over the saint. On the side of the altar, the monk showed us a simple stone monument which was erected for the man who found the body of the saint somewhat further into the cave, resting in the exact position in which she is presented in the tomb. Finally they led us to a marble spring embedded in the cave wall, into which an arc of cold and clear water was dripping in such abundance that it was diverted from the church down the slope into the valley and city below. In the monastery there was nothing particularly of note except for the affection of the monks who lead here a solicitous but wantless life. At all times, they are obliged to hold services for the incoming pilgrims. Their penitence is extraordinarily severe: I met one who had heavy chains on his arms, legs and neck. In rags, barefoot and with an uncovered head, he dragged them behind him with great strain. A mask hid his face and many asked: 'who could this be?' The monastery receives offerings of great sums from the pious, which is why the monks I saw here were very fat and those at prayer were very skinny.

## The Chinese House

In the northern region of the valley five or six *versta*s [5.33-6.4 km] from Palermo stands the king's country home, referred to as the Chinese House. The beautiful pavement leading to it is lined with trees and on both sides could be seen the gardens and manors of the aristocracy. The king spent most of the summer on this estate, and we held tickets for entry. As soon as we reached the gate, the porter rang a bell and a few servants opened the gate, followed by a crowd of them in green coats and livery who ran out to greet us, took the horses and immediately sent for the steward. An old man soon appeared with a heavy bunch of keys who hurried us to approach and bowed deeply before us from afar, being short of breath. When we came before him, he did not ask us for our tickets. He assured me that the king was very fond of the Russians and that he was greatly honoured to receive us and show us every interesting sight. We persuaded him not to worry; the kind old man handed the keys to the servants and directed us to an official, asking that we visit him again after our tour.

Atop a square marble foundation, an octagonal house was placed, all in glass, surmounted with a curved roof and decorated with a weathervane designed as a dragon instead of a cockerel. The roof droops down lower than the walls with festoons and hanging bells, with lacquered columns for support, which form the gallery around the house. Nothing is correct in the architecture, but the diversity of elements placed between the light and pleasant architecture of European buildings to represent a Chinese house have a miraculous effect like magic. The interior layout of the rooms is completely novel. To move from one to another, one must climb up curved and spiralling staircases. The furniture, porcelain dolls and precious wallpaper were defaced with disfigured chimeras that bear no likeness to man, bird or beast and employ neither chiaroscuro shading nor perspective but the colours of the dyes, the landscapes full of Chinese houses, temples, bridges, arbours and so on have a pleasing variety immediately on sight. When looking on all of these effigies, one imagines being genuinely transported to China.

The garden near the palace is truly royal. Those tending it do not overlook anything for decoration. It begins with topiaries, flower beds, marble pools and fountains. Further on, various hillocks are covered with fruit trees, bushes and flowers. Lavender everywhere fills the air. On one side is a grove, on the other runs an avenue of blooming fruit trees. On squares and platforms stand gazebos. Still further one finds a smooth path, a carved boat on a pond, a magnificent fountain, a quiet stream bubbling under rocks and so on.

## The Royal Assembly

This is the name given to a society consisting of the most elite nobility, amongst whom the king is premier. In the manor of this assembly, one or two balls are given each week and salons are held every evening. On the first day of the year 1808, Tatishchev introduced our captain and four officers to the king and queen. When the ambassador led us into the royal presence, His Majesty quit a game of cards, stood up and said: 'I love Russians. I hope you will not be bored here'. He stepped out into another chamber, made a sign to the queen, and said to her: 'I introduce to you these gentlemen; they are Russian officers'. Her Majesty spoke very kindly to the ambassador, then to the captain and finally to the other officers. Following the example of such a benevolent reception, the lords in sashes and breast stars and their ladies in silk robes came one after another to bestow their magnificent greetings upon us. Walking around this courtly circle and hearing all manner of politeness, the acting director of the society, the Count of Sangiovanni, led us into other rooms where he also introduced us to some lords, gave us tickets to return at any time and finally, when the contradances began, he introduced us to some ladies and placed us in the first pairs.

An hour after midnight, the ball ended. The royal family departed and the court staff began to board their coaches. The director invited us to stay for dinner. Soon the doors opened, the orchestra played a march and everyone entered the dining hall. It was beautifully lit and the brilliance of the crystal, bronze and silver blinded the eyes. In the windows there were transparent illustrations. One was of a sea battle at night, another was a burnt out village, a third depicted a rising sun and dawning sky; the best of them was of the ruins of Baiae (an ancient town near Naples) under the light of the moon. The ladies and gentlemen sat down together at a common table but we were seated at a special one. Someone in a silken, embroidered coat, top hat, shoes with massive rhinestone buckles and with powdered hair approached us and asked with the air of a noble lord: 'how might I serve our Russian gentlemen?' A servant handed us a long menu and we guessed that the man in the silken coat was the owner of the establishment. He asked us to choose dishes from the menu, of which more than 20 were identified by names I had never heard before. We ordered dishes with the most magnificent titles: *boeuf à la mode* revealed itself to be beef; a *bombe de Sardanapale* was a sweat cabbage stuffed with meat. Even the bread here had an *à la* appellation! In the end, the host himself served us cakes with a truly breathtaking presentation, for which we paid him well. The servant, receiving a gold coin, was enchanted by our generosity and escorted us to the carriages where on the front steps he divulged in secret that his master had charged us three times the usual prices.

On typical days where there are no balls held, they assemble for salons. By the meaning of such a word, I had expected to be engaged only in conversations, but when I entered the first hall, I did not recognize it; everything had been changed. Large tables occupied both sides of the hall with piles of gold casually laid out on top and bags underneath. On one were large cards for playing faro and on another spun a roulette wheel. On one spin, winning bets had been placed on 31 and 36; red won first and then black; even and then odd. Different bets paid out different multiples based on their odds, so that a handful of coins could become thousands in no time. On one side, '*gioco fatto!*' (the game has concluded) was loudly repeated, and on the other were heard 'black', or 'even', or '25' and whatever the outcome, gold coins were then pushed about the tables by the croupiers' rakes. The ladies and gentlemen bustled around the tables noisily, putting down handfuls of coins on the layout's numbers or colours and then quietly walk along to other chambers as if disinterested in the game, sending someone else over to inquire on whether they won or lost with neither joy nor regret for the outcome.

Passing through several rooms, I stopped at one where it was not so boisterous and sat down on a couch by a door and fireplace so that everyone had to pass me by on entering. The room was furnished with sofas and armchairs; on one, someone drew several monograms with chalk; on another, with cards in their hands, they wrote double entendres; close to me, someone muttered about love; another pair passing by whispered about something similar; in the corner at the window, a laugh came from behind the curtain. They began to recite poetry and one exclaimed: 'beautiful, perfect!' One lady dropped her glove beside me, intentionally of course; I picked it up and she and her friend sat down on the sofa. She thanked me and invited me to join them. The conversation began and though I was not timid or at a loss for words, I was carried away with politeness and indulgence. As the sofa was very small for three, we moved to another and for some reason I cannot remember, we moved again to a third and I suddenly found myself in the company of a duchess, princess and countess. I was then handed a stack of coins to run over to the card tables and several kind words for my part. The women I first met engaged with the others and they took me on. The conversation, perhaps to the surprise of many, I must say was not limited to trifling pleasantries, judgements of fashion, local news and the like; on the contrary, the very young and beautiful ladies here analysed literature and told intricate and sharp jokes. No one deliberated on their answers and the conversation was simple as if between close friends and everyone generally spoke from the heart. If the ladies should wish to please, the gentlemen would be pleased with them, but it was very clear that the former were concerned with the dexterity of the mind and the latter only paid attention to youth and beauty. What was more surprising for me was that they spoke very bravely: 'you're very kind! Ah, how sweet he is. *Vi vogli bene*', which should mean 'I wish you well' if translated literally, but effectively means 'I love you'.

At twelve, a bell rang, the coins returned to their owners' pockets and the games ended. The bank did not pay out for those games partially in session. After the salon, the people typically went for a stroll in the Flora garden, along the waterfront or down Cassero Street, for which such a walk is called *Cassariata*.

## The Palace

Thick walls, sometimes cracked and blackened by time, small windows, two quadrangular sections on the edges like towers above a solid three-storey structure and between them a terrace decorated with flower vases and small fruit trees comprising the roof of the palace provides an excellent view of all the buildings of Palermo. The viceroys of Sicily who lived in the palace modified the ancient building at various times and built new structures around it, creating an ugly motley of styles with the remnants of Arab architecture and Norman towers visible. The courtyard was covered with white marble and four water fountains murmur ceaselessly. Beyond the front stairs, dark passages and open galleries led us to the palatial chapel. The dome and walls are decorated with Greek mosaics as in Monreale. The choice, beauty and value of the stones deserve special attention. An artist will not find anything superb in it as this work belongs to the age of Gothic barbarism when art was in decline; but so many centuries have not degraded this work at all. Of all the arts, only mosaics can withstand blows and heat and survive the centuries. The church is poorly lit but this darkness, amidst a wealth of golden and silver ornaments slightly tarnished over time, will be pleasant for the devout. Whoever does not like the heavy sight of antiquity must visit this church for its Correggio; his painting of the Mother of God, the young Jesus and Saint Catherine alone surpasses all the mosaics and chandeliers. The Saviour lies on a pillow, surrounded not by a subtle glow but by radiant light which proved his divinity. Mary stands before him on her knees with her hands folded and in her eyes, a motherly tenderness and awe can be seen in her gaze, along with her prayer. One cannot doubt her love for her child and that she is praying for the Son of God. The infant looked at his mother with a smile and she smiles back at him; their expressions are not at all like those I have seen in many other images – they are divine and inimitable. Saint Catherine, with her head bent, looks at the child with lively delight. Her feelings flow through the viewer, whose soul is shocked by the presence of the shrine, does not dare to admire the physical beauty of Saint Catherine, marvels at the emotion of the virgin and rushes directly to Christ's face. The image of Saint Placidus attracts attention: the shading and colours have excellent accuracy, vivacity and clarity.

From the chapel, we passed several rooms decorated with heavy silks and carved furniture, all antique and without taste. We stopped in one chamber to look at two statues carved from stone and we were told they were works by the glorious Archimedes; they were large and nothing more. On the walls were hung portraits of the kings and viceroys who ruled Sicily. In these, except for old coats, helmets, plates and ruffled cuffs, there was nothing interesting. In the next room, paintings were veiled by curtains, promising something greater. The caretaker reading off the names of the viceroys with each portrait, noticing our inattention, drew the curtain and spoke coldly: 'Titian's *Danaë*, Carraci's *Venus*, Guido's *Cupid*, Albani's *Rachel*, *Philanthropy* by Scidoni, an apprentice of Correggio, and here is Correggio himself'. We stopped, fixed our eyes, and I will simply say that no matter how I saw girls and children, lovely and sweet, I could not imagine that they were alive on the canvas without the artistic perfection of Correggio. The child laughs as if from her gentle heart. Naturally no mother could pass it by or leave its side without wishing to caress it. The maiden's smile is enough to give even the cold-blooded Quaker pause to ponder. Correggio painted from nature and from the heart, he was a sensitive man and naturally he loved, which is inimitably transferred into his paintings. The pride of all the oldest and latest painters must be reconciled before his works.

My comrades went to see a collection of medals and coins while I stayed in the gallery and continued to view the pictures, noticing in them such ready and conspicuous impressions that I then began to hastily record my thoughts. These will of course be unsatisfactory for artists, as I only describe what I enjoyed. Several times later I rewrote my thoughts, tried to memorize the whole impression, but was not happy with everything and finally returned to what I intended in my notebook's first draft. In Titian's *Danaë*, only the body is beautiful; there is no soul in her. Carraci's *Venus* was full, white and tender, but her nudity and inflamed, passionate eyes were those of an ordinary woman, of which there are many in the world and in paintings. I saw a print very similar to this, though I cannot recall where, under the authorship of Portofranco. Guido's *Cupid* slept peacefully but his pink lips retained a dangerous and cunning smile; if he woke and opened his eyes, the beauties in the gallery would flee with fear, but in his present state, none of them would avert their gaze from his nudity. Albani's *Rachel* has a perfection of earthly beauty and technique. The young Rachel is innocent and simple, her beautiful eyes are half-closed with long black lashes; her chastity can be seen in all her features. The covering thrown on her head is so delicate that through it her hair is visible which would seem as soft and thin as silk if it could be touched. With one glance at Scidoni's *Philanthropy*, you can see that he was the pupil of Correggio. The young woman is portrayed, to the surprise of the viewer, without any beauty. She gives pieces of bread to a child with mercy and kindness, but cannot a charming woman be just as good? Does Scidoni believe that beauties are very rarely without vanity? By her facial features, one can conclude that he painted this portrait in England. The kindness in her gaze and expression, the only charms in her face, shone brightly from her clear, blue and stirring eyes and was portrayed in her smile. In the child, expectation and joy are not wholly extinguished but there is something missing. It would not require much more mastery for Scidoni to become equal with his master.

Near these great monuments of the visual arts, two small pictures painted by one of Palermo's nobility were on display. The first depicted butterflies and the second was of a grapevine. A child would try to catch these butterflies as if they were standing on the wall, and Praxiteles himself, looking at these grapes, would say that they are ripe and fit to eat.

In a collection of rare manuscripts, they showed us one ancient text written on papyrus and another on vellum. The latter contained a service to the Mother of God in Latin. Some illuminator adorned her with miniature vignettes and after three centuries, those roses and peaches have yet to wither. Another manuscript, burned in Herculaneum, deserves special attention. They found a means to separate the scorched sheets and managed with extraordinary difficulty to copy several pages over many years. Glory to the patient scholars engaged in this tedious work!

Among the vessels, statues, busts and various instruments of the Romans, Greeks and later eras, a portion of which were brought to the king after the discovery of Herculaneum and Pompeii,[6] each item shows either a successful vision, an elegant artistry or a rare, precious material. The vessels and especially the censers, lachrymatories and candlesticks were very fine. The bronze busts and statues of Greek works were of the finest style. Of these, the faun and two wrestlers are the very best. The faun truly slumbers and the naked wrestlers preparing to spar, no matter how small they are compared to life, make the viewer feel genuinely threatened. In the many toys or miniatures, different animals were reproduced with surprising accuracy, giving life to their bronze and marble. Among the musical instruments lies a flute which the Polynesians play with their noses, carved from bamboo or the wood of coconut trees. In the same room many large books were exhibited containing descriptions and sketches of unfinished paintings from the best painters of the ancient and modern eras. I enjoyed the images of the Greeks most of all. One was of a nymph plucking a flower; another was of a sleeping dryad being discovered and embraced by a faun; a third depicts the elderly Silenus holding in his hands an infant who stretches out its arms to reach a grapevine held cheerfully over the head of an old man by a young girl. Is it not true that with these images of beauty, love and the three ages of man, the Greeks were able to explain their thoughts in the tenderest way? I end my review of the rarities and curiosities with three trifles: a small chariot harnessed by two bees while a mottled butterfly stands in place of the coachman and holds the reins with its legs. Another, slightly larger, is drawn by a parrot and driven by a locust. The third chariot contained a jug entwined with roses as its cargo and two small, laughing nymphs are making off with it in haste. This was how the Greeks animated their favourite dreams and fantasies.

Descending to the lower floor and entering the armoury, in three halls I saw all the murderous weapons from the baton of Cain to the Italian dagger, saw the

---

6     The ancient cities of Herculaneum and Pompeii, buried by an eruption from Mount Vesuvius in 79 AD, were rediscovered in the 1720s during the digging of wells and other routine constructions. Smith, *A New Classical Dictionary*, s.v. 'Herculaneum'; Ibid., s.v. 'Pompeii'.

cudgels of the Iroquois, the darts of New Zealanders, all the weapons by which the Romans, Greeks and Scythians conquered one another, and on the whole, one could see the incremental steps of mechanical craftsmanship toward perfection which further and further enabled man's anger and refined the art of fratricide. The king, as a passionate hunter and sharpshooter, collects weapons from the most famous master craftsmen and his muskets can truly be called royal. The best of them are distinguished by the immaculate finish, the intricacy of their mechanisms and the strength of their metal. They were decorated with gold, mother of pearl and precious stones and were laid in expensive cases. Hunters will find many worthy objects of admiration here. I noticed just three: the first was a double-barrelled musket which could fire 24 shots in rapid succession with the use of a mechanism that fed the barrels with a magazine of 24 cartridges; the second was an air gun hidden in a walking cane; and the third was a dagger which splits and widens its blade when driven into the victim's body and then fires a shot from a small pistol barrel concealed in the handle.

## Hospice for the Poor

This building has a simple but massive appearance. Magnificence here is sacrificed for the greater good. Outside the building there is a garden with a beautiful fountain. Rising up a gently inclined staircase, decorated with fountains and decent statues, we entered the central storey. Men and women are divided into separate wards. Some of the residents were convalescing, some were severely ill, others were incurable and dying and some were insane. In a large chamber, at a common table, over 300 patients eagerly swallowed pieces of bread floating in soup; they asked for our charity out of habit. The rooms are always unclean and if the windows were not opened, the air could be harmful. Here they are treated with the simple means of rest, food and lemon juice, which is especially useful in the local climate. The doctors are famous for their prowess and the sick, I was assured, do not die here prematurely. In the reception room is a life-sized portrait of Ferdinand IV. It was a very close likeness and I looked upon him with respect. Ferdinand was loved by his subjects and as a kind sovereign who defended the poor and orphaned, he was worthy of his people's gratitude and devotion. On the lower storey, on both sides of a long corridor are series of cells with low, vaulted ceilings where on one side, the incurable live out the last minutes of their lives and the other are occupied by the insane. One of them in the hall under the great arcades was lashed to the wall by a chain around his torso. His arms and legs were held with leather straps, his head was shaved and covered in stubble. Upon our appearance, he rushed at us and began to jump about like a fierce hyena, gnawing on his chain and hands and uttering indistinct noises in a hoarse voice. But when the caretaker entered the room, he threw himself into a corner and burrowed into the straw that lay there. This unfortunate person rejects the usual food and constantly begs for raw meat. His rabid spells strike every three months and last for two or three weeks. Entering another corridor, we came to a chamber labeled No. 1. A cardinal lay on a bed who blessed us with all the import of his office. 'This is a beggar', said the caretaker. In chamber No. 2, was a 20-year old student who was mad with ambition and called himself a general, constantly drew up plans and dispositions for his armies to carry out in battle. His kindly caretaker reported our arrival and took his orders, even addressing him as 'your excellency!' In the third chamber, a destitute baron was obsessed with the fact that he only had on him one of his hundred waistcoats, the other 99 being elsewhere. Most of the mad interred here had delusions of grandeur and more were female than male.

'Do you have anyone mad from love?' I asked the doctor.

'There isn't anyone now; we had in the past, but they quickly recover with us. Our women are philanthropic', the doctor continued jokingly, 'they do not like to drive others crazy and rarely give reasons to despair. As Pangloss rightly said: "everything in the world is for the best", and within evil itself there is good enclosed'.[7]

Lastly we were showed a mad girl. I asked then: 'from love, of course?'

'No', the doctor replied coldly. 'She had the misfortune of losing her father who was publicly executed for a proven crime. She accompanied him onto the scaffold, no matter how much she was persuaded to come down, and stayed with him until his final moment. Her firmness and calm spirit persuaded them to relent in trying to talk her down, but when her father's head rolled across the platform and the man's blood splashed his daughter's face, this unfortunate girl picked it up, kissed it and wrapped it in her shawl. She then fainted and went mad. A year later she regained her senses but as soon as she left the hospital and encountered a soldier, she recalled the execution and again lost her mind. Now she is recovering and when she has returned completely, the queen has ordered that she be removed to a village where she will be provided with a sufficient pension from Her Majesty'.

## The Field of the Dead

When I was a little unwell, on one red day I left my apartment in the suburb of Saracen near Porta Nuova in only my undress frock coat so that I could take a quiet walk along the street. Crowds of people with prayer books in their hands walked

---

7    In Voltaire's novel *Candide or Optimism*, the worldview of the character Professor Pangloss is that we live in the best of all possible worlds and that all things that we perceive as arbitrary, evil or malicious serve some greater cosmic purpose which is ultimately good, even if an individual man cannot perceive it. His mantra that 'all is for the best' has been used as a subtitle in some publications. Voltaire, *Candide or All for the Best*, trans. Walter Jerrold (London: George Redway, 1898), pp.1-17.

with me along the road on their way to attend mass. After about a *versta* [1.07 km], I reached a wall with a dilapidated gate and an avenue of cypress trees that led to a monastery; I changed my mind about my destination and decided to enter the church to pray. This pious disposition was rewarded by an unexpected occurrence; curiosity is satisfied with a terrible kind of death. The alley along which I walked was intersected by another and there the cypress trees stood sadly over countless simple tombstones. The slabs of marble were covered with verses and inscriptions. The green meadow separated the monastic structures from a garden. I asked a pedestrian nearby: 'what is this monastery called?'

'You are on the field of the dead', he said. The name surprised me but it was confirmed by strangers telling me the same thing. The monastery's bell rang out a few dull blows to announce the arrival of the deceased. I stopped, turned to the gate and saw several sedans with a black wooden cross on a long pole being paraded before them. The porters were in mourning clothes and their litters had the skull of Adam painted on them. I fell in with the retinue and entered the church with them to find quite a shocking sight. In the centre of the church, on a hearse upholstered in black cloth, there lay more than 20 bodies without coffins. Some were dressed in fine clothes but without shrouds and some were simply wrapped in course cloth. I had seen death in many forms, and by my duty and honour I did not fear her, but I will admit that this new scene caught me off guard and astonished me. Their weakness after illness, the lamenting psalms and music that tore at the soul, and the woeful faces, cries and tears surrounding the hearse made me feel as if I could not withstand the sad rite of burial, but curiosity compelled me to stay. The liturgy ended, the relatives gave their last kiss to the dead, everyone departed and the church was locked up. I had nothing else to do but to ask the Capuchin monk as he walked past to explain their rites of burial.

The monk was a terrible sight: barefoot, in a thick reddish brown cassock and very unkempt. By this appearance, I did not expect him to be polite but the opposite turned out to be true; he was even very indulgent. To my first question, the Capuchin kindly promised to satisfy my curiosity. He then asked with whom he had the honour of speaking and when he heard that I was Russian, he bowed and continued, 'It is very pleasing, my good sir, to have an opportunity to do some service for a Russian'. He immediately ordered his keys be brought to him and we walked over to the long structure of the monastery's left wing where he unlocked the door and threw it open. Dear God, what I saw there! Thousands of human skeletons were standing and tied to the walls, stacked on tables and lying across the floor. I turned pale, shuddered, reproached myself for my vapid curiosity but, being ashamed to back away, I still continued to follow the Capuchin into the long, low gallery, lit weakly from above. On the chest of each skeleton was hung a black placard bearing the name of the deceased and the date of their death. Continuing further, I saw several coffins or rather chests of silver and bronze in which the remains of the high nobility rested. These tombs were locked and the key is usually kept by the closest relative. The inhabitants of Palermo often visit this monastery of death, choose their place in the galleries and cry over the coffins of their ancestors who died over 200 years ago. We stepped out into the garden only for viewing monuments, but I was very glad that we were soon out of the galleries and catacombs. The Capuchin took me to another structure enclosed by a high wall in the corner of the compound and a fair distance from the living quarters. A servant opened the iron gate for us. In the middle of the courtyard stood a low building no more than two *arshins* [1.42 m] tall and covered by a thick arch. The small windows around it were locked up with iron shutters. This is the common grave of all those who have died in Palermo. The cellar is filled with lime. Bodies are fixed to iron peels or shovels with shafts of an approved length and lowered into the lime and once it is reduced, the remaining skeleton is then placed in the gallery. The bodies of the most notable lords, being disembowelled in advance, are mummified in a small cave and their remains retain their skin and likeness for a long time.

In the hot climate, such burial is very prudent; the pestilence that killed half the inhabitants of Palermo prompted this practice. For more than 200 years, it has been decreed by law that the dead are not buried in the city's churches and are immediately taken from their homes without ceremony to the Capuchin monastery where, after the burial rites, the bodies are first taken to the lime pit and left for five to seven days as a precaution to prevent the accidental burial of people unconscious from prolonged fainting spells. Before this five day period, autopsies are also prohibited.

## The Noble Assembly

Our five-month stay in Palermo made us many acquaintances. In the garden, we already travelled through the most magnificent society like locals and people bowed to us from afar; at the ball, we did not sit in the corner without attention and the ladies gladly danced with us; in the theatre, instead of engaging in the performance, we walked from box to box and visited the other spectators as was the custom here. We were invited to a noble assembly as if we were relatives. We were all the more eager to mingle with this society when our friends, the officers of the guard, and all the young military men were typically in attendance, and every day brought an invitation to some new function: a gathering of ladies in the Flora garden, a masquerade, a church concert, a gathering of literati at a coffee house, a recital organized by lovers of music, or a function at the town club. Do you make a hasty conclusion, reader? If you judge by your own customs, you can be mistaken and unjust. The burgher community here, consisting of toiling merchants, simple artisans and craftsman, is not like that which we have in our country. Here, the daughter of a tailor or even a cobbler can dance the minuet, quadrille and twirl in a waltz and does not speak in the local tongue but rather the noble Tuscan dialect. Although here there are no diamonds and lace of great cost as in the royal assembly, the girls are all dressed cleanly, cheerfully and respectably. They all blossomed like roses in May, white and pink, with not one ugly face, no pallor to be seen or any tired eyes which one tries to avoid. For that reason, we could more often be found among the burghers and lower nobility than with the royal assembly. The girls treated us very affectionately. They had become used to the Spanish pride in their nobility (who still willingly mingled with them however) and were grateful for the slightest attention paid. Mothers left every freedom to their daughters and were not at all obstructive; it even so happened that some of them preferred Russians for their daughters over the local gentlemen. They eagerly and often presented us their daughter's hand for a dance and sincerely thanked us for the honour given.

In the continuation of the carnival holidays, we rushed about in a whirlwind of light. For several days we were invited to various concerts, balls, masquerades and park gatherings. The masquerades in particular demonstrate the character and temper of the playful Italians. I will speak about the carnival entertainments later, but now I will describe in a few words the masquerade, called a *veglione*, which lasts all night. After the theatre, the chairs and benches were removed from the stalls and a scene as extensive as the hall was set in half an hour. While these preparations were being made, people dined in the theatre boxes and an orchestra performed a symphony. The king and his family were in the state box without any guard; he was protected instead by the people's love. His presence did not dampen the gaiety of the crowds but rather further animated them. Once the hall was ready, a timpani began to boom, the orchestra played a march and suddenly characters in grimacing masks and matching clothes began to stream in from all sides. The hall was soon full and bustling, shrieks and laughter were abound and everyone was speaking in the voice of their persona; one person mooed like a cow, another sang an aria, from here came the meowing of a cat and over there a poet struck a strange pose and recited verses. Everyone was rushing about, affecting characters, twirling and posing and straining their voices and it was so entertaining for everyone that the spectators were laughing heartily. The masked figures dispersed into the boxes, even entering the royal box and amusing His Majesty with jokes, intricate verse, witty remarks or just their outlandish attire. The king was indeed very indulgent and merciful and was clearly consoled by this revelry.

## Grimaldi

'Tell me, who plays the violin at the San Ferdinando Theatre so beautifully?' I asked the Professor of Music Ciciliano.

'That is Grimaldi', answered the professor, 'our most glorious artist and chamber musician. A genius of the likes Italy rarely possesses, despite being a lazy and careless eccentric. Have you not already heard him? His life and oddities attract attention to him. He is very famous and respected by all; loved most of all by the king. I'll tell you a story about him', continued Ciciliano.

'He has such a gift that in the theatre, when he must play a solo, suddenly by inspiration he dazzles the whole public and surprises the other musicians more so by thinking up some of the finest music without any preparation. He sometimes writes notation from memory without the use of an instrument or dictates notes to another and loses patience for the musician trying to follow behind with his pen. He later took on a blind student who has a rare sense of hearing and became accustomed to understanding his teacher and could record long fantasias from him at once. Grimaldi does everything by the first impulse, never forces himself to do anything and even performs for the king when he pleases. Although he is not wealthy, he never performs for anyone for money and does not accept gifts from anyone; meanwhile, he lives at someone else's expense and donates his salary to the poor. He does not value gold nor does he care about himself. Unmarried, he led a disorderly but mostly serene life.

'The king, wishing to keep him at court, ordered him to marry. Finding a bride, Grimaldi was placed in her family's home and the rumours circulating that he was eligible were dismissed. The king greeted him and the surprised eccentric bowed, asking: "does Your Majesty wish to make me a cuckold?"

'"It would be better than absent-minded and lazy," replied the king.

'"I agree to whatever you wish." The king ordered that the wedding ceremony be concluded on the next day, generously awarded Grimaldi and increased his salary. What Grimaldi did – listen – after dinner he met somewhere with his friend whom he had not seen for a long time and they went to a coffee house for a lively and friendly conversation, forgetting all about his bride waiting for him at the church. When he came home at dawn, he responded coldly to the reproaches of his acquaintances: "I saw my friend of long estrangement and now I will get married"'.

'How I would like to hear him in person', I said.

'That is very difficult', answered Ciciliano, 'however, I will try to arrange it for you'. After his instructions, my comrade N. went to the coffee house where Grimaldi often visited, met him very briefly and brought him to his apartment where he stayed for a meal and after the theatre that same day, Grimaldi returned for supper and promised to visit us more often. He kept his word. For our part, we never asked him to do anything, but one day Grimaldi found the five best virtuosos in Palermo at our apartment and after dinner, being touched and inspired by one of Ciciliano's plays, he sent for his violin and the student; finally I heard him play. I do not know who was more surprised, him or his blind student who stood next to the one musician who played the same thing and in the same way as the sheet music laid before him. The pleased Grimaldi praised his blind transcriber, finally took up his violin and tuned it, played a few test notes, and then began in earnest. The musicians surrounding him tilted their ears toward his instrument or jotted down notes on their pages, and only Ciciliano dared to quietly accompany him on the mandolin. The blind man only played when ordered. An adagio began and the violin took on a living voice, all the sounds merged and the minor notes touched the heart. The musicians staring at their Orpheus[8] did not dare to breath and if that sad minor were to continue, we would have begun to cry, but he then smoothly transitioned to cheerful rondo and a folk song, rolling on the strings, which revitalized and delighted us. The musicians took up their instruments and all played together and then performed solos one after another in the manner of Grimaldi's fantasia. After he suddenly changed the tone, a new allegro began, the musicians gradually faded into the niches and in the distance we heard oboes, then a harp, the creaking of a gate, the barking of a dog, and imitations of various bird songs. We were amused for easily more than two hours by these wondrous musical arts and all of it was poured out on the spot from his head or, better said, from his soul.

## Fishing

Over the course of the summer, catching tuna fish is the most pleasurable pastime of the nobility. This fish comes from the Atlantic in large schools, usually staying close to the coasts, and make fishing very profitable. Their catches are salted and then exported, constituting a major portion of Palermo's trade. The tuna has a length of three *arshins* [2.13 m], is disproportionately thick and contains a juicy red flesh similar to salmon. The method of fishing is rather intricate and unknown in other parts of Europe. I rode to Mondello, north of Palermo, to see the construct called the *tonnara*, which consists of thick nets occupying a space of two to three or more *verstas* [2.13-3.2 km], divided into several chambers which are named according to a house's plan, for example: the first is called the hall, the second is the dining room, the third is the bedroom and so on, but the final chamber is always called the room of death. This network, which I helped to load, sinks to the bottom and is held by anchors. When the fish enter the first chamber, the small entrance is closed by a special net and the man on watch sends a signal to several dozen boats to approach. They form a square around the *tonnara* and when the

---

8    In Greek mythology, Orpheus was a legendary musician wielding the lyre of Apollo and taught by the Muses. He could enchant any person, animal or even inanimate objects with his music. Smith, *A New Classical Dictionary*, s.v. 'Orpheus'.

fish begin to circle the walls without an exit, they find a new hole and enter the next chamber. The fishermen begin to beat the water starting in the first chamber to drive the fish through the whole system into the room of death. When the final chamber is full of fish, they cautiously and gradually pull it ashore, careful not to agitate the strong fish within. Here a final signal is given and the fishermen and spectators attack with their spears, some jump into the water and swim together with the fish; some hit them with small darts and others drag the dead fish onto land. The joyful exclamations, shouts and usual din greatly entertain onlookers. The owner of the fishery invites guests and entertains them in tents spread out along the shore. The fishermen participating in the catch receive rewards, dance and sing and turn the affair into a cheerful and simple rural holiday. I was assured that sometimes a thousand or more fish are caught in a single *tonnara* and although they are sold very cheaply during the fishing season, with the five fisheries around Palermo combined that belong to the king and four prominent nobles, their income reaches 800,000 rubles per year.

The catching of swordfish as well as many other small creatures such as moray eels, gold fish etc., gives spectators an even grander spectacle, especially since it resembles the catching of whales in miniature. After the setting of the sun, in calm weather, several boats suddenly cast off from the shore and spread out across the bay. On the bow, one fisherman holds a lit torch near the water while another with a sharpened harpoon stands on his feet ready to strike a mortal blow. The light of the torch attracts fish that come up to the surface and are instantly stuck with the harpoon. As the swordfish is very large and strong, the fishermen chase after it for a rather long time and strike it with the harpoon and a few darts with every appearance. Injured in this fashion, the fish fights close to the boat, stabbing it with its solid, sword-like bill roughly two *arshin*s [1.42 m] long and pouring water into the boat with its tail as if to flood it. Eventually it tires and bleeds to death. The fishermen haul it into the boat or tie it to the stern with a rope. On a bright and quiet summer night, the great number of boats that set out on these expeditions, lit by their torches, appear like a large illuminated town on the water. This method is used throughout Italy and the fishermen wielding the harpoons are very adroit and skilled in this technique, enjoying the general respect of their peers.

## A Day in Fashionable Society

In Palermo the people live in public, always among strangers, and return to their homes only to sleep. The life of high society is one of eternal wandering; it seems none of the nobles here likes peaceful domestic privacy, live in luxuriant excess and do not think at all about their finances. They seek out pleasure everywhere, they laugh and rejoice over everything, console themselves for every trifle, never engage in important debates about politics, religion or government, do not condemn anyone, and always joke, sing, dance, compose poetry and the most gentle of them recite these verses before the ladies. Both sexes are concerned with the same thing: whatever should prove to be the most entertaining. It can be said that the Sicilian nobility, in the theatres, masquerades, church festivals, folk shows and gatherings, spend their time in perfect bliss, ceaseless ecstasy and the highest of happiness.

To give an idea of how time passes for this society, we will follow a fashionable baron, a young man of fine breeding and a gentle admirer of the fair sex who lives by kindness, sweetness, and wisdom. In the morning, before 10, not a carriage can be heard, only the crowds of merchants, artisans and other people in the streets and as Palermo is very crowded, the streets and squares are always like a fairground. At noon, carriages begin to clatter and half-asleep servants draw the blinds and open the windows. Our young baron, not getting up, drinks hot chocolate in bed at this time and if the weather is not too hot, he sets out to visit his friend the marquis, for example, who receives him while still lying in bed in casual clothes and under a silk blanket. Modest readers, blushing at reading these lines, will complain that I have planted this immodest habit. In justification I will say that this was the fashion here, and fashion is law everywhere. This lifestyle is already seductive for the ordinary among us, but even the reserved among the local men do not see anything wrong with it and the most timid of women with the strictest morals soon become accustomed to it and even learn to enjoy it. From the marquis, the baron visits a duchess who has already risen and sits at her dressing table, sorts through the pages of new compositions and listens with a smile to the clever hairdresser who tells her the city's latest news. The baron adds some from his own knowledge, praises her hair, finds that the blue or pink colour is the best compliment for her face, rushes about and fusses over her instead of a servant, handing the duchess her perfume, lipstick, hairpins or a handkerchief, helps her dress, argues with the maid, and praises her black, mischievous eyes. The duchess narrows her eyes with cunning and laughs almost discontentedly; finally she arises and bids 'addio, caro' (farewell, my dear). After these morning visits, the baron browses in the shops and the studios of the sculptor and painter who usually live on the ground floors and complete their works in the open street. The baron, as a connoisseur, notices the shortcomings and gives some advice before leaving with a hearty exclamation for a splendidly-maintained coffee house which he visits more often than any other.

Here the numerous throngs begin to surge and acquaintances and strangers alike become a single boisterous family. They argue, joke with each other, take no offence to a sharp word and repel them with intricate speeches, they play pranks on each other and chase after romantic adventures both fortunate and unfortunate. Poets, literati, professors and abbots in the corners read their writings and if they are poor, the other guests yawn; if they are good, they clap their hands and shout:

'unbelievable, incomparable!' Crowds move ceaselessly from one door to the other, including peddlers of haberdashery, toys and trinkets and ruddy villagers with baskets of flowers who offer a bouquet with a bow to anyone who makes eye contact. A Capuchin monk with a cross in one hand and a small plate in the other and a wilting countenance reads a prayer and while glorifying mercy to the poor, he receives spare change in the smallest denominations with humility! Hungry beggars stand at the open doors and windows, crying and begging. A servant carrying a censer through the halls forces them to remain silent or even drives them away from the door. Our baron, as a noble gentleman, sits casually on the sofa and orders a servant to bring him a small cup of coffee or frozen desert and glances over the newspapers without reading them, eavesdropping on the conversations around him. He admires his diamond ring or the shapeliness of his legs, frequently checks his watch with feigned impatience, and kills time by examining the poor prints on the walls, adjusting his cravat and cuffs in front of a mirror, and finally caresses the lovely maid who sits behind the sideboard in a gilded armchair and flirts. This is how he ends his morning.

At 5 o'clock, the baron returns home, redresses, rides to a better restaurant to dine and tries to sit at the common table beside any beautiful woman he can, but not having time to pleasantly converse with his two unfamiliar neighbours, they are served and everyone pays for themselves. After dinner, the baron disrobes and rests in bed typically until 7. As soon as the street lights are lit, a terrible noise begins. Coaches, carriages, gigs and phaetons lit by torches shake the pavement, skip on stones, push one another, collide and break away from each other. They ride off to variously attend a tragedy, an opera, a national *divertimento* and so on. At 9 o'clock, the baron goes to the royal assembly, from which his wife departs and visits noble and burgher clubs alone. He plays card games, eagerly listens to and accepts the tender words of his fellow gentlemen, wins a dear glance with a witticism and courteously arranges a rendezvous. At midnight, the noise grows to the extreme. In Palermo, this time of day is as busy as our noontime. The whole public flocks to the waterfront and the Flora garden. The embankment (*marino*) has an even better view than the Palatial or English Quays in St. Petersburg. On one side is the vast bay, always covered by warships and merchant vessels, and on the other is a part of the city walls and a long building with a wide terrace covering its ground floor. In the middle of the embankment is a round pavilion with a dome and a beautiful colonnade which hosts symphonic concerts performed by an orchestra. Pedestrians walk along the sidewalk and the carriages squeeze in between the footpath and the walls. It should be noted that here the carriages are even more luxurious than in our capitals. Generally all the carriages, even the hired taxicabs, are in the latest English style. The nobleman, if he dared to appear on foot in the street, would have been mocked. Besides the queen and the archbishop, they all travel with a pair of coachmen covered with rich golden livery, and some even use footmen running alongside. The horses, especially the riding horses, are of the most beautiful Barbary and Sicilian breeds.

After making a few laps of the *marino* in their carriages, they head to the Flora for a walk while their carriages return to Porta Felice and the lackeys extinguish the torches. No one is allowed to enter the garden with torches or lanterns and beggars or anyone poorly dressed (with the exception of musicians) are barred as well. In the four gazebos in the corners and in the central square of the garden, five wind orchestras pour out sweet harmonies. A more entertaining venture cannot be imagined for everyone in general but they are all the more beneficial for young men, especially lovers. The brilliant dresses of the ladies, their beauty and gentle treatment of even strangers represent the pleasing deception for both the eyes and the heart. I did not see anyone sitting and lost in thought; a quiet whisper, a rustling of the feet, a smile or a sigh are enough to captivate even the most absent-minded person. The Flora could be more properly called the garden of Venus; it truly was a temple of love and courtship. Princes and counts, army officers, civil servants and the clergy, marquises, baronesses, actresses, maids and the best beauties of the commons were out looking for adventure, pleasure and merriment. One cannot distinguish who is pursuing whom, with everyone looking for something and their hearts seemingly burning with impatience. Two female friends sit in a broad shadow and two gentlemen timidly approach them. If the girls smile benevolently, the young men immediately take them by the hand and go together down the broad alley where they serve cooled treats that seem to only worsen the heat. In the darkness of covered lanes, there are sometimes disguised individuals; they whisper a password to nearly every passerby which only one lucky person will recognize. In the large straight paths, with an open face and an unassuming smile, wives and innocent maidens walk into the shadows to disguise their vices and debauchery. From here, wrapped in long cloaks and placing a hat over their eyes, lowering their veils and tilting their heads down as far as possible, couple after couple walk out of the garden through the gate where, with concealed lanterns, *servitore di piazza* offer their services. In an alley, light carriages await to take them into the centre of town at a gallop to the backdoors of those houses where good-natured matrons and the keepers of the fashion shops, out of compassion for the wives of jealous husbands, rent out beautifully decorated rooms for an hour, where in silence and liberty one can 'cavare il capriccio' (indulge in a fantasy), as they say.

After 2 in the morning, the music ends, the baron looks for his wife and does not ask where she has been or what she has done, because he would rather not answer such questions for his own activities. This is why such husbands are very lenient and willingly allow their wives all kinds of liberties. At sunrise, some people go home, others find a restaurant, and little by little the rumbling of carriages and coaches dies down and everyone retires.

In the great heat of summer, the nobility live in their country homes in Bagharia and Il Colle, however the Marino is never wholly vacated. In the winter, on cloudy and rainy nights, instead of walking through the gardens, the carriages drive their clients up and down Cassero Street and it sometimes becomes as crowded as the carnival games during a festival. On clear winter evenings, a walk in the garden begins at noon but high society does not assemble there before 6.

## Habits and Customs

The Sicilians are perceptive and quick-witted, love idleness and amusements, have skill in deception and by their Greek heritage they are not inferior to them in cunning and subtlety. The sky, though temporarily clouded by darkness, is almost always a bright azure, and the seasons are so similar here that in the winter and summer alike it is possible to live in the open air, from which the body gains flexibility, the imagination is broadened with more ideas and the intellect benefits most of all from a moderate and fruitful spark. Therefore, perhaps, the character of the Sicilian is clearly written in his intelligent, sparkling eyes. By their excessive liveliness, they do not brag about the improvements of their minds, as they do not like profundity, and they do not have the coolness that is necessary for finishing difficult and time-consuming works. In crafts and the fine arts like architecture, music and painting, they are the most practiced. Their artists choose fine subjects in their works but in execution the finish is not always precise. They have no affinity for mechanized labour and if they engage in it, it is very mediocre. Being disposed to restlessness, impatience and heatedness, they are excessive in both their vices and their virtues. They are gentle in love and indulgent to their spouses, but if one has cause to be jealous, his revenge is terrible. In hard misfortunes, they firmly tolerate losses without despair and, loving their king, are submissive to the authorities, but the slightest oppression cannot be carried without open grumbling. Their piety is superstition, good nature seems to them to be a deceit of the mind, sincerity is only contributing to liveliness, cunning is the art of living, forgery takes on the appearance of generosity. Courage is a mixture of cruelty and magnanimity. In the rest of Italy, Sicilian robbers are famous for their passion and nobility of spirit; if the government wished to direct this spirit to a proper goal and use it to bring honour to their fatherland, the military prowess of the people could be raised from the unremarkable to the truly heroic.

The Sicilians have an affable appearance, are very attentive to foreigners and always cheerful. Whoever sees their pantomime for the first time will be surprised and amazed by the agility of their theatrical movements. If the good and gentle German with all his inflexibility and phlegmatic temperament were to suddenly resettle in Sicily, he would not notice the gradual alacrity observable among the people in his new southern habitation and would have thought at first that he was living among jesters whose eternal delight would, probably very soon, compel him to move more quickly and eventually he would learn to dance, sing wildly and laugh with a kind heart as they do. The very lowest of the Sicilian mob are much better skilled in the pantomime than the Neapolitans. The Sicilians, without saying a word, but by the movement of their eyes, hands, legs and whole body, can convey their thoughts so clearly and strongly that even a foreigner who does not know their language will easily understand what is being said. The birth of this custom is attributed to the tyrants of Syracuse who forbade everyone from speaking to one another at gatherings for fear of conspiracies. This, so they say, gave rise to silent signs and lively expressions which were honed to perfection by the fiery imagination of the Sicilians. Their signals are elaborate enough to substitute speech and writing, for example: putting a finger on the upper lip means 'man'; showing the length of a dress with both hands means 'woman'; miming a queue or lock with one hand means 'girl'; closing the fingertips together and kissing them means 'beautiful'; kissing the palm of the hand and blowing across it means 'I kiss you'; placing the hand on the heart and sighing means 'I love you'. These have responses as well: if someone wipes their mouth with a handkerchief, it indicates rejection or refusal; to lower one's eyes conveys doubt; shaking the head after doubt means 'I don't believe you love me', but before doubt it means 'I don't understand' or 'what is that?'; jealousy is signified by biting one's fingernails; biting on a finger expresses anger or is a threat. To these and other gestures, flourishes could be added, with its own meaning and special kind of telegraph made by the fingers. In the course of romantic relationships and to communicate thoughts and desires, all possible means are invented.

The women in general are lovely. In Italy, especially the people of Palermo and Catania, they are considered beauties. They are called 'bel boccone' (a beautiful morsel) and there is something of the Greek preserved in both the sexes. The Sicilians are genuinely striking; they are quite tall, stately, full of liveliness, have fiery black eyes and surprisingly, for such a hot climate, they are very pale. Naturally they owe this to the purity and freshness of the air. To that end (speaking of the women of Palermo with which I am more familiar) they are all agreeable, clever, always cheerful and sweet in the full sense of the word. Despite the fact that girls as young as 11 and 12 are married to men, and despite the fact that they are beginning to feel too much love here too early, even despite immodesty and waste, the women at the age of 30 are still just as fresh and lovely as they were at 18. On the contrary, the girls around that age are very pale and languid. Beauty, that gift from heaven, is preserved of course by the blessed air; in Sicily it seems to me to contribute all the more to the splendour and the image of the idle, carefree life, with a passion for all manner of pleasure, comfort and the satisfaction of the heart. The women here have almost secured the same rights of men, love is dominated by their wilfulness, whims and sometimes fashion, seldom vanity, and even less often by avarice; on the contrary, the men are not ashamed to live off of their fading charms. Love in high society is a great flame that only lasts a short while, rarely burns for several months, and even less often for a year or two; it typically lasts only three weeks. A man's infidelity is considered a greater crime here than a woman's. It is not permissible here for a man to abandon his love before she has dismissed him, though not many people complain about this impermanence, as the tastes of both sexes are equally variable. The fashionable ladies freely talk about their lovers; the husbands favourably receive their wives' friends; mothers kindly admit that their daughters are in love and pronounce this without blushing just as one might say 'she has a headache'.

Matrimonial duties have no price. Happy marriages occur more often among the lower class and rarely if at all among the nobility. Taking concubines is nearly universal in the middle class. Fathers, mothers, husbands and brothers do not cherish the honour of their daughters, wives and sisters and many even openly trade them. Parents marry their daughters during minority and do not allow choices of the heart to be made. When signing wedding contracts, it is pronounced that she subsequently elect a cicisbeo or one of her cousins might be appointed to this post immediately with her consent. These gentlemen servants are a legitimate intermediary between husband and wife, a trustee and a petitioner in all her affairs; the husband must secure the bride's dowry by the pledge of his estate. For these connections, the cicisbeo, having some power over the husband, is certainly in a more convenient position than other competitors to gain favour with the wife, but the desires of the heart are not subject to law and the cicisbeo does not mean concretely anything more than a relative or friend participating in domestic affairs. We interpret the cicisbeo incorrectly. In Russian we use the word to mean an ardent admirer who is not always admired. Under the common name of cicisbeo there might be five or six individuals who make up the circle of acquaintances of a fashionable lady, each of which has his own position or role. For example, an old man famous for maintaining connections and rich for his money-lending had served as a 'cicisbeo' as a tutor, poet or musician. If there is a handsome young man or two or three on this domestic staff, then the real cicisbeo can be mercifully distinguished by the habit of reclining on the sofa, spitting on the silk carpet or whistling an aria of double-entendres. Lastly, one of the cicisbei is called *Il Patito* (the sufferer). The fate of this Céladon is worthy of true pity: sighing and burning with passion in vain, he must bear the ridicule of the other companions. This crowd of rivals, most of whom are satisfied with one affectionate look, live peacefully and do not dare quarrel. Deftness is a common property among the local women. If they are free and bored with this system, not even the most guilty wife resorts to deceit and lies, as infidelity is not regarded here as a mortal sin and this corruption need not be augmented by further crimes. But one still asks: what is a cicisbeo, what are his rights and to what extent are they limited? The comedy entitled *The Wife of Two Husbands* is the best answer. There are as many wives with two husbands as there are women. It is equally indecent for a lady to appear in public without a cicisbeo as to appear at a gathering with her husband. The companion is obliged to accompany the lady everywhere, must entertain or bore her everywhere, make himself available for her at any time, and this does not worry the husbands at all. These semi-marital ties may be for love, but most often are calculated arrangements. The fashionable husband has his own circle and while the wife is surrounded by young people, he is looking for conquests outside the home and opportunities to take advantage of someone else's property. For this reason, it is fair for the wife to repay him likewise. Simply put, the spouses live independent of one another. Everyone follows their own inclinations, which is why silence within the household and social life is no great dilemma for them.

This custom has great inconveniences however. A father cannot call his wife's children his own and this uncertainty is often accepted without the slightest scrutiny; coldness toward the children is the result. In those marriages made for decent appearances and continued by necessity, in which love has no part, there is no pleasure in being married; they are bound together by their children when only the wife can call them hers and not the husband. It is difficult to find a union that has neither the sweetness of love nor the consolation of marriage but the Italians have found it and they call it cicisbeismo.

However, some fashionable ladies surround themselves with cicisbei only in accordance with what is customary and employ the same coquetry simply to turn heads and fool the older men whom they occasionally choose for the vacancies in their circle of gentlemen servants so that they might protect them from insolent people. Despite all that and with such a decline in morality, true love still finds a way here; contrary to the general debauchery, the immaculate torch of passion still ignites the hearts and the happiness of such spouses lasts just as long here as it does everywhere it blossoms.

Noble girls are raised by tutors under the supervision of their mothers; only fathers of inadequate means, following the custom typical in Italy, give their daughters over to the monasteries for education. Sicilian baronesses,[9] having a good upbringing, are very courteous in public. They are accustomed to society from childhood and have complete freedom in conversation. The transgressions which were so frequent in the monasteries cannot be heard or are very rare in the

---

9    Bronevskiy's note: 'Here, the nobility generally appropriates the dignity of baronage'.

larger world. Parents here are not afraid that their daughters might disappear, for this misfortune happens only with those who do not allow their daughters to say a word and do not dare to let them out of sight; in society, they are only put on display. Such parents certainly do not believe that nothing excites young people to flee so much as banning all innocent amusements. The girls sent to the monastery therefore, in their strict imprisonment, think of nothing more than escaping as soon as possible, indulging in daydreams like a child dressing up dolls, and when they are finally free, they fall in love with the first living doll they meet.

Poetry here is so respected that although brides might be sure that the proclamation of love with prose is more sincere than in verse, the bridegroom who delivers his speech in verse gains an advantage over the rival who would speak only in prose. Sicilian poetry, like their fiery sky, breathes with tenderness and voluptuousness and is adorned with charming inventions that reveal the spirit of a people who are passionate for the elegant. The Sicilians for their outpourings of flattery so popular with the fairer sex should justly be honoured as natural and amazing poets. In the weddings of the nobility, there are no superstitious rites, but the splendour and lavishness at their receptions are commanded by the laws of fashion more than any superstition could. Among the commoners there is the following superstition: after a wedding, a female friend gives the bride and groom a large spoonful of honey, saying: 'live in harmony and love and be as fortunate as this honey is sweet'. It would be beneficial if something bitter were mixed with the honey in order to impress on the youth that there are rarely marriages without any troubles, that the road of life is strewn with pitfalls and every rose has its thorns. After leaving the church, the newly christened couple are put on donkeys decorated with flowers and ribbons while a rural orchestra consisting of bagpipes, clarinets, flageolets or guitars begins to play a humorous song. The matchmaker and friends, in order to ensure that the couple will have many children, throw wheat on the youths without interruption all the way to the groom's doorstep. This divination is fulfilled by reality, as Sicilian women are very fertile; many have up to 20 children each and some, as Fazella and Carrera assure us, have as many as 40. The custom of sprinkling newlyweds with wheat has been preserved from pagan times, as the same practice was used during the rites of Ceres, who was revered as the chief deity of the island of Sicily. Finally in commemoration of their patience and moderation, the young couple must not eat and after the meal, in order to remind the husband that he is taking on in his new wife years of difficulties and cares, the father of the bride gives him a leftover bone and says 'pick this clean and know that the bone you need to gnaw is much stronger and harder to swallow'. To be married in May is regarded as unfortunate and they try very hard to avoid it. This superstition has passed from the Romans to many European nations and although they do not heed it as stalwartly as the aversion to the First of April, it is still in general use.

The Sicilians are moderately tempered in their diet: meat is consumed very little while green vegetables and fruits, fish and all sorts of sweet dishes make up the most luxurious items on their table. Heavy consumption of iced deserts and lemonade in such a hot climate serve to keep them cool and, as doctors assure, to strengthen the stomach, but the excesses of various cool foods seasoned with spices produce the disease known as Umori Salsi[10] from the accumulation of acids in the body. The sale of ice and snow is very profitable, as the preservation of it is quite troublesome. In the winter when the snow falls on the mountains, lying for only a few hours, the peasants sweep the precious manna into caves in the mountaintops and pack it into icy masses with the help of water and salt which can last for a rather long time when carefully shielded from the sun. But as snow does not fall every year, it is not surprising that ice is sometimes as expensive as sugar. Drunkenness is considered a vice and although at first glance, the delight and gaiety of the people might seem to a foreigner to be a result of drink, but I never happened to see anyone, not even a member of the mob, drunk in the street.

The men of the nobility dress like the English; the ladies follow Parisian fashions. The commoners of Palermo and generally of all the coastal towns wear a sailor's attire with a red woollen cap. The peasantry, even in the worst heat, never shed their thick cloaks with large Capuchin hoods, which are very comfortable in inclement weather. When it is cold, they don an additional cloak or two. Such clothing protects them from the danger of catching cold in this climate, as in the mountains during intense heats reaching 70 degrees, or even 80 or more during the sirocco, the warm wind can suddenly become frigid. In the women's attire, something Greek has been preserved. The villagers very cleverly wear bedspreads and gird themselves with sashes like cummerbunds.

The Sicilians, both in features and character, retain some severity; judging by their actions and appearance, this is still the very same people who bloodied their hands during the Sicilian Vespers. In 1800, when the French Army returned from Egypt under treaty, one transport vessel stopped at Augusta and 93 French soldiers, who would not tolerate the cruel ridicule of the people, were massacred with stones and daggers. In Palermo, there was a similar misfortune with the Turks and if it were not for Admiral Ushakov who commanded the combined Russian and Turkish fleet at the time, the infuriated Turkish sailors – among whom there was a thief

---

10    Italian for 'salty humours'. Hippocrates's theory of the four humours asserted that the balance and mixture of four bodily fluids – blood, phlegm, yellow and black bile – were responsible for good health or illness. David Rothman, Steven Marcus and Stephanie Kiceluk (eds.), *Medicine and Western Civilization*, 3rd Ed. (New Brunswick, NJ: Rutgers University Press, 2003), p.43.

who stole from a shop in broad daylight – would have caused terrible bloodshed. Although the people are reliant on the nobility and clergy, the fear of daggers restrains injustice and oppression and makes their masters meek and lenient. The people of the villages are not so lazy as some travellers have described. This vice belongs to the rabble roaming in the large towns; their murder and robbery do not come from passions or deprivation, but from the habit of an isolated and depraved life. Many criminals confessed that they had committed murders solely in order to enjoy themselves for an evening. These so-called *lazzaroni* roam the streets begging and if occasionally out of necessity they secure employment at the docks, they bring all of their money to the tavern, hire a female companion, of which there are many, drink with her, sing and dance and 'enjoy the life', as they say. The sad thought that illness and old age will deprive them of their livelihood never disturbs their imaginations; for the state of an old pauper, due to the laudable piety of the rich, is the most carefree in matters of food and shelter. The government, having no means to employ so many destitute, cannot prevent the many murders they commit, although they do not happen so often as before in Palermo since the king's residence. At night, through all the streets and alleys, there are dragoons on horseback with loaded muskets; at 10 o'clock they spur their horses and drive the mobs back into the cellars and prevent anyone from walking the streets without a lantern. Under the rule of the viceroys, it cost no more than 100 or 150 rubles to hire a killer, but now, by the severity of the police, it is rarely possible to buy such villainies for a thousand.

The Sicilians, despite their many traditions of pleasure and idleness, have not yet lost their military spirit like the other Italians. They love amusements but do not lose sight of their fatherland and although military ranks do not hold the same respect as they should, the king could hope on the courage of the soldiers and the zeal of the populace in the event that he should need to take advantage of them.

## Religious Rituals on Holy Week and Easter

The people are pious and the churches are always full, but as the services are performed in Latin, being a diligent Catholic means confessing and attending services and never missing a mass or vespers, especially during illuminations and concerts. As the majority of the people have not read any of the Scripture, the clergy deems it necessary to occupy them with external rituals such as marches, fireworks and musical performances. Every town has a special ceremony of its own invention and is not a part of the established church celebrations. If such faith does not enlighten the people, then in this external blasphemy everything necessary can be found to be Christian in their simplicity of heart and without false reasoning.

In Palermo, besides the 46 male and 25 female monasteries, there are 121 churches, which belong to various monastic orders. On the holidays of the patron saints of each church, there is celebratory gunfire and a procession through the city during which the monks of that parish decorate the church or play music. The best virtuosos are among their singers and they try to attract more people into the crowds in order to compete with or surpass the richest monasteries; great sums of money are spent on these displays. I will not talk about many of the festivities like the celebration of the Body of the Lord (Corpus Domini [or Corpus Christi]), Christmas and the Washing of the Feet, common to all Catholics, not to mention the glorious celebration of Saint Rosalia, but I will discuss only the rituals of Holy Week and Easter which have yet to be described by any traveller.

In the first week of fasting, is announced during the daily agenda firstly the necessity of repentance, the prohibition or permission to consume meat or dairy products, then they announce the arrival of some glorious or famous preacher in the city who will speak in a particular church on a particular day and recite a particular text. Sermons begin from the second week and complete a circuit of all the churches each day. As these are spoken in the Italian language, the gatherings of people are tremendous. One preacher from Messina whose name I cannot recall truly has a gift for speech. He always spoke from the depths of his soul so convincingly and so eloquently that the listeners were frequently brought to weep. In the first speech on repentance, he threw himself onto his knees before the crucifix and pressed it to his chest with such passion, bursting into tears and sobbing, that I, being unaccustomed to such bold gestures never used on our cathedrals, fell to my knees before the pew. On the subject of bold gestures, I add that if these were employed only during the excitement of the sermon, they would be decent; but as the Italian preachers consider it necessary to use pantomime in all circumstances, it seems inappropriate to the holiness of the ground on which they stand. For example, when a preacher turns to the altar or to the crucifix, he pretends to walk around the throne for five or six paces; if he speaks to the servants, sometimes he completely loses his balance over the railing or threatens the sinners by waving a handkerchief at them; if he addresses an individual, he places his cap on the person's head and, pretending to sit down, he leans in and converses with an altered voice… Should the preacher not be skilled in his office, such theatrics would be not only improper but entirely impermissible.

On Holy Thursday in the city, a great movement begins in the morning. At several churches and along the large avenue they display wax statues in groups depicting the Stations of the Cross; here Judas sells Christ to the soldiers, there He is led to trial before Pilate, and so on. Apostles, bishops, scribes, Roman soldiers and crowds in ancient attire all seemed to be alive in the present through the perfect craftsmanship of the statues. When the archbishop read from the Gospel and said: 'the veil of the temple was rent in twain from top to bottom and the earth did quake'[11] the bell in the cathedral rang to begin the mourning. From this time until the Resurrection, no one is allowed to travel in carriages, ringing of bells is suspended, all the ladies and gentlemen appear in deep mourning and black sheets and carpets are hung from the windows. The king with an uncovered head and the entire royal family in mourning clothes, accompanied by the court staff, visit the cathedral and other churches on foot, listening to the vespers in the convent of Saint Cecilia. A choir of young pupils hidden from a curious glance behind an impenetrable curtain delight every listener. At 9 o'clock, I left the church located in the centre of the city and was amazed by the brilliant illumination along the two main streets. Between the sidewalks were set up arcades with pyramids and pillars between them at equal distances; the former were decorated with hung coloured lights and the latter were lit by braziers. In the distance, the four gates of Palermo sparkled with continuous fire. Until 2 in the morning, there was such congestion in the streets that it was necessary everywhere to wade through the people. The nobility was accompanied by a multitude of servants carrying lit torches before them. The services continued until dawn and all the churches were filled.

On Friday at 4 in the afternoon, a grand procession for the Entombment of Christ began. This ceremony was pious and magnificent. I was amazed at the illumination of the cathedral, admired the singing and orchestra, and was touched to the depths of my soul by the burial. From the palace to the cathedral, soldiers in black attire were arranged in two lines with banners, cannons and drums. The road where the king and his family were supposed to proceed was lined with a red carpet. Although I came to the cathedral two hours before the service, I could hardly push through the crowd to find a good spot to watch. The church was decorated and lit in a fashion like I have never seen, I must confess. Turning around bewildered, it seemed to me that I was in the hall of heaven where the sun and all the planets in the vast vaults of the church illuminated the room. The gigantic vaults were fixed with mirrors, the windows were covered with transparent paintings depicting the suffering of Christ, the walls were covered in black cloth dotted with stars made of gold and silver foil and the columns were covered with white and black taffeta. In the centre, opposite the main altar, stood a tomb carved from stone in which lay the Savior with a crown of thorns and was carried by cherubs and angels on a velvet carpet under a canopy covered with pearl and precious stones. The virgin at the foot of the tomb in deep sorrow fell prostrate at the steps of the catafalque, and likewise Joseph mourned at the head and two apostles on the sides. With this decoration, one must imagine at least 10,000 wax candles burning under the vaults in crystal chandeliers, at thirteen altars and

---

11    Matthew 27:51.

surrounding the funeral party in large candelabras. This light, reflected from the mirrors, spread such a dazzling brilliance that the church seemed to be enveloped in flames. A thundering of drums announced the king's procession, the archbishop met His Majesty in the portico and the service began. I was beside myself with the music I heard, but when they sang the verse 'The Noble Joseph', I was so touched I could scarcely hold back my tears. At the end of the service, the coffin was taken out of the church and placed on a funerary carriage. The king, archbishop and two princes of the blood lifted a precious shroud of diamonds and pearls from the throne and laid it over the tomb of the Saviour. The procession began in the following order: in front came the guilds of artisans with banners; followed by the nobility and mayors; then the clergy; a squadron of Roman horsemen; a crowd of Jews and Roman soldiers encircling a massive chariot pulled by twelve horses; behind the body walked the king with his family; a detachment of the guard and finally the common people followed behind. Imagine several thousand torches, the melodic sounds of thousands of instruments and voices, over 100,000 people crowding the street, standing at the windows and on the roofs. You can imagine the reverent impression that must be produced in the Christian soul by such a sacred procession, reminding us of the death of our Saviour. Due to the extreme crowding, I could not join behind the coffin which rounded the main streets and returned to the cathedral where the ceremony ended. The service, as on Thursday, continued all night; the people moving from church to church clutched the shroud to themselves and the very poorest gave something to the alms for the poor, even if it meant giving away the very alms they received; the clergy, to their credit, not only abstain from using this significant collection but add to it themselves so that on Easter Sunday, they are able to distribute it to all the poor of their parishes.

On Saturday at 3 in the afternoon, the booming of guns from the ships and fortresses and a terrible rumbling Martian fire at every church announced the resurrection of Christ. In Italy, cast iron mortars called *mascoli* are used for the celebratory fire. They are charged with a small measure of powder and stopped up with a wedge of soft wood; they are laid in one or several rows with one large barrel between every nine small ones so that when they are set off, they accurately resemble musketry and artillery fire in tandem. For the firing, they place the *mascoli* in a spiralling pattern or squares converging into a single centre and distanced from each other to control the timing and pattern of their ignition, and as the fire converges into the centre, it intensifies. The conductor lays out soaked fuses plugged into the touchholes and lights them from a distance. Where cast iron barrels cannot be procured, clay mortars are used. Due in part to poor weather and more so out of fear of hurting my wounded arm, I did not see the ceremony on Easter Sunday. The lighting, continuing through all of Holy Week, was in an excellent style and taste. On Cassero and Maqueda, in every chamber of every house were placed transparencies lit from behind by lamps, transforming both sides of the street into picture galleries that would have you believe you were standing in the Hermitage.

On Monday, passing from church to church, I observed the decorations and could not decide which I preferred, although the cathedral's was superior. Its columns were embroidered with garlands of artificial flowers, the altars had depictions of fragrant flowers and the walls were covered with greenery of coloured paper intermixed with reflective foil. Over the course of the seven days of Easter, charity for the poor is gathered in all the monasteries and parish churches, a custom worthy of imitation. Before the end of the liturgy and during the concert, the three most beautiful girls, either out of their own piety or by choice, I do not know, approach the altar; the priest gives one a silver plate, covers it with a veil and blesses a flower wreath placed on her head; the other two are decorated over the shoulder with garlands of roses and all three proceed together around the church and bow before anyone who places a coin on the plate. Following this custom, I prepared a few copper pieces, but I must admit that as the girls approached, I switched to silver and when they finally reached my place, I laid gold on the plate, which caught the eye of all three of them. While these alms are being collected, the poor were invited in the courtyard or behind the monastery for a communal meal which is concluded by the three girls, like angels, heading out and sharing the sums equally among the people. Another method of collecting donations afforded the poor a significant allowance: noble ladies of the greatest regard accept the responsibility to invite all who wish to subscribe to this noble cause. In that year, such donations were collected by the Princess Paterno. I met her once riding along Toledo in an open coach with a team of six horses, dressed in a black veil and holding a crucifix before her; the people followed her with blessings and she often stopped, went into the houses and took even from those passing through all sorts of trifles. I was assured that in a single week she collected 100,000 rubles, which were distributed to the poor on Sunday along with another donation of clothing and bread. In addition, she treated 3,000 beggars in the courtyard of her estate.

On Holy Saturday, instead of statues depicting the Passion of Christ, in the rich alcoves were placed excellently crafted waxworks of the Mother of God with fine taste and splendid attire. Before the alcoves from morning until night, during the week of Easter, orchestras of Calabrian bagpipes blew ceaselessly between choirs of the poor singing hymns and begging for mercy. Theatrical, regimental and church musicians, like ours on New Year, go to their homes to ring in the holiday. In conclusion, I will note a ritual worthy of special attention. On Saturday, the king, on the proposal of the criminal court, pardons several offenders (except murderers). This ceremony is called the Cleansing of Crimes and is accomplished as follows: in the square opposite the prison is erected a gallows surrounded by soldiers. Twelve selected criminals in chains and behind an escort are brought out of the prison in the very same fashion as if they were to be executed. The court official reads the death sentence to them and the executioner places a linen hood over each man's head and one by one brings them to the gallows to place the noose around their necks. On a signal, the rope is pulled and the hood is removed from the criminal's head. It is then declared that the king took his crime upon himself and granted a pardon. The soldiers present arms, strike a beat on the drum and join the people in shouting 'long live the King!' After this ceremony, the criminals go to church, repent, pray on their knees and take the sacraments. They are admonished to remain honest citizens useful to society, deserving of royal mercy. In the church, white shrouds are placed on them and they drive around the city in the company of musicians to collect alms.

## The Nobility

Count Roger in 1130 was recognized by the pope as King of Sicily and divided the realm into three parts: the first was given to the clergy, the second to the commanders of his army and the third he kept for himself. He laid the foundation for a feudal system which has long ceased to exist in Europe but survives to this day in Sicily. The nobility or baronage, as it is called here, comprises the military estate, for their rights of possession bring the obligation to take to the field with a certain number of vassals at the king's first request and this duty enjoys the privilege of *mero et mixto imperio*, the jurisdiction to sentence one's own subjects to death, with the only restriction being that the king must be notified before such a sentence is executed. There are 378 persons who possess these baronial privileges. The eldest son takes the father's title, while the younger sons are called 'don' and daughters are 'donna', which correspond to the German 'von' or the English 'lord' and 'lady'. In Sicily, there are many nobles who do not have these advantages, which is why a great deal of importance is placed on genealogy; the titles they use are as follows: prince (*principe*), duke, count and marquis. Although the first two are revered as superior to the latter, those with princely and ducal dignity were elevated in the modern era by Phillip II and Charles V, King of Spain, whereas the counts can trace their lineage to the original nobility of Norman Sicily and the marquises were entitled in the 15th century by King Alfonso; so the prestige of a Sicilian title is nearly the inverse of its rank.

The Sicilian nobility, like the English lords, love to wander in strange lands. Taking on useful offices and customs abroad, the nobles return home without prejudice and as much of the clergy are engaged in the sciences, the nobility more specialize in literature. With such an upbringing and way of life, they do not have the arrogance of Spanish pride in conversation; on the contrary, they are very attentive to foreigners and their courtesy is equal with the French, while their hospitality is equal with the Russians. Their generosity to the poor is worthy of universal praise, the luxury in decoration of their houses or rather their palaces in the collections of statues, paintings, libraries, museums and especially their passion for possessing the finest carriages and livery surprise every traveller and it must be truthfully said that they have more taste and knowledge in such things than their neighbours the Neapolitans.

## The Clergy

In Sicily, there are three archbishops and eight bishops. The Archbishop of Palermo, Primate of Sicily and head of the clergy in parliament, has an annual income of 16,000 thalers and in his archdiocese are the following bishops: Agrigento, Mazara, and Malta. The Archbishop of Messina has the largest archdiocese but a smaller income, containing the Bishops of Cefalu, Lipari and Patti. The Archbishop of Monreale has the smallest archdiocese but is the richest prelate in the kingdom with an annual income reaching 72,000 thalers. The Bishops of Catania and Syracuse are his subordinates. The governor of Monreale is appointed by the archbishop.

The clergy, receiving a third of the island from King Roger, possesses a great sum of capital, which does not bring any benefit to the state. Among the 1,700,000 total inhabitants of Sicily, 500,000 are initiated in one of the holy orders. In Palermo, out of 180,000 people, 40,000 are monks. In Messina, roughly half of the 40,000 citizens are monks. It should therefore not be surprising that the city streets are constantly darkened by black and brown cloth. Such a multitude of idle people, almost without any occupation, levying every corvée and living at the expense of the people, contributing nothing to the government and being partially responsible for maintaining the throngs of beggars who live off of the alms this estate collects can not only be called useless members of society, but also the tremendous number of monks is the reason for the weakness of the government and the many subsequent disorders in their society. The secular power of the clergy, which was the cause of many evils, is now very weakened however and although it can resolve private quarrels in its estates like a noble family, its sentences have no power.

## The People

By the small population of Sicily and its sparse production, it is possible to judge the extreme oppression of the people, who are not as lazy as generally imagined. The people pay the nobility a significant tribute. The affluent peasants lease their estates and the other peasants live on such land; contracts for such leases are for periods at least 20 years long. If, under this condition, the means to acquire and grow properties were not difficult, then the Sicilians could have considered themselves fortunate, but the nobility appropriated the grain trade by countless intrigues throughout history and became monopolists, ruining the agriculturalists. Although since the time of the king's residence in Palermo all means have been employed to exterminate this deeply rooted evil, the king's good intentions are hindered by the ongoing war and an impoverished people cannot quickly recover. With all the incentives employed, the farmer has experienced over the course of several years that the prohibitions and permissions to export grain are not subject to permanent law and now, as the British government and court have intervened, policy sometimes changes instantly. This uncertainty of supply produces profits which prompts the villager to make no serious effort to improve agriculture. Laziness and negligence are the natural consequences of the weakness of the government and abuses of power by their senior officials.

The people living on fertile land but experiencing extreme poverty look for other means to feed their people. Idleness, as the mother of vices, engenders atrocities. The government does not eradicate them at the very source and the slowness of proceedings, in some respects, encourages crimes; numerous gangs of robbers operate with impunity in the interior provinces of Sicily. In the counties belonging to the nobility and clergy, there are no local police; for these rulers regard themselves in their palaces as safe. Besides the coast, there is not one company of soldiers in the interior towns and the small detachments of criminal investigators in the towns belonging to the king are unable to prevent robberies. For that reason, being a robber or a watchman here is regarded as a lucrative trade. A traveller can save his life and property by hiring for himself one of the hearty youths who are numerous in every village and whose honesty and courage are absolutely dependable. Many of the local inhabitants pay the leader of the bandits for safe passage and receive a written note that will take them a certain distance unharmed. If they are robbed and present their note of passage, then they will be returned or compensated their money without the slightest loss or delay.

## The Government[12]

After the expulsion of the Saracens from Sicily, King Roger entrusted supreme authority in a parliament consisting of three estates: the first was the landed nobility whose present leader, Prince Butero, is the hereditary president and captain-general of the army; the second was the clergy, consisting of three archbishops, all the bishops, abbots, priors and deputies of the various orders numbering 70; the Archbishop of Palermo was the head of this party; the third were the representatives

---

12   Bronevskiy's note: 'This section is borrowed from a brief description of Sicily by an unknown writer which, in a French publication, is augmented with the letters of Mr [Patrick] Brydone on Sicily and Malta'.

of the people, 42 deputies appointed from major towns and 310 smaller settlements owned by the barons. Every citizen who owns property casts a vote when electing the deputies. The head of this estate (*Braccio Domaniale*) is the praetor or mayor of Palermo. This dignity is highly respected, as in the absence of the president, the praetor takes his place and as the head of the people's representatives, he controls a large share of the government. This parliament is the supreme court and all the authorities are subordinate to it; it imposes taxes and assigns the sums for disbursement. The king has the right to convene and dissolve the parliament at will and proposes new laws to them through a chancellor. The chancellor (*il Protonotaio*) proposing the designs of the king and 12 chosen deputies called the 'defenders of the people' are outside of the government. Despite these formalities, the power of the king's authority renders the parliament ineffectual.

Civil rule consists of four tribunals. The first, the Royal Chamber, is divided into a civil and criminal court which decides all cases with finality. The second, the Tribunal on the Royal Property (*Patrimonio del Re o della Regia Camera*) which governs the royal income. The third, called the *Giunta*, is the municipal government of Messina which was established when that city was deprived of its great privileges for its rebellion [against the Spanish in 1674]. The fourth, the consistory, reviews appeals or considers the decisions of the first two tribunals. The advisors of these four tribunals, the judges, presidents, advocates and investigators are appointed by the king.

The Pope Eugenius III granted King Roger II the rights of his legate, by which the kings of Sicily have long regarded themselves independent from the Pope in spiritual and secular matters and some of the Catholic Monarchs [of Spain] have inherited this. In consequence of this privilege, the rulers of Sicily appropriated the papal legate to establish a clerical tribunal for trying cases, which is called *la Monarchia Sicula* and consists of four spiritual ministers: a doctor of Catholic law, named the *Monsignore della Monarchia*; an advocate, investigator, and a procurator. Appeals in spiritual cases are concluded ultimately by this tribunal. Another spiritual court is called the Tribunal of the Crusades. In 1095, Pope Urban II granted to those subjects of the Christian sovereigns who would go to Palestine to secure the grave of the Lord many privileges, one of which being the allowance to consume dairy during fasts. Pope Alexander VI confirmed this privilege by papal bull as a favour to Ferdinand the Catholic for his domains in Spain and Sicily. The Archbishop of Palermo, as the primate of the clergy, is the head of this tribunal and institutes others for all the other towns. For granting the consumption of dairy during the fasts, this tribunal receives an annual income of 600,000 rubles which is used for the maintenance of galleys or for ransoming Christians held in Turkish captivity.

The Inquisition exists in name only; the authority of this court is very limited and all of its abuses are thwarted. Despite this, no one dares to publicly boast of his unbelief or misinterprets the accepted rites. This court, after its initial establishment by the kings of Spain, was not so bold as to employ the same cruel methods as were usual in Spain and Italy; the people resisted this and the nobility could not stand the control exercised over them by the Spanish monks. All exceedingly zealous inquisitors were assassinated for the slightest offence, especially when they dared to intrude on the affairs of the nobility.

The city of Palermo, according to its ancient privileges, is governed by a senate consisting of a praetor and six senators. The praetor moreover manages the economy and is the head of the people's representatives in the parliament. The senators, elected from the Spanish grandees of the highest degree, don purple togas like the senators of Rome. The so-called captain of justice (*capitano di giustizia*) presides over the criminal court and is also the leader of the nobility. In the praetorian court there are three judges appointed annually from the citizens of Palermo; they are also present at the criminal court and, participating in the dispensation of the municipal revenues, are under the jurisdiction of the praetor.

## Laws and Proceedings

The laws of Sicily are scattered in many old, thick volumes and bundles of new decrees, and in the hands of judges take upon themselves every colour and change like a chameleon, as the one authority above all laws does not judge them but merely agrees that every colour is good. This power sometimes sees that disorders are mounting day after day and that sickness has taken root in the body of the state, it hears the cries of those who suffer, and knows that to suppress this evil is to take upon itself a laborious task or expense, but assuming that some exertion of its authority will cause more harm than good, no effort is made at all. Thus, struggling between assumptions and realities, the disorders and outcries are ignored and the sickness is normalized. It expects the problem to resolve itself or delegates the task to individuals who have an interest in simply perpetuating the sickness.

Judicial proceedings in Sicily are woefully inadequate and are the most intricate part of the people's government. Before a case reaches the throne, it must pass through a baronial court and then six others and often it occurs that the state secretary (*Maestro Secreto*) finds even the slightest deviation from decreed procedures and sends the case back to be reconsidered; in this fashion, the pleas of the just and unjust alike remain unresolved for ages. Ongoing litigation is countless and slanderers play the game of forgery and cunning trickery; all nobles of meagre means engage in these activities in order to occupy themselves. They are frequently discharged from military service where one cannot profit from the passions of the rich without first needing to know the person and establish a history of conflict for a slander to succeed in court.

The solicitors here are called doctors of law and this name is very proper for them, they treat the mischievous just as our physicians treat malingerers, taking their money and only giving them a drink of water with sugar. Despite the fact that there are many competing doctors here, each of them earns the equivalent of 20-30,000 rubles a year via legal contracts. If a case is doubtful or convoluted, other legal experts are invited onto the council, reach a consensus and undersign the entrusted doctor's case. The concern of the doctors is to win over the judges who can be easily convinced of anything so long as they receive proportionate financial compensation for their labours. The judges and even secretaries on whom the proceedings revolve like the earth on its axis have long since become accustomed to receiving large sums, some collecting no less than 60,000 rubles a year for their sins. They rush to fill their pockets by every means possible, because the king replaces their posts every two years. Judges and secretaries earn small salaries and are elevated to their positions from among the solicitors.

I once visited the Royal Chamber. Such noise, congestion, filth and suffocation! It is a temple to falsehoods where all the slanderers, twisted interpreters of the law and dishonest clerks seek to distinguish themselves in the field of deception. The president, the advocate-investigator and three judges sat around a table and they all must have had a combined age of 400 years. One of them was sweating under the weight of a large wig, another was cooling himself with a fan, a third yawned and the fourth was asleep. The solicitor stood on his toes, holding a thick notebook in his hands, and shouted all the time: *'la senta! la senta!'* – 'listen to this, listen to this!' and no one was listening, because his documents were undiscovered and outside the submitted form. Judgements of the court, based on inconsistent and questionable laws, are powerless and only the singular will and prerogative of the king are enforced. The judges who are obligated to give an account of their opinions to the higher officials who are reliant on arbitrary power cannot be impartial custodians of the law and they are never afraid of punishment for non-compliance; for should the laws be clear and precise, there would be no need to so often ask for royal arbitration and the judges at every step would not dare to be mistaken. The most cunning lawyer there would not be able to extract his justification from the contradictions of the decrees, for a punishment would immediately follow his crime.

The words of the orderly are learned and inflated, full of extraneous repetition and eccentricities, constant use of 'aforementioned' and 'undernamed', 'for so long as', 'once again', 'consequently', 'most especially', and voluminous citations to Roman law and precedents from ancient and ecclesiastical history that leave very little of the actual case in a case's proceedings. Nothing is communicated, their words have no force, and their eloquence is entirely pedantic, because their arguments are written solely in order to bore the judges with a long and ruthless rant and force them to sign a ruling as quickly as possible, which they do. As they know that the case will be considered several more times and that they will not say a word in their confusion, even the most blatant abuses are ignored. They do not look into the circumstances of the case or even listen to common sense, but sign only those cases which have put the ringing of coins in their ears.

In the criminal court, cases are as slow as in the civil administration. They imprison men indiscriminately and as a result, sometimes innocent men die in unsanitary conditions before their cases are properly investigated. Compared with the murders committed here, the death penalty is very rare. In a criminal offence, despite doubtless evidence and testimony, the law requires voluntary confession and until the criminal confesses, he will be imprisoned. If he should sit in that tomb, deprived of light and air, for four years, then he will be sent to the galleys. To the misfortunate who has already been read the death sentence, a delay of a month is given for justification; here one cannot help but notice the beneficial purpose of the laws. In this terrible postponement for the condemned, a so-called 'solicitor for the poor' comes to his defence – a person on whom he can genuinely and honestly depend, as the king draws special attention to this venerated position and selects only the most unselfish, meek and generous people to occupy it.

With so many shortcomings in this chaotic civil administration whose disorders can only be exceeded in their oppression of the subject populace by the ravages of external war, there is still something positive. I refer to the class of solicitors who, without imitating or following the rule of their fellows to love the slanderer and live off of the ruin of the parties, have their own ambition and glory. The solicitors of the finest quality earn the great respect of society through their good deeds. They take the younger men under their guidance and endeavour without being petitioned to protect the poor from the falsehoods of the rich; they take on all the costs of the legal proceedings and do not accept signs of gratitude under any circumstances. Others do not otherwise take on the petition for a case unless they are certain of the accuracy and fairness of the petitioner and after they have received a negotiated fee, but they can be proud of the name of 'the defender of innocence' as much as the former group. The announcement of judicial sentences raises an amazing competition and is the basis of that honour and righteousness that seeks to win approval and praise of well-wishers, which boldly uplifts the voice of truth in the courts and often sharply criticizes the decisions of the government in incendiary terms. To the king's credit, I must say that he respects these worthy people and tries to distinguish them with his favour and affection. An example of this behaviour of the best solicitors having a beneficial effect is that their subordinates see that to profit in an honest way is to earn the trust of the public, which is not as easy to acquire as diligence, knowledge and selflessness. Their work does not go unrewarded and the most famous doctors have significant estates.

## The Power of the King – Revenues – The Army

The power of the king is unlimited; it is supported by the love of the people and now, since his stay in Sicily, hardly a shadow of the old feudal system remains. The power of the nobility for many reasons has weakened and the king has been presently impeded by the legitimate legal rights of the barons, his dependence on the British and most of all by the fact that the deprivation of the nobility coupled with all their privileges would inevitably ruin the people; the throne would be deprived of strong support, the treasury would lose most of its income from the freewill of idle people, and the king, instead of the disorders caused by the meagre number of nobles, would have to fight the riots of ignorant mobs which until now have been kept in check by the power and prudence of the nobility. To free the people from any subordination to which they were already accustomed means arming them against the very autocratic power he seeks to expand, and moreover, the liberty of the people is incompatible with autocracy.

The state's annual income, consisting of different taxes and fees, approaches 5,000,000 rubles. The regular army, including the royal guard, numbers 22,000 men. The soldiers do not march so straight or so deftly but they do fire very accurately and in good order. The cavalry are nimble and mounted on beautiful horses. The army is dressed smartly and even richly, receives all necessities and is even more animated by a courageous spirit. Many believe that the Italians are generally incapable of military service, but this is largely unfair. Italy has always been renowned for its fine generals and although the Italians do not resemble the Romans and are pampered to the point that the soldiers do not have a warlike appearance, if they are nonetheless subordinated to a skilful general, they will match any nation in courage. The Italian forces under Napoleon so distinguished themselves in various battles, especially at Wagram[13], that the opinion of their inability can be completely refuted. The Sicilian grenadiers under the Landgrave of Hesse-Philippsthal defending Gaeta also deserved recognition for bravery, even from the French who do not always willingly give justice to their enemies.

In the beginning of 1808, when an enemy expedition was being prepared in Naples for the conquest of Sicily, Ferdinand announced this threat to the fatherland. The commons, nobility, clergy, all the classes in general expressed a

13    The battle of Wagram was fought on the 5-6 July, 1809 between France and its client-states against the Austrian Empire. The decisive French victory prompted the Treaty of Schönbrunn and the end of the Fifth Coalition. Ward et al., *Cambridge Modern History*, vol. 9, pp.352-360.

willingness to die for the king which was unexpected by many. At the same time, the Sicilians' entrenched hatred for the Neapolitans was revealed. The people publicly asked to be given commanders from among natural Sicilians and when the king indulged in this request, a militia of 52,000 volunteers was mobilized in three weeks, being already uniformed at the expense of the nobility and armed with weapons provided by the British. We were pleased to see that the uniform and exercises of this militia were nearly the same as our infantry had in the reign of Catherine II.

For some time, rumours were circulating that the British government intended to take advantage of the king's impotence and offer him a pension for the crown, but as soon as the militia were standing under arms, all unpleasant news was silenced and naturally they were unfounded. The British who occupied Messina, Catania, Syracuse and Milazzo were too few in number to defend those fortifications from the French and required the preservation of Sicily for their retention of Malta. All the fortifications opposing Calabria were handed over without the slightest resistance to the royal forces and the British, their former masters, became their guests as auxiliaries. The British parliament also subsidized the king for maintaining the readiness of his entire army. It is possible to say with all probability that Napoleon, in conquering Sicily, would encounter many obstacles and fail to find his confederates here; for although there are those dissatisfied with the present government, they fear his dominion more so. The Sicilians have not yet forgotten the tyranny of the Norman despots and were poised to again bath their hands in the blood of the French as they did during the Sicilian Vespers.

The navy of the King of Naples consisted of only one ship, three frigates and 20 gunboats.

Ferdinand IV is the most kind; his clear and always cheerful face depicts all the mercy of his soul. Fate would have burdened him with many misfortunes and losses but he is not discouraged, he places his hope in God and endures all troubles with an unshakable firmness. When Napoleon prophesized to his army their occupation of Naples and the speedy conquest of Sicily, the good Ferdinand jokingly said: 'Napoleon will not be able to drive me off the globe, with a weapon in my hand and my *Borboni*, I will always be king'. His Majesty wished to say that he will defend himself as the king and die with the honour of the Bourbons.

The people adore the king. He once drove through the city toward his favourite site to hunt birds and the people crowded the sides of the street so tightly that his coach could hardly move. The king kindly let the closest *lazzarone* kiss his hand and scarcely had time to calm them down and ask for passage before the people cleared the way and cried: 'long live our father!' They fell silent and as soon as the king began to advance, I saw the crowd turn to that pauper who had the honour to kiss the royal hand and everyone sought to embrace him as if he were anointed.

Naturally I thought to myself that no victory in war could make this king more beloved than he already is by his misfortunes. The king always rides without his entourage in a simple coat, rarely in uniform. He is so close to the people and so accessible that his charity sometimes makes the poor too bothersome and impudent. Once, when the price of bread soared in Naples, the people chased after the king's carriage and shouted: 'our father, bread is too expensive!'

The king aborted his plan to go hunting and ordered his driver to take him to the municipal board where he asked: 'why has bread risen so much in price?' The president explained that the price was very moderate for the market and it was not possible to lower it any further. 'Very well', replied the king, 'reduce the shares by half an ounce per pound and announce that the price of a half-loaf has been decreased'.

Ferdinand, already advanced in years, has for some time given most of the concerns of government over to Queen Maria Carolina who, possessing the high mind of her mother Maria Theresa as well as her character, rules Sicily as her sister Marie Antoinette had ruled France. Adroitly and tightly she holds the reins of government, intervenes everywhere, gives orders to the ministers, directs the movements of the army, and disarms the nobility with tokens of merit, caresses and audiences in the court. The whims of the Palermo mobs are curtailed by the strict police and the queen knows everything that happens around her, what people are thinking and doing in Naples, and understands their actions from their circumstances and through her secret contacts with former subjects. She worries the King of Naples more than his armies worry her. Being visibly dependant on the British government, she bears with what is necessary before dignity. In relations with the enemy, she was adamant. Napoleon proposed through a marriage of her daughter with Murat to unite through their offspring the inheritance of the crowns of both Sicilies.[14] The queen expressed her disagreement in such a tone that in a fit of anger, the humiliated victorious knight sought any means to subdue Sicily and stooped to indecent language in his proclamations to his Neapolitan army.

Despite the notion that it is not possible to stealthily land a force with fishing boats without the transports and protection of a military fleet, a sufficient number of soldiers to seize Messina or some other fortified town defended by significant forces and a fleet of galleys were amassed and Napoleon gave a decisive command to fulfil his intention. Out of a corps of 10,000 men transported from Reggio to land south of Messina at night during a dead calm, scarcely a third were saved.

---

14    Joachim Murat was already married to Caroline Bonaparte, sister of Napoleon, since 1800. Andreyevskiy et al., *Brockhaus and Efron Dictionary*, s.v. 'Мюрат, Иоахим'. [Andreyevskiy et al., *Brockhaus and Efron Dictionary*, s.v. 'Murat, Joachim'.]

Several gunboats, being without protection, were sunk in the strait and very few men were taken prisoner.

The actions of the queen with regards to the French were exactly proportionate and reciprocal with their conduct and this concept disturbed Napoleon, for he feared that his other enemies would also become obstinate with him and force him to concede many advantages. Fra Diavolo, the glorious partisan of Calabria, was taken prisoner after an unfortunate turn in 1806 and the King of Naples determined to subject him to a terrible punishment as a criminal. When the queen learned of this, she warned that for the death of her 'general', she would order the execution of six French field officers who were held in Sicilian captivity. Joseph did not listen and Fra Diavolo was broken on the wheel and quartered in Naples. The six misfortunate French officers were promptly hanged in Palermo like criminals. Murat, who replaced Joseph, identified all the soldiers and officers who were native Neapolitans and remained in the service of King Ferdinand before being captured, and shot them as traitors. The queen notified him that she would likewise shoot the French in her possession, number for number, rank for rank...

## Mineral Springs – Production and Trade

There are many mineral waters in the whole of Sicily; some are too hot and others are too cold, even reaching as low as the freezing point, though they never turn to ice. There are springs throughout the island with oil floating on their surfaces, which farmers burn in their lamps and find many other uses for. The spring at Nicosia called Il Fonte Canalotto deserves special attention: it is always covered with a thick resin or tar which the villagers use as a greatly effective remedy for severe rheumatism and other ailments. The water of the small lake at Naso, despite being as clear as glass, dyes black anything submerged in it. There are several sulphur baths in Sicily with those in Termiti considered the best. These baths were famous in the time of the Romans. On some of the smaller islands surrounding Sicily, vapours rise from deep in the earth. At a great distance from Etna one finds lava, pumice and porous stones erupt from the fire-breathing mountains and it should be concluded that Sicily and the Aeolian Islands originated from subterranean fire. Three *verstas* [3.2 km] west of Palermo, near the shore, there are many hot springs which erupt from the depths of the sea with such force that hot water is thrown up two *arshins* [1.42 m] into the air but comes down as cold as ice. Where the depth is not great, vapours emerge from the cold waters rather than the warm.

The primary product and the bounty of Sicily is wheat. The soil, even without fertilizer or judicious cultivation, is so fruitful that a single harvest of an average crop provides food for the whole population for seven or eight years. The Sicilians thresh their grains with horses like our Crimean Tatars do and store it in the same special way. In dry pits dug in the ground, the wheat is immediately dumped after threshing and covered over to keep out the air and rain, and the grain is preserved within much longer than ours.

The salsola soda plant, which produces an ash that is considered ideal for making glass, is cultivated in Sicily with great care and brings profits to the villagers. Wild honey is harvested especially around Etna and is preferred over domesticated bee honey and highly priced. Sugar is not yet an object for foreign export but sufficient quantities are produced for domestic consumption. Licorice root and its syrup is another commodity profitable for industrialists. The manna ash tree is the most useful product of Sicily; a precious medicine is extracted from incisions in the bark in July during the most intense heat, flowing out like a thick, whitish sap and soon hardens in the sun. These grains of manna gum are carefully broken off and collected in small boxes. The peasants only cut one side of the tree per season and leave the opposite side for the next summer. Each tree produces half a pound per year which can last for a whole century.

Trade, despite the war, has improved so much since the king's residence that manufactured goods and raw commodities have already doubled since before the loss of Naples. The Sicilians have a sufficient number of vessels but due to the privileges given to the British, the majority of these remain in harbour without any use.

Sicily is indisputably the finest country in Europe; it can be called the 'garden of Europe'. The soil is exceedingly fertile from the abundance of volcanic ash. The provinces of Val di Noto and Val di Mazara are rich with grain and Val di Demona with fruits. The finest grapes, sugar cane, dates, pistachios, olives, oranges and lemons grow everywhere and average examples abound of peach, almond, fig, silk trees etc. in the forests which need no cultivation. The amazing multitude of sources and springs which irrigate and decorate this charming country certainly contribute no small part to its bounty. The pastures in the vicinity of Mount Etna close to Catania are so lush that the cattle that graze there are bled to prevent them from becoming too obese. The meadows and forests all year long are covered with flowers and aromatic shrubs: lavender, rosemary, lily, jasmine and many others grow here in the open air. Etna is the chief cause of such amazing fertility.

The sea surrounding Sicily delivers abundant catches of fish. In Messina eels, in Palermo tuna, and in all ports the sturgeon, mackerel, sword fish and many others are caught to great esteem. Rivers and small springs are also richly populated. Among game, the wild peacock and partridge are regarded as delicacies.

The realm is also very rich with minerals: there are 31 varieties of marble alone. The golden-coloured, green, and black with gold veins are considered the finest. Jasper, agate, porphyry, carnelian, lapis lazuli and other precious stones are recognized in over 300 variations. In the depths of the mountains are kept the richest veins of metals and metalloids. The king has recently paid special attention to mining operations which were largely neglected under the old viceroys. Sulphur, alum, cinnabar, pumice and other products of volcanic peaks bring significant profits. Rock salt excavated near Castrogiovanni and sea salt from Marsala constitute the most profitable mineral exports. Soapstone, like ours in Crimea, is used by the peasantry in place of soap due to its characteristics.

In short, Sicily's abundance of all the necessities of life and luxuries, in the hands of that naval power which always pay the greatest attention to foreign trade and industry, could quickly reach its deserved greatness. Its population is presently so small in proportion to its space that it would quickly increase and Sicily, having no need to seize land from anyone, would acquire great riches through the utilization of her surpluses. The king's residence in Palermo has certainly brought considerable benefits, but the many abuses in government require gradual correction. War with a strong neighbour requires investment incommensurate with available revenues and the king's good intention to improve all aspects of the people's government is no easy task to fulfil. The Sicilians then can only consider themselves to be fortunate when trade is freed from restraining, unpredictable and variable tariffs; when roads are constructed for better internal communication, especially in those mountainous regions only accessible by pack donkeys; when the civil government will be founded on a strong and permanent code of laws; when the powers of the king will be unimpeded to do good and the rights of the nobility and clergy will be curtailed by proper limits; and when the wealth of the nobility and the poverty of the common people will come to some proper balance.

# 105

# War with Britain – The Surrender of the *Venus* to the Sicilian Government

On the 20th of November [2nd of December], 1807, to our extreme regret, it was found after an inspection that the frigate had so many critical defects that she could not sail in the open sea without repairs. The frigate's commander, Captain-Lieutenant Andreyanov, presented to the Russian ambassador to the Sicilian court, Privy Councillor Tatishchev, a report on the need to immediately repair the vessel and asked for a speedy conclusion to this task with the port's assistance. As a result of the negotiations with the Sicilian government, the frigate entered the harbour to unload its stores of gunpowder into the royal arsenals and by the 10th [22nd] of December, the rudder had been replaced, and the mainmast, bowsprit and beams which were cracked during the storm were reinforced with new pillars. The holes suffered in battle were filled and sheathed with new copper, the hold was restocked, the powder magazine was repaired and the whole frigate was rejuvenated inside and out.

After such repairs and receiving provisions for two months, we were preparing to sail to Portoferraio where Commodore Baratynskiy stood with the *Svyatoy Pyotr* and *Moskva* when the rumours of a rupture between Russia and Great Britain were confirmed by official messages received by the British minister to Palermo, William Drummond, from his associate in Vienna. This news deeply saddened the court and especially those residents who were equally committed to both the Russians and the British. At the same time, the British squadron cruising off the island of Marettimo returned to Palermo to prevent a French squadron's return to Toulon from Corfu.[1] Our minister instructed a trusted person to ascertain

---

1   Bronevskiy's note: 'The French admiral [Count Honoré] Ganteaume, having delivered ammunition to Corfu, escaped the vigilance of the British cruisers and fortunately returned to Toulon'.

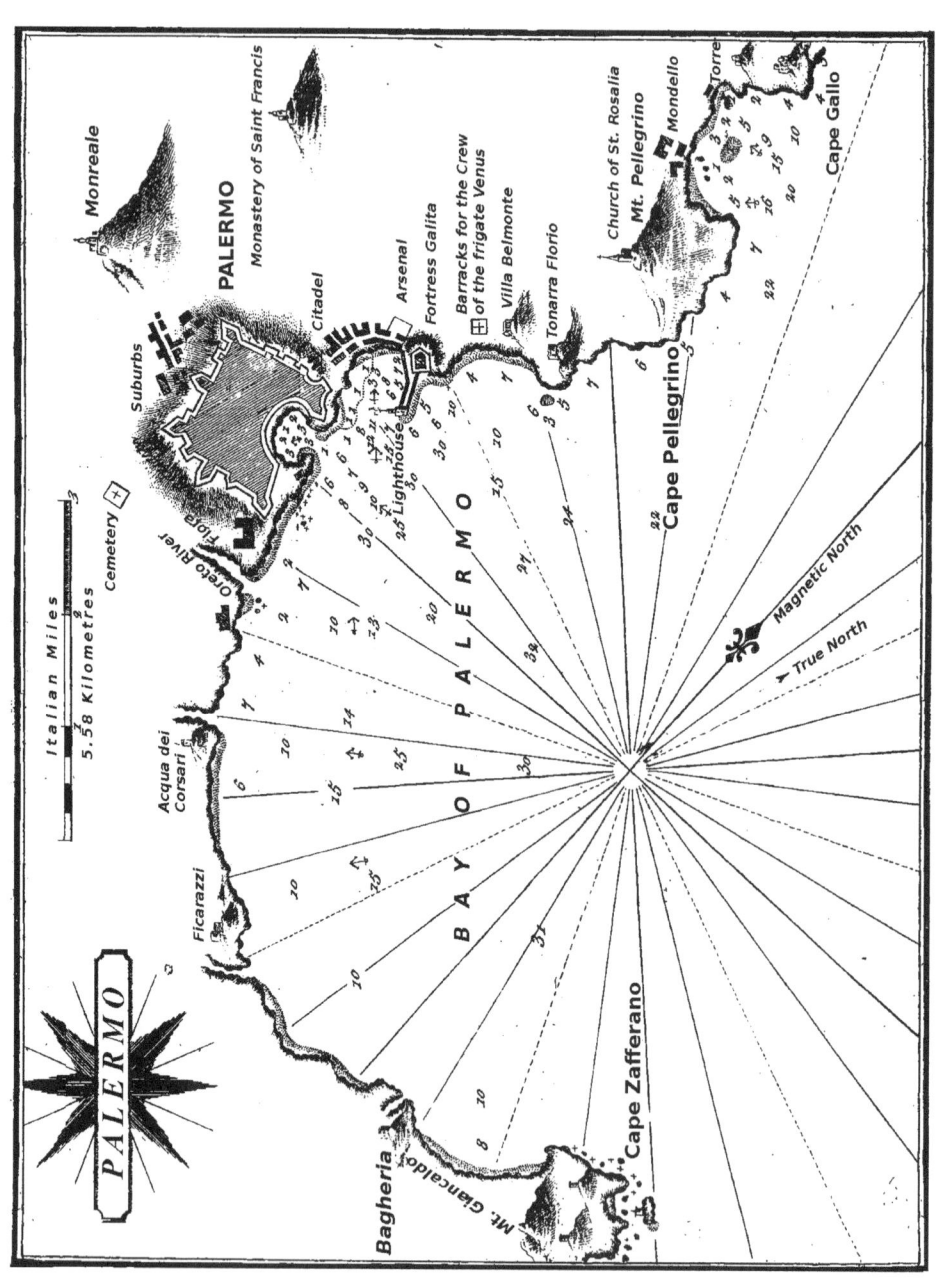

whether the British would honour the law and begin hostile military action based on the word of a single letter from their ambassador in Vienna. Drummond positively announced that a war would certainly follow, that Vice-Admiral Edward Thornbrough would take possession of our frigate, send it to Malta and then further instructions could be expected from the Lords of the Admiralty regarding whether or not the officers and crew would be prisoners.

The clear and decisive announcement made it impossible for our frigate to depart. Tatishchev tried to learn from the Sicilian foreign minister, the Marquis of Circello, how his court intended to act during the beginning of hostilities between Russia and Britain[2]. His answer was at first ambiguous, but when asked if, in the present circumstances, the Russian frigate could safely remain in the port of Palermo, he gave a satisfactory answer. Wanting better proof of the court's feelings, Tatishchev asked the queen, who answered: 'be sure that His Majesty will never raise arms against Russia. Emperor Alexander was always our patron and we will not forget it'.

Dmitriy Pavlovich Tatishchev. Vasiliy Tropinin, 1838, oil on canvas, St. Petersburg, Museum of the Russian Academy of the Arts.

2    Tommaso di Somma, Marquis of Circello, served as Naples and Sicily's minister of foreign affairs from 1804 to 1822. *Dizionario Biografico degli Italiani* (Rome: Istituto dell'Enciclopedia Italiana, 1991), s.v. 'Di Somma, Tommaso'. [*Biographical Dictionary of Italy* (Rome: Institute of the Italian Encyclopedia, 1991), s.v. 'Di Somma, Tommaso'.]

Meanwhile, although the Russian mission received on the 17th [29th] of December official intelligence from St. Petersburg about hostilities between Russia and Britain, it was kept secret in the hope that some unexpected event forcing the British squadron to set out for the open sea would give the frigate an opportunity to sail un-harassed to Portoferraio, Naples or any other friendly harbour. This expectation was in vain; the British minister was very adamant in his intention to seize the *Venus* and all Russian merchant vessels residing in Sicilian ports. The king, amazed by such a bold demand, resolutely and with displeasure refused an act so contrary to his feelings yet the British began to insist and issue threats. Drummond refused to continue the subsidies paid by his court and the commander of the British forces, General Moore, threatened that he would not protect Sicily from the attempts made by Joseph Bonaparte to annex the island to his Kingdom of Naples. The Russian ambassador saw that he could no longer remain passive and wrote to the Sicilian minister with a facsimile of the manifesto in which the causes for the declaration of war on Britain were set out, demanding a direct and accurate statement on which side the King of Sicily would choose to support in this war. The Marquis of Circello said that his sovereign could not separate the interests of England from his own, that His Majesty's ports would henceforth be closed to the Russian flag and that the presence of the *Venus* in Palermo could not continue during the present circumstances.

This answer clearly revealed the impotence of King Ferdinand and that it was impossible for him to defy the will of the British, whose army occupied Messina, Syracuse and almost all the major ports and fortifications in Sicily. The behaviour of the Sicilian court was a consequence of its position and unfortunate for its needs, as an alliance with the Emperor of Russia would be just as useful to Ferdinand as the severance of that union was harmful. Russia however needed neither to seek friendship nor avert a break with a powerless ally. Only the desire to save the frigate *Venus* and deliver those who served aboard her to save the honour of the Russian flag motivated our venerable ambassador to act with zeal. Seeing that the Marquis of Circello, for all his prudence, loyalty to his sovereign and devotion to Russia, could not throw off the British yoke, our minister turned directly to the king and queen for his objective. The marquis however despatched a new missive at the insistence of the British ordering the frigate to leave Palermo within 24 hours. Our minister replied that the frigate could not leave port when there was an enemy squadron standing on the roadstead; that the battle between such unequal forces that would result could not be doubted; that the frigate which arrived in port under friendly relations would depart likewise; and finally that His Sicilian Majesty would be responsible to the Emperor of Russia for any insult inflicted on his flag.

During these negotiations, our captain saw that the patronage of the king, in light of his dependence on the British, was very unreliable and decided to wait for a strong tailwind to leave Palermo at night. Exploiting the speed of the frigate, he could reach another, safer, allied port. To this end, he demanded that our stores of gunpowder be returned to the vessel. The Sicilian harbourmaster, having at first made some contrived delay, finally had our powder loaded onto one of his gunboats, but the British admiral gracelessly and without probable cause detained the boat at his ship. Soon after this act of coercion, on the 27th of December [8th of January, 1808], an official at the embassy, State Councillor Pyotr Ivanovich Karpov, coming aboard the frigate, informed us that the British intended to attack the frigate at night and asked the captain on the minister's behalf to give him our secret signals and orders for the sake of security.

On the roadstead, five British ships of the line stood within grapeshot range of our frigate, two of them were 100-gun vessels and two frigates deliberately sailed toward us at the entrance of the Bay of Palermo. In this extremely troublesome situation, when it was impossible to either leave or procure a stock of gunpowder, the captain invited the officers to a council and presented all the measures and means that might serve to protect the frigate, we agreed and by a unanimous signing the council approved: to remain within the mole; to purchase from our personal cash enough gunpowder from the city to supply the upper deck of guns; and if the British attack the frigate with a ship of the line and not with boats attempting a boarding action, then we would fire off every charge we have and set fire to the frigate ourselves.

Lieutenant Matvey Nasekin was sent to notify the minister that the captain, officers and all the crew were resolved to defend the frigate to the last and blow themselves up rather than surrender the vessel to the British squadron. Tatishchev, upon receiving this notification, shook Nasekin's hand and said: 'tell your captain that I recognize the Russian in him! Your intentions are most heroic, but I hope to ward off the death of your brave men in any way which would not dishonour them. If I run out of time, I will be on the frigate myself and conclude my diplomatic assignment for the good fortune of being able to share in your danger'.

The main obstacle of fulfilling this decision was procuring powder. It was already evening and we had not more than three hours left. We dispatched our every acquaintance to buy powder for us in the city. The captains of the Bokez corsairs, the two brothers Petrović, were the first to return with three barrels, then the Danish and Greek skippers came one after another to deliver as much as they had. In a short time, we had enough powder to supply the whole upper deck and four guns below. The Danish skippers began to help us with their men and the Bokez became jealous. Having no need for sailors, we refused these offers and requested that they only provide us with boarding weapons. They fulfilled this request so thoroughly that every shooter had three muskets and two pistols each and in order to increase their rate of fire, 40 men were assigned to exclusively reload and hand off ready muskets to the shooters. The Bokez, Greek and Danish skippers gave us their word that in the event that the British boats come alongside the frigate, they would attack with their own and as soon as the frigate was lit on fire, they would burn their own ships and withdraw directly to the city.

After sunset, the frigate was turned into a fortress, so to speak, with its sufficient store of powder and abundant small arms. On the upper deck, for the rapid shooting of muskets, scaffolds were built and parapets were added to the tops and chains out of the officers' beds; the portholes for the guns on the lower deck which could not fire were hammered shut; between the lower yards on ropes were hung ballast stones which would be dropped through the enemy's boats from directly above after they closed in to our hull. Pistols, sabres, spears, halberds, crowbars, boat hooks and every other implement of death were laid out within our reach. In such a defensive condition, we hoped that it would not be easy to take us in a boarding action. After some demonstrative training, when everyone knew what he would have to do in battle, the captain ordered all the men to be assembled on the quarterdeck and asked the officers to impress upon them how necessary it was in the first battle with the British before the eyes of foreigners to sacrifice life for the salvation of the honour of the Russian flag and if we should perish in an unequal battle, the British will at least be deprived of the right to brag that they conquered us or seized our *Venus*. Our brave sailors, some of whom distinguished themselves in the Swedish war [of 1788-90],[3] readily answered: 'we are prepared to die, Your Nobleness! Do not give up our *Venus* while we still live'.

The intention to burn the frigate caused great unrest in the city and everyone crowded the shore and embankment to see if the British would attack us and if all the vessels in the harbour could be engulfed in flame. The Marquis of Circello did not at first believe these rumours, but when our minister told him in person that a British attack on the frigate would be the signal for a general fire in the port, he was so distressed that he immediately went to Drummond and notified him of the threatened disaster. Both ministers, wishing to avoid these events, conveyed the intention to burn the frigate to Admiral Thornbrough. He was just as amazed as the ministers and to be certain of it, he inspected the frigate at around midnight. He must have considered it impossible to take the frigate by boarding, as two hours later, the *Kent* and assembled boats with soldiers and marines crept closer but when our drummers struck an alarm, they regained their distance.

---

3    Being originally a Swedish frigate captured by Russians, the *Venus* would presumably be regarded as a treasured trophy by the veterans of that war and worthy of a strong defence. Veselago, *The List of Russian Military Vessels*, p.745.

At dawn on the 29th of January [10th of February], Captain Charles Rowley of the 74-gun ship HMS *Eagle* brought a letter which is presented here as a word-for-word translation:

January 10th [New Style], 1808
His Britannic Majesty's Ship
*The Royal Sovereign*. Palermo.
My Lord!
The declaration of war between Great Britain and Russia affords me the right to demand that you surrender the Russian Imperial frigate *Venus* under your command to the squadron of His Britannic Majesty which I command.

In the present circumstances, escape and resistance are clearly not possible and the consequence of a vain defence will only be the total loss of the brave men under you. I therefore hope that you will not force me to support my claim with a regretful force of arms. I await an immediate response and am,

your most obedient servant,
Edward Thornbrough.
Vice-Admiral of the Blue Flag and
Commander of His Britannic Majesty's
squadron in the Bay of Palermo.

Captain Rowley, having delivered the letter, casually told our captain that he had been ordered by the admiral to give no more time for deliberation than noon and that if the frigate were not surrendered on that day, the British squadron would then be obliged to use force. Captain Andreyanov took Rowley's hand and said to him: 'I will not write a reply, but here you have my word of honour that my frigate will never be yours!' He then stepped aside and turned to the officers and men gathered on the quarterdeck to say: 'Gentlemen! Men! We heard one another's opinions this evening and now, when the decisive moment comes, we will certainly not back down from it'. To this the officers and the whole crew replied that they would all die without surrender. The English captain was surprised by this outcry and without asking what it meant or conversing further, he bid us a good morning and left.

I was ordered to take Thornbrough's letter to our minister. When I came to his house in the early morning, I woke up some of the staff, but Tatishchev was already awake and immediately received me when he heard the commotion. The minister rushed through the admiral's letter and asked what we were going to do next. 'The captain requests that Your Excellency write a reply in English or French reading that we will not surrender under any circumstances'.

'To his missive in French', answered the minister, 'we will reply in Russian, let him work it out himself[4] and thereby I will win you four hours at least and save you from danger and hopefully keep the frigate out of enemy hands. Ask the captain to try to negotiate and delay in any way possible and I shall petition the king and queen as a last resort to save the frigate, the honour of our flag and yours. Be calm and firm in your decision and perhaps we will share a laugh with the English tonight'.

Here is the response which I was instructed to take to the British admiral, dated 27th of December, 1807 in the Old Style [8th of January, 1808]:[5]

> Your Excellency,
> Being in the harbour of His Majesty the King of Sicily, allied and friendly to us, and knowing the rights of neutrality and hospitality which hitherto are regarded by all enlightened nations as sacred and inviolable, I consider myself safe from you. I am honoured to be,
>
> your Excellency's humble servant,<br>Kondratiy Andreyanov.
>
> Captain-Lieutenant of my most merciful Sovereign, His Imperial Majesty, and Commander of the frigate *Venus* in the Harbour of Palermo.

Aboard a boat flying a white flag, I approached the *Royal Sovereign*. The captain of the ship met me on the stairs and prevented the officer on watch from blindfolding me. He shook my hand and said: 'circumstances here are turning to pitch us now as opponents, but nevertheless we will certainly not be enemies; the English and Russians will always love and respect one another'. Meanwhile, we approached the cabin door and six sentries with an officer saluted me as I entered. The admiral stepped forward, bowed, grabbed the packet out of my hand, opened it, furrowed his brows and brought the letter closer to his eyes. He went over to the window and scrutinized it again, smiled coldly and then handed it over to his flag captain saying: 'they look like Greek letters'. Then he turned to me and continued: 'I cannot read Russian but you speak English, so to quickly conclude our business, explain to me, what is the meaning of your letter?'

'I have been instructed only to give the letter to Your Excellency', I answered.

'So you want to correspond diplomatically', he said and I remained silent. The admiral saw that I did not want to answer, threw his hands behind his back and

---

4    Bronevskiy's note: 'This was all the more fair, since the British kept all correspondence with foreign powers in their own language'.
5    The letter was deliberately antedated to correspond with the date of the captain's discovery of the hostile intentions of the British in Palermo.

began to walk out of the cabin. At every turn he looked me up and down with a stern gaze while I glanced out the window or lowered my eyes. He stopped and thought for a moment before finally abruptly saying: 'Please wait, I will call you when needed'. I bowed, stepped out of the cabin and was escorted to the wardroom where the officers that recognized me closed in around me.

'What did you conclude?' they asked.

'Nothing', I said, and the conversation moved on to other subjects. We were served tea, breakfast, and newspapers. Each officer invited me to his cabin and took me on a tour of their ship, counted how many balls struck them during Trafalgar and finally showed off their fine armoury on the orlop deck. Muskets, sabres, pistols, clean and bright as glass; nails, rings, blocks and every other item were arranged on the walls just like in a haberdashery. Coming out onto the weather deck, I looked at a watch and saw four hours had already passed. As the British and their minister could not find someone who would translate the letter, they again called me to the admiral in his cabin.

'Have a seat'. Thornbrough began. 'You do not wish to surrender? And naturally you think that I have no right to take your frigate by force or you hope for something?'

'At first we thought', I began, 'that for just one frigate you would not violate the respect due to the king who it seems cannot put us in the hands of an enemy. We hoped that His Majesty would not tolerate the flag of our emperor who twice returned him to his throne being disrespected in his harbour, under his watchful eye. But now we know your intentions and his thoughts and do not expect anything from anyone or any salvation and we consider it our duty to fulfil what we are ordered to do'.

'Let's leave the arguments aside', objected the admiral, 'and conclude that you must surrender because our negotiations will not end otherwise'.

'The only means afforded to me by my captain is to dare to offer to Your Excellency that your men and ours can avoid reproach thus: "let the frigate leave Palermo and allow us to take advantage of maritime law so that after 24 hours of amnesty, without any insult to the king, we might decide on the open sea and not in the harbour who shall strike their colours for whom"'.

The admiral was not in any way surprised by this offer and, looking at the *Venus* through the window, said: 'a bird in the hand is worth two in the bush. Is it not true that your frigate is very quick under way? But you wouldn't be thinking of escaping from the whole squadron'. Pondering a little, the admiral continued: 'I could not however agree to your proposal. Firstly, I would have to answer to my government for the unnecessary bloodshed when I could have achieved my objective without it; secondly, out of personal respect for Russian courage and to spare the lives of your brave men, who could better serve their country in other circumstances. I will not deprive you of the honour of surrendering to the whole squadron and not just a single ship'.

'Your Excellency already knows that I am entrusted only to deliver to you a letter and return with your reply', I said.

'Very well', said the admiral. 'I will give you a reply but it will be the last, after which I will not accept any objections or offers'.

The ship's captain, having invited me to his cabin, seemed to have been instructed to persuade me. Here is my conversation with him. 'You don't really want to defend yourself against five first-rate ships; this is not the time for courage. A man who loves his country must save his life for better prospects. Surrendering to an enemy of superior strength is not at all dishonourable. I could give you many examples but I will only say one: in the last war, two of our ships in the fog stumbled on the Spanish fleet and surrendered without a fight'. I answered that Russians never surrender without a battle. But in the present situation, the captain objected that one of us must relent and that naturally it would be our side. 'If the captain and officers agreed', the captain continued, 'to surrender without a fight, then they would have no reason to complain about their captivity. In England you would be treated like guests and well received everywhere. I would especially invite you to my home in London'.

'Being free and not captive, I would have to thank you for your hospitality, captain. I must repeat however that I am not authorized to conduct negotiations and, so as not to waste words, I ask that I be allowed to return to my frigate'. The captain was then told that their minister, Drummond, was on his way.

I walked about the quarterdeck with the officers when suddenly they received a signal and quickly boarded all of the ship's boats with hooks or anchors and headed to the *Eagle*. This meant that they decided to seize the *Venus* by force. Approaching the captain, I asked him to ascertain whether the admiral would like to give me an immediate reply. 'His Excellency', began the captain, 'wants you to remain here but you may leave on your boat'.

'Remain here? Do you already intend on detaining me, captain? His Excellency should be reminded that I am here under parley and who would believe that I was being detained? My comrades would think that I remained on the ship of my own will. I hope that your admiral does not want to dishonour me without cause or reason'.

'Calm down', said the captain, shaking my hand, 'go. Seeing as you're already wounded, I would regret it very much if you did not save yourself from this avoidable danger'.

During this time, while I was on the British admiral's flagship, our captain visited our minister and asked him not to quit his assistance. Tatishchev answered that he was bound by duty to do everything in his power. 'I will visit the king this very hour and petition him with the last of my means to save you from the hands of the English, but you are military men and if my proposal is accepted by the king, you cannot judge what follows'.

Upon my return to the frigate at 2 in the afternoon, when the British *Eagle* began already to make deliveries to the harbour, galloping cavalry appeared out of the city, followed by the artillery and infantry of the King of Sicily's royal guard. Flags were raised over all of the fortresses not already flying them. Countless sailors were standing along the shore and the windows and terraces of all the homes were full of curious spectators. As the frigate stood at the extremity of the mole and could be attacked from the port side, we pulled closer to the dock in order to cover the stern and set the bow against the *Archimedes*, ensuring by our position that that Neapolitan ship and two frigates behind it would inevitably be blown into the sky along with us should the *Venus* be burned down. Our minister, taking advantage of the slow negotiations, managed to save us from the avarice of the British. He convinced the king that it would be better if he took our frigate than if we surrendered it to the British in the harbour. His Majesty, gripped by fear and wishing to maintain amicable relations with both of his powerful allies, gratefully accepted Tatishchev's proposal. At three in the afternoon, when the *Eagle* was already within range of the harbour, the chief of police for Palermo, Giuseppe Castroni, came aboard the *Venus* along with our ambassador's secretary, Aleksandr Yakovlevich Bulgakov. First, the king announced that the frigate and all of its accoutrements would be taken and upon the conclusion of peace, it would be returned to our government; the officers and men, after agreeing to surrender without fighting a battle that would be disastrous for the whole port of Palermo, would not be considered as prisoners but as guests; and after receiving permission from the Emperor of Russia, they would either remain in Palermo until the conclusion of peace with Britain or return to Russia. The king would cover the costs of the maintenance and transportation of the Russian complement. The secretary confirmed that Tatishchev had asked for this surrender and we could seize this opportunity. The captain summoned all the officers and men to the quarterdeck to announce the king's proposal and demanded their agreement. The sailors replied that they agreed if the proposal was accepted by the captain and officers as well. As the conditions were most satisfactory, the captain announced with unanimous consent to the chief of police that the frigate would be given to the King of Sicily. The lord Castroni summoned 10 soldiers from the *Archimedes* and at the same time, when the British *Eagle* turned its side to the *Venus* to open fire, we hauled down our colours and raised instead the Sicilian flag. Leaving a guard[6] on our

---

6    Bronevskiy's note: 'The frigate afterward was given to the Sicilian government and placed on the roll by a general signing by the officials of the port authority, our captain, the

frigate, we evacuated onto the mole, taking our flag with us and saluted it with a volley of muskets and a cry of *'ura!'* Prince Leopold and the Landgrave of Hesse-Philippsthal were the first to greet our crew standing in formation and kindly conversed with the captain and officers, thanked us for having saved the king from a terrible anxiety and immediately ordered the brigadier who commanded the port to put up our sailors in the abandoned monastery close to the mole and to rent a house in the city for the officers.

The British, seeing themselves so skilfully deceived, turned their indignation toward the Sicilian court and especially to the queen, whom they called the soul of the Russian party. Drummond, hurt by this failure, complained to Her Majesty but the queen replied: 'we quarrelled with Russia for England and must bear the burden of war with this mighty power. Justice demands that we take advantage of the war and take a side, so we have demanded that the frigate *Venus* surrender to us. Who can dispute this prize of ours?'

Our minister, returning from the king and queen at the same time the Sicilian flag was hoisted on the *Venus*, sent a note to the Marquis of Circello which said, among other things: that the proposal made this morning to the captain of the *Venus* by the British admiral and two notes from the Sicilian court serve as evidence that he has acted with Britain united against us; that no matter how great the bravery of the Russians, the frigate without even powder cannot resist against five ships of the line and cannot resist the naval and ground forces of an entire state; that the shedding of blood in this case would be reckless and so the Russian frigate has been handed over to His Sicilian Majesty. The minister ended the note with a resignation of his post as ambassador and took down the Russian coat of arms[7] from his residence, remaining in Sicily as only a private citizen.

The king sincerely thanked Tatishchev for having delivered to His Majesty the means to give our Sovereign Emperor a proof of his unhypocritical devotion without subjecting him to the vengeance of the British. 'What could our islanders do?' asked the king. 'Wherever there is a great deal of water, there are a great many Englishmen too!' Although several days later, at the insistence of Mr Drummond, a Sicilian guard was sent to the monastery where our sailors were quartered and offered to lay their arms in the magazine at their barracks. The soldiers were still permitted to wear their swords. In the instructions to the officer of the guard, it was said that they were to protect us from the British, to prevent anyone suspicious from entering the quarters and to be at the complete disposal of the Russian officer on duty at all times. At the changing of the guard, the Sicilian officer reported to

---

inspector and the embassy secretary A. Ya. Bulgakov'.

7   Bronevskiy's note: 'In all of Italy, diplomatic agents typically display the coat of arms of their respective states on the gates of their homes'.

ours and his soldiers who stood sentry at the gate of the monastery obeyed our sailors, performing guard details alongside them. In short, we were treated like friends and not as prisoners. Thus the matter ended to the pleasure of both sides, averting the disastrous consequences which might have transpired, were it not for the presence of mind of the Russian minister and the determination of Captain Andreyanov. For such a feat, Privy Councillor Tatishchev was awarded the Order of Saint Ferdinand upon the renewal of friendly relations and the Secretary to the Embassy Bulgakov was awarded the Constantinian Order [of Saint George].

Before departing, Tatishchev treated us very indulgently and all of the pleasures which we enjoyed during our stay in Palermo are owed to the honourable minister. He introduced us to the king and queen, recommended us to some of the persons of the court who could satisfy our needs in his absence, loved to share our company frequently and tried to provide us with wondrous pastimes. After the minister's departure, we now felt that we had lost our solicitor and defender. No sooner had he left Palermo, than the men were reduced to their entitled rations and occasionally those were withheld so that our men would need to work for their livelihood. Joseph Ventimiglia, the Prince of Belmonte, whose country home was near the barracks, was left with a strong impression of the Russians, as the work he expected them to complete in a year was finished in two months. The stone cliff was blasted, rebuilt and transformed into an English garden which, according to the intended design, is the best decoration in the whole surroundings of Palermo. The officers were not given any salary and the sailors were covertly and indirectly coerced into British service.

One disorder followed another. Private Yepifanov of the 3rd Naval Regiment accompanied an English sergeant, an old acquaintance of his, into a tavern and drank one glass too many. The Englishman remarked that his fellow was quite cheerful and offered him to sign on to the British service, giving him a few gold pieces as an earnest payment. Yepifanov understood why he was so eagerly entertained. Taking the coins, he threw them in his face, poured the rest of the wine over the astonished sergeant's head and threw him through the doors of the tavern into the street. The British recruiters who had not managed to bribe or trick any of our sailors, finally dared to take them by force onto their ships. In one case, they seized three of our sailors but did not have time to abscond with them as the guard mounted at the arsenal intervened on our behalf. The British received aid from their brig and drove the Sicilian soldiers away, but more of our sailors ran out of the barracks and a fight broke out in the street, which fortunately ended with the offenders driven off and their abandoned dinghy smashed to pieces. In another incident, they seized one of our sailors but the local crowd beat them off of him, nearly turning to daggers and stones in the fight, but luckily the police arrived in time and prevented bloodshed. These events could not be hidden from the king and aroused in him a powerful indignation. His Majesty ordered the guard at our barracks to be doubled and to prevent the British sailors from coming any closer than the arsenal. We were compelled by necessity, with the exception of the work in the Prince Belmonte's gardens, to forbid our people from leaving the barracks. They lost many benefits in this fashion, but not only did they not grumble at these deprivations, they refused offers made to them. Offers to join the British service were made even through the Sicilian sentries, so that by the end of our stay in Palermo, our captain did not even permit the men to go past the front gate. When they indirectly gave word to the sailors that if they wanted, they would be allowed to leave for their work details regardless of the captain's orders or that they would even be given transport back to Russia without their officers; it must be said that, to their credit, the entire crew took offence and rejected these offers, announcing that they would not disobediently leave their leaders or return to Russia without them. After this unsuccessful experience with our men, under the pretense of a lack of money, they offered the officers their salaries alone in lieu of paying everyone, but we also announced that we would not seek any benefits or advantages over our subordinates and although we were suffering from a lack of cash, we refused to accept it.

We believed that all of our troubles stemmed from the Marquis of Circello, acting in favour of the British. When he heard that our pay was being withheld and feared that our complaints might not be able to reach the queen, he called for Lieutenant Nasekin, who was recommended to him by Tatishchev due to his fluency in Italian for all necessary relations between us and the government. He affectionately suggested that the captain and officers be sent on a vessel which is already prepared for them, while the men will be sent later once a vessel or vessels are made available for them, on the condition that we officers give our solemn pledge to abstain from serving in the ongoing war against the British. Nasekin understood the implications of the proposal: 'the officers without the men and vice versa should not and cannot agree to travel anywhere separately and we will not only swear no oaths against serving in this war against the English, we will not promise to avoid fighting even you. We did not surrender to Sicily, we are not prisoners here and the king's word to let us go at the first occasion, without any conditions, must be upheld reverently'. The minister, disappointed by such a response, began to threaten him. Nasekin repeated that he and his comrades, no longer fearful of death, would certainly not be intimidated by the threats of a foreign minister who should know that any violence against Russians made by his government would be unjustified and ungrateful, and that he, relying on the righteousness of the king and queen, would henceforth boldly reject any similar proposals.

The marquis was so flustered and angered by these last words that upon leaving his office, he said: 'if that is so, then I can assure you that you will change your

Roman tone come tomorrow; I have means of making you do what I need'. These threats did not promise anything good for us. The captain, knowing that the minister could incriminate us before the queen in favour of the British and treat us any way he pleased, invited all the officers to his quarters in order to reach a consensus on how to repel the marquis's attacks. The officer on watch sent messengers to summon us all to the barracks. This surprised us. The captain was not feeling well and asked the senior lieutenant, Aleksey Melnikov, to find out who first dared to make such an offer and punish him as an example to the others.

But imagine our indignation when the Sicilian officer on watch outside the gates of the monastery rushed in and announced with great fear that our sailors would not listen to him or our officer on duty, that they unlocked the magazine without authority and disseminated the arms within and that he did not know what to do. As soon as we entered the barracks, the disorderly noise ceased upon the first sound of an officer's voice and all the men immediately fell into formation without the slightest reluctance on Melnikov's order. When, naturally, we began to angrily reprimand them and asked who dared to voice their disobedience and rebellion, the Seamen Koptyev and Afanasyev and Private Yepifanov were the first to step forward and behind them followed a boatswain and ten of the best men, usually well-behaved and righteous. The first of them, Koptyev, began to explain: 'Your Nobleness calls us mutineers falsely, please listen and you will see that we never thought to escape your authority. We know very well that without commanders we are like a body without a head and here on foreign soil, we would all perish. True, we took muskets and powder without permission, but we took them to protect you and nothing else. You know that we refused to go to Russia alone without you, now we hear that all the gentlemen officers are even to be imprisoned and we will be put on English ships by force. We are afraid of either coming true and as your quarters are in the city and separate from ours, we dare to ask you to join us in either defending ourselves against oppression or to go to jail together. Whatever you command, we are all ready to obey'. After our threats, when everyone was poised for the strictest punishment against the offenders, the amazing transition from anger and grief to joy and relief is impossible to imagine or describe. When Koptyev explained the thoughts of all of his comrades in simple but bold words and some of the officers expressed the same, he took off his cap, dropped it on the ground and said: 'I am the instigator, punish me alone'. The strictest of us involuntarily lowered their eyes.

After several minutes of expressive silence during which on one side they were struck by the fairness of the speech and on the other side, with humility, they waited for the commander to declare a sentence and administer the punishment. I could hardly resist embracing Koptyev and waited impatiently for what the superiors would say to me and when they then suddenly, as if automatically, said:

'Koptyev! You're right'. I then approached him and said: 'Koptyev, you're a clever lad, a glorious sailor and have a noble spirit'. All the officers changed their tone, softening their voices, as if not daring to give orders to such a detachment which deserved our gratitude for their noble determination and devotion. We tried to persuade them that it would be foolhardy to take up arms, that such an act would be harmful to us and that we must remain in the monastery barracks until our fate is decided, opting not to return to our quarters in the city. After this, the sailors laid down their arms in their original places without the slightest objection. The Sicilian officer who was expecting the worst but now was in awe of such a swift turn and incomprehensible subordination, clapped his hands and exclaimed '*o, che gente!*' – 'oh, what a people!' When the brigadier arrived upon the notification of the officer of the guard, we informed him of the threats of the minister and announced our intention to remain in the barracks with the sailors.

'Remain calm', said the brigadier, 'the king and especially the queen respect you enough that the minister would not dare to use force against you. Out of vexation for our dependency on the English, he has tried to threaten you with some kind of disorder in order to present it to the king and separate you from your people so that he might please Drummond and even more so Thornbrough, who greatly desires Russian sailors on his ships'.

In order to continue to protect ourselves against the attacks of the Marquis of Circello, on the next day, five officers in lieu of our ill captain went to court with a petition. The queen honoured us by receiving us first. When we were brought into her study, Her Majesty was already waiting for us at the doors and taking the paper without reading it, graciously said: 'explain to me what you need and I will gladly satisfy you in every way'. Nasekin briefly repeated his conversation with the minister and the queen replied: 'I do not understand why you were given this trouble, however it seems when the captured French officers were released, they very willingly gave their word of honour, yet in truth they never keep their promises'. Nasekin in response dared to submit to Her Majesty that during the reign of Catherine II, there was an example of one officer being held in captivity by the Swedish and giving his word not to serve against them when released, he returned to Russia and was discharged from service as a result. Her Majesty listened favourably and replied: 'I very much believe you and I praise this custom of yours of not giving pledges of honour, but you are not my prisoners. I hope that you do not regard yourselves as such, I would fear to distress you with anything more than words for it is not possible for us to regard the Russians as our enemies. Only God and your emperor are my sole hope. Only Alexander', she continued passionately while turning her eyes to heaven, 'he alone is a firm buttress for the oppressed and only he alone is capable of stopping this chaos… Have no fear, I will let you depart without any conditions as my friends; choose a harbour to which it might be possible to deliver you and you shall immediately depart'.

The queen's promise was exactly fulfilled. We were given everything required in excess of what the naval regulations prescribed. For the kind and exemplary behaviour of our men who stayed in Palermo for five months, which deserves general praise, the king especially granted us expenses for travel. Finally, after much displeasure, we hired two Austrian merchant vessels to transport us to Trieste where Commodore Saltanov stood on the 12th [24th] of April, 1808. Thus with honour, arms and rolling drums, we boarded the vessels and hoisted the Russian colours on the mainmast, with a white flag of parlay for a jack at the bow.

**106**

# En Route from Palermo to Trieste – A Note on Messina

During a calm breeze and cloudy weather, we left Palermo. The vast city seen from some distance presented the finest view. The harbour filled with ships, the magnificent buildings and city walls and all the surrounding countryside for miles around was the most beautiful locale. In the evening, we passed the island of Ustica, reminiscent of the courage of the Berber pirates and the weakness of the Neapolitan government. Corsairs typically harassed this island which housed soldiers in fortresses for guards. Despite this force, the Algerians frequently captured ships in the very harbour of Palermo before the British occupied Sicily.

The night was beautiful, we sailed on a fair wind and expected to arrive in Messina in the morning, but the sky and sea chose to contradict us. At dawn on the 13th [25th] of April, when we were between the Aeolian Islands and Sicily, the wind became strong and foul, throwing up great waves and covering the horizon in a gloom of clouds. We tacked windward by Lipari where it was said that Aeolus trapped the winds in a cave, but on this day they roamed free. Our skipper came very close to the shore and from the force of the waves he did not have time to tack through the wind, nearly crashing the vessel on a rock. From this danger, the skipper lost his mind, cursing and shouting and not knowing what to do. His sailors took *La Madonna* (an icon of the Virgin Mary) and placed her on the mast, praying for the storm to end, but in fact the wind was not that strong. The distress of the sailors and the haste of the skipper produced an unnecessary din. Our captain drove the skipper into the cabin, the Italians left him to pray, and our sailors were ordered to take up their duties. By noon, the wind had relented and became fair. We were enjoying a speedy course and were able to look off either side with pleasure at the froth that bubbled up around the boat, white like snow. Toward evening, the wind began to die out and we nearly coasted along the green coast of Sicily. On one side passed images of towns, villages and monasteries while on the other stood the blue Aeolian Islands, four of which spewed smoke like censers set out across a smooth table. The night was dark but quiet and pleasant. Stromboli occasionally flared in the distance. This view painted an image the likes of which are difficult to find from any artist. The eruption of a volcano leaves a strong impression on those who are not yet accustomed to it. It is incomprehensible how the Italians can joke and cheerfully sing with it nearby. What could be more terrible in nature than the rumbling of the earth? The hard granite of the mountain which touches the clouds before falling to the ground can change the appearance and lay of the area; and yet man spreads across this globe ceaselessly despite its almost annual destruction and quietly enjoys life at the feet of such mountains. It can be agreed that there is nothing braver than habit.

On the 14th [26th] of April, when we entered the Strait of Messina and were over the abyss, the fresh wind suddenly died. Our boat kept close to the Faro and managed to escape the whirlpool safely, but the other vessel with Lieutenant Melnikov and the other half of the crew was thrown by the current toward the coast of Calabria. The French battery built there, despite the fact the boats were flying the Russian and white flags for safe passage, opened fire first with solid shot and then with canister. For the defence of our boat, the British at the lighthouse began to fire from a single gun of a large calibre and each of their shots landed directly in the French battery. Thus our allies received us as enemies and our enemies, respecting the white flag, defended us like allies. I leave it to you, dear reader, to judge what we felt in this situation. Although the ship was already on the rocks and consequently in the hands of the French, they did not stop shooting, for which Captain Andreyanov sent Lieutenant Lasekin on a launch to demand an explanation from the French. The lieutenant, despite the musket and canister fire, reached the shore and then the batteries ceased firing. The French officer in command apologized and explained that he mistook our third squadron ensign[1] for a British one. A fine excuse! The boat was damaged in its masts, two Italian sailors hiding in the hold were killed by a shot, but not one of our men on deck were wounded or killed during this fire.

Arriving in Messina, the captain sent me with a letter to the British general commanding the garrison and fortress, asking that he allow us to send several boats pulling our second vessel from the shallows. If that were not possible, then our detachment would proceed to Messina and hire another merchant vessel to take them to Trieste. I came first to the fire watch. The captain of the frigate on fire watch told me that he had not yet permitted us to go ashore but he would pass the letter on to the general and bring a response back immediately to our captain. The English captain soon returned and told me that the general willingly agreed to satisfy our requirements, but doubted that the French would also favourably accept our offer because they disrespect every flag and seize every vessel which

---

1    A red ensign with a blue saltire on white in the canton.

should unfortunately fall on their shore. It was necessary then to ascertain in advance the opinion of the French general commanding the vanguard in Reggio. Lieutenant Nasekin was given a boat and was sent to Reggio that same day, returning on the 18th [30th] of April with an unfavourable response. The French general did not believe that the British would provide their services with good intentions and thought that for such indulgences, they would detain both vessels while in Messina and take us prisoner; furthermore, he alone could not satisfy the requests of our captain. The courier who was sent to their headquarters in Cosenza brought back the decision of the commander-in-chief of the French army in Calabria:[2] 'the Austrian vessel is to be detained and the passengers on it are to be sent via Naples, Rome and Ancona to Venice where the Russian squadron stands'. A French officer was assigned to Lieutenant Melnikov for escort and was under orders to carry out any necessary tasks on his behalf. In this uncomfortable situation, the motivations and actions of the British and French were revealed in various ways. The hatred between these two nations comes from pride and rivalry. Whoever thinks only of himself cannot be fair to others and here lies the reason and source of the long, murky hate that degrades both peoples. The British blame the French, the French scold the British; both are right and wrong. In some cases, however, the British should be defended, as they occasionally recognize common rights and are respectful in conduct. The French, imitating Napoleon, neglect all the charters and treaties and are respectful only in words.

As soon as we entered the harbour, Count Kaunitz, Austrian envoy to the Sicilian court, was the first to visit us and offered his services.[3] The captain accepted it gratefully as although our consul, Manzo, remained in Messina, he did not dare to appear to us as a private citizen. The next day, we ourselves looked up his address and found he was in a poor financial situation and the count's aid was very helpful.

The French preparations to conduct a landing on Sicily arrested trade. The British merchants were greatly anxious. Some of them sold their colonial goods at meagre prices; others, being more foresighted, bought them up in the hopes of turning a profit later. Napoleon made great preparations in Calabria for the conquest of Sicily, precisely with the same purpose as he had at Boulogne during

2    Marshal Jean-Baptiste Jourdan commanded French forces in Naples until June 1808, when he accompanied Joseph Bonaparte to Spain. Louis-Gabriel Michaud (ed.), *Biographie Universelle Ancienne et Moderne*, vol. 21 (Paris: Madame Desplaces, 1854), s.v. 'Jourdan, Jean-Baptiste'. [Louis-Gabriel Michaud (ed.), *Universal Biography Old and New*, vol. 21 (Paris: Madame Desplaces, 1854), s.v. 'Jourdan, Jean-Baptiste'.]

3    Aloys Wenzel von Kaunitz-Rietberg served as Austria's minister plenipotentiary to Naples and Sicily from 1806 to 1808. *Genealogisches Staats-Handbuch*, vol. 66, part 2 (Frankfurt: Verlag von Franz Varrentrapp, 1835), pp.513-515. [*Genealogical State Handbook*, vol. 66, part 2 (Frankfurt: Press of Franz Varrentrapp, 1835), pp.513-515.]

the Peace of Amiens, without having ships of the line at his disposal but simply gunboats (and possibly hot air balloons), he appeared to intend on landing forces in England only to suddenly turn to Austria with the whole army; likewise, Sicily was a diversion for an offensive in Spain.

By the subsidies and labours of the British, all the fortifications of Messina have been brought up to a better state. Instead of taking a walk, I went to inspect the port and the fortress. The harbour of Messina is shaped like a ladle and presents the most beautiful sight. It is the safest refuge and of course can be regarded as among the best in the world. Along the Palazzata, which is a semi-circle, stand military and mercantile vessels moored with countless ropes. The floor is muddy everywhere and the depth close to the town's shoreline is 8 to 35 *sazhen* [17.07-74.68 m], while around the centre of the harbour it approaches 60 *sazhen* [128.02 m]. A narrow sandy cape or sickle, as the Greeks once called it, bending opposite the shore in a semi-circle forms an extensive pool with a single entrance 220 *sazhen*s [469.4 m] wide. The whirlpool of Charybdis sometimes makes entry into the harbour difficult by its strong currents, but ships that drop anchor outside need to reinforce themselves with mooring lines to the shore more so against the wind than the currents. The quarantine building, according to its purpose, was built in a central position in the harbour and connected to the cape by a lengthy draw bridge. The lighthouse of Messina is lit every night and stands to slow vessels as they approach the Tangora shallows, which should be done with extreme caution as the Charybdis, locally called Garofalo, is very strong here. The fortifications facing the sea constitute a strong defence but against land, though the town is surrounded by a wall and dry moat and features a citadel constructed on a hill, a proper siege would reduce the place quickly.

The people of Messina are revered in Italy for being the best swimmers and they achieve incredible feats in this sport. Their boys, diving down 30 *sazhen*s [64 m], pull up oysters from the bottom of the sea. Here they speak of some Nicolas the Fish, a native of the town, as if he could walk on the seabed against the current, live off fish and remain for several days without touching dry land. If this occurrence is affirmed by many Sicilian writers, then it can be safely regarded as a fable of the Greek imagination. King Frederick, while visiting Messina, they say, wished to witness these feats. Nicolas gave two demonstrations and amazed his audiences with his lengthy bouts under the water. The king's curiosity finally cost the poor Nicolas his life when he ordered a large golden cup be thrown into the abyss of the Charybdis as the man's reward. Nicholas dove in and never returned.

Messina's surroundings are very pleasant and wonderful festivals can be seen all around the town. The roads to Palermo and Taormina are lined with shady trees. Returning from the citadel to the town, I ascended to the top of one hill and stopped in order to enjoy the charming panoramic view which opened up before me. The town was laid out underfoot. The strait appeared to the eye as a majestic river slowly flowing between two mountain ranges. Both banks were covered with rich fields of grain and vineyards, towns, villages, monasteries and handsome lighthouses. On each side, the horizon was curbed by high peaks draped in natural groves of fruit trees. All the fields, meadows and hills near Messina are covered with clovers, fragrant plants, bushes of roses and other flowers that fill the air with a lovely perfume. In the harbour itself, there are virtually no offensive odours from the sea water that ordinarily disturbs the air in seaside towns. The strong currents of water in the strait are the cause for this.

Passing the city, I went to an old Gothic church on the square where there stood a monument to Charles III, father of the present King Ferdinand IV. This church is decorated with a Greek mosaic in a very mediocre style but several statues seem to be modern and somewhat handsome. On the mosaic floor, various numbers and a celestial axis were drawn which divided the signs of the Zodiac. In the wall of the church, a narrow loophole was cut which let in the rays of the sun, indicating the month, date and position of true noon in Messina.

In Italy, every town has its own special church holiday. Messina is distinguished by the celebration on the day of the Assumption of Mary, the 15th of August New Style. One of my comrades was an eyewitness of this strange rite and I reproduce here his remarks. On the hill, at the end of the large street, a wooden machine is built in the form of a cone, 7 *sazhen*s [14.94 m] tall. The base of the machine is suspended on wheels, which drive gears that spin the various platforms of the cone in a single axis, one after the other. The base of the carriage is decorated with orange branches, potted flowers and coloured papers. Nearly a hundred boys in long white robes with wings tied on their shoulders representing the angels sit among the flowers on the spinning platforms, representing the circles of heaven. On the upper tier, above the choir of the cherubim, an elder in purple and a fake beard represents the Almighty. Beside him there is a young maiden clothed in precious garments as the Mother of God and for this role they choose a virgin of 10 or 11 years from the poor, as she must be beautiful and innocent. As many people as could fit in the street dragged the machine with ropes downhill to the cathedral. As the wheels roll along the street, the platforms spin around the centre. Some of the angels sing, eat oranges, frolic about on their platforms, and many fall asleep. Cannon fire announces the beginning of the procession and the people crowd the main street where the machine is dragged. The devout rush to the edges of the path and throw themselves prone on the ground while the procession passes. From the windows of the houses hang multicoloured silk coverings and women shower flowers down onto the massive carriage which resembles a moving castle filling the whole width of the street. This process stops at every hundred paces and the people kneel before the girl on the summit. Orchestras play hymns in honour of the Mother of God. At the end of mass, when the girl steps out of the cathedral, she is honoured with a volley from young boys dressed as martyrs. She goes to all the churches and houses and the people give her money or gifts as a dowry. On this day, the girl has the right to pardon a criminal, even if he had been sentenced to death. She also visited the Russian ships. Although such a visit was forbidden by Peter the Great, this one could not be denied and she received much more in alms than her predecessors in previous years. Those who accompanied her said: 'Our Mother of God is happy that the Russians have come to her feast'. The next day, two paper giants walked about the city depicting a man and woman in strange attire. The people, and especially the women, bowed to these moving sculptures. On the creation of the celebration, the following is said: when Count Roger drove the Saracens out of Sicily, one of his commanders stayed in Messina and his wife of gigantic proportions became a beloved icon of the people. This procession was thus established in their honour. It is incomprehensible that such hijinks are allowed from the rabble in the Catholic world, but such customs are everywhere and cannot be judged.

On the 19th of April [1st of May], we left Messina and rounded the Cape of Spartivento, staying close to the shore. The winds were gentle and the weather was clear. Etna was visible for three days, surrounded by a dense cloud of smoke. The steep and high mountains of Calabria with crooked peaks touching the clouds, wild cliffs overhanging the sea, slopes and valleys between them covered with greenery, fruitful oak forests, vineyards, castles, villages, monasteries and fortresses all made for an alternatingly cheerful and terrible view. Nature was here in all its splendour and bounty and pleased the eye amidst the terrors of desolation, but living in these Gardens of Eden is another matter. I admit that I feel a great aversion to the earthquakes and volcanism here; how could I stand on such a land that shakes almost ceaselessly beneath my feet? What can you compare with the fear of being crushed by your own house?

On the 23rd of April [5th of May], we passed the Otranto and entered the Adriatic Sea. Since at night the winds blow here from the shore, we held as close to the coast as possible. A quiet night and full moon made for a beautiful voyage. As our vessel floated along with a light breeze filling its upper sails, the bobbing and shimmering lights in the huts along the shore flashed in and out of existence. Sometimes we approached so close to the shore that we could hear people speaking. Our sailors, being unoccupied, gathered in a circle on the deck and sang melancholy songs. The sad sound of these songs, merging with the quiet murmur of the water around our hull reminded me of our dear homeland. Who is not charmed by the familiar sounds and the simple expressions of folk songs and transported to their fatherland, forgetting for a moment their separation from it?

I went below deck at midnight but could not fall asleep from the heat and humidity and soon went back on deck. A person accustomed to sailing on a warship will not find a merchant vessel accommodating. The former can be compared to a large house with all of its conveniences and benefits while the latter is a low hut, crowded and dirty. By morning on the 24th of April [6th of May], the wind did not freshen much. The waves rolling up on the shore and sinking into the sand reminded us by their noise that we were veering too close to land. The scarlet glow of dawn opened before us a spectacular vista. In the east, gloom yielded to the light and the sky burned with purple fire. The sea was as smooth as a mirror and to the west nearby could be seen a low-lying beach of red sand. We passed Brindisi, belching out swirling smoke from its chimneys appearing like straight pillars. A fog lay in the low, remote fields, but as the sun appeared on the horizon, the view began to change. The vapours rising off the land and the warmth of the upper layers of the sea intermixing with the cool air formed a light mist in the sky. The golden rays of the sun expanded through the fog as through a floral curtain, illuminating distant objects gradually. The darkness receded and the shore was revealed to us.

Under all sails, we slowly and smoothly floated along the shore, tacking about and then cruising around the cape to enter a small strait. The Kingdom of Naples from the side of the Adriatic appeared like a vast plain divided by fields and meadows. The chain of the Apennine Mountains was blue in the distance. The province of Puglia, which we passed, was very fruitful and rich with fields of grain. With great anxiety, we wished to visit Bari where the relics of Saint Nicholas the Wonderworker rest. We passed this small town very closely and in honour of the great saint, patron of sailors, we fired three shots and the monastery replied with the ringing of their bell. The Italians fell to their knees and all of our sailors joined them in prayer. We were very sorry that we could not stop to perform a thanksgiving prayer to the saint. Past Bari, villages and towns passed without interruption, interspersed with curious sites of antiquity, but the wind was rather refreshed and we only saw the town of Cannae where the Romans defeated the glorious Hannibal. The valley where the battle was fought is now called the field of blood (*pezzo di sangue*). In Manfredonia, the plain ends at the foot of the mountain of Sant'Angelo, whose high peak is an excellent landmark for seafarers.

From the bay beside Manfredonia, we set out into the Adriatic Sea, passing the islands of Pelagosa (Palagruža) and turning north between Sveti Andrija and Lissa. We began to follow the Dalmatian Archipelago. The island of Pomo (Jabuka), lying in the centre of the sea, deserves special attention for its appearance and position. When the sea is calm, it appears as a small floating ball and by its shape, it resembles an apple. It is located north of Sveti Andrija and west of Lesina at equal distances of 30 Italian miles [55.8 km], though on many maps it is signified as being further or closer. In cloudy weather or at night, extreme care must be taken not to miss it. The islands of Incoronate, Lunga, Premuda, Sansego, Unie and Ossero appear as only bare stones from the sea but occasionally show signs of vegetation and habitation. There is no port for ships but there are many for smaller vessels. On these islands in ancient times lived the Liburnians who were famous for their light boats and rampant piracy. Strabo narratives that the morals of these Liburnians and generally all the Illyrians were not distinguished from other barbarians; they fought like the Getae, were very brave and long resisted the Romans. When they were forced to move to the mainland in Dalmatia and then further into the mountains, they engaged in agriculture for their livelihood. The majority grew grapes and some brewed a strong beer from oats called *sabaja*. From this, Emperor Valentinian, a native of Illyria, was mockingly called Sabaiarius.

Passing Pola in Istria, near which the remains of a Roman theatre are still visible, we met with a British tender[4] blockading Venice. The British wished us a good journey. The island of Lissa, occupied by the British, provides a greatly advantageous site for observing the entire Adriatic Sea, being in the centre of the sea and having a very sheltered harbour (San Giorgio) and a small fortress which can be defended by only a company of soldiers. When we went around Cape Salvore (Savudrija) and when the Tyrolean Alps appeared, which so grandly surmounted Italy, we saw a French gunboat departing from Pirano. On the 30th of April [12th of May], after quiet and variable winds during nearly our whole voyage, we dropped anchor in Trieste. In the anchorage stood the squadron under the command of Captain-Commodore Ivan Osipovich Saltanov. This included the following ships: 1) *Svyataya Paraskeva* of 74 guns under the commodore; 2) the *Uriil* of 80 guns under Captain M. Bychenskiy; 3) the *Sedd-el Bahr* of 80 guns under Captain Sulmenev; 4) the *Aziya* of 66 guns under Captain Giorgio (Yegor) Borozzi; and the frigates: 5) the *Lyogkiy* of 44 guns under Captain Povalishin; 6) the *Mikhail* of 44 guns under Captain Snaksaryov; and the corvette 7) *Diomid* of 24 guns under Captain Palaiologos.

---

4    Bronevskiy's note: 'A small military vessel with a single mast'.

**107**

# Trieste

---

## Port and Fortifications

The Viennese court, wishing for a long time to possess a military port, was searching for any and all means to become a maritime power. Their policy constantly was to assert authority by naval power and foreign trade, but this beautiful ambition long remained unfulfilled due to circumstances. Finally the Empress Maria Theresa decided to take advantage of the convenient position of Trieste, which was then a small town. In 1750, a shipyard was established with a barracks, hospital and magazines for sailing supplies. In a short time, the Austrian flag appeared on the Mediterranean, heralding the rise of Trieste. During the reign of Joseph II, the town was declared a free harbour and a multitude of foreign and Austrian merchants with considerable capital settled there. The products of southern Germany, the Levant, Egypt, Italy and Sicily began to pour in, enriching and decorating the settlement and making Trieste into a dangerous rival to Venice, whose trade began to falter.

The bay formed by Cape Salvore on one side and the Venetian shore on the other is called the Bay of Trieste. The town sits at the very corner of the Adriatic Sea and according to the surveys of General Baron Zach made in 1806, it has a latitude of 45 degrees, 38 minutes, 8 seconds North, and a longitude of 11 degrees, 26 minutes, 56 seconds East, counting from the Parisian meridian.[1] A stone embankment was built on the shoal with an artillery battery on the extremity, adjoining the old quarantine buildings, to cover the harbour against sea winds which stir up large waves and can cause considerable damage. Every year, the strong southwesterly winds wreck 20 to 30 vessels. The *bora*, due to the high mountains surrounding Trieste, blows directly from the shore with such terrible force that despite its

---

1    From the modern prime meridian through Greenwich, this becomes 13°46'10" E.

shallow depth and firm floor, ships sometimes tear off three anchors and lose their masts. In the winter, the *bora* lasts for two weeks continuously and although the winds howl violently and the surface of the sea is covered with grey foam with spray reaching up to three *sazhen*s [6.4 m] in height, there is no choppiness in the harbour. In the vicinity of Trieste, this wind causes terrible devastation, tearing roofs off the houses and overturning carriages in the streets. The new quarantine, otherwise called Santa Teresa, is set aside for ships coming in from plague-infected places. In the basin of the harbour, which is divided into three sections, no more than 20 ships can stand. Its depth is three *sazhen*s and the entrance is very narrow. In the canal in the middle of the town the depth is two *sazhen*s [4.27 m] and vessels load and unload their cargo there. Several guns are distributed along the mole of the old quarantine and around the basin toward the new one, protecting the town and harbour from the sea. Two dilapidated fortifications called the citadel were built on a steep hill overlooking the town but neither can protect the town or resist an enemy over land; there are nearby heights which dominate it and the town is almost completely open all around. Touring the fortifications of Trieste, one can say that they are built only for appearances.

## Quarantine

Each time we passed from country to country, a small obstacle delayed us. The moment we arrived in Trieste, we were greatly frustrated by the fact that we could only look on from a distance. As soon as we dropped anchor, the quarantine officer and our consul, Mr Pellegrini, announced to us the unpleasant news that we should sit in quarantine for three whole weeks and not communicate with anyone. The gunboat performing fire watch approached us and the watchman – called a *guardino* here – came aboard our vessel and ordered the skipper to take it into the basin while we and the crew went ashore to the old hospital. We obeyed and immediately began to disembark. In the first yard where we were brought, there were quite a few people already and everyone fled from us. Our watchman himself, with a desperate cry, reminded us not to approach strangers. At first, we were amused but then boredom set in, following on our heels, so to speak. The chief of the quarantine asked us to patiently submit to the quarantine regulations as one who violates these laws even slightly is subject to execution. In fact, what could be worse than the plague? From one inflicted person, the whole city or even the whole state could suffer; thousands of people can die from a single touch. The excessive caution and strictness in this case is, therefore, prudent.

   In 1812, rightly called the year of tribulation, when our dear fatherland was being tormented by fierce enemies, a plague struck Odessa and Feodosia at the same time the French occupied Moscow. Serving then in the Black Sea Fleet, I unfortunately witnessed the sad consequence of this scourge on the human race.

Ghastly ulcers gradually infect every part of the body and the result is almost always fatal. The infected person first feels nauseous, then light-headed and dizzy, begins to vomit and breaks out in red spots which then turn black. When black carbuncles appear in the groin, a fire burns in the intestines and death inevitably follows. During the first seizures, the person becomes delirious and the spirit loses strength and from it the body seems to derive new vigour, allowing the patient to suffer through the severe cruelty of the disease completely relaxed. Violent convulsions, vomiting, a ceaseless cough and insomnia torment the patient, in addition to an insufferable heat that burns within with inflamed eyes, tightness of the chest, pallor in the face, exhaling fetid breath and sputtering soiled blood on their lips. They desperately call for water or ice. Unable to satisfy their thirst, they tear off their clothes, bite themselves and rabidly writhe on the ground. Most of the sick I saw died on the fifth to seventh day, a few died in only one or two days and some even within three or four hours. Those who recover from this disease are reduced to a wretched spectre of their former selves. The Anatolians who volunteered to treat the sick went without fear into the lazarettos and discovered which medicines did harm and which brought relief; many sick patients were brought back from the brink of death and none of these generous people died. When there were obvious signs of plague and the city was surrounded by a military cordon severing all communication with the surrounding area, no pen could possibly describe the horror strangling the people. At first there were visible examples of maternal tenderness, filial piety and generous donations worthy of imitation. Out of many examples, I will recount just one. Colonel Rebok, noticing that his child was showing signs of the infection, hastened to get help for him and washed him with vinegar with every kind of protective gear. Soon though, he began to suffer from seizures. He announced this to the police, locked himself in his room, lit the stove and burned his clothes and everything else that might be contaminated, and died the next day. After such a sad experience, as soon as the plague was found in a household, the police in leather suits and smeared with tar would immediately divide the healthy from the sick or questionable. Could anything be more pitiful than to see a babe torn from its mother's breast, a son from his father, and the most sacred of bonds disrespected? Many tragic and heart-moving episodes unfolded. The healthy were locked up alone in their homes while the others lived outside the city in tents and dugouts. The city turned into a desert; some of the homes were burned, others had their windows knocked out. No one dared to go out into the street and were afraid to meet with friends and acquaintances. There were only the mobs of the poor crying out in piercing voices for food. In those unfortunate days, the dying had no one to close their eyes and brutal death became common enough to no longer draw tears.

After many unfortunate events resulting from the poor segregation of quarantines in the large trading cities of Italy, France and Spain, built inconsistently, it can be said that the quarantine in Trieste, both in terms of accommodations and in the order and precision observed, is fairly regarded as among the best in Europe. Everything here is conceived for the better. The division of rooms for people and stores for goods are made in such a way that even during the actual attempt, it is not possible to move from one section to another; everywhere there are gates, high walls, chevaux de frise, open yards, fences and locks. I believe several details about the design of the Trieste quarantine would not be useless to many readers. They are built on the extremities of the town and each is surrounded by a high wall. The new quarantine is divided by walls into two sections. The plague section with the cemetery is wholly unique. In different yards of the plague section, the detained people and their goods are separated. The cargo and crew of a given vessel are segregated from those of the other vessels. Sailors and passengers, if some of them are suspect, are each placed in a separate hut with a small courtyard locked with an iron gate until they can be safely declared to be healthy. Near these gates a window is provided through which the guards serve food on an iron peel or shovel with a long handle. In short, the plague section is a prison. When the skipper of an arriving ship declares that the plague is onboard, the vessel is immediately unloaded in the basin and the goods are hung up in barns of lattice. The people are stripped of their clothes, which are burned, washed, shorn of hair and fumigated. Each one is taken into a room where they find new clothes, a censer, wood for a fireplace and everything else essential. The ship remains empty, all its hatches are opened and the hull is cut to let air flow easily into the hold, with sea water being poured in and over the vessel each day. With loads of cotton, the most contagious material, great caution is exercised. Each bundle is broken down and unravelled on tables and hung up on hooks under open-air magazines, surrounded by fences. They turn the cotton every day without entering the magazine by means of long-handled iron pitchforks. This dangerous work, as well as the unloading and fumigation of the the vessel and its goods, is paid for at the owner's expense. The improper unloading of cargo from a quarantined vessel by its crew is a criminal offence potentially carrying the death penalty.

The second section, divided into two yards, is assigned to ships coming from plague-infested regions and has all the same housing and magazines as the former but with the difference that the crew of a vessel, if they show no signs of the plague, are housed in one large room. In the second section there is a chapel, a well with drinkable water and a special yard designated for gardening. The quarantine officials live in a separate section. They enter the first and second sections through special entrances, keep order everywhere, deliver food, and never approach the sick or quarantined too closely; always with the utmost vigilance. The guards and attendants of the plague section, upon the cessation of an infection, do not immediately return to the town, as they need to undergo quarantine themselves.

The old quarantine, located on the south-western edge of the town, is designated for passengers and people arriving from ports in which there is no known contagion. In the first half, a two-storey house was built which was divided into eight sections, each floor having four quarters. The yard is divided into four sections and accessible by four gates. The windows of the lower floor face a gallery inside these yards. The entrances to the rooms on the ground floor also exit into the yards. The entrances on the upper floor and its windows face a street. Thus, the eight compartments can accommodate passengers from eight vessels and, if necessary, each section can be divided into two parts with all 16 sections having its own exit. Inside the yard, a small church is attached to one wall and has only one priest. Those who live in the house can pray from their gallery facing the yard. In every section, water is piped in. In the second half of the old lazaretto, another two-storey building was raised which was divided into four large rooms which each could house a single ship's crew. After rotation, they allow you to go out for a walk in the yard, observing that the people of each term do not mingle with the people of another who have been interred before or after them. No one is deprived of the right to see their friends and acquaintances, however. The meeting place is a long, narrow square where one side is separated from the other by three *sazhens* [6.4 m]; one side opens to the town and the other to the quarantine. Those who wish to speak privately can enter a house partitioned by meshes and the townsman must be examined upon exiting. A tavern is built outside the quarantine walls, which serves the interred people food and drink by extending a long-handled peel through a small window. Items confiscated are not released from quarantine before a thorough cleansing.

During our confinement, although we were not deprived of anything material, we suffered tremendous boredom by the loss of our freedom. After 10 days, Consul Pellegrini secured our release and announced it to us personally. We rejoiced like a family and embraced the consul and quarantine director like old friends long estranged. Some boats were sent to us from the squadron and the whole crew and officers save for two were transported to the *Sedd-el Bahr*, the ship to which we were then assigned.

## A View of the Town

A branch of the Alpine mountains called the Julians, whose exposed peaks, steep cliffs, and green foothills adorned by country homes, create a magnificent amphitheatre that descends down to the harbour. Few towns and cities are as active as Trieste. Large wagons move ceaselessly along the streets and convoys ascend and descend the great slopes to and from the town. At the *Sanita* (the quarantine canton), where the ships load and unload their cargo, and in the customs warehouses where everything is packed for shipment throughout the empire and beyond, one can see almost all the products of Italy, the Levant, Britain and Germany. The bustle and commotion of exchanges is such as one cannot imagine. Merchants in a hurry to sell their goods lose patience with the sluggishness of the German coachmen. Crowds of curious people filling the square, animated and intermixing, coalesce into a single mass. I noticed that the day labourers here carry goods from the pier to the wagons with excellent dexterity. Two or four of them can raise heavy barrels and move in lockstep, seemingly running with a light burden. Free trade has enriched the citizens hear in every manner, especially the craftsmen and working classes of the people. Poor people cannot be found in Trieste and everything exudes abundance. As the city permits every sort of product to be traded, merchants of contraband cannot profit by prohibition and secret sales; merchants do not need to resort to tricks here and the customs inspectors, if necessary, collect[2] and hand over everything in full to the state treasury, which by prudent regulations enjoys this income and does not share it with anyone.

Trieste differs from the cities of Italy in its neatness and simplicity. The appearance of the houses are in the latest fashion and not inferior to the best buildings in St. Petersburg. The blinds they close instead of shutters when it is hot give their houses a unique look. The yards here are very small and many homes do not have them at all, which forces the owners to keep their carriages and horses in a common stable built outside the town. Trieste is divided into the old and new town. The former is located on the hill surrounded by the citadel, its streets are narrow and dirty and the houses are low and small. Most of the Jews and poor people live there. The new town is built around the curve of the harbour on level ground. Its streets are wide, paved and always very clean. The main street, which runs down the length of the town, is called *Strada del Ponte Rosso* – the street of the red bridge. The square of Saint Anthony is decorated with a fine fountain. A Corinthian column surmounted by a statue of Saint Anthony sits on an octagonal base which is surrounded by several marble figures that continuously spout water. On another square near the channel, a fountain in a statue of Neptune strikes the water. These two fountains supply the residents with drinkable water, which is carried out by underground pipes from a reservoir located near the town on the road to Boschetto. The theatre, the commodity exchange and the Palazzo Carciotti are distinguished from the other buildings in both their vastness and elegance of architecture. The exterior of the theatre is simple but the interior and the masquerade hall with choirs are worthy of any great capital. The exchange, where merchants gather every day for their business, is a massive and magnificent structure. On the dome can be seen a burning phoenix surrounded by symbols of trade. Among

2    Bronevskiy's note: 'Duties on goods leaving Trieste are collected only when they are sent to the inner cities and towns of Austria'.

the beautiful colonnade of the portico facing the square are two colossal statues of reasonable craftsmanship. The nose on one is unfortunately damaged. The Palazzo Carciotti occupies a whole block along the canal and embankment. It has a simple and pleasing appearance, its ornaments being just two porticos supported by Ionian columns. In 1770, when Count Orlov commanded the fleet, Demetrio Carciotti escaped the vengeance of the Turks and left his homeland by sea with 100 piastres to his name, settling in Trieste and beginning to trade in hooded cloaks before later serving as a courier and a labourer. By his diligence he amassed a considerable sum of capital in 30 years, becoming someone now regarded as the richest merchant in Trieste.

The Cathedral of Saint Justus, recognized as the patron saint of the town, is located on a height near the citadel and built in the old Gothic style, quite simple and unadorned. Here all faiths are tolerated and every confession has its own temple, but they are not very rich at all. I did not notice anything distinguishing among them.

Merchant vessels are always being built in Trieste. The slope of the shore replaces the slipways and the ships are launched fully armed. The local craftsmen and shipwrights build large sloops and brigs which are very beautiful and durable. The masting houses are filled with sawn lumber, mostly maple and oil-bearing species which are much harder and lighter than our oak. The mountain oak that is brought here from Dalmatia is also very heavy and strong. The vessels of Trieste, in addition to their beautiful appearance that rivals military vessels, are light to manoeuvre and carry more cargo than the Hydriots but less than the Danish and English.

The residents of Trieste constitute a mixture of peoples containing Germans, Italians, Greeks, Slavs, French and Jews. Everyone lives in their own fashion and is generally very self-interested. Besides a few noble families and some immigrants from every corner of Europe who have settled here, the populace are engaged in trade. Everywhere, the countless shops are full of merchandise. Labour and industry here walk with a cheerful countenance. The merchants resemble the nobility in fashion and way of life and their children are raised in the best manner. The very poorest have a fair appearance and demeanour. Young people of honest conduct and diligence to their position very quickly acquire an independent estate. They are first employed by rich *negozianti* (shopkeepers) as clerks, and when they learn the order of affairs and good accounting, they take on the cargo of a single vessel and claim one tenth of its value instead of a salary. After one successful turn, they already have a small fortune which increases with each subsequent *Reise*.[3] It

---

3    Bronevskiy's note: '*Reise* refers to a vessel's departure from and return to its home port; a complete voyage'.

happens that after ten years or so, a man who started without a kopeck to his name can build an account of 100,000 rubles.

Our two-year stay in Trieste afforded us time to become acquainted with many people; but besides the Slavs, who received us as relatives, we were rarely invited by the others. In the best noble houses where there are evening gatherings, a new guest not even briefly acquainted would find it boring. Old folks here sit down to play lotto or cards while the young people talk about the weather or the theatre. This affair is so rigid that if a pair of lovers did not have a complete, genuine and strong love for one another and become enraptured in one another during these assemblies, ignoring everyone else around them, they would surely suffer to ensure such boring entertainment. The most surprising thing is that the host, hostess and their children retire to a separate chamber to silently dine, while the guests are served nothing but water. O blessed Mother Russia! If you were not my homeland, I would always praise your hospitality! Vainly are we looking for it in foreign lands where there is not a shadow of Russian geniality. Travelling is undoubtedly useful and provides countless different pleasures, but to live only in one's homeland is proper and contentful.

Invitations to someone's home for breakfast or dinner here is uncommon, so there are instead many taverns, restaurants and coffee houses established. They are filled with people from morning until evening. Each variety of merchant and tradesman has their own casino (coffee house) where they go to read the latest newspapers, drink coffee and chocolate, play cards and billiards and discuss politics and current events. Here, as in Italy, it can be said that the people lead the tavern life. Not many keep a table at home; whole families dine at restaurants. Women also follow this custom and do not think it indecent; on the contrary, they find many benefits in it. Here their charms are always on display, coquetry is well employed, and their minds acquire that flexibility and worldliness which teaches them not to blush at everything but to riposte with a joke and laugh. These beauties are raised with some kind of common expression which aids their ordinary conversation in becoming entertaining.

From the way of life that women lead here, there is another custom which I consider worthy of note. To be rid of the terrible noise and crying and to be freer, some mothers (but not all, I think) will leave their children with a paid nanny and do not collect them again until evening. I loved to observe these magazines of children. Imagine a group of beautiful babies of three, four or five years, crawling and jumping on a softly carpeted floor, and so that they can never hurt themselves, even the first *arshin* [71.12 cm] of the walls from the floor up are carpeted. The older girls engage in needlepoint in another room under the supervision of a madam while the others frolic or play with dolls.

## The Boschetto and Sant'Andrea

In Triste, we had all the same pleasures that can be found in big cities. The theatre, balls, masquerades and strolls in the Boschetto and Sant'Andrea follow one after another through the whole course of a year. Hired carriages and coaches, although very cheap, are only employed in rainy weather, as the ladies are not ashamed of walking here. So as not to tangle the threads of time, I will begin by describing the summer walks and finish with the winter amusements.

In the summer, at sunrise, the merchants in marvellous starched caps spread out tables and benches on the square and lay on them greens, fruits, cream, oils and every sort of bread imaginable. The hostesses in their morning gowns and accompanied by maids with baskets and jugs in their hands come out to make their purchases. Behind them follow the young folk and the square soon turns into a meeting hall. Back and forth they walk and talk, gentlemen offer fresh fruit to the ladies or invite them to the coffee house and often a cup of chocolate is delivered to an unexpecting acquaintance. It must be admitted however that they prefer to chase after the pretty servants who are very skilful at enjoying a meal at a philanderer's expense. The blonde, blue-eyed, rosy-cheeked Germans, with their coldness and modesty, win the attention of many men over the lively and cunning Italian girls but would rather seek out the shepherd boys instead. Neither one nor the other, as far as I could see, returns home with an empty basket. Every holiday, a great many people gather in the Boschetto, a small grove located two *versta*s [2.13 km] from the town. Some sit in a circle and enjoy iced deserts, fried chicken, asparagus and sweet cakes, smoke tobacco and drink beer. Others walk along the paths with their families. Some sit under the shade of the trees and read, not gracing the passer-by with their glances. Some of the young villagers sell fresh cream, oil and fruits while others swirl about the meadows in circle dances or waltzes. Girls in red bodices bring bouquets of flowers to whom they please. Music hums in various places and dancers pay the musicians two groschens for a song. In the taverns, people read the papers, joke, drink wine or play billiards. All of this together resembles a simple rural holiday. Those not strolling through the Boschetto shoot muskets at targets; the garrison officers here, most of whom are obese, with a proud and philosophical expression, instruct the shabbily dressed young shopkeepers how to hold the musket, take aim and so on.

In the daytime, ladies and gentlemen walk only one behind the other, silently and content with only a glance. In the evening, when the greater part of the public departs, conversation begins among the remainder and a happy accord is quickly established. When the music falls silent and the twilight of the evening darkens the shadows in the grove, a pair appears followed by another, and they hurry in different directions. Some go up the slope, others go downhill; some return to town and others climb into a hired carriage and ride deeper into the woods. The less fortunate bow deeply before the beauties as if they were shot in the heart with an electric shock and if the girl does not have any immorality in her thoughts, she blushes, puts on airs of importance, glances downward or turns away and eloquently expresses her refusal. If she looks affectionately, then he offers to escort her home or dine together at a tavern. The most memorable charmers here do not otherwise surrender except to the ones they like or when a suitor's determination simply wears them down. In Trieste there is a kind of Bacchant,[4] but they do not attack like the furies on passing; rather, they have their own tone, taste and pickiness and they can be regarded as possessing true humility. Here, the liveliness and ardour of the Italians are noticeably tempered by the coldness of the Germans. The locals of Trieste or visitors from the surroundings are so fresh-faced, white and blushing that even a captive will rejoice if he is fortunate enough to cross their path.

In Sant'Andrea, people stroll every day; in the evenings during summer and at noon in winter. There is no garden, no grove and no greenery. A simple road near the shore provides a good view of the sea, for which reason the best company can be found there. Besides freshly caught oysters, a young wine called Refosco, ham, cheese and beer, which are served in a small two-storey tavern, nothing else can be obtained; there are no other amusements. People come here only to stroll, see the sea and watch the ships come and go.

The surroundings of Trieste are very handsome; all around one can see gardens and cozy country houses. In some gardens I saw many statues. In one place, they seemed more numerous than the trees. There is no luxury in the decoration of the homes however; the taste of the local gentlemen is limited to precision and simplicity. I often went out of town to admire the wonderful location. The green hills with the wild, bare mountains behind them on one side and the majestic town and formidable sea visible on the other comprise a magnificent view. Here a great many picnics are held. A small number of friends agree on a day and some nearby village to meet. Everyone assembles at the appointed time and place with cloth bundles containing a roast or cake, wine and confectionaries. The ladies are obliged to bring only what they can cook themselves. The gentlemen must deliver wine and the like. Huts, gardens and meadows are popular sites for these picnics. One of the women is elected the hostess and commands everyone. Everyone does whatever they can, from carrying water and chopping wood to setting the table and roasting vegetables. In these chores the beautiful lady is fully animated and everyone tries to please her. From her eyes, it seems, even a garden without shade or a meadow without grass takes on new charms.

---

4 The female followers of Bacchus or Dionysus, also known as the maenads (the ravers), who worked themselves up into frantic ecstasy with dance and drink during their rites. Smith, *A New Classical Dictionary*, s.v. 'Bacchae'.

## Theatre

To be in Italy and not say anything about the theatre and its charms, which is the finest and most fulfilling pastime, would be unforgiveable. Italy, in fairness, should be called the fatherland of theatrical spectacle. They honour a glorious singer here more than a skilful and fortuitous general. Actors are divided into classes. They are educated in theatrical academies and the first-class serve as a model of good treatment. The prominent lords receive them in their homes with the utmost respect and all others consider it an honour to have actors in their social circles. In Italy, it is rare for a town to have no theatre and the best are owned by the government, while the others are built and maintained either by subscription or by private patronage. The latter are almost always in disrepair; as a result, renting boxes and seats is very cheap. In Trieste, when a *chervonets* is exchanged for 18 florins, the porter takes 48 kreuzers[5] at the door, a box of the first tier costs just 5 rubles and does not rise in price during gala spectacles but instead one pays the actors at the entrance how much they feel they have earned. Due to the low price of entry, the theatres run all day long and the most mediocre actors still receive sufficient salaries. The very best of them, however, can acquire a fortune proportionate to their craft in a short span of time from a single benefit. This is why a talented singer can rarely be heard outside of Italy, since this kingdom of the fine arts values and encourages such geniuses.

Tragedies are limited to performing the operas of Metastasio and from them, arias are excerpted. The works of other authors are poor imitations or translations. The tragedies of Metastasio are filled with high thoughts and tragical beauties; his verse is noble and majestic and there is such tenderness in it that his operas serve as a model for poets of delicate and refined taste. Despite how glorious the creations of Metastasio may be, if tragedy should touch or terrify the soul with the thrill of adventure and the extraordinary but not romance, then the Italian Melpomene[6] must yield to the English and German. It seems that the cold air of the north better produces true tragedies than the healthy air of the south. To this day there are no good actors in Italy for the tragedies of Metastasio and it seems there never will be; they are born for operas. No matter how many actors I saw which are well regarded here, they were all very mediocre. Most of them spoke very tensely and there was something noble in their postures and movements,

---

5    Before decimalization in 1857, the Austrian *Gulden* or florin was divided into 60 *Kreuzern*. Leopold Bleibtreu, *Handbuch der Münz-, Maaß- und Gewichtskunde* (Stuttgart: J. Engelhorn, 1863), pp.460-461. [Leopold Bleibtreu, *Handbook of Coinage, Measures and Weights* (Stuttgart: J. Engelhorn, 1863), pp.460-461.]

6    The muse of tragedy in Greek mythology. Smith, *A New Classical Dictionary*, s.v. 'Melpomene'.

but they were too lively as if they were in a hurry to finish. The Italian public do not respect tragedies and dramas very much and they do not come to the theatre during performances to listen, but to visit friends and acquaintances. Usually at the end of a performance, the theatrical director runs a lottery and retains for himself a fourth or fifth of the collected pool. Those in the audience who have had their numbers called become actors themselves.

The comedies of Carlo Goldoni, called the Italian Molière, have much passion and chemistry in their performance, but for the Italians, as they themselves note, there is little comedic in them. Works by other authors are also fine, but they are pale in comparison with Goldoni. In Italy, generally there are very few actors with true talent but there are many fools of the most ridiculous and amusing quality. Original and marvellous farces, wherein the harlequin plays the main role, are the strange works of a merry mind. In these national comedies, there are generally only four characters: Sior Pantalone, a rich Venetian merchant in a mask with a large red nose; Brighella the servant; Harlequin, in a foolish, colourful gown with a bonnet on his head, a black half-mask and a wooden sword tucked in his belt; and Colombina, his constant companion. The role of Harlequin is difficult due to the fact that as a beloved child of the public, he must deliver every manner of joke in the corrupt local dialect of Italian and give the audience whatever they might find funny and, to their credit, the local actors are quite effective in the role. During these performances, the applause is nearly ceaseless and the Harlequin is quite deserving of it, acquiring it by the sweat of his brow, so to speak. For the most part, these actors improvise their roles and derive little from the writer. This however is not as difficult as it first appears; the Harlequin memorizes two or three dozen of the most stupid, low and common jokes, proverbs and insults which are so full of double entendre and misogyny that I do not know how they have the patience to hear them all. Such jokes would naturally have been banned by our carnival theatres. For example, Harlequin expresses his love to Colombina in the most unusual way and when she rejects him, he wants to kill himself. Struggling to decide how best to end his life, as usual for Harlequin, he pretends to always be hungry, stupid and trembling and writes himself a grave stone with the most obscene inscription... His treatment of Colombina is too brusque, he embraces her and beats her with his wooden sword or his hands for the slightest reason, and his insults are mostly limited to comparisons of the worst sort. Telling Brighella how he once stole a cloak lying on the bed in a house, he likens the item to a woman and the audience applauds him. However, such shamelessness from the actors is not surprising as they speak very freely in society, though still with some restraint; the Italian nobility observe the strictest decency in their conversations. I dare not mention the sort of remarks that make the ladies in the audience cheer without the least embarrassment. Many Harlequins are skilled and light dancers and quite ridiculous and amusing in these movements. The role truly commands comedic farces. It is more fun to see him as the king. Imagine that Harlequin sits on a throne, judges the people and issues orders, but as soon as a plate of pasta is carried past him, he leaps down to the ground and forgets his crown, eating what he can of it and putting the rest in his pocket for later.

The passion for theatrical performances in Italy has since spread and has nearly supplanted Catholicism itself. Its Great Lent is comprised of comedies, dramas and tragedies; I rightly do not know what to call them, as they are neither one nor the other. These plays are borrowed from the Bible or from the lives of the saints. I saw Saint Theresa at the theatre and the contents of the play were the most sinful and contrary to taste and morality. It is unclear what the purpose and intention of these tragic-comedic-dramatic chimeras are. It would be very useful if Christian virtues and the sincere penitence of the saints were described in the best possible way by the most skilled pen, but the vices and errors of worldly people brought to the stage before the public eye offend the faith and the faithful. It is possible, without disregarding proper respect for the shrine and without the indecency of seeing a dissolute woman burning with a vicious passion who repents only after her sin has exhausted itself, to see the saint conversing with her lover in the first act only to later reject the vanities of the world and finally on her deathbed be surrounded by angels, devils and harlequins. Of course, such plays are the product of freethinkers and constitute the most malformed generation.

In their tragic operas, Italian music is in full splendour and every emotion sought is made enchanting. The scenery and costumes employed are so close to reality that they are truly magnificent. There are few cities that could cover the necessary costs accrued by such productions. Giovanni Velluti, the greatest soprano, received a thousand florins for a single performance in Trieste and after 40 such performances and two benefits, he could afford a carriage, a table for six people and a wardrobe. No expense was spared on the scenery and costuming. Unfortunately, the richest costumes are not always appropriate for the character being portrayed. The major drawback of these operas is that the castrati-sopranos who occupy the first rank in the theatre are incapable of representing the famous heroes of antiquity due to their bodily disorder and feminine voices. It is all the more strange until you get used to it that the hero being stabbed and dying continues to sing so loudly that his voice overtakes the orchestra and thunder of applause. This cruel and useless custom was born out of a passion for vocal talent. Parents, disregarding nature and humanity and seeking to enjoy fame and fortune through their children, hand over their sons to a theatrical academy where, out of twenty victims, scarcely two will produce excellent voices. These half-men have all the strength and sonority of a man's voice with all the tenderness and flexibility of a woman's. Velluti, a pupil of the San Carlo Theatre in Naples and first-class soprano, astonished Trieste with his heroic arias. In tenderness and love, he attained the zenith of artistry. His roulades, trills, depressions and elevations of his voice were so unusual in their power, pleasantness and expression that at the end of his best arias, the stage was always showered with flowers, candy and purses full of gold. I did not always agree with this enthusiasm from the parterre; it seemed to me that if Velluti sang with a more ordinary voice during some of his antics, he and his art would better touch the hearts of his listeners. Velluti gained fame not only by singing but also for his acting; two talents that rarely come together in a person. Not even the best singers dared to sing with him in the theatre. Lorenza Correa, likewise in the first class, decided to compete with him at last and perhaps I am wrong again, but I believe that no castrato could sing with such soul and feeling as she did when she sang the aria 'No, non ti lascio; io moro / Se a te non vivo unita; / Dipendo la mia vita, Idolo mio, da te'[7] from *Aureliano in Palmira*. Imagine Correa, a tall, stately and full woman in magnificent royal clothes sprinkled with pearls and precious stones, in sorrow and tears, with a sweet, gentle and expressive voice, and judge whether any half-man could so touch and arouse your heart. Can Velluti himself not concede to the advantage of Imperatrice Sessi when she sings the aria from *Merope*: 'Cari miei figli, venite!' – 'My dear children, come to me!'

Opera buffa is perhaps the finest feature of the Italian theatre. In these operas, they bring to the stage all the stratagems of love and seduction conjoined. One flaw they have though is that the conversations which are sung like a chant (*recitativo*) are tiresome and boring. The lyrics in the arias often do not make any sense but with the thunder of beautiful music, fortunately, no one can hear them. Several scores by the most glorious composers have been written for these librettos. The dignity of the music in these operas and ballets is so great that it alone surpasses all others. The Italians are born musicians; they have by nature a tender feeling for music and what we acquire by training, they possess instinctually, even among the ordinary people. This Italian talent cannot be contested; their music depicts tenderness, love, sadness, fear and jealousy excellently, but in other more heroic passions, there is something languid and effeminate in their works and although the Italians are inferior to the French in military marches and to the Germans in technically difficult works with variations, they still far exceed them in other areas of music.

The ballet does not yield to the glory of the opera. Brilliant costumes, excellent scenery, and above all, inimitable heavenly music enchant the audience. The best dancers fascinate the eyes with their lightness and gracefulness of movement. Their pantomimes are movingly expressive. Their *grottesco* dances are nimble, bold and

7 Italian: 'No, I shall not leave thee; I should die / If I could not live with thee; / My life depends, my idol, on you'.

powerful; they are astonishing and praised everywhere they are performed, but I do not like their so-called deadly leaps (*salti mortali*). They interfere with the enjoyment of the second-rate dancers. These theatrical graces are beautiful, slender, half-naked and very dangerous for the heart. One's gaze glides from subject to subject and the heart cannot choose one over the other; each feeling which touches the imagination is equally beautiful. Rosina is the first singer of the opera buffa and Carolina is the first dancer, like a rose and a lily among other flowers, distinguished from the others by their beautiful and altogether immaculate behaviour. No rule is without its exceptions and in Italy there are lovely 17-year-old actresses who dare not love. Luigi Bassi, the foremost *buffo*, is an excellent actor, something Italy is lacking. He is a phoenix in his role. His jokes are full of witticisms and none of them are obscene; he does not rely on double entendres with ambiguous words, his eloquent pantomiming complements his dialogue in the best manner and the charming girls can admire his performance and laugh with all their heart without any reason to blush with embarrassment. During our stay in Trieste, the best and most expensive troupes were in town. Coming out of the theatre, which I visited every day, I always felt elated.

Theatrical companies are usually hired for two or three months, during which time they perform the same play 40 times in a row, excluding comedies and tragedies, and in this fashion, some new plays chosen for their benefit performances enjoy a lengthy run. Each troupe has its own professor of music, choreographer or poet. The third is a most miserable and poor creature. I dare not declare the ordinary fee paid for their opere buffe, or I would be forced to say that they were not worth it. They usually select several acts from the best works and quickly stitch them together. Excellent music overcomes all these shortcomings. Here, people are not even curious about the name of the writer of the new opera, but instead ask whose music is being used. The authors of comedies and tragedies receive even higher fees, but as dramatic creations are not highly respected, a new composition is only received well by virtue of being new and the best of them rarely enjoy two or three performances, almost never appearing on the stage again.

## Carnival

Carnival amusements continue from Christmas to Lent. The masquerade, the main amusement of the carnival, is made only for loving pranks and every kind of foolishness. During these days of shamelessness, the youth have every encouragement to satisfy their passions; debauchery is not made more proper by being concealed with a mask. The women are busy preparing their costumes in the shops from morning to evening and choose the most deceptive disguises and think of nothing but how to attract the most attention. As soon as evening comes, the perfectly illuminated costume stores are filled with ladies and gentlemen. The masquerade ball opens at the end of a theatrical performance, but typically the crowds come at nightfall and dissolve again into nowhere with the break of dawn. Only in Italy can you see such a variety of intricate clothing. William Hogarth's caricatures are a weak imitation of the Italian masquerade. Nothing can be more amusing than to see all the peoples of the world in their native costumes intermingling: Romans, Greeks, monks of every order, Indians, wild Americans, gods and goddesses, cupids and devils, amongst which wander windmills and towers and Charon rowing his boat across the hall. Out of the characters adopted, the noble gentleman with a grand entourage plays the first role. His staff consists of various dignitaries: a poet follows him with couplets and verses and occasionally recites amusing satires; Harlequin and Pagliacci are distinguished by cutting barbs selected from the best works; musicians with the heads of turkeys; a master of horse, a hunter and a cook each play their part and are made to speak by their lord like in some kind of comedy made up of different ridiculous scenes, to the amusement of the spectating public. Every mask transforms the wearer's voice and generally matches their clothing. The doctor gives out ambiguous prescriptions for all manner of illness and behind him follows a pharmacist who offers medicines to either ignite or extinguish the flames of love. The oracle carries an urn from which people pull out papers on which their fortunes have been written in advance. One character in the carnival in particular garners a thunderous applause: a woman dressed in the latest fashion and holding a mirror in her hands. Holding pink ribbons tied to their noses, she leads seven men dressed as a dandy, philosopher, warrior, merchant, doctor, judge and king.

At midnight, the masquerade hall is filled to the point where one can hardly move. In such a cramped space, people come together and separate in different directions, surging about, and may give free rein to their hands. Women walking unaccompanied do not take offense at all, supposing that such obscenities should be tolerated in a masquerade. Those who want to avoid assaults do not wear masks and they are given due respect for this. The free conduct in the masquerades extends even to women under the humble garb of nuns boldly saying what could never be expected from their sex. The men are not embarrassed in the slightest and accept or reject proposals in the heat of the moment. The disguised soon find their friends and retire to another room to drink coffee or change outfits at a mask shop and go for a ride in a hired coach, or retire to a special room rented at the theatre's restaurant… At two o'clock in the morning, the masked figures return to the hall in their previous attire and search for their friends. Neither mothers nor fathers, much less husbands, worry at all about where they were and what they were doing. This, I believe, is the real reason why people look forward to the carnival. We take solace in the fact that all of our amusements are alien to this depravity and relaxation of morals.

During the carnival season there is the general masquerade which is very strange and amusing. After lunch, the whole town is in masks, on foot, riding in carriages, or on the backs of donkeys and cows. Regular carriages and ones for the masquerade ride up and down the main street, two or three abreast. The latter sort of carriage is fixed to absurd teams such as a bull beside a goat or a cow and a horse, all of which are draped with blankets and flowers, and every sort of bauble is hung between their two heads. The balconies and windows, decorated with hanging corrals, are occupied by ladies. Gentlemen are stocked with small dry confectionaries, beans, flowers and memorized rhymes, throwing out one or the other (depending on their beauty and respect) directly at the ladies' faces. The heavy hail of candies is preferably strewn onto the beauties as it spares them from weeping. At the approach of evening, the disguised ladies go from house to house and visit, trying their hardest to be unrecognizable even to their closest friends. At this time, acquaintances are made without ever seeing one another's face. These deceptions are quite amusing and always leave a pleasant memory.

During the carnival, magicians entertain the people with various displays. Ballets and comedies are enacted with dogs on miniature stages. Cabinets containing wax statues are exhibited in the square. Acrobats, fire-swallowers and the like sometimes show their crafts in the theatre. I enjoyed the training of the canaries most of all. A Tyrolean could make them march with a band and had them storm a paper fortress, from which they fired tiny cannons. Having taken the fortress, a deserter was mock-executed with a toy gun and fell over as if dead, but when the Tyrolean picked him up and laid him on his arm, the canary suddenly flew into the air and sang. It is amazing how such a small bird can be conditioned to obedience and learns various movements unusual to its species. It is all the more amazing when there are a thousand of them gathered and sing together with an organ and then all suddenly stop when the Tyrolean pretends to threaten them with his cane.

## The Underground Grotto at Lipica

The astonishing underground grotto at Lipica, 24 *verstas* [25.6 km] from Trieste on the road to Fiume, aroused much curiosity. Agreeing to hire carriages, we travelled in a group of eleven to the grotto early in the morning. The road first led us past beautiful country houses and between handsome gardens but we were soon forced to climb a high, stony and completely bare mountain. Under the baking sun, the heat was unbearable and we paused during our ascent to let the tired horses rest. We hid under the shadow of three or four trees with pipes and beer. This was the most relaxing rest. The view around the mountain featured various subjects. To the east stretched a range of mountains occasionally powdered with small forests, through the land facing us was barren stone. The poor inhabitants of these mountains make their livelihood from the sale of charcoal, for which they are called *carbonari*. To the north, in the distance, was the grey ridge of the mountains of Fiume, which were also as bare as the ones on which we stood. Near Trieste, a portion of the sea surrounded by high rocks shone like a mirror by the light of the sun. Before the village of Basovizza, there was no sign of habitation. Only flint rocks and desolation could be seen everywhere and a gloomy silence reigned around us. After crossing the village of Basovizza, I was suddenly transported from hell to paradise. Fruitful gardens, beautiful groves and numerous herds grazing along green meadows unfurled. I did not notice from the scorching heat how finely kept and straight the road was that led to the small village of Lipica. After coffee and ordering dinner, we went to the cave with a guide.

On a level clearing with many stones, the guide showed us a deep pit surrounded with small shrubs and dry grass. One by one, we began to descend into the cave. Going only a few steps, the impenetrable darkness forced me to carefully slow down, grasping at the irregular outcrops of stone, and not putting my foot down ahead of me before feeling the next step with a stick. Hearing voices but not seeing anyone, I was afraid that whoever was above me might slip and take me down into the abyss as he fell, and the two of us would crash into whoever was ahead. I began to anxiously call out to my fellows. The guide then lit a torch and suddenly we were surrounded by light. For half an hour, we walked through winding passages and the walls of the cave first converged and then diverged so far that the light of the torch no longer illuminated the far corners. Finally we reached the bottom of the cave at a depth of 90 *sazhen*s [192 m] and our eyes were struck by a wonderful and magnificent spectacle. The walls of the cave were coated with scales of petrified water which sparkled by the torch into a blinding, inimitable light which only the wise hand of nature could achieve. We were in a subterranean, perfectly illuminated crystal chamber. The ceiling of the cave at points rose to such a height that the torchlight did not reach the vault and its vast size seemed to be supported by only a few thin pillars of pure crystal, while other pillars hung down from the ceiling as if threatening to fall. Nature's playful games have formed many figures on the walls like busts, birds and animals. In the centre of the grotto, a pile of stones, clear and transparent like glass, resembled a colossal statue set on a round pedestal. These stalactites and stalagmites split the light so brightly that they seem to burn and it is impossible to look at them for very long. The cold and dampness coming from the water dripping from the ceiling was so severe that we all soon shivered and hurried out of the caves. The scorching sun quickly compelled us to take off our coats and when we returned to the tavern, we again sought out coolness to dine comfortably.

## The Deeds of the French in Trieste

When Napoleon succeeded in depriving the Bourbons of their last throne, the righteous Spanish people, being unable to bare such an insolent grievance, resolved to take up arms in the name of King Ferdinand VII to defend their rights and freedom. The revolution was brutal in its conduct but justified by the outrages suffered and aroused heroic courage in the hearts of the noble Spanish. Upon the announcement of Joseph Bonaparte as King of Spain, there was no longer any doubt that Napoleon, having destroyed one kingdom after another, intended on conquering all of Europe. The Emperor of Austria, to secure his independence, found it necessary to create a strong militia (*Landwehr*) which could beneficently serve alongside the regular army in a war. The nobility, clergy, merchants and common people did not withhold their donations and willingly carried out the will of their emperor. On the 18th [30th] of June, 1808, Archduke John arrived in Trieste to form the local militia and His Highness honoured our ships with a visit, being received with all the dignity due to his honour.

Napoleon, being unable to conquer Spain in a single campaign, demanded in March of 1809 that the Austrian Emperor dissolve his militia and the rumbling of war rang out close to us. At the opening of the military operations, the Austrian arms were crowned with brilliant successes. The archduke defeated Prince Eugene, Viceroy of Italy, at the Fontana Fredda (in Friuli) and drove the French across the Adige River. The inhabitants of Italy[8] were glad to receive the Austrian forces and it seemed assured that the Kingdom of Italy would be liberated in a short time, but fate dictated otherwise. Napoleon's fortune soon compensated him for this loss. Hastily supporting the troops retreating to Bavaria with several new corps, he defeated the Archduke Charles, the commander-in-chief of the main Austrian army, at Regensburg on the 11th [23rd] of April. The loss of Vienna and the withdrawal of John from Italy to Hungary were the result of that unfortunate battle. On the 6th [18th] of May, the French occupied Trieste with the provision that they would not raise any contributions besides 800 portions per day for the maintenance of their forces; as soon as the Austrian forces withdrew from the area, however, the French began to increase their demands a little day by day: first they needed horses, then wine, then sugar and so on. The regiments began to arrive, each worse than the last. Soldiers in tattered uniforms or barefoot and wrapped in rags with only a musket on their shoulder demanded clothes from the locals. When the citizens of Trieste lost their patience and the Austrian civil officials who

---

8     Bronevskiy's note: 'Andreas Hofer in Tyrol, Major Ferdinand von Schill in Westphalia and numerous mobs in Italy rose up against the French; an unquestionable proof of their tyrannical rule'.

remained in the town and were reaffirmed in their posts by the new government reminded the French of the terms by which the town was surrendered, the French then dropped their façade and began to seize everything they needed by force. First, they announced that the inhabitants would hand over all their weaponry to the arsenal and once they prevented an uprising by disarming the people, they began to demand 50,000 florins, followed by 100,000. Then, with weapons in their hands, they seized wool and linen, canvas, and cobbling supplies from the shops and detained all the tailors and shoemakers under guard at the barracks until two whole regiments were outfitted. In the previous war of 1800, André Masséna devised a better method for the quick clothing of soldiers. For any sort of celebration or festival, entrance to the masquerade was allowed without a fee. When the hall was full, grenadiers with fixed bayonets drove the gentlemen out of the room and the unmasked women were made to start sewing shirts instead of the expected entertainment. The noble ladies were not let out of the hall until they could produce servants for their stead and made a cash donation. The poor women sat in that hall under guard for a week and then were sent off to the barracks...

Every general who came for a short time to Trieste imposed an indemnity for maintaining his forces. One of the generals, upon receiving this, invited the Austrian officials to his quarters for dinner and when, after the meal, the president of the magistrates bowed before the general and left, he was stopped by the adjutant on the stairs and handed a bill to be paid for the meal and dessert. The officers were not far behind their generals, taking everything they liked from their hosts except occasionally those things which they could not easily take with them. One officer of a party passing through, seeing ladies on a balcony, went into the house and frankly told the host that he admired his beautiful women and therefore would spend the night there. The host of the house, the advocate Rossetti, asked him if he had a letter for quartering in the house. 'What do I need a letter for', answered the Frenchman. 'Prepare a meal for six with champagne and Burgundy wine'. The next morning, the French officer filled his pack with linen from the house and took the host's fine new boots, leaving his own worn-out pair as a token of his friendship.

When Louis Joubert, the French intendant general for the region, arrived in Trieste, the calamities were still great and the poor inhabitants were burdened with hitherto unheard oppression. I would rather remain silent on these predatory actions, which do a disservice to the honour of a nation calling itself great and enlightened and as such atrocities always arise from the government or rule of a despot, I should not flog a dead horse, as the proverb says, and would drape a veil over an event which I witnessed and which tore at my heart then; but I consider it necessary to give my compatriots an idea of what we could suffer if, like the Germans, we remained in our homes. What would the residents of Moscow expect if our civil officials had stayed in office and were obliged to rob their friends and neighbours, fathers, mothers and even surrender their own property to the enemy? Comparing the calamities of all Europe with our own losses or those of the Spanish, let the readers themselves say whether it was better or worse that they set fire to their own homes and left nothing for the enemy to occupy; and finally, did we not defeat the invulnerable Napoleon and did our government, like the courageous Spanish, not take various measures to resist him?

The day after Joubert's arrival in Trieste, the French confiscated British merchandise, as well as a portion of German merchandise which was labelled as British by the French commissars. In order to liquidate these goods, a portion was sold off in an auction. The purchasers were given bills of credit and permission to transport or sell such goods without duties in France's territories. The capitalists of Trieste, who thought they could enrich themselves by this trade, were deceived in the most unusual way. On the border of the Kingdom of Italy, their goods were withheld. The certificates given by Joubert were declared void by the customs officials and the unfortunate merchants were grateful that they could sell their goods to Marshal Masséna and several other French generals. Naturally, the goods belonging to the marshal were immediately admitted.

After the capture of Vienna, Napoleon imposed on Trieste indemnities worth 50 million florins. Although at first they believed that the town could scarcely pay a quarter of this amount, Joubert proved the opposite; in two months, he collected more than 20 million in cash, provisions and other necessities. Joubert gradually and systematically drained the town of its money. First, a small contribution was levied, then under various pretexts three more levies were taken, and when there was nothing left to seize from the impoverished province, he began to employ compulsory loans, which is to say that the rich had half of their capital seized thanks to their magistrates to balance their allocation and subsequently to collect from their fellow citizens. During these forced loans, if someone refused to pay, they would administer a so-called military punishment: on the first day, five soldiers and an NCO would be quartered in the house and the host would have to pay each man 5 florins that same day, in addition to their meals; on the next day, five more soldiers would be added and extort 10 florins each from the host; on the third day, 15 soldiers were given 15 florins each and so on. If, after five days, the master still could not pay the contributions, then on the sixth day a commissar would take from him all of his silver items and other valuables that might be conveniently liquidated. Almost never or very rarely could anyone withstand the rudeness and unruliness of the soldiers for five days. They usually took up the best rooms, hung their muskets and pouches on the walls, ruined the furniture, forced the inhabitants to clean their boots and wash their linens, took whatever they liked, gave the women no rest and the most cruel insults went without punishment.

When the shops were looted, barely anything was left in the homes to eat and only half of the original 40,000 residents remained. Joubert then used the following means to squeeze out a considerable sum: 20 of the richest capitalists were detained and it was announced that if they did not bring in a new forced loan in ten days, they would be shot. No one had any money and these unfortunates were sent to the fortress-town of Palmanova in order to be executed. I cannot describe the despondency and despair with which this news was received by the people of Trieste. Some of the French nobility sympathized with the woes of the people and some even indignantly condemned the cruel acts which greed provokes. Louis, Duke of Narbonne-Lara,[9] a divisional general and the governor of Trieste at the time, tried as much as possible to alleviate the suffering of the people, but as the full authority to recover the indemnities levied rested with Joubert, his noble efforts were mostly unsuccessful. As much out of obligation and a sense of duty as with his own natural despotic character, Joubert seemed to be completely unmoved by their plights and used measures of extreme cruelty with surprisingly cold detachment. Here is an example: Carciotti, an 80-year-old man, was sent to Palmanova along with several other merchants. His son petitioned Joubert, saying that the estate belonged to him and not his father and asked the general to allow him to be put to death in the old man's place. Joubert answered indifferently and with a mocking smile, saying to this decent son: 'your intentions are commendable; suitable for a tragedy. If you pay a contribution of 20,000 florins in addition to the sum owed by your father, then I will order you be shot instead of your venerable parent'. Fortunately, peace was soon concluded and the victims languishing in prison were released.

Such were the means used to raise contributions, but there were still other more infernal deeds which the most violent bandit chiefs or even Attila himself would hesitate to employ. Before the arrival of the French in Trieste, the crown's income and all state property were removed, but the capital of minors and widows living under care remained. Joubert did not hesitate to demand these sums in order to fulfil his contributions. The president of the municipal government protested for a long while and Joubert did not want to use obvious violence, resorting to tricks then to extract this money. He found a man who had no qualms with losing his honour and dignity to take the place of the president and divert cash with the acts of his office. The previous, righteous president was sacked and the orphans and widows were then deprived of their daily bread. In order to have a reason to oppress

9    Bronevskiy's note: 'The duke was among those émigrés who returned to France and entered military service. His mother and sister, having lost all of their possessions, lived in Trieste in severe poverty and uncertainty. His mother rejoiced when she accidentally met him again, but she forbade him from visiting her in his French uniform'.

the people and seize their money, it was finally published that denouncers would be duly rewarded. The innocent suffered and were forced to pay for unfounded charges and not even false witnesses were required to testify. This was how the French obfuscated their forceful conduct, which at times seemed even to them as unacceptable.

In the wake of one army came another into Trieste consisting of sutlers, loose women, card players, craftsmen, entertainers, spies with lofty titles, secret policemen and every other type of person who are alien to all morality and dare to praise the philanthropy and selflessness of Napoleon and consider it an honour to marvel at his exploits. At every step, their base character tarnishes their hero with cowardice and predation and they involuntarily exhibit his low birth.

The card players, having paid a substantial sum for the privilege to win fairly, came under the auspices of the law. The croupiers were distinguished by a broad tricolour sash worn over his shoulder like a chivalric order. From morning until night, the theatre hall was filled with players. I sometimes visited this place to feed my soul with disgust and to note the desperate faces of the players who either blush or turn pale with every turn of the roulette wheel. The gloomy silence of the hall was interrupted only by curses and sighs and the clatter of the wooden rakes with which the dealers pushed and pulled money across the tables. The women who did not have any more cash would lose their rings, earrings, combs and scarves or hastily sell their goodwill in the theatre's restaurant. These swelled the ranks of the French nymphs of shame who were made into spies and received salaries from the police for the task. The army's sutlers, also paying their fees for the privilege, bought up seized goods at the auction at the contributions depot. In one shop, it was possible to buy something for a groschen, like a single shoe or a patch of an old dress, for example, and then in another a scrap of cloth could be bought for nearly nothing. Someone who purchased goods for 100 rubles might then sell them off for 150 after the latest valuation. This was how seized goods were liquidated. On holidays, during good weather, the so-called cash lottery was played in the square. To the advantage of the treasury, half of the collected sum was withheld and the rest was allotted for prizes; but as soon as someone won the largest prize, he is imprisoned under the pretext that he did not attain the winning numbers from the proper lotto officials, so eventually the people would not even risk a few groschens for the prospect of winning more. The corrupt mores of the victors crept into the hearts of the vanquished. Crowds of players from the lower classes, having nothing to eat, began to steal, which was not the case under the previous Austrian administration. The Machiavellian politics of Napoleon allowed such a corruption of the people intentionally; for a man who is in extreme poverty cannot regret his freedom lost and would willingly search for it on the battlefield as an alternative to starvation. In Trieste, a few recruits were taken by force and these unfortunate conscripts would have been compelled to fight against their own fatherland if peace had not soon been concluded.

After the battle of Aspern-Essling,[10] the French sought to conceal their loss and invented circumstances in their favour, lying without any restraint or credibility. One officer who visited the house of the Baroness Zanka, who received Russian guests graciously, with a confident and proud demeanour, relayed the most authentic information that one wounded French colonel travelling in a carriage was suddenly surrounded by a 6,000-man strong column of the Austrian militia and declared to be a prisoner of war. 'But our brave colonel', continued the braggart, 'by his word alone forced the 6,000 Austrians to lay their arms at his feet'.

'Please do not finish', jokingly retorted the Countess Vojnović (née Pisani). Turning to the other guests, she continued: 'gracious lords, I would claim to you that there is no woman more talkative than me, so be grateful that I am now retiring to Vienna and I assure you that I will force the entire French army to lay down their arms by the force of my chatter'.

At the conclusion of peace in Vienna, Auguste de Marmont, now a marshal, was made the governor of the Illyrian provinces. Their new subjects gave an oath of allegiance with bitter hearts. Their hope that fate would save them had dampened their despondency, but unfolding events soon proved otherwise. Every owner of a house or land had to play 10 to 20 percent a year not of their income, but from the amount of their property's value, which included furniture, staff, etc. From the many burdensome taxes and duties strictly collected, as well as the military's contributions, the richest people were bankrupted. In Venice, one of the theatres was sold for 60,000 livres but as soon as the money was delivered, the municipal government demanded from the buyer prior arrears reaching 140,000 liras and when he could not produce that sum, the theatre was forfeited to the treasury within a year. In this fashion, it was sold off three times and reacquired without any expense.

The continental system completed the ruin of Trieste. Napoleon's personal hatred for the British stretched to the point that, having no fleet that could avenge the British for their bold, unbearable ridicule of his poor character and so boiling with impotent rage, he did not hesitate to impoverish millions of his best subjects in order to deprive the enemy of their industry and business. The Milan Decree proves how little Napoleon thought about the welfare of his people. According to this decree, any merchant who might send his cargo by sea must pay the value of

---

10    Aspern-Essling was fought on 9-10 [21-22] May, 1809. The bloody battle cost over 20,000 men on both sides and killed the French Marshal Jean Lannes, but the victorious Austrians failed to exploit their victory and decisively destroy Napoleon's army in Germany. Ward et al., *Cambridge Modern History*, vol 9, pp.350-352.

the ship and its cargo in either cash or reliable collateral and if it comes to light that the vessel was inspected by British cruisers and released, then it was seized by the French as a fair prize. The customs officials, for the slightest suspicion and without any evidence, could seize any vessel and its corresponding collateral for the benefit of the treasury. Despite the vigilance of the French coast guard, British goods were sold in large quantities even in Paris itself. Napoleon, aiming to eradicate the trading of contraband which was enriching British merchants, ordered all colonial goods in his territories to be burned. This reckless policy, as we know, did not stop the black markets; what loss could the British suffer when they were already paid for the goods being destroyed?

# 108

# Incidents during the Squadron's Stay in Trieste – Our Return to Russia

On the 10th [22nd] of June, 1808, a British frigate came to Trieste under the flag of parlay carrying news that the experienced and virtuous George III had decided to spare no expense in lending aid to the Spanish and Portuguese as they were rising up with the sword of revenge against Napoleon. Despite the protests of the French consul in Trieste, whose notes were as good as commands hitherto, when the Archduke John arrived in Trieste for the formation of the militia, the British warships stopped near the harbour and took on a convoy of Austrian merchant vessels, accompanying them apparently past Istria, whose ports were reinforced by the French with a flotilla of galleys. The Austrians, out of respect for our flag, did not allow the British to approach our squadron within cannon range, but we met with them quite often in the town and treated each other amicably. On the 27th of August [8th of September], the first Spanish merchant vessel arrived and several Austrian merchants departed from Trieste for Spain. The alliance of Austria and Britain with Spain, although it was not made public, was undoubted by everyone due to their apparently friendly relations. On the 9th [21st] of November, Major-General Aleksandr Bibikov, who was appointed ambassador to the court of Joachim Murat, the new King of Naples, travelled through Trieste and visited our ships. On the 13th [25th] of December came into port the former ambassador to Madrid, Baron Grigoriy Aleksandrovich Stroganov, aboard a Spanish frigate. When he came ashore, the Spanish frigate saluted him with 15 shots. If the whole Spanish fleet could be judged by this frigate, one's opinion of the whole would not fare well. The construction of the frigate was not beautiful but it sailed lightly and was heavily armed. The crew were not agile with the sails, were dressed poorly and the whole vessel was very unclean.

On the 26th of January [7th of February], 1809, to our common sorrow, the honourable and beloved Commodore Ivan Osipovich Saltanov died. All the

Austrian forces stationed in Trieste were present at the burial. The procession according to our military regulations was quite magnificent. Banners, cannons and drums draped with veils; a long line of clergymen dressed in stupendous garments; choral and military music which rent the heart and impressed an impeccable sadness on the faces surrounding the coffin and hearse; ships with cockbilled yards[1] and their ensigns and pennants at half-mast; and the rolling cannon shots that followed one after another for five minutes – all of this in equal measure both touched the audience and amazed them with a splendour that they had never seen before in a funeral. Despite the poor weather, the streets were nearly impassable with crowds. By seniority, command of the squadron fell to Captain First Rank Mikhail Timofeyevich Bychenskiy.

On the 31st of January [12th of February], for the birthday of the Austrian Emperor Francis I, our ships were bedazzled with flags and each one fired off 31 shots in salute. On the 12th [24th] of March, the anniversary of our Emperor's ascension to the Russian throne, the Austrians fired off all the guns along their fortifications. On Easter Sunday, the 28th of March [9th of April], we held a truly Christian ceremony. Matins was held in the Slavonian Church of Saint Spyridon. The ship chaplains joined in the parish's own clergy in performing the service. Our singers stood on the right wing and their singing was admired by the local Slavs, but when the first cry of 'Christ is risen' was heard in the dead midnight air and our illuminated ships fired off a thunder of cannons, then the delight of the Slavs was indescribable.

The triumph of faith, of course, leaves an impression more pleasing than any other. The good Slavs confessed that they never rang in the great holiday with such joy and they would never forget that day they spent with us. The foreigners, especially Catholics, admired our church rituals; they admitted that with all the splendour of the Greco-Russian service united with a proper elegance, a sacred veneration is poured into the soul. Yet for all that, they call us schismatics and apostates and sometimes represent our rites completely inaccurately. Here is a striking example. One traveller who witnessed an Easter in St. Petersburg described the triumph of that day by saying: 'it was moving for me to see when all the courtiers and soldiers who were in the church, without distinction of rank, peasant and general alike, would began to embrace one another and kiss each other, saying: "*Krestovskiy ostrov*" and "*Vasilevskiy ostrov*,"' confusing the greetings of 'Christ is risen' and 'indeed he is risen'[2] with two islands in the city.

---

1    To slant the yards vertically so that one end is pointed at the water or deck and the other is up into the air.

2    'Христос воскресе – Khristos voskrese' and 'воистину воскресе – voistinu voskrese' respectively. These phrases are traditionally used as greetings on Easter by Eastern Orthodox, Eastern Catholics, etc.

At the end of March, the long and eagerly awaited war between Austria and France began. The squadron commander, Captain Bychenskiy, being without orders with respect to whether we should consider ourselves on the side of the French or the Austrians, sent Lieutenant Karl Rosenberg to St. Petersburg to receive the necessary instructions. After the occupation of Trieste by French forces on the 6th [18th] of May, the position of our squadron became difficult because the French and Austrian generals alike constantly assured us that we were allied with them. This confusion continued until the arrival from Vienna of the former ambassadors to the Sicilian court and the Ottoman Porte, Privy Councillors Tatishchev and Italinskiy.

On the 10th [22nd] of May, despite the multitude of British cruisers, 10 French gunboats managed to sneak out of Venice and arrived in Trieste. On the 13th [25th], the Italian Kingdom's war minister, Marie-François de Caffarelli, visited our commander and was saluted by 13 shots. That same day, due to the rotten state of the *Uriil*, half of the guns were removed and placed on the mole of the old quarantine. The Austrians did not leave a single gun in Trieste. This situation served to our advantage or rather it spoiled the opportunity to successfully fight the British. At dawn on the 17th [29th], a British squadron consisting of three ships, three large frigates and a brig appeared at Cape Salvore and came to Trieste under all sails.[3] Our squadron changed its position and stood so closely to the shore that it was impossible for the enemy to pass between our vessels and attack us from both sides.[4] The line, consisting of 4 ships, 2 frigates and a corvette was closed into a crescent and protected on both sides by coastal batteries such that the British would find it very difficult to approach under the fire of some 250 guns and stand against us on springed anchors. Assuming our new position, taking down the topmasts and yards, mooring and preparing for battle in all took three hours. The danger of being attacked in disorder was our best aid in these endeavours as it motivated our officers and sailors to act quickly. The French were no less active in constructing coastal batteries and they were finished and ready by noon. The enemy's squadron, without coming into range, dropped anchor and stood as the wind died out. At 4 in the afternoon, when a fresh wind picked up, the British weighed anchor and set every sail to approach us and several shots were fired from the old quarantine; we eagerly and greedily counted the minutes when the enemy would close within our range but to our extreme regret, the British commander, after examining our situation closely, did not dare to commence the attack and

---

3    Captain William Hargood approached Trieste with the *Northumberland* (74), *Excellent* (74), *Montagu* (74), *Spartan* (38), *Amphion* (38), *Thames* (32), and brigs *Imogene* and *Redwing*. Joseph Allen, *Memoir of the Life and Services of Admiral Sir William Hargood* (Greenwich: Henry Richardson, 1841), pp.188-189.

4    Bronevskiy's note: 'Our position is illustrated on the diagram of the port of Trieste'.

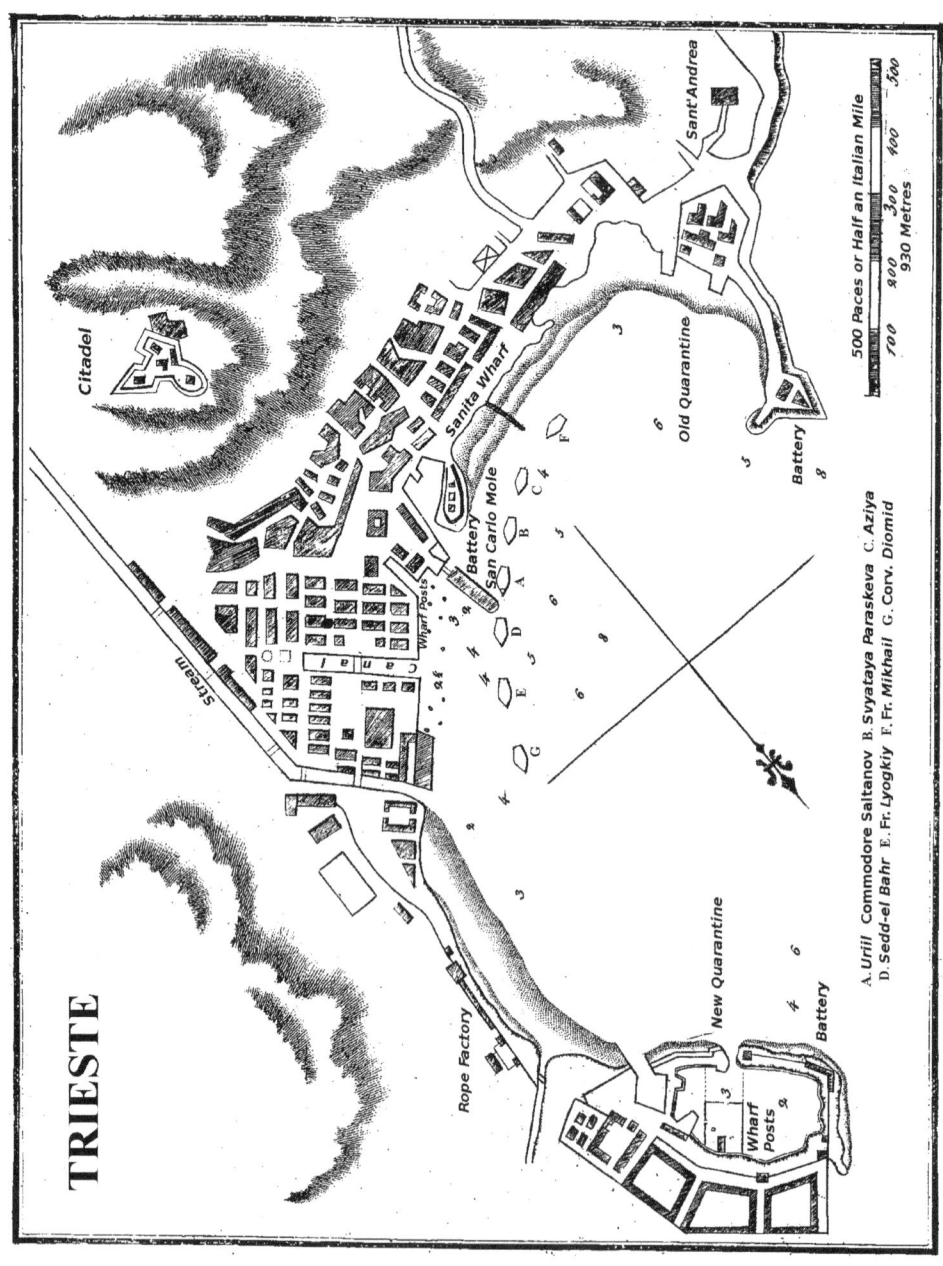

turned back, dropping anchor in the same place as before. We were irritated since we had been placed in such a favourable position that we could not even be sunk (which would be likely with such dilapidated vessels) as there was barely an *arshin* [71.12 cm] of water below our keels. An attack against us here would be reckless and its perpetrators would fall into our hands as prisoners.

The enemy squadron remained in view of Trieste for more than a month and seemed to have been looking for a chance to attack and meanwhile, we were constantly ready for battle. Upon a shot of grape from the line, a series of booms[5] tethered on anchors was deployed and every day the men were drilled in cannon and musket firing with powder and hand-to-hand fighting on the boats in the event of a boarding action.

On the 9th [21st] of June, the British attempted to procure water near Trieste at night, but our galleys and the French pickets prevented them. On the 24th of June [6th of July], when a detachment of the Austrian militia skirmished with the French on the way to Fiume, the British squadron then approached the harbour and greatly imperilled us; the Austrians fought stubbornly and the sound of their guns approached closer and louder. Our situation was difficult, for if the Austrians took the town, we would either have to perish without glory, or surrender without a battle. One of the British frigates began to fire bombs from the Bay of Muggia, which landed near our vessels. Our officers forced the frigate to retire with a few well-aimed shots from a 48-*funt* [23.6 kg] gun taken from the *Uriil* and laid on the height of Sant'Andrea. The French galley flotilla left the harbour in pursuit but the wind freshened and the British frigate managed to escape and reunite with her squadron.

The next day, that frigate repaired a breech below the waterline. The Austrians also retreated and did not approach Trieste again. During the night, the British fired several Congreve rockets into the town and one of them pierced a house, but without doing any further harm. On the 17th [29th] of July, a British frigate and brig, having learned that a French flotilla was making its way from Venice to Trieste close to the shoreline, attacked it at night so effectively that it was completely destroyed and 7 gunboats and 4 trabaccolos were captured. This was the last military action near Trieste. At the conclusion of peace, the British withdrew.

After the Battle of Aspern, Napoleon had a need for skilled sailors to serve on the gunboats and batteries arranged on the island of Lobau and decided to take advantage of the British attempt to attack our squadron in the harbour, but in order to conceal his intentions and knowing that our stay in Trieste was

5    Bronevskiy's note: 'They were constructed from old masts and bound together with iron chains, serving to keep the enemy ships at an appropriate distance'.

unpleasant since the French occupied the town, he sent the following message to Captain Bychenskiy:

> Believing that the position of the Russian Imperial squadron in Trieste is endangered from the attack of the British, I suggest to you, Captain, sir, to take advantage of the enemy's withdrawal from the coast or whatever opportunity presents itself and relocate yourself and the squadron entrusted to you to Ancona, where both the maintenance of the people and the strong protection of the well-fortified defences will be provided. If however the current campaign does not present such an opportunity, I am sincerely obliged for the sake of the honour of the flag of my ally and friend to suggest that you disarm your vessels and hand over all accoutrements to my commissars and relocate your crews to Udine where they can be formed into battalions and expect further instructions for returning to your fatherland.

On the 10th [22nd] of June, returning from St. Petersburg, Lieutenant Rosenberg was sent to Vienna with the following reply:

> Due to their dilapidation, it is not possible for the ships of the squadron to relocate from Trieste to Ancona without great danger. I hope that the flag of my August Sovereign might be better honoured by fighting with the enemy than to leave my ships behind as a sacrifice without firing a shot. In such circumstances, to leave my post without precise orders from my Sovereign is forbidden to me by honour and duty.

As the war continued, the hope of the Austrians to receive our aid was so widespread that even after the battle of Wagram, rumours were told confidently that 100,000 Russians would soon unite with the army of Archduke Charles.[6] So many Germans are used to regarding us as the friends of the oppressed and helpers of the weak. It is not possible to describe the feelings of sadness and despondency of the people of Trieste at that moment when the bulletin was published which described the

---

6    Worse than remaining neutral, Russia in fact joined the War of the Fifth Coalition on France's side and sent a small force into Austrian territory, as the Treaty of Erfurt bound Russia to aid France and her client-states in the event of a war with Austria. Sergey Fyodorovich Golitsyn commanded a corps of 32,000 to aid the forces of the Duchy of Warsaw in Austrian Galicia, but the Russian commanders were more interested in curbing Polish expansion than doing damage to the Austrians. For this participation, Russia received the eastern portion of Galicia containing Tarnopol via the Treaty of Schönbrunn. Alexander Mikaberidze, 'Non-Belligerent Belligerent Russia and the Franco-Austrian War of 1809', *Napoleonica - La Revue*, vol. 10, no. 1 (2011): pp.4-22.

articles of peace concluded between France and Austria. The misfortunes of Francis I were washed in the bitter tears of all his subjects; the sorrow of those people who were deprived of his gentle and fatherly government was truly pitiable.

When the Archduchess Maria Louise of Austria was betrothed to Napoleon, a ray of sweet hope was rekindled for a short time in Trieste. There was a rumour that the Illyrian provinces would be returned to Austria but when everything remained as it was, all the disasters of the Austrian Emperor began to be attributed solely to the Russians. Napoleon's good fortune, as they thought, was no longer surmountable. His marriage with Maria Louise reassured the disappointed Austrians that an alliance with France was now possible and indeed built on a solid foundation. These new subjects of Napoleon, displeased by the failure to relieve them, dreamed together with the French about further conquests, about the ruin of their neighbours, and finally it was clearly spoken that the theatre of war would soon move into the heart of Russia. The political opinion which had once been so flattering for the Russians had completely changed; the love and respect for our righteousness had become very cold. Our long absence from our home, inactivity, impotence and now the tension with the locals who no longer wished us well all turned our pleasures into boredom and weariness. In general, the unknowable questions of whether we would remain helpless here for such a long time and the premonition of a coming tempest that was gathering over our fatherland from seemingly all sides made our continued stay in Trieste agonizing.

Finally, to the inexplicable joy of all, we received Imperial orders from the 27th of September [9th of October], 1809: the ships and all their cargo and accoutrements were to be sold to the French government and their crews residing in Trieste, Venice and Corfu were to unite in one of the towns neighbouring Trieste where they would reside at the behest of local authorities until further orders for their return to Russia. In determining the price of the vessels and their supplies, the French commissars made great difficulties; for example, guns were taken only for their metal, gunpowder for its saltpetre, and other items that were still usable were estimated at only a 24th of their proper current value. One act of the squadron commander forced them to be more just. The ships' masts, which are very expensive in such places with no or few trees, despite the fact that some were quite strong and others were not damaged in any way, were determined to be cut up for firewood. Under the pretext of lightening the ships for floating them in the basin of the new quarantine, the French commissar suggested that all the masts be taken out by our men and placed into a warehouse in their entirety, but as there was no crane in the port, to take the masts as required, Captain Bychenskiy ordered them to be cut down. We hardly had time to cut down one mast before the commissar urgently asked us to leave the rest intact and so he was forced to begin treating our masts, as well as the guns and other things according to their full value. By the

20th of October [1st of November], the ammunition, sails and tackle were packed away into various magazines and storerooms, the empty ships were brought into the basin of the new quarantine, and the men were moved into a barracks assigned for them in the town.

Captain-Lieutenant Saltiy, the commander of the squadron remaining in Venice, having relinquished his vessels to the arsenal and leaving several officers and a small number of sailors for the appraisal and sale of their various materials to the French government, left Venice at the behest of Captain Bychenskiy in November and took up quarters in Oberlaibach (Vrhnika) assigned to him and his men by Marshal Marmont who was now the Governor-General of the Illyrian Provinces. Lieutenant Nikolay Kulomzin, who stood in the Bay of Cattaro with two transports and having handed over his vessels and received a note of credit for their value, arrived in Trieste in December by way of Dalmatia. Lelli, now a commodore,[7] who had remained at Corfu all the while, encountered considerable obstacles in the surrender of his ships, prizes and magazines and especially in relocating from Corfu to Italy. Despite the vigilance of the British cruisers, however, the detachments were all safely transported without losses on small crafts and from Lecce, where an assembly area was assigned, they continued overland. Meanwhile, the General-Adjutant Count Pavel Shuvalov, at the behest of the Sovereign, asked for aid from the Austrian government and when Commodore Lelli's detachment arrived in the vicinity of Venice, we finally departed from Trieste in six columns on the 24th of March [5th of April], 1810. The detachments of the Baltic Fleet under the command of Captain First Rank M.T. Bychenskiy were to march through Carinthia, Styria, Hungary and Galicia to then head straight to Kronstadt. The detachments of the Black Sea Fleet under the command of Captain-Commodore Lelli were to head on to Nikolayev after passing through Radzivilov.

Despite the changing political circumstances, the residents of Trieste parted with us sadly. During our two-year stay, there was not a single incident about which the citizens could complain. The strict subordination of our sailors and their gentle conduct earned them respect and their agility and courage in extinguishing a burning boat in the canal which runs through the centre of town was deserving of a common gratitude. This fire demonstrated to the residents of Trieste the selflessness of the Russian people. Shops full of merchandise stood on both sides of the canal and their destruction would have ruined the richest merchants. The police did not have enough men to extinguish the fire, the merchants each thought about only his own property, the commoners would not risk their lives without payment and while they were bargaining, the late Commodore Saltanov

---

7    Fyodor Panteleyevich Lelli was promoted to captain-commodore on the 12 [24] December, 1807. *Complete Naval Roster*, vol. 3, pp.231-232.

dispatched a third of each ship's crew to the shore. Immediately one portion of our sailors rushed to the burning ship while another cut the mooring lines and evacuated all the other vessels from the canal. Being unable to stop the fire, which had spread to the masts and sails, the sailors cut through the hull and sunk it in the harbour, thereby saving the others from certain destruction. To the surprise of the merchants, who had collected a cash reward to repay the sailors, our men each drank a glass of vodka from whoever had brought it to them, without bragging or demanding anything, and then immediately departed. Ties of friendship and family somehow subjected the French officers to an oppressive misery from the hosts of those houses where Russian officers had previous been quartered or entertained. Prior to our departure, the municipal government expressed to our commander the general gratitude of all the classes of the people and their desperation for keeping the good order, accord and exemplary behaviour of both our officers and enlisted men.

**109**

# The Departure of the Prince Regent of Portugal for Brazil – Negotiations in Lisbon

When the Prince Regent of Portugal decided to leave for Brazil, and the elderly queen, his mother, who had hitherto considered it impossible to abandon Europe for America, encouraged him to go as soon as possible, the unexpected arrival of the Russian fleet in Lisbon on the 3rd [15th] of November, 1807 produced a whole new anxiety in the court. Our alliance with France, the mystery of what orders our admiral had and what his intentions were in regards to the Portuguese fleet incited ill-advised rumours in Lisbon. The people, frightened by the approach of French forces and the preparations for the departure of the royal family, demanded weapons and the common hatred for the French could have had sad consequences. But on the eve of the departure, the following proclamation calmed the people and convinced them of the necessity for evacuating the royal family:

> Having sacrificed that which is most preciously beneficial to the people, I entered into an alliance with the powers of Europe, fulfilled all the demands of the Emperor Napoleon[1] and proposed only the condition that foreign armies should never occupy the frontiers of Portugal, but it was not accepted and now the French Army enters my domain and I, being unsure of my own safety, am retiring to Brazil, in which I will govern from São Sebastião [do Rio de Janeiro]. Departing from the country, I ask my subjects to endure with patience and obedience the fate that befalls them. Any effort to resist would be blood shed in vain. Withhold, my loyal subjects, your indignation against that powerful enemy who defeats the mightiest nations. God, who occasions us with temporary misfortunes,

---

1 Bronevskiy's note: 'The Regent issued a proclamation on 8 [20] October forbidding entry to British trade'.

will sooner or later punish the unjust. Bidding you farewell, my beloved and loyal subjects, I do not lose hope that I will see you again.

On the 17th [29th] of November, at 9 in the morning, Queen Maria Francisca Isabel, her son the Prince Regent and the whole royal family departed for their fleet. In their journey through Lisbon, the people fell to the ground, pierced with sorrow, and did not bellow out loud exclamations but expressed their devotion with a desperate and heavy silence. At the pier, the regent stepped out of the carriage and bid farewell to the remaining officials with a certain emotion, instructed them to try to keep silent upon the entry of the French and admonished them to submit without complaint to their unfortunate circumstances. He ordered that portion of the army which could not be fitted on the vessels to disband and return to their homes. After receiving a blessing from the archbishop, he boarded a boat and departed for his ship. At 11 o'clock, when the French appeared in the vicinity of the capital, a cannon shot gave the signal to set sail and the Portuguese fleet, consisting of 8 ships, 6 frigates, 9 brigs and 10 large transports, weighed anchor. Countless merchant vessels, fearing to lag behind their navy, cut their ropes and hastily rushed out over the open ocean. The solemn cries of 'vivat!' with wailing cries from the crowds running along the embankment behind the queen and regent's ship and the some thousand boats following in its wake created such a spectacle that any heart would ache for the humiliation of that royal house and the sorrow of their people. The British squadron under the command of Sir Sidney Smith blockaded Lisbon and stood on anchor at the mouth of the Tagus, meeting the prince regent with all due respect. All day long, Portuguese merchant vessels packed with people, so to speak, took on whole families from boats leaving the river, hoping to be accepted on either their own vessels or the British ones, but the cramped confines of the military ships and transports could not afford any more passengers. The confusion and despair of those who had to return into the hands of the French went unsung. The authorities struggled to contain the excitement and will of the Lisbon mobs who intended on resisting the enemy's entry into the city and were poised to invite a new catastrophe. Many families sought refuge on the ships remaining in the Tagus, for fear of a rebellion in the city. To exasperate their horror, a violent storm arose that very day, catching the departing fleet on the open water. The poor condition of many of their vessels made us fear for the most painful of losses.

During the departure of the Portuguese fleet, there was a rumour in Lisbon that the prince regent would be detained by the Russian admiral. The ties between our court and Napoleon, whom we owed support in all of his enterprises via the Treaty of Tilsit, inspired this rumour and was confirmed by one French gazette. Being spread by malicious people, even general opinion among the good and proper people believed that Senyavin would not miss an opportunity to win Napoleon's favour. When the Portuguese fleet passed the Russian one and all the merchant vessels were left to pass freely, the anxious expectations and vague suspicions of the people turned to joy. This simple act earned for Senyavin the love and confidence of the Portuguese, the reverence of the well-intended French and the amazement of those who blindly followed the Napoleonic philosophy and regarded such acts of virtue and magnanimity to be extraordinary; they believed that the sacred rights of hospitality and even honour itself could be violated for the sake of the treasures stored in the holds of those Portuguese ships. The consequence of this righteous feat was that Senyavin deserved the respect of even his foes and prepared for himself the indulgence of the British admiral, which saved the honour of our flag and relieved Russia of the grief of seeing her fleet forced to surrender without glory or even destroyed.

On the 20th of November [2nd of December], a French army up to 20,000 strong gathered on the outskirts of Lisbon but fearing the indignation of the residents in such a populated capital, it was not until 6 in the evening on the 22nd [4th] that it entered the city and began to occupy the fortifications along the Tagus river over the following days. On the 25th [7th], 4 ships, 10 frigates and 8 smaller military craft[2] in the dockyards and all the fortresses and batteries hauled down the Portuguese flag and hoisted the French colours.

Despite the fact that Portugal was taken without any resistance, she was treated like the territory of a vanquished enemy. The first acts of the French government were: seizing for the treasury all British goods and crown property, imposing burdensome indemnities on the state and all the other measures to suppress and ruin the people, which greatly hampered Senyavin's orders for procuring provisions for his squadron.

Not having any instructions from our cabinet regarding the military occupation of Portugal, hitherto a Russian ally, and as our fleet came to Lisbon while the prince regent was still in power and assuming at the time that the port of Lisbon was neutral for the Russian flag, Senyavin decided not to take any part in the affairs of our new ally of France in order to secure himself from any poor turn that they might suffer, to evade any sort of hostile acts that could offend the people of Portugal, and finally to limit himself in actions against the British so that he might repel an attack at any time with his whole force. The admiral took up a heaven burden, needing extraordinary sharpness and prudence in order to win the patronage of Jean-Anchoche Junot, Duke of Abrantès without insulting or provoking the British and to keep the trust of the Portuguese. Fortunately, Junot, being a benevolent and magnificent Frenchman, was moreover a kind, simple and frank man and Senyavin had previously found that the general would, in so far

---

2    Bronevskiy's note: 'Merchant craft in the river numbered nearly 300'.

as Napoleon's strict orders allowed, alleviate the fate of those British long since settled in Lisbon. On the other hand, Admiral Sir Charles Cotton received from Sidney Smith, whom he replaced, a favourable opinion on Senyavin's character, although the dispatch to Russia of Rear-Admiral Greig and the other British officers[3] serving in our fleet was the reason for Cotton's hostile reception, to whom this generous measure by our state seemed bitterly opposed to Britain. After this, however, the relations between the two admirals were repaired by mutual respect and proper courtesy.

In April of 1808, Senyavin received orders to put himself and his squadron at Napoleon's disposal. But this treacherous ally used his authority maliciously: every order from them contained cunning motives aimed at the destruction of the Russian fleet. No matter how hard he tried to avoid such instructions under various pretexts, Senyavin was finally put in a dangerous predicament. In these circumstances, Senyavin rejected personal enrichment and ambitious flattery and was guided by his complete devotion to his sovereign and his love for the fatherland, and if Napoleon was dissatisfied with the delayed execution of his whims, then it is to Senyavin that we must credit the preservation of our honour. Here is an example: in order to reinforce our squadron with a Portuguese ship and frigate that remained in Lisbon, Napoleon ordered that the crew of the *Shpitsbergen*, which found itself in Vigo, be withdrawn and reassigned to that ship and frigate with a supplement of Portuguese and other foreign sailors who were forcibly pressed into service. Under the pretext that he needed to be careful of unexpected attacks and to be able to give proper resistance to the British, Senyavin began only by repairing his ships and gave word that when he was ready to depart for open waters with his squadron and give battle to the enemy, then he would proceed to arm the Portuguese ship and frigate.

On the 13th [25th] of May, at 5 in the afternoon, the mainmast on the admiral's ship was set on fire by a lightning strike. The fire spread so far down that it was not possible to salvage it. The admiral ordered the mast be cut down and when a new one was prepared, it was delivered from the docks, planted and rigged to the

---

3    Bronevskiy's note: 'This was done on the 9 [21] February, 1808'. Translator's note: Aleksey Samuilovich Greig was second generation Scottish-Russian (his father, Samuel, was born in Inverkeithing, Fife) and had served in the Royal Navy and East India Company from 1789 to 1796. Unlike other foreign officers like French émigrés who might be relied on to oppose the revolution and Bonapartist regime on ideological grounds, Greig and other 'British officers' were withdrawn from active service during the Anglo-Russian War rather than risk a conflict of interest. Greig returned to active service on the staff of Admiral Chichagov in 1812 when Russia was again allied with Britain and at war with France. *Complete Naval Roster*, vol. 3, p.433-440.; 'Memoir of Sir Samuel Greig', *The Dublin University Magazine* 44 (July 1854): p.156.

ship in no more than four hours, for which the captain and the officers were given a sign of gratitude and the sailors were each awarded a glass of wine.

In the beginning of 1808, a people's war spread across all of Spain. Already the patriots who fought with fierce courage for their precious honour and freedom, despite their disorder, succeeded in some places and all relations with Russia ceased. The hope of receiving money for the squadron's supply and maintenance was absolutely extinguished. The admiral, having credit and personal respect, could receive money for repairs and other needs of the squadron from agents but decided to use the prize money rather than risk the accumulation of interest at staggering rates which would only accrue losses for the treasury. But as this sum was the property of those who earned it and according to the laws of Peter the Great, reconfirmed by the reigning emperor, this constituted inviolable private property. The admiral suggested to the possessors that if they did not agree to donate their cash to the squadron's needs, they would only spend it on foreign wares and return home with countless trivial baubles, but assured them that if they did volunteer their prize money, the sovereign would naturally reward such zealous generosity with his good favour and everyone would be compensated upon their return to Russia. Could Senyavin's subordinates, who so often saw how he sacrificed his own bounty to the treasury in all of his endeavours, dare not to follow his example? The whole fleet unanimously agreed and the treasury and the bankers of the commissary possessed some 250,000 *chervontsy* exchanged into foreign currency; all of the prize money and even personal salaries donated then grew the squadron's available cash to 600,000.

The example of the Spanish people awakened the fallen spirit of the Portuguese. On the 8th [20th] of June, they raised the banner for the honour and freedom of their nation. On the 25th [6th], in Oporto, the commander of the regular Spanish forces captured the French general François Quesnel and his staff, appointing Luis de Oliviera in his stead as governor, and soon a junta was established under the chairmanship of the bishop. Assuming full authority, the junta proclaimed that peace and friendship had been renewed with Spain and Britain and that the Kingdom of Galicia and other bordering Spanish regions were ready to join the British in a patriotic war. Soon the landing of British forces and the delivery of muskets, cannons and powder reinforced the universal uprising. Junot, having received word of this, disarmed all the Spanish men in his corps and confined them to the hulked ships moored in the Tagus. Napoleon's legions acted successfully at first and managed to restore calm, but the mobs of patriots multiplied unceasingly, desperately defended themselves in advantageous positions, yielding sometimes to the excellent order of the French regiments, but never losing heart. They dispersed, rallied again, attacked, sought death, fought stubbornly, sacrificed their lives and did not ask for or give any mercy. The spirit of heroism enlivened the peaceful peasantry, vengeance became their watchword, death and wounds in the defence of the fatherland were their promise. The bloody and cruel war spread across the two states, from the Pyrenees to Cadiz and from the Ebro to the Tagus. The whole people, old and young, even women, armed themselves and swore an irreconcilable hostility against the French. The brazen and unprecedented insult in the face of the Spanish and Portuguese kings embroiled the faithful people with outrage and wild heroism, and so Napoleon took the first steps toward his fall. The Hand of God on the Iberian Peninsula prepared for him a punishment commensurate with his tyranny. The French forces saw that for the first time, people dared to expunge them as if they were robbers and who could only be confused, discouraged and defeated in their *Moniteur*. In each battle, they lost men without any benefit and moved from action to action, wandering as if in an enchanted forest. They drove the patriots out of the city and then left to suppress another, returning, conquering and conceding the same city several times in a single month. Hunger and fatigue reduced their forces more than combat; the wounded, sick and stragglers who could not keep pace perished without replacement and those who fell into captivity were mercilessly killed by the people. The French took revenge with torchings and executions while they themselves burned on the fires of the enemy, died at the hands of the night assassin and choked on poison.

General Louis Loison was sent from Lisbon with a strong detachment to pacify the patriots in Oporto and after brutal, fruitless blunders, he was forced to turn back for fear of being cut off from the main corps. The line of communications with the French army in Spain was severed and danger mounted. Finally, the French in Portugal were surrounded by numerous mobs who were still disorganized but now quite accustomed to the smoke and thunder of military action. In this state, the Duke of Abrantès issued an admonitory proclamation to the inhabitants of Lisbon full of shameless threats, but it had little effect, the course could not be reversed and the people were already sharpening their daggers in secret with an infernal smile. At the same time, in order to strengthen the protection of the fortresses along the river Tagus and to make a useful impact on the Portuguese and Spanish, Junot urged Napoleon to demand that Admiral Senyavin land several of his marines and sailors ashore. Senyavin, determining to remain neutral for as long as possible, replied to the French general in much more courteous terms that in accordance with Napoleon's orders and the demands that honour placed on him, he needed to conserve and concentrate all of his forces in order to repel an attack from the enemy, referring to the British and not the Portuguese, and therefore he unfortunately could not lend any of his men without weakening his position and furthermore, the language barrier would make his sailors and marines more of a burden than a boon.

Soon after this, Junot was compelled to assemble his troops in one place and attack the British with all of his available resources on the 5th [17th] of August at Roleia or Roliça and on the 9th [21st] at Vimeiro but after stubborn battle, he was defeated and fell back to Lisbon where a rebellious people placed him in a troubling position. On the 12th [24th], Junot invited Senyavin to Cascais for the conclusion of a general capitulation to the British commander-in-chief of their ground and naval forces, but on the 16th [28th], he was informed that an agreement had not been reached. On the 19th [31st] of August, Junot reported the capitulation concluded at Cintra between himself and the British general Sir Hew Dalrymple, which was greatly advantageous. Among the articles of this surrender, the seventh was as follows:

> The neutrality of the port of Lisbon shall be recognized for the Russian fleet: that is to say that when the British army or fleet shall be in possession of the city and port, the Russian fleet shall not be disturbed during its stay nor stopped when it wishes to sail, nor pursued after setting sail until after a time fixed by maritime law.

By the force of the other articles of this treaty, which were accepted by the British government and people with great displeasure, The French had to be transported on British ships to the nearest French port, without any conditions on their future service and the Portuguese fortresses were immediately surrendered to the British.

On the 22nd of August [3rd of September], Admiral Cotton, disapproving of the seventh article of the convention, announced to Senyavin that it was impossible to recognize the port of Lisbon as neutral neither in its present state nor after the evacuation of the French. The next day, British flags were hoisted over the fortresses of São Julião and Bugio, and then the Tower of Belém[4] was also occupied by the enemy. In this dangerous circumstance, where our squadron was surrounded on land and blockaded from the sea by superior forces, the admiral called a council of the captains and asked for their opinions on what should be done. The ship captains unanimously announced to the admiral that they agreed to follow anything he ordered. Senyavin, thanking them for their flattering confidence, answered: 'I will offer to negotiate with the English admiral, but with the situation being how it is, it's unlikely that any agreement besides an unconditional surrender could be accepted. In that case, I see no other choice but to fight to the best of our ability'.

Our squadron stood between the Tower of Belém and the southern shore in two semi-circular lines so that an enemy ship attacking one of ours would have to

---

4    Bronevskiy's note: 'After the treaty was concluded, Portuguese flags were then raised over all the fortresses'.

engage two or three simultaneously and passing through would expose them to the collective fire of nearly the whole Russian squadron. In this position, everyone was confident in the opportunity to give a strong rebuff to the British, despite the fact that the coastal batteries were within canister range of our ships. The officers and men, animated with courage, did not think about the danger and prepared with some cheer for death, keeping their eyes on the enemy and hungering for the first shot. For the duration of the negotiations, everyone was tormented by uncertainty and burned with an impatience to fight. With each slight movement among the enemy's vessels, someone would exclaim: 'the British are withdrawing at last, thank God!' After three days of this fruitless and agonizing waiting, the commander-in-chief ordered the following:

The twisted state of the Kingdom of Portugal has finally afforded the British complete control of the port of Lisbon. Admiral Cotton announced to me that he does not recognize the neutrality of the port before or after the withdrawal of the French. The French commander-in-chief, the Duke of Abrantès, on the 19th [31st] of August concluded to withdraw and capitulate the city to English forces and thus our squadron's position is made dire both from the sea and even more so from the land by the superiority of the enemy.

Everyone clearly understood at that time that the salvation of the squadron had no other means than to agree to entreaty with the enemy, which would be commensurate with the honour and benefit of the Sovereign Emperor, the fatherland and our own persons. To that end, I gave them proper warning of the gentlemen commanders of the ships and frigates who have agreed to follow my orders. The articles of the treaty that I have drafted have been approved by the English admiral on the 22rd of August [3rd of September]. The commands so required are hereby attached:

### The Articles Concluded between Vice-Admiral Senyavin, Knight of the Order of Saint Alexander Nevskiy[5] and other Russian Orders and Admiral Sir Charles Cotton, Baronet

1. The ships of war of the Russian Emperor now standing in the Tagus as specified in the annexed list shall be delivered up to Admiral Sir Charles Cotton immediately, with all of their stores as they now are, to be sent to

---

5     Senyavin was awarded the Order of St. Alexander Nevskiy on 18 [30] September, 1807 for the victory against the Ottomans at Mount Athos. *Courtly Menologium for the Year of Our Lord 1808*, p.121.

England and there held as a deposit of His Britannic Majesty and to be restored to His Imperial Majesty within six months after the conclusion of a peace between His Britannic Majesty and the Emperor of All Russia.
2. Vice-Admiral Senyavin, with the officers, sailors and marines under his command, shall return to Russia without any condition or stipulation respecting their future services; to be conveyed there in men of war or other proper vessels at the expense of His Britannic Majesty.
Done and concluded aboard the ship *Twerdy* [sic] in the Tagus and aboard His Britannic Majesty's ship *Hibernia* off the mouth of that river, on the 3rd of September, 1808.

-Senyavin
-Cotton

Countersigned at the behest of the Vice-Admiral
-L. Zass, Collegiate Assessor.
Countersigned at the behest of the Admiral
-James Kennedy, Secretary.

The next day, in addition to these articles, the following two orders were approved by the squadron commanders:

3. The colours of His Imperial Majesty on board the flagship or on board any of the others are not to be struck until the admiral quits the ship or until the respective captains do the same.
4. At the conclusion of a peace, the ships and the frigate will be restored to His Majesty the Emperor of All Russia in the same state in which they are actually delivered up.[6] Of the nine ships, the *Yaroslaf* [sic] and *Rafael* [sic] will remain in the Tagus and their crews will be distributed amongst the other seven ships that proceed to England.

The above two articles will be regarded as forming part of the convention concluded and signed on the 3rd of September, 1808. In witness thereof we undersign two completely identical copies. Given and concluded on board the *Twerdy* in the Tagus and on board the *Hibernia* at the mouth of the said river, 4th of September, 1808.

---

6   Bronevskiy's note: 'The *Silnyy* and the *Moshchnyy* arrived in Kronstadt in 1813. For the other five ships and frigates, despite their completely rotten condition (which they still would have suffered in Russia, naturally) the English government paid a sum worthy of newly launched vessels. Their guns and ammunition were delivered on our fleet as it departed from England in 1813'.

## The Vessels Included in the Convention

| Vessel | Commander | Number of Guns | Size of Crew |
|---|---|---|---|
| *Tvyordyy* | Capt. 1st Rank Maleyev | 84 | 736 |
| *Skoryy* | Capt. 1st Rank v. Scheltinga | 64 | 524 |
| *Svyataya Yelena* | Capt. 1st Rank Ivan Bychenskiy | 74 | 598 |
| *Selafail* | Capt. 2nd Rank Rozhnov | 74 | 610 |
| *Yaroslav* | Capt. 2nd Rank Mitkov | 74 | 567 |
| *Retvizan* | Capt. 2nd Rank Rtishchev | 66 | 549 |
| *Silnyy* | Capt.-Lt. Malygin | 74 | 604 |
| *Moshchnyy* | Capt.-Lt. Razvozov | 74 | 629 |
| *Rafail* | Capt.-Lt. Aleksey Bychenskiy | 84 | 646 |
| *Kildyuin* | Capt.-Lt. Durnov | 32 | 222 |

In total 700 guns and 5,685 men.

The preservation of the honour of the flag and the glory of the Sovereign is necessary, an object of great importance, and precious to every general, soldier and son of the fatherland. In the circumstances in which our squadron found itself, my readers can clearly see the danger looming over the honour of the Russian flag and if those who have served in the military branches will know what it means to lose a banner or standard, they will read with pleasure this memorable Lisbon Convention. Naturally they will understand from the fact that the singular determination, art of negotiation and most especially the enemy's respect commanded by Senyavin were our salvation and are owed the credit of saving the honour of the flag for which we willingly sacrifice our lives and seek death with joy. In military operations, the benefits gained are measured by the enemy's losses but often both sides claim victory, which is why the comparison of the public acts of the belligerent powers is the true measure of their relations. In respect to this, my fellow countrymen can take pleasure from the discontent of our enemies. I present here an excerpt from the public English papers[7] presented for judgement in parliament.

The account of the victories in Portugal, obtained by Sir Arthur Wellesley on the 17th and 21st of August, were received by people of all ranks with the most generous enthusiasm, but the dissatisfaction which afterwards pervaded the public

---

7    Bronevskiy's note: 'See *Naval Chronicle*, volume 20, pages 229 to 235 and 362 to 369'.

mind on the appearance of the *Extraordinary Gazette*, relating to the evacuation of Portugal and the surrender of the Russian fleet is indescribable.

That the evacuation of Portugal is an object of importance must not be denied, but that a proudly victorious army of 32,000 should suffer a routed enemy of only 15,000 to depart with their arms in their hands, with 800 horses, with all their artillery, with 60 rounds of ammunition, with all their baggage and with all their private property, of which they had plundered from the wretched people whose country they had been ravaging; and that they should even furnish the means of conveying these marauders to their own country, in order that they might again be immediately employed against ourselves or our allies, is indeed passing strange.

The acceptance of the Russian fleet as a mere temporary deposit to be restored unconditionally at the period of peace seems no less astonishing. That all its officers and seamen should be conveyed to their own shores, giving them an immediate opportunity of acting against our gallant ally, the King of Sweden, is an act unprecedented in history.

The terms of the armistice or provisional convention on which the definitive one was founded appear even more infamous and more disgraceful than those which were ultimately agreed upon. According to those, the Russian fleet would have totally escaped. Our admiral has been praised for having refused to accede to the seventh article of the famous French armistice, that he might be enabled to try his own skill at negotiating with the Russian admiral. [...] I am of the opinion that if that seventh article had been abided by, we should have been immense gainers in comparison with the naval convention afterwards agreed upon. The case stands thus: The Russian fleet had entered the Tagus while the Prince Regiment was power. It was then a neutral port and at the time of the naval convention we might surely fairly deem it the same. In short, it continued to be a Portuguese port, although the French army occupied the city by force. Suppose then, from a sense of honour carried to a Quixotic height, the Russians had been permitted to sail and were not pursued for 48 hours, one of the following would have been the consequence. Our fleet would have pursued and perhaps taken them, or our Channel fleet, or our fleet in the North Seas, or the Swedes might have encountered them; and if, in defiance of probability, they had escaped all these lets, and we suppose them to have arrived in safe at Kronstadt, still they would have taken their 7,000 men home at their own expense instead of ours. As the Russian hulks were at all events not to have rewarded the toil of our gallant tars with some small recompense, we should also have been gainers by their rotting in Russian ports instead of British, and our hospitals would not have been crowded with sick enemies, who had come into our port as if in triumph with flags streaming.

Are we, in the course of a few short years, to see Sir Robert Calder[8] tried and reprimanded after a decided victory over our enemies, and the man who had been so completely vanquished by Admiral Senyavin to retain his power without censure? The honour of the navy is deeply at issue, and if, at the meeting of Parliament (a measure the ministers seem unwilling to try), no inquiry shall have been made into the conduct of the naval commander-in-chief, I do most earnestly entreat our naval members of Parliament to take care that his honour may be cleared, or his crimes punished, after a fair and impartial investigation.

According to this submission by the Lord Mayor, Dalrymple was handed over to a court martial and replaced by Wellesley (now the Duke of Wellington), who commanded the vanguard of the army. Wellesley, having undersigned the capitulation by the order of the commander-in-chief, protested it. An example of such an exact obedience to authority was the first step on the Duke's path of glorious feats in Portugal and Spain. The dispatch of Cotton in the present circumstances and the reasons given are so curious that I do not think it unnecessary to provide a brief extract here.

The prosperity of England and Russia are inextricably linked. Peter the Great and William Pitt thought so, the wise lovers of their countries in both nations agree, and experience has shown us the benefit of our alliance with Russia. I hope as well that experience will show that the current war will not bring Russia any glory or benefit and England even less so. Russia and England, by geographical and even moral condition, cannot and should not be rivals and should be like sisters only bound in mutual love and respect. True patriots accepted with great regret this change in policy which was so contrary to our political connection with Russia; we lost our long and loyal friend. The Russian people, shedding their blood to protect a common cause with such selflessness, have procured such an entitlement to our gratitude that, despite the break of our friendly relations, it would be unwise to alienate from ourselves the good disposition of a powerful nation. Nations that once were at war can

8    Bronevskiy's note: 'Calder, having defeated a French squadron, was court marshalled for failing to capture or destroy them all and letting so many escape at the Cape of Finisterre [on the 10 [22] July, 1805]'.

never be sincere friends thereafter. Spilled blood sews the seed of enmity between the victor and vanquished which will grow and bear terrible fruit; with time, a rivalry in glory turns into hatred.

Having served until my old age with complete zeal for my nation, I am sure and I hope that no one will reproach me for evading an attack on the Russian squadron, which, despite the praiseworthy courage of the combatants and despite the resoluteness of their leader who declared he was ready to defend himself to the utmost, he should undoubtedly have yielded to a superior force or bury himself in the Tagus. The timely evacuation of Portugal did not allow any delay; the firmness of the enemy admiral made him expect the dire consequences of his desperate courage; the battle that would occur in Lisbon itself would have wrecked considerable losses on the inhabitants, and the capital might have been destroyed by a battle between our two fleets. For these reasons, I approved the contract sent by Senyavin, and without reproaching my conscience, I did not doubt to sign the two additional articles on the immunities and respect owed to the Russian flag. Senyavin's noble and prudent behaviour over the course of his ten-month stay in Lisbon, the unhindered passage afforded to the Prince Regent to Brazil and the trust he earned amongst the Portuguese people, myself and the captains under my command persuaded me to agree out of respect for his virtues. The honour to the Russian flag, to our enemies shown before the face of Britain, ruler of the seas, will be a sacrifice paid for the gratitude of the English people to the Russians. Let us prove the enlightened character of the Britons has not changed yet and that we lay down our lives for justice even to our enemies! But the cries of the people accuse me – I look forward to an impartial trial resigned and hope that the enlightened patriots, while observing the future changes of our political situation, do not tarnish my honour and my zealous service to the country.

Cotton, as it is known, was acquitted and did not soon lose his command, but he was reassigned and Vice-Admiral Sir George Berkeley took his place. Only the Admiralty Board on the 17th of September New Style, probably before his acquittal, remarked to him that he should not have signed two additional articles after the capitulation was already concluded.

# 110

# The Russian Squadron in Portsmouth – Presentation of a Vase to Senyavin – Arrival in Riga

According to the Lisbon convention, the crews from the *Yaroslav* and *Rafail* were stationed on other vessels. At a congress of the captains, the flags and pennants were lowered with proper honours. For the surrender of these two ships, the store-masters and a ship's secretary with 30 sailors were left on board. On the 31st of August [12th of September], the Russian squadron left Lisbon. The British admiral's flagship approached our vessels with her men standing on the shrouds and all the British vessels following saluted our admiral in this fashion. At the mouth of the Tagus, the British squadron, which was under the command of Rear-Admiral Sir Charles Tyler, and consisted of seven ships, two frigates and a brig, united with us and formed a line leeward of our squadron. During the voyage, Senyavin's squadron streamed the imperial flags; the British admiral yielded to Senyavin's seniority and gave him the honours of command. On the 26th of September [8th of October], beating windward and approaching Portsmouth, flags were raised on our vessels. Tyler's squadron did the same, but on the vessels standing on the roadstead and on the fortresses, the flags were lowered. On the next day, the ship of Admiral Montagu, commander-in-chief of Portsmouth, our vessels and all the other British ships hoisted their colours with drummers rolling. The unusual sight of enemy flags waving in their port did not please the proud English people. That the naval officers would show such respect to the Russian flag was regarded as a humiliation for Britain's domination of the seas. The government, in order to appease the people, did not publish the latter articles amended to the convention, but when London learned of the arrival of the Russian squadron under their own colours in Portsmouth, they could not believe that it happened. The disclosure of this and the grievous gossip brought forth an obvious murmur, and King George III, following the unpleasant rumours brought to him, sent Senyavin the following note through the Minister of Naval Forces:[1]

> Admiral Cotton, after the conclusion of the first two articles of the Lisbon convention, did not have the right to sign two additional articles amended to it. His Britannic Majesty does not recognize these two articles as valid and cannot allow an enemy's flag to wave in his harbour. For this reason, the Russian squadron must haul down their colours and shall not raise them again until their departure for Russia, which will soon follow. Your Excellency is invited to London and your captains have permission to go ashore or reside on their ships before the return to Russia.
>
> -Mulgrave<br>-R. Ward<br>-W. Domett

Senyavin could not help but realise that the British government, having rejected part of the treaty, intended on taking advantage of his stubborn tenacity and then gain a cause for dissolving all of the articles. To that end, he answered the Lord Mulgrave with the following:

> I could never doubt that the signatory of the Lisbon convention had the proper authorization from the English government. That His Britannic Majesty does not recognize the validity of the last two additional articles, which were ratified by Admiral Cotton together with the first two and form a part of the present treaty, I accept all the more with surprise and regret. For my part, I have fulfilled all the conditions sacredly. Being in the port and in the possession of the English, I cannot but fulfil the will of His Royal Majesty, and so the further fulfilment of the treaty depends on the British government; any other explanation on this subject is superfluous. I cannot use the invitation to come to London, nor can my captains find proper quarters ashore.
>
> -Senyavin

Admiral Montagu, either by zeal of service or per instruction, demanded the immediate compliance with regard to Lord Mulgrave and threatened that if

---

1    Britain's equivalent to a Ministry of Naval Forces was the Admiralty Board with the First Lord of the Admiralty joining the cabinet as the political head of the navy. Between 1807 and 1810, the post was held by Henry Phipps, Baron (later Earl) of Mulgrave. Lewis Namier and John Brooke, *The House of Commons 1754-1790* (London: Secker and Warburg, 1985), s.v. 'Phipps, Hon. Henry (1755-1831), of Mulgrave Castle, Yorks'.

Senyavin did not strike the ensigns on his flagship and all the other vessels under his command before sunset, the admiral would be sent ashore and should never hoist his colours again. Senyavin answered: 'I cannot resist the will of the king within his domain. As it is typical for a ship's flags to be lowered with due respect after sunset, my ship's will be hauled down at night. If Your Excellency has the right to threaten me, violating the sacredness of the convention, you force me to inform you that I am not a prisoner here yet, I have not surrendered, I shall not give up now, I shall not strike my flag today and will hand it over only along with my life'. Montagu did not dare to insist more – without the government's orders to force the lowering of the flags, there would be a clear violation of the treaty, even more derogatory for Britain than the assertion itself. So after his threats, he was silent... As a result of these exchanges came the following order:

> From the English naval minister I have received news that as a consequence of the Lisbon Convention, His Majesty the King of Great Britain would like to send us to Russia as soon as possible; and as His Majesty finds it indecent that our flags would flutter in his ports, being those of an enemy, he suggests that I and the captains should go ashore with our ensigns and pennants with us and give the assurance that before our departure for Russia, no device will be raised on our ships. I do not find it necessary that I go ashore, nor the gentlemen captains; but having no possibility to resist the requirements of the King of England, all the more so being in his ports and possession, I must tonight haul down my flag and so order the gentlemen commanding the ships and frigate to remove their pennants as well this night. The ships' flags are to be lowered after the beating of the tattoo as usual. Given aboard the *Tvyordyy*, 29th of September [12th of October], 1808.

Montagu gave the residents of Portsmouth an opportunity to expect that Senyavin would strike his flag as done by prisoners of war who have surrendered with military honours. When this did not happen, however, the journalists attacked Cotton with all of their might and gave justice to Senyavin. Caricatures distributed in public all praised the latter and for several days, Senyavin's name was passed from mouth to mouth and many curious people wished to see him; those who did kind-heartedly congratulated him on his triumph. One who knows the character of the English will not be surprised that Senyavin deserved such respect in the general opinion. If Senyavin agreed to go to London during this continued enthusiasm, it was very likely that the people would have met him with applause and carried him in their arms with cheers. During the first break with Britain in 1801, Nelson sailed with a fleet to Reval; and when peace negotiations opened, he asked for permission to visit St. Petersburg in anticipation of an excellent reception. Senyavin, for the same reason, refused to see London. Such arrogance and such modesty can be seen in the characters of both admirals.

On the 1st [13th] of October, per Lord Mulgrave's directive, a commissioner Mackenzie was appointed to Senyavin by the British government to carry out the details of the Lisbon convention and oversee the maintenance of the squadron. Firstly, the ships' powder was stowed ashore and then the squadron proceeded to the Isle of Wight where each vessel stood on a pair of anchors. For the winter, to facilitate the ships and the free placement of their servicemen, the sails and artillery were removed to storehouses.

Senyavin's requests for additional accommodations to the maintenance of the officers and enlisted men, the acceptance of patients in the hospital and similar needs were easily granted, but the prompt for a speedy departure to Russia cost him many troubles, great anxiety and produced a lengthy and delicate correspondence lasting all the while until his departure from England. At first they rejected departure for a lack of vessels, then they opted to take the crews to Arkhangelsk instead of the Baltic, and then they made inconsistent proposals such as leaving behind a sufficient number of men for the safekeeping of ships and supplies until peace could be concluded. Ultimately, the British government postponed the departure because of the ongoing war with Sweden.[2]

In late 1808 and early 1809, the British sent troops to Spain. Almost ceaselessly, 200 and 300 transports came from and went into the sea. On the 1st [13st] of February, 1809, the officers and sailors of the *Rafail* and *Yaroslav* who had remained in Lisbon arrived in England. On the 18th [30th] of April, a British frigate ran aground off the Isle of Wight while manoeuvring through the Needles against a fresh, westerly wind. She signalled for rapid aid from Portsmouth and was nearly under the water with only a few minutes remaining before disaster. At the same time, a signal from *Tvyordyy* conveyed that aid needed to be given. With considerable difficulty and danger, our men quickly removed the frigate from the shallows. Admiral Roger Curtis was instructed to thank Senyavin on behalf of the government. The venerable elder arrived on board the *Tvyordyy* and

---

2   The Russo-Swedish War of 1808-09 or otherwise called the Finnish War began on 9 [21] February 1808 when three Russian divisions crossed the frontier in Finland, but war was not formally declared until 16 [28] March. The war ended on 5 [17] September, 1809 with the Treaty of Fredrikshamn. Having a common enemy in Russia, British and Swedish naval forces operated as allies in the Baltic Sea. Александр Михайловский-Данилевский, *Описание Финляндской Войны на Сухом Пути и на Море в 1808 и 1809 годах* (St. Petersburg: Штаб Отдельного Корпуса Внутренних Стражи, 1841), pp.19-76; Ibid., pp.127-148; Ibid., pp.502-515. [Aleksandr Mikhaylovskiy-Danilevskiy, *Description of the Finnish War on Land and Sea in the Years 1808 and 1809* (St. Petersburg: Staff of the Separate Corps of the Interior Guard, 1841), pp.19-76; Ibid., pp.127-148; Ibid., pp.502-515.]

gladly expressed their gratitude to Senyavin on behalf of the people and, among other things, told him that Britain considered him a friend. Senyavin received this flattering and greatly valued gratitude with all the reverence it deserved.

Here is another sign of the special gratitude the English government had for Dmitriy Nikolayevich Senyavin. The frigate *Speshnyy* was sent from Kronstadt with money and various supplies for the army and navy formerly in the Mediterranean Sea. The frigate's captain, upon arrival in Portsmouth and being informed that our squadron was returning to Russia, stopped to wait for us there. During that time, we broke with the British and the frigate was captured. On board was a set of silver dinnerware addressed to Admiral Senyavin. The British government, on the basis of personal respect, ordered that it be excluded among the prizes seized as Senyavin's property and delivered to him. The British officers who had the opportunity to deserve the attention of Senyavin sought his patronage with great respect and were given a reward or token of some kind. On the 28th of April [10th of May], the ships began to take on deliveries of their inventory and on the 18th [30th] of May, 36 transports were assigned for taking detachments to Russia.

Before leaving, some officers offered to convey to Senyavin the general gratitude with a public act. 'Will we really', they said, 'part with our glorious commander indifferently? No, a mere word of thanks is not enough; we will present him with a vase that would be worthy of it and commensurate with the zeal and gratitude we wish to express before the fatherland and the whole world'. This decision was accepted with great joy and unanimity. Immediately they began to execute on it: they collected a sufficient sum from each man equally, elected deputies to write a speech, draft a diagram of the object, decide how it should be decorated, etc. Until the vase was ready, they kept quiet to keep the gift a secret surprise and prevent the commander-in-chief from suddenly and pre-emptively rejecting it. Collegiate Councillor Lyev Waxell, who was in London, was asked to choose or compose the best from among many drawings and according to the advice of notable artists, sparing no effort. Mister Waxell willingly took on all the duties and enrolled the help of many of the officials of our embassy and travellers who remained in London. Drawing up a picture, he entrusted the creation of the vase to the most outstanding academics and jewellers in the capital. In recognition of one of them, our vase far exceeded the one offered to Lord Nelson in its style, decoration and central emblem. The gift is not only memorable as an excellent token of devotion of subordinates for their commander, but more notably is the first example of this kind in the Russian Navy, an example important for posterity and equally so for the honour of that commander to which it was given by these men. Many cases may be more elaborate and expensive, but the gift bestowed on Senyavin is adorned with the very best thoughts and feelings of such a rarely deserved collective gratitude, love, respect and devotion. Discovering that the vase could not be finished before departing to Russia, they decided to exhibit a detailed drawing of it.

On the 1st [13th] of June, when Senyavin was least expecting any spontaneous revelation, he saw the captains and officers of all the vessels in full dress uniforms riding toward his ship. Taken unawares, Senyavin asked 'what could this mean?' The elected deputies Captain P.M. Rozhnov, F.K. Mitkov and R.P. van Scheltinga suddenly entered the cabin and behind them followed as many officers as would fit in the room. One of the deputies, to Senyavin's pleasant amazement, greeted the admiral on behalf of the whole party with the following speech:

Your Excellency!
Over the course of your four-year term as our commander-in-chief, in every case you have shown us your excellent leadership. As a skillful warrior in repeated battle with the enemy, you have always made us, your subordinates, to triumph. Like a kind father, you cared about us like family, we did not know deprivation and our concerns and labour became amusements; you can see it on our merry faces.

By your example and exhortations encouraging goodness and punishing moderately where guilty, our mores were purified and all the vices of youth were driven out; therein lies the source of our behaviour. Being harried by misfortunate circumstances, you turned us away from every shortcoming and even brought about cases for rejoicing – with you, we are and have always been in good spirits.

Now the time for returning to our beloved fatherland and the end of our long voyage is near; perhaps, if necessary, we will lose our commander. Therefore it remains for us only to thank you for all your good deeds, but with what token? Do we glorify you with our praise? We know that an honourable person dismisses his praise and will not listen. Do we show you our respect and love? But they have dwelled long in our hearts; they are obvious to you and who could doubt them? Do we try to assure you of our obedience and devotion? You saw them both in practice.

When a people are unenlightened and having no law but war and no authority above themselves but the church, that people[3] voluntarily obeyed you, honoured you and loved you; so, are we equal to them? No, this is unsatisfactory for us! We wish to build a monument in which you and your descendants might see and remember the unforgettable good you have done. We also wish for you to equally see in this monument a worthy example of good governance and for our most gracious Sovereign, knowing our loyalty to you, to see how great is our gratitude to him for placing us under such a worthy commander. Lastly, you yourself might

3    Bronevskiy's note: 'The Montenegrins'.

remember when looking upon it, not without pleasure, the thousands of hearts attached to you.

This monument will consist of a vase with appropriate images on it. The speed of our departure does not allow us to wait for its delivery from London, where it is being made, but after our arrival in Russia, it will be delivered by entrusted parties to St. Petersburg where we will have the pleasure to present it to Your Excellency.[4] Our impatience is so great that we, in anticipation, ask you to favourably receive a drawing instead which represents the design of the vase with a description of its appearance, that will give you some idea of the finished item. This is accompanied by a list of officers who express their gratitude to you. In conclusion, it remains for us to wish that Your Excellency would kindly receive all of this from us and not consider any of this as mere flattery but solely a demonstration of our zeal, love and appreciation.

The description of the vase is thus: the vase was in an Etruscan style, standing one and a half feet [45.72 cm] tall, cast from silver and decorated with pure gold. On the lid was a golden eagle with the Imperial crown on its heads, sitting on a round shield and holding in one of its claws the Turkish moon while the other gripped the shield which has the following inscription: 'In memory of the victory won by the Russian squadron over the Turkish fleet near the island of Lemnos in the Archipelago on the 19th of June, 1807'.

Four writhing snails symbolizing wisdom and eternity comprised both arms of the vase and their heads supported a wide golden belt on which was inscribed in enamel: 'Presented to His Excellency Vice-Admiral and Knight Dmitriy Nikolayevich Senyavin by the Russian officers of the squadron under his command in an expression of zeal, love and gratitude. 1809'.

In the centre of the vase were two golden branches, one of oak and the other of laurel, representing steadiness and glory, with one side encircling the image of His Imperial Majesty with the inscription: 'Alexander I, 1807, in memory of the victory at Lemnos during the prosperous reign of this monarch'. On the other side, the branches encompassed the personal arms of Vice-Admiral Senyavin.[5]

---

4    Bronevskiy's note: 'The vase was finished before their departure and was presented in Portsmouth'.
5    The arms of the Senyavins were a pale blue shield charged like a fess by a wavy river, with a six pointed silver star in the centre of the upper half and a golden crescent moon with its points turned upward in the lower half. *Общий Гербовник Дворянских Родов Российской Империи*, vol. 2 (St. Petersburg: 1797), pp.67-68. [*The General Heraldry of the Noble Families of the Russian Empire*, vol. 2 (St. Petersburg: 1797, pp.67-68.]

The lower half of the vase was decorated with leaves and lotus flowers. On the base were three anchors entangled in ropes and converging into one in the centre as if to support the vase.

The admiral did not expect such a thing and as the speech went on, his humility wrestled with a heartfelt pleasure; at the end, when they presented him with the illustration of the vase, he could hardly answer through gasps: 'My dear fellows – this is too much – your noble feelings touch me to the depths of my soul – I have no words – I cannot express to you my gratitude… but I cannot accept such an invaluable gift – it will be my treasure and the most cherished inheritance for my children'. As soon as Dmitriy Nikolayevich received the image of the vase, the men cried '*ura!*' across the whole squadron. The officers then asked to share a meal. 'I am at your disposal', said the admiral. Everyone then stepped out of the cabin and the quarterdeck was turned into a hall, beautifully decorated with ensigns and flags. When they sat down at the table, a choir of singers accompanied by an orchestra sang an acrostic verse composed for the occasion:

See ye the one who is welcome
Ever making our hearts happy?
Now crowned that chief glorisome,
Yea, to us all a father savvy.
A victor over Russia's foes
Vaunted author of our fair fate,
In our hopes a patron fixed and froze,
Never dimming in memories great.

On the 5th [17th] of June, the admiral threw a ball and dinner for the officers in appreciation. The holiday lasted all night. The *Tvyordyy* looked quite unusual at this time. Illuminated by lanterns, it seemed like a huge pillar of fire emerging from the sea. The quarterdeck was turned into a magnificent hall decorated with plants, vases, paintings and colourful flags. The officers' mess and the upper deck until the mainmast comprised two halls decorated in the same manner. A buffet was specially arranged with barrels of rum, lemonade, porter, sherry, port wines and other spirits hung on chains. A Bacchus crowned with grape leaves poured glasses through a tap and served the guests. On the lower deck, the battery officers' mess was turned into a theatre. Thus the whole ship became a three-storey manor in which everything nautical was transformed. In addition to English women, the ball was joined by those Russian women who came from London for joining the crews in their return voyage to Russia. The fare was truly Russian: the pleasure of the host and his affection and attention paid to everyone present was truly and sincerely merry; everyone happily danced and frolicked until dawn. Choirs and Russian and Gypsy dances made for diverse entertainments and the guests, especially the English, admitted that they had never seen anything like it.

On the 12th [24th] of June, the detachments which were aboard transports returned to their ships after fulfilling what the British required of them. Soon 20 ships, 15 frigates, 23 brigs and 280 transports with ground forces aboard sailed for Spain. Finally on the 31st of July [12th of August], detachments of the squadron transferred onto 21 transports. For the commander-in-chief was allotted the frigate *Champion*. On the 5th [17th] of August, they left Portsmouth.[6] They passed Dover on the next day and shortly after turned to Deal and Yarmouth. On the 18th [30th], arriving in the Kattegat, they dropped anchor between the islands of Anholt and Hesselo. Passing through the Belt, due to frequent dead calms and shoals, the vessels alternated often between standing on anchor and exploiting the slightest of breezes. On the 25th of August [6th of September], the convoy standing off the island of Romso was met by another consisting of 250 English and Swedish vessels. The British rear-admiral who was commanding this convoy into the Baltic offered our admiral the best frigate from his squadron, the *Tartar*, onto which Senyavin and his staff moved that same day. On the 28th [9th], they encountered another convoy of 200 vessels returning from the Baltic. On the 5th [17th] of September, in view of Swedish Pomerania, several vessels hoisted Prussian flags and detached from the convoy to go in different directions. In this manner, despite the vigilance of the Napoleonic coast guards and customs, the mutual benefit of the merchants or better still, the people, who cannot do without trade, have always found ways to conduct their business through secrecy.

On the evening of the 9th [21st] of September, the convoy arrived in Riga and the detachments came ashore. This was the end of that campaign so memorable for the Russian Navy. After four year of trials and tribulations, contending not only storms on the ocean or enemy navies bristling with guns, but also with the confluence of unfavourable political affairs, the Russian sailors finally returned to the safety of their own harbours. The preservation of such a large number of brave, experienced sailors, in any case, is very important for Russia. Senyavin tried to keep the naval forces entrusted to him out of the hands of her enemies, both covert and overt, and returned them to the Sovereign and fatherland with honour and glory.

---

6    Over the course of the Russian squadron's quasi-captivity in England, 668 Russians were admitted in the Haslar Naval Hospital for a variety of ailments, scurvy being predominant. 126 of the patients died, including Colonel Phillipe Boissel of the 2nd Naval Regiment. Eric Birbeck and Robert Goetz, 'The Admission of Russian Military to the Royal Hospital Haslar from November 1808 to August 1809', *Haslar Heritage Group*, http://www. haslarheritagegroup.co.uk/index.php?option=com_content&view=article&id=95, accessed 20 June, 2018.

# 111

# The Squadron of Captain Hetzen in Toulon

Captain First Rank Hetzen, taking over command of the two ships *Svyatoy Pyotr* and *Moskva*, received a letter of salutation from the Viceroy of Italy, Prince Eugene, and an official notification of the declared war on Britain from the French Minister of the Navy, Denis Decrès, along with advice from Emperor Napoleon, then at Padua, proposing that the captain's squadron should relocate from Ferraio to Toulon to be better secured against the enemy. Captain Hetzen waited for Highest confirmation from our court before executing on this proposal and in order to receive word as quickly as possible, he wrote to the Minister of Naval Forces in St. Petersburg, Pavel Vasilyevich Chichagov, and to our ambassadors Prince A.B. Kurakin in Vienna and Count P.A. Tolstoy in Paris. The ambassadorial secretary A.Ya. Bulgakov, who had been sent from D.P. Tatishchev in Palermo to St. Petersburg with a report on the surrender of the *Venus* to the Sicilian government, had orders to deliver this news to the commander of the ships at the port of Ferraio. Bulgakov went first to Cagliari and then to Corsica. After 55 days of difficult travel by sea on small boats and on horseback over land, in constant danger of British cruisers and highwaymen, he finally reached the port of Ferraio and very opportunely assured Hetzen of the accuracy of the reports on our complete diplomatic break with Britain. In respect to the captain's inquiry, Prince Kurakin said that his reports to St. Petersburg were sent and if any supreme order came, they would be conveyed to him expressly from Vienna.

In early April of 1808, an imperial order was received which placed Captain Hetzen's detachment and all naval forces outside of Russia at the disposal of Napoleon and instructed him to execute his orders precisely and immediately. Together with the rescript, the French naval minister sent an order to sail to Toulon and the commander there, Admiral Honoré Ganteaume, sent a brig and schooner with pilots to escort Hetzen and instruct him on the French signals and other necessary instructions. In consequence of these orders, on the third day after receiving them, his detachment left the port of Ferraio. On the first day, they were held up off of Livorno by a dead calm, but by the third day of travel, the ships exploited a strong tailwind at 20 *versta*s [21.34 km] per hour and safely arrived in Toulon, despite being in view of an English squadron of 14 ships no more than 5 *versta*s [5.33 km] away. A French fleet standing on the anchorage consisted of 13 ships (including two of 100 guns), 5 frigates and several smaller craft.

Hetzen's ships were immediately placed in the line and mended whenever possible.[1] Admiral Ganteaume and generally all of his subordinates welcomed and entertained the Russians lavishly. The unusual and hitherto unseen union between the French and Russian navies was of course pleasant for them and they treated us with every sort of luxury in a kind and gentle disposition. However, at the slightest change of circumstances, suspicions and subtle movements of the political barometer disturbed the mutual concord and good candour. This change was especially felt in 1809 when the war between Austria and France broke out and after Napoleon became betrothed to the Archduchess Maria Louise. After this, all the gestures of external courtesy from the French were acceptable. Over the course of the long stay in Toulon, lasting 22 months, amidst hopes for a speedy return to their beloved fatherland, especially when the ships were dilapidated, the French government repeatedly suggested exchanging them for new vessels. A fear was held that according to their granted authority, our detachments would be taken off of their ships and sent God knows where. Languishing in uncertainty, idleness (though with cheerful diversions) and lastly being separated from their home for so long, many of the sailors and officers fell into a bored and despondent depression. Some comments delivered to me by one of the comrades who was in Toulon regarding the organization and shortcomings of the French fleet, would be very entertaining and even useful to reproduce, if I did not fear that such a description would resemble a criticism written in a bad faith... It is enough to say that the French fleet goes to sea only in order to run from the British and meets them only to strike their colours.

Finally, in regards to the ships' poor condition rendering them unfit to sail, an imperial order came from the 27th of September [9th of October], 1809: after the appraisal of the value of all accoutrements, the ships were to be transferred to the French government and their crews were to return to Russia. This joyous command, despite some difficulties in the transactions involved in the sale of the ships, was executed and the crews of both vessels left Toulon in the beginning of 1810. Admiral Ganteaume expressed to Hetzen his satisfaction and praised the

---

1    Bronevskiy's note: 'From the 1st [13th] of January, 1809, all naval forces stationed in
     French ports, according to a special agreement, were to be restocked at the expense of
     the French government according to the regulations of our admiralty, but besides the two
     ships sheltered in Toulon, the other squadrons which found themselves in French ports
     were denied aid from the French government via various pretexts'.

good and exemplary behaviour of both the officers and enlisted men. On the 1st [13th] of April, the crews arrived in Mainz and from there they marched through Frankfurt to Weimar. Her Highness the Grand Princess Maria Pavlovna[2] honoured the seafarers with her special attention. She personally met them and entertained them to a Russian dinner. A spectacle unusual for the people of Weimar, and an unexpected honour and good fortune for sailors travelling over land! The pleasure felt by the Grand Princess, to be surrounded by Russians for the first time since leaving Russia, to talk with them and remember together their dear homeland, was certainly not small. His Majesty the King of Prussia also honoured them with his gracious attention in Beeskow. On the 17th [29th] of May, 1810, the crews and naval infantry of the *Svyatoy Pyotr* and *Moskva* finally crossed our frontier.

'Russian Naval Soldiers and Sailors in Leipzig, 7th of April, 1810', Christian Geißler, 1810, painted print from copper engraving, Leipzig, Municipal Museum of History. Left to right: Four sailors, at least one from the naval artillery (black collar and cuffs), a fleet captain, another sailor, two officers of the naval infantry (sashes and gorgets; red shoulder straps from the 1st Regiment, white from the 2nd), a fleet officer, a petty officer (golden tape on the collar and cuffs), and two musketeers of the 1st Naval Regiment.

2    Maria Pavlovna, sister to Emperor Alexander I, married Charles Frederick, heir to Saxe-Weimar-Eisenach in 1804 and resided with him in Weimar. In 1828, with the accession of her husband, she reigned as Grand Duchess Consort until his death in 1853. Andreyevskiy et al., *Brockhaus and Efron Dictionary*, s.v. 'Мария Павловна, Дочь Императора Павла I'. [Andreyevskiy et al., *Brockhaus and Efron Dictionary*, s.v. 'Maria Pavlovna, daughter of Emperor Paul I'.]

# 112

# The *Shpitsbergen* in the Port of Vigo

After leaving Corfu on the night of the 26th and 27th of September [8th and 9th of October], 1807, the sloop *Shpitsbergen* was thrown off course and away from the fleet during strong winds off the island of Marettimo. Throughout October, the sloop withstood two cruel storms, fought constantly against strong winds and finally had to enter Gibraltar on the 2nd [14th] of November for lack of fresh water. Captain John Gore of the British 74-gun ship *Revenge* sent an officer to the sloop to congratulate them on their arrival and offered his services. With this greeting also came the captain of the port aboard the sloop. After his departure, the sloop's commander, Captain-Lieutenant A.R. Kachalov, went to thank Captain Gore and together they visited the Governor, Lieutenant-General Dalrymple, who politely offered his assistance.

On the 6th [18th] of November, the sloop left Gibraltar. They met the *Venus* on the 10th [22nd] off the Cape of St. Vincent and having received word that the fleet was standing in Lisbon, they arrived at the mouth of the Tagus on the 15th [27th] of November. A British squadron of 7 ships, 2 frigates and a brig under the command of Rear-Admiral Sidney Smith sent a lieutenant to the sloop with word that Lisbon was being blockaded and they could not be permitted to enter into the river. Kachalov personally went to Admiral Smith but he was again told that it was impossible to unite with the Russian squadron, though he allowed him to send an officer to Senyavin in order to obtain instructions on where to sail instead. The next day, Midshipman Aleksandr Zavalishin took a boat to the *Tvyordyy* and Admiral Smith sent provisions and charcoal to the sloop. On the 17th [29th] of November, the Portuguese fleet left Lisbon, Smith saluted the Prince Regent from all of his vessels, and lent one ship and brig of his to the Portuguese. The night was marked by such a violent storm from the south that the sloop could not see the united fleets through the rain and darkness. The storm lasted three days and broke every sail on the sloop, damaged the rudder and produced a dangerous leak in the cutwater of the bow; fortunately, on the fourth day the wind abated somewhat and on the 25th of November [7th of December], during a foul wind and choppy waves, the sloop managed to enter the Bay of Vigo.

The Spanish authorities, on receiving the captain's word of honour that there were no sick people aboard, freed the sloop from quarantine. The governor of Vigo, Brigadier Don Nicolás Mahy, received Kachalov very politely. He accepted the request to send papers to Senyavin in Lisbon and to Baron Stroganov in Madrid and proposed that the sloop proceed further into the bay and anchor at the port of Redondela by the village of Portela. The sloop saluted the fortress with 13 shots and received 14 in reply. On the roadstead stood 3 Spanish ships: the *Santiago*, the *América* and the *España*; the frigate *Sabina*, six gunboats and the French ship *Atlas*, which saluted the sloop with 21 shots and an equal number was returned. After mutual visits, the Spanish enthusiastically offered their aid, sent provisions and assigned a shipwright to repair the rudder, cutwater and all the other many damages discovered on the sloop.

On the 21st of May [2nd of June], 1808, the people swore their allegiance to Ferdinand VII and a general resistance to the French was declared. The captain of the French ship, the *Atlas*, after punctual negotiations, was forced to surrender without a fight and his crew became prisoners of war. On the 23th of July [4th of August], the people celebrated the alliance of Spain with Britain and Portugal and all day were heard shouts of: '¡Viva Ferdinando! ¡Viva España!' – Long live Ferdinand! Long live Spain! On the 2nd [14th] of August, the British frigate *Diana* arrived and her captain, Grant, paid a visit to the sloop. On our Emperor's name day,[1] the Spanish ships and fortresses saluted and the *Shpitsbergen* gave reply. On the 15th [27th] of September, word was received from Admiral Senyavin that he sailed with his squadron to Britain and ordered the sloop to remain in Vigo until circumstances changed. On the 20th of September [2nd of October], Captain Richard Hawkins of the British frigate *Minerva* sought to attack the sloop at night, but the Spanish authorities announced to the English captain that the Russian sloop was under the auspices of the Spanish people and the daring captain was forced to give up his plan. On the 1st [13th] of October, Lieutenant Prince Aleksandr Putyatin was sent with dispatches to the ambassador in Madrid. Baron Stroganov, after requesting that the Spanish government repair and resupply the sloop, departed for Trieste on the 23rd of October [4th of November]. Even before the departure of the minister, the delivery of provisions ceased and although Kachalov alluded to the order of the Prince of the Peace,[2] the governor

---

1    30 August [11 of September].
2    Manuel Godoy served as Prime Minister of Spain for a second time from 1801 until 1808, being ousted in March amidst the anti-Bonapartist rebellion. He had earned the title 'Prince of the Peace' for negotiating the Franco-Spanish Treaty of Basel in 1795. Ward et al., *Cambridge Modern History*, vol. 9, pp.428-433.

of the province of Tui responded that he had no means of enforcing the order but offered the services of two merchants who would deliver provisions so long as they were paid in cash. On the 16th [28th] of November, 145 transports arrived in Vigo carrying British ground forces who immediately landed and marched off. On the 29th of December [10th of January, 1809], those same British, now retreating, hastily boarded the squadron under Rear-Admiral Sir Samuel Hood containing 7 ships, 2 frigates and 305 transports and departed for open waters.

On the 2nd [14th] of January, 1809, owing to the mistrust expressed by Admiral Hood and fear that the sloop could aid the French in occupying Redondela, the commandant of Vigo and the governor of Tui suggested that Kachalov relocate to the shore under the battery of Cape Elena. Captain Kachalov, remaining in place and preparing for a fight, responded to the Spanish that he, according to the existing union between Spain and Russia, would not take any part in the actions of the French; that he would observe strict neutrality in the Spanish port; and moreover that one sloop could not inspire any reasonable suspicion for a British fleet. On the 12th [24th], the people in Redondela and Ronda revolted. The commandant of Vigo, in order to curtail the violence of the mobs, again suggested that the sloop relocate to Vigo under its guns, but as the French army approached, the people soon reconciled themselves and the sloop continued to remain at Redondela. On the 19th [31st] of October, when a small detachment of French cavalry appeared, the armed villagers fled and Vigo was occupied without resistance along with all of its fortifications.

On the 25th of January [6th of February], 1810, the French general Baron César de Belle came aboard the sloop under a salute of nine guns, and this general took it up himself to deliver reports from the vessel to Russia. On the 28th [9th], Marshal Soult, passing Vigo, sent his adjutant to offer all manner of aid, which in reality he could not spare. The people, recovering from their initial fear, again armed themselves. The French, wandering about the region pacifying the locals, soon had to seriously consider their own safety. On the 5th [17th] of March, the people of Vigo revolted. The French were driven from the town in a stubborn battle and were besieged in the fort. The next day, the British frigate *Venus* came to blockade it. The captain of this frigate, James Crawford, brought to the sloop an announcement from Vice-Admiral Berkeley that peace negotiations had been opened between Russia and Britain. On the 7th [19th] of March, Colonel Jacques Chalot, the French commandant in Vigo, surrounded on all sides, asked Captain Kachalov to supply him with provisions to feed 800 people for 10 days, promising that the King of Spain (Joseph Bonaparte) and Emperor Napoleon would reward such aid with their gracious generosity. The situation that the *Shpitsbergen* found itself in was very precarious, there was nowhere to procure money or supplies and only the prudent precautions of Captain Kachalov could save the crew from perishing. He replied to Chalot with the following terms: 'since my arrival, I have not received from my government any command. Therefore, I do not know whether we are allied with you or not. The provisions you request exceed the quantity needed for keeping my crew for three months and I only have enough for one month. I cannot help you in your dire situation, in any event, as it would violate my necessary neutrality with Spain and put me at risk of being captured by the British who, in regards to the same neutrality, have not harassed me yet. Do not be upset with this refusal and have faith that in any other case, I would be pleased to be accommodating to your King and Emperor'. On the 15th [27th] of March, patriots numbering at least 4,000 and reinforced by 200 regulars attacked the French, who, in order to avoid the fury of the mob, surrendered to the two British frigates and on the next day, they were transferred onto merchant vessels standing in Vigo.

On the 18th [30th] of March, the Spanish governor, Bernardo González, requested that he be supplied with a certain quantity of bread, powder, cannons and muskets. Captain Kachalov again refused on the grounds of maintaining neutrality and notified the governor that his insistence suggested an inclination to sever the agreements hitherto preserved. Over the course of the siege of Vigo, many famous Spaniards, including the former minister of justice, lieutenant-general and canon of the Cathedral of Santiago de Compostela, Don Pedro Acuña Malvar, for fear of the mob's rage, sought refuge on the Russian sloop and was permitted aboard and saved. George McKinley, captain of the British frigate *Lively*, also sent two individuals to the sloop, assuring that he had a command from his superiors to regard the Russian flag as friendly. After the people calmed down and the wandering French detachments were eliminated, the noble González confirmed in the name of the Central Junta that the people of Spain would, in all circumstances, honour the Russians with their friendship and thanked Kachalov for the shelter given to eminent persons on his sloop. But this kind consent was soon violated by the following action: before the liberation of Vigo, the French abbot was admitted aboard the sloop to serve as an interpreter and was left at the disposal of Captain Kachalov with the knowledge of the Spanish government. Despite the people's hatred for the French, the abbot dared to appear in the town in the belief that being in Russian service would shield him. The crowd immediately surrounded him and hauled him to the governor who just barely saved him from death and returned him to the sloop. The next day, a rumour spread in the town that the Russian sloop was keeping a treasure belonging to the French and also harbouring a dangerous spy. Gonzálaz, in order to temper the will of the mobs on which the defence of his country depended, demanded that the abbot be taken away to the British frigate. Kachalov was forced to extradite the abbot and gave assurances that he was not carrying any French property, soothing the resentment of the people. In the meantime, the supply of provisions to the crew was almost impossible. Fortunately, a good and honest merchant named Abalaira was found, who personally volunteered to pay for a loan and, despite all the difficulties, kept his word as a noble and selfless Spaniard.

On the 2nd [14th] April, a passing detachment of French troops 4,000 strong razed Redondela. The villagers fought back desperately. On the 18th [30th] of the month, the French tried to take Vigo in greater numbers but were repulsed with losses. On the 30th of April [12th of May], 5,000 Spanish regulars arrived in the town and the French also reinforced their presence in the vicinity. Throughout the month of May, the battle raged ceaselessly and the fires never died down. Finally, the French were completely defeated and forced to withdraw with only small remnants of their force. In early June, military operations in the vicinities of Vigo ended; the province of Tui and other neighbouring areas cast off the French yoke. Over the course of the hostilities, by different demands made by the Spanish commanders, Captain Kachalov was put in the most difficult position. On the 12th [24th] of May, his refusal to lend two guns and powder to the governor of Vigo to protect a bridge leading into the town where stubborn fighting flared up three times upset the Spanish and they sought an opportunity to enforce their demands with a strong pretext. The captain of the frigate *Ifigenia*, Juan Carranzo, on the 26th of May [7th of June], having been notified of a supposed Russian declaration of war against France and about the Austrian victory won against Prince Eugene in Friuli, suggested that the captain of the sloop should take part in the protection of Vigo from the French. 'The lasting accord', he wrote in his letter, 'assures me of your good disposition towards Spain, under whose protection you have remained for so long. I accept that you have no hostile intentions'.

'Since my arrival here', Kachalov answered, 'I have not received from the government any news of the renewal of friendly ties with Britain nor of the interruption of peace with France. Naturally, judging by your service, you cannot disagree with me that I am not at liberty to take any action without waiting for precise instructions from my superiors. I look forward to this command with impatience; I hope that this will soon be sent to me, and then with great pleasure I will prepare everything in my power to oppose our common enemy'.

All such demands came from an extreme lack of powder, guns and frequently provisions. Justice should be paid to the Spanish government that it was so magnanimous and indulgent to the Russian flag at a time when we were allied with France and although our ambassador left Madrid, they never changed their disposition towards us. Naturally, another government would not have suffered for a single day in their ports such an ally who was bound to their enemies and did not want to take part in any of their affairs. The Spanish government has always been distinguished for its special nobility. The policy of their court has always been the most righteous. For example: in 1796, British cruisers captured two Spanish frigates departing Cadiz for America with gold and silver before a declaration of war; all Spanish vessels in Britain were detained, yet all the British vessels in Spanish ports were released and the property of the British merchants was declared inviolable.

When a complete silence was restored around Vigo, the consul in Oporto delivered 37,000 Spanish dollars. From that point on, the many anxieties about shortages, at least as far as provisions were concerned, were put to rest and the crew was safeguarded. At the end of the year, Captain Kachalov withstood the last offensive mounted by the Spanish government and again he was put in a precarious situation. Here is the letter from the captain of the Spanish ship *Héroe*, dated 11th [23rd] of December:

> My lord!
> The King, my sovereign, has decreed that the sloop you command be detained. In execution of this supreme command, my divisional adjutant was ordered to remove your powder to a gunboat for storage ashore, as the singular rite in such cases. Your sloop is to be disarmed. However, you may fly your colours and your officers and crew may stay on the sloop and enjoy complete freedom. Your kindly conduct and the experience you have endured deserve all of our attention and alleviation. I am honoured to be at your service.
>
> -Tomas Romari

> Gracious lord!
> I had the honour of receiving your letter from the 11th / 23rd of December in which you propose to disarm the Imperial Russian sloop placed under my command. Allow me, Captain, sir, to note that the poor condition of the sloop and the ongoing war with England do not allow me to withdraw from this port without precise orders from my government. I gave you my word of honour that I will not leave here without notifying you. I cannot execute your order to unload my powder, for this would serve as a stain on the Imperial flag, which honour commands to defend to the last drop of blood. I hope that you will not force me into a reprehensible act. I assure you that I will not change my behaviour and will act according to the friendship and union that exists between our highest courts. I have the honour to be yours, etc. etc.
>
> -Aleksey Kachalov

The Spanish captain, as can be seen from the consequences, had no command from the government to take the sloop and its crew captive. Rather, he only had a need for powder and had intended on procuring it by a cunning ruse.

The years 1810 and 1811 passed in nigh complete inactivity. Such a long estrangement from the fatherland, the uncertainty of how this unpleasant situation would end, the constant danger of being seized by the British or Spanish, and lastly the lack of instructions from Russia for four years were firm grounds for an insufferable boredom. The death of the priest aboard, Pyotr Andreyev, also deprived the last consolation of faith. This venerable elder, feeling his end approach, decided to confess to the *batailleur*[3] and after taking communion, he sighed, pressed the chalice to his heart and died like a righteous man. Captain Kachalov sent an officer to the town of Tui to ask the local bishop if he could allow the burial of the priest in the monastery or another church and if he could order his clergy to perform the burial rites with due honour. Unfortunately, the bishop said that he was unworthy of the dignity. He refused to bury the priest for the sole reason that the deceased did not recognize the authority of the Pope and was independent from His Holiness. Such a reply reveals to what extent superstition pervades the Spanish clergy; but nevertheless, the intolerance of the Roman Church towards others is always the same. By necessity, the burial ceremony was performed as well as was possible by the *batailleur* and the body was placed in a special cemetery reserved for dead sailors.

In 1811, after the inspection of the sloop by a Spanish shipwright sent from Ferrol, it was revealed that a keelson and the internal planking had completely rotted, and all 64 of the frames were found unfit. Therefore, the master refused to repair the sloop as it was too far gone to be made capable of service again. At the beginning of 1812, the first papers from Russia were received and Captain-Lieutenant Kachalov, by Highest decree, was promoted to Captain of the First Rank.[4] Finally on the 21st of June [3rd of July], the order to return to Russia was received with inexpressible joy. That same day, the sloop crossed to Vigo and began to prepare for departure. On the 5th [17th] of July, in the home and company of the governor and other officials, the sloop was auctioned off for 10,000 Spanish dollars. On the 16th [28th] of July, the crew boarded two merchant vessels hired by our general consul in Lisbon, Andrey Dubachevskiy, and departed for Russia.

Thus was the fashion by which our fleet, after the conclusion of the Peace of Tilsit, being deprived of communication with Russia and any hope of assistance, left among enemies and false friends who sought openly and secretly to destroy the honour of our glory, was fortunately preserved. One portion of the fleet safely

---

3    Bronevskiy's note: 'The assistant commissar who looked after the supply of provisions'.
4    Kachalov had been promoted to Captain 2nd Rank in 1808 but the detainment of the squadron and separation of the *Shpitsbergen* complicated communications such that he had already been promoted a second time before word arrived. *Общий Морской Список* (St. Petersburg: Морская Типография, 1808), p.11. [*The Complete Naval Roster* (St. Petersburg: Naval Press, 1808), p.11.]

reached allied harbours in view of the enemy commanding the seas; another, consisting of those ships which had seen many battles and weakened by a lengthy voyage and nearly broken by a storm in the terrible, late days of autumn was evidently saved by the Hand of God. After that, oppressed by the enemy's superior strength and resources and threatened equally by friends as by foes, the commander-in-chief's prudence, caution and firm spirit sheltered his men from the flames and not one vessel fell into the hands of the enemy. Every crew, by their experience and renowned courage, labour and subordination precious to the fatherland, returned to Russia without critical losses. Lastly our government, for the old vessels incapable of service which would have rotted in our ports without benefit, received through their sale compensation large enough to pay for the construction of new ships.

# Afterword

Vice-Admiral Dmitriy Nikolayevich Senyavin did not receive a hero's welcome when he returned to Russia. After a brief report to the Admiralty in St. Petersburg, he was appointed commander of the port of Reval. During the French invasion, he requested an active combat posting, even offering to take command of a militia detachment on land in order to participate in the campaign, but his requests were rejected. Being passed over and snubbed during the nation's most critical hour, Senyavin tendered his resignation and on the 21st of April [3rd of May], 1813, he was expelled from the service on half-pension. He would remain retired, languishing without property or prize money to augment his meagre pay, until 1825, when Nicholas I ascended the throne and not only rehabilitated Senyavin's reputation, but appointed him to the post of general-adjutant, making him an attendant and courier for the Emperor. After a promotion to full admiral, a few minor commands sailing to England and around the Sound, and an award of diamonds to his cross of the Order of St. Alexander Nevskiy, Senyavin retired again from the service due to illness and died in 1831.[1] The vessels left behind in England were all sold to the British in 1813 except for the *Moshchnyy* and the *Silnyy*, which would return to Russia and eventually be broken up in Kronstadt in 1817 and 1819 respectively.[2] They were purchased at a price exceeding the actual condition of the craft in order to effectively subsidize Russia in their war against Napoleon. After the Congress of Vienna, the Bay of Cattaro or Kotor was returned to the Austrian Empire and the Ionian Islands became a British protectorate.

Although the admiral had won the Emperor's favour in 1806 when he wisely stalled and rejected the hasty treaty negotiated by d'Oubril which would have surrendered the Bay of Cattaro without a fight, he overstepped his authority in the negotiations at Lisbon. Despite the fact that he managed to guarantee a safe passage for his crews without the shame of surrender, and secured financial compensation for any vessels that the British might retain after the conclusion

---

1   *Complete Naval Roster*, vol. 5, pp.58-61.
2   Veselago, *The List of Russian Military Vessels*, pp. 48-51.; Ibid., pp.206-207.; Ibid., p.748.

of the Anglo-Russian War, rather than simple seizure, Alexander characterized the loss of the squadron as 'vessels ... remaining in enemy hands as prizes' and refused to award the participants for their voyage. This strained relationship was not soothed any when Senyavin requested an active post in 1812 and was asked by Alexander 'where will you serve and in what manner?' As if wounded by an insult, Senyavin replied 'I will serve exactly as I have always done and as any true Russian officer typically serves'. His request then went unanswered.[3]

It is notable that Bronevskiy, publishing between 1818 and 1819, went to great lengths to explain the rationale of Senyavin's decision-making and defend his reputation in context, but never once alluded to the admiral's fate and ended his narrative as soon as the men and officers arrived in Riga. With the patronage of the Russian Academy, Admiralty and even a donation from the Empress Consort, it would certainly not have been possible for him to express a biting criticism of the Imperial prerogative, should he have held such an opinion. It is also notable that the Treaty of Tilsit is praised as a prudent strategic and geopolitical manoeuvre, despite all the calamities that immediately followed in its wake. Within the confines of decorum and under the thumb of the censor, Bronevskiy found the careful route by which he could heap praise on his commander-in-chief and his sovereign at once and in equal measure, despite the contradictions and despite the former being disgraced. In this translation, I have done my best to remain out of Bronevskiy's way and let his words speak for themselves, biases and all, and I trust that the reader can sort fact from agenda with the benefit of context and hindsight. At the end of the game, the king and the pawn return to the same box and posterity has a levelling effect on justice and reputation, when the pieces disposed cannot control the narrative.

Darrin Boland<br>2019

---

3    Евгений Тарле, 'Экспедиция Адмирала Сенявина в Средиземное Море 1805-1807', *Академик Е. В. Тарле – Сочинения*, vol. 10 (Moscow: Академия Наук СССР, 1959), pp.352-354. [Yevgeniy Tarle, 'The Expedition of Admiral Senyavin in the Mediterranean Sea 1805-1807', *Academic Ye. V. Tarle – Works*, vol. 10 (Moscow: Academy of Sciences of the USSR, 1959), pp.352-354.]

# Appendix I
# Russian Officer Rank Comparisons

| Class | Naval Fleet | Army and Naval Infantry | Civil Service |
|---|---|---|---|
| I | Генерал-Адмирал<br>*General-Admiral*<br>General-Admiral | Генерал-Фельдмаршал<br>*General-Fel'dmarshal*<br>General-Field-Marshal | Канцлер<br>*Kantsler*<br>Chancellor |
| II | Адмирал<br>*Admiral*<br>Admiral | Генерал от Инфантерии<br>*General ot Infanterii*<br>General of the Infantry | Действительный Тайный Советник<br>*Deystvitel'nyy Taynyy Sovetnik*<br>Actual Privy Councillor |
| III | Вице-Адмирал<br>*Vitse-Admiral*<br>Vice-Admiral | Генерал-Лейтенант<br>*General-Leytenant*<br>Lieutenant-General | Тайный Советник<br>*Taynyy Sovetnik*<br>Privy Councillor |
| IV | Контр-Адмирал<br>*Kontr-Admiral*<br>Rear-Admiral | Генерал-Майор<br>*General-Mayor*<br>Major-General | Действительный Статский Советник<br>*Deystvitel'nyy Statskiy Sovetnik*<br>Actual State Councillor |
| V | Капитан-Командор<br>*Kapitan-Komandor*<br>Captain-Commodore | - | Статский Советник<br>*Statskiy Sovetnik*<br>State Councillor |
| VI | Капитан Первого Ранга<br>*Kapitan Pervogo Ranga*<br>Captain First Rank | Полковник<br>*Polkovnik*<br>Colonel | Коллежский Советник<br>*Kollezhskiy Sovetnik*<br>Collegiate Councillor |
| VII | Капитан Второго Ранга<br>*Kapitan Vtorogo Ranga*<br>Captain Second Rank | Подполковник<br>*Podpolkovnik*<br>Lieutenant-Colonel | Надворный Советник<br>*Nadvornyy Sovetnik*<br>Court Councillor |
| VIII | Капитан-Лейтенант<br>*Kapitan-Leytenant*<br>Captain-Lieutenant | Майор<br>*Mayor*<br>Major | Коллежский Асессор<br>*Kollezhskiy Asessor*<br>Collegiate Assessor |
| IX | - | Капитан<br>*Kapitan*<br>Captain | Титулярный Советник<br>*Titulyarnyy Sovetnik*<br>Titular Councillor |
| X | Лейтенант<br>*Leytenant*<br>Lieutenant | Штабс-Капитан<br>*Shtabs-Kapitan*<br>Staff-Captain | Коллежский Секретарь<br>*Kollezhskiy Sekretar'*<br>Collegiate Secretary |
| XI | - | - | Корабельный Секретарь<br>*Korabel'nyy Sekretar'*<br>Ship's Secretary |
| XII | Мичман<br>*Michman*<br>Midshipman | Поручик<br>*Poruchik*<br>Lieutenant | Губернский Секретарь<br>*Gubernskiy Sekretar'*<br>Governorate Secretary |
| XIII | - | Подпоручик<br>*Podporuchik*<br>Second Lieutenant | Провинциальный Секретарь<br>*Provintsial'nyy Sekretar'*<br>Provincial Secretary |
| XIV | - | Прапорщик<br>*Praporshchik*<br>Ensign | Коллежский Регистратор<br>*Kollezhskiy Registrator*<br>Collegiate Registrar |

Shepelyov, *Titles, Uniforms and Orders*, pp.108-120.; Ibid., pp.138-144.; Ibid., pp.150-162.

# Appendix II

# Timeline of Events

---

## 1805

20 Aug / 2 Sept - Fleet of Admiral Tate takes on ground forces at Oranienbaum
25 Aug / 6 Sept - Alexander I bids farewell to Vice-Admiral Senyavin's Mediterranean squadron
28 Aug / 10 Sept - Bronevskiy transfers from the *Gavriil* to the *Svyatoy Pyotr*
10 / 22 Sept - Senyavin's squadron departs from Kronstadt for the Mediterranean
11-12 / 23-24 Sept - Senyavin's squadron reaches Reval
30 Sept / 12 Oct - Senyavin's squadron reaches Copenhagen
9 / 21 Oct - Senyavin's squadron reaches Portsmouth
9 / 21 Oct - Battle of Trafalgar; French and Spanish navies crippled
20 Nov / 2 Dec - Battle of Austerlitz - Coalition forces defeated
3 / 15 Dec - Senyavin's squadron departs Portsmouth; Admiral Nelson's body saluted
14 / 26 Dec - Treaty of Pressburg; Austria becomes neutral to France
14 / 26 Dec - Senyavin's squadron reaches Gibraltar
17 / 29 Dec - Senyavin's squadron departs Gibraltar - *Argus* left behind
29 Dec / 10 Jan 1806 - Senyavin's squadron reaches Cagliari

## 1806

11 / 23 Jan - Senyavin's squadron reaches Messina and unites with squadrons of Admirals Greig and Sorokin
12 / 24 Jan - Frigate *Nazaret* and Brig *Letun* run aground by Messina lighthouse
19 / 31 Jan - Senyavin's squadron arrives in Corfu
30 Jan / 11 Feb - Bronevskiy transfers from the *Svyatoy Pyotr* to the *Venus*
30 Jan / 11 Feb - *Venus* sails to Ragusa
2 / 14 Feb - *Venus* rescues civilian boat at Ancona
9 / 21 Feb - Captain Baillie occupies Bay of Cattaro (Kotor)
13 / 25 Feb - *Letun* confronts French corsair at Preveza
14 / 26 Feb - *Venus* returns to Corfu

16 / 28 Feb - Lieutenant Sytin captures French xebec *Azard*

21 Feb / 5 Mar - *Venus* arrives at Castelnuovo (Herceg Novi)

21 Feb / 5 Mar - Austrians evacuate Bay of Cattaro

23? Feb / 7? Mar - Bronevskiy leads small observation unit on Sipan Island

6 / 18 Mar - *Venus* arrives at Fiume

13-15 / 25-27 Mar - Admiral Senyavin arrives in Bay of Cattaro and city proper

15 / 27 Mar - *Venus* returns to Cattaro

21 Mar / 2 Apr - Bronevskiy entrusted with taking prizes back to Cattaro

27 Mar / 8 Apr - Bronevskiy turns in prizes at Castelnuovo

29 Mar / 10 Apr - Captain Baillie takes a squadron to occupy Dalmatian islands

30 Mar / 11 Apr - Curzola (Korčula) captured

5 / 17 Apr - Bronevskiy visits the Cetinje region of Montenegro

17 / 19 Apr - Baillie besieges fortress on Lesina (Hvar); lifts the siege on the 25 Apr / 7 May

6 / 18 May - Austria begins detaining Russian and allied vessels in Trieste and Fiume

14 / 25 May - General Lauriston crosses Turkish frontier with French corps

15 / 27 May - Senyavin assumes full command of Russian forces in the Mediterranean

16 / 28 May - Republic of Ragusa occupied by French

21-25 May / 2-6 June - Skirmishes between Old Ragusa (Cavtat) and New Ragusa (Dubrovnik)

21 May / 2 June - Skirmish at Capodistria and liberation of detained vessels from Trieste

27 May / 8 June - Senyavin returns to Cattaro

5 / 17 June - Assault on the Bergetto Heights above Ragusa; General Delegorgue killed; siege begins

6 / 18 June - Landing on San Marco

10-12 / 22-24 June - Four guns and 3 mortars placed on the heights to bombard Ragusa

16 / 28 June - French sortie from Ragusa and are repelled

20 June / 2 July - *Venus* sent to patrol Ragusan coast, takes up position at Curzola

21 June / 3 July - French sortie again from Ragusa, again repelled

22 June / 4 July - *Henri* and *Tremenda* captured by *Avtroil* and *Venus*

24 June / 6 July - General Molitor marches to relieve Ragusa; Russian-Montenegrin retreat; siege lifted

8 / 20 July - D'Oubril signs armistice with France which would surrender Cattaro to France

9 / 21 July - *Venus* patrols the Bay of Narenta

27 July / 8 Aug - D'Oubril's treaty is confirmed for Senyavin

31 July / 12 Aug - Emperor Alexander refuses to ratify d'Oubril's treaty

2 / 14 Aug - Curzola evacuated

26 Aug / 7 Sept - Senyavin receives Imperial orders to resume hostilities

31 Aug / 12 Sept – Commodore Ignatyev's squadron arrives at Corfu

2 / 14 Sept - *Venus* covers coast from Budva to Molonta

13-14 / 25-26 Sept - Russian-Montenegrin force drives French back to Old Ragusa

17 / 29 Sept - Marmont counterattacks; destroys Petar I's camp

19-20 Sept / 1-2 Oct - Battle of Castelnuovo; French are repelled

24 Sept / 6 Oct - Senyavin publically praises and thanks the Bokez and Montenegrins

25 Sept / 7 Oct - *Venus* returns to Castelnuovo

2 / 14 Oct - *Venus* sails to Corfu

2 / 14 Oct - Battle of Jena; Prussia crippled

4 / 16 Oct - 13th Jägers and Montenegrins raid Old Ragusa

14 / 26 Oct - *Venus* reaches Syracuse

23 Oct / 2 Nov - *Venus* reaches Palermo

11 / 23 Nov - Russian forces invade Moldavia and Wallachia; Russo-Turkish War begins

12 / 24 Nov - *Venus* reaches Malta

29-30 Nov / 11-12 Dec - Assault and capture of Curzola

27 Nov / 8 Dec - *Venus* reaches Cagliari

12 / 24 Dec - Skirmish between Russian brig *Aleksandr* and French tartane *Napoleon*

21 Dec / 2 Jan 1807 - *Venus* returns to Palermo; American trade ship *Triton* is rescued

27 Dec / 8 Jan 1807 - Corvette *Flora* crashes on the coast of Albania and captured by Ottomans

## 1807

7 / 19 Jan - *Venus* returns to Messina

15 / 27 Jan - *Venus* returns to Castelnuovo

31 Jan / 12 Feb - *Venus* returns to Corfu

7 / 19 Feb - British Admiral Duckworth attacks the Dardanelles

10 / 22 Feb - Senyavin's squadron departs Corfu for the Greek Archipelago; Commodore Baratynskiy in command of Cattaro

15 / 27 Feb - Senyavin's squadron reaches Hydra

23 Feb / 7 Mar - Russian and British squadrons unite at Tenedos

1 / 13 Mar - Duckworth departs for Egypt

8-10 / 20-22 Mar - Russian siege of Tenedos (Bozcaada)

23 Mar / 4 Apr - Froberg Regiment mutinies on Malta

2-16 / 14-28 Apr - *Venus* stationed to observe the Dardanelles

2 / 14 Apr - Failed excursion into Herzegovina

3 / 15 Apr - Bronevskiy travels with party to Imbros to purchase provisions

21 Apr / 3 May - *Venus* stationed off the Rumelian coast

2 / 14 May - *Venus* docks off Skyros for provisions

7 / 19 May - Turkish squadron in the Dardanelles sets sail

8 / 20 May - Turkish aborted assault on Tenedos

9 / 21 May - *Venus* reunites with the fleet off Tenedos

9 / 21 May - Captain Baillie attacks Ali Pasha's flotilla at Patras

10-11 / 22-23 May - Battle of the Dardanelles; Commodore Ignatyev dies

12 / 24 May - Baratynskiy places detachment at Curzola; Dalmatian uprising breaks out

16 / 28 May - *Venus* returns to Tenedos

17 / 29 May - Ottoman Sultan Selim III deposed; Mustafa IV seizes power

21 May / 2 June - *Venus* searches for French corsair

28-30 May / 9-11 June - Skirmish at Almissa (Omiš)

31 May / 12 June - *Venus* blockades Chesme

2 / 14 June - American brig *Hector* captured; Bronevskiy assigned to sail her to Tenedos

2-5 / 14-17 June - Admiral Greig lands a force on Lemnos; aborted siege and skirmishing

2 / 14 June - Battle of Friedland; Fourth Coalition defeated

4 / 16 June - *Hector* arrives at Tenedos

7 / 19 June - *Venus* returns to Tenedos

10 / 22 June - Turkish fleet leaves the Dardanelles again

11 / 23 June - Russian fleet departs to intercept

12 / 24 June - Battle of Obileşti; Turkish field army repelled over the Danube

15-17 / 27-29 June - Turkish assaults on Tenedos

16 / 28 June - Bronevskiy is shot in the left shoulder

16 / 28 June - Russian fleet stands on anchor between Imbros and the continent

17 / 29 June - Russian fleet returns to Tenedos

18 / 30 June - Russian fleet pursues the Turkish fleet; *Venus* left at Tenedos

18-27 June / 30 June - 9 July - Turkish siege of Tenedos continues

19 June / 1 July - Battle of Athos; *Sedd-el Bahr* captured

25 June / 7 July - Treaty of Tilsit signed, Franco-Russian alliance established; Russia to evacuate the Ionian Republic and Cattaro

18 / 30 July - *Venus* returns to Corfu

29 July / 10 Aug - British Admirals Martin and Collingwood arrive at Tenedos

29-31 July / 10-12 Aug - Lauriston occupies Bay of Cattaro

4-24 Aug / 15 Aug-5 Sept - British bombardment of Copenhagen; destruction of Danish fleet

7-12 / 19-24 Aug - General Berthier arrives in Corfu

22 Aug / 3 Sept - Ionian Republic abolished and annexed to France

4 / 16 Sept - Senyavin and the fleet return to Corfu

9 / 21 Sept - 15th Division transported to Venice

18 / 30 Sept – Senyavin awarded the Order of Alexander Nevskiy

19 Sept / 1 Oct - Senyavin leaves Corfu for Gibraltar

23 Sept / 5 Oct - Bronevskiy awarded the Order St. Vladimir 4th Class

30 Sept / 12 Oct - Senyavin's squadron reaches Sardinia

2 / 14 Oct - Baratynskiy leaves Corfu with the *Moskva* and *Svyatoy Pyotr*

4 / 16 Oct - *Venus* sent ahead to Gibraltar to retrieve pilots

5 / 17 Oct - Senyavin's squadron passes Gibraltar

17 / 29 Oct - Baratynskiy arrives in Portoferraio

26 Oct / 7 Nov - Russia declares war on United Kingdom

27 Oct / 8 Nov - Storm hits Senyavin's squadron

30 Oct / 11 Nov - Senyavin's squadron takes shelter in Lisbon harbour

9 / 21 Nov - Andreyanov takes command of the *Venus*; sent back into the Mediterranean

20-22 Nov / 2-4 Dec - French occupy Lisbon

22 Nov / 3 Dec - *Venus* arrives in Palermo

25 Nov / 7 Dec - *Shpitsbergen* arrives in Vigo

10 / 22 Dec - *Venus* completes repairs

Dec - Baratynskiy is recalled and Hetzen commands the *Svyatoy Pyotr* and *Moskva*

## 1808

1 / 13 Jan - Bronevskiy meets the King and Queen of Naples and Sicily

9 / 21 Feb - Rear-Admiral Greig recalled to Russia

9 / 21 Feb - Russia invades Swedish Finland

29-30 / 10-11 Feb - *Venus* blockaded by the British in Palermo harbour; surrendered to Sicily

12 / 24 Apr - Crew of the *Venus* depart Palermo on Austrian boats

Early Apr - *Svyatoy Pyotr* and *Moskva* relocate to Toulon

19 Apr / 1 May - *Venus* crew leaves Messina

20 Apr / 2 May - Dos de Mayo Uprising, war in Spain begins

30 Apr / 12 May - *Venus* crew arrives in Trieste and quarantined

10 / 22 May - *Venus* crew released and transferred to *Sedd-el Bahr*

18 / 30 May - Archduke John of Austria arrives in Trieste and raises Landwehr

28 July - Ottoman Sultan Mustafa IV deposed; Mahmud II seizes power

19 / 31 Aug - Convention of Cintra signed; French evacuate Portugal

22-23 Aug / 3-4 Sept - Cotton and Senyavin renegotiate Russian safe passage

31 Aug / 12 Sept - Senyavin's squadron departs from Lisbon without the *Yaroslav* and *Rafail*

26 Sept / 8 Oct - Senyavin's squadron arrives in Portsmouth

## 1809

26 Jan / 7 Feb - Commodore Saltanov dies

1 / 14 Feb - Crews of the *Rafail* and *Yaroslav* arrive in England

3 / 15 Apr - Battle of Fontanafredda

11 / 23 Apr - Battle of Regensburg

6 / 18 May - French occupy Trieste

17 / 29 May - British squadron blockades Trieste

23-24 June / 5-6 July - Battle of Wagram

17 / 29 July - British engage a small French flotilla near Trieste

5 / 17 Aug - Senyavin's squadron leaves Portsmouth

5 / 17 Sept - Treaty of Friedrikshamn; Russo-Swedish War ends

9 / 21 Sept - Senyavin's squadron arrives in Riga

27 Sept / 9 Oct - *Svyatoy Pyotr* and *Moskva* sold to France

2 / 14 Oct - Treaty of Schönbrunn; France annexes Austrian Trieste and Dalmatia

20 Oct / 1 Nov - Squadron in Trieste is sold to the French

## 1810

24 Mar / 5 Apr - Russians withdraw from Trieste and Venice

17 / 29 May - Crews of the *Svyatoy Pyotr* and *Moskva* return to Russia

4 / 14 June - Crews from Trieste reach the Russian frontier

19 / 31 Dec - Russia relaxes embargos on 'neutral' trade, de facto trades with Britain

## 1812

16 / 28 May - Treaty of Bucharest; Russo-Turkish War ends

12 / 24 June - The Grand Armée invades Russia

5 / 17 July - *Shpitsbergen* auctioned off in Spain

6 / 18 July - Treaty of Orebro; Anglo-Russian War formally ends

16 / 28 July - *Shpitsbergen* crew leave Vigo on merchant vessels

14 / 26 Dec - Grand Armée expelled from Russia

# Appendix III

# Russian Vessel Names

Dimensions and armaments derived from Veselago's *The List of Russian Military Vessels* and Tredrea and Sozaev's *Russian Warships in the Age of Sail*. When their gun numbers differ from Bronevskiy's, 'nominal' is prefixed. Hull sizes are given in the *fut* and *dyuym*, equal to Imperial feet and inches, with metric conversions in brackets.

*Avtroil* – Автроил – Af Trolle; after the Swedish admiral
> Rowing frigate, nominal 24 guns, length 115'6" [35.2 m], breadth 31' [9.45 m], depth in hold 7'5" [2.26 m].

*Azard* – Азард – Hazard; from the French 'Hasard'. Also written *Gazar* – Газар
> Xebec, 14 guns, unknown dimensions.

*Aziya* – Азия – Asia
> Third-rate ship, nominal 66 guns, length 160' [48.77 m], breadth 44'4" [13.51 m], depth in hold 19' [5.79 m].

*Aleksandr* – Александр – Alexander
> Brig, 16 guns, unknown dimensions.

*Altsina* – Альцина – Alcina; also *Altsinoe* – Альциное
> Corvette, 18 guns, unknown dimensions.

*Amfitrida* – Амфитрида – Amphritrite
> Frigate, 44 guns, length 151' [46 m], breadth 38'4" [11.68 m], depth in hold 18'11"[5.77 m].

*Argus* – Аргус – Argus
> Brig, 12 guns, length 76' [23.16 m], breadth 19' [5.79 m], depth in hold 10' [3.05 m].

*Akhill* – Ахилл – Achilles
> Foreign corsair, unknown class and dimensions.

*Bogoyavlensk* – Богоявленск – from 'Богоявление', the Theophany
> Brig, 16 guns, unknown dimensions.

*Bonasorte* – Бонасорте – Good Fortune; from the Italian 'Bona Sorte'
> Brig, 16 guns, unknown dimensions.

*Dyerzkiy* – Дерзкий – Daring, Bold
> Corvette, 28 guns, unknown dimensions.

*Diomid* – Диомид – Diomede
Corvette, 24 guns, unknown dimensions.

*Dnyepr* – Днепр – Dnieper
Corvette, 18 guns, unknown dimensions.

*Ekspeditsion* – Экспедицион – Expedition; from the French 'Expédition'
Schooner, 16 guns, unknown dimensions.

*Feniks* – Феникс –Phoenix
Brig, 18 guns, length 70' [21.37 m], breadth 20' [6.1 m], depth in hold 9' [2.73 m].

*Flora* – Флора – Flora
Corvette, nominal 22 guns, length 106'8" [32.51 m], breadth 28'9½" [8.78 m], depth in hold 13'10" [4.22 m].

*Gavriil* – Гавриил – Gabriel
First-rate ship, 100 guns, length 188' [57.3 m], breadth 51'9" [15.77 m], depth in hold 20'6" [6.25 m].

*Grigoriy* – Григорий – Gregory
Armed transport, 24 guns, unknown dimensions.

*Grigoriy Velikoy Armenii* – Григорий Великой Армении – Gregory of Greater Armenia
Frigate, 50 guns, length 158' [48.16 m], breadth 44'6" [13.56 m], depth in hold 18'6"[5.64 m].

*Irida* – Ирида – Iris
Foreign corsair, unknown class and dimensions.

*Kherson* – Херсон – Cherson
Corvette, 24 guns, unknown dimensions.

*Kildyuin* – Кильдюин – Kilduin
Frigate, 32 guns, length 135' [41.15 m], breadth 35' [10.67 m], depth in hold 14'6"[4.42 m].

*Kur'yer Arkhipelazhskiy* – Курьер Архипелажский – Courier of the Archipelago
Foreign corsair, unknown class and dimensions.

*Lavrentiy* – Лаврентий – Laurence
Brig, unknown armament, length 75' [22.86 m], breadth 20' [6.1 m], depth in hold 9' [2.74 m].

*Letun* – Летун – Flyer
Brig, 12 guns, unknown dimensions.

*Lyogkiy* – Лёгкий – Light
Frigate, nominal 38 guns, length 141'8" [43.18 m], breadth 40' [12.19 m], depth in hold 13'6" [4.11 m].

*Melpomena* – Мельпомена – Melpomene
Corvette, 22 guns, length 106'8" [32.51 m], breadth 28'9½" [8.78 m], depth in hold 13'10" [4.22 m].

*Merkuriy* – Меркурий – Mercury
   Cutter, 22 guns, unknown dimensions.
*Mikhail* – Михаил – Michael
   Frigate, 44 guns, unknown dimensions.
*Moshchnyy* – Мощный – Mighty
   Third-rate ship, nominal 66 guns, length 168' [51.21 m], breadth 45'6" [13.87 m], depth in hold 18'6" [5.64 m].
*Moskva* – Москва – Moscow
   Third-rate ship, 74 guns, length 170' [51.82 m], breadth 46'8" [14.22 m], depth in hold 20' [6.1 m].
*Nazaret* – Назарет – Nazareth
   Frigate, 44 guns, length 159'2¾" [48.53 m], breadth 42' [12.8 m], depth in hold 12'8" [3.86 m].
*Oryol* – Орёл – Eagle
   Brig, 16 guns, unknown dimensions.
*Pavel* – Павел – Paul
   Corvette, 18 guns, unknown dimensions.
*Panagiya* – Панагия – All-Holy, from the Greek 'Παναγία'
   Foreign corsair, unknown class or dimensions.
*Pobyeda* – Победа – Victory
   Third-rate ship, 66 guns, length 160' [48.77 m], breadth 44'4" [13.51 m], depth in hold 19' [5.79 m].
*Pomona* – Помона – Pomona
   Corvette, 22 guns, length 106'8" [52.51 m], breadth 28'9½" [8.78 m], depth in hold 13'10" [4.22 m].
*Rafail* – Рафаил – Raphael
   Third-rate ship, nominal 82 guns, length 182', breadth 49'6", depth in hold 21'.
*Retvizan* – Ретвизан – Justice; from the Swedish 'Rättvisan'
   Third-rate ship, 64 guns, length 163' [49.68 m], breadth 46'8" [14.22 m], depth in hold 18'3" [5.56 m].
*Schastlivyy* – Счастливый – Joyous or Fortunate
   Frigate, 44 guns, length 151'6" [46.18 m], breadth 38'10" [11.84 m], depth in hold 15'9" [4.8 m].
*Selafail* – Селафаил – Selaphiel
   Third-rate ship, 74 guns, length 178' [54.24 m], breadth 48' [14.63 m], depth in hold 19'3" [5.87 m].
*Sfinks* – Сфинкс – Sphinx
   Brig, unknown armament or dimensions.
*Shpitsbergen* – Шпицберген – Spitzbergen or Svalbard
   Sloop, 32 guns, length 110' [33.53 m], breadth 30' [9.14 m], depth in hold 14'1" [4.3 m].

*Silnyy* – Сильный – Strong
   Third-rate ship, 70 guns, length 148' [45.11 m], breadth 48' [14.63 m], depth in hold 19'3" [5.87 m].

*Skoryy* – Скорый – Quick
   Fourth-rate ship, nominal 60 guns, length 176' [53.64 m], breadth 46' [23.16 m], depth in hold 20' [6.1 m].

*Speshnyy* – Спешный – Urgent
   Frigate, 44 guns, 159'2⅔" [48.53 m], breadth 41'6" [12.65 m], depth in hold 12'8"[3.86 m].

*Strela* – Стрела – Arrow
   Cutter, 18 guns, unknown dimensions.

*Svyataya Yelena* – Святая Елена – Saint Helen
   Third-rate ship, 74 guns, length 170' [51.82 m], breadth 48' [14.63 m], depth in hold 20' [6.1 m].

*Svyataya Paraskeva* – Святая Параскева – Saint Parascheva
   Third-rate ship, 74 guns, length 176' [53.64 m], breadth 47' [14.33 m], depth in hold 19' [5.79 m].

*Svyatoy Pyotr* – Святой Пётр – Saint Peter
   Third-rate ship, 74 guns, length 170' [51.82 m], breadth 46'8" [14.22 m], depth in hold 20' [6.1 m].

*Svyatoy Mikhail* – Святой Михаил – Saint Michael
   Fourth-rate ship, 50 guns, length 159' [48.46 m], breadth 42' [12.8 m], depth in hold 15'9" [4.8 m].

*Tvyordyy* – Твёрдый – Steady
   Third-rate ship, 74 guns, length 186' [56.69 m], breadth 49'6" [15.09 m], depth in hold 21'4" [6.5 m].

*Uzhasnaya* – Ужасная – Dreadful
   Demi-xebec, 2 guns, unknown dimensions.

*Uriil* – Уриил – Uriel
   Third-rate ship, nominal 80 guns, length 186' [56.69 m], breadth 49'6" [15.09 m], depth in hold 21'4" [6.5 m].

*Venus* – Венус – Venus
   Frigate, 44 guns, length 115'6" [35.2 m], breadth 38'10" [11.84 m], depth in hold 15'9" [4.8 m].

*Versona* – Версона – Versona
   Corvette, 22 guns, unknown dimensions.

*Yaroslav* – Ярослав – Yaroslav
   Third-rate ship, 74 guns, length 170' [51.82 m], breadth 46'8" [14.22 m], depth in hold 20' [6.1 m].

*Zabiyaka* – Забияка – Quareller, Fighter, Rabble-rouser
   Xebec, 14 guns, unknown dimensions.

# Bibliography

Anon. 'Atlantic Herring (Clupea Harengus)', *Newfoundland and Labrador Department of Fisheries and Aquaculture*, accessed 20 October, 2017. http://www.fishaq.gov.nl.ca/research_development/fdp/pdf/herring.pdf

Anon. *Biographical Dictionary of Italy* (Rome: Institute of the Italian Encyclopedia, 1960-2017). [*Dizionario Biografico degli Italiani* (Rome: Istituto dell'Enciclopedia Italiana, 1960-2017).]

Anon. *Book of the Naval Regulations*, 6th ed. (St. Petersburg: Imperial Academy of Sciences, 1780). [*Книга Устав Морской*, 6th ed. (St. Petersburg: Императорская Академия Наук, 1780).]

'Claims against Russia', *Nile's Weekly Register* 34 (March-September 1828).

Anon. *Complete Collection of Laws of the Russian Empire* (Moscow: II Department of His Imperial Majesty's own Chancellery, 1830). [*Полное Собрание Законов Российской Империи* (Moscow: II Отделение Собственное Его Императорского Величества Канцелярии, 1830).]

Anon. *The Complete Naval Roster* (St. Petersburg: The Naval Press, 1806). [*Общий Морской Список* (St. Petersburg: Морская Типография, 1806).]

Anon. *The Complete Naval Roster* (St. Petersburg: The Naval Press, 1808). [*Общий Морской Список* (St. Petersburg: Морская Типография, 1808).]

Anon. *The Complete Naval Roster* (St. Petersburg: Press of V. Demakov and Press of the Naval Ministry, 1885-1907). [*Общий Морской Список* (St. Petersburg: Типография В. Демакова and Типография Морского Министерства, 1885-1907).]

Anon. *Courtly Menologium for the Year of Our Lord 1808* (St. Petersburg: Imperial Academy of Sciences, 1808). [*Придворный Месяцеслов на Лето от Рождества Христова 1808* (St. Petersburg: Императорская Академия Наук, 1808).]

Anon. *Dictionary of Serbo-Croatian Literary and Folk Language* (Belgrade: Institute for the Serbo-Croatian Language, 1959-2010). [*Речник Српскохрватског Књижевног и Народног Језика* (Belgrade: Институт за Српскохрватски Језик, 1959-2010).]

'Documents upon the Peace of Tilsit', *The Napoleon Series*, accessed 15 February, 2018. https://www.napoleon-series.org/research/government/diplomatic/c_tilsit.html

Anon. *Genealogisches Staats-Handbuch* (Frankfurt: Verlag von Franz Varrentrapp, 1748-1839). [*Genealogical State Handbook* (Frankfurt: Press of Franz Varrentrapp, 1748-1839).]

Anon. *The General Roman Calendar* (Vatican City: Vatican Polyglot Press, 1969). [*Calendarium Romanum Generale* (Vatican City: Typis Polyglottis Vaticanis, 1969).]

Anon. *His Imperial Majesty's Military Regulations on the Field Infantry Service* (Smolensk: Provincial Government Press, 1797). [*Его Императорского Величества Воинский Устав о Полевой Пехотной Службе* (Smolensk: Типография Губернского Правления, 1797).]

Anon. 'Historical Affairs', *The Scots Magazine and Edinburgh Literary Miscellany* 68 (1806): pp.778-800.

Anon. 'Memoir of Sir Samuel Greig', *The Dublin University Magazine* 44 (July 1854): p.156-167.

Anon. *Menologium with a List of the Ranking Individuals or a General State of the Russian Empire in the Year of Our Lord 1806* (St. Petersburg: Imperial Academy of Sciences, 1806). [*Месяцослов с Росписью Чиновных Особ или Общий Штат Российской Империи на Лето от Рождества Христова 1806* (St. Petersburg: Императорская Академия Наук, 1806).]

Anon. *Menologium with a List of the Ranking Individuals or a General State of the Russian Empire in the Year of Our Lord 1807* (St. Petersburg: Imperial Academy of Sciences, 1807). [*Месяцослов с Росписью Чиновных Особ или Общий Штат Российской Империи, на Лето от Рождества Христова 1807* (St. Petersburg: Императорская Академия Наук, 1807).]

Anon. 'The Monthly Register for November 1805', *The Scots Magazine and Edinburgh Literary Miscellany* 67 (1805), pp.868-888.

Anon. 'On Budding and Grafting or the Influence of the Stock Upon the Scion and Vice Versa', *Journal of Horticulture, Cottage Gardener and Home Farmer* 5, series 3 (1883): pp.173-206.

'The Nature of Water-Spouts', *The Universal Magazine of Knowledge and Pleasure* 7 (July 1750): p.154.

Anon. *Service Regulations for the Imperial-Royal Infantry* (Vienna: I.-R. Court and State Press, 1807). [*Dienst-Reglement für die Kaiserliche Königliche Infanterie* (Vienna: K.-K. Hof- und Staats-Druckerei, 1807).]

Anon. *Speech on the day of the Holy, Blessed and Grand Prince Alexander Nevskiy, on the Name-Day of the Pious Sovereign Emperor Alexander Pavlovich, Blessed Sovereign Grand Prince Alexander Nikolayevich, and on the Birthday of the*

*Blessed Sovereign Grand Princess Olga Nikolayevna* (St. Petersburg: Press of the Department of Medicine of the Ministry of Internal Affairs, 1825). [*Слово на день Святого Благоверного и Великого Князя Александра Невского, на Тезоименитство Благочестивейшого Государя Императора Александра Павловича, Благоверного Государя Великого Князя Александра Николаевича, и на Рождение Благоверной Государыни Великой Княжны Ольги Николаевны* (St. Petersburg: Типография Медицинского Департамента Министерства Внутренних Дел, 1825).]

Anon. *The Three Constitutions of the Seven Ionian Islands* (Corfu: Press of Nicolaides Filadelfeo, 1849). [*Le Tre Constituzioni delle Sette Isole Jonie* (Corfu: Tipografia di Nicolaides Filadelfeo, 1849).]

Anon. 'The Treaty of Copenhagen, 27 May 1660', *Danish History – Aarhus University*, last modified 25 August 2011. http://danmarkshistorien.dk/leksikon-og-kilder/vis/materiale/freden-i-koebenhavn-1660/ ['Freden i København, 27. Maj 1660', *Danmarkshistorien – Aarhus Universitet*, last modified 25 August 2011. http://danmarkshistorien.dk/leksikon-og-kilder/vis/materiale/freden-i-koebenhavn-1660/]

Anon. *The World Fact Book: 2010 Edition* (Washington D.C.: Potomac Books, 2010).

Abbott, Evelyn, *A History of Greece* (New York: G. P. Putnam's Sons, 1888-1900).

Abélard, Peter and Héloise, *Letters of Abelard and Heloise with a Particular Account of their Lives, Amours and Misfortunes* (Chiswick: Whittingham, 1824).

Aikin, J. (ed.), 'Narrative of the Late Mutiny at Malta', *The Athenaeum* 2 (1807): pp.343-347.

Allen, Joseph, *Memoir of the Life and Services of Admiral Sir William Hargood* (Greenwich: Henry Richardson, 1841).

Alston, Charles, *Lectures on the Materia Medica* (London: Edward and Charles Dilly, 1770).

Andreyevskiy, I. E., K. K. Arsenyev and F. F. Petrushevskiy (eds.), *Brockhaus and Efron Encyclopedic Dictionary*, 1st ed. (St. Petersburg: Efron, 1890). [Андреевский, И. Е., К. К. Арсеньев and Ф. Ф. Петрушевский (eds.), *Энциклопедический Словарь Брокгауза и Ефрона*, 1st ed. (St. Petersburg: Ефрон, 1890).]

Beamish, Richard, *Memoir of the Life of Sir Marc Isambard Brunel* (London: Longman, Green, Longman and Roberts, 1862).

Beskrovnyy, Lyubomir (ed.), *M. I. Kutuzov: Collection of Documents* (Moscow: Military Press of the War Ministry of the USSR, 1950-1956). [Бескровный, Любомир (ed.), *М. И. Кутузов: Сборник Документов* (Moscow: Военное издательство Военного Министерства СССР, 1950-1956).]

Bezotosnyy, Viktor (ed.), *The 'Patriotic War of 1812' Encyclopedia* (Moscow: Russian Political Encyclopedia, 2004). [Безотосный, Виктор (ed.), *Энциклопедия 'Отечественная Война 1812 года'* (Moscow: Российская Политическая Энциклопедия, 2004).]

Bharatdwaj, K., *Physical Geography: Atmosphere* (New Delhi: Discovery Publishing, 2009).

Birbeck, Eric and Robert Goetz, 'The Admission of Russian Military to the Royal Hospital Haslar from November 1808 to August 1809', *Haslar Heritage Group*, accessed 20 June, 2018. http://www.haslarheritagegroup.co.uk/index.php?option=com_content&view=article&id=95

Bleibtreu, Leopold, *Handbook of Coinage, Measures and Weights* (Stuttgart: J. Engelhorn, 1863). [Bleibtreu, Leopold, *Handbuch der Münz-, Maaß- und Gewichtskunde* (Stuttgart: J. Engelhorn, 1863).]

Bonsma, Madeleine, 'Weird and Wonderful Manifestations of Electromagnetism: Past and Present', *University of Waterloo Phys13 News* 149 (Fall 2014): pp.3-5.

Bostock, John and H. T. Riley (eds.), *The Natural History of Pliny* (London: George Bell and Sons, 1893).

Bronevskiy, Dmitriy, 'Bronevskiy's Recollections', *Russian Antiquity* 6 (1908): pp.537-576. [Броневский, Дмитрий, 'Воспоминания Броневского', *Русская Старина* 6 (1908): pp.537-576.]

Bronevskiy, Vladimir, *Journey from Trieste to St. Petersburg, 1810* (Moscow: Moscow University Press, 1828). [Броневский, Владимир, *Путешествие от Триеста до С.-Петербурга, 1810* (Moscow: Московская Университетская Типография, 1828).]

Bronevskiy, Vladimir, *Memoirs of a Naval Officer in the Continuation of the Campaign in the Mediterranean under the Command of Vice-Admiral Dmitriy Nikolayevich Senyavin from 1805 to 1810* (St. Petersburg: Naval Press, 1818-19). [Броневский, Владимир, *Записки Морского Офицера в Продолжении Кампании на Средиземном Море под Начальством Вице-Адмирала Дмитрия Ноколаевича Сенявина от 1805 по 1810 год.* (St. Petersburg: Морская Типография, 1818-19).]

Brown, Culum, Kevin Laland and Jens Krause (eds.), *Fish Cognition and Behavior* (Oxford: Blackwell Publishing, 2006).

Cardarelli, François, *Encyclopedia of Scientific Units, Weights and Measures,* trans. M. J. Shields (London: Springer, 2004).

Carpenter, Kenneth, *The History of Scurvy and Vitamin C* (Cambridge: Cambridge University Press, 1988).

Catafago, Joseph, *An English and Arabic Dictionary* (London: Bernard Quaritch, 1858).

Charavay, Noel, *The Generals who Died for the Fatherland* (Paris: Noel Charavay, 1893-1908). [Charavay, Noel, *Les Généraux Morts pour la Patrie* (Paris: Noel Charavay, 1893-1908).]

Church, Alfred, and William Jackson (eds.), *Annals of Tacitus* (London: Macmillan and Co., 1876).

Ćirković, Sima (ed.), *History of the Serbian People* (Belgrade: Serbian Literary Society, 1981). [Ćirković, Sima (ed.), *Istorija Srpskog Naroda* (Belgrade: Српска Књижевна Задруга, 1981).]

Dalrymple, Hew, *Memoir written by General Sir Hew Dalrymple of his Proceedings as Connected with the Affairs of Spain and the Commencement of the Peninsular War* (London: Thomas and William Boone, 1830).

Dennis, George and John Murray, *A Handbook for Travellers in Sicily* (London: Murray, 1864).

Denton, William, *Montenegro: Its People and their History* (London: Daldy, Isbister and Co., 1877).

Derzhavin, Gavriil, *The Compositions of Derzhavin with Explanatory Notes by Yakov Grot* (St. Petersburg: Imperial Academy of Sciences, 1864). [Державин, Гавриил, *Сочинения Державина с Объяснительными Примечаниями Якова Грота* (St. Petersburg: Императорская Академия Наук, 1864)]

Dummett, Jeremy, *Palermo, City of Kings: The Heart of Sicily* (London: I. B. Tauris, 2015).

Elsie, Robert, *A Biographical Dictionary of Albanian History* (New York: I. B. Tauris, 2012).

Elsie, Robert, *Historical Dictionary of Albania*, 2nd ed. (Landham, Maryland: Scarecrow Press, 2010).

Elting, John and Herbert Knötel, *Napoleonic Uniforms* (Rosemont, Illinois: Emperor's Press, 2000).

Eton, William, *A Survey of the Turkish Empire*, 4th ed. (London: T. Cadell and W. Davies, 1809).

Fieffé, Eugène, *History of Foreign Troops in the Service of France* (Paris: Military Library, 1854). [Fieffé, Eugène, *Histoire des Troupes Étrangères au Service de France* (Paris: Librairie Militaire, 1854).]

Ford, Richard, *A Handbook for Travellers in Spain and Readers at Home* (London: John Murray, 1845).

Frilley, Gabriel and Jovan Vlahović, *Contemporary Montenegro* (Paris: E. Plon and Co., 1876). [Frilley, Gabriel and Jovan Vlahović, *Le Monténégro Contemporain* (Paris: E. Plon et Cie., 1876).]

Ganado, Albert, 'The Froberg Mutiny at Fort Ricasoli in 1807', *Times of Malta*, last modified October 16, 2016. https://www.timesofmalta.com/articles/view/20161016/life-features/The-Froberg-mutiny-at-Fort-Ricasoli-in-1807.628162

Gerli, E. Michael (ed.), *Medieval Iberia: An Encyclopedia* (New York: Routledge, 2003).

Gilly, William O. S., *Narratives of Shipwrecks of the Royal Navy between 1793 and 1857,* 3rd ed. (London: Longman, Green, Longman, Roberts and Green, 1864).

Gordon, Patrick, *Geography Anatomized or a Complete Geographical Grammar,* 15th ed. (London: Knapton, Midwinter, Bettesworth and Hitch, Ward, Birt, Longman, Brotherton, Ford and Clarke, 1737).

Guthrie, William, *A New Geographical, Historical and Commercial Grammar,* 21st ed. (London: Hamilton, Weybridge and Surry, 1808).

Guthrie, William K. C., *A History of Greek Philosophy* (Cambridge: University of Cambridge, 1981).

Haddock, Steven, Mark Moline and James Case, 'Bioluminescence in the Sea', *Annual Review of Marine Science* 2 (2010), pp. 443-493.

Halpenny, Francess, and Jean Hamelin (eds.), *Dictionary of Canadian Biography* (Toronto: University of Toronto Press, 1966-1994).

Hayes, A. Wallace (ed.), *Hayes' Principles and Methods of Toxicology,* 6th ed. (Roca Raton, Florida: CRC Press, 2014).

Hertslet, Edward, *The Map of Europe by Treaty* (London: Buttersworths, 1875).

Jacoby, Tim, *Social Power and the Turkish State* (London: Frank Cass Publishers, 2002).

James, William, *The Naval History of Great Britain* (London: Conway Maritime Press, 2002).

Kamenskiy, Evgeniy, *History of the 2nd St. Petersburg Dragoon Regiment of Field-Marshal Menshikov 1707-1898* (Moscow: Wilde's Press, 1900). [Каменский, Евгений, *История 2-го Драгунского С.-Петербургского Генерал Фельдмаршала Князя Меншикова Полка 1707-1898 гг.* (Moscow: Типография Вильде, 1900).]

Kekewich, Margaret, *The Good King: King René and Fifteenth Century Europe* (Basingstoke, UK: Palgrave MacMillan, 2008).

Keltie, John (ed.), *History of the Scottish Highlands: Highland Clans and Regiments* (Edinburgh: Grange Publishing Works, 1887).

Kibovskiy, Aleksandr and Oleg Leonov, *300 Years of the Russian Naval Infantry* (Moscow: Russian Knights, 2008). [Кибовский, Александр and Олег Леонов, *300 Лет Российской Морской Пехоте,* vol. 1 (Moscow: Русские Витязи, 2008).]

Lieber, Francis (ed.), *Encyclopaedia Americana* (Philadelphia: Lea and Blanchford, 1849).

Llorente, Jean Antoine, *The History of the Inquisition of Spain* (London: G. B. Whittaker, 1826).

Macaulay, Neill, *Dom Pedro: The Struggle for Liberty in Brazil and Portugal, 1798-1834* (Durham, North Carolina: Duke University Press, 1986).

Malone, Thomas (ed.), *Compendium of Meteorology* (Boston: American Meteorological Society, 1951).

Marmont, Auguste Viesse de, *Memoirs of the Marshal Duke of Ragusa from 1792 to 1832* (Paris: Perrotin, 1857). [Marmont, Auguste Viesse de, *Mémoires du Maréchal Duc de Raguse de 1792 à 1832* (Paris: Perrotin, 1857).]

Marshall, John, *Royal Naval Biography* (London: Longman, Rees, Orme, Brown and Green, 1823-1835).

Mas Latrie, Louis de, *Treasure of Chronology, History and Geography* (Paris: Library of Victor Palmé, 1889). [Mas Latrie, Louis de, *Trésor de Chronologie, d'Histoire et de Géographie* (Paris: Librairie Victor Palmé, 1889).]

Michaud, Louis-Gabriel (ed.), *Universal Biography Old and New* (Paris: Madame Desplaces, 1854). [Michaud, Louis-Gabriel (ed.), *Biographie Universelle Ancienne et Moderne* (Paris: Madame Desplaces, 1843-1854).]

Mikaberidze, Alexander, 'Non-Belligerent Belligerent Russia and the Franco-Austrian War of 1809', *Napoleonica - La Revue*, vol. 10, no. 1 (2011): pp.4-22.

Mikhaylovskiy-Danilevskiy, Aleksandr, *Description of the Finnish War on Land and Sea in the Years 1808 and 1809* (St. Petersburg: Staff of the Separate Corps of the Interior Guard, 1841). [Михайловский-Данилевский, Александр, *Описание Финляндской Войны на Сухом Пути и на Море в 1808 и 1809 годах* (St. Petersburg: Штаб Отдельного Корпуса Внутренних Стражи, 1841).]

Mikhaylovskiy-Danilevskiy, Aleksandr, *Description of the Second War between Emperor Alexander and Napoleon in 1806 and 1807* (St. Petersburg: Staff of the Independent Corps of the Interior Guard, 1846). [Михайловский-Данилевский, Александр, *Описание Второй Войны Императора Александра с Наполеоном в 1806 и 1807 годах* (St. Petersburg: Штаб Отдельного Корпуса Внутренних Стражи, 1846).]

Mikhaylovskiy-Danilevskiy, Aleksandr, *Description of the Turkish War in the Reign of Emperor Alexander from 1806 to 1812* (St. Petersburg: Staff of the Independent Corps of the Interior Guard, 1843). [Михайловский-Данилевский, Александр, *Описание Турецкой Войны в Царствование Императора Александра, с 1806 до 1812 года* (St. Petersburg: Штаб Отдельного Корпуса Внутренней Стражи, 1843).]

Mortier, David (ed.), *The Flags or Banners which most Nations Have at Sea* (Amsterdam: David Mortier, 1718). [Mortier, David (ed.), *Les Pavillons ou Banniéres que la Plûpart des Nations Arborent en Mer* (Amsterdam: David Mortier, 1718).]

Namier, Lewis and John Brooke, *The House of Commons 1754-1790* (London: Secker and Warburg, 1985).

Narochnitskiy, Aleksey (ed.), *The Foreign Policy of Russia of the 19th and Beginning of the 20th Century* (Moscow: State Press of Political Literature, 1960-1970). [Нарочницкий, Алексей, *Внешняя политика России XIX и начала XX века* (Moscow: Государственное Издательство Политеческой Литературы, 1960-1970).]

Nikčević, Tomica, 'Governorship as a Political Force in Montenegro', *Matica* 43 (Autumn 2010), pp.191-210. [Nikčević, Tomica, 'Guvernadurstvo kao Politička Struja Crne Gore', *Matica* 43 (Autumn 2010), pp.191-210.]

Nilus of Sinai, 'On the Eight Evil Spirits', *Philokalia*, 2nd ed., vol. 2 (Moscow: Type and Lithographic Press of I. Yefimov, 1895), pp.238-249. [Нил Синайский, 'О Восьми Духах Зла', *Добротолюбие*, 2nd ed., vol. 2 (Moscow: Типо-Литография И. Ефимова, 1895), pp.238-249.]

Oersted, Hans Christian, 'On Water-Spouts', *The American Journal of Science and Arts* 36 (July 1839), pp.250-267.

Oliva, Narciso (ed.), *Historical Dictionary of Universal Biography* (Barcelona: Antonio and Francisco Oliva, 1833). [Oliva, Narciso (ed.), *Diccionario Historico o Biografia Universal* (Barcelona: Antonio y Francisco Oliva, 1833).]

Olofsson, Magnus, 'The Swedish Army in the Napoleonic Wars – Regular Army Units in 1805', *The Napoleon Series*, last modified April 2008. http://www.napoleon-series.org/military/organization/Sweden/Army/Organization/c_swedisharmy2.html

Palmer, George, *A History of England* (Boston: Robert S. Davis and Co., 1861).

Paracer, Sirindar and Vernon Ahmadjian, *Symbiosis: An Introduction to Biological Associations*, 2nd ed. (Oxford: Oxford University Press, 2000).

Perrin, William, Bernd Würsig and J. G. M. Thewissen (eds.), *Encyclopedia of Marine Mammals*, 2nd ed. (Burlington, Massachusetts: Academic Press, 2009).

Pisani, Paul, *Dalmatia from 1797 to 1815* (Paris: Alphone Picard and Sons, 1893). [Paul Pisani, *La Dalmatie de 1797 à 1815* (Paris: Alphonse Picard et Fils, 1893).]

Podmazo, Aleksandr, *Chiefs and Commanders of the Regular Regiments of the Russian Army (1796-1825)*, last modified 18 December, 2006. http://www.museum.ru/1812/library/podmazo/ [Подмазо, Александр, *Шефы и Командиры Регулярных Полков Русской Армии (1796-1825)*, last modified 18 December, 2006. http://www.museum.ru/1812/library/podmazo/]

Popov, Sergey, *Army and Garrison Infantry of Alexander the First* (Moscow: Russian Knights, 2010). [Попов, Сергей, *Армейская и Гарнизонная Пехота Александра Первого* (Moscow: Русские Витязи, 2010).]

Popovic, Tanya, *Prince Marko: The Hero of South Slavic Epics* (New York: Syracuse University, 1988).

Porter, Whitworth, *A History of the Knights of Malta* (revised ed.) (London: Longmans, Green and Co., 1883).

Porter, Whitworth, *Malta and Its Knights* (London: Pardon and Son, 1871).

Rafferty, John (ed.), *Plate Tectonics, Volcanoes and Earthquakes* (New York: Britannica Educational Publishing, 2011).

Redhouse, J. W., *An English and Turkish Dictionary* (London: Bernard Quaritch, 1856).

Rhoades, Rodney and David Bell (eds.), *Medical Physiology: Principles for Clinical Medicine*, 3rd ed. (Philadelphia: Lippincott Williams & Wilkins, 2009).

Richards, William (ed.), *Early Stages of Atlantic Fishes* (New York: CRC Press, 2005).

Rothman, David, Steven Marcus and Stephanie Kiceluk (eds.), *Medicine and Western Civilization*, 3rd ed. (New Brunswick, NJ: Rutgers University Press, 2003).

Russell, Jeffrey, *Inventing the Flat Earth: Columbus and his Modern Historians* (New York: Praeger, 1991).

Sanxay, James (ed.), *Aristophanic Lexicon, Greek-English* (London: H. Woodfall, 1764). [Sanxay, James (ed.), *Lexicon Aristophanicum, Graeco-Anglicum* (London: H. Woodfall, 1764).]

Selin, Helaine (ed.), *Encyclopedia of the History of Science, Technology and Medicine in Non-Western Cultures* (Dordrecht, Netherlands: Kluwer Academic Publishers, 1997).

Shepelyov, Leonid, *Titles, Uniforms and Orders of the Russian Empire* (Moscow: Tsentrpoligraf, 2005). [Шепелёв, Леонид, *Титулы, Мундиры и Ордена Российской Империи* (Moscow: Центрполиграф, 2005).]

Skalon, D. A. and N. P. Mikhnevich (eds.), *Centenary of the War Ministry 1802-1902* (St. Petersburg: 'Prudence' Press, 1902-1914). [Скалон, Д. А. and Н. П. Михневич (eds.), *Столетие Военного Министерства 1802-1902* (St. Petersburg: Тип. 'Бережливость', 1902-1914).]

Smith, William, *A New Classical Dictionary of Greek and Roman Biography, Mythology and Geology* (New York: Harper and Brothers, 1871).

Solovtsov, Anatoliy, *Book of Russian Opera* (Moscow: Young Guard, 1960). [Соловцов, Анатолий, *Книга о Русской Опере* (Moscow: Молодая Гвардия, 1960).]

Staël-Holstein, Anne Germaine de, *Corinne, ou l'Italie* (London, M. Peltier, 1807).

Johann Stritter, *History of the Russian State* (St. Petersburg: Fyodor Brunkov, 1800). [Иван Штриттер, *История Российского Государства* (St. Petersburg: Федор Брунков, 1800).]

Tarle, Yevgeniy, 'The Expedition of Admiral Senyavin in the Mediterranean Sea 1805-1807', *Academic Ye. V. Tarle – Works*, vol. 10 (Moscow: Academy of Sciences of the USSR, 1959), pp.233-362. [Тарле, Евгений, 'Экспедиция Адмирала Сенявина в Средиземное Море 1805-1807', *Академик Е. В. Тарле – Сочинения*, vol. 10 (Moscow: Академия Наук СССР, 1959), pp.233-362.]

Tooke, William, *View on the Russian Empire during the Reign of Catherine the Second* (London: Longman and Reese, 1799).

Tredrea, John and Eduard Sozaev, *Russian Warships in the Age of Sail, 1696-1860* (Annapolis, Maryland: Naval Institute Press, 2010).

Twiss, Travers, *The Laws of Nations considered as Independent Political Communities* (London: Oxford University Press, 1892).

Tyndale, John, *The Island of Sardinia* (London: Richard Bentley, 1849).

Urfé, Honoré de and Balthazar Baro, *L'Astrée* (Paris: Witte and Didot, 1733).

Veselago, Feodosiy, *The List of Russian Military Vessels from 1668 to 1860* (St. Petersburg: Naval Ministry, 1872). [Веселаго, Феодосий, *Список Русских Военных Судов с 1668 по 1860 год* (St. Petersburg: Морское Министерво, 1872).]

Vialla de Sommières, Jacques L. C., *Historical and Political Voyage to Montenegro* (Patris: Alexis Eymery, 1820). [Vialla de Sommières, Jacques L. C., *Voyage Historique et Politique au Montenegro* (Paris: Alexis Eymery, 1820).]

Voltaire, *Candide or All for the Best*, trans. Walter Jerrold (London: George Redway, 1898).

Ward, A. W., G. W. Prothero and Stanley Leathes (eds.), *Cambridge Modern History* (Cambridge: University Press, 1902-1912).

Wornum, Ralph (ed.), *The Biographical Catalogue of the Principal Italian Painters* (London: John Murray, 1855).

Wright, George, *The Shores and Islands of the Mediterranean* (London: Fisher, Son and Co., 1840).

Zyablovskiy, Yevdokim, *The Latest Geographical Description of the Russian Empire* (St. Petersburg: I. Glazunov's Printing House, 1807). [Зябловский, Евдоким, *Новейшее Землеописание Российской Империи* (St. Petersburg: Типография И. Глазунова, 1807).]

# Index

# From Reason to Revolution – Warfare 1721-1815

http://www.helion.co.uk/published-by-helion/reason-to-revolution-1721-1815.html

The 'From Reason to Revolution' series covers the period of military history 1721–1815, an era in which fortress-based strategy and linear battles gave way to the nation-in-arms and the beginnings of total war.

This era saw the evolution and growth of light troops of all arms, and of increasingly flexible command systems to cope with the growing armies fielded by nations able to mobilise far greater proportions of their manpower than ever before. Many of these developments were fired by the great political upheavals of the era, with revolutions in America and France bringing about social change which in turn fed back into the military sphere as whole nations readied themselves for war. Only in the closing years of the period, as the reactionary powers began to regain the upper hand, did a military synthesis of the best of the old and the new become possible.

The series will examine the military and naval history of the period in a greater degree of detail than has hitherto been attempted, and has a very wide brief, with the intention of covering all aspects from the battles, campaigns, logistics, and tactics, to the personalities, armies, uniforms, and equipment.

## Submissions

The publishers would be pleased to receive submissions for this series. Please contact series editor Andrew Bamford via email (andrewbamford18@gmail.com), or in writing to Helion & Company Limited, Unit 8 Amherst Business Centre, Budbrooke Road, Warwick, CV34 5WE

## Titles

No 1 *Lobositz to Leuthen. Horace St Paul and the Campaigns of the Austrian Army in the Seven Years War 1756-57* Translated with additional materials by Neil Cogswell (ISBN 978-1-911096-67-2)

No 2 *Glories to Useless Heroism. The Seven Years War in North America from the French journals of Comte Maurés de Malartic, 1755-1760* William Raffle (ISBN 978-1-1911512-19-6) (paperback)

No 40　*So Bloody a Day: The 16th Light Dragoons in the Waterloo Campaign* David J. Blackmore (ISBN 978-1-912866-66-3)

No 41　*Northern Tars in Southern Waters: The Russian Fleet in the Mediterranean 1806–1810* Vladimir Bogdanovich Bronevskiy, translated and annotated by Darrin Boland (ISBN 978-1-912866-71-7) (paperback)

No 42　*Royal Navy Officers of the Seven Years War: A Biographical Dictionary of Commissioned Officers 1748-1763* Cy Harrison (ISBN 978-1-912866-68-7) (paperback)

* indicates 'Falconet' format paperbacks, page size 248 mm x 180 mm, with high visual content including colour plates; other titles are hardback monographs unless otherwise noted.